fP

ALSO BY DOUGLAS WALLER

The Commandos

The Inside Story of America's Secret Soldiers

Air Warriors

The Inside Story of the Making of a Navy Pilot

Big Red

The Three-Month Voyage of a Trident Nuclear Submarine

A Question of Loyalty

Gen. Billy Mitchell and the Court-Martial That Gripped the Nation

WILD BILL
DONOVAN

The Spymaster Who Created the OSS
and Modern American Espionage

Douglas Waller

Free Press

New York London Toronto Sydney

A Division of Simon & Schuster, Inc.
1230 Avenue of the Americas
New York, NY 10020

First Free Press hardcover edition February 2011

FREE PRESS and colophon are trademarks of Simon & Schuster, Inc.

For information about special discounts for bulk purchases,
please contact Simon & Schuster Special Sales at 1-866-506-1949 or business@
simonandschuster.com.

The Simon & Schuster Speakers Bureau can bring authors
to your live event. For more information or to book an event
contact the Simon & Schuster Speakers Bureau at
1-866-248-3049 or visit our website at
www.simonspeakers.com.

Book design by Ellen R. Sasahara

Manufactured in the United States of America

7   9   10   8   6

Library of Congress Cataloging-in-Publication Data

Waller, Douglas.
Wild Bill Donovan: the spymaster who created the OSS and
modern American espionage
p. cm.
Includes bibliographical references and index.
1. Donovan, William J. (William Joseph), 1883–1959. 2. Intelligence officers—
United States—Biography. 3. United States. Office of Strategic Services—
Biography. 4. World War, 1939–1945—Secret service. I. Title.
JK468.I6D638 2010
940.54'8673092—dc22
[B]   2010024986

ISBN 978-1-4165-6744-8
ISBN 978-1-4165-6805-6 (ebook)

To Thomas and Jack

Contents

Prologue 1

PART ONE: PRELUDE

1. First Ward   9
2. The Great War   21
3. The Prosecutor   32
4. Politics   38
5. Family   45
6. War Clouds   50
7. Envoy   58
8. Spy Service   69

PART TWO: WAR

9. Pearl Harbor   83
10. The Beehive   92
11. Adolf Hitler   106
12. Enemies   112
13. The Embassies   120
14. Torch   129
15. Bern   145
16. The Neutrals   153
17. Infiltration   164
18. Sicily and Italy   172

19. The Balkans 183

20. Peace Feelers 190

21. Asia 200

22. The Russians 220

23. Normandy 235

24. Intelligence Failures 249

25. The Plot 259

26. The Sideshow 274

27. Stockholm 283

28. The Vatican 292

29. The Leak 303

30. Harry Truman 315

PART THREE: AFTERMATH

31. Nuremberg 341

32. Recovery 349

33. Thailand 360

34. Walter Reed 374

Epilogue 385

Selected Bibliography for Source Notes 391

Source Notes 401

Acknowledgments 443

Index 449

WILD BILL DONOVAN

Prologue

———❧❧❧———

A S FRIDAY EVENING fell, more than seven hundred members of America's clandestine service trooped quietly into the Riverside ice skating rink. They were undercover spies, battle-hardened commandos, and intelligence analysts, along with an assortment of secretaries, cable clerks, receptionists, and telephone operators from headquarters. The converted skating rink, one of many in Washington whose ice had been melted and floor covered with plywood for much needed federal office space during the war, was just a short walk for them down the hill from their headquarters on E Street.

It had been a hot, muggy day that September 28, 1945, typical for the beginning of fall in Washington. But the capital, like the rest of the nation, had come alive now, barely two months after atomic bombs dropped over Hiroshima and Nagasaki had ended World War II. Transport ships had just deposited another six thousand war-weary troops from overseas at East and West Coast ports, the services promising to beat deadlines for processing them out of uniform. Washington's government workers were being given time off to attend a parade for Fleet Admiral Chester Nimitz, hero of the Pacific. Paced by surging auto production, the stock market set a new high. The University of Maryland football team, led by a new coach named Paul "Bear" Bryant, trounced the Guilford College Quakers 60 to 6 at Byrd Stadium north of the capital. Military bands filled the amphitheater near the Lincoln Memorial with music. Newspaper classified sections bulged with employers begging for employees. Downtown store shelves and racks began filling up with consumer goods—sport jackets at Kann's for $19.75, Gershwin albums at Hecht's for $1.25.

Mixed emotions filled the men and women who filed into the Riverside rink Friday evening. They were there to mark the peace but also the end of the country's first national spy agency, the Office of Strategic Services. The

1

new president, Harry Truman, had ordered the service disbanded by the end of the month, its intelligence functions that would be needed after the war to be scattered among the State Department and military. That morning each of the OSS employees had been given a certificate and offered a gold lapel pin with "OSS" stamped on it to commemorate their service, but it did little to lift their spirits. They had to pay a dollar for the pin.

After they settled into the rows of chairs, Major General William J. Donovan, their leader the previous four years, stood up. He fiddled with a gold Hamilton pocket watch given to him by the crew of the USS *Enterprise* aircraft carrier, on which he had once landed, and unfolded his notes before a lectern. Not a particularly tall man and, at sixty-two, somewhat overweight with a face grown pudgy, Donovan hardly fit the nickname, "Wild Bill," which he had earned over the years. Elizabeth MacDonald, one of his propaganda officers in Asia, had been captivated as all women were by Donovan's piercing blue eyes, but he now appeared "penguin-shaped" to her. Mary Bancroft, one of his operatives in Switzerland, thought he looked more like a "kewpie doll" than a glamorous spymaster.

Donovan's life up to that point indeed had been storybook. A poor Irish Catholic kid from Buffalo, New York, he had worked his way through law school, married into a wealthy Protestant family, and marched off to World War I, where he earned a Medal of Honor for heroism on the battlefield. After the war he made headlines as a crime-busting prosecutor, earned a fortune as a corporate lawyer on Wall Street, then finally caught the eye of Franklin Roosevelt, who tapped him to head a new national spy agency in the summer of 1941. Over the next four years, Donovan built that agency, the Office of Strategic Services, into a worldwide intelligence organization with over ten thousand operatives, a remarkable achievement by itself considering he started with just one person—Donovan.

Friends found the spy chief a rich personality. He slept five hours or less a night, could speed-read at least three books a week—mostly on military history and politics but also Shakespeare plays (his favorites)—and filled notebooks with lines he wanted to remember. He was fearless under fire; Father Francis Duffy, his chaplain in World War I, believed Donovan was one of the few men who actually enjoyed combat. He was deeply religious—at one point seriously thinking about becoming a priest. A football player in college, he was an excellent ballroom dancer, loved to sing Irish songs in his baritone voice, and bought up sheet music to learn the latest Broadway tunes. He didn't smoke, rarely drank alcohol, but enjoyed fine dining, which added weight. He spent lavishly with little concept of the value of a dollar; aides who traveled with him always carried cash because he did not. He was witty, often breaking into a broad grin over something he found amusing, but he seldom laughed out loud and rarely told a dirty joke. He hardly ever showed anger, letting it boil inside him instead. He had a quiet unassuming manner that charmed most people instantly and he was a charismatic leader who inspired nearly blind devotion from his OSS agents. Most of the time he asked, rather than commanded, and they followed him loyally.

"We have come to the end of an unusual experiment," Donovan now told the audience in the skating rink, his voice deep, soft, patrician, almost singsong. "This experiment was to determine whether a group of Americans constituting a cross section of racial origins, of abilities, temperaments and talents could meet and risk an encounter with the long-established and well-trained enemy organizations. How well that experiment has succeeded is measured by your accomplishments and by the recognition of your achievements." He went on to describe how they had been able to "fuse" themselves "into a team—a team that was made up not only of scholars and research experts and of the active units in operations and intelligence." Yes, they had made mistakes but only "because we were not afraid to try things that had not been tried before." Though they were being disbanded, the men and women in this room could leave knowing they "have made a beginning in showing the people of America that only by decisions of national policy based upon accurate information can we have the chance of a peace that will endure."

Donovan's speech was short, and given the emotions swirling among the men and women in that room, it was uninspiring. After pinning medals on fourteen OSS commandos lined up by the lectern, he shook the hand of every person in the rink. The bland farewell to his troops, however, masked a deep disappointment and burning anger that Donovan felt toward Truman for breaking up the OSS. Resentment simmered as well among many of Donovan's agents overseas. The White House even received hate mail from one—written, oddly, in Latin, with a picture of an OSS gravestone drawn on it. Truman had returned American intelligence gathering "to the Eighteenth Century," just when the country needed a modern one for future threats, Donovan wrote the *New York Times* Washington bureau chief, Arthur Krock, who had been a favorite for his leaks in the past. The Soviet Union would now be the principal threat, likely allied with China, Donovan's analysts warned. The atomic bomb had radically changed the nature of future warfare, they also warned. Once Russia obtained the bomb, and Donovan was sure it would, large-scale wars between nuclear-armed countries would be inconceivable because they assured mutual destruction. Donovan's analysts were already preparing a classified report on a hostile power one day able to sneak in atomic devices by diplomatic pouch, deliver a "declaration of war a few minutes before the first bomb explodes in some remote town," then demand that the U.S. government surrender or face bombs detonating "in our largest cities"—a far-fetched notion in 1945 when the Hiroshima bomb weighed 8,900 pounds, but one the government would worry about in decades to come.

Truman was hardly naive to future threats. He realized he needed a worldwide intelligence service—he just did not want Donovan or his OSS to be a part of it. Donovan's bureaucratic enemies in Washington, as determined as his admirers, saw him as a power grabber as dangerous as Adolf Hitler. The sleaziest attack came from J. Edgar Hoover, whose Federal Bureau of Investigation had spied on Donovan and his OSS as if they were Nazi agents. Hoover, whose hatred of Donovan was matched only by the OSS director's hatred of him, had an FBI agent pass along to Truman a vicious rumor that Donovan was sleeping with his daughter-in-law Mary. There was no evidence that was the case. Mary had been devoted to Donovan, filling in as hostess for many of his social functions, and Donovan had been as close to her as he would be to a daughter—but only as a daughter. Even so, the story had been given credence among gossips by the fact that Donovan had cheated on his wife, Ruth, many times.

The ugly rumor was not the final straw for Truman, who signed the order closing the OSS on September 20. Piled on his desk were other derogatory reports about the spy service that disturbed him as much. A White House military aide, collaborating with intelligence operatives in the U.S. Army, had slipped the president the most scathing memo—fifty-nine pages accusing Donovan of running what amounted to a rogue operation, plagued throughout the war by intelligence failures and all manner of hidden scandal. It all built an animosity in Truman toward Donovan that never diminished over time. Three years later, an aide sent him the draft of a speech he was to deliver for a Sons of St. Patrick Society dinner, which listed Donovan among the country's Irish American heroes. Truman crossed out his name.

Closing down a spy operation as large as Donovan's and parceling out what remained to other agencies became a complicated job. Snitches on the payroll and foreign officials who had been bribed for information now came forward with promises of cash and special favors they claimed OSS officers had made in the heat of war, but no way to vouch for them. Tens of thousands of spy gadgets and sabotage weapons—code pads, submachine guns, pistols with silencers, bomb detonators, limpet mines, pocket incendiaries, suicide capsules, knockout pills, lock-picking sets, matchbox cameras, stilettos—all had to be rounded up and trucked to responsible agencies in the Pentagon. Donovan worried about the hardware falling into the wrong hands, particularly the more dangerous items such as chemical and biological agents the OSS had been developing for assassination weapons. Millions of pages of intelligence documents, spy reports, and secret cables had to be inventoried, boxed up, and shipped to classified storage facilities. Donovan passed the word quietly to selected officers in the field: Destroy any embarrassing documents, such as currency transactions in fast-moving operations where corners had to be cut. "They'll come back to haunt you."

The day after the Riverside ceremony, Donovan turned his government car over to the White House, which agreed to hire James Freeman, his African American chauffeur who had loyally driven him around Washington the previous four years, many times to rendezvous with secret sources. He later dropped by an OSS studio to record a propaganda record promoting a future CIA, which his agents hoped to entice radio stations in the United States to broadcast. "The national policy of the United States in the postwar world will be shaped by our knowledge or ignorance of our fellow nations," Donovan spoke into the microphone wearily. "America cannot afford to resume its prewar indifference. And here's a fact we must face. Today there's not a single permanent agency to take over in peacetime certain of the functions which the OSS has performed in wartime."

Donovan also spent every spare moment he could find locked in his office with a few trusted aides and a technician from the OSS photo unit, who set up a tripod and camera on his conference table. Day and night, they frantically photographed tens of thousands of classified documents from Donovan's personal files before trucks carted the papers to the Pentagon. He had the photos—many of them grainy or out of focus because of the rush—transferred to microfilm and driven to his law office in New York. Harry Truman would not be in the White House forever. Perhaps the next president would be friendlier toward him and appoint him director of a central intelligence service. He would have copies of his sensitive files to jump-start the organization.

Donovan also wanted the microfilm as a historical record to tell his and the OSS story the way he thought it should be told. A publisher had approached him during the war about writing his autobiography. Donovan was intrigued with the idea but never followed up. He was, however, intensely interested in how his OSS would be portrayed in the future. He carefully edited official histories of the organization that were written later. Eager to cash in on the OSS story, Hollywood put into production three movies extolling the agency: *Cloak and Dagger* starring Gary Cooper, *OSS* with Alan Ladd, and *13 Rue Madeleine* with James Cagney. Donovan and his aides screened their scripts. They found *Cloak and Dagger* and *OSS* tolerable, but *13 Rue Madeleine* so technically inaccurate and its plot so far-fetched (Cagney wins the war single-handedly as a spy) that Donovan threatened to organize a boycott of the film if studio executives did not change the script. To shut him up, 20th Century-Fox just removed references to the OSS in the film. All three movies were hits at the box office.

Hollywood could be expected to hype history. Donovan's own story was far more nuanced. Friends and enemies tended to paint him in broad strokes, white or black. His real life, however, had far more shades of gray.

PART I

PRELUDE

Chapter 1

———✿———

First Ward

SKIBBEREEN, a coastal town on the southern tip of Ireland in County Cork, had a reputation for producing cultured people, or so went the lore among county folk. Timothy O'Donovan, who had been born in 1828, fit that stereotype. Raised by his uncle, a parish priest, Timothy had become a church schoolmaster. It was too humble an occupation, however, for the Mahoney family, who owned a large tract of land in the northern part of Cork and who took a dim view of their daughter, Mary, spending so much time with a lowly teacher eight years her senior. But the Mahoneys could not stop Timothy and Mary from falling in love. Attending the wedding of another couple they decided they would do the same—immediately. They eloped that day.

Growing poverty in Ireland and the promise of opportunity in America were powerful lures for the O'Donovan newlyweds, as they were for millions of young Irish men and women. They landed in Canada in the late 1840s with money Mary's father grudgingly had given them to resettle and made their way across the southern border to Buffalo in western New York.

A boomtown, Buffalo was fast becoming a major transshipment point in the country for Midwest grain, lumber, livestock, and other raw materials dropped off at its Lake Erie port, then moved east on the Erie Canal to Albany and on to the Eastern Seaboard. The O'Donovans, who soon dropped the "O" from their name, settled in southwest Buffalo's First Ward, a rough, noisy, polluted, and clannish neighborhood cut off from the rest of the city by the Buffalo River, where several thousand Irish families packed into clapboard shanties along narrow unpaved streets.

Timothy could walk to the grain mills along the river, where he found employment as a scooper shoveling grain out of the holds of ships for the mills. Scooping was considered a good job, which made Timothy enough money to feed Mary and the ten children she eventually bore. He became a teetotaling layman in one of First Ward's Catholic churches and allowed his home to be used by local Fenians, a secret society dedicated to independence for the Irish Republic.

The Donovans' fourth child, Timothy Jr., who was born in 1858, proved to be a rebellious son who often played hooky from school and defied his father's pleas that he attend college and make something of himself. Instead, "Young Tim," as he had been called at home, went to work for the railroad, becoming a respected superintendent at the yard near Michigan Avenue. At one point the Catholic bishop of Buffalo called on him to calm labor unrest at the docks, which Young Tim succeeded in doing. He continued to display an independent streak, becoming an active Republican in his ward, a rarity for Irish Americans of his day, who voted practically lockstep with the Democratic Party.

In 1882, Young Tim married Anna Letitia Lennon, a brown-haired Irish beauty the same age as he (twenty-four), who had been orphaned when she was ten. Her father, a watchman for a grain elevator, had fallen off a wharf and drowned in the Buffalo River. Her mother had died the year before from an epidemic sweeping through First Ward. Anna had gone to live with cousins in Kansas City, but returned to Buffalo by the time she was eighteen, now a mature young woman with a love for fine literature.

To save money, the newlyweds went to live with the older Donovans at their 74 Michigan Avenue home; "Big Tim" (as the father was called) lived on the first floor with his family. Young Tim's family took the second floor and the house's enormous attic that had been converted into a dormitory. By then, Young Tim had come to regret profoundly that he had not studied in school and gone to college. He began to read widely, stocking hundreds of books in the library of the nicer two-story brick home he and Anna later bought outside of First Ward on Prospect Avenue. Tim also eventually left the rail yard to take a better job as secretary for the Holy Cross Cemetery. He and Anna became "lace curtain Irish," the term the jealous "shanty Irish" of First Ward used for families that moved up and out. By the time he was middle-aged, Tim and his family were even listed in the Buffalo Blue Book for the city's prominent—no small feat considering that as a young man looking for work he saw signs hanging from many businesses that read "No Irish Need Apply."

It was while they were living with his father that Tim and Anna had their first child, whom they named William Donovan. He was born on New Year's Day, 1883, at the Michigan Avenue home, delivered by a doctor who made a house call. Mary chose "William," which was not a family name. The young boy picked his own middle name, "Joseph," later at his confirmation. His parents called him "Will."

Anna had another boy, Timothy, the next year and Mary was born in 1886. Disease killed the next four children shortly after birth or in the case of one, James, when he was four months shy of his fourth birthday. Vincent arrived by the time Will was eight and Loretta (her siblings called her "Loret") came when the family had moved to Prospect Avenue and Will was fifteen.

From Anna's side of the family came style and etiquette and the dreams of poets. From Tim came toughness and duty and honor to country and clan. At night the parents would read to Will and the other children from their books—Will's favorites were the rich, nationalistic verses of Irish poet James Mangan. Saturday nights, when the workweek was done, Tim would often take the three boys with him to the corner saloon (practically every corner of First Ward had a saloon) to listen to the men argue about the Old Country and sing Irish ballads. Fights often broke out; a young man who walked into a First Ward pub always looked for the exit in case he had to get out fast. Tim, who like his father abstained from alcohol and also tobacco, sipped a ginger ale while Will and his brothers snitched sandwiches piled high on the bar.

Will adored his mother and tried to control his violent temper for her sake. But there was an intensity to the oldest Donovan son; he rarely smiled and fought often with other boys in the neighborhood (who could never make him cry) or with his brothers, who tended to be milder mannered. Tim, who could be hotheaded at times himself, finally bought boxing gloves and set up a ring in the backyard to let the three boys punch until they wore themselves out.

Both parents were stern disciplinarians and insisted that their children have proper schooling. When he was old enough to start, Will awoke early each morning and spent an hour taking the streetcar and walking to Saint Mary's Academy and Industrial Female School on Cleveland Avenue north of First Ward. The school, which became known as "Miss Nardin's Academy" after its founder, Ernestine Nardin, offered classes for working women in the evening; during the day, boys and girls attended for free. Will, who attended the academy until he was twelve, proved to be an erratic student. His spelling grades were poor. He earned barely a C in geography. But the nuns who taught him found him unusually well read for a child his age with an almost insatiable appetite for books. He also was not shy about standing in front of the class and reading stories or orations.

At thirteen, Will enrolled at Saint Joseph's Collegiate Institute, a Catholic high school in a downtown suburb run by the Christian Brothers. Saint Joseph's charged tuition but James Quigley, the six-foot-tall bishop of Buffalo, who knew the Donovan family well, paid Will's fee from a diocese fund. The school stressed public speaking, debating, and athletic competition. Will Donovan thrived. He acted in school plays, won the Quigley Gold Medal one year for his oration titled "Independence Forever," and improved his grades. He also played football for Saint Joseph's and was scrappy and ferocious on the field.

In Irish Catholic families, it was assumed that one of the boys would enter the priesthood. Tim and Anna never even hinted at the notion with their sons, but Will expected he would be the one when he graduated from Saint Joseph's in 1899. To make up his mind he enrolled in Niagara University, a Catholic college and seminary on the New York bank of the Niagara River separating the United States from Canada. The school was founded to "prepare young men for the fight against secularism and . . . indifference to religion," as one university history put it.

Donovan, however, soon disabused himself of a religious calling as he plunged into his studies at Niagara. Father William Egan, a professor at the university who became another of Donovan's religious mentors, gently advised him that he did not seem cut out for the cloth. Donovan also concluded "he wasn't good enough to be a priest," Vincent recalled. But for someone who had decided to take the secular road, Donovan still had a lot of fire and brimstone left in him. He won one oratorical contest with a speech titled "Religion—The Need of the Hour." In florid prose he condemned anti-Christian forces corrupting the nation—a theme pleasing to the ears of the Vincentian fathers judging him. "We stand in the presence of these evils which threaten to overwhelm the world and hurl it into the abyss of moral degradation," Donovan railed.

After three years of what amounted to prep school at Niagara, Father Egan convinced Donovan that the legal profession might be his calling (he certainly had the windpipes for the courtroom) and wrote him a glowing recommendation for Columbia College in New York City—which helped get him admitted in 1903 despite mediocre grades.

He continued to be an average student at Columbia, but the college gave him the opportunity to widen his intellectual horizon and explore ideas beyond Catholic dogma (though like Donovan, a large majority of his classmates professed to be conservative Republicans). At one point Donovan even questioned whether he wanted to remain in the Catholic Church and started attending services for other denominations and religions, including the Jewish faith, to check them out. He finally decided to stick with Catholicism.

Donovan soaked up campus life. He won the Silver Medal in a college oratory contest, rowed on the varsity crew squad, ran cross-country, and was the substitute quarterback for the college football team. Football elevated him to near campus-hero status by his senior year, when the coach let him in the game more often. (His gridiron career ended abruptly during the sixth game of the 1905 season when a Princeton lineman hobbled him with a tackle.) In the senior yearbook his classmates voted him the "most modest" and one of the "handsomest."

Donovan *was* handsome, his dark brown hair brushed neatly to the side, his face angular but with soft features that showed manliness yet gentleness, and those captivating blue eyes. Young women found him irresistible and at Columbia Donovan began going out with them, gravitating toward girls with highbrow pedigrees. He dated Mary Harriman, a free spirit who attended nearby Barnard College and whose father was railroad tycoon Edward Henry Harriman. His most serious romance developed with Blanche Lopez, the stunningly beautiful daughter of Spanish aristocrats resettled in New York City, whom Donovan had met at a Catholic church near Columbia.

Donovan graduated with Columbia's Class of 1905, earning a bachelor of arts degree. He immediately enrolled in Columbia Law School, which took him two years to complete. Donovan became a serious student. He caught the eye of Harlan Stone, a highly respected New York lawyer and academic who taught him equity law. Stone, who never looked at notes or raised his voice at students during class, was impressed by the kid from a rough Irish neighborhood, who asked and answered questions in such a thoughtful, measured tone. Stone was Donovan's favorite professor—and over the years, a close friend.

One of Donovan's classmates was Franklin Delano Roosevelt. The two never mingled, however, because they had absolutely nothing in common. Roosevelt came from a wealthy New York family, he had attended the country's best schools (Groton, then Harvard), he was never particularly good at sports, he was not too serious a law student, and he was already married. Roosevelt saw Donovan on campus frequently but paid him no attention. Donovan, for his part, had no interest in the dandy from Hyde Park.

DONOVAN RETURNED to bustling Buffalo, worried that he had rushed through college and law school, that he wasn't truly educated, not fully prepared for the courtroom. He moved back in with Tim and Anna at the Prospect Avenue house and seemed to them aimless at first. They were uncertain how their son, with all his fancy schooling, would now turn out. He mulled entering politics, an idea that horrified friends and relatives as a perfectly good waste of a fine education. After more than a year of indecision, Bill Donovan (only his parents and siblings still called him Will) finally joined the venerable law firm of Love & Keating on fashionable Ellicott Square in 1909, earning almost $1,800 a year as an associate—a respectable enough salary that guaranteed him the "promise of future success," as one local newspaper noted. Two years later, Donovan struck out on his own, forming a law partnership with Bradley Goodyear, a Columbia classmate from a prominent Buffalo family. Setting up an office in the Marine Trust Building downtown, they specialized in civil cases, which ranged from defending automobile drivers and their insurance companies in lawsuits (their bread-and-butter work) to settling a dispute (in one case) among neighbors over the death of a dog. Donovan and Goodyear took on associates. Three years later they merged with a firm run by one of Buffalo's most well-connected lawyers—John Lord O'Brien, who had advised President William Howard Taft and would have the ear of future presidents on intelligence and defense issues.

Goodyear and O'Brien opened doors for Donovan in Buffalo society and among the exclusive clubs and civic organizations, where more important business contacts were made and lucrative deals were hatched. Donovan was admitted to the Saturn Club on Delaware Avenue and to the Greater Buffalo Club, where the city's millionaires hung out. He joined the sailing club, organized a tennis and squash club with Goodyear (a magnet for business contacts), bought property with his spare cash, ordered his suits from a tailor in New York City, and began donating to the local Republican committee (required for a businessman on his way up).

As he moved up in Buffalo society, Donovan did not forget his roots. He paid Timothy's early bills in setting up his practice in Buffalo after he graduated from Columbia's medical school and covered Vincent's education expenses at the Dominican House of Studies. (Vincent, not Will, would be the priest in the family.) But his generosity was not without strings—big brother soon became preachy about how his siblings were so freely spending his dollars. Seminary students who swear oaths of poverty tend "to forget the significance of money," he wrote to Vincent in one of many nagging letters. "It doesn't grow on trees." And "don't get too self-righteous," he added in the note. Donovan sent his sister, Loretta, an allowance to attend Immaculata Seminary in Washington, D.C., but he had the seminary's sisters send him Loretta's grades and they were "horrible," he complained: Fs in Latin and geometry, a D in music harmony.

In the spring of 1912, Donovan began a major diversion. He and a group of young professionals and businessmen, many of them Saturn Club members, organized their own Army National Guard cavalry unit, called Troop I. It started out more as a drill, riding, and camping club for well-to-do city boys, most of whom, like Donovan, had never marched in a line, mounted a horse, or slept outside. They soon became known as the "Silk Stocking Boys"—and even Donovan found his comrades at first to be a provincial collection of military neophytes.

Drilling every Friday night, the "Business Men's Troop" (the nickname they preferred instead of the Silk Stocking Boys) was an egalitarian bunch. They wrote bylaws for their organization (officers wore uniforms to drills while enlisted men did not have to) and elected their own leaders. Donovan was made captain of the troop. He took his command seriously, buying dozens of books on military strategy and attending Army classes two nights a week on combat tactics. Despite grousing from the men because they had to buy their own horses and equipment, Troop I soon became a popular

Buffalo pastime for adventurous spirits. In four years, it had a hundred cavalrymen in uniform with another thirty-six being trained and a waiting list of more wanting to join.

AS HIS FORTUNES rose in Buffalo, Donovan also developed a reputation as a man with an eye for the ladies—though in polite company that kind of talk was always whispered. Privately, Donovan thought prostitution served a useful function for young hormone-charged men—although he never bought sex because he didn't have to. He was considered one of Buffalo's most eligible bachelors and had young women swooning over him, sometimes married ones. One of them was Eleanor Robson, a glamorous, English-born star of the New York City stage who had met Donovan (three years her junior) when he was a law student at Columbia and found that in addition to being an exciting romantic partner he also had acting talent. After Donovan returned to Buffalo, he continued to make occasional trips to New York for more drama coaching from Eleanor. But tongues started wagging in Buffalo when the private lessons continued after the thirty-year-old actress married August Belmont, a wealthy fifty-seven-year-old widower, in 1910. Between train rides to New York, Donovan in 1914 also met a smart, sophisticated, and fashionable blonde from one of Buffalo's wealthiest families at the city's Studio Club, where both were acting in amateur productions.

Her name was Ruth Rumsey. She was the daughter of Dexter Phelps Rumsey, a multimillionaire who had operated several Buffalo tanneries and leather stores, plowed his profits into real estate, and built a grand mansion on fashionable Delaware Avenue. Ruth, who was born in 1891 when Rumsey was sixty-four, was sent to Rosemary Hall, an exclusive boarding school in Greenwich, Connecticut, where she performed better in field hockey and class plays than in dreary subjects such as Latin and algebra. She was quick-witted, fast to assimilate facts, and not shy about speaking her mind around boyfriends. She spent summers traveling the world—Europe, Asia, the Middle East—and always first class. Back home she hunted foxes in Geneseo, sailed on the Great Lakes, and rode horses as well as any man. And when Dexter Rumsey died in 1906, the estate he left would one day make Ruth a millionaire.

Ruth's mother, Susan, who was thirty years younger than her husband

and herself a beautiful socialite and political activist on behalf of women's suffrage, was not pleased with her daughter's interest in this handsome young lawyer. Susan was an enlightened woman who had opened her home to artists and liberal causes since Dexter died, but Donovan had strikes against him. He was Irish Catholic for starters (even Ruth had a schoolgirl prejudice against Catholics) and he came from First Ward, not Delaware Avenue, despite his respectable bank account. Friends also had passed on to Susan the rumors that he played around—and was continuing to do so while he dated her daughter.

But Ruth had always been adventurous. Many rich girls of Buffalo found the tough, wild Irish boys of First Ward alluring. And one like Donovan—who had been a college football star, attended a prestigious law school, and was heart-thumping handsome—that kind of man proved irresistible. Ruth quickly fell in love with him and Donovan was smitten with her. During their first dates, "my heart was in my mouth," he told her later. "I wanted you so much and yet thought you would choose someone of your own class."

Ruth heard the rumors about other women in Donovan's life, about the acting lessons he was taking from an old flame in New York, and she didn't like them. The Robson affair came to a head one evening at a soirée the All Arts Club of Buffalo organized after Ruth's and Bill's engagement had been announced. Eleanor, who was in town visiting friends, performed Robert Browning's poetic play *In a Balcony* for guests at Mrs. Hoyt's new house on Amherst Road. Her leading man for the show was Donovan. Ruth leaned against a wall behind the audience silently steaming with jealousy. A column in the society page later made note of the "gala performance" and the fact that the young lawyer had been on the stage with the famous actress, which sparked more gossip in Buffalo. Afterward, Ruth delivered Donovan an ultimatum: Choose her or the acting lessons. Donovan chose his fiancée.

Bill and Ruth were married late Wednesday afternoon, July 15, 1914, in the conservatory of the Rumsey mansion. Fewer than a dozen friends and relatives attended the quiet, low-key ceremony—a signal to the rest of social Buffalo that Susan was not completely sold on this union. Donovan, however, soon won over his mother-in-law, who found him to be conscientious and hardworking. By the end of 1914, he was serving as her personal attorney for financial matters. When they returned from their honeymoon

Ruth and Bill bought a comfortable home on Cathedral Parkway with money from Ruth's trust. Susan bought them a car.

Donovan had definite ideas about marriage. Love was a reason to marry, but also a reason not to, he thought. A man and woman must be compatible in their interests, but there must also be "strong degrees of independence between them," he told a friend. He thought he and Ruth were compatible and he hoped she would not be the clinging type. Most important, a man must find an unselfish woman, one not interested in dominating him. Donovan had no qualms about using Ruth's money and social standing to get ahead. A man should not marry a woman because she is wealthy, he believed, but he should not refuse to marry a woman because she has money. A wife is an important asset and wealth does not make her any less important. He also continued to be a flirt. To a law firm colleague about to be married he advised: "Don't give up your women friends. They'll tend to improve your manners."

THE STATE DEPARTMENT cable reached Donovan toward the end of June 1916, while he was in Berlin. Five months earlier the Rockefeller Foundation had commissioned him to be one of its representatives in Europe convincing two belligerents, Great Britain and Germany, to allow the foundation's War Relief Commission to ship $1 million worth of food and clothing into famine-plagued Belgium, Serbia, and Poland. The position paid only expenses, but Donovan, who had grown increasingly interested in news stories he read about the European War, jumped at the chance to tour the continent and its battlefields, and, perhaps, scout future overseas clients for his law firm. But now Troop I had been ordered to the Texas border to join General John "Black Jack" Pershing's expeditionary army hunting revolutionary leader Pancho Villa and his band attacking Americans across the border.

Donovan took the first ocean steamer he could book in July and sailed back to the United States to join his unit being deployed to McAllen, Texas. Ruth, who had been home alone caring for their firstborn for almost four months, was not happy her husband would be absent months more. The baby had arrived July 7, 1915. Instead of an Irish name, Donovan wanted a biblical one for his son, so they called him David. But Donovan had left when David was just eight months old and Ruth soon became overwhelmed caring for an infant and managing a house, where appliances always seemed to be breaking. Now David had just turned one year old and he had barely seen his father.

Troop I arrived at McAllen, a border town at the southern tip of Texas just north of the Rio Grande River, toward the end of July 1916. It was miserable duty, with temperatures soaring past 100 degrees during the day and Gulf storms turning their chigger-infested camp into a muddy swamp. Soon promoted to major, Donovan drilled his men relentlessly to toughen them, but they ended up battling the elements more than the Mexicans.

As fall stretched into winter, lonely Ruth began to suffer bouts of depression in Buffalo, which made her physically ill. Donovan thought she was being a hypochondriac and his response was harsh. In one early October letter he threatened to stop writing her if she did not start sending him cheery love notes. She should take a vacation "and not 'mope' around any longer," he wrote. "You need to be in very good condition when your husband gets there," he lectured in another note. "You had better make up your mind to get well."

Troop I finally returned to Buffalo in March 1917, but Donovan remained with Ruth only long enough to make her pregnant again. His career once more took priority over family. He joined the 69th "Irish" Regiment of New York City to train for the war he was sure the United States would enter in Europe. The regiment, parts of which traced its lineage to the Revolutionary War, had more than three thousand of New York's finest Irish sons, including the critically acclaimed poet Joyce Kilmer. They wanted Irish American officers to lead them in battle—no one more so than their chaplain, Francis Duffy, a liberal Catholic priest from a Bronx parish who recruited Donovan to head the regiment's 1st Battalion with visions of him one day commanding the entire 69th. Donovan, who shared that ambition, came to worship the lanky chaplain with the gaunt face, who was devoted to the spiritual welfare of his soldiers.

In August, the 69th moved to Camp Mills on Long Island to begin training for war. It was redesignated the 165th and became part of the 42nd Division with an up-and-coming regular Army major named Douglas MacArthur as its chief of staff. Donovan, who soon discovered his ragtag group was a long way from being fit for trench warfare, had his men run three miles each morning, then strip to the waist and fight one another barehanded to make them mean. It made him an unpopular but respected commander. "I hate Donovan's guts but I would go anywhere with him," said one bruised but loyal soldier.

On August 13, 1917, Ruth delivered a baby girl, whom they named Patricia. Father Duffy baptized her with water from his canteen and she was officially designated the Daughter of the Regiment. Desperately missing his wife and children, Donovan moved the family to a bungalow outside Camp Mills for his final months there. He was delighted that Ruth seemed to be coming out of her depression.

Late in October, Donovan's battalion boarded a troop train for Montreal, where the *Tunisian* passenger liner awaited to take them to Europe. He did not expect to come back alive. "I am glad so glad that you are happy," Donovan wrote Ruth in a poignant letter. "Dearest, the knowledge that we are both making sacrifices in a good cause will bring us closer." His wife's love "is what keeps me going. I cannot be depressed. I will not be downhearted."

Although they did not realize it then, October 1917 was the last time they would be truly man and wife.

Chapter 2

—⟨ᴓᴓᴓ⟩—

The Great War

Dawn, Monday, October 14, 1918

I N HIS QUARTERS at the northern French village of Exermont, Donovan cinched his polished Sam Browne belt with its shoulder strap over his tunic. He made a final check of the bright-colored service ribbons over his left breast pocket and the shiny silver oak leaf clusters pinned to his epaulets. The month before, he had been promoted to lieutenant colonel. It was a reward for being one of the best battalion commanders in his division, but it ended up being almost as much a headache when he had to fight higher headquarters' attempts to move him up to a staff job.

Officers preparing for battle usually stripped their uniforms of rank insignia to make them less inviting targets for German snipers, but Donovan this morning dressed as if he were marching in a Sunday parade for a pragmatic reason. Half of his 165th Regiment was now made up of nearly raw recruits brought in to replace the dead or wounded and their lack of training appalled Donovan. He decked out in his finest hoping that these young replacements, sure to panic under intense fire, saw him clearly and followed his orders in the fog of battle that would unfold that day.

Donovan had already been wounded in the leg from shrapnel and nearly blinded by sickening gas in previous rounds of intense combat. He had been awarded the French Croix de Guerre for rescuing under fire comrades buried under tons of earth after German artillery had unleashed heavy *minenwerfer* mortars on the regiment's position at Rouge Bouquet in March. (He refused to accept the award until a Jewish sergeant at his side during the attack, but who at first was denied the medal, got his as

well.) General Pershing, the commander of the American Expeditionary
Forces, had pinned on Donovan's chest the Distinguished Service Cross,
the Army's second highest decoration, for leading his battalion in a late
July assault to drive German infantrymen back near the shallow Ourcq
River during the Aisne-Marne campaign northeast of Paris. That battle's
cost to the Irish Regiment had been staggering: 1,571 killed, wounded, or
missing—almost half its men. Donovan had lost all of his company commanders, as well as the poet Joyce Kilmer, who had been serving as his
acting adjutant.

Donovan had been curious about how he would react the first time
under heavy fire, but discovered he had "no fear of being able to stand up
under it," he wrote Ruth. Growing "easily accustomed," as he put it, to
Germans shooting at him and he firing back, Donovan had no intention
of being a dugout commander. He was thrilled by the danger of combat
like "a youngster at Halloween," he told Ruth.

Since his battalion had arrived in Europe in November 1917, Donovan
had trained his men relentlessly. He was a strict disciplinarian, keeping
drinking to a minimum and the village whores away from his enlisted soldiers, and reprimanding junior officers when security was breached or a
few dollars were unaccounted for in the battalion's cash box. He had his
platoon leaders memorize six questions they should be prepared to answer
anytime he showed up or risk his wrath:

1. Do I know my particular job here?
2. Do I know the amount of reserve ammunition I have on hand?
3. Do I know the use and purpose of each and every signal at this
   post?
4. Have I instructed my men in and do they know the place of each
   in time of attack?
5. Am I doing my utmost in looking out for the men in my platoon?
6. Can I conscientiously say that I am giving the best attention to
   the feet of my men?

After once running them in full packs on a three-mile obstacle course
over walls, under barbed wire, through icy streams, and up and down hills,
the men collapsed gasping for air. "What the hell's the matter with you
guys?" demanded Donovan, who had just turned thirty-five and carried the

same load. "I haven't lost my breath." A trooper in the back who Donovan couldn't see shouted: "But hell, we aren't as wild as you are, Bill." From that day on, "Wild Bill" stuck. Donovan professed annoyance with the nickname because it ran counter to the quiet, intense image he wanted to project. But Ruth knew that deep down he loved it.

Donovan's cool and firm leadership under fire had won him praise from higher-ups at 42nd Division headquarters like MacArthur—although MacArthur sniped he had been "running wild" during the September Saint-Mihiel offensive, racing his battalion ahead of slower-moving units on the front line. Soon, however, Donovan had become a legend in the entire AEF and a celebrity back home for his heroics. Ruth retyped his letters (editing out personal items) and sent them, with their vivid details of each battle, to New York's influential senator, James Wadsworth, who was impressed and became an important Donovan political mentor. She also sent the letters to New York newspapers, which eagerly published them.

But Ruth was also desperately lonely once more, plunging again into bouts of depression and paralyzing fear that her husband would be killed in battle. She begged Donovan to let her travel to Paris so she could see him on leaves. Donovan wouldn't hear of it. He had enough on his mind at the front without worrying about German shelling and aerial bombing of the French capital endangering his wife.

Ruth turned to Vincent for emotional support. She had leaned on Timothy during Donovan's months on the Mexican border, but he was now in Europe with the Army Medical Corps. Friends believed Donovan's caring brothers were better matches for Ruth than her always absent husband. The best Donovan could offer his wife was pep talks in his letters, praising her for her "pluck" and suggesting she take in the sea air "and read." Unfounded gossip even spread during the Mexico expedition that the handsome Timothy, a ladies' man himself who had been constantly at Ruth's side for comfort, was having an affair with her. Now Ruth poured her heart out to Vincent, who became her confidant. A crisis of faith grew in her. "Religion is fine for those who need it," she told Vincent. "I don't feel I need it." Vincent sent her books on Catholicism and long letters pleading with her not to abandon God.

Donovan eventually did give up his battalion and was made chief of staff of the 165th, but he considered it a plum assignment because he would be the forward ground commander for the entire regiment in the battle that would soon begin the morning of October 14. The overall commander, a competent low-key colonel named Harry Mitchell, remained at the headquarters dugout in the rear. Donovan would be at the front, leading his men into what he knew would be a meat grinder.

No sooner had Pershing disengaged his forces from the Saint-Mihiel battle than he mounted a final American offensive to punch like a battering ram through German lines on the Western Front between the Meuse River and the dense Argonne Forest with more than a million men. The offensive soon bogged down as cold rainy weather settled in over dense woods, deep ravines, and high ground that the Germans fiercely defended. Donovan's 42nd Division was to relieve the 1st Division to the right of the Argonne Forest and break through the Kriemhilde Stellung, which consisted of belts of barbed wire, tank obstacles, minefields, cement pillboxes, machine gun nests, dug-in infantry, and artillery on high ground. The terrain was rolling and dominated by one hill, Côte de Châtillon, on the right. If the 42nd could break through the Kriemhilde Stellung and overrun the two heavily defended villages just north—Saint-Georges and Landres-et-Saint-Georges—the American army would have the less defended valley beyond to pour through forces.

Although Donovan did not realize it as he prepped that Monday morning, the inexperienced generals above him had crafted a tactically complex plan, which did not have much chance of breaching the Kriemhilde Stellung as quickly as they envisioned. Major General Charles P. Summerall, the new 5th Corps commander, was a hard-charging and vindictive artilleryman with little experience in infantry tactics. Summerall had approved a wildly unrealistic attack plan drawn up by the 42nd's lackluster commander, Major General Charles Menoher. Menoher's two brigades—the 83rd on the left, which included Donovan's unit, and the 84th on the right now commanded by MacArthur, a newly minted brigadier general—lined up their four regiments to attack abreast even though the Kriemhilde Stellung was not a straight line. Brigadier General Michael Lenihan, who was popular with the Irish soldiers but indecisive in combat, commanded the 83rd Brigade, whose mission was to clear Saint-Georges and Landres-et-Saint-Georges on the left. But before he moved out, MacArthur's 84th Brigade on the right was to take Côte de Châtillon in three hours. If he had had no German guns pointed at him, MacArthur's force could not have walked the distance in that short a time. But the can-do and overdramatic

MacArthur did not protest. Neither did the taciturn Lenihan, whose brigade depended on MacArthur taking out the hill's artillery and machine guns in time to protect Lenihan from enfilading fire on his right flank.

With rain pouring down, chilling the men in the summer uniforms they still wore, Donovan's regiment moved out quickly Monday morning from the sunken road north of the forest of Maldah. Extra bandoleers of cartridges hung over their shoulders, which he knew they would need. A rolling artillery barrage cratered the ground three hundred yards in front of them. The terrain ahead (littered with American and German body parts from previous assaults) sloped up to the first line of barbed wire and was largely open and flat save for small clumps of trees. As poorly trained soldiers of the regiment bunched up at the first line of wire, however, enemy fire cut them down from the north and from Donovan's right flank, whose enfilade was supposed to be suppressed.

"Where the hell is that coming from?" Donovan shouted to a battalion commander. MacArthur's brigade predictably had not taken Côte de Châtillon in the three hours allotted. Germans from Châtillon aimed their machine guns cruelly low to strike Donovan's men first in the feet, then their heads when they fell.

Donovan, often leading at the front of companies to get men to move, pushed his regiment on toward Landres-et-Saint-Georges, deciding it could not be as bad ahead as it was where they lay. Tactically it was rash to press forward when his right flank was so exposed, but Donovan had little choice. He did not know exactly what MacArthur was doing on his right (conflicting reports came in during the day on whether Côte de Châtillon had been captured) and he wasn't about to give up ground paid for with so many casualties.

By afternoon, however, the advance had stalled. With more intense fire coming from two sides, the battalion commanders, unable even to shuttle their wounded to the rear, had their men crawl into shell holes for the evening, popping up to fire when they could. Donovan, who remained at the front as night fell for fear green troops might bolt in retreat, ordered another assault at the line of wire, hoping the German machine gunners would not see the wave coming in the darkness.

"The Germans remained silent until the front wave reached the first line of barbed wire," recalled a company commander. Then "a terrific machine gun fire and artillery fire was suddenly let loose by the enemy, and German flares transformed night into day." With his regiment perilously far ahead of the others, with MacArthur's slow-moving brigade unable to halt the enfilade fire, and with no artillery support coming from his own Army, Donovan dug in for the night, five hundred yards from the German line. He munched a raw onion and chewed on hardtack for his dinner.

Charles Pelot Summerall was angry. The detailed plan Menoher had so laboriously crafted, to which the corps commander had given his stamp of approval, had not been followed. The 42nd, which was known as the "Rainbow Division" because it was an amalgamation of National Guard units like Donovan's, was to have broken through the Kriemhilde Stellung quickly the first day. But by Tuesday morning, October 15, not a single brigade had breached the German defenses south of Saint-Georges and Landres-et-Saint-Georges. Donovan had advanced the furthest but he had conquered only a mile and a quarter of land, suffering an appalling number of casualties.

As a heavy mist hung in the air early Tuesday, Donovan sprinted from shell hole to shell hole realigning his forces and pumping up men exhausted and hungry. The regiment's attack began promptly at 7:30 A.M. Ten minutes later, as German machine gun fire raked the field, Donovan raced back to the hole where his telephone man lay.

It felt to him like someone had struck the back of his right leg with a spiked club. A machine gun bullet had slammed into his knee just below the joint, traveling clean through, shattering a hole in his tibia. Donovan fell like a log. He recovered a few minutes later from the shock and searing pain, clawing the dirt with his hands to crawl to his telephone hole. A machine gun lieutenant ripped open his breeches, poured antiseptic powder over his gaping wound, and bandaged it tightly to stop the bleeding.

Nauseated from the pain, Donovan refused to be evacuated and continued directing the attack, barking orders into the phone or scribbling them on a bloodstained message pad to be delivered to his battalion commanders. But the phone line to rear headquarters went dead. Messengers sent out were wounded or killed so messages remained undelivered. An enemy artillery shell exploded in a foxhole that had three men next to him, showering his hole with dirt and torn flesh. Thick, nasty clouds of gas poured in. The artillery barrage ended after an hour. Twenty-five tanks were supposed to arrive to roll over the barbed wire and make a hole for the infantry, but a combination of mechanical failure, hostile fire, and wounded drivers caused them to arrive late and eventually to turn back.

By 9 A.M., the assault had stalled once more. The corpses of two entire companies that had managed to advance near the barbed wire now lay dead before it or hung on the wire. MacArthur's brigade still had not halted flanking fire from Donovan's right and it now raked behind him, threatening to cut him off from rear elements.

With Summerall breathing down his neck, Lenihan at 10 A.M. issued a second order—a ridiculously unrealistic one considering the reality at the front. An artillery barrage would begin in fifteen minutes and end at noon when Donovan's regiment was to resume the attack. Mitchell tried to relay the order to Donovan, but the phone line to him remained cut and runners were delayed in reaching him with a written message.

Meanwhile, Donovan, carried by men from foxhole to foxhole to continue his command, decided his position was untenable—which it was. He had to move his regiment back or be completely cut off and wiped out. Mitchell's attack order finally reached Donovan at 12:05 A.M., but he considered it overtaken by events. The artillery barrage, which did not halt enemy frontal and flanking fire, had already ended. The remnants of the tank battalion had long since retreated. Donovan countermanded Mitchell's order. He continued pulling back his infantry to a more defensible position for the Germans' counterattack.

"I will assume the responsibility for you not going," he shouted to a battalion commander preparing to move his force forward.

Growing groggy from loss of blood, Donovan finally turned command over to a major and allowed four men to lug him back, slung in a blanket. One of them was wounded along the way when a machine gun bullet ripped through the blanket and struck him.

At a battalion first aid station a medic treated his leg and tied a tag to his toe identifying him. Stretcher-bearers hauled him by foot to the regimental dressing station about a mile to the rear where his wound was rebandaged. Duffy found him among the rows of litters.

"Father, you're a disappointed man," Donovan said with what cheer he could muster through the pain. "You expected to have the pleasure of burying me over here."

"I certainly did, Bill," the chaplain answered, "and you are a lucky dog to get off with nothing more than you've got."

Medics eventually hoisted his stretcher into an ambulance for a bumpy and painful ride over potholed roads to a rear hospital. Nurses there stripped off his uniform, gave him a tetanus shot, and rubbed his body with a warm sponge. It felt glorious.

At the operating table, surgeons decided they did not need to cut into him since the bullet had gone clean through and instead put his leg in a splint. Back in the ward, orderlies lifted him onto a bed with clean sheets. He could not remember the last time he'd slept in one. Beside him, an officer lay dying with a stomach wound; across from him, soldiers coming out of anesthesia asked nurses to hold their hands and smooth their brows. In the next ward was "a bedlam of delirium," he later wrote Ruth, from men wailing with painful wounds.

There was bedlam, as well, back at Donovan's unit. Enraged that for a second day the Kriemhilde Stellung had not been breached, Summerall on Tuesday evening stormed into the field headquarters for the 83rd Brigade and 165th Regiment and fired Lenihan and Mitchell. Both officers, Summerall concluded, had kept themselves too isolated in their command posts and had lost their aggressiveness to press the attack. (Ironically, Summerall did not find fault with the flashier MacArthur, who in this case had been a passive dugout commander.)

Would Donovan, who on his own halted the assault, have been fired if he had been at the command post? Summerall, who could be intimidating when he smelled indecisiveness in officers like Lenihan and Mitchell, probably would not have bullied the steely Donovan, who had faced far greater dangers in this war than a blowhard general and whose press clippings had earned him powerful political friends in New York.

But while Donovan lay in a hospital recovering from his wound, Menoher (who also conveniently escaped blame for his faulty battle plan) launched a formal investigation to determine whether the lieutenant colonel should be court-martialed for countermanding Mitchell's attack order. Lenihan and Mitchell protested their firings and in affidavits blamed the failed offensive on MacArthur dragging his feet for two days in securing their right flank. Mitchell also took a swipe at Donovan, hinting in his affidavit that Donovan's "painful wound" likely dulled his enthusiasm to continue the attack.

The 42nd Division cracked the Kriemhilde Stellung on October 16.

Duffy and the soldiers of the Irish Regiment remained bitter over Summerall's shabby treatment of them. After forty-seven days, Pershing finally drove through the Meuse-Argonne defenses, but at a cost of 120,000 casualties; the Irish regiment suffered another 1,110 killed or wounded. Germany's will to continue fighting soon broke; an armistice was signed November 11. Lenihan and Mitchell did not get back their commands. But the Army dropped its investigation of Donovan, concluding that he had received Mitchell's attack order too late to carry it out.

March 1919

DONOVAN, who had recovered from his leg wound by January, took his evening stroll with Father Duffy. He now walked with just a slight limp. The two men sauntered along the road paralleling the Rhine, which wound ahead through the gorge of the Siebengebirge mountain range near Bonn. The ruins of the Drachenfels castle looked down upon them and vineyards terraced along mountainsides.

Occupation duty the past four months had been boring. Donovan had been stuck in a staff job with the AEF's provost marshal general, which made him a glorified cop, managing military police and keeping idle American soldiers out of brothels and other assorted trouble spots in Germany. The martinets now put in command over the Irish Regiment and other fighting units showed little regard for the men who had survived such horrible combat, Donovan complained in letters to Ruth. He joined several dozen other officers in Paris to organize the American Legion, which would lobby for veterans' benefits and advocate a strong national defense. Donovan realized the allies had won the World War by the slimmest of margins. The German army that marched back to the Fatherland and surrendered its rifles numbered more than two hundred divisions "and they are in general the Prussians who do not approve of the armistice and who wish to continue the war," he wrote Ruth. He worried they would bide their time to fight again.

War had brought Donovan and Duffy together as close as brothers. They would often tease each other, as they did again during this evening's walk, over who had the most news stories written about him back home (both had a lot). Donovan thought Father Duffy was as close to a saint as he

would ever see, a man of God who had braved dangers as great as any infantryman to minister to his flock on the battlefield. Father Duffy thought
Donovan was the bravest leader he had ever met.

The chaplain maneuvered to have higher headquarters make Donovan,
who had just been promoted to full colonel, the commander of the Irish
Regiment. Duffy also mounted an intensive lobbying effort behind the
scenes to have Donovan awarded the Medal of Honor for the controversial battle at Landres-et-Saint-Georges. He collected affidavits from more
than a dozen regimental officers and noncommissioned officers attesting
to Donovan's heroism on October 14 and 15 and submitted them to AEF
headquarters.

The Army thought otherwise. In previous wars, more than 2,600 Medals of Honor had been passed out like candy, but by World War I the service had elevated the standard for the award considerably. It could now
go only to an officer who had "performed an extraordinary act of heroism, above and beyond his duty, of such brilliancy that the gallantry of the
deed stands out clearly and strikingly above those acts of his comrades."
Donovan's performance October 14 and 15 did not reach that bar. He had
fought heroically and as a senior officer had led from the front instead of
from the safer rear, refusing to be evacuated after a painful wound. But that
was his job. Donovan had performed no more heroically than other soldiers in the regiment who made that bloody assault and did not turn back.
(Pershing blocked a similar move to have MacArthur awarded a Medal of
Honor for his leadership at Côte de Châtillon, which the AEF commander
considered unremarkable.) Donovan also had the cloud of the countermanded order hanging over him. Instead of the Medal of Honor, Pershing
approved another second highest decoration, an Oak Leaf Cluster for the
Distinguished Service Cross he had earned at Ourcq River.

Donovan was ready to go home. Ruth had sent him news stories that
floated his name as a future candidate for governor of New York. That possibility excited her and at first intrigued Donovan. Ruth "would be a very
attractive and gracious" first lady of New York, he wrote her. But not now,
he decided.

He wanted to make money. He wanted to buy a grand house in Buffalo
to entertain friends. He wanted to hire a French governess for the children
and shop for fine clothes so he could "be a dandy," he wrote Ruth. He also
made clear to her that he wanted a "gladsome bride" when he returned.

"I know that your condition is due much to your mental state, but keep thinking that I am coming home, coming full of love and eagerness," he wrote. He urged her to be fitted for the latest diaphragm device doctors were prescribing (they should have no more children for a while) and buy "lots of fluffy lingerie. You must remember I have been a very righteous old man and it will be your duty to cheer and allure."

Donovan admitted he had been "a difficult husband," as he wrote Ruth in another letter, and he didn't know "of any other who could handle" him "so expertly" as she had. But he would change, he promised her. From now on he would be totally devoted to her. Nothing would come between them. He promised her a second honeymoon when he returned. "Pick where you would like to go and what you'd like to do." He would follow.

Escorted by a noisy flotilla of steamers and tugboats, the *Harrisburg* transport ship carrying Donovan and the first elements of the regiment docked at Hoboken on April 21, 1919. Ruth and Vincent stood at the pier to greet him. The days that followed were filled with welcoming ceremonies, a regimental parade up Fifth Avenue, and a key to the city from New York's Mayor John Francis Hylan. Broadway stars, such as opera soprano Lilian Breton and vaudevillian Sophie Tucker, entertained the men at evening banquets. The gaggle of reporters always following Donovan shouted questions: "Colonel, do you know they are all talking about you as a possible candidate for governor?"

"Governor!" Donovan exclaimed, pretending to be surprised. "Don't even think about it. I'm a lawyer and my chief aim in life just now is to get back to Buffalo and resume my practice."

Ruth rented a room at the Vanderbilt Hotel for the week, but Donovan spent little time there because festivities and the chores of garrisoning his men at nearby Camp Mills consumed practically every minute. As Vincent drove his brother to the camp the evening after the April 28 parade, emotions churning inside Donovan suddenly overwhelmed him. Fewer than half the regiment's men who had sailed to France returned. "When I think of all the boys I have left behind me who died out of loyalty to me, it's too much," he told Vincent. He lowered his head and wept.

Chapter 3

——◈——

The Prosecutor

T HE HIRED CAR, with Donovan and his wife in the back seat and their luggage piled in the trunk, sped along the Tokai-do High-way from Yokohama to Tokyo. Peering out the window, Donovan made mental notes of the activity he saw along the way: convoys of trucks hauling cedar logs from the interior, workers by the hundreds toiling in muddy rice fields wearing only loincloths, small carts on the road drawn by women, even children, delivery wagons attached to rubber-tired bicycles, young Japanese men in kimonos playing baseball in makeshift fields. Their automobile finally pulled up to the Imperial Hotel in Tokyo, where the couple checked in for the first stop on their second honeymoon.

Ruth, who left Patricia and David with her mother, had selected Asia for the trip Donovan had promised her. Donovan was only too happy to follow her. Asia was a burgeoning market for the West; he arranged business meetings along the way to explore opportunities his law firm might lucratively exploit.

For the next month, Bill and Ruth toured Japan, Korea, and China. Embassy officers in Peking briefed him on China's vast market awaiting Western business. Like America, Japan had emerged from the World War strengthened. But resentment toward the United States was building "because Japan felt that America was thwarting her in her ambitions in the Pacific," a U.S. diplomat told him. Hostility toward the United States was particularly intense within her military, warned a Japanese diplomat. Donovan filled notebooks with details.

When he was not playing intelligence agent, Donovan and Ruth saw the sights and toured museums. They attended elegant dinners at the U.S. embassies in each country, where diplomats made a fuss over Ruth—and slipped Donovan confidential business and political intelligence in private meetings. Then in mid-July, Donovan reneged on the promise he had so fervently made to Ruth in his war letters. He dumped her and took off for Siberia. Roland Morris, the U.S. ambassador to Japan, and General William Graves, the U.S. commander at Vladivostok, had been dispatched to Omsk to size up whether the White Russian forces led by Admiral Aleksandr Vasilyevich Kolchak had any chance of success in their war with Vladimir Lenin's Bolshevik army. Exactly how Donovan got on this trip remained a mystery. He claimed that John Lord O'Brien, his law partner and Woodrow Wilson confidant, asked him to go as a secret envoy at Wilson's behest because the president needed objective intelligence on Kolchak from a trained military man. But Graves had the military training and Donovan, a Republican hostile to Wilson, seemed hardly the ideal secret agent for the Democratic president. Morris claimed Donovan begged to join the mission and he finally relented since Donovan agreed to pay his own way. After two months in typhus-infested Omsk, Donovan concluded that Kolchak's government was cruelly corrupt but Washington's only hope for holding Siberia together against the Bolsheviks. He also warned that Japan had designs on the region. (Wilson's State Department paid little attention to Donovan's warnings when he later made the rounds in Washington.)

Ruth sailed back to the United States by herself, a bitter wife. Vincent noticed that she became "a different woman" after the Asia trip and he warned Donovan so. Ruth realized Donovan would not be the husband, or the father, that she had imagined she would have. She resolved to make her own life with her children, knowing that he would be only occasionally in the picture.

Buffalo was perfect for Donovan's ambitions. It had become the "Queen City of the Great Lakes," the eleventh largest in the country with a growing Roman Catholic and Republican population. With Bradley Goodyear, Donovan formed a new law firm whose clients included insurers from the old practice plus railroads and corporations from other parts of the state. Donovan bought a large home on fashionable Perry Street and went in with Ruth's brother, Dexter, on a summer cottage along the North Shore.

But Donovan's main focus, which often left his law partners breathless, was on making his Buffalo firm a national and international powerhouse rivaling the best in New York City. In the spring and summer of 1920, for example, he sailed to Europe as J. P. Morgan & Co.'s counsel to scout out foreign corporations for a Morgan-owned trading consortium and to collect intelligence on the Communist International. Donovan found economic and political turmoil in Germany, but no Comintern threat to the investment giant's billion-dollar plans.

His foreign travel regularly making the society pages, Donovan toyed with the idea of moving his family to London for a couple of years so he would be nearer to European business. It would do Ruth good to know the important people he'd met in Europe, to "loosen up a bit," as he wrote in one letter, and "above all get confidence in yourself and believe in the devotion of your husband." Ruth already was developing the confidence (she began taking foreign trips by herself, to exotic places like Tibet). It was the devotion of her husband that she wasn't so sure of. In their first eight years of marriage, Donovan had been home only eighteen uninterrupted months. He also continued to be solicitous and charming to female clients who found him such a good listener. Gossip persisted in Buffalo that Donovan offered more than his ear. Even Vincent began to worry about his brother's "erring" tendencies, as he once delicately put it.

AT THE BEGINNING of 1922, Donovan took another detour from corporate law. Senator Wadsworth, by now a close political friend whose campaign coffers Donovan regularly filled with checks, engineered his appointment as United States attorney for Buffalo and western New York. Donovan replaced a prosecutor who had run afoul of the state Anti-Saloon League. Donovan had never been particularly moralistic about alcohol but he now vowed to strictly enforce the Volstead Act. In Buffalo it was a hot topic. The city's crime rate had increased. Buffalo was a smuggling haven for rum and heroin runners from Canada. The local Ku Klux Klan, which allied with the Anti-Saloon League, set aside its anti-Catholic bigotry and praised Donovan's dry stand. On the other side, the Irish and other ethnic groups in Buffalo detested Prohibition and routinely violated it. What's more, Francis X. Schwab, a brewery owner and the city's mayor, backed the immigrants and fought the liquor ban. Donovan became a zealous prosecutor. He went after bootleggers, who sent him and his family death threats, he raided a Chinese opium kingpin who was paying off Buffalo cops, cracked down on coal profiteers, prosecuted strikers who had dynamited a rail line, and even had Schwab in court on liquor violation charges.

Being a U.S. attorney was not a full-time job. Donovan remained a partner in his law firm with Goodyear. In August 1922, state Republican leaders talked him into running for lieutenant governor with incumbent Governor Nathan Miller, but the Democratic ticket headed by Alfred E. Smith easily defeated them. Donovan also continued to roam Europe, taking a three-month Mediterranean excursion with Ruth in early 1923. He made a side trip to inflation-wracked Berlin, where diplomats briefed him on a young extremist named Adolf Hitler who was leading the National Socialist German Workers' Party in Munich.

Before he left for Europe, Donovan squeezed into his colonel's uniform, which he could still do at age forty, to attend a ceremony at his old regiment's armory in New York City. Father Duffy had not given up his lobbying to have his friend awarded the Medal of Honor and the stars now lined up in Donovan's favor. As Army chief of staff, Pershing had become more liberal about awarding the medal. Republican Warren Harding was in the White House. Donovan's patron, Wadsworth, chaired the Senate Military Affairs Committee and had been pestering the War Department to bestow Medals of Honor on members of the regiment. John Weeks, Harding's war secretary, approved the award—four years after the armistice.

Some four thousand World War veterans crowded into the armory. When Major General Robert Lee Bullard draped the Medal of Honor around Donovan's neck they broke into a long and loud cheer. Donovan was now the only man to win the Army's top three awards in the World War. Even more so, this medal was vindication for the regiment's humiliation at Landres-et-Saint-Georges. Donovan recognized as much. His face flushed, he pivoted on his heel and called the regiment to attention. He unsnapped the ribbon from his neck and presented the medal to the unit. "It doesn't belong to me," he said quietly. "It belongs to the boys who are not here, the boys who are resting under the white crosses in France or in the cemeteries of New York, also to the boys who were lucky enough to come through." He left the medal with the armory.

———

DONOVAN STOOD BY the switchboard outside his U.S. attorney's office, his shirtsleeves rolled up. It was a muggy Thursday night, August 2, 1923. Federal liquor agents gathered around waiting for him to give the order for the raid. Among the many Buffalo establishments that routinely ignored Prohibition was the prestigious Saturn Club on Delaware Avenue. Its members, the city's wealthy and powerful, kept their liquor stored in private lockers, taking the bottles out to mix their own drinks in the men's grill room and bar. Or they hauled up cases of booze from the basement for lavish Roaring Twenties parties. The Saturn Club's flouting of the law was the worst kept secret in Buffalo. The city's lower-class griped: Why were federal agents always raiding their saloons while ignoring watering holes for the rich? It put Donovan in an awkward position. He had not given up his membership in the Saturn Club when he became U.S. attorney—though he should have—and he knew the imbibing was going on there. Donovan had warned the club's leaders he could not ignore the illegal drinking much longer and was finally forced to act when a bootlegger he had hauled before a grand jury testified he was the club's supplier. The jurors expected Donovan to raid Saturn along with the other saloons the bootlegger listed as customers.

"Go ahead, boys," Donovan ordered, signing the search warrant application. "I've warned these fellows three times. For all their prestige, they are no better than East Side saloons."

Shortly before 11 P.M., as its members had their nightcaps in the grill room, black cars screeched to a stop in front of the Saturn Club and a half dozen liquor agents rushed in, confiscating twelve quarts of whiskey, twenty quarts of gin, several bottles of champagne, and five gallons of cheap grain alcohol. The federal men then launched a second raid at the Buffalo Country Club on Main Street, where they confiscated $5,000 worth of liquor. Donovan also belonged to that club.

Both clubs eventually plea-bargained a settlement, which resulted in $500 fines for each and no one sent to jail. But a political firestorm erupted, which shocked Donovan. Newspapers carried banner headlines on the raids. Donovan was praised or cursed. Working folks were delighted to see the upper crust served with the same justice. But Donovan became a pariah among the city's elite. He quickly learned who his real friends were and they weren't many. Both clubs now received him with stony silence and hostile stares. Goodyear, who was a Saturn member and livid over the raid, pulled out of their law firm, which deeply hurt Donovan. A delegation from the club went to another younger partner, Frank Raichle, and told him he had better leave Donovan's firm or he would "never get anywhere as a lawyer." Raichle told them "to go to hell," and stuck with Donovan. But he was jeered when he entered the club.

Dexter was furious with his brother-in-law for putting the Rumsey family in this awkward spot. So was Ruth. The whispering campaign—always out there among many who were jealous that Donovan had achieved a social status they didn't think he deserved—now intensified. Donovan had no right to be holier than thou on liquor considering his womanizing, detractors sniped. "He is just a cheap Irish nobody from the wrong side of the railroad tracks, who only became of some importance when he married a socially prominent woman with lots of money," sneered one. "He is interested in nothing but chasing women and having a good time." Ruth heard the talk and it infuriated her. She never fully forgave her husband for the raid.

Chapter 4

$\approx$

Politics

DONOVAN'S POLITICAL CAREER in Buffalo was over after the Saturn Club raid. His law practice there was nearly ruined. He wasn't run out of town but he might as well have been. His prospects looked dim until Calvin Coolidge came to his rescue a year later. A humorless former Massachusetts governor picked as Harding's vice president, Coolidge was nevertheless a good government politician who, when he assumed the presidency in 1923 after Harding died, quickly cleaned house of Harding holdovers tainted by the Teapot Dome scandal. Among the men he cashiered: Attorney General Harry Daugherty. At one point, Donovan, whose Saturn raid had made him a celebrity outside Buffalo, was rumored as Coolidge's choice to replace Daugherty. That sent the politically powerful Klan to battle stations over the prospect of a Roman Catholic being in the cabinet. Coolidge instead made Harlan Stone, Donovan's mentor from Columbia Law School, his top legal officer and Donovan Stone's assistant attorney general over the department's criminal division.

The aloof New England academic and the Irish glad-hander proved a perfect match. Stone wanted an assistant to crack down on what he believed was growing lawlessness across the country from bootleggers and drug traffickers. Donovan had earned his spurs as a crime-busting prosecutor. A Buffalo newspaper reported that the city's underworld was as glad to see him go as high society.

Donovan, who won easy Senate confirmation, bought a stately brick two-story in Georgetown that looked like an English country manor. His starting salary at Justice was only $7,500 a year, and the couple decided to keep their home in Buffalo, to which Donovan planned to return often for his law firm business. Ruth also later bought a sprawling lodge in the upper-class resort village of Nonquitt, Massachusetts. It had nine bedrooms and a wide front porch that offered a perfect view of Buzzards Bay. Nonquitt became her and the children's refuge from Washington's oppressive heat each summer. Donovan at first spent many weekends there sailing and playing tennis but soon tapered off because he found the beach house boring.

With his usual vigor, Donovan plunged into his new job. He filled his staff with bright young attorneys with strong opinions (he did not want to be surrounded by yes-men) and hired women lawyers, which was rarely done. Any chance he could, he fled Washington to join in liquor raids around the country, one time flying in a Navy dirigible over the Caribbean to track rum runners. Ruth reveled in Washington's social life and became as politically ambitious for Donovan as he was. Weekends were filled with dinner parties and luncheons at their Georgetown home for economists, authors, poets, entertainers, and assorted cabinet officers like Commerce Secretary Herbert Hoover (a regular invitee who became a close friend of Donovan's). Ruth proved to be a delightful hostess, although more shy and self-effacing than her extrovert husband. Quickly the rakishly handsome Justice man and his classy wife became favorite invitees for media, congressional, and embassy parties.

No senior official could work in Washington and not make enemies, and it wasn't long before Donovan began accumulating his share. But although he did not realize it at the time, his most implacable foe in the future would be a somewhat neurotic young attorney who had just taken over the Justice Department's Bureau of Investigation.

John Edgar Hoover could not have been more different from Donovan. He was a bachelor, obsessed with cleanliness, and sensitive about being short. He lived with his mother, was never talented in sports, went to night school to earn his law degree, and got a draft exemption from the Army to serve as a Justice Department clerk. A stylish dresser (one trait he did share with Donovan), Hoover had ascended quickly in the department, showing a flair for hunting down suspects and keeping meticulous files. Daugherty had made him assistant chief of the Bureau of Investigation, a collection largely of political cronies, alcoholics, and incompetent detectives who investigated white-collar crimes and spied on suspected communists or sometimes the department's political enemies. Hoover convinced the newly arrived Stone, who knew the bureau had an "exceedingly bad odor," that he was the man to clean it up. Hoover did just that, professionalizing the force. But Stone first kept him on a short leash, making the twenty-nine-year-old lawyer only the acting director and putting Donovan over him to keep watch.

Hoover, who had scoped out Donovan before he even arrived at Justice, considered his new boss an empire-building dilettante, not too skilled in the courtroom, and a poor administrator. Instead of leaving Hoover alone to run his own show, Donovan began meddling in his bureau and overturning decisions with which he disagreed. Donovan considered Hoover an unimaginative civil servant, good on detail but sorely lacking in vision. It was not long before both men began keeping files on each other—Hoover maintained his dossier, filled with dirt and gossip, for the rest of Donovan's life.

J. Edgar Hoover soon had Donovan out of his hair, however. Stone moved to the Supreme Court in March 1925 and Coolidge replaced him not with Donovan, as Ruth wanted and many news stories speculated he would do, but rather with John Garibaldi Sargent, a fellow New Englander who turned out to be fairly lazy. As a consolation prize Donovan was made the third highest official at Justice as assistant to the attorney general and head of the antitrust division. Hoover then deftly maneuvered to have his bureau report directly to the attorney general. For long stretches, however, Donovan ended up being the de facto attorney general. Sargent spent more time at his Vermont home than in Washington and the number two man, Solicitor General William Mitchell, was consumed with Supreme Court cases, which left Donovan to run the department. Like his president, Donovan was a free marketer who tried first to cajole corporations to eliminate unfair trade practices instead of taking them to court. Even so, he prosecuted sixty-five major Sherman and Clayton antitrust act cases during the next four years and proved adept with the high-profile ones before the Supreme Court. No one would accuse him of being a legal scholar, but Donovan argued well, almost with boyish enthusiasm, before the High Court, which impressed the justices.

Donovan quickly became a favorite of the Washington press corps; he delighted reporters with colorful, on-the-record quotes and juicy gossip off the record. Wadsworth and home state newspapers talked him up in 1926 as a New York gubernatorial candidate. (Donovan at first was eager for the GOP nomination but eventually begged off when he did not have the convention votes, which was just as well. Incumbent Al Smith had a lock on reelection.) The *New York Times* next floated his name as a vice presidential candidate in the 1928 election. Douglas MacArthur, who now commanded the Army's 3rd Corps in Baltimore and had become a Donovan pen pal, wrote him that his "old friends in the Army" wanted him to be secretary of war.

Donovan, however, was angling for a much more important cabinet post in the next administration. He had become a key campaign adviser and speechwriter for Herbert Hoover, the Republicans' presidential nominee. In the summer of 1928, Hoover had pulled Donovan aside in the garden of his Georgetown home and said "of course you're going to be the attorney general" if he won. But after Hoover trounced Al Smith in the election, he reneged on his promise and put Mitchell, Coolidge's solicitor general, in charge of Justice. Powerful forces had lined up against Donovan: Southerners who would not stand for a Catholic attorney general, prohibitionists who considered him a closet wet despite his Saturn Club fame, Democratic enemies in the Senate poised to fight his nomination, and J. Edgar Hoover, who had buttonholed the president-elect's press secretary to bad-mouth him. Herbert Hoover, who became incensed over news stories accusing him of anti-Catholic bias, also claimed he rejected Donovan because he lacked administrative experience. The best he would offer him was governor of the Philippines. Insulted, Donovan considered it political exile and refused the post. Ruth believed her husband's greatest disappointment ever was being denied the attorney generalship. For as long as he lived, Donovan harbored a grudge against Hoover for double-crossing him.

DONOVAN RESIGNED FROM the Justice Department in March 1929 and moved to New York City, where, with $100,000 in seed money, he formed a new law firm with his Buffalo partner, Frank Raichle, and staffed it as he had at Justice with energetic young lawyers, many from the Coolidge administration. The stock market crash eight months after he opened shop and the Great Depression that followed drained hundreds of thousands of dollars from his personal portfolio and caused the firm to struggle at first, but Donovan soon found a niche, handling legal details for the many mergers, acquisitions, and bankruptcies that come with an economic downturn and working the other side of the fence defending trade associations, oil companies, and coal mine owners facing government antitrust suits. Donovan also accumulated Hollywood clients, such as Jane Wyman and Mae West, many of them introduced to him by Vincent, who was ministering to stars in Los Angeles. Within ten years his firm, which eventually moved into two floors of offices at 2 Wall Street, was grossing more than $800,000 annually with over forty associates on the payroll, making its founder a millionaire. Donovan, who hated the drudgery of legal work and concentrated mostly on bringing in business or arguing the big cases that went to the Supreme Court, worked in regal style. A barber came in every morning to shave him and clip his hair, lunch was served to him in one of the city's exclusive clubs, a tea trolley rolled by his office in the afternoon with Earl Grey, and a chauffeured limousine brought him home at night.

DONOVAN HAD RUTH meet him at the pier when he returned from Germany in the summer of 1932. He had traveled to Berlin to scout business opportunities but prospects there seemed grim. Germany had been hammered even harder by the worldwide depression and the Nazi Party controlled the largest number of seats in the fractured Reichstag. But Donovan had politics at home on his mind. Rumors circulated in New York political circles that he and Ruth were separated, which could be damaging just now. He wanted her at his side to be framed in the shots photographers were taking of him at the pier. Ruth was more than willing to pose with him. She, too, wanted the prize he now sought.

As his law practice built up, Donovan had hit the lecture circuit, delivering red-meat speeches before Republican audiences, accusing New York's governor, Franklin Roosevelt, of being a "crafty" politician who ignored corruption in state government. He caught the eye once more of New York GOP leaders, who approached Donovan about running for governor. This time he was interested. A New York governor was always one of the country's most powerful political figures outside of Washington. The position had been the launching pad for national campaigns. Roosevelt, who Donovan thought had compiled a lackluster record in Albany, was now running for president. Donovan as well saw it as the best stepping-stone for what he wanted most—to be the nation's first Roman Catholic president.

Donovan privately bet that FDR would beat Hoover, who he thought had been politically inept in dealing with the depression. Winning the governorship might be sweet revenge. It would prove he was electable and Hoover was not. Donovan's Republican allies believed Hoover had calculated as much and warned him of rumors that the president was pressuring the New York party to deny him the nomination.

If Hoover did in fact lean on the state party, he wasn't successful. Donovan was nominated by acclamation at an enthusiastic GOP convention in October with New York assemblyman F. Trubee Davison as his running mate. Donovan knew he faced an uphill fight. His opponent was Roosevelt's liberal lieutenant governor, Herbert Lehman, who was popular in the state and benefited from the anger that depression-weary voters nationwide felt toward the Republican Party. He began barnstorming New York, papering the state with flyers that urged voters to "put a fighting man in the governor's chair." Ruth always kept a smile on her face for photographers and hosted an obligatory tea for six hundred Republican women at her mother's Delaware Avenue mansion. But though she wanted to be New York's first lady, she spent much of the fall with the children in Nonquitt instead of at her husband's side.

Political friends assured Donovan he was a shoe-in. His campaign even composed a victory song—"Wild Bill Donovan, there's magic in the name," went one verse. Donovan should have been leery of the optimists. He was "an awful campaigner," a horrified Davison said after appearing at several events with him. "The minute he'd get up on the platform he'd lose his great charm and his Irish wit," Donovan's running mate complained. "He just kind of froze up and got to be a statesman and that wasn't what they were looking for." His political organization also began hopelessly disorganized. Edward Bernays, a New York public relations consultant brought in to draft a campaign plan, left after a week when he couldn't pry Donovan away from the horde of county chairmen and party patrons he seemed to always want around him, who were pulling him in every direction. Donovan was "busy being busy," Bernays said. His idea of running for governor was "having a cavalcade of cars go from place to place" for speeches, but with no thought given to a strategy for winning.

Donovan nevertheless campaigned nonstop for a month, attacking Lehman as Roosevelt's "Siamese twin" who would sink state government in debt. Like all good Republicans of his day, Donovan believed low taxes, budget cuts, and the free market would pull the country out of the depression, not Roosevelt's New Deal. Donovan also began to go after FDR, calling him a Hyde Park "faker" claiming to be for the working man but really a "new kind of red, white and blue dictator" with "delusions of grandeur." He ridiculed Roosevelt's claim in one speech that the two had been friends in law school. "I was a youngster earning my way through law school and he never knew me," Donovan sneered.

Roosevelt fired back, accusing Donovan of being in bed with New York public utility interests he had represented as a lawyer. FDR also had surrogates rough him up. Eleanor Roosevelt took pot shots at Donovan while stumping for Lehman. James Farley, chairman of the Democratic National Committee, sniped that Donovan "is evidently losing his head" by attacking FDR. Labor unions accused him of "persecuting" their movement when he had prosecuted union agitators as U.S attorney.

Donovan, exhausted, woke up early Tuesday morning November 8 and with Ruth walked across the street from the Delaware Avenue mansion to a polling station to vote. Party leaders believed that in the closing days of the campaign he had narrowed the gap with Lehman and overtaken him. The evening before he had delivered his final radio address to the state from Buffalo, then paid a visit to First Ward. A huge crowd had gathered on Elk Street to cheer him, many of them friends he had known since boyhood.

"I am just a First Ward boy who has been nominated for the highest office of the state," Donovan said, choked up with emotion, his voice hoarse from so many speeches. "I have received some mighty nice receptions, but there has been none that has made me happier than this."

Shortly before nine o'clock Tuesday night, Donovan sent a congratulatory cable to Lehman at Tammany Hall. State party leaders blamed the sweep on Hoover, not Donovan. Lehman had soundly beaten him by 18 percentage points, slightly better than Roosevelt's margin of victory over Hoover in the state. Donovan won upstate but Lehman swamped him in New York City. Even more humiliating for Donovan, he lost Buffalo by more than seventeen thousand votes. The Saturn Club raid had not been forgotten.

Chapter 5

—⟋⟋⟍—

Family

WHEN THEY MOVED to New York, Bill and Ruth had bought a pricey duplex at One Beekman Place overlooking the East River, staffing it with servants and filling it with expensive furniture selected by a professional decorator. Fine china and silver always graced their dinner table. A grand piano in the living room was played for the many parties. Donovan, who always traveled first class, had no more concept of a family budget than he did a business one. Ruth's money paid for Beekman Place and she began to quarrel with him over the huge amounts he spent. But it was the least of their problems. By the 1930s, their family had begun to go its separate ways, coming together only for holidays, which were more quick drop-bys for Donovan, who was always on the go.

As a teenager, David was packed off to boarding school at Saint Georges in Newport, Rhode Island, where he was indifferent about his studies and resentful at being separated from his parents. In 1938, Ruth bought the Chapel Hill farm near the town of Berryville, which was part of Virginia's upper-crust horse country west of Washington. Its Federal-style farmhouse, which sat atop a gently rising hill with a spring running through it and a spectacular view of the Blue Ridge Mountains, had been built in the mid-1820s with native stone quarried from its five-hundred-acre farm. Donovan hired a Washington architect for extensive renovations, which included adding a library, joining outside slave quarters to the main building, and installing a ten-foot-high, walk-in bank vault in the basement, where Ruth could keep jewelry and Donovan could store secret documents. But Ruth bought the farm not for her or her husband, but rather for their son.

Shy and sensitive like Ruth, David by the time he began college was far closer to his mother than to his father, whom he considered practically a stranger. David was proud of his father but he wanted no part of the high-powered life he led. Instead David wanted to be a simple farmer.

Though he professed to Ruth that he was just as proud of his son, Donovan was disappointed with him. He had sent him to Harvard hoping he would follow him into the law, but David dropped out after two years (the university politely termed it an "honorable dismissal") and enrolled in Cornell, where he stayed only a year to learn enough about agriculture so he could start growing wheat and breeding Angus cattle at Chapel Hill.

Donovan was far closer to Patricia, who had his strong-willed, outgoing personality, and who had always loved sports, the outdoors, and riding horses with her father. As a teenager she attended Rosemary Hall (Ruth's alma mater) in Connecticut. Later as a young woman, she began filling in for Ruth as hostess for her father's parties.

It was while Patricia was attending Wellesley College that she often brought home to Chapel Hill or to the Beekman Place apartment in New York her best friend from Rosemary Hall, Mary Grandin. The daughter of a prominent family in Warren County, Pennsylvania, Mary now went to Mount Holyoke College. She was a smart, beautiful, and vivacious brunette, who spoke fair French, enjoyed English literature and photography, and was a good shot with a rifle. And it didn't take many visits to the Donovans before she became smitten, as many young women were, with Patricia's glamorous father—so much so that gossip spread in New York circles and Berryville that she was one of Donovan's girlfriends. That was not the case. To Donovan, Mary was just Patricia's best friend—and soon to be his daughter-in-law.

By the beginning of 1939, Mary had fallen in love with David. They married on June 17 in Warren County. Patricia was the maid of honor and Vincent helped officiate. Afterward, the young couple settled into Chapel Hill with Ruth to run the busy farm. But malicious gossip continued that Donovan had married Mary to his son to continue his affair with her.

Her hair beginning to turn prematurely gray by the early 1930s, Ruth continued to be treated by Timothy for illnesses and insomnia caused by loneliness. She was only infrequently at her husband's side during parties and vacationed almost always without him. During a six-month tour of Europe with Patricia in 1930 she received "electric treatments" that doctors there had begun to use for depression cases, but wrote Donovan that "so far" she had felt "no result from it." The electroshock therapy was not helped by the fact that Donovan wrote her infrequently, which made her sad, and canceled a trip to join them because of business.

After David's wedding, Ruth boarded the *Yankee*, a two-masted, ninety-two-foot schooner home-ported in Gloucester, to sail around the world. She had sailed on the *Yankee* two years before for the Asian leg of its world voyage and enjoyed the rugged life on board, manning the sails and even cooking in the galley. David had joined her for that voyage before entering Cornell. He worked as a crewman in the boat's small engine room and discovered he had mechanical aptitude.

Donovan was delighted with his wife's independence. "I am proud of what you have done," he wrote her during her voyage. Striking out on her own, he believed, not only "will bring you great contentment," it will make the two of them appreciate each other more.

But the separate lives Donovan was comfortable with came at a price. He was furious when Ruth decided to have a risky hysterectomy in 1939 without consulting him—although he had no grounds for complaint considering he was not around much to consult. "I had two objections," he wrote her in an indignant letter. "First that you did not think enough of me to mention it and, second, that you used some rotten judgment and so utterly disregarded consequences with anyone else."

Donovan loved Ruth, but he loved his dalliances as well. Among New York society ladies—married and unmarried—Donovan became a darling. He occasionally took their divorce cases, such as Helen Astor's split from Vincent, always charming the aggrieved wife with his empathy. He became close friends with activist journalist Dorothy Thompson. At the "21" Club he partied with Marion Davies, a film actress and William Randolph Hearst's mistress. Much of it was innocent. Unlike his chauvinistic colleagues, Donovan liked having women as friends and treated them as equals, which made him all the more attractive to them. Ruth joked with him about the gossip he stirred. But she was sure that he took some of these friendships a step further—which he sometimes did—and it understandably angered her. She confided to her friends about "his girls," as she derisively put it. She resented the "damned fool" women who threw themselves at Bill. And it was during the late 1930s that her husband pursued his most serious affair.

The midnight reception that Donovan threw at his Beekman Place apartment for New York's glitterati made the society columns. Poets, politicians, business tycoons, and the wives of the powerful gathered around the pianist entertaining them and enjoyed lobster Newburg at the candlelit buffet. Patricia served as Donovan's hostess in Ruth's absence. As the black-tie party got into full swing, the beautiful and glamorous Becky Hamilton made her entrance, sweeping down the circular staircase into the living room wearing a stunning off-the-shoulder black gown with swirling inserts of lace.

A Wellesley graduate and now an editor at *Harper's Bazaar*, Rebecca Stickney Hamilton had married Pierpont Morgan Hamilton, a nephew of J. P. Morgan, in 1930. She had a reputation for being "a little bit fast and a touch cheap," recalled Mary Bancroft, who as a young teenager had swooned when Donovan marched by her with his regiment during the Fifth Avenue parade after the World War and who now was a close friend of Becky's. "She wore red suits and she was one of the first girls I knew to use a certain kind of matching red lipstick," a clear sign of the times that she would play around. Mary also found that "there was really something tough and calculating about Becky for all her good looks and cheerful charm." Becky, Mary thought, used people and no one more so than Mary, who helped arrange her trysts.

By 1939, Becky's marriage to Pierpont was headed for the rocks and she was having a steamy love affair with Donovan. When Donovan was in Europe the two would meet in Switzerland. Becky would use the excuse that she was visiting Mary, who was living there with her husband, Swiss financier Jean Rufenacht. After one rendezvous Mary set up for the lovebirds, Becky had sent her a black lace nightgown as a thank-you gift, which the jealous Rufenacht was sure had come from a man. He threw it into the furnace.

Becky had fallen madly in love with the manly Donovan. At one point she wanted him to divorce Ruth and marry her. With Becky's driving ambition and Donovan's star power, she was convinced she could put him in the White House. Donovan, who had fallen hard for Becky as well, realized that would never happen if he divorced and remarried. By the end of the 1930s the two lovers had drifted apart.

Ruth learned of the affair. This time, she had a serious talk with Donovan about whether they should divorce. Donovan, who was over Becky, did not want one. And in the end neither did Ruth. She was from the old school; when you married you were supposed to stay married and put up with all the problems. Marriage was as sacred as a business contract and you do not break a contract.

Chapter 6

—✺—

War Clouds

DONOVAN BROUGHT THE rifle to his right eye and squinted through its sight to take a bead on the ram some seven hundred yards away. He exhaled softly, then gently squeezed off a round. The Indian guide crouched next to him peered through his binoculars and confirmed a likely kill. It was a triumphant end to an adventurous expedition Donovan had taken with Sears, Roebuck chairman General Robert E. Wood and two other business executives into Canada's Yukon Territory. For three glorious weeks the four men had ridden horseback (with attendants leading a long mule train of supplies behind them) through the Yukon's rugged mountains with their snow-capped peaks, cliffs serrated by glaciers, winding icy rivers, and gusty winds blowing siltlike dust through canyons. By day they had hunted Dall sheep, moose, and grizzly bear. Donovan had already bagged another ram at three hundred yards and a nine-foot grizzly. At night cooks prepared feasts of fresh lake trout, roasted wild duck, lamb cutlets, hot fluffy biscuits, ears of corn, and cole slaw, topped off with lemon pie, glasses of Scotch, and cigars.

Near midnight, the exhausted men sat in a tent at a card table playing their last round of bridge (Donovan usually lost and owed money). Early the next morning they would begin the four-day ride by horseback to a landing field, where a plane would take them back to civilization. An Indian guide opened the tent flap, pulled an envelope out of his pocket, and handed it to Wood. The cable inside was dated September 1, 1939, from Juneau, Alaska. "Warfare started today between Poland and Germany," it read. That Friday morning, September 1, German planes and tanks employing novel blitzkrieg tactics had stormed across the border and quickly overrun poorly prepared Polish forces.

Donovan and the other three had been in a news blackout the past three weeks, but around campfires they had discussed often the territory Hitler had been grabbing in Europe. His rearmed army had reoccupied the Rhineland in March 1936. In March 1938 he had marched German troops into Austria for the *Anschluss*. He annexed the Sudetenland in western Czechoslovakia six months later and six months after that his tanks rolled into Prague. England and France, which had done little more than protest up to that point, finally threatened military action if Germany conquered any more small states. Donovan and the three others, nevertheless, were startled by the cable that lay before them on the card table. Up to that point, Donovan had felt that Hitler was Europe's problem, that the United States should remain neutral and on its side of the Atlantic. But with England and France declaring war on Germany—which they did that day, September 3—Donovan knew it would be only a matter of time before America intervened.

Europe and the threat of war had been engaging more of Donovan's time and travel. His secretary always kept in his office a bag packed with his passport so he could take off on just twenty minutes notice, which Donovan did often in the 1930s. He took Pan American Airways' first transatlantic flight to Marseilles by its giant Dixie Clipper seaplane, dining on turtle soup, steaks, and ice cream and receiving a silver cigarette case to commemorate the maiden trip. Before he boarded the plane, however, Donovan had a rigger come to Beekman Place to show him how to use a parachute. During his European and Asian trips he studied rearmament among future belligerents, becoming part of an informal network of American businessmen and lawyers who closely tracked and collected intelligence on foreign affairs. Donovan, recalled a friend, also was "not happy if there is a war on the face of the earth, and he has not had a look at it."

One such foray occurred in November 1935 as he tended to legal work, which included a boring coal mine lawsuit and a more interesting dispute a client had with retired actress Mary Pickford. Donovan was eager for a break to tour the Ethiopian front. Italy's fascist dictator, Benito Mussolini, had invaded Ethiopia the month before with grand visions of restoring the Roman Empire. Donovan's law partners were not enthusiastic about the trip. But he aggressively lobbied Italy's ambassador to Washington, arguing that he wanted to tour the war zone as a Republican representative, so if the GOP beat Roosevelt in 1936 his party "would be accurately advised" on the Abyssinian conflict. Mussolini agreed to meet Donovan, not completely buying his line that he was a party envoy but believing the Italians could milk some propaganda from the trip. Douglas MacArthur, now Army chief of staff, thought the excursion had some value, as long as his old friend paid his own way (which Donovan was more than willing to do, drawing from the law firm till). MacArthur's Military Intelligence Service had been unable to get its spies to the Italian front and had a long list of questions for Donovan to answer.

The day after Christmas, an elderly usher in a black Prince Albert coat opened the doors to a large ballroom with high ceilings in Rome's Venetian Palace. At the furthest end sat Mussolini at a plain table, a lamp on it lit, not looking up from papers he was reading. Donovan made the long walk toward him, the clicking of his heels on the marble floor echoing in the huge chamber.

Il Duce finally glanced up as Donovan neared the desk. His chin jutting out, his dark eyes bulging from his shaved head, the dictator rose from his table. He strutted around it to greet the American, pointed to a seat, then returned to his own chair.

"You were in France during the war?" asked Mussolini, who spoke English.

"Yes," Donovan replied.

"For how long?"

"Nineteen months"

"Wounded?" Mussolini asked, lifting his eyebrows.

"Yes."

"How many times?"

"Three times."

Mussolini seemed impressed. "What is your impression of Italy?" he asked.

"Tranquil," Donovan said simply, with a smile.

"Oh, yes," the dictator agreed, "it is quiet."

"Unity of spirit," Donovan added, trying to slather on the charm.

"Yes! Yes!" Mussolini agreed, becoming somewhat excited.

But "of the spirit of the soldier I cannot tell," Donovan hedged.

"Oh, you will see that," Il Duce assured him. Donovan now knew he would be allowed into Ethiopia. He had not been completely sure up to that point.

Donovan wanted to see Mussolini's forces in action now, he told the dictator, "because I did not think much of your troops in the World War—neither the discipline of the men nor the quality of the officers."

"It is different now and you will see a vast change," Mussolini said, eyes blazing.

"If Italy is to have a new empire she must have a new Tenth Legion," Donovan said, knowing that would push his hot button. On the voyage over he had read this would-be Caesar's autobiography.

"That is right!" Mussolini said, almost shouting.

The dictator probed Donovan on American public opinion toward Italy and its invasion of Ethiopia. He also picked Donovan's brain about the political climate in the United States, inquiring whether he thought Roosevelt would be reelected.

"I cannot tell," Donovan answered. "The next few months will decide."

"Mr. Roosevelt is popular?"

"Yes."

"With whom."

"The left of labor, the left of the farmers, and the great mass of those who want something for nothing."

"And recovery now comes to you by reason of the New Deal policies?"

"In spite of them," Donovan gave him the partisan Republican answer.

"Oh!" Mussolini said, rising from his chair, laughing and repeating: "In spite of them."

The dictator approved clearances for Donovan to inspect Italian forces in Ethiopia. "We are not afraid to have an impartial observer," Il Duce insisted.

Donovan toured Ethiopia for two weeks inspecting front lines, arms depots, artillery positions, motor pools, field hospitals, and airfields. He interviewed hundreds of Italian officers up and down the chain of command, spent hours with Marshal Pietro Badoglio, whom he had already met during one of the general's visits to the United States and who was now busy trying to drive back a Christmas counteroffensive by Ethiopian Emperor Haile Selassie. Donovan wrote detailed reports on everything he saw and heard, concluding that the Italian army was "vastly improved" from the World War with superior equipment and soldiers who would easily conquer Ethiopia.

British defense officials who read Donovan's report thought he exaggerated Italian military prowess. The War Department, however, was delighted with his intelligence. (Donovan also managed to work in a little business on the side, hooking up Italian diplomats with American businessmen who still wanted to invest in Italy.) His prediction of an Italian victory proved to be the case. In fact, Donovan seemed almost too effusive in his forecast, praising Badoglio's generalship to reporters and sending him a gushy private note congratulating him on his "great victory"—which took the marshal five months to achieve with Italian planes dropping poison gas on the helpless Ethiopians. But more importantly, Donovan was establishing himself as a player in international affairs—and honing his skills as an intelligence gatherer overseas.

FBI agents, who tracked the Ethiopian venture, sent J. Edgar Hoover regular reports on Donovan's overseas travel, which by 1939 had been extensive, particularly to Germany. Hoover suspected that Donovan, who often went to Berlin representing clients, was collaborating with the Nazis. Donovan, who signed a petition in 1933 protesting German government dismissals of Jewish judges, was actually trying to protect clients, such as Rothschild bankers in Austria, from the Nazis.

Donovan also developed a network of German informants, such as Berlin lawyer Paul Leverkühn, who slipped him political intelligence and set up meetings with key German officers. One important appointment Leverkühn arranged on a Berlin trip Donovan made shortly before his Yukon expedition was with Walter Warlimont, a handsome and energetic colonel on the German General Staff who would eventually become a top Wehrmacht general. The two men spent hours in a Berlin apartment, with Warlimont talking freely about Hitler's strategic aims in Italy and the Balkans. Donovan quietly listened.

NEAR THE END of January 1940, Donovan sat in a New York radio studio with actor Pat O'Brien plugging the Warner Brothers release of *The Fighting 69th*, an overdramatized movie about the regiment in the World War. Donovan loved Irish star George Brent, who played him in the film. O'Brien played Father Duffy, who had died in 1932. The release of *The Fighting*

69*th* had made Donovan once more a national celebrity, whom FDR was becoming more interested in using for his own political purposes.

Donovan had been a persistent critic of Roosevelt's first term in office, accusing him in speeches before GOP faithful of being an undemocratic, destructive, big-spending liberal. His New Deal was a "racketeering attempt" to create prosperity, which unfairly soaked the rich with more taxes, threatened family values, and bordered on being communistic. But by the beginning of 1940, Roosevelt was quietly moving the country to a war footing and fighting isolationists who denounced him as a warmonger. He realized that the New York Republican who had savaged him on domestic issues the past eight years could now be his ally. Heavily influenced by his European travels, Donovan by 1936 had begun publicly branding Hitler, Mussolini, and Soviet dictator Joseph Stalin as Europe's axis of evil and warned that "this is not time" for America to shrink from its obligations as a world power. He stopped short, as Roosevelt did, of advocating U.S. military intervention in Europe. Before Hitler invaded Poland he still privately advised clients not to bet on war. But he called for a military buildup and by 1940 backed a draft not only for young men but also for older ones like him, who he thought were smarter and still had fight left in them.

FDR and Donovan began to warm to each other; they were two canny politicians who were beginning to see an opening for a common cause. Donovan began exchanging notes with the president on his observations from trips abroad and on foreign policy initiatives, such as the private Polish relief fund he now headed with the help of actress Greta Garbo. The two men came from divergent backgrounds and disagreed on domestic policy—Donovan thought the differences far more profound than Roosevelt did—yet they had a lot in common. Both were energetic and supremely confident of America's potential power, both had charisma and insatiable intellectual curiosity, both were enigmatic and played people off one another, both had courageously overcome tremendous obstacles (Roosevelt over polio and Donovan on the battlefield). Each also respected the other's political skills. Donovan sensed he was dealing with a powerful man in FDR. Roosevelt, who thought Herbert Hoover had cheated Donovan on the cabinet appointment, believed that if Donovan had been a Democrat he might well have been sitting in the White House.

After Germany invaded Poland, Roosevelt began to consider forming a coalition cabinet for the bipartisan support he would need if the country must go to war. He began to sound out Colonel Frank Knox, the Republican publisher of the *Chicago Daily News* and an internationalist like Donovan, for the navy secretary's job. Knox, the GOP's vice presidential nominee in 1936, was interested but wanted company; he urged FDR to consider his "very dear friend" Bill Donovan for secretary of war. Having two prominent Republicans controlling all the armed forces of a Democratic administration might be more bipartisanship than either party could bear, Roosevelt worried. Others in FDR's inner circle, such as Interior Secretary Harold Ickes, were cool to the idea. Donovan's name was still being floated for high office in a future Republican administration. The last thing FDR aides wanted was their cabinet becoming a farm team for the GOP's stars.

"Let us let the whole matter stand as it is for a while," Roosevelt finally wrote Knox as 1939 came to a close. This would be a tricky political move. He wanted more time to think about bringing in the Chicago publisher and any other Republicans.

A HEAVY RAINSTORM pounded the East Coast on Monday afternoon, April 8, 1940, as Donovan's daughter drove her convertible north on Route 1, hardly able to see much ahead of her even with the windshield wipers on. Patricia had been visiting a friend at Duke University in Durham, North Carolina, and was returning to Washington. She had transferred from Wellesley to George Washington University in the District and planned to graduate from there in two months.

Thirty-five miles south of Fredericksburg, Virginia, her car hydroplaned on a patch of water. It spun around twice and slammed into a tree on the side of the road, throwing the driver's door open and hurling Patricia fourteen feet away. An ambulance evacuated her to a nearby hospital. She was unconscious with a crushed shoulder and hip and massive internal injuries. Mary and David rushed from Chapel Hill to the hospital and found her still clinging to life.

Rain pelted the windows of Donovan's Wall Street office Monday afternoon when a phone rang in the hallway. A doctor at the hospital had called the firm's Washington office with the news of Patricia's accident. Thomas McFadden, one of the lawyers there, relayed the report to Donovan that his daughter was in a coma. He nearly collapsed with fear.

The rainstorm made it impossible to fly south so Donovan took the train to Washington and then a car to Fredericksburg. But he was too late. Patricia died at 6 P.M. that day. Even worse, Ruth was somewhere in the Pacific aboard the *Yankee*. Donovan succeeded in reaching her on the boat by shortwave radio, but it would take Ruth more than three agonizing weeks just to reach Hawaii. Roosevelt had been informed of the tragedy and had overseas embassies help arrange her voyage back.

Donovan seemed to crawl into his own shell and lose all interest in the pressing family matters. David had to make the funeral arrangements and with Mary he flew to Honolulu to meet his mother. Donovan did fly to Los Angeles to greet the three of them when they finally arrived on May 13. He and Ruth would never discuss divorce again. They would remain married forever. Donovan was now fifty-seven, and his hair seemed to turn white almost overnight without Patricia. After her death he drifted further away from his family. Only Mary grew closer to him, taking the place of the daughter he lost.

Chapter 7

—⚬⚬⚬—

Envoy

THE SUMMER OF 1940 was a foreboding one. Germany, which would soon sign the Tripartite Pact with Italy and Japan, had successfully invaded Norway, Denmark, Belgium, Holland, Luxembourg, and France. The Battle of Britain had begun. U-boat submarine packs prowled the Atlantic waters to strangle her lifeline from the sea, the Luftwaffe ranged over her southern coast, and Hitler had ordered planning for a German invasion. The only thing that stood between the Nazi dictator and the United States, FDR knew, was the British and American navies.

The garrulous and combative Winston Churchill, who became prime minister after Neville Chamberlain's government fell in May, intended to defend the homeland to the last man, while bombing and blockading Germany and stirring revolts in the territories Hitler occupied. To do so he desperately needed American aid and wanted U.S. military intervention. But anti-British sentiment, whose roots traced back to the Revolutionary War, ran deep in the United States and a broad array of isolationists argued fiercely against America being sucked into another foreign war to save Europe from itself.

By June, Roosevelt decided to bring Frank Knox into the administration as navy secretary. Instead of Donovan, he nominated for war secretary a less politically ambitious establishment Republican, seventy-two-year-old Henry Stimson. Donovan was not thrilled with being edged out by a man he considered a milquetoast, but he nevertheless worked to quell a Republican revolt over the two nominations and prepped Knox for what turned out to be a rancorous confirmation hearing.

Roosevelt believed Great Britain would survive, but it was only a vague impression at this point. The military's intelligence services, which were tiny underfunded operations, had filed conflicting reports. The new British prime minister who was sending FDR assurances was still an unknown quantity to him. The Democratic convention was about to nominate Roosevelt for a third term and he was walking practically blind into a controversial and complex American aid initiative for Europe, which could derail his reelection if he got it wrong. Roosevelt, who already had dispatched a number of emissaries to scope out the war, was eager to have Donovan's seasoned eyes and ears there as well to assess whether England could withstand the Luftwaffe and a cross-Channel invasion. Knox also thought a London trip would help his friend get his mind off Patricia's death.

Reporters staked out a New York waterfront Sunday afternoon, July 14, 1940, where Donovan boarded a Pan Am Clipper flying to London. He insisted to the press he was on routine business. Just before leaving the dock he had phoned Ruth in Washington and told her, for the first time, that he was flying to London but could not explain why.

He arrived in the British capital on July 16. Knox also ordered Edgar Mowrer, the *Chicago Daily News*'s top foreign correspondent then in Lisbon, to join Donovan in London and help investigate German fifth column espionage and sabotage operations in Great Britain and Europe. At first, the British Foreign Office was leery about opening doors for this latest emissary, an Irish American lawyer from the opposition party whose sidekick was a reporter. But Lord Lothian, Britain's ambassador in Washington, had cabled London that Donovan was a close Knox adviser, who "may exercise considerable influence" over Washington's decisions to ship arms. That was hardly the case at this point, but Lothian convinced the Foreign Office that Donovan could be a political ally. Whitehall scrambled to arrange ministry appointments for him and wedged fifteen minutes into Churchill's busy schedule for a get-acquainted chat.

Donovan ended up receiving unprecedented access befitting a high-level visitor. Britain's top sea lords of the Admiralty, senior air commanders, and government economists gave him secret briefings on ships and planes in her arsenal, on output by her industry, and on food supplies from her farms. He inspected a fighter squadron at Essex and a naval officers training camp in Portsmouth. Churchill had to assign seven men working overtime to prepare for Donovan answers to all the questions he left behind from each visit. Even more important, he received highly classified briefings, normally not given to foreigners, on British intelligence and propaganda operations overseas. The counterintelligence arm, MI5, slipped him reports on the 16,300 aliens in the country who had been detained as suspected subversives. Over dinner at the Royal Thames Yacht Club, Admiral John Godfrey, the ruthless and normally reticent director of Naval Intelligence, told Donovan that London was eager to collaborate closely with Washington on spying. Britain's Secret Intelligence Service chief, Stewart Menzies (known in MI6 simply as "C"), took Donovan under his wing and loaded him down with bulky reports—hoping like Godfrey to shape a future American spy organization after His Majesty's services. The gentle, charming—and very secretive—Menzies, who liked to brag to American visitors that he gave Churchill his intelligence briefing each morning while the prime minister was still in bed, came from a wealthy family close to the royals. He did not reveal Ultra, which could intercept and break Germany's coded radio messages. But he made clear to Donovan he was confident the Luftwaffe's moves over British skies could be anticipated.

Donovan told delighted British officials he would lobby hard for U.S. aid back in Washington. He thought the best place for Britain to go on the offensive was up through the southern periphery of German-controlled territory in the Mediterranean region (Churchill believed as well that it was Hitler's soft underbelly). London diplomats hinted to the State Department that Donovan would be an ideal replacement for the current U.S. ambassador, Joseph Kennedy, whom they despised because he was convinced Britain was doomed. On August 3, the Air Ministry booked priority passage for Donovan on the flying boat *Clare*, which was camouflaged in green and blue and leaving the town of Poole on the southern coast for New York. Officers put a bottle of champagne and a volume of Edmund Burke by his seat for the thirty-four-hour flight. The Foreign Office, which Donovan had already briefed on his conclusions, wanted him back in Washington with his message as quickly as possible. Though he put the odds lower than the British briefers pitching him, Donovan believed England could beat back a German attack (even so, he underestimated how weak the British army was). But to do so, Britain required American military equipment and desperately needed U.S. destroyers to protect supply convoys in U-boat–infested sea lanes.

Back in Washington Donovan briefed Knox and other cabinet officials, who were impressed with his upbeat assessment as well as the British
reports he had collected to answer hundreds of questions they had submitted to him before his trip. Columnist Walter Lippmann gushed that
his findings "almost singlehandedly overcame the unmitigated defeatism
which was paralyzing Washington." Even the normally reserved Stimson
noted in his diary that the colonel "told a very interesting story."

Friday night, August 9, Donovan and Knox boarded the armor-plated
presidential train at Hyde Park, which carried Roosevelt and the large
White House entourage of aides, Secret Service agents, and reporters
always following him. The train chugged east overnight to the Portsmouth,
New Hampshire, Navy Yard. Roosevelt inspected it for an hour, then
boarded his presidential yacht, *Potomac*, for the sail south (followed by a
destroyer for protection) to the Navy Yard at Boston and another tour.

Donovan briefed Roosevelt on the overnight train ride and the sail
from Portsmouth to Boston, which became a challenge in itself. The president was easily distracted by the hundreds of memos and foreign cables
his secretary, Grace Tully, fed him along the way, and by the striped bass
he trolled for off the *Potomac*. Roosevelt also had a penchant for launching
into monologues instead of listening, which Donovan found irritating. But
over the day and a half, Donovan thought he had convinced the president
that Britain could hold out. He pressed FDR for the military hardware, for
which Churchill was desperate: seaplanes, bombers, the Sperry bombsight
for British warplanes, and above all the destroyers. Roosevelt worried the
massive arms package, particularly the destroyers, could sink his reelection,
but he still felt it should be sent.

Roosevelt had Donovan spread his upbeat prognosis with the media.
But with the dozen reporters following him on the trip FDR was evasive,
having Knox say only that Donovan had visited Europe "to see what he
could find."

Walter Trohan always found that caginess irritating. In fact there was
not much the conservative Trohan and the isolationist newspaper he
worked for, Colonel Robert McCormick's *Chicago Tribune*, liked about
FDR. Roosevelt, who found McCormick contemptible, tried his best to
remain friendly with the *Tribune*'s White House correspondent. Press Secretary Stephen Early, who got along well personally with Trohan, occasionally even fed him derogatory information on administration black sheep

like Joe Kennedy. Donovan now was on Trohan's radar screen. The New York lawyer had been a reliable Republican—but he now warranted closer watching, Trohan decided. Although Donovan did not realize it at the time, Trohan was a reporter he would come to know well in several years.

IN SEPTEMBER, Donovan and Knox flew to Hawaii for three weeks to observe naval fleet maneuvers. The two had a grand time aboard the aircraft carrier *Enterprise,* where Donovan's coat with his watch and wallet inside it were blown off the flight deck. Donovan appreciated the crew replacing his watch, but he was not impressed with the Navy's Pacific performance. "The maneuvers here have disclosed our weaknesses in all their nakedness," he wrote a friend.

After briefing Roosevelt in August, Donovan had delivered a nationwide radio address over the Mutual Broadcasting System warning that the United States had better prepare militarily or face the scary prospect of joining "the nations of Europe that have fallen." With Mowrer he penned a wildly exaggerated series of articles warning that a $200-million-a-year German propaganda and sabotage program worldwide, which had undermined the will of conquered countries like France to resist, now had hundreds of thousands of hostile agents or Nazi sympathizers inside the United States. There was no evidence that was the case, but FDR believed it and had ordered J. Edgar Hoover to ruthlessly investigate Nazi, fascist, and communist subversion in the country.

Donovan hoped that by winter he would be back in uniform, training an infantry division in Alabama and leading it in the war he thought the United States would eventually join. But Britain's top spy in the United States considered a division command a waste of Donovan's talent. He had bigger plans for the New York lawyer.

Bill Stephenson and Donovan were remarkably similar. Stephenson, a low-key Canadian, was another man others found impossible not to like. As athletic and fearless as Donovan, Stephenson had been an amateur boxer who had performed heroically in World War I as a British fighter pilot. He became a millionaire entrepreneur afterward, and, like Donovan, occasionally fed his government intelligence by dealing with German businesses. In the summer of 1940, Menzies and Churchill had sent Stephenson to the United States to take over British intelligence operations there.

He set up his organization on the thirty-sixth floor of Rockefeller Center in New York, eventually giving it an innocuous-sounding cover name, the British Security Coordination Office, and casting out lines to Washington's powerful through old American pals like Vincent Astor, who was close to Roosevelt, and professional boxer Gene Tunney, who hooked him up with J. Edgar Hoover.

One of Stephenson's principal jobs was to mount covert operations against American isolationists trying to thwart war aid to Britain and to make sure that the aid Washington approved was not sabotaged by German agents before being shipped. His embassy had kept him posted on Donovan's London trip. Stephenson began having long martini lunches and dinners with the New York lawyer at the St. Regis Hotel and "21" Club, talking up the need for the United States to have a worldwide intelligence service like Great Britain's—an idea that intrigued Donovan. Stephenson also soon realized Donovan could be useful for another mission Churchill gave him—to help bring the United States into the war.

KEYED UP BY the publicity after his first visit, the press staked out No. 10 Downing Street and clicked photos when Donovan arrived at noon on December 18, 1940. He said nothing to the reporters, walking quickly past the helmeted guard at the entrance. German intelligence also had Donovan on its radar screen. It's best "to discreetly observe him and see what he is up to," a German Foreign Office memo advised.

Churchill booked more than an hour with the New York lawyer. Stephenson, who accompanied Donovan on the flight over, had urged him to make the second visit to collect material in London to justify U.S. Navy convoys protecting merchant shipping and then to take a tour of the Mediterranean region, which was critical to British war interests. The peripatetic Donovan hardly needed persuading and convinced Knox and Roosevelt to sign off on the trip. Like Lord Lothian, Stephenson dialed up Donovan's importance, telling Menzies that he had a "vast degree of influence in the administration." Churchill should "be completely frank" with this unofficial envoy, Stephenson advised. He could "contribute very largely to our obtaining all that we want of the United States." That whet Churchill's appetite as the two men tucked into a table in his study for their private lunch.

The Mediterranean region—the southern front in this war—was far more strategically important than Americans realized, Donovan stressed as they began their lunch. Churchill agreed, but said nothing yet.

"It's time for both us—your people and our own people—" to study "the economic, political and military implications of the Mediterranean," Donovan continued, and for both countries to come up with a "common" game plan for denying Hitler the region.

That was exactly what the prime minister wanted to hear. Normally Churchill would never reveal to a foreign civilian his secret war plans—particularly not an Irish American who might be a closet Anglophobe. But he now opened up, as aides had urged him to do, rising from the table and sweeping his finger over a nearby map. Hitler already had Hungary and Romania in his orbit. The prime minister told Donovan what he now feared most: Germany would slice through the rest of the Balkans, taking Yugoslavia and Bulgaria through alliance or conquest, then aim for strategically placed Turkey with its important access for his army to the south and east. Churchill's war plan was to set the territories Hitler now controlled "ablaze" with resistance movements to tie down his divisions and form a British and American alliance with Yugoslavia, Bulgaria, Turkey, and Greece against Germany in the south. Churchill's critics would accuse him of being naive in thinking he could mount an effective Balkans movement against Hitler, but with the British army far too weak to confront Hitler head-on in France, he was convinced his "peripheral strategy," as it came to be called, was the only way to go on the offensive. Donovan agreed.

Cables went out to British embassies and military commands in the Mediterranean: Donovan "has been taken fully into our confidence," show him everything. For more than two exhausting months, Donovan toured the southern front. Menzies's service paid his expenses, the Royal Air Force flew him from country to country, and trusted British military officers (on one leg it was a Naval Intelligence aide named Ian Fleming, the future author of the James Bond novels) served as escorts, cabling London detailed reports on his movements. Donovan intensely interviewed everyone he met at each stop, filling leather pouches with secret war planning documents to take back to Washington.

This time, however, Donovan was far more than a fact finder. In effect, he became a diplomatic envoy for both the United States and Great Britain—unprecedented considering he had no official standing in either government. In closed-door meetings with fence-sitting leaders in Bulgaria, Yugoslavia, Turkey, Spain, and the Middle East, he delivered the same blunt message: Franklin Roosevelt did not intend to let Great Britain lose this war.

Hoping to block or at least delay Hitler's move into the region, British diplomats and generals there were delighted with the pressure he applied. "I must thank you for the magnificent work done by Donovan in his prolonged tour of the Balkans and the Middle East," a grateful Churchill cabled FDR. "He has carried with him throughout an animating heartwarming flame." Aides to Cordell Hull, the turf-jealous secretary of state, investigated whether Donovan's strong-arming Balkan leaders violated the Logan Act, which made it a crime for private citizens to negotiate with foreign countries.

Berlin grew increasingly alarmed over Donovan's meddling in the region. The Abwehr, Germany's foreign intelligence service, began to follow his every move. Nazi propaganda denounced his tour as an "impudent" act. Paranoid that Donovan might even be preparing the ground for a U.S. invasion, German diplomats buttonholed friendly foreign leaders he had met to find out what he said. One was Bulgaria's Tsar Boris III, whom Donovan thought was "a very frightened man" (understandable considering German forces from Romania had already infiltrated into his northern hills). Boris was dismissive of this American trying to convince him not to join the Axis. Donovan was "naive," the swarthy Bulgarian told a German envoy, with "not the faintest notion of the political conditions and the history of the Balkans."

Berlin decided to play rough. As Donovan relaxed in a Sofia nightclub with a British intelligence officer and George Earle, Roosevelt's colorful ambassador to Bulgaria, Abwehr agents sneaked into his room at the Bulgarie Hotel and stole his traveling bag (his British handlers kept his pouches of secret documents in a separate room). German propaganda claimed that Donovan lost the bag in a night of drunken barhopping with Earle. That was an outlandish tale for the abstemious Donovan, but not so far-fetched for Earle, who enjoyed carousing in Sofia's nightspots with chorus girls.

Donovan, who was notorious for losing personal items like wallets, pooh-poohed the theft to reporters, insisting the bag had only his passport and papers of no value to the Abwehr. Angry British and U.S. security officers weren't so sure. The bag contained a sensitive list of questions from the U.S. Navy for Donovan's trip. When Bulgarian police finally found the pocketbook and returned it to the embassy, only the list was missing from inside it.

RUTH AND MARY, in full-length mink coats to ward off the chill, stood at New York's La Guardia Field Dock for flying boats to greet Donovan on his return March 18, 1941. David was there as well but stayed in the background to avoid the photographers. He did not enjoy New York's hectic pace. He also did not have good news for Donovan that day. Despite Knox's intervention, the Navy had just rejected David's application for a reserve commission (relatives suspected he chose the sea service so he would not follow his father into the Army). David had poor eyesight and the naval reviewing board found his academic record decidedly undistinguished.

The photographers framed Donovan's wife and his pretty daughter-in-law in all their shots. Mary liked being in front of the cameras. She wanted more than just a farm life. As free-spirited and assertive as she was stylish and beautiful, Mary enjoyed throwing parties and being the center of attention at them playing the piano. She smoked Lucky Strikes and sometimes shot birds in an elm tree from her bedroom window. To break the tedium of Berryville, she painted floral works, designed jewelry, and often was the leading lady in local productions by the Blue Ridge Players. And unlike her husband, Mary liked the fact that Donovan was a celebrity.

Donovan had already sent Knox, Hull, and the White House lengthy cables on his findings and recommendations. Roosevelt should erect "a Balkan barrier against Germany," he urged in one report. Donovan also sent Knox a detailed letter on how London organized its intelligence and unconventional warfare operations. Menzies and British commandos had been even more forthcoming during Donovan's latest stopover in London. He began forming in his own mind how a new American intelligence operation should be assembled for this war. "It should be headed by someone appointed by the President, directly responsible to him and to no one else," Donovan wrote Knox. Funding for this unit "should be secret and made solely at the discretion of the President."

Roosevelt, who had easily defeated Republican Wendell Willkie four months earlier for a third term, seemed no more preoccupied with the

Mediterranean at the moment than Hitler was. He told his scheduler to give Donovan only fifteen minutes in his White House study on March 19 before he headed out on a vacation cruise to Florida. Donovan managed to extract a few minutes extra for a hurried-up pitch on war equipment the British needed in the region. Harry Hopkins, a close Roosevelt confidant not only on domestic policy but also on defense and foreign affairs, sat in on the meeting and cabled Churchill afterward that the White House was "moving rapidly to get [the] materials required."

TREASURY SECRETARY Henry Morgenthau Jr., another one of Roosevelt's closest advisers, liked to convene his daily senior staff meeting at 2:30 P.M. to see who took a long lunch and to begin it by trading the latest political gossip with his aides. Washington on March 20 was chattering about Donovan. Morgenthau, who despised the Nazis and had encouraged Hoover to bug the phones of Axis envoys in the United States, wondered if Donovan was replacing Hopkins as FDR's favorite private emissary to Churchill. None of the staffers had picked up that morsel.

Morgenthau thought Donovan was an up-and-comer and had ordered Treasury to give him any help he requested. Donovan had been to England twice, he had met practically every leader in the Balkans and Middle East, and had been "in the trenches" at different fronts, Morgenthau told the dozen young men around his conference table. "I think he knows more about the situation than anybody I have talked to by about a thousand per cent."

"That is all good preparation for Washington," said an aide, chuckling. "He ought to be at home in all the fighting that is going on."

Donovan did quickly join the political combat. Armed with talking points the War Department and the British slipped him, he went on the speech circuit and took to the radio airwaves once more, denouncing "defeatists" like famed pilot Charles Lindbergh and pacifists who called for "peace at any price." But though the country's mood had begun to shift more toward aiding Britain and he had Roosevelt's support, Donovan could not escape personal attack. Hate mail over his speeches poured in. The vision he and Churchill had of a united Balkans alliance also soon went up in smoke. Succumbing to German pressure, Boris in Bulgaria had joined the Tripartite Pact on March 1. To squelch a coup Belgrade officers launched to block their government from joining the Axis, the German army invaded Yugoslavia in April. Axis propaganda claimed Donovan had met with one of the Belgrade coup plotters and encouraged the officers to launch their foolhardy revolt. Donovan dismissed the charge as "poppy-cock," which it was, but conservative reporters in the United States picked it up and accused him of making promises of U.S. military aid in the Balkans that he had no authority to make.

J. Edgar Hoover was miffed as well over his European trip. Hoover had already sent two of his best agents to London to review the entire British intelligence setup and had sent their report to the White House two weeks before Donovan had returned home. But now Donovan was running around Washington passing himself off as the first to discover intelligence's Holy Grail. By any measure Donovan's European tour had been the most wide-ranging and in-depth that any American had taken up to that point. Hoover, however, sent FDR a report from an unnamed (and hardly reliable) source "close to the German embassy" in Washington. Because Donovan was "not schooled in the art of diplomacy," his European mission had been a "failure," Hoover's report concluded. It would be one of many poison-pen memos soon targeting Donovan.

Chapter 8

---————oഉ/o————

Spy Service

D ONOVAN HAD PASSED an Army physical in May 1941 so he could command a combat division. But the British kept nudging him into a different direction. Stephenson had been intensely lobbying the Roosevelt administration on the need for a coordinated American intelligence service partnered with the United Kingdom. So had Admiral Godfrey, Britain's Naval Intelligence chief, and his aide, Commander Ian Fleming. By May both naval officers were guests in Donovan's Georgetown home. They joined Stephenson in talking up the intelligence idea with him. Forming a new spy service had been in the back of Donovan's mind. He had the credentials for it, with his military experience and his world travels informally collecting secrets. Donovan told Knox that America, too, needed an organization of spies and saboteurs like Britain's with "men calculatingly reckless with disciplined daring."

Knox pressed Roosevelt on Donovan's ideas for a new intelligence service, but it soon began to ring alarm bells in other parts of Washington. Hoover and the State Department's intelligence chief, Adolf Berle, were convinced that Stephenson's vast operation—it included spying on American opponents of Britain and breaking into hostile embassies—violated U.S. espionage laws. Brigadier General Sherman Miles, the Army's well-connected intelligence chief, warned the service's chief of staff, George Marshall, in a memo that Donovan was scheming "to establish a super agency" that would take over the Army, Navy, and FBI spy services. Marshall agreed.

Roosevelt, however, was interested in Donovan's ideas. Secretive by nature, even with his closest advisers, FDR had been enamored since his youth with subterfuge and intrigue. Donovan much later would call him "a real cloak-and-dagger boy." Roosevelt had already set up his own private network of spies because the traditional intelligence system left him so much in the dark on what was happening overseas that it made him physically ill at times. The primitive and parochial intelligence units in the Army, Navy, and State Department were underfunded and undermanned dumping grounds for poor performers. No one was at the top coordinating these separate, often feuding fiefdoms, Donovan realized. No one analyzed the bits and pieces of information coming in to give Roosevelt a clear picture of events abroad.

At Roosevelt's request, Donovan on June 10 sent him a memo, with a crudely drawn organizational diagram enclosed, explaining how he would set up a centralized spy service. "Strategy, without information upon which it can rely, is helpless," Donovan's memo began. "Likewise, information is useless unless it is intelligently directed to the strategic purpose." In other words, information needed to be both collected and used as a weapon. Donovan's new unit would gather intelligence overseas by itself or through the existing organizations in the Army, Navy, State Department, and FBI. This unit would then be responsible for analyzing the information that came in from everywhere and reporting it in a coherent fashion directly to the president. "But there is another element in modern warfare," Donovan argued, "and that is the psychological attack against the moral and spiritual defense of a nation." The other mission for Donovan's "coordinator of strategic information": Wage propaganda warfare against the enemy, which he thought the Nazis had "effectively employed."

Shortly after noon on Wednesday, June 18, Donovan and Knox walked into the Oval Office to meet with Roosevelt. With Menzies keeping a close watch from London, Stephenson had continued feeding Donovan reports on British espionage while Godfrey had left Fleming behind for advice on fleshing out his intelligence plan. Donovan was well aware of the dangers in depending too much on the British, whose agenda, he knew, did not always jibe with Washington's. He accepted suggestions from Fleming he considered useful and ignored the ones he thought wacky, such as putting the headquarters of this new organization in the FBI's offices, Hoover's lair. Berle, a formidable economist who had been part of FDR's New Deal brain trust and still had his ear over at the State Department, nevertheless worried that Donovan's spy operation would be an adjunct of Stephenson's. Even Roosevelt privately questioned whether the package he was being pitched was Donovan's or London's, although he kept his uneasiness to himself as Donovan and Knox settled into their chairs before his desk.

Donovan told the president he did not really want the intelligence job (he still hungered for combat with a division) but he would take it on three conditions: First, he reported only to FDR. Second, Roosevelt paid for the operation out of a secret, and unaccountable, White House fund Congress had approved. And third, FDR instructed all other government departments "to give me what I want."

A bureaucratic firestorm erupted behind closed doors over Donovan's intelligence plan. Tipped off early by informants, Hoover began lobbying the White House against it before Donovan had even put it on paper for Roosevelt. Hoover had built a massive domestic counterespionage operation in the thirteen years since Donovan had left Justice. The FBI had fingerprint cards on more than ten million Americans, confidential files with embarrassing personal information on hundreds of politicians, and now read thousands of pieces of international mail the British shared from their secret letter-opening facility in Bermuda. The FBI had rounded up most Nazi subversives. The bureau also oversaw spying in Latin America. Hoover, who suspected Donovan had continued to try to get him fired after he left Justice, did not want him meddling in his operations now.

Neither did George Catlett Marshall. Dignified and aloof with an obsession for proper order, Marshall also had an explosive temper, which erupted whenever he caught anyone trying to play politics with him or his Army. Marshall was now furious with what he saw as a naked ploy to usurp his power as chief of staff and give another man control over his intelligence arm with direct access to the president. Marshall demanded that Stimson, who was inclined to agree with Donovan on this idea, strangle the plan in the crib.

But Roosevelt, who had so far been successful at picking the right men for jobs, felt he had nothing to lose with this appointment and Donovan was the only forward thinker in town with a plan for fixing the intelligence mess. With the press now buzzing about the bureaucratic battle, Roosevelt finally signed the executive order on July 11 designating a new "Coordinator of Information." Stimson had managed to water it down, making it an unpaid position. Donovan's duties were described so vaguely it left other cabinet officers scratching their heads over exactly what his job was. He would "collect and analyze all information and data, which may bear upon national security," and perform other unspecified "supplementary activities" for FDR (which Donovan took to mean psychological operations and sabotage). Other departments were ordered to cooperate with him, but Donovan could not "interfere" with Army or Navy intelligence operations.

London was delighted with the appointment. The German embassy in Washington, which had been following closely the bureaucratic maneuvering, cabled Berlin that Donovan and his gang of "notorious German haters" had been organized to promote FDR's "political and economic war measures" among Americans and to "counter strongly the effective propaganda by the Axis powers."

With so many powerful men in Washington's political snake pit lined up against him, Donovan either will "give up in disgust or fight his way through," Interior Secretary Harold Ickes, a key New Dealer, wrote in his diary. "Probably he will be able to do the latter, as he is a fighter." Ickes's prediction would prove true.

AROUND THE DINNER table of his Georgetown home, Donovan, Elmo Roper, and Robert Sherwood began sketching out the new intelligence agency. Roper was a public opinion pollster skilled in gathering information overseas and an administrative gadfly brimming with ideas for how the organization should be set up. Sherwood was a Pulitzer Prize–winning playwright Donovan had met at the premiere of one of his New York productions and now a rabid New Dealer who wrote speeches for Roosevelt. Tall, angular, and artistically temperamental, Sherwood also was a bon vivant who enjoyed fine wine and women. He was now eager to join Donovan as his chief propagandist.

For days in Georgetown and at Donovan's New York apartment, the men scratched ideas on notepads, crumpled sheets, and threw them into the wastebasket. They grappled with complex questions about exactly how a spy operation should collect, analyze, and report information and use it as a weapon. Stephenson continued to feed suggestions. Sherwood was dispatched to New York to acquire radio-transmitting stations and recruit broadcasters and journalists, like *Chicago Daily News* foreign correspondent

Wallace Deuel, who were eager to leave the newsroom and join Donovan as spies or propagandists. To analyze intelligence, Donovan knew he needed a research department immediately. "If we get into this [war], and we probably will," he told Roper, "we want men who can tell us more about France than anybody now knows . . . and we've got to know the same thing about every single country in Europe and probably Asia." Archibald MacLeish, the voluble poet and librarian of the Congress, agreed to lend the library's scholars. Donovan recruited James Phinney Baxter III, the erudite president of Williams College, to head the research and analysis section.

With $450,000 from Roosevelt's secret fund, Donovan soon moved the operation to government quarters, first to an empty barnlike conference room in the State Department offices next to the White House, then to the Apex Building near the Capitol. Donovan got the Navy to loan him a Buick sedan, eventually with one of Zenith's new portable shortwave radios installed in it so he could talk to FDR and other key administration officials on the road.

Donovan made a number of politically astute hires. Estelle Frankfurter, Justice Felix Frankfurter's brilliant and Washington-savvy sister, came on board to make sense of complicated government reports for him. Marine Captain James Roosevelt joined to cajole other departments into cooperating, a chore Donovan detested and knew FDR's son would have more clout doing. More senior aides were brought in, such as Edward "Ned" Buxton (a World War comrade) to be an assistant director and organize a unit to interview foreigners arriving in the United States with useful intelligence, David K. E. Bruce (a courtly Virginia lawyer and world traveler) to head the intelligence collection operation, and William Whitney (a pro-British American lawyer) to set up an office for the new agency in London.

Early in September, Donovan moved his operation to its permanent headquarters, a three-story granite building with long stone columns in the front that the Public Health Service was abandoning at 25th and E Streets atop Navy Hill. Donovan took the high-ceilinged corner office on the first floor of the "Kremlin," as staffers soon nicknamed the East Building. From its tall windows, which he liked to keep open even in winter, he could see the Potomac River far off. His room number was 109, which he now made his code number for message traffic. The top third floor still had caged lab animals the health service had used for syphilis research. Berlin radio mocked it as the new home of "50 professors, 10 goats, 12 guinea pigs, a sheep, and a staff of Jewish scribblers." For several weeks Donovan's aides gagged on the putrid smoke from animals carted out and incinerated nearby.

The German embassy in Washington was not so contemptuous of the Kremlin. It fired off a coded cable to the Foreign Office warning that "as soon as the Donovan organization is on track," Hitler should expect American agents organizing "acts of sabotage against the occupying army." Donovan indeed commanded Roosevelt's premier espionage organization—but not his only one, the lawyer quickly learned to his great annoyance. He stumbled across another one almost by accident as he tried over a breakfast to recruit Chicago anthropologist Henry Field, a relative of department store magnate Marshall Field. Henry told a startled Donovan he could not join his organization because he worked for another secret White House spy agency.

John Franklin Carter was a brainy and passionate Washington columnist, easily excitable, who tended to feel self-important and have harebrained ideas. But he had worked for a while as an administration speechwriter and had known Roosevelt since he was governor. While Donovan was roaming the Balkans in February, Carter, who also thought U.S. intelligence was "loused up," had convinced Roosevelt he needed a small, off-the-books operation for discreet spying that the White House could deny existed. With $10,000 in start-up money from FDR's secret fund, Carter hired a dozen informants, many of them businessmen overseas, who fed him tips on military and political developments abroad, which he passed to Roosevelt. Carter also spied on FDR's political enemies at home. Donovan complained to FDR, and even vented to Hoover, about being kept in the dark on what Carter was up to. But Roosevelt encouraged rivals and he never let one person know everything he was doing. After Carter's money ran out in June, FDR approved another $30,000 for the rest of the year. Carter also continued to take pot shots at Donovan in the syndicated column he still wrote, never mentioning to his readers that he was a bureaucratic competitor.

THE COORDINATOR OF Information office became a reflection of Donovan's creative and eclectic mind—constantly exploring, expanding, experimenting. He launched new projects, rearranged priorities, and shuffled

personnel—so fast his harried staff was forever catching up with his direc-
tives. Donovan's idea of management, according to Buxton: "Put a lot of
strong men in a pen and let them fight it out, on the theory that the strongest ones would emerge at the top." He hated bureaucracy and its rules,
refused to follow a chain of command. Anyone could walk into his office;
sometimes, all they had to do was walk by and he would shout at them to
come in and assign them a job that had just popped into his head. When
Early, FDR's press secretary, asked Sherwood one day at the White House
for an organizational diagram of the Coordinator of Information, the playwright grabbed a sheet of paper and sketched a notional one as best he
could remember. It was as accurate as any of the printed charts they had.

Donovan and his secretive organization became the talk of Washington. The "celebrated man of mystery" was running "one of the wisest
emergency moves the administration has made," enthused the *Washington
Star,* whose comic page ran a strip on "The Exciting Adventures of 'Wild
Bill' Donovan." At the end of October 1941 the British embassy cabled a
cheery note to London: "Donovan is proceeding slowly in the exercise of
his power" so as not to alienate other departments and "he appears to be
building up amicable relationships."

That was not the case, however. Knowing this was one of Roosevelt's
pet projects and Donovan had direct access to him, other departments at
first promised to cooperate. Even Hoover was helpful, trading tips with
Donovan on Nazi subversives. But tensions quickly mounted. War Secretary Stimson became increasingly irritated with Donovan's end runs to
Roosevelt with off-the-wall ideas that infringed on the War Department's
turf. Miles, the Army's intelligence chief, who was called its G-2, was leery
about sharing the service's intelligence with Donovan's untrained civilians
and furious that Donovan had gotten FDR's okay behind his back to have
agents overseas pretend to be military attachés. Secretary of State Cordell
Hull complained to FDR that Donovan was secretly making foreign policy.

Soon, everywhere Donovan turned he was irritating someone. Nelson
Rockefeller, the young and dapperly dressed White House coordinator
responsible for commercial and cultural relations with Latin America,
controlled propaganda for that region. Donovan and Sherwood thought it
ridiculous that Central and South America, which were infested with Nazi
agents, were carved out of the world propaganda operation the Coordinator of Information was supposed to oversee. But when Donovan made a

play for that turf, an angry Rockefeller, who was a member of one of the country's richest families and had far more clout with the White House, easily beat him back. Roosevelt ordered Donovan to stay out of Latin America.

Harold Smith, Roosevelt's tight-fisted Budget Bureau chief, thought Donovan was an empire builder. A Kansas engineer with wire-rimmed glasses perched always on his beaklike nose, Smith envisioned Donovan having a small $1 million a year operation; he was shocked when in two months Donovan was demanding ten times that much. Donovan's personal expense vouchers became a bean counter's nightmare: a thousand dollars for unspecified secret meetings in unnamed Washington hotels and restaurants with the sources never identified. Even more annoying to Smith, Donovan wasn't shy about griping to Roosevelt when the Budget Bureau tried to trim his requests. By November, Roosevelt had approved almost $13 million for his operation the next year. Donovan grumbled that it was $1 million less than what he wanted. Smith grumbled that it was far more than he deserved.

Hoover quickly became convinced that Donovan's organization was the biggest collection of amateurs he had ever encountered, which at the outset it was, and riddled with enemy agents, which it wasn't. Hoover suspected that much of the classified material he sent Donovan ended up in British hands. Columnist Walter Winchell, a Hoover pal, published an article, which looked suspiciously like a Hoover leak, claiming FBI agents had found a Hungarian American with fascist ties in Donovan's organization. The story was false.

Hoover distanced himself from one press report. *Collier's* magazine quoted an unidentified FBI agent in November 1941 who bragged: "Donovan knows everything we know except what we know about Donovan." The day the magazine hit newsstands an embarrassed Hoover sent Donovan a letter, insisting "the Bureau does not possess any information concerning you."

That was a lie. Not only was the FBI file on Donovan growing, Hoover had begun an intensive spying operation on his organization. He had a mole in Donovan's message center feeding him information and FBI agents began to compile dossiers on members of Donovan's senior staff. At one point Hoover wrote Donovan innocently suggesting that whenever he was traveling in the country he should drop by the local FBI office and get acquainted with their agents. Donovan knew he just wanted to track his movements and ignored the suggestion. In another letter Hoover tested Donovan's gullibility further, asking him to send the names and addresses of all his secret agents—just in case a person walked into an FBI office and claimed he worked for Donovan, the bureau could check the list to see if he was an impostor. Donovan refused.

By the end of the year, however, the only person who mattered to Donovan—Franklin Roosevelt—thought "Bill was doing a pretty good job," as he put it. Donovan never cared to be a Roosevelt intimate or to socialize with his old political rival. Roosevelt still kept a short leash on his intelligence chief, although Donovan did not always realize it. The White House was not unmindful of the fact that the high-powered bankers, lawyers, corporation executives, and society friends Donovan brought in gave his intelligence agency a decidedly Republican color. But Roosevelt admired Donovan's boldness (he had already begun talking up FDR and Stimson on the idea of forming a guerrilla warfare force to fight alongside the regular Army).

FDR also enjoyed reading tidbits of inside information from around the world. In the first six months, Donovan flooded him with phone calls, visits, and more than two hundred memos with intelligence on the war. Some reports misjudged German armament production, but others, such as studies of German casualties and supply problems on the Eastern Front, were on target. Much of the intelligence came from the British, which Donovan sent to FDR without attribution. Roosevelt suspected he was getting London's reports under a different wrapper, but never complained. Donovan's, he began to tell friends, are "my secret legs."

SATURDAY AFTERNOON, NOVEMBER 29, 1941, a military attaché in the Reich's embassy, a dreary nineteenth-century brick mansion on Massachusetts Avenue, finished typing his report to Berlin on the war as seen in Washington. It contained the usual vitriol the Nazi leadership wanted to hear about Roosevelt "dilettantes" like Hopkins and Donovan. At the end of his report the Oberleutnant shifted to the Far East. Washington, he advised, was building up its forces in Asia "to woo and intimidate Japan" but "America needs time. All the dangers that threaten Japan will only materialize if Japan gives the Americans time."

Saturday evening, December 6, Roosevelt with Hopkins at his side in the lamp-lit study on the second floor of the White House read a lengthy Japanese diplomatic message just delivered by a Navy lieutenant. The U.S. military's Magic code breakers had decrypted it. The thirteen-part message to the Japanese embassy in Washington rejected a final American diplomatic offer to relax economic sanctions if Japan withdrew its troops from China and Indochina. The fourteenth part of the message, which Tokyo delayed sending until overnight, formally broke off negotiations, but Roosevelt could tell where the two countries were headed after quickly reading the sheaf of papers before him. "This means war," he said quietly to Hopkins.

Roosevelt, however, was blind to when and where. The Japanese military command had already deployed its army and a combined fleet of six aircraft carriers and 360 warplanes to their attack stations, ordering strict radio silence to mask the movements. The president had seven intelligence agencies (including Donovan's) reporting to him but none knew the timing of the most important strategic event about to happen to the United States in the Second World War. The take from Magic, the military's Japanese code-breaking capability in place since 1940, was distributed in a cockeyed manner with no single person in charge of making sense of its raw intelligence. Because of interservice rivalry, the Army sent FDR reports from Magic on odd-numbered months, the Navy sent them on the even-numbered ones.

Donovan's researchers were focused mostly on the European war. He worried about Japanese aggression in Asia and tried to cultivate Saburō Kurusu, Japan's special envoy sent to negotiate with Hull. But much of Donovan's interest in the country was Eurocentric, requesting studies, for example, on German activity there. Most of his agents overseas were still unreliable and few of them were in the Far East. As a stopgap measure in early December, Bruce asked the Asian representatives for the International Harvester and International Telephone and Telegraph companies to send him any intelligence they ran across. Donovan also paid Mowrer $1,880 in the fall to spy on the Japanese in the region, but the reports the journalist filed were little better than newspaper features.

At 1 P.M. Friday, December 5, Donovan boarded the train at Union Station for New York. He continued to practice a little law on the side and allowed other senior aides, who had left lucrative jobs in the private sector, to tend to business work. The weekend trips to New York soon became a headache for Eloise Page, Donovan's secretary. He constantly changed his travel plans, which sent Page rushing to the phone to plead with the Pennsylvania Railroad to find him a last-minute seat on a train. One Friday after Donovan had changed his mind about traveling to New York four times and finally announced "I'm not going," Page looked at him steely-eyed and said, "Oh, yes you are."

"What did you say?" Donovan asked, glaring.

"You are going to New York," Page said. "I got a special car put on for you and if you don't take this train you'll never get on that train again." She grabbed his coat from the rack and draped it over him. "Now, you go!" she ordered.

"Yes ma'am," Donovan said meekly, and went.

Page was the only secretary who could talk back to him and get away with it. Donovan developed a complicated relationship with his female employees. About 4,500 eventually joined his agency, with 900 serving overseas. Donovan welcomed them as spies; they became known as "Donovan's girls." He pressed to have the women paid salaries higher than they would earn in other government jobs and routinely showed unusual acts of kindness toward them. But there was still a glass ceiling. Few women broke through the clerical ranks to be research analysts. Practically all of the secretaries, who gave Donovan the code name "Sea Biscuit" because he always raced about, found him to be an intimidating taskmaster, which he was. He once threw a cup full of pencils across the desk at Page in a fit of anger.

For this weekend, Donovan had tickets for the Sunday pro football game in the Big Apple. He settled into a seat in the train's drawing room car that he always took because it offered privacy and pulled out a stack of office papers from his briefcase. An aide back in Washington had put a memo in Donovan's in-box proposing a quickie pamphlet titled "Japan's Road to War" to distribute among Asians and Americans. "This pamphlet done factually can definitely establish that the Japanese military has brought on this war—not the United States, not FDR," the memo advised. Like Roosevelt, Donovan was convinced the Japanese would attack. When and where remained a mystery. A memo in his bag from MacLeish outlined a propaganda campaign if Claire Chennault's Flying Tigers, who were part of the Chinese air force, soon began fighting the Japanese. Donovan had already had Cheney Brothers, a textile manufacturer, plant rumors that

Japan's silk trade with the United States would end permanently if she went to war—hardly a concern of Tokyo's at the moment. Donovan also flipped through a draft speech Sherwood had edited for FDR to deliver after the war began, assuring Japanese Americans that the U.S. government had faith in their loyalty and that the United States "feels no enmity toward the Japanese people, but only toward the dangerous clique of military leaders who have betrayed" Japan. Roosevelt never delivered that speech.

PART II

WAR

Chapter 9

~*o/o/o*~

Pearl Harbor

DONOVAN SAT BUNDLED up in a heavy coat as a cold wind swept through the Polo Grounds in New York Sunday afternoon, December 7, 1941. The stadium was packed with more than 55,000 fans watching the National Football League's final regular season game between the New York Giants and the Brooklyn Dodgers. The Giants had already clinched the Eastern Division title but their crosstown rival now was clobbering them 21 to 7. In the press box above, sports reporters began fielding phone calls from their editors in Washington and not paying attention to the game. Suddenly a voice on the stadium loudspeaker announced: "Attention please! Here is an urgent message. Will Colonel William J. Donovan call operator nineteen in Washington immediately."

Donovan, startled, climbed down from the stands and finally found a phone booth under the bleachers. Jimmy Roosevelt came on the line. The Japanese have attacked Pearl Harbor, he told the boss. The president wanted Donovan back in Washington as quickly as possible. At 5:15 P.M., he boarded an Eastern Airlines plane at La Guardia, refusing to comment to reporters at the terminal. Vice President Henry Wallace, Labor Secretary Frances Perkins, and Postmaster General Frank Walker boarded the next flight out twenty-five minutes later hoping to make the cabinet meeting Roosevelt had set for 8:40 P.M. Hoover, also in New York for the weekend, hopped on a charter flight at La Guardia. An FBI agent from Honolulu had called him, holding the telephone out his office window so the director could hear for himself the sound of exploding bombs. An excited Churchill, joyful that Britain would survive with America now in

83

the war, phoned Roosevelt in the afternoon. "We are all in the same boat now," the president told the prime minister.

A car was waiting at the Gravelly Point airfield on the Virginia bank of the Potomac when Donovan's plane landed and sped him quickly to headquarters, which already was scrambling. The news flash of the Japanese attack had come in at 2:35 P.M., and the entire propaganda staff had been summoned along with Donovan's Asia analysts. Donovan had no agents or saboteurs for striking back. All he could throw at the enemy at this point were words. His agency's Foreign Information Service, which Sherwood ran on New York's Madison Avenue, had shortwave propaganda broadcasts reaching Europe and the Far East, with a staff of twenty-one researchers, ex-reporters, and editors in Washington churning out radio copy and leaflets. While Donovan bought transmitters for his own stations, NBC and CBS executives had made their shortwave broadcasting facilities available, along with newsmen and technicians plus private overseas surveys for targeting audiences. A man had already been put on a plane that Sunday to San Francisco to join technicians at a shortwave station now under police guard. A Schenectady, New York, transmitter had been shifted from Latin America to the Far East broadcasts so the agency had two shortwave beams hitting Asia with propaganda. An hour after the news flash, four thousand words of copy had been put on the air for overseas audiences. By 6:30 P.M. it totaled sixteen thousand words. The American line: "Again, the Axis has misjudged world opinion. Shooting doesn't frighten but unifies [the] United States."

Donovan walked into Roosevelt's dimly lit oval study at midnight. Cable messages from the Navy and Pearl Harbor were stacked on one corner of his cluttered desk, which was surrounded by more than a dozen empty chairs from the 8:40 cabinet meeting. Miserable with a stuffy nose and headache from a cold, Roosevelt was exhausted from nonstop meetings since midday.

The president now munched on a sandwich and sipped a beer. Donovan found Edward R. Murrow already in a chair chatting with him. Murrow and his wife had been guests for the scrambled eggs dinner Eleanor always fixed Sunday nights when the White House cooks took the evening off and Roosevelt had asked the CBS correspondent to stay behind on a bench in the outside hallway until he finished his meetings. Donovan did not mind Murrow intruding on his time. The two were old friends. Just the month before, Murrow had confided that he wanted to join the Army "to do more in this war" than just talk about it. Donovan thought that would be a terrible waste of a newsman whose European broadcasts had been so important in shaping American public opinion. Within a month he would be broadcasting Murrow's military commentaries from an agency radio station.

Pearl Harbor's planes had been caught "on the ground, by God, on the ground!" Roosevelt said in anguish, pounding his fist on the desktop as Donovan walked in. Had the Germans been in on this operation, the president asked? Donovan said he didn't know but guessed that Hitler had been as surprised by the strike as Roosevelt. The three men wondered how the attack would affect American public opinion. Donovan assumed it would be galvanized behind war, the message his propagandists had been broadcasting the past nine hours. "It's a good thing you got me started on this," Roosevelt finally told Donovan, referring to the intelligence agency.

AT NOON ON Monday, Roosevelt delivered one of the most powerful speeches of his presidency, asking Congress to declare war on Japan. December 7 will be "a date which will live in infamy," he began to thunderous applause. Donovan spent the busy day pressing the military for more radio transmitters, deciding propaganda themes for Japan, arranging with United Press for the loan of one of its reporters to set up a broadcast station in China, and tightening security at his headquarters. "The use of telephones for discussing secret matters should be avoided," a memo ordered. That evening, he attended a dinner party at the home of Atherton Richards, a wealthy landowner in Hawaii who had been in Army intelligence and now was one of his senior aides. One of the guests, Donovan's friend Arthur Krock of the *New York Times*, broke away from the table at one point to take a phone call. "My God!" Krock said, ashen-faced, when he returned. "Ninety percent of our fleet was knocked out at Pearl Harbor." Heads turned to Donovan. "Arthur has very good sources," the spymaster said almost in a purr.

As details of the devastation leaked to Congress and the press, the Navy quickly came under fire for being caught napping. Fingers began pointing at the military, and even at Hoover, accusing them of a massive intelligence failure. Donovan "had a little explaining to do also," Berle at the State

Department wrote in his diary. Donovan, however, escaped blame because he still had no intelligence assets to speak of that could have failed. He spent the week scouring West Coast businesses and foreign embassies in Washington for information on Japanese military and industrial targets that might be bombed.

Tuesday morning, Donovan flipped through the newspapers for reaction to Roosevelt's declaration of war speech, then scanned the foreign radio news summaries his office prepared daily. One rumor, Donovan noticed, had not worked so far. A dispatch from Tokyo reported that trading at the "silk exchange in Yokohama was firm."

Donovan sent Ruth to Chapel Hill, worried as many senior government officials were that Washington and other large cities would be bombed. Paranoia that blinded better judgment gripped Donovan's agency as it did John Franklin Carter's and J. Edgar Hoover's. Donovan and Carter warned Roosevelt that Japanese planes were attacking or would soon bomb Los Angeles. Hoover sent the White House a secondhand tip (the source turned out to be a hardly reliable young secretary in one of Washington's foreign embassies) that the Axis planned a full-scale invasion of the East Coast. Donovan even passed to FDR an unconfirmed report that five thousand Japanese saboteurs had landed on Mexico's Baja California peninsula, poised to raid San Diego. A Donovan agent sent to San Diego to check it out later cabled that the report was bogus. But Roosevelt, Donovan, and other top national security officials realized that Pearl Harbor laid open America's strategic vulnerability. Two days after the attack, William Langer, a distinguished Harvard historian who had taken over for Baxter as research director, outlined for Donovan a scary scenario from the best minds in the agency: The Japanese catch up with the Pacific Fleet that has escaped Pearl Harbor and destroy it, the Panama Canal is attacked and disabled "by Axis air or naval forces or by sabotage," "the Hawaii disaster . . . discourage[s] the Russians from joining forces with us," freed from the Eastern Front, Germany invades North Africa to gain "control of the Western Mediterranean," the Battle of the Atlantic intensifies, choking off Great Britain.

Midday Tuesday, Nelson Poynter, a former Florida newspaper editor now on Donovan's staff, sent suggestions for Roosevelt's fireside chat that evening, which Sherwood was helping draft. "The President must brutally warn the American people that we may fight alone," Poynter wrote. "This is FDR's blood, sweat and tears speech." Roosevelt should also promise to fire admirals and generals who "stand in the way of victory," the memo advised. The final script did tell Americans it would be a long and hard war. FDR decided to leave out the part about firing senior officers.

Donovan that same afternoon asked the State Department to cable its attaché in Berlin to see if his propaganda broadcasts were reaching the German capital. But he was too late. Attaché operations quickly shut down. Germany and Italy declared war on the United States on Wednesday. Hitler included Donovan in his Reichstag speech, dismissing him as "an utterly unworthy character." Tipped off by Stephenson, Donovan had alerted FDR on Tuesday that Germany would declare war first rather than wait for the United States to do so.

DONOVAN SOON HAD a delivery system set up for the White House. Couriers lugging locked pouches made deliveries three times a day, seven days a week. The 8:30 A.M. delivery, when most of the senior staff were not yet at their desks, went to the White House usher, who made sure it got to Roosevelt's bedroom, where he was usually reading the morning papers. For the noon and 6 P.M. deliveries the courier went directly to Grace Tully and exchanged the bag's contents for the papers FDR had read or notes he wanted sent back to Donovan. Donovan succeeded in charming Tully, who made sure every document went to her boss's in-box. If a report was particularly sensitive, a senior aide took the bag and waited in the Oval Office as FDR read it.

By the end of December the courier bag for each drop bulged. Donovan's research analysts began producing more accurate studies of German military strength. Other reports, however, had forecasts that did not pan out or contained half-baked intelligence, such as a memo predicting that Germany would invade Sweden (she didn't) and a warning that Spain's Washington embassy was burning its papers possibly as a prelude to joining the Axis (the smoke seen at the compound came from a boiler room explosion). Still other reports were entertaining but inconsequential: a memo to FDR on four South American diplomats attending a cocktail party the German ambassador in Chile hosted, another note that Axis radio was now calling him a *Klinkenputzer*—roughly translated, a door-to-door salesman.

Roosevelt rarely sent back comments on the reports, to indicate that he had read them all carefully, or called Donovan to task over faulty intelligence. He also welcomed all ideas from Donovan and his other intelligence mavens—even the offbeat ones. Many from Donovan made sense, such as organizing the collecting of European newspapers and journals to sift for useful intelligence. But Donovan also proposed an "out of the blue" commando strike by the remaining U.S. Pacific Fleet against the Japanese home island of Hokkaido to rattle Tokyo. He suggested fitting every home radio with an "Alert Receiver" so Roosevelt could "press a button" from his desk and reach Americans with war instructions. The Army had no commandos to raid Hokkaido. Roosevelt never had an alert button. But FDR approved Colonel James Doolittle's symbolic air raid over Japan four months later to demonstrate her vulnerability.

Roosevelt had the good sense to have many of Donovan's schemes run by other agencies before approving them. One proposal forwarded to the Navy: $100,000 for an intelligence team infiltrating Japanese conquests in the South Pacific and headed by Guy Richards, a Yale man and military feature writer for the *New York Daily News*. Richards had sailed in the region thirteen years earlier and, according to Donovan, was "highly intelligent . . . with a pronounced audacity." The Navy, which oversaw the area, rejected what it believed would be nothing more than a "newspaperman's junket," according to its memo.

Donovan, who soon won military approval for a two-thousand-man commando force in his agency, begged Roosevelt to let him fly to the Philippines and personally lead guerrilla operations against the Japanese. "This is an appeal from a soldier to his Commander-in-Chief," Donovan pleaded in a memo to FDR.

"I would want to do the same thing if I were in your place," an amused Roosevelt wrote back. "Talk to General Marshall about it." Marshall wrote Donovan that his eagerness to see combat "is typical of you," but MacArthur wanted no interlopers. All Mac would accept were broadcasts and leaflets from Donovan's men to counter Japanese propaganda urging Filipino soldiers to defect.

Donovan became convinced that a powerful German subversive operation lurked in the United States and the fact that no one could find it did not dissuade him. He warned FDR that Nazi saboteurs now planned a massive "frontal attack on New York, synchronized with general Nazi organized revolution in all South American countries." He suggested that Polish, Czech, and Yugoslav Americans, whom he thought reliable because the Germans brutally occupied their countries, be organized in factories to watch for Nazi sympathizers among ethnic groups he considered unreliable, such as Ukrainian Americans, because elements of their old country had allied with the German invaders.

Donovan was far less worried about Japanese Americans. He believed a mass relocation of them was a bad idea and tried to dissuade Roosevelt, sending him reports from his West Coast representatives who concluded there was no sabotage threat and internment camps would just make enemies of loyal Americans. "We are about to create dangers where little exist," Buxton wrote Donovan, who agreed. He met with author Pearl Buck, who sent him a long memo, which Donovan condensed and forwarded to Roosevelt, warning that the Japanese would exploit in their propaganda American racism toward Asians. Roosevelt ignored Donovan and ordered the internment.

SPORTING A NAVY pea jacket and yachting cap that made him look like an admiral, Winston Churchill landed at the Gravelly Point airfield the night of December 22. The prime minister arrived in Washington determined to settle with the Americans the strategic debate over where the new alliance should attack first. Donovan kept Churchill and his staff supplied with daily news bulletins from London newspapers, which he appreciated. But the British leader appreciated even more Donovan's lobbying for Churchill's peripheral strategy. Before the prime minister arrived, Donovan flooded FDR with memos advocating a beachhead on North Africa before Hitler seized it and proposing American intelligence and guerrilla operations to soften up the battlefield prior to an Allied invasion. Roosevelt was interested. With Marshall's approval Donovan launched a $500,000 covert operation to have an anti-Nazi Portuguese shipper infiltrate an intelligence and special operations team into the Azores nine hundred miles off Lisbon's Atlantic coast. If the Germans captured Portugal's archipelago they could threaten American convoys to North Africa. Marshall approved another half-million-dollar plan to recruit commandos to take over the Cape Verde Islands, another Portuguese possession off the northwest Africa coast.

Over the twenty-four-day Christmas conference in Washington, which was code-named "Arcadia," the second floor of the White House became Downing Street West with Churchill ensconced in the Rose Suite and his staff occupying the Lincoln Study and other adjoining bedrooms. The Monroe Room had been converted into a map room like the one Churchill had at home. Roosevelt became so enamored of Churchill's setup that he had a replica built in a ladies' coat room on the ground floor of the White House with battle maps covering its walls. Roosevelt later would visit the room daily to read secret military reports in its safes and overseas cables off its clattering Teletypes.

Late Sunday afternoon, January 11, Donovan cut short a New York trip and flew back to Washington for a private dinner Roosevelt hosted at the White House for Churchill and a few members of the British traveling party. Averell Harriman, the U.S. ambassador to England, who had accompanied Churchill, and Hopkins also attended the convivial meal. Churchill and Donovan traded stories about the days they rode as gallant cavalry officers in wars past. The talk soon turned to the present war and Churchill, fueled by Scotch and sodas, proclaimed with a flourish: "This is the stage of history that will be important—the time to make sure the deed is recorded." Donovan had begun to find Churchill's "curtain raising of history" monologues, as he called them, annoying. "All we were thinking at the moment was how to get more guns and ammunition in where we needed them," he told a friend later, and Churchill kept making everything out to be a grand epic with him at center stage. "Very few get their names into history who don't see to it that their names are included," Donovan noted.

The day after the White House gathering, Donovan attended another dinner Churchill hosted at the British embassy for the senior members of FDR's administration. Over coffee and dessert, the talk drifted to the direction of the war. Churchill argued vigorously for an Allied landing at North Africa as the first step. Stimson quickly became irritated with Knox's and Donovan's loose tongues; both men chimed in on Churchill's side, even though they knew Marshall and other senior U.S. commanders strongly backed a cross-Channel invasion of France first. Donovan, however, had become just as convinced as Churchill that attacking northern France now would result in the German defenders delivering "a terrific lacing" to the far weaker Allied force. The only realistic move, he believed, was to invade North Africa first and use it "as our aircraft carrier" for launching operations into Europe. Roosevelt and Churchill eventually agreed to set up a Combined Chiefs of Staff with the defeat of Germany first as the priority. Under political pressure after Pearl Harbor to quickly begin fighting somewhere, FDR by late July also agreed to postpone a cross-Channel invasion and attack North Africa first. A bitter Stimson, and practically every senior American officer except for Donovan, saw it as a wasteful diversion of forces to a strategic sideshow, just to keep Americans "entertained," as Marshall later put it.

Donovan's backing had not tipped the decision Churchill's way. If anyone had it was FDR's closest confidant, the physically frail but always irreverent Harry Hopkins, who became his de facto national security adviser shaping his defense and foreign policy priorities in long memos immediately after the Pearl Harbor attack. Hopkins's clout grated on Marshall and his senior aides. They resented having to give secret military briefings to someone they considered a political hack pretending to be "a great strategist," as one general grumbled. Even so, Roosevelt depended on Marshall, air Lieutenant General Henry "Hap" Arnold, and fleet admirals like Ernest King and William Leahy to run the war. Donovan was not part of the war council. He was Roosevelt's idea man, his secret daredevil, his spark plug for thinking outside the box. Knowing the military would refuse to send his map room secret reports if political cronies were allowed inside it, Roosevelt gave only Hopkins access. He never invited his intelligence chief to that inner sanctum.

Chapter 10

—◦◦◦—

The Beehive

T HE LEADER OF America's first strategic intelligence organization—
the man the Washington press called "Hush-Hush Donovan"
and Berlin reviled as a "monstrous" conspirator—was stuck in his
driveway. A cab waiting on the street for a fare blocked the main exit from
headquarters on February 18 and the driver refused to move to let Donovan's limousine pass. Donovan's driver, James Freeman, tried to shoo the
taxi away, but the cabbie started hurling racial insults at the black chauffeur. Incensed as much over Freeman's treatment as being delayed for his
1 P.M. appointment, Donovan climbed out of the limo and ordered the
driver to move. He also scribbled down the cabbie's name and sent it to the
District of Columbia police, who hauled the terrified man into the station
for a tongue-lashing.

Donovan was now totally in his element building a spy organization.
During weekend trips to New York he would drop by for only a few hours
at his law firm, which shrank as many of its lawyers joined the military.
Occasionally he visited Chapel Hill but found he hated the country and
rarely stayed overnight. Ruth visited the Georgetown home only occasionally when Donovan needed her as a hostess for official functions. Otherwise she lived in "Little House," the renovated slave quarters now attached
to Chapel Hill's main structure where David and Mary stayed. She rode
sidesaddle in fox hunts, tended a large garden in scruffy overalls and straw
hat, sipped Coca-Cola with girlfriends on the back porch, and threw occasional teas and dinner parties for Berryville's social set. For the war effort
she rolled bandages for the Red Cross and helped man a hilltop tower at

nearby Woodley Farm to look out for German planes that might approach the capital.

Donovan had people around him for practically every waking moment of the day, which usually stretched from 6 A.M. to midnight. In his office, maps marked "Secret" hung from its walls. Two telephones to patch him into the White House and military sat on his desk, piled each morning with overnight cables from the spies whose numbers abroad began to grow. For meetings close by or lunches at the F Street Club, he often walked briskly for exercise, with Freeman following in the car. His loyal chauffeur, who drove him to clandestine meetings around Washington at all hours, often was the only one who knew where the chief had disappeared to. Where Donovan is, "that's where [he wants] to be," Freeman would tell frustrated aides trying to track down the boss for a missed appointment. "Where [Donovan] ought to be, that's just a little bit of never-mind."

By the end of 1941, Donovan had nearly six hundred people on his payroll. Most knew little about spying but they included some of the country's best and brightest: Wall Street banker Junius Morgan, Academy Award–winning movie director John Ford, labor lawyer Arthur Goldberg, Rhode Island governor William H. Vanderbilt III, author Stephen Vincent Benet, historian Arthur Schlesinger. Hire on the spot anyone "of great ability," was Donovan's rule, "later on we'll find out what they can do." Smart people can handle any job, he believed.

Donovan's "league of gentlemen," as he liked to call them, also included a healthy share of social misfits, spoiled rich kids, and military castoffs. Everyone from Ickes to retired General Pershing to Eleanor Roosevelt to even his brother Vincent tried to foist friends or relatives on him, many the Army had rejected as physically unfit. (Donovan usually found a place for referrals from Eleanor, whom he did not want to alienate.) His headquarters soon earned the nickname "bad eyes brigade" because so many wore glasses. Society WASPs who were fit for combat but hoped to stay out of it also gravitated to Donovan. Reporters began to call the agency a "draft dodger haven." Generals called them the "East Coast faggots." Though he professed to want honest upstanding souls he could teach the shady black arts, Donovan took many who already knew the latter. He accepted safecrackers, men with prison records who could be useful as burglars, and occasionally Mafia thugs for paramilitary operations. Steve Early visited a training camp Donovan set up for German and Italian Americans he wanted to infiltrate as saboteurs and was struck that they were a bunch of "tough-looking hombres . . . not the kind of guys you would like to meet in a dark alley."

In Donovan's rush to build up, early applicants were hired with no more security check than someone vouching for their family connections. It resulted in Nazi sympathizers slipping in, who had to be weeded out later when they were more carefully screened. Communists were a dilemma. Donovan wanted them to work with him but not necessarily for him. With Roosevelt's blessing he had Buxton meet regularly with Eugene Dennis, the leader of the Communist Party USA, who fed him intelligence on Axis agents in the United States and abroad. Donovan relayed the tips on the agents to Hoover, but didn't tell him from where the information came. Yet when he discovered employees in his own agency with communist sympathies, Donovan could be ruthless in getting rid of them, particularly when they were outed by Hoover or congressional witch hunts. When forty-two members of his propaganda staff signed a letter protesting that his firing of two writers was based on flimsy evidence of communist affiliation, Donovan indignantly threatened to fire the petitioners as well.

But handing out pink slips posed its own dangers, Donovan soon realized. The discharged left angry and more willing to spill secrets they had learned. With thousands needed for a worldwide intelligence organization, Donovan began screening applicants more carefully at the outset so he wouldn't have to fire them later. In addition to security checks, he eventually set up assessment units on the East and West Coasts, where teams of psychiatrists and psychologists put applicants through an exotic battery of tests to determine if they were suitable for clandestine work.

By June 1942, Donovan had set up espionage and sabotage schools at vacant Civilian Conservation Corps and National Parks Service camps in Maryland and Virginia. After a sixteen-week espionage course, the students took final tests called "schemes." They fanned out to cities to try to infiltrate defense plants with false identities to steal secrets—and also to practice talking their way out of a jam if guards caught them. The trainers usually alerted the local police or military authorities when a scheme was in their area. Even so, Hoover became incensed when he found one of Donovan's students in San Diego posing as an FBI Academy graduate. He threatened to prosecute any impostors his agents nabbed. Donovan ignored the threat and continued the schemes.

From the beginning Donovan recognized he was starting from "minus zero," as he put it. To launch sabotage and guerrilla attacks, he set up what was code-named the "L activity," run by Lieutenant Colonel Robert Solborg, an Army intelligence officer born in Warsaw who had fought in czarist Russia's cavalry during World War I. But L was a unit in name only; Solborg had no saboteurs or guerrillas to command. Fortunately the military was willing to dump what little espionage capability it had on Donovan. In October 1941, the Navy gave him American businessman Wallace Banta Phillips and the thirteen agents he controlled around the world gathering information on foreign shipping the sea service found only occasionally useful. A longtime London resident, Phillips became the chief of "K activity" to collect intelligence and counter Axis spying.

By mid-November 1941, Phillips had forty-two agents scattered in a dozen countries, but they were an odd lot with questionable spying skills: an ex-Treasury officer in Bulgaria, a museum curator in Iran, a *National Geographic* editor in Afghanistan, an American roaming France whose only qualifications were that he had lived there many years and spoke "perfect French," Phillips told Donovan. But the only espionage operation Donovan had overseas was Phillips's and he gave him a blank check to draw from a $2.5 million secret account Roosevelt's Bureau of the Budget eventually agreed to set up for it.

Like a player in a pickup basketball game, Donovan looked for other amateurs he could use for now. The Philips Company, which sold lamps overseas, agreed to have its representatives in neutral and Axis-controlled countries feed him information they ran across on their sales calls that might be militarily useful. The Eastman Kodak Company canvassed its five thousand amateur camera clubs around the country for photos of enemy installations its members might have taken on foreign trips before the war. Pan American Airways loaned employees at its hubs throughout Africa; one sent reports, code-named "Cigar," on German U-boats prowling off the Ivory Coast. Working through his old friend, Francis Cardinal Spellman, the archbishop of New York, Donovan also cast lines out to the Catholic Church. An apostolic delegate in Washington secretly promised that Vatican envoys posted in Axis countries would discreetly supply him with political intelligence they collected.

America's foreign-born and first-generation population—some 46 million—became a pool for information and agent recruitment. While the

Oral Intelligence Unit he had set up in New York interviewed thousands of newly arrived refugees, Donovan cultivated a number of the high-profile émigrés. Prince Serge Obolensky, a tall and handsome former White Russian cavalryman who had worked his way up the New York National Guard, offered his expertise on the Soviet Union. Donovan's kind of guy, the prince was hired immediately. Count Carlo Sforza, an aristocratic Italian antifascist and occasional Ickes dinner partner, became an informant. Donovan was also captivated by Eve Curie, the enchanting daughter of Nobel Prize–winning scientists Marie and Pierre Curie. She had dark almond eyes and spoke with a sultry French accent. Donovan helped her arrange a world tour as a newswoman and from the North Africa war zone and Russian front she sent him private reports, which he passed on to FDR.

Many of Donovan's early amateur spies ended up a waste of money. He convinced Roosevelt to approve $5,000 to send explorer and nature filmmaker Armand Denis to roam central and southern Africa to spy on German espionage and military activity, using the cover that he was scouting a future movie on primates. The Belgian American shot a lot of footage on apes, caught several tropical diseases, and filed what amounted to a long travelogue with no useful military or political intelligence. He finally admitted in a letter to David Bruce that he was a hopeless secret agent: "I cannot see the forest for the trees."

But at least Donovan's unit was going on the offensive, fanning out across the country and around the world to begin collecting intelligence. In wartime Washington that was something new. By mid-1942, he had organized his agency into four branches: Secret Intelligence, to send undercover spies abroad collecting information on Axis forces and the economies that sustained them; Special Operations, to spread propaganda and organize sabotage and guerrilla warfare in occupied countries; Foreign Nationalities, based in New York to mine ethnic groups in the United States for political intelligence abroad and recruit foot soldiers for covert operations; Research and Analysis, which became known as the "Chairborne Division," to make sense of the fire hose of information pouring in. Donovan realized the mundane business of intelligence would be the most important, the gathering, analyzing, and interpreting of "many minute bits of evidence," he said. "A half hour spent with the brakeman of a freight train running into occupied France would produce more useful information than Mata Hari could learn overnight."

The administrative chores of running an intelligence organization, however, bored Donovan. He brought more men into his inner circle for that: Duncan Lee, a tightly strung lawyer from Donovan's firm, to be an executive secretary and troubleshooter; Edwin Putzell, another law firm colleague, to manage Donovan's schedule and the paper flow to him; Ernest Cuneo, a Democratic Party operative who took over Jimmy Roosevelt's job cajoling cooperation out of the FBI and other agencies; and Otto "Ole" Doering Jr., the son of a top Sears, Roebuck executive who also left Donovan's law firm and ended up his chief of staff. Self-effacing yet meticulously efficient, Doering's principal job became making sure Donovan's agency survived, which was not a given with the State Department, military, and FBI lined up against him. Donovan wanted $135 million for the 1943 fiscal year. The Budget Bureau's Smith wanted it slashed to $50 million. Donovan, he groused, had "sold the President a bill of goods."

DONOVAN ALSO NEEDED front companies to hide parts of his organization. Stephenson transferred to him Western Continents Trading, a phony export-import firm British intelligence had used, along with its head agent, George Muhle, who had been the American representative for a German-controlled pharmaceutical before Pearl Harbor. From an office in the RCA Building at Rockefeller Plaza, Muhle and five staffers collected intelligence on companies important for the Nazi war machine, such as I. G. Farben, and tracked German business activity in Latin America, which Donovan knew treaded on Hoover's and Rockefeller's turf. He kept Western Continents secret even from many in his own organization. "Project George," as the operation came to be called, compiled index cards on thousands of German businessmen linked to espionage and prepared hundreds of reports for the State Department and other agencies on Berlin companies in Latin America and elsewhere. Among its odd jobs: finding a bottle of German Bayer Aspirin the Navy wanted so it could be imitated and reproduced.

Setting up dummy corporations, however, could get complicated, Donovan quickly discovered. He had to evade nosy inquiries from Dun & Bradstreet, which wrote profiles on companies. Workers had to waste time pretending to do what the sign at the front door said they were supposed to do. No guards or night watchmen could be posted to protect secrets in the office; it would be a tip-off that the company was conducting more than just routine business.

Donovan also began to have a bad feeling about a major the Army's Military Intelligence Service had loaned him for another one of his front companies, FBQ Incorporated, which was setting up two radio listening stations in New York and California. John "Frenchy" Grombach was a burly West Point graduate and former boxer. He had left the service during the interwar years to dabble in radio broadcasting but had returned to the Army in 1941. Donovan thought he was a gabby conspiratorial type, not the kind of man he wanted organizing these highly sensitive stations. They would be intercepting not just German and Japanese propaganda broadcasts but also coded military messages and Gestapo dispatches that Donovan hoped his men could decipher. That decryption work would give him a capability like Magic's, whose raw take his agency was not allowed to see. He knew Marshall would not appreciate the overlap. Grombach also had gotten his wife a job at FBQ as a radio technician, which raised nepotism alarm bells with agency lawyers. Frenchy and Mrs. Grombach were soon edged out of FBQ, which left the major nursing a bitter grudge against Donovan. He would soon become a troublesome rival.

DONOVAN'S HEADQUARTERS quickly became frenetic with activity. Julia Child, a young public relations woman from New York who joined the agency as a file clerk in Donovan's outer office and later would transfer to Chungking, remembered the boss as little more than a blur, who "constantly passed by our door as he saw people in or out of his office. And when in it his door was usually open and we could overhear an occasional loud remark or command." The aging headquarters building itself soon began to strain under the hectic pace. An incinerator exploded in the basement because too many classified documents had been stuffed into it for destruction. Another day, aides scrambled to save valuable papers when pipes burst, flooding the first floor. Even Donovan began to complain that half-eaten late-night meals piling up in trash cans gave the place a malodorous pall when he arrived in the morning.

Donovan found that putting secret agents in the field posed a host of practical problems. They all had to have code numbers, but so many were passed out (one memo called it a "numbers racket") headquarters soon had difficulty keeping track of who was who on documents that just listed the numbers. Spies wanted life insurance, understandable considering their profession's hazards. But insurance companies refused to write policies unless they knew a client's name and what his job was, which would blow an agent's cover. Donovan decided to pay death benefits from his unaccounted-for money.

Transportation became a hassle. With military support personnel pouring into Europe, space on ships and planes for Donovan's agents became scarce. He had hired Ruth Shipley's brother, hoping it would make the State Department's top passport official friendlier to his agency. It didn't. The officious Mrs. Shipley balked at allowing Donovan's agency to make its own American passports for agents with phony details on them. In the beginning, she had stamped on the ones she issued for Donovan's men that the passport holder was traveling abroad "on Official Business" for the Coordinator of Information. They might as well wear buttons on their lapels reading "American Undercover Agent," a memo to Donovan complained. He finally got the policy rescinded.

Even riding around town could be a problem. Interior Secretary Ickes, who had a quick temper, sent Donovan an angry letter in September after his National Parks police caught an overeager agency courier speeding forty-six miles per hour on the Arlington Memorial Bridge to rush film to the airport for a West Coast flight. It was a "reprehensible" offense, Ickes wrote. Donovan apologized. But Ickes continued to send the spy chief angry notes when his park police caught couriers speeding, which started Donovan's aides wondering if the cabinet officer had anything better to do than play traffic cop.

Donovan hired a banker to manage the secret funds he received from the White House. Spies had to have money to live on while in the field. Dollars obviously would give them away so a complex system had to be set up to quietly buy foreign currencies. The Treasury Department had over $175,000 worth of foreign gold coins available, while Paramount Pictures held foreign currency reserves for their overseas films, which Donovan could purchase. German marks and French francs were bought on the black market. So they wouldn't stand out for an agent using them, new bills had to be aged by spreading them out on an office room floor and walking on them for a day. Donovan also scoured the country for engravers, printers, graphic artists, and special paper stocks to produce difficult-to-find currencies as well as foreign passports, rations cards, and other documents agents needed in the field. The Treasury Department, nervous about this collection of forgers, demanded that they all be drafted into the Army and closely watched so they didn't counterfeit on the side.

Donovan became a stickler about holding employees accountable for the White House's unvouchered funds. He set up detailed expense account rules; a station chief overseas was allotted $300 a month to wine and dine sources. Donovan, however, had looser rules for his own spending. He always kept $2,000 in the top right drawer of his desk to buy information from his personal sources.

WITH A FERTILE MIND Donovan was willing to launch practically any project, no matter how unconventional. Roosevelt approved $15,000 for a confidential geographic study Donovan wanted Arctic expert Vilhjalmur Stefansson to prepare on Alaska, northern Canada, Greenland, and Iceland, where the United States might have to fight Germany or Japan. He hatched an idea for an air-conditioned, high-tech briefing room at his headquarters with situation maps and the latest audiovisual gadgets (including a new one called television), which FDR could visit daily for a picture of the worldwide war. Roosevelt was intrigued and approved $2 million, but the Budget Bureau complained it was a useless toy and the Secret Service, horrified at the thought of carting a wheelchair-bound president to it daily, objected. The military brass eventually grabbed the project so they could watch the war through multimedia.

Ideas poured in from outsiders and Donovan entertained them all. A New York art appraiser proposed flooding Germany with counterfeit marks to create economic chaos. (Donovan worried Berlin would retaliate and flood the U.S with phony bills.) John Steinbeck wrote suggesting air-dropping tiny grenades over occupied countries so children could toss them from rooftops at German soldiers. (Donovan didn't reply to the novelist.)

Yet he was willing to try almost anything—even if it had little to do with spying—and to stick his nose into anyone else's business. Donovan agreed to have his agency sponsor an Australian dental officer making a U.S. speaking tour on "Dentistry in Total War." He sent memos to FDR proposing that a road be built to Alaska to truck in supplies for new military bases there to attack Japan—with a route he thought the road should take. Another memo to FDR proposed that he declare a national day "of fasting, humiliation and prayer." Stimson told him to butt out; the War Department already had its own route for the Alaska road project. Roosevelt joked that the fasting and prayer day would do his overweight press secretary, Steve Early, more good than it would the American people.

STANLEY P. LOVELL was a short, round-faced, and unpretentious man, orphaned since childhood, who was fifty-two when Donovan hired him in early 1942. Lovell had already established himself as a respected commercial chemist and New England inventor. Donovan called him his "Professor Moriarty." From a cramped basement room in the headquarters building, Lovell headed the Office of Scientific Research and Development, with free rein to develop any spy gadget he could dream up.

For that mission, Lovell had a mind even more creative than Donovan's. Thousands of pistols with silencers, lightweight submachine guns, miniature cameras, agent radios, exotic knives, and special explosives were manufactured and shipped out to operatives. Invisible ink was developed to write secret messages on paper or even an agent's shirt. Explosives shaped like lumps of coal (nicknamed "Black Joe") and pocket-sized incendiaries with time-delayed fuses to start fires were sent to Europe. Bombs fashioned with explosive powder made to look like flour, which could be kneaded and baked into bread, were produced and sent to Asia.

Lovell and Donovan brought Marshall to the Congressional Country Club to demonstrate the power of "Aunt Jemima," their nickname for the flour. A batch of the deadly dough was placed under a thick armored plate and detonated. Ordnance officers, however, misjudged its explosive force. Shards of steel flew in every direction. One crashed through the window of Marshall's car. Another chunk narrowly missed Donovan's head and embedded into a tree behind him. Lovell, trembling, picked himself up from the ground next to Donovan. "What's next on the program?" the spymaster asked him in a calm voice, oblivious to his near-death moment.

Some of his gadgets were comical. Lovell had gland experts produce female sex hormones an agent could inject into the vegetables Hitler ate to make the hair from his mustache fall out and his voice turn soprano. Other ideas flopped. A chemical called "Dog Drag" to confuse bloodhounds chasing an agent did not work; the hounds never lost the scent. But Lovell had other gadgets that were deadly serious, such as tasteless poisons that could be slipped into food and drinks. More than twelve thousand knock-out pills, called "K tablets," were manufactured for American and British agents. DuPont Company also produced the "L tablet," a poison pill spies could take if captured that caused quick death. Donovan kept one when he traveled overseas. He had a gag he liked to pull on his aides, taking two white pills out of his pocket for a headache and saying: "I don't know which is the L tablet and which is the aspirin." But once when a plane carrying him to Europe strayed too near the French coast and came under German antiaircraft fire, Donovan reached into his coat pocket for his L pill in case the aircraft was forced down over enemy-occupied territory.

With Donovan's blessing, Lovell also conducted highly secret research into how chemical or biological agents could be used as mass destruction weapons—or for discreet sabotage operations. Lovell's scientists investigated poison gases that could kill draft animals and researched a rare bacterium, designated "peach fuzz," that had "tremendous possibilities" as a lethal biological weapon, according to one memo.

SMOKE SWIRLED AROUND Little Augie's head as he took another long drag on the cigarette. His real name was August Del Gaizo, a middle-aged New York gangster who had been in and out of prison for assorted assaults and murder charges and who now ran the mob on New York's Lower East Side. Little Augie lounged on a couch in the apartment of George White, a roly-poly former New York cop who had busted him several times but kept in friendly contact with the mobster over the years. Augie's driver waited impatiently in the car on the street below, but the crime boss was in no hurry. And the more he sucked on the cigarette the chattier he became. He bragged about the bribes he had given to cops over the years. He offered details about his loansharking operation that was raking in hundreds of thousands of dollars. He shared gossip about Lucky Luciano's battles with other underworld bosses like Meyer Lansky and Frank Costello. "Whatever you do, don't ever use any of the stuff I'm telling you," Little Augie said with a silly grin on his face.

White smiled and just listened. The ex-cop now worked for Donovan. Little Augie didn't know that the cigarette White had offered him was laced with tetrahydrocannabinol acetate. The highly secret truth drug experiment seemed to White to have worked.

Donovan, who had collected research papers on truth drugs and had kept close track of the Little Augie test, had ordered Lovell in September 1942 to find a potion that could be used on high-value war prisoners, enemy agents, or even American officials suspected of betraying state secrets. It had to get them to talk—without the person knowing he'd been slipped it. The Army also was eager to have a reliable drug for its interrogations. Lovell had tried scores of concoctions on unwitting soldiers, who were told they were part of a research project to find a treatment for shell shock: mescaline, various barbiturates, scopolamine, Benzedrine, and marijuana. None produced the desired results with the subject unaware that he was being doped. But the drug that showed promise when injected into food or cigarettes was tetrahydrocannabinol acetate, an extract of Indian hemp.

White had Little Augie back several more times for smokes and chats. The gangster gabbed about bribing a congressman and his opium smuggling business, which along with his other revelations could have put him back in prison. (Augie's secrets were safe with Donovan, who did not want the "TD" project revealed in a trial.) But the drug's effect was uneven and Augie sometimes complained of being woozy, which meant an agent might be tipped off if he was slipped it. Tetrahydrocannabinol acetate, Lovell's scientists wrote Donovan, "is not a perfect 'truth drug,'" and "is probably not adaptable for mass interrogation." But Donovan persevered, secretly enlisting the Surgeon General's Office and Cornell University's Medical College to continue the experiments.

SOME AIDES IN Donovan's inner circle began to grumble that their director was becoming too creative, jumping at too many jobs and offbeat ideas. Donovan invited self-criticism—he sent his senior staff a memo in February ordering "a review of all projects now under way"—but he wasn't always happy with the feedback. Bill Whitney, his London representative, wrote him a lengthy and pointed memo complaining that the agency was spread too thinly and Donovan was micromanaging too many extraneous details. Instead of "dabbling in some of this and some of that," choose one core mission, such as spying, "and let the others go," Whitney advised. Donovan, who had already decided that Whitney was a self-centered eccentric, had no intention of slimming down his organization. He sent a curt note back to Whitney that he was all wet. His London chief resigned in April.

Donovan's deepest rift came with his propaganda director, Robert Sherwood, who ran his Foreign Information Service. Sherwood turned out to be a poor administrator and Donovan became increasingly annoyed that the playwright wasn't keeping him in the loop on what his propaganda operation was doing. But a deeper philosophical difference began to divide them. Sherwood believed propaganda should be based on the truth and that his service should educate the world on "the American way of life." Donovan saw information as a weapon and had no qualms about spreading lies to subvert the enemy. By March the feud between Donovan and his playwright had grown so bitter the two men weren't speaking to each other. Eventually, Sherwood privately urged Roosevelt to shut down Donovan's entire spy agency and fold its work into the Army and Navy.

Roosevelt, who let the bickering fester, did not intend to do that. The president and his spy chief had developed their own, somewhat peculiar, rapport. Donovan sent Roosevelt documents from France in their original French, knowing FDR liked to exercise his fluency in the language. Roosevelt was as open to weird ideas as Donovan. When his spymaster sent him a slightly bizarre suggestion that oil pipelines could be built with plywood, FDR had him run it by the War Production Board. The board thought it too risky to try. Roosevelt even sent Donovan his own wild suggestions, such as one Eleanor passed on from a Pennsylvania dentist who claimed that bats fitted with tiny time-delayed incendiary devices could be powerful terror weapons if dropped from planes over Japanese homes. The bats would fly into the eaves of the wood and paper houses and their charges would ignite to burn them down. Donovan ordered Lovell to test the idea. But when the Air Force released the poor creatures from planes with the devices clamped on their backs they dropped to the earth like stones.

Roosevelt also liked the fact that Donovan was eager to take on unconventional diplomatic missions his stodgy State Department wouldn't touch. In July, Donovan dispatched Count Ilya Tolstoy (the grandson of the Russian novelist) and explorer Brooke Dolan to scout a route from India to Tibet and on to China as a possible supply corridor for Chinese fighting the Japanese. The two agents (code-named "Mud" and "Slug") also were to report on enemy espionage and sabotage along the route. It was a politically tricky mission because the Tibetans in the middle had been warring with the Chinese, who wanted to control them. But Tolstoy and Dolan managed to carry it off and came back with a warm letter to FDR from the Kashag, Tibet's governing council. Roosevelt, who didn't have a clue what a Kashag was, penned Donovan a playful note:

> Thank you for sending me the letter from the Kashag. I never saw a Kashag. I never want to see one. But this I know, and know full well, I would rather see than be one!

The President not only did not mind Donovan's branching out, he enjoyed his adventures.

Chapter 11

—❦❦❦—

Adolf Hitler

D ONOVAN'S COORDINATOR of Information office became a favorite target for Fred Kaltenbach. The German American from Iowa was now a radio anchor in Berlin for Joseph Goebbels's Ministry of Public Enlightenment and Propaganda.

With Donovan's appointment as a spy chief, Roosevelt has turned "his attention to propaganda on a large scale," Kaltenbach began one of his English-language shows, broadcast on shortwave to the United States.

"Oh, Donovan!" responded "Fritz," his straight man in the booth. "Isn't he the man of the nightclubs in the Balkans?"

"At any rate, he's going to spread the desirable information," Kaltenbach said. "His department is called COI."

What does that stand for, the two asked each other—"Center of Ignorance" or "Corporation of Idiots"?

Goebbels's propaganda machine was now vilifying Donovan almost as frequently as Roosevelt. Stephenson sent him a Nazi document British agents in Holland had captured warning that Donovan was plotting to subvert German morale with a wide-ranging propaganda and espionage program.

Donovan aimed to do exactly that. A 1939 attempt on Hitler's life by a German dissident had failed. Among the German high command there were a few skeptics of the führer's western and eastern offensives, but most senior military officers (whom he had bought off with bribes and large estates) backed him, the rank-and-file soldiers were even more loyal, and the German public overwhelmingly approved. But from the first day he became Coordinator of Information, Donovan began plotting how to topple Adolf Hitler, a man he personally viewed as the incarnation of evil.

Donovan formed a team of psychoanalysts to study the führer's mind from afar. He wanted "to know what Hitler was thinking before he thought it," Baxter recalls. The psychological and personality reports the shrinks eventually produced on Hitler took up 392 pages. The leader of the Third Reich is well read and "a veritable demon for work," the reports noted. His physique is frail but his bright blue eyes have a "depth and glint which makes them appear to have a hypnotic quality." He has "underlying inferiority feelings." "Sexually he is a full-fledged masochist," who when "smitten with a girl, tends to grovel at her feet in a most disgusting manner." The psychologists found no evidence he was homosexual, but he displays "feminine characteristics" and "derives sexual pleasure from looking at men's bodies and associating with homosexuals." "But, underneath," the reports concluded, "he is every inch the Führer." Hitler will never surrender or allow himself to be captured, the psychologists predicted. If he is not assassinated beforehand, he will wait "until the last moment" as the enemy is closing in and commit suicide. Donovan ordered propagandists to publicize a "spiced-up" version of the studies, emphasizing the sex.

An important contributor to Hitler's psychological study was a Harvard man like FDR, who had once been the führer's press secretary. The son of a Munich art dealer and an American mother from a prominent New England family, Ernst "Putzi" Hanfstaengl was a tall heavyset man from two opposite worlds. After graduating from the Ivy League college in 1906 he had sat out World War I minding his father's art shop on New York's Fifth Avenue. But he returned to Munich in 1921 and soon fell under Hitler's spell. When Hitler took power in 1933, he made the cosmopolitan Hanfstaengl his foreign press secretary and glad-hander for Americans checking out the new chancellor. But by 1937, Hanfstaengl had fallen out of favor with Hitler and his inner circle of fanatics, who never trusted the American half-breed. He fled to England.

John Franklin Carter, FDR's personal spy, discovered Hanfstaengl languishing in a British internment camp in Canada and convinced Roosevelt that his fellow alumnus could be a valuable window into the Nazi regime. Hanfstaengl, who was now eager to switch sides and gossip about his old boss, had an encyclopedic memory for intimate details of Hitler and key henchmen, such as Hermann Göring, Goebbels, and Interior Minister

Heinrich Himmler. In July 1942 a U.S. Army plane flew Hanfstaengl to Washington, where he was put under armed guard in quarters at Fort Belvoir, Virginia. The dubious British agreed to release their prisoner only on condition that he be kept under wraps and not allowed to stray.

Putzi became a pain. The Army found him to be a demanding, arrogant, and racist houseguest. When rumors began circulating in Washington that a top Nazi was living the high life at Fort Belvoir, the post commander demanded that he be evicted. Putzi, who had been given the pseudonym "Ernst Sedgewick" after his mother's maiden surname, was relocated to a secluded estate in Bush Hill, Virginia, where he kept his ear glued each day to a shortwave radio set receiving German propaganda broadcasts.

Hanfstaengl had volumes of Third Reich tales to unload. Hitler, he told his interrogators, considered Churchill and Roosevelt parlor patriots, while he stayed at the front "sharing the Spartan life of the Army." Donovan's analysts who interviewed Hanfstaengl complained it took a herculean effort to organize his disjointed thoughts into coherent reports. Donovan found them valuable more for their peek into the regime's insider politics than for military intelligence. Roosevelt also enjoyed reading Putzi's papers. He called them his "Hitler bedtime stories."

Donovan looked for ways to create anti-Hitler unrest. His broad targets were German civilians and soldiers. "Our propaganda must be convincing," a strategy memo advised. "It must carry the ring of truth" to their mind-set and play on their assorted paranoia, such as fear of inflation making their marks once more worthless. Some propaganda lines his brain trust dreamed up made sense: German soldiers are freezing on the Eastern Front because they were issued only summer clothing, while Hitler is snug and warm at his Berchtesgaden retreat. Others ideas were silly: planes dropping leaflets over Germany with "pictures of succulent, appetizing dishes that would make a hungry person almost go mad with longing."

Donovan became almost frenetic with schemes to topple Hitler. On one day alone (September 30, 1941) he shuttled from his office to his home for secret meetings on three different plots—the final one of the day by a Quaker named Malcolm Lovell who proposed to be an intermediary in an unusual gambit.

A peace activist and a bit of an airhead, Lovell had struck up a friendship the past three years with Hans Thomsen, Germany's acting ambassador to Washington. Over long dinners he urged the envoy and the Nazi regime "to pursue paths of love rather than hatred." Tall, suave, and well educated, Thomsen (half-Norwegian on his mother's side) was a good conversationalist and clever at eliciting information on the diplomatic cocktail circuit. He would even have his wife burst into tears at designated times about "those awful Nazis" so sympathetic Washington women would spill their husbands' secrets to her.

Lovell was convinced Thomsen wanted to defect. During a dinner two weeks earlier, the ambassador confided that he would be willing to lead a coup against Hitler and take over the government if he had "financial backing." He told Lovell to convey the offer to Donovan.

A chargé d'affaires in a faraway embassy was hardly a prime candidate for seizing the German government. Donovan, nevertheless, was intrigued enough by the approach that he directed the Quaker to tell Thomsen he would put up $1 million if the ambassador would renounce the Nazi government and come out publicly in favor of the western alliance. That was a healthy sum for just a propaganda coup. Thomsen, however, never bit on the bribe. When it served his diplomatic purposes, the ambassador portrayed himself simply as a loyal foreign service officer, but in reality Thomsen was a loyal Nazi and a Hitler friend.

Hoping to glean intelligence, Donovan nevertheless continued to have Lovell dine with Thomsen and file reports on their conversations, which he forwarded to Roosevelt. But by November 1941 Thomsen was often feeding Lovell Nazi disinformation—one line he peddled: "Russia has already been permanently eliminated as an offensive factor"—knowing it would get back to Donovan.

The failure of the Thomsen affair did not discourage Donovan. He hunted for secret bank accounts Nazi leaders might have in Latin America and the United States that the State Department could seize. The British sent him details gleaned from a Hungarian diplomatic source on the special train Hitler rode as his mobile headquarters, the planes at his disposal when he flew by air, and the type of meals he liked to eat when he visited military canteens—all helpful for planning an assassination.

New York as well as Washington became a hub for Donovan's early schemes to topple Hitler. Using his union contacts, Arthur Goldberg looked for ways to organize what remained of the German labor movement. Allen Dulles, a New York lawyer with diplomatic experience who had left the city's prestigious Sullivan and Cromwell law firm to join Donovan's agency, was convinced a dissident movement remained in Germany waiting to be exploited. Donovan agreed. He and Dulles began hatching their plots among the royalty, the clerics, the intelligentsia, the business wealthy, the politicians, and the retired military officers who had fled Germany, Austria, and other European countries and who now sat in fancy salons in New York and Washington dreaming up ways to return to power.

They were an odd cast of characters for overthrowing Hitler. Finding levelheaded operatives among the often feuding exiles proved difficult. All brimmed with biases or personal agendas. Paul Hagan, an Austrian author Dulles at first thought was "a revolutionary with fire in his eye," proposed a daring plan to infiltrate a small team into Europe to link up with the German underground movement; but Hagan soon became worthless as a secret agent when he publicly bickered with other expatriates who accused him of being a communist Lothario. Father Odo, who had arrived in Washington in 1940, offered to send Donovan detailed reports on conditions in Germany. The good father had been the former duke of Würtemberg and a major on the German General Staff, but after his testicles were shot off during World War I he became a Benedictine monk. Donovan found him fanatically anti-Nazi but temperamental and his reports "highly colored and inaccurate," he finally wrote Roosevelt.

Then there was Archduke Otto of Habsburg, one of the most voracious eaters on Washington's dinner party circuit, who roamed the State Department with grand visions of assuming the Habsburg throne of the old Austro-Hungarian Empire. Otto's offer: Set up a spy network for Donovan in Hungary and work his Budapest contacts to convince the government to desert the Axis. Though his aides believed Otto might be the silver bullet, Donovan was unsure. "Let me know what you wish done," he wrote FDR. Climbing into bed with Otto, the horrified State Department warned, would paint Roosevelt as favoring restoration of the washed-up Habsburgs, not a popular idea with the Russians or other Balkan countries Washington wanted as allies. The president ordered the Otto contact severed. Later Donovan had to tamp down false rumors spreading through Washington that his brother Vincent would be "court chaplain" when Otto became emperor of Austria.

Donovan thought he had a fighting chance with Gottfried Treviranus, a former communications minister to Heinrich Brüning, who had been German chancellor from 1930 to 1932. Treviranus, who had fled Germany to escape Hitler's purges, knew Göring and other top Nazis. But of more interest to Donovan: Treviranus claimed to have ties to anti-Nazi terrorists among the Freikorps, the paramilitary bands of disgruntled German soldiers that sprouted after World War I. The operation became known as the "T Project" and Donovan ordered little put on paper for the highly secret plan. Treviranus, his wife, and daughter were moved from Canada to a New York apartment, which Dulles's partner, Donald Downes, had rented. The German would be paid $10,000 a year to organize an insurrectionist movement inside Germany from his Freikorps and dissident contacts. But backbiting became fierce among the exiles. Hagan claimed Treviranus had no real following inside Germany and had been unusually chummy with the Nazis before he fled. What finally sank Treviranus, however, was his big mouth. Before leaving Canada he blabbed openly to friends that he was organizing a coup in Germany for the Americans. Donovan cut a $3,750 severance check for the German, hoping it would keep him quiet, and shut down the project.

Donovan's research analysts warned him that the exiles he consorted with were, for the most part, an unreliable lot with no followings in their countries. But espionage meant operating in this "strange netherworld of refugees, radicals and traitors," Downes argued in one memo. "There is neither room for gentility nor protocol in this work. Utter ruthlessness can only be fought with utter ruthlessness; honor, honesty, carefulness and sincerity must be left to the fighting forces and the diplomats." Donovan agreed.

Chapter 12

❦

Enemies

THE ACCIDENT HAPPENED, of all days, on April Fool's 1942. Freeman raced the limousine to Union Station so Donovan could make the 1:05 P.M. train that Wednesday to New York. But as the car neared the station a cab slammed into it, throwing Donovan from the back seat to the front and painfully wrenching his right leg, the one injured in World War I. The leg was likely broken, but Donovan insisted that Freeman and a porter carry him into the drawing room car of his train. New York has the best doctors, he told Freeman. He would have one there check him if the leg still hurt.

The pain was excruciating by the time the train reached New York's Penn Station. But Donovan had a porter and Wayne Nelson, a Dulles aide who had clerked in his New York law firm, lift him into a cab, which took him to his suite at the St. Regis Hotel.

Back in Washington the next night, Evalyn Walsh McLean hosted her weekly dinner party at her Georgetown mansion for Washington's political and diplomatic elite. It was always a glittering black-tie affair with fine silver candelabras and McLean presiding with the forty-five-and-a-half-carat Hope Diamond dangling from her neck. The spoiled daughter and widow of publishing magnates, McLean was a rabid Roosevelt hater. FDR ranked her among Washington's most prominent "parasites," but key people in his administration went to her dinners to hear whom she was trashing. Tonight Vice President Henry Wallace sat next to McLean as she ranted about one of her pet hates: "Wild Bill." The dowager was convinced Donovan was plotting to become the vice president with Frank Knox as the presi-

112

dent. McLean assured Wallace she had the goods on the colonel: "He is a very bad egg." Wallace thought Evalyn talked too much, as always. But he kept it to himself.

Colorful stories about "Wild Bill" became chitchat fare at Washington parties. To show off what his unit could do, he had agents steal secret documents from the office of an admiral he was having drinks with at one social event, then bring the papers to him to give them to the astounded officer before the party broke up. But the trail of bruised egos Donovan left behind was growing longer. Admiral Harold Train, the Navy's intelligence chief, was irked when he denied Donovan the loan of an officer and within minutes received a phone call from Knox asking him to deliver the man. Train stood his ground and refused to transfer the officer.

Washington also was a fairly libertine city filled with many extramarital affairs. Even so, Donovan's dallying raised eyebrows. He was often seen driving around the capital with a beautiful woman in the back seat of his limo who seemed to have no official function. His aides routinely talked behind his back about the affairs. Army intelligence picked up the rumors. Some of the wives of Washington's powerful took notice and did not appreciate how he treated Ruth. He cannot be trusted, some whispered into their husbands' ears.

Laid up with his broken right leg encased in a plaster cast, Donovan within days set up his two-room suite at the St. Regis as his office. "I am still in the ring," he cheerily told friends. A stream of visitors trooped in at all hours of the day and night: advisers to receive his orders and relay them to Washington, secretaries to take dictation for letters and memos, agents returned from overseas to brief him on their operations, visitors from British intelligence to check his condition and report back to London.

Donovan had hoped to return to Washington within a week after his accident but the injury turned out to be more serious than he realized. A blood clot had formed in his leg and had traveled to his left lung causing a dangerous embolism which was life-threatening. Doctors ordered him to bed, where he remained for six weeks. He was lucky to escape death once more. But Donovan was not sure his agency would survive. "I have greater enemies in Washington than Hitler in Europe," he told Fisher Howe, whom he had sent to his England station. And they were circling now.

FRANK KNOX DROPPED by the St. Regis on April 26 to see how the patient was doing and to pass along two bits of news from Roosevelt. The president had told him Donovan's accident had probably left him physically unfit to lead a force in combat. Donovan, who still hungered for action at the front, insisted there was "nothing permanently wrong" with him and he was in fine shape for a field command. But Knox's second piece of news almost gave him another embolism. Undersecretary of State Sumner Welles had told FDR that Donovan had ninety agents prowling Mexico in clear violation of the president's ban on him putting spies in Latin America. Donovan thought he had buried that rumor when Welles brought it to him the month before. "It was a well worn lie," he angrily wrote Roosevelt the next day—which it was.

After almost a half year of Donovan pestering to get his men into Latin America, Roosevelt finally signed an order on January 16 siding with Hoover and ruling that the FBI would control spying in the region. Donovan abided and ordered Wallace Phillips to transfer agents he had watching ship movements along Mexico's coast back to the Navy. But a good rumor can always find a way to survive. Hoover suspected Donovan still had spies there and Donovan's men suspected he kept alive the tale, which they began to call "the famous ninety humpty-dumpties." "I only hope that the German Army will melt away as rapidly as my alleged force of ninety agents in Mexico melts under investigation," Donovan wrote FDR in a long memo rebutting the charge, adding, "You should know me well enough to know that I do adhere strictly to my orders and make no attempt to encroach upon the jurisdiction of anyone else."

FDR did know Donovan well enough and suspected he was conducting intelligence operations in Latin America. Donovan never openly violated the ban—he did not put spy stations or intelligence-collecting officers in Latin America—but he cheated on the edges. Latin America—"our South rear," as he told his aides—was important in the espionage war with the Axis. Hoover refused to share what his men collected there. Donovan's agency might be banned from operating in the region but "we cannot be prohibited from thinking about Latin America," he argued.

Donovan did more than just think. He had friends from United Fruit Company and National City Bank feed him intelligence their executives touring the region picked up. He huddled privately with a Mexican labor leader to arrange for him to supply information he ran across traveling through the continent. A year later, Donovan began one of his most secret

Latin American projects, code-named "Kangaroo." Its records were kept in London instead of Washington to reduce their chance of leaking to the FBI. With $50,000 from his unaccounted for funds, Donovan had about a half dozen Chilean diplomats feed him intelligence on the Axis from Santiago and from European and Asian capitals where the envoys were posted.

Hoover, nevertheless, picked up whiffs of the Kangaroo Project. State Department officials, who noticed Donovan's men spending an unusual amount of time snooping in their Latin America files, also did not believe his claims that he was following Roosevelt's January 16 order. In one heated confrontation, Nelson Rockefeller accused him of being a "liar" when he denied he had agents in South America. Donovan lost his usual self-control and threatened to throw Rockefeller out the department window they were standing next to. The two men cooled down and tried to remain cordial to each other after that. But Rockefeller still thought Donovan was lying.

LIMPING FROM HIS sore leg, Donovan took up another important piece of business with FDR when he returned to Washington in May—moving his agency to the Joint Chiefs of Staff. Roosevelt thought he was committing bureaucratic hari-kari. "They'll absorb you," he warned.

"You leave that to me, Mr. President," Donovan answered confidently. He knew the Joint Chiefs wanted nothing better than to kill his unit, but if he didn't move under their wing he would likely be scuttled anyway. His outfit was too vulnerable sitting out as a lonely White House agency with the military, State Department, and Justice now at his throat. Moreover, the military controlled the war and Donovan believed his spies and guerrillas had little chance of operating in the combat theaters unless they did so under the control of the Joint Chiefs. Smith at the Budget Bureau was eager for the military to take over what he considered a rogue agency and clamp down on its freewheeling spending. The Joint Chiefs, however, wanted nothing to do with what they considered a disorganized bunch of civilian spies and disreputable saboteurs run by a political appointee who had amply demonstrated he was no team player willing to follow the chain of command. But Roosevelt insisted that the move be made. Marshall finally agreed to take Donovan's organization, realizing it did have talent within its ranks and he did need covert operatives for subversive activities in this war. Better to have Donovan under his control than not.

The transfer came at a painful price for Donovan. Smith convinced Roosevelt to consolidate most propaganda operations under a new Office of War Information directed by Elmer Davis, a conscientious former *New York Times* reporter who spoke through his nose with an Indiana twang. Donovan could not convince Roosevelt that ripping out Sherwood's Foreign Information Service "would tear the tissue of our whole organization," as he declared in one pointed memo. Sherwood backed the move, which made sense to other Donovan aides. What business did an espionage organization have broadcasting slanted news and Roosevelt's speeches to foreign countries? On June 13, Roosevelt signed another executive order, this one moving Donovan and his agency to the Joint Chiefs of Staff, minus the Foreign Information Service. But with the Joint Chiefs' approval, Donovan continued to wage his own "black" psychological warfare abroad, broadcasting lies to disrupt the enemy. It ensured two years of warfare with Davis when the two agencies' propaganda operations bumped into each other overseas.

Roosevelt also gave Donovan's agency a new name: the Office of Strategic Services. Donovan liked the title. But London still put its odds of survival at low. "It was not clear what Col. D would now be looking after," a secret Foreign Office memo concluded two days after Roosevelt's order.

WHAT DONOVAN WOULD now be looking after if Marshall had his way was a guerrilla training camp in the sticks with a general's star to keep him quiet and the Office of Strategic Services' functions scattered among the Army and Navy. Roosevelt, however, would not allow the OSS to be dismembered. Donovan kept his organization intact, but it quickly became bogged down in the military's vast bureaucracy with a gauntlet of procedural hurdles he had to clear before launching any intelligence or sabotage operation overseas. The OSS nearly ground to a halt.

To be sure, Marshall and the other chiefs had far more pressing things on their minds than Donovan's dirty tricksters. America's military-industrial complex had to be organized for war. Priorities had to be set. Marshall was juggling a lot of balls. Guerrilla and espionage units were flyspecks on his to-do list. At the same time he and the other military chiefs did not want Donovan going off half-cocked with clandestine operations that might spark a battle they weren't yet prepared to fight. The days of covert games run out of the White House had passed. Roosevelt had turned the war over to his generals and admirals. Donovan's organization now had to fit into the military's machine.

Yet the cultural chasm between Donovan's novel organization and the brass was gaping. When he tossed out ideas for subversive plots and psychological warfare and exotic espionage, "the Joint Chiefs of Staff didn't really know what Bill was talking about," Roper recalled. FDR had finally ordered that Donovan be paid $10,000 a year, more than $132,000 by today's standards although it hardly matched his law firm earnings. Donovan, however, began to find the backbiting not worth any salary.

He soon discovered an adversary in the Pentagon as cunning and ruthless as Hoover in the FBI. Major General George V. Strong, who replaced Sherman Miles as Marshall's G-2, had earned the nickname "George the Fifth" for his gruff and imperious manner. Strong was a professional soldier from head to toe with a cerebral side—he once wrote a Japanese-English military dictionary—and he was intent on improving Army intelligence. Like Donovan, Strong had visited London's MI6 and returned brimming with ideas for putting G-2 on a wartime footing. He also had the ear of Roosevelt, who considered him an authority on battlefield intelligence. Strong had decided that the OSS was a band of civilian amateurs that had to be broken up or it would take over his agency. He began referring to the OSS director as "Wildman Donovan."

Donovan thought Strong was an idiot. But the general chaired powerful committees in the military and he began a one-man guerrilla operation to shut down Donovan's agency. He tried to block the OSS from setting up intelligence-sharing agreements with the British and the Free French forces led by Charles de Gaulle. He prevented enemy cables the Army intercepted overseas from going to Donovan. He even took control of businesses Donovan had enlisted for spying overseas, such as the Philips Lamp Company.

Donovan persevered and soon even the service chiefs recognized the value in having his civilian organization control subversive warfare, considered unsuitable duty for men in uniform. They eventually ordered Strong to scale back his attacks. But George the Fifth remained determined to supplant Donovan. Convinced the OSS was infiltrated by the British, French, and Russians, Strong set up with $350,000 his own small espionage unit, whose existence he kept secret from Donovan and all but a few top officials in the government. The unit eventually became known as "the Pond" and like Donovan's OSS began infiltrating spies overseas under State Department and commercial cover. It was run by the man who had not forgotten that Donovan had fired him from the FBQ front company—Major John Grombach.

STRONG DID SUCCEED in blocking Donovan's access to Magic. Donovan protested his agency being walled off from radio intercepts. Marshall and Admiral King had also shut down the small decoding unit Donovan set up to decipher Axis transmissions that FBQ's radio receivers picked up. How could his spies operate in the field and his researchers analyze Axis moves if they were deaf to what the enemy was saying over the airwaves? But Strong prevailed. All the OSS would receive were paraphrased copies of selected Magic intercepts that the Army and Navy deemed pertinent to the agency's mission. Marshall feared security in Donovan's organization was still not tight enough to be granted direct access to Magic, one of the U.S. military's most closely held secrets.

Donovan had done a lot to improve security in his outfit. Information was compartmentalized so no one person knew everything about an operation. Even secretaries typing secret research reports were assigned every third page so no one person in the pool read the entire document. But the organization was still infected with security breaches. Over a two-week period in June security officers roaming the headquarters building at night found seventeen safes open—an "epidemic," one internal memo complained. Screening of employees still needed improvement and Donovan had just begun to organize counterintelligence agents to vet foreign sources.

Donovan could be a stickler with others about security. But he was notoriously lax himself. Aides always became nervous when he chatted about operations in front of the barber who shaved him in the morning or Freeman during car rides. One time he left a briefcase filled with secret papers in a cab. Dulles was shocked when he once found the door to the St. Regis suite wide open, secret papers spread over the bed, and Donovan on the john. He scooped up the documents, went downstairs to the lobby, and phoned Donovan, casually saying: "Bill, I'd like to talk to you about that memorandum I sent up to you yesterday." There was a long pause from the other end of the line. Dulles began to laugh. But Donovan didn't think the joke was funny. He always became testy when aides suggested he might be more careful with sensitive material.

One of his most serious breaches—although Donovan never realized it—came shortly after he returned to Washington from his convalescence at the St. Regis. The Polish embassy was a favorite haunt for Donovan. He visited it often to milk the ambassador for information from Eastern Europe. Chatting one day with Count Mohl, the Polish secret service chief, Donovan casually told him not to expect an invasion of Europe that year; the Allies did not have the ships for it. He also revealed that Russia had over 360 divisions for the coming summer offensive. A German informant in the embassy overheard those two morsels and passed them on to the Abwehr. Fortunately for Donovan, the leak did not reveal much new news to the German army. The Wehrmacht did not expect an invasion of Europe in 1942 because it also knew the Allies lacked the shipping and its count of Russian divisions on the Eastern Front nearly matched Donovan's.

Roosevelt refused to overrule Marshall's decision to deny Donovan direct access to Magic. He thought he now had Donovan in the right spot conjuring up his spy intrigues. Donovan would not be happy, Roosevelt joked with Adolf Berle, unless he was on an "isolated island, where he could have a scrap with some Japs every morning before breakfast." But the president also told Ernest Cuneo he did not want his spy chief "horsing around" making problems for the military or the White House.

Donovan continued to cultivate Roosevelt to keep his ear. He had his agents pick up stamps from around the world that he forwarded to FDR for his collection. He sent him movies a Dutch photographer had taken of the Roosevelt ancestral home in the Netherlands just before the Nazi invasion and a large world globe the OSS commissioned, which FDR kept next to his desk. But his appointments with the president tapered off as he became enmeshed in military work—although Donovan still encouraged gossip that he had direct access to Roosevelt because it bolstered his political clout. But though he still believed FDR was the shrewdest politician he had ever met, Donovan was coming to the conclusion that he was not a great wartime leader.

Donovan's judgment was likely clouded because he also realized that his drive to centralize intelligence under his control would not succeed. Roosevelt would not let it be successful.

Chapter 13

⟩❦⟨

The Embassies

CYNTHIA ROSE FROM the couch in the hall outside the naval code room of the French embassy. She lifted her dress over her shoulders and threw it on the floor. Then she wiggled out of her slip and girdle, unhooked her bra, and removed her panties and silk stockings. Cynthia stood naked in her high-heeled shoes with just a string of pearls draped from her neck. It was a warm night in Washington on June 23, 1942, so the air wafting in from the nearby open window did not chill her. Charles Brousse, the embassy's press attaché, looked up at her gaping.

"Suppose someone should come in!" he whispered with a gasp. "What are you thinking?"

"I am thinking of just that," Cynthia answered coolly. They had already convinced the embassy's night watchman they were lovers using the hall for late night trysts. The guard would be suspicious if he walked in on their burglary and they did not look like they were having sex. She ordered Brousse to strip.

Sure enough, as the attaché pulled off his coat the door to the hall suddenly opened and the guard beamed a flashlight on Cynthia's naked body.

"I beg your pardon a thousand times, madame," the flustered guard apologized. "I thought . . ." He flipped off his flashlight and beat a hasty exit so the couple could continue their lovemaking in private.

Cynthia put just her slip back on. The curious guard might return. She rushed to the window and signaled the "Georgia Cracker" to climb up the ladder. That was the nickname she had given the locksmith Donovan's men had paid $1,000 for the job. He had cracked safes before for the British. Cynthia also had been a British agent, but since January her burglary and the other black bag jobs had been taken over by Donald Downes, Donovan's New York operative who had been hatching anti-Hitler plots.

The Georgia Cracker quickly picked the lock to the code room. It did not take him much more time to break into the room's antique safe; he had already spent a night earlier there carefully spinning the dial to figure out the combination. Cynthia and Charles scooped out the large cipher books, which told the French radio operators how to code and decode classified messages, and carried them to an OSS agent at the bottom of the ladder outside. Then they waited for two agonizing hours as Donovan's men photographed the hundreds of pages in the cipher books in a nearby hotel room. Donovan's officers finally returned at 4 A.M. with the books. Cynthia and Charles stuck them back in the safe. They checked the room to make sure nothing looked out of order, locked it, then scurried quietly down the embassy's front steps before the first employees arrived for work.

The Asia war Americans read about in their newspapers had been largely grim. There had been American victories, such as the Battle of Midway in early June, where the U.S. Navy destroyed four Japanese carriers. But Tokyo's forces had overrun the East Indies, FDR had ordered MacArthur to evacuate from the Philippines on March 11, Corregidor had surrendered on May 6, and the rest of the islands had been conquered by June 9. Behind the headlines, however, a private war consumed Donovan's secret force. It was being waged against the Vichy French and Spain, both of which were cozy with the Germans. In Washington, the battleground for the OSS became the embassies of the two. But this secret war would produce the deepest rift yet between Donovan and J. Edgar Hoover.

While German forces occupied Paris and northern France, Marshal Philippe Pétain, the World War I hero of Verdun, had negotiated an armistice with Hitler that left remnants of the defeated French army, headquartered in Vichy, controlling southern France plus her colonies in Indochina and West and North Africa. Donovan had ample evidence the Vichy French were collaborating with the Nazis. He had already begun planning with Hull a broad propaganda campaign to destabilize Pétain's government if it continued to cooperate with Berlin and to convince his navy and his army in North Africa to join the United States and Britain in fighting the Germans. George Marshall's intelligence officers were now eager to get their hands on the copies of the French embassy's code books so they could decipher from Vichy radio messages intelligence critical for the Allied invasion of North Africa.

Roosevelt, who could be ruthless when it came to fighting foreign enemies on American soil, had given Hoover wide latitude to wiretap, open diplomatic pouches, and burglarize the embassies of hostile, neutral, and even friendly countries. Donovan saw Washington's diplomatic community as a rich target for his agents as well, even though FDR had explicitly made domestic spying the FBI's responsibility. Donovan knew his breaking into embassies was probably illegal, so he kept it secret from Hoover. He thought he could get away with the trespassing on a technicality. Under international law an embassy was considered foreign territory so penetrating it would be no different than Donovan's agency spying overseas.

Roosevelt was not particularly bothered by Donovan's trying to exploit the obviously questionable loophole. He had alerted Roosevelt, Hull, and the Joint Chiefs in April that he was launching a highly secret operation to steal the ciphers in the French embassy. Donovan knew the penetration "must be handled with great care and discretion," he wrote Roosevelt. If the French discovered the burglaries, it could "jeopardize" the U.S. military's winning Vichy cooperation with the North Africa landing.

Donovan had inherited the French embassy job from Bill Stephenson. Earlier in the year, Tennessee senator Kenneth McKellar had introduced a bill requiring that foreign governments, including Great Britain's, disclose to the Justice Department all their agents and activities in the United States. An angry Stephenson knew it would close him down. Donovan, whose organization depended heavily on British help, realized the McKellar bill would be a body blow for him as well and lobbied Roosevelt to veto it. Roosevelt did, though he was furious when he learned of covert British operations being waged in the United States. A different version later became law, which exempted the British, but Stephenson knew his freewheeling days in America were over. He transferred to Donovan Cynthia and his other burglary jobs.

Cynthia was the code name for Amy Elizabeth Thorpe Pack. The daughter of a U.S. Marine Corps major, she had grown into an enchanting and sexually promiscuous beauty. In 1930, Betty Thorpe had married a British diplomat named Arthur Pack, who turned out to be a cruel husband. Betty took on lovers and by the end of that decade had begun working for British intelligence plying sex for secrets among foreign officials when Pack was away. Divorced by 1940, Betty had moved to Washington with orders from Stephenson's men to penetrate the Vichy French embassy, posing as a free-lance journalist looking for stories. Pack soon began a heated romance with Brousse, a married man who had had a number of affairs and was eager to start another. Soon Cynthia had Brousse, who she discovered harbored a private hatred for the puppet regime in Vichy, passing her telegrams his deceitful ambassador, Gaston Henry-Haye, received and delivered.

The press attaché finally agreed to an even more daring operation to steal the embassy's cipher books. Brousse had convinced the compound's night watchman he needed the hall outside the code room for lovemaking that he wanted to keep secret from his nosy wife. On a previous visit the couple had shared a bottle of champagne with the guard. Cynthia slipped Nembutal into his glass, and while he snored away the Georgia Cracker sneaked in to case the safe.

Cynthia eventually fell in love with Brousse and the two later married after the attaché obtained a divorce. But for now she was a coldly calcu-lating agent handler. "Australia," Cynthia's code name for Brousse in her agent reports, "has no secrets from me," she told her new American boss, Donald Downes. Cynthia even urged her lover to continue having sex with his wife so the woman wouldn't become suspicious of his extracurricular activities. Downes was just as coldly calculating with Cynthia. He had other moles in the French embassy slipping him floor plans for the safe's loca-tion along with schedules for the arrival times of workers to check against the information Brousse provided his mistress.

Donald Downes was one of Donovan's true oddballs. He wore a corset for a bad back and had an assortment of phobias—snakes, stray dogs, and yellow paint to name a few. His biographers have written that he was a homosexual, although he never openly acknowledged being gay. A Yale graduate, Downes had traveled through Europe as a professor in the late 1930s mastering several foreign languages and picking up a yen for for-eign intrigues. In 1940 he applied to Army and Navy intelligence to be a spy, but he seemed to them nothing more than a quirky amateur and both turned him down. So Downes approached the British, who thought he might be useful. After a stint overseas performing odd jobs for MI6, whose officers found him a bit insecure, Downes returned to New York in 1941. By September, he was snooping on isolationists and casing foreign embas-sies for Stephenson. Doing so broke a number of U.S. laws forbidding citizens from spying for other countries, as well as Stephenson's promise to Hoover that he would not hire Americans. After the Pearl Harbor attack, however, Downes asked Donovan if he could join his team. Dulles and other senior aides were leery; the agency already was filling up with misfits and Downes's résumé had the extra baggage of his having been an illegal spy for the British.

But Donovan had a soft spot for this thirty-nine-year-old overweight professor, whom the British had already taught how to crack a man's skull by silent killing. Downes believed as fervently as Donovan that "extracurricular warfare," as Downes euphemistically put it, would be key to winning major military campaigns. Donovan first kept Downes in New York dreaming up covert operations with Allen Dulles and Arthur Goldberg, but by March he had moved him to Washington to take over Stephenson's embassy jobs.

By the time he went on Donovan's payroll, Downes had come to Hoover's attention. The FBI director reserved a special loathing for Downes, whom he considered a traitor for spying for the British (it had not taken Hoover long to discover that Stephenson had reneged on his promise) and for being a "sex deviate," as the bureau's many surveillance reports on Downes described him. Downes, who believed FBI agents constantly tailed him, detested Hoover as much as Donovan did.

Not knowing what Cynthia was up to irritated Hoover as much as Downes now working for Donovan. His agents on routine stakeouts had soon spotted a fashionable young lady they identified as Mrs. Arthur Pack making an unusual number of visits to embassies in Washington, particularly the Vichy compound. A snitch told a bureau agent that Mrs. Pack was having an affair with a Charles Brousse in the French embassy. The bureau's wiretap of Brousse's line certainly turned up conversations that sounded like the two were talking in codes: "The little boy has spoken to the boss," Brousse told Mrs. Pack during a June 23 call. Hoover on August 14 ordered his men to put Room 215-A of the Wardman Park Hotel under watch. Mrs. Pack and the French press attaché seemed to spend a lot of time there. The FBI agents also tapped the room's phone line.

SPAIN INTENDED TO remain neutral for the moment, but its dictator Francisco Franco favored Germany and if Hitler won he wanted to join the Nazis in reaping the spoils of war. It did not take long for Donovan's men to uncover evidence of how Franco was deviously positioning himself and secretly helping the Third Reich. With the North Africa invasion just eight months away, the U.S. military, which feared a German flanking maneuver through the Iberian Peninsula and Spanish Morocco, wanted every scrap of information it could find on Spanish intentions. Stephenson's men had regularly burglarized the Spanish embassy in Washington to steal the books with the ciphers the Spaniards changed often to frustrate decoders. With General Strong and the Joint Chiefs eager to acquire the codes, Donovan had Downes add Spain's to the list of embassies he was breaking into.

Since he had no inside employee like Brousse, Downes had to devise a more complex plan to penetrate the Spanish embassy. He had agents follow and compile full dossiers on the private lives of practically every employee in the embassy from the senior counselors to the cooks and chauffeurs, looking for sympathetic moles to approach. Agents wrote down the license plates of cars around embassy parties to check if their owners could be used as informers. Downes also arranged for Sidney and Eleanor Clark, a wealthy Philadelphia couple, to approach the embassy posing as producers who were planning expeditions to the Iberian Peninsula to record color films of folk dances for American museums. They began throwing parties for embassy employees in a luxury suite at the Wardman Park Hotel and filed detailed reports on each one who attended.

To infiltrate one of his own agents into the embassy, Downes went to a Northeast women's college and recruited "Ella," his code name for a young student who spoke perfect Spanish and could type and take dictation. He rented Ella a room in a boardinghouse off Connecticut Avenue where the embassy's secretaries lived so she could become friends with them. To create a job opening in the embassy for Ella, Downes arranged for International Telephone and Telegraph Company to post an ad in the *New York Times* looking for a Spanish-speaking secretary and offering $400 a month. He knew that was more than an embassy secretary made. Ella, who had already identified one of her new girlfriends, María, as the most eager to leave the embassy for big-city life, innocently showed her the ad and told her she ought to apply. María did, and as Downes had arranged, IT&T promptly hired her. A grateful María then helped Ella get her old job in the embassy in April.

After just a week in the compound, Ella had drawn detailed sketches for Downes of the floor plan and the location of the code book safe in the senior counselor's office, where she worked as his secretary. By early May, she had made pencil drawings of the safe, built by the Shaw Walker Company, and memorized the dial numbers and turns she thought the counselor made when she watched him behind his back opening it. Inside the vault, she saw a circular leather box, ten inches in diameter, which spooled out tape with numbers printed on it, plus four leather-bound encoder books for converting the tape's numbers into words. But when no one was around and Ella tried to open the safe with the combinations she thought she had seen, the door wouldn't budge.

Downes finally had her whack the dial one night with a leather-headed mallet. When the counselor couldn't open the damaged safe the next morning he phoned Shaw Walker to send a locksmith to repair it. Downes had already arranged for Shaw Walker to dispatch G. B. "Sadie" Cohen, a safecracker who had been in and out of Sing Sing. Downes had hired him with the help of a New York policeman. Cohen fixed the safe and recorded the combination that would open it.

On July 29, Cohen and two antifascist Spaniards Downes had recruited sneaked into the embassy at 10:30 P.M. The Clarks threw a party that night for the embassy employees at a Maryland roadhouse to keep them occupied. It took Cohen just minutes to open the safe. They grabbed the spool box and the four leather books, which were spirited to an apartment near the embassy where a team of OSS technicians hurriedly took 3,400 photographs of the spool and pages the next two and a half hours. The code material was back in the safe by 1:45 A.M.

Donovan, who waited nervously for a report on the operation, was "practically delirious with joy" over the haul, Ernest Cuneo recalled. The code book copies were delivered to Stephenson and the War Department so both countries could read Spain's diplomatic messages. The risky burglaries, however, had to be repeated each month when the embassy switched out the code books. In October the operation came to a crashing halt.

The phone in Donovan's bedroom jarred him awake in the middle of the night. Downes was on the other end of the line and relayed the story the burglary team had just given him. Cohen and the two Spanish American agents were about to open the safe when they heard police sirens outside waking up the neighborhood. When they looked out the window they saw FBI agents approaching the embassy. Hoover's men intended to arrest them, Downes told Donovan. Downes suspected that Hoover knew the OSS was breaking into embassies. He told Donovan that Hoover intentionally launched this raid to catch them. Fortunately, the team scampered away and no one was caught. Downes recalled later that he did not "believe any single event in [Donovan's] career enraged him more" than this incident.

Hoover, however, had a different story. FBI agents , who were also breaking into the Spanish embassy on a regular basis, had spotted one of the OSS burglars earlier in the summer, casing it late at night, and shooed him off. Hoover's men said they warned Downes the next day that the OSS had no legal authority to sneak into Washington embassies. That should have settled the matter, the FBI agents thought, but apparently not. Downes continued his black-bag jobs. But Hoover insisted he had not raided Donovan's men in retaliation. The sirens Downes's excited team heard that night came not from the FBI but rather from District of Columbia police squad cars. The local cops had arrived at the Spanish embassy in response to calls from a neighbor who thought he had seen a prowler there. Fortunately, the Spaniards never discovered all this activity in and around their compound.

Donovan and Hoover, each furious at the other, rushed to the White House the day after the botched burglary to protest. Roosevelt settled the dispute by ordering that from then on the FBI would break into all embassies, but would have to share what it stole with the OSS. (Hoover later refused to provide Donovan copies of what FBI agents took.) Donovan turned his operations and his burglars over to Hoover. The FBI director finally learned what Cynthia had been up to. Donovan eventually sent Downes out of the country, fearing Hoover might look for any excuse to arrest him if he stayed in Washington.

After the Spanish embassy incident, a visceral hatred grew between Donovan and Hoover. Intelligence exchanges between the two agencies began to taper off and Donovan's aides considered much of what the FBI still provided the OSS worthless. Both men also stepped up their espionage war against the other. Hoover had his agents investigate the personal lives of senior aides like Dulles and even kept tabs on Donovan's brother Vincent. The bureau opened overseas mail addressed to Donovan. Donovan had his home phone routinely checked for taps, which he suspected might be placed by Axis agents or Hoover. FBI agents, who catalogued for Hoover every derogatory comment they heard on Donovan from his political and press enemies, had no trouble uncovering the talk in Washington about his extramarital affairs.

Donovan also had his moles inside the FBI. He assigned an officer to investigate the bureau and compile a dossier on its blunders. It also did not take long for Donovan's men to accumulate reports that Hoover was gay. FBI officers were routinely sent out to try to squelch rumors around the country "that the director was a 'fairy,'" as internal bureau memos always indelicately put it. From then on, each man treated the other as if he were the Axis foe. The rivalry detracted from the war both agencies were supposed to be fighting against the real enemy.

Chapter 14

———※———

Torch

D AVID BRUCE MET Donovan's plane when it landed at London's Hendon Airport on the afternoon of June 12, 1942. An Anglophile like Donovan, Bruce had an aristocrat's taste for fine wines and expensive antiques (both of which he had to be enterprising to find in bomb-damaged London). The Virginian was immensely popular among Britain's senior leadership—one reason Donovan would soon make him chief of the OSS station in London.

Stephenson followed Donovan down the plane's ladder. The British agent, whose code name was "G," had already sent long memos to London on "G.50,000" (London's code name for Donovan) and the new OSS organization ordered by "G.60,000" (Roosevelt's code name). Though he was still bogged down in bureaucratic warfare at home, Donovan had managed to set up five OSS stations in London, Chungking, Lisbon, Cairo, and Lagos by the summer of 1942. He had fifty-seven espionage projects either underway around the world, about to get underway, or awaiting approval from the Joint Chiefs. The intelligence sharing between Donovan and the British had grown regular and intimate. Donovan's was still a small operation by British standards, but Stephenson's bosses wanted G.50,000 in town to make sure it did not invade London's networks as it grew.

Donovan settled into a suite at Claridge's, his favorite London hotel. After obligatory visits to the king in Kensington Palace and the War Cabinet, which met in a secret chamber buried deep under Whitehall, he got down to important business in a family flat at 64 Baker Street. It was the unlikely headquarters for the Special Operations Executive, Churchill's commando organization whose mission was to set occupied Europe ablaze with sabotage and guerrilla attacks. Sir Charles Hambro, a large man who had been a wealthy international banker, now headed the "Baker Street Irregulars," as the SOE became known. Donovan and "CD," the code name always given to the SOE director, divided up the world for their commandos. Neither completely trusted the other not to poach territory, but they agreed that the British would oversee operations in India, the Balkans, the Middle East, and for the moment Western Europe. They would jointly operate in Southeast Asia, Germany, and Italy. Donovan got control of mostly table scraps, such as China and Finland. But he would also run the region most important to him and CD just now: North Africa.

"Torch," the code name for the Allied landing to capture French North Africa in November 1942, would be the U.S. Army's first major test in the war. The American force could not have been more unprepared for the complex and risky operation. Torch would also be the first large-scale test of Donovan's OSS. But flying back to Washington on June 26, he knew his spies and saboteurs were as unprepared as the conventional soldiers. In North Africa "we have neither the trained agents nor any great reservoir of dependable potential agents susceptible of being trained," warned a blunt memo from one of his aides. Even for simple items like photos of North Africa, Donovan's men had to go to the National Geographic Society and rummage through their archives.

His mission for Torch was threefold: keep Spain neutral, ensure that the French fleet that Vichy controlled did not join the Axis in attacking Allied forces, and prevent a war between the Vichy French and the United States when American GIs landed in North Africa. Spain intended to remain neutral, although Donovan did not realize it at the time. He proposed beaming shortwave radio broadcasts at French navy ships to convince their officers to resist any German takeover of their vessels. Roosevelt approved the plan. Admiral King thought it was a dumb idea. The French navy, like most sea services, restricted the broadcasts its ships received and their senior officers were still loyal to Vichy. But if it would keep Donovan busy, King saw no harm in his trying.

Donovan's most difficult mission was keeping the eight Vichy divisions in North Africa from fighting the Allied landing. If they did, General Dwight Eisenhower, commander of the Torch invasion, feared it might take him three months to subdue them before he could march toward

Tunisia. He wanted to occupy that country within two weeks and before the Axis could rush in reinforcements from Sicily and Italy. Roosevelt and Churchill ordered Donovan to do all he could to entice the French authorities to cooperate in North Africa. But if carrots did not work—and neither Roosevelt nor Churchill trusted that they would—the OSS had the green light to subvert Vichy control there with its covert operatives.

Churchill and Roosevelt did not trust de Gaulle, the maverick and abrasive French general who had denounced Vichy collaboration with the Nazis and declared himself leader of the Free French resistance force. He now demanded command of the North African invasion. But Washington and London excluded the Free French commander from Torch. His presence would only antagonize the Vichy defenders in North Africa to put up a fight, they feared. That left Donovan the collection of leaders in Vichy to woo. They ran the gamut from the feckless to the opportunistic to those traitorous to the Allied cause.

With no espionage and sabotage network of his own in North Africa, Donovan had to cobble one together from the natives on the ground. He gave that assignment to William Eddy, a hulking Marine lieutenant colonel who limped on a squeaky prosthetic because his right leg had been shot off in fierce World War I combat. A scholar, Eddy had taught English literature at Princeton in the interwar years and served as president of Hobart College. Born in Lebanon, he was also fluent in Arabic and French. Donovan had recruited him from Cairo where Eddy, who had rejoined the Marines before Pearl Harbor, served as a military attaché. Wallace Phillips, who ran Donovan's first spy network, found the hard-drinking marine temperamental and prone to bouts of "extreme depression" if not handled carefully. Donovan believed Eddy was his Lawrence of Arabia.

With $1 million from the White House secret fund, Eddy had set up his headquarters in Spanish Morocco's Tangier by January. He kept another apartment in Algiers, for operations in the French Algerian capital, which was filled with secret agents of all stripes along with tens of thousands of French refugees.

Eddy joined forces with Robert Daniel Murphy, whose title as the State Department's consul general in Algiers masked a far more important job he had in North Africa. A gregarious career diplomat whose Milwaukee Irish background was considered lower-middle-class by State Department elitists, Murphy had nevertheless had important postings overseas. He had

been in the American embassy when the Germans marched into Paris and
had taken charge of the U.S. mission in Vichy in July 1940, soon with a
direct pipeline to Roosevelt, who considered him his personal spy. More
importantly, in February 1941 Murphy had negotiated an agreement with
the Vichy regime to allow its North Africa colonies to import American
food and consumer items in exchange for twelve U.S. control officers he
would supervise at five port cities there to make sure the goods weren't
slipped to the Axis. Those officers were soon known as Roosevelt's "Twelve
Apostles," collecting intelligence on French forces and the Axis presence
in North Africa. De Gaulle distrusted Murphy and some OSS officers
thought he had developed an unseemly affection over the years for French
right-wingers. His control officers were a mixed lot of mostly upper-class
Ivy Leaguers with little or no spy training. But by October 1941, Donovan
had been given control of Murphy and his Twelve Apostles. Eddy managed
the espionage and sabotage operations. Murphy hunted for French officers
who might be sympathetic to an invasion.

By the time Donovan flew home from London in late June, Eddy had
clandestine radio stations in Tangier, Algiers, Tunis, and Casablanca.
The transmitters would broadcast messages to the Torch invaders as they
neared the shore. Intelligence chains had been set up in Tunisia, Algeria,
and French Morocco manned by an odd collection of foreign agents with
comical code names like "Pink Eye" for a former legionnaire organizing
midlevel French officers who hated the Nazis.

To support an Allied invasion, Eddy thought he could count on six
sabotage cells in Morocco to turn out some two hundred European-born
guerrillas and potentially ten thousand native tribesmen, although few had
arms at the moment. He believed the large French garrison of 35,000 soldiers and irregulars in Algeria was poised to defect. Carleton Coon, a middle-aged and overweight Harvard anthropology professor, who had studied
Spanish Morocco's Muslims, arrived in Tangier in May. With Gordon
Browne, a Boston importer who also had lived in Tangier and now worked
under diplomatic cover as a vice consul, the two began secretly cultivating
tribal chiefs among the Arab Moors and Berber adventurers.

Eddy had begun some minor vandalism jobs, such as pouring iodine
into the fuel tanks of German trucks in Tunisia to ruin their motors.
Coon, who had a bawdy side, developed the "explosive turd"—a charge to
blow vehicle tires, which looked like a mule dropping. Donovan enjoyed

reading cables on their antics. But his demand for intelligence to pass to the Torch planners also became insatiable. Murphy's control officers sent hundreds of reports on Vichy forces and fortifications along the Algerian and French Moroccan coasts, on fuel and equipment stockpiles for their armies, on the sea and beach conditions Eisenhower's amphibious assault would face. Coon and Browne even set out in a car to clock travel times on Spanish Moroccan roads that Ike's forces might use.

German intelligence soon planted a Spanish cleaning woman in Eddy's Tangier office. She pawed through papers left out in the open at night until OSS counterespionage officers finally caught her. Gestapo thugs had little difficulty identifying Murphy's control officers. They considered them rank amateurs. But Hitler's diplomats there were not so smug. "The activity of the American Murphy in Algeria must be considered as very dangerous for Germany," one cabled Berlin.

The covert operation Eddy and Murphy launched under the nose of the Gestapo hinged on organizing a nascent French underground in North Africa to back an Allied landing. Their key intermediary became a mysterious Algiers peanut oil magnate named Jacques Lemaigre-Dubreuil. Lemaigre-Dubreuil had floated between Vichy and Nazi circles but now led what became known as the "Group of Five," a collection of right-wing French monarchists and industrialists plotting to seize power in North Africa and then invite in the Americans. Murphy believed Lemaigre-Dubreuil, whose code name became "Peanuts," was a "courageous, patriotic Frenchman" and now a German hater eager to work with the allies. Many of Donovan's senior advisers were wary. The Group of Five seemed to them a French version of Ku Klux Klansmen. They had all been connected with the Cagoulards, a French fascist organization whose members wore hoods at their meetings. Eddy and Murphy, however, convinced Donovan and the Joint Chiefs that Lemaigre-Dubreuil and his Group of Five were the only game in town. But suspicious that Lemaigre-Dubreuil had not given up all his Nazi ties, particularly to the pro-German banks and industrialists grouped under Banque Worms et Cie, Donovan ordered that Peanuts know as little as possible about Allied plans.

For the insurrection among French officers in Algeria, Morocco, and Tunisia, Murphy and Eddy needed a supreme leader. They thought they had found their "noble puppet," as Murphy came to call him, in Henri Honoré Giraud, a sixty-three-year-old French general the Germans had captured when they overran his 7th Army headquarters in the northern France offensive. Giraud in April had managed to slide down a rope from the window of his castle prison and make his way back to Vichy, where his old friend, Marshal Pétain, kept the Nazis from recapturing him. A French journalist had slipped Donovan a heartfelt letter Giraud had written to his children two years earlier urging them to join the rebellion against the Nazis. "The sentiments he expressed from his prison camp are both poignant and significant," Donovan wrote FDR, enclosing a copy of the letter in its original French.

Roosevelt approved an approach. Lemaigre-Dubreuil, whom the Germans allowed to travel in and out of unoccupied France, had once served under Giraud during his army duty, so Murphy dispatched him to Lyon in southern France to sound the general out about leading a revolt as the Allies landed. Giraud appeared interested, but he soon was not the only senior French officer receiving American feelers. Pétain's senior naval officer and the commander of his Vichy forces was Admiral Jean Louis Xavier François Darlan, a stump-sized and often foul-mouthed egotist who became a Hitler enthusiast to climb the ladder in the Vichy government. But after the United States entered the war, Darlan, whom the Americans called "Popeye," could feel the wind shift and he had begun sniffing out collaboration with the Allies. The admiral now sent a message through an intermediary that he also might be willing to join Giraud and bring the French navy with him. Donovan's agents also picked up intelligence that Darlan's son had entered an Algiers hospital suffering from polio. Roosevelt approved another approach.

In July, Eddy flew to London to pitch his covert plan to Eisenhower's command. George Patton, who would lead the western task force landing at French Morocco, was impressed. "The son-of-a-bitch has been shot at enough," the general wisecracked when Eddy walked into a dinner with him at Claridge's wearing his Marine uniform that had five rows of combat ribbons from World War I. Strong, the Army's G-2, who was with Patton in London, at first was skeptical, but he left the dinner persuaded that Eddy could win over the French officers in North Africa. Eddy did so by inflating the number of guerrillas he could count on at that point. Eisenhower, who was smoking three packs of Camel cigarettes a day worrying about the Torch invasion, nevertheless welcomed Donovan's OSS and believed that Eddy might just deliver the French.

Friday evening, August 21, Donovan gathered Eddy and his headquarters brain trust at the St. Regis in New York to review where their covert operation for North Africa stood. Donovan was not as optimistic as Eddy that Giraud, Darlan, and other senior French officers would be won over. We should plan for the worst, he told his aides. "We should look at it as if there were not any French help, that there would be some resistance," he said. He wanted more ideas from his men, more "considered thought."

DONOVAN SLIPPED INTO London unnoticed on Thursday morning, September 10, to review the OSS covert operations for Torch with Eisenhower. He had not been impressed with Ike so far. The general was not his idea of a great wartime leader. He had no combat experience and to Donovan his career up to this point seemed unremarkable as a staff officer. But Eisenhower's genial manner masked a razor-sharp intellect and command of detail.

For Ike one important detail became Donovan's softening up the battlefield for his landing force. Eddy and Donovan had come up with more ambitious ideas, which Donovan outlined for Eisenhower. Murphy's apostles would be paired with landing force commanders to hook them up with dissident French elements when they hit the shore. The Joint Chiefs first balked at Donovan's unconventional proposal to pay the salaries and pensions of French navy and army officers who join the Allies. They decided the $36 million cost was too high. Eisenhower thought the bribe a small price to avoid fighting the French. When he returned to Washington, Donovan lobbied Marshall to reverse the decision and approve the payoffs.

The heart of the OSS plan that Donovan briefed to Ike remained Lemaigre-Dubreuil's Group of Five organizing a coup d'état in North Africa backed by U.S. arms with Giraud leading that force to welcome in the Allies. But after another skull session at the St. Regis with his inner circle four days before he flew to London, Donovan still was unsure that the complex political scenario would play out as Eddy and Murphy envisioned. There were deep misgivings among Donovan's aides. Leaders like Giraud and the generals in North Africa who would follow him "think with their heads" not their hearts, one OSS memo warned.

Two days after Donovan left London, Murphy slipped into Telegraph Cottage, Eisenhower's hideaway outside the city, to brief the supreme commander on the byzantine political factions in North Africa that the ambassador and Eddy hoped to muster behind the coup. It made Ike's eyes water. Murphy, however, was confident and suggested Eisenhower send a senior officer to Algeria to scope out for himself the potential of the French military there. Ike decided the scout would be his deputy, Major General Mark Clark.

Before his mission to Algiers, Clark lunched with Donovan and Murphy in Washington on September 28. He plopped down on the lunch table a long list of artillery and antiaircraft emplacements Eisenhower wanted Eddy's saboteurs to take out in North Africa before the Torch invasion. Clark was a lanky general other men found to be short-tempered, aloof, and a publicity hound. But Donovan found him to be open to unconventional ideas. When the Allies landed, Clark had approved an Eddy plan to assassinate all Axis agents and members of the German and Italian Armistice Commission, which monitored the Vichy government in North Africa. Eisenhower later ruled the plan "out of bounds" and quashed it.

Clark would grow to despise the Vichy generals he dealt with in North Africa, giving them a private code in memos to Ike: YBSAS for "yellow bellied so and so." But he came away impressed after a clandestine meeting October 22 that Murphy arranged for him at a seaside farmhouse west of Algiers with General Charles Emmanuel Mast, Giraud's North Africa representative. A short stocky man in his mufti, Mast in fluent English promised that Giraud would unite all of North Africa in revolt. Clark, who had been sneaked into Algeria with the help of a British submarine that deposited him at the coast, sent a coded message to Ike from Gibraltar afterward: "Anticipate that the bulk of the French army and air forces will offer little resistance."

AS D-DAY NEARED, Eisenhower became increasingly edgy about security leaks tipping off the Germans to Torch. By the end of August, he barred Donovan from bringing more OSS officers into North Africa, fearing it would arouse suspicion among German intelligence there. A month later, Ike and Marshall were livid when they learned that Eddy had smuggled to London René Malvergne, an anti-Nazi and the retired chief pilot at Port Lyautey, to guide the U.S. Navy when it reached the French Moroccan coast. It had been a daring escapade. Given the cover name Victor

Prechak, Malvergne had been hidden under a blanket in a truck trailer that carted him from Casablanca to Tangier, where he was spirited off to Gibraltar. But if the Nazis discovered the pilot missing it shined a spotlight on Morocco as a landing site, Ike worried. Donovan was irked as well. Patton approved the operation but Eddy had not alerted Donovan, who came under fire and did not appreciate being blindsided.

On November 6, Eddy moved to Gibraltar, where Eisenhower had relocated his Torch headquarters to the British underground fortress tunneled into the two-and-a-half-square-mile limestone rock. Murphy remained in Algiers to tend to senior French officers, but Ike wanted Eddy in his command post to advise him on the covert operations that were to unfold. Eisenhower's staff also feared the Gestapo might try to capture Eddy at the first sighting of the Allied armada.

From a cramped underground office, Eisenhower began the agonizing wait for Torch to begin. Sending messages around the clock to operatives on the ground, Eddy had intelligence networks in place at all the major cities along the North Africa coast. Clandestine radio stations funneled their reports to his main listening post in Tangier. He was counting on resistance groups in French Morocco, Algiers, and Tunisia taking over the local governments for long enough to let the invaders in with minimal fighting. Agents sat at the beaches with flares to guide in landing parties. Carleton Coon, who had joined him in Gibraltar, expected some eighty thousand Muslims in Spanish Morocco to join the revolt. Gordon Browne drove to a bleak plain south of Oran to assemble "Rebecca," the code name for a radio beacon device and its bulky nine-foot antenna that would guide in planes dropping 556 paratroopers, who were to capture the Tafaraoui and La Sénia airfields.

His nerves fraying, Ike still worried that the French would fight, his fear heightened when Murphy sent a frantic cable to Washington on November 1 pleading for a two-week delay in the landing. General Mast and Lemaigre-Dubreuil, who had expected the invasion much later, complained they did not have enough time to organize the cooperation of French forces. They might battle the Americans at the beaches if Eisenhower came too early, the intermediaries warned. Delay at this point was impossible, Ike told Murphy.

Donovan the week before had asked the Budget Bureau to rush more money from the White House secret account to Eddy's covert force. Suspi-

cious that Donovan was inflating his role in Torch to justify these emergency funding requests, a Budget Bureau aide earlier had asked Milton
Eisenhower, who had gone to work for Elmer Davis's Office of War Information, to snoop around his brother's London headquarters for any complaints about the OSS. Milton reported back that he could not find anyone
who knew much about the agency's secret operations. Torch, Donovan
told his aide Otto Doering, "may be a test of whether we survive or not."

DONOVAN'S WASHINGTON headquarters was bustling Sunday evening,
November 8. No one had left through "crash weekend," as it came to be
called. Consumed with monitoring the Allied invasion of North Africa,
branch chiefs, research analysts, office clerks, and secretaries had caught
just brief minutes of sleep on cots by their desks. The excitement over the
invasion kept them awake and charged.

The early reports from the region seemed to Donovan to indicate that
Torch was rolling out smoothly. "Thank God, all well," Eddy cabled him.

But it soon proved not to be the case.

Eddy and Coon munched on ham sandwiches and sipped beers at
their office on Gibraltar Saturday night, November 7, when the French-
language BBC broadcast: "Allo, Robert. Franklin arrivé." It was the signal,
which Eddy's clandestine stations in North Africa heard as well, that the
Torch invasion was on time for the next day.

Eddy's first all's well cable to Donovan bore some truth. Parts of the
OSS operation proceeded splendidly. Eddy's clandestine radio stations in
Casablanca, Oran, Algiers, and Tunis stayed on the air throughout the
invasion transmitting agent reports to him in Gibraltar on last-minute
beach defenses and the movements of French forces that they spotted while
driving their cars through the cities. By 2 A.M. Sunday, some four hundred
young guerrillas Lemaigre-Dubreuil had trained captured the French 19th
Corps headquarters (which controlled Algerian troops), Radio Algiers
(where Giraud was to broadcast a message to North Africa), and the main
post office and military telephone exchange (where they cut telegraph
and phone service for the city). Murphy's officers aboard command ships
directed the task forces to their beaches, where in most instances the GIs
were met by Eddy's French guides—although at Oran neither side knew the
other's password. Even Malvergne, the pilot Eddy had caught so much heat

for smuggling out, succeeded in steering the USS *Dallas* destroyer through a narrow channel from Port Lyautey off the Moroccan coast, dodging sandbars, sunken ships, and Vichy shore fire so seventy-five U.S. Army rangers could debark and seize the nearby airport.

But only a small fraction of the French partisans Eddy expected to battle Vichy forces ever showed up for the fight. Rifles and machine guns promised for rebels in Casablanca and Algiers never arrived. Meanwhile, gutless French officers who were to lead revolts, such as General Mast, went missing, refused to fight, or were arrested. Rebels failed to capture the critical French naval headquarters in Algiers, while the facilities Lemaigre-Dubreuil's guerrillas had seized early Sunday morning were soon surrendered back to Vichy loyalists.

Early Sunday morning Lemaigre-Dubreuil dressed in his crisply starched French major's uniform and left for the Blida airfield at Algiers to greet Giraud, who was supposed to land at dawn. Giraud never showed up. A British submarine had sneaked the French general to Gibraltar on Saturday. He arrived in a wrinkled herringbone suit, unshaven with a handlebar mustache drooping over his lip. Murphy fully expected that Giraud would fly to Algiers the next day, order the Vichy forces to allow the Allies in, then take over France's North Africa army after Eisenhower had established his beachhead. But in a tense first meeting with Eisenhower, Giraud balked at leading the French insurrection unless he also was supreme commander of the invasion force. Ike, who had put off the touchy command issue when Giraud had raised it before with Murphy, now adamantly refused to give up his job. If that is the case, "Giraud will be a spectator in this affair," the general stubbornly announced. Eisenhower, who had his fill of self-centered French officers, later grumbled to an aide: "What I need here is a damned good assassin." Hours ticked by, as the two men waited for the other to blink. Giraud finally "decided to play ball," Clark recalled, but precious time had been wasted.

In a Tuesday press conference, Roosevelt warned Americans that in any war "there are peaks and valleys." Eisenhower began his Sunday invasion in a canyon of pandemonium. Murphy's vision of the Allies being welcomed by the locals had quickly blown up in smoke. Americans were fighting Frenchmen. The landings at Algerian beaches near Oran and Algiers were chaotic with transports off course or lost in the dark night, tank-carrying vessels stuck on sandbars, green American soldiers staggering to shore with hundred-pound packs on their backs, and French soldiers waiting for them who chose to fight though they were far outnumbered. Browne waited with his Rebecca beacon kit set up south of Oran. But no paratroopers had arrived by their 5 A.M. deadline so he blew up the set and left; navigation errors had scattered the aircraft and their commandos all over the region. Patton's landing was just as sloppy at Morocco, where Vichy French resistance near Casablanca and Mehdia further north stiffened. Had the Germans been defending instead of the French, "we would never have gotten ashore," Patton later admitted.

Back in Washington, Donovan began his morning staff meetings reading aloud from a chapter of a War of 1812 history. "They haven't burned the White House yet," he said each time after closing the book. True, but the recitals lifted spirits only briefly until another discouraging cable came in from North Africa.

Giraud finally arrived in Algiers on Monday, November 9, to proclaim himself the leader of French forces resisting the Axis. But French officers, still loath to break their oath to Pétain, ignored him and continued fighting. Events, it turned out, had already overtaken Giraud. Shortly after noon the day before, Murphy had discovered, much to his surprise, that the hated Darlan was in Algiers visiting his polio-stricken son, who was near death in the hospital. Murphy quickly began talks with Darlan, who unlike Giraud *was* in command of French North Africa forces, and tried to persuade him to order a cease-fire. Clark joined the negotiations Tuesday, pounding the table and telling Darlan point-blank that his North Africa army would be destroyed and he would be arrested unless he halted the fighting.

By November 12, a tenuous cease-fire finally was in place across North Africa. In response to Torch, German forces quickly swept through southern France and Vichy, making Pétain, who had disowned Darlan's armistice, irrelevant. Eisenhower arrived at the St. George Hotel in Algiers on November 13 to close the rest of the agreement with Popeye. In exchange for the cease-fire, Darlan would be the Allies' "Head of State" for North Africa.

Murphy believed the accord was far better than the alternative: Eisenhower, who had suffered 2,225 casualties in four days of fighting, bogged down longer in a bloody battle with the French. But an international firestorm erupted. Elmer Davis's propagandists complained that the pact with a notorious collaborator like Darlan was a public relations nightmare. "Are we fighting the Nazis or sleeping with them?" Edward R. Murrow asked sarcastically. Roosevelt, who had held his nose in agreeing to the deal with Darlan, assured Americans it was "only a temporary expedient." The arrangement troubled Donovan, whose aides feared it would be used by overseas rivals to discredit American influence in Europe. But for the moment, the American Army command was thankful just to have survived its first test of fire in the war. Torch had blooded the GIs and provided some relief for the Soviets fighting the Germans on the Eastern Front.

Torch, however, exposed serious shortcomings in the American war effort. FDR privately questioned Ike's judgment. Patton had been derelict with logistics. Murphy proved naively blind to the political deviousness of French reactionaries, such as Lemaigre-Dubreuil. Donovan suspected that Peanuts had revealed Torch to Nazi collaborators with the Banque Worms et Cie so they could transfer 25 billion francs to North Africa before the invasion and reap a windfall from a better exchange rate for dollars and pounds there. Within OSS, a secret internal assessment sent to Donovan concluded that while the agency had provided valuable intelligence for the Army on French forces in North Africa, its covert operation to win them over had failed miserably. Donovan bristled at the second-guessing. In truth, the OSS had done no worse—nor better—than the rest of the Army.

AS AMERICAN AND BRITISH ground forces rolled east toward Tunisia, OSS officers watched their back for any German counterattack from Spanish Morocco. Donovan's men also tracked German espionage agents who sneaked into Tangier or remained in Casablanca and Algiers to monitor Allied ships off-loading military cargo. Meanwhile, Charles Hambro moved a large contingent of British subversive warfare operatives into Algiers, under the code name "Massingham." It sparked angry complaints from Eddy that Hambro was taking over North Africa, which he had agreed in June would be Donovan's territory, and making the OSS there "window dressing." American and British generals from the beginning had been critical of the quality of each other's army and leaders. That same tension quickly crept into the American and British secret services. Confidential memos from his field officers began landing on Donovan's desk complaining that British intelligence agents pouring into North Africa were snobs who held themselves "aloof" from the OSS. London's station chief for Tangier was so unscrupulous he "should have been killed a long time ago," one OSS report complained. A Cairo OSS agent considered his British counterpart "the scum of the earth."

Donovan also thought he was being muscled out of North Africa. "The trouble with you British," he vented to one of Hambro's officers in New York, "you always try to seduce your partners for your own advantage." The officer relayed the remark to Hambro, who did not appreciate being called a whore. He thought Donovan was an ingrate. Nevertheless, Hambro realized Donovan was upset and had to be treated with kid gloves. He ordered Massingham to be more deferential to their temperamental American cousins.

Like the conventional generals, Donovan was looking ahead to the next fight. For almost a year he had been mulling ambitious plans to make North Africa his aircraft carrier for launching future covert operations into southeastern Europe. Roosevelt could go down in history as the "great liberator" of Axis-occupied Greece and the Balkan states, he wrote the president. Donovan now planned to expand his OSS bases in Algiers and Cairo to three hundred operatives. To infiltrate fascist Italy, he asked the Army to send him 230 Italian-speaking soldiers to begin sabotage training. He also proposed organizing Italian, Greek, and Yugoslav guerrilla brigades recruited from their ethnic communities in the United States. Donovan began getting the Italian American officers, but Marshall nixed the special ethnic armies. They would divert soldiers from the regular force, the chief of staff feared.

To plunge into the next war zone with his covert operatives Donovan also found that he needed two things in short supply: transportation and British cooperation. He begged Marshall to order American commanders in the field to provide him planes and ships to infiltrate his agents and supplies into Southern Europe, but Marshall refused to micromanage his generals in the field. Donovan would have to join a long line of units pleading for cargo space. Under the agreement he had signed with Hambro, the British oversaw covert operations in southeastern Europe. They were eager to have Donovan pony up arms for the region and join the covert force Hambro ran there. But the British, who kept as close a watch on Donovan's moves in the Mediterranean as the Germans did, wanted no OSS rookies barging in by themselves and blowing operations Hambro's guerrilla warriors or Menzies's MI6 spies had spent years setting up.

London's operations may have been more seasoned but they did not dazzle Donovan. So far, "the quality of the British intelligence in Greece left much to be desired," one secret report sent to him complained. What's more, his OSS officers thought they had a better chance of succeeding in the Balkans because as a rule Americans were more popular there than the British. Donovan knew what Hambro and Menzies were up to with all their talk of joint Anglo-American operations. As his OSS grew they wanted it swallowed into their secret service so it never achieved independence in the field. Donovan was "determined," he angrily told Hambro's New York agent, "not to be nobbled"—British slang for fixing a horse to lose.

MARSHALL SENT DONOVAN a kind note on December 23. The Army chief had wanted no part of his spy outfit at the outset, but in the end he had saved it from a premature death. Marshall finally had his deputy, Major General Joseph McNarney, hammer out a lengthy formal charter delineating the duties of the OSS. Donovan would not coordinate Army and Navy intelligence—his goal from the outset—but he would be an equal partner with the two services. The thicket of red tape was cleared so his OSS could launch espionage and sabotage operations overseas, and Donovan finally won approval to form his guerrilla and commando forces. Now Marshall, who had been impressed with the intelligence the OSS had produced for Torch, offered in his note to bury the hatchet. "I regret that after voluntarily coming under the jurisdiction of the Joint Chiefs of Staff your organization has not had smoother sailing," he wrote.

Donovan planned to spend Christmas at Chapel Hill with Ruth, Mary, and his new granddaughter. David and Mary had their first child the year before and named her Patricia, after Donovan's daughter, who had died in the car accident. With the war begun, the Navy was not so picky about personnel and commissioned David as an ensign to operate landing craft—not as glamorous as sailing the high seas on a warship, but the service thought it suitable for the small boat skills he had picked up aboard the *Yankee* schooner. David had been aboard an amphibious ship for Torch and was now earning glowing fitness reports as a lieutenant junior grade training landing craft crews on the base the U.S. Navy set up at the port of Arzew along the Algerian coast.

As Donovan drafted a response on Christmas Eve to Marshall's note, an aide rushed in with a cable from North Africa: Darlan was dead.

Fernand Bonnier de la Chapelle, a fanatic recruited by French monarchists bent on eliminating the hated admiral, had gunned down Darlan in his office at Algiers's Palais d'Été. Suspicion turned first to the British being behind the assassination (Bonnier had received guerrilla training at their Äin-Taya camp west of Algiers) and then to the OSS (Carleton Coon had been detailed to Äin-Taya and taught Bonnier). Donovan had no qualms about "wet" jobs. His men had been prepared to kill Armistice Commission members in North Africa and in OSS reports after Torch agents wrote in clinical language of using "extra-legal" means to eliminate Axis sympathizers. Donovan had been dreaming up schemes to assassinate Hitler. Coon had also prepared a lengthy memo proposing that after the war the OSS retain an elite team of assassins who would roam the world eliminating future Adolf Hitlers before they could start conflicts. Neither the British nor Coon had any role in the Darlan assassination, however. Even so, Eddy thought it prudent to send Coon undercover to the Tunisian front until Algiers calmed.

Giraud, who served as Darlan's military chief and now took over as high commissioner, had Bonnier executed the day after Christmas, which ensured that the extent of the plot never would unravel. Nobody was particularly interested in a full investigation. The murder was "an act of providence," Mark Clark admitted. "His removal from the scene was like lancing a troublesome boil." As commissioner, Darlan had surrounded himself with Vichy officers who like he had once backed the Nazis. He was despised by de Gaulle's Free French. "All over North Africa," one OSS report noted, "the habitants raised their Christmas wine glasses to the Admiral's assassin."

Chapter 15

Bern

AT THE STATION in Annemasse, the last stop in southern France before the train crossed the border into Geneva, Allen Dulles handed his diplomatic passport to gendarmes behind the desk. A Gestapo man stood behind the French officers, watching. With the Allied landing at North Africa the day before, German intelligence was even more interested in who was entering the neutral country. The Gestapo agent huddled with the gendarmes out of Dulles's earshot. He had been smart enough not to carry any OSS documents to reveal who he really was, but the Gestapo would certainly become suspicious if they searched his bag and found the $1 million letter of credit for a Swiss bank in it that he planned to use to set up his operation in Bern.

The chief gendarme at Annemasse finally returned and told Dulles they would have to consult Vichy before they could allow an American diplomat to cross. Dulles drew the gendarme aside and in whispered broken French pleaded with the man to let him pass, at one point pulling out his wallet stuffed with ten one-thousand-Swiss-franc notes Donovan had bought for him in New York five months earlier. The gendarme refused the bribe. Dulles considered grabbing his bag and running across the countryside to the border. But at noon, as engineers stoked the train's steam engine for the last leg to Geneva, the Gestapo man left for lunch at a nearby pub. The gendarme handed Dulles his passport and told him to board. "Now you see that our collaboration is only symbolic," he said with a slight smile. Using the code name "Burns," Dulles messaged "Victor," the code name for the OSS radio receiving station in London, when he arrived in the Swiss capital on November 10. The German army swept into southern France that day. "I was the last American for a year and a half to cross legally into Switzerland," Dulles later proudly wrote.

Dulles had debated whether even to attempt the train trip from the Spanish border through southern France, not knowing if the Nazis had begun to move in. But Donovan was anxious to put him in Switzerland before the Germans sealed the Swiss border and had booked priority passage for him on a plane to Lisbon. Penetrating a closed totalitarian state like Germany with his agents could take years and Donovan did not have the time. Neutrals such as Switzerland for the moment would be his porthole into the Third Reich.

Dulles knew that he was made for the Bern assignment. Born with a clubfoot to an upstate New York Presbyterian minister whose father-in-law had been secretary of state, Allen Welsh Dulles joined the State Department in 1916, serving first as an embassy secretary in Vienna and then in Bern. He found his ambition, curiosity, and affable charm useful in collecting World War I intelligence on Germany, Austria-Hungary, and the Balkans. He served as an adviser later to the Versailles peace conference and helped reopen the Berlin embassy, prowling communist cell meetings to collect intelligence and striking up acquaintances with Weimar Republic backbenchers who would prove useful later, such as Gerhart von Schulze-Gaevernitz. After earning a law degree, Dulles left State in 1926 and joined his brother, John Foster, at Sullivan & Cromwell. There he made his fortune in international finance and wrote foreign policy treatises for the prestigious Council on Foreign Relations until he joined Donovan's outfit after the Pearl Harbor attack.

Donovan occasionally played tennis with Dulles and found him a fierce competitor on and off the court. Dulles believed he was more qualified—and sophisticated—to run the OSS than any of his colleagues, including Donovan. He had jumped at the chance to set up the agency's secluded outpost in Bern so Donovan would not be looking over his shoulder. Other OSS officers complained that behind the outward charm he was insufferably patronizing, rigid, self-centered, and devious. But Dulles proved to be the perfect man for setting up what amounted to a separate OSS organization in isolated Bern.

Switzerland was a spy haven for the Allies and the Axis. Some 150,000 Germans lived there, at least 1,500 of whom the OSS considered hostile

Nazi agents. Within five days of his arrival in Bern, Dulles had begun cabling to London tidbits of intelligence picked up from other embassies. He settled into an old burgher's mansion at Herrengasse 23 that came with a butler, regrew his mustache, and had a Swiss tailor sew him tweedy sports jackets to give him a country look he thought more congenial for cultivating sources in his wood-paneled study. Dulles kept a revolver at his bedside table in case of emergencies and before long a mistress lay in the bed next to him: Mary Bancroft, who had arranged Donovan's trysts with Becky Hamilton and who joined Dulles's operation to analyze German news reports. Dulles's marriage to his wife, Clover, had become loveless by the 1930s. Donovan learned of the affair and pestered Mary for details when she later traveled out of the country.

Dulles, whose code number became 110, turned Herrengasse 23 into a lint trap for informants. He welcomed anyone with tips: chatty diplomats from other embassies, Swiss intelligence officers, journalists, German dissidents, and complete strangers off the street. He set up weekly radio-telephone calls to the OSS message center in Washington. Because the Germans had cut off Swiss mail and courier service with the Allies, a friendly engineer tucked microfilms of Dulles's longer written reports in an engine compartment for the Geneva train run to Lyon, where a bicyclist carried it in a backpack to Marseille, where it eventually made its way by boat and plane to the OSS station at Algiers. The circuitous delivery took about twelve days.

Donovan soon began sending Dulles's reports to the War Department and White House as well as to the British embassy. But much of the early material proved to be uncorroborated gossip the British and American military found false when they cross-checked it with Ultra or Magic intercepts. On April 20 Donovan had an aide send Dulles a stinging cable warning him "that all news from Bern these days is being discounted 100% by the War Department."

Dulles developed a curious collection of walk-ins, but several of the contacts proved exceedingly valuable. Ten days after arriving in Bern, he was introduced to Gero, the handsome and debonair son of Gerhart von Schulze-Gaevernitz, his friend from Berlin twenty-two years earlier. Now forty and an international investment broker, Gero had taken up residence in New York but maintained a home in Switzerland. When he met Dulles in Bern, he was committed to overthrowing the Nazi regime and had a wealth of insights for the American on dissident military officers and government officials he knew from his years in Germany. Hoover, whose agents had kept tabs on Gaevernitz in New York, warned the White House that he had an "unsavory reputation." But Dulles soon became close friends with the Weimar legislator's son, who found him important contacts in German industrial, banking, and diplomatic circles and even interviewed many of them for him.

Among the Germans Gaevernitz screened and introduced to Dulles was Hans Bernd Gisevius, a stern and haughty Abwehr counterintelligence agent over six feet tall (Dulles referred to him as "Tiny" in reports) who literally looked down on Hitler as a common criminal. Gisevius operated undercover in the Germans' Zurich consulate. Admiral Wilhelm Franz Canaris, the Abwehr's chief, who had also grown disenchanted with the war, had posted Gisevius there to contact the Allies on behalf of opposition elements among German government and military intellectuals. British intelligence believed Gisevius was a Nazi plant sent to flush out regime opponents meeting with Dulles, but Dulles believed Tiny was genuine and stood by the intelligence he fed on opposition elements, which largely proved accurate.

In August, Dulles met his most valuable contact, Fritz Kolbe, a short, wiry, baldheaded man who worked in the bowels of Joachim von Ribbentrop's Foreign Office and had refused to join the Nazi Party. Kolbe made trips to Bern or Stockholm periodically as part of his job and had access to the secret cables that came into the Foreign Office from its embassies. What the Prussian idealist read of Nazi "wickedness" overseas sickened him. He first approached the British offering to deliver to them the Foreign Office documents that crossed his desk, but the MI6 officers rebuffed him suspecting he was a double agent. Donovan also at first was skeptical this source was too good to be true. But over the next two years, Kolbe, whom Dulles gave the code name "George Wood," delivered him 1,600 ministry documents smuggled out of Berlin. To save space, Kolbe at night condensed long reports into handwritten letters that he photographed with a camera Dulles gave him, then hid the microfilm rolls in a clothes trunk he had a Berlin courier service ship to Switzerland for his visits. He narrowly escaped capture when a Nazi official at the courier service one time began searching his trunk. Kolbe gripped the revolver he always kept in his pocket, ready to shoot as many Nazis as he could before killing himself. But the inspector became distracted when another official entered the room and let the trunk pass.

The British eventually conceded that they were wrong about Kolbe. "The Wood traffic . . . is one of the greatest secret intelligence achievements of this war," Stephenson concluded.

Dulles had his problems. Donovan had approved his operating somewhat in the open in Bern to attract sources, but that made him vulnerable to Axis penetration. Within weeks of his arrival the Gestapo began following him, believing—incorrectly—that he was collecting only economic secrets. But even with heavy enemy surveillance, within a year of planting his flag in Bern, Dulles had made his station "the hub of intelligence from Germany, Italy, occupied countries, and the Balkan satellites," an OSS report concluded. Donovan considered Dulles's operation one of his greatest successes in the war—although he always remained wary of his ambitious protégé, who was not shy about taking credit for successes.

ROOSEVELT AND CHURCHILL gathered at Casablanca's Anfa Hotel on January 14, 1943, to plot their next move. The prime minister succeeded in pressing the British position that the war should continue in the Mediterranean with the invasion of Sicily by July as the stepping-stone for attacking Italy. Donovan sent Roosevelt stacks of travel guides his aides could use to see the sights in the Moroccan city during their ten-day stay. The OSS also developed thirteen thousand feet of movie film taken at the conference, which was distributed to newsreel companies to show in American theaters. Donovan backed Churchill's Mediterranean strategy. But another announcement Roosevelt made at a press conference after the meeting left him and Dulles worried.

Tender after the international uproar over the Darlan deal, Churchill and Roosevelt wanted to reassure the public that the alliance would strike no more sweetheart deals with fascist French admirals or any Nazis now popping up peddling offers to halt the war in exchange for their taking over the government from Hitler. From Germany, Japan, and Italy, the alliance would accept nothing less than "unconditional surrender," Roosevelt told reporters.

Donovan wanted total defeat of the Axis as much as Roosevelt, but he feared that FDR's stark announcement could backfire. It offered proud

German soldiers no alternative than to continue fighting. Dulles worried as well that FDR's edict put a straitjacket on his covert maneuvers in Bern to encourage internal dissidents to topple Hitler. Donovan tried to convince FDR to take a more nuanced approach so German officers could be enticed to work for the Allies. Roosevelt refused. Donovan's agents could meet with Axis intermediaries to milk them for intelligence, but not to negotiate peace deals. Unconditional surrender demands ended up having no effect one way or the other on the German government, but Goebbels at the time was delighted with such announcements. The more the Allies talked about "a disgraceful peace for Germany," he wrote in his diary, "the more easily I succeed in toughening and hardening German resistance."

While Goebbels had a seasoned propaganda operation to put out his message, Donovan's psychological warfare program was still struggling to get off the ground. Morale Operations, a new branch started in January 1943 and staffed with a number of decidedly unmilitary journalists and artists, concocted a mixed bag of propaganda ploys. Rumors were spread out of London that senior Nazis had gone into hiding. Leaflets were eventually dropped over German soldiers claiming their wives and sweethearts back home belonged to the "League of Lonely Women" having sex with their comrades on leave. Fake German mailbags, stuffed with poison-pen letters whose addresses were copied from prewar German phone directories, were air-dropped in the hopes that German civilians would give the sacks to postmen to deliver the phony mail.

But Morale Operations mired Donovan in another ugly bureaucratic battle that once again threatened to sink his organization. Elmer Davis was outraged that the Joint Chiefs let the OSS play these psywar games when Roosevelt had clearly ordered that his Office of War Information ran propaganda at home and abroad. Davis lined up powerful allies, such as General Strong, to try to convince Roosevelt to strip Donovan of propaganda. George the Fifth still considered Donovan "high and mighty" and his OSS "a hydra-headed organization." On February 18, the general stumbled into his best chance ever to take Donovan down.

As Strong told the story, Roosevelt had summoned him to the White House that afternoon and when he walked into the Oval Office, Davis was sitting there badgering the president to transfer the last of Donovan's propaganda operations to his Office of War Information. Roosevelt was already nervous about politically sensitive propaganda being in military hands. Strong claimed that FDR ordered him to draft another executive order to transfer not only Donovan's psychological warfare functions to Davis but also to move the rest of the OSS under Strong's Army intelligence office.

Donovan never pinned down whether this was FDR's idea or Strong had put it in his head, but that didn't matter. He considered it a major betrayal by the president. The executive order that Strong rushed back to his office to draft allowed Strong to do what he wanted with the agency when it came under his wing and he intended to break it up into small pieces. Furious, Donovan considered resigning. His aides scrambled for time to head off a confrontation. Ernest Cuneo phoned a White House friend to see if he could take Strong's draft order off Roosevelt's desk. Impossible, the aide told him. "Well, put it at the bottom of the pile!" Cuneo shouted into the phone.

Donovan sent Roosevelt a protest letter, which he tried his best to word diplomatically. But it warned that the order FDR was about to sign would "be a valuable gift to the enemy." That was pretty strong stuff. Donovan was now charging that the bureaucratic move Roosevelt contemplated was treasonous. The Joint Chiefs sided with Donovan so Roosevelt backed off. He signed an order on March 9 giving Davis overall control of propaganda but allowing Donovan to keep his secret psywar operations like the sex leaflets and the rumor campaigns. Donovan also got Strong off his back; the order did not move the OSS to Army intelligence.

Roosevelt tried to smooth Donovan's ruffled feathers. He asked him to join him at a Sunday service at St. John's Church on Lafayette Square across from the White House. More importantly, he made Donovan an Army brigadier general on March 24. But as everything was with Donovan, his promotion came with controversy. He had expected and wanted to be made a major general, a rank higher, but the Army balked. In fact, the Army would have preferred his being named an admiral so the Navy would have to deal with him. Doering suspected that Roosevelt and the Joint Chiefs wanted the boss back on active duty as a general so he could be subject to court-martial if he got out of line with his operations.

Donovan told old friends to keep calling him "Colonel"—but that was an act. He liked being a general. The War Department issued him a black leather general officer's belt with two holsters for pistols. Donovan went to Wetzel tailors in New York to have his uniform custom-made with silver stars embroidered on its epaulets. He also knew how to manipulate his new wardrobe before military rivals. He would show up—often late—for meetings with generals and admirals with only the ribbon designating the Medal of Honor he had won pinned to his chest. It subtly reminded the flag officers adorned with their rows of ribbons that he had the only award that counted.

Chapter 16

—∽∾∽—

The Neutrals

W AR RATIONING DID not crimp Donovan's fondness for dinner parties, which always had a business purpose to them. He had choice cuts of beef from the Chapel Hill farm sent to the Georgetown home for his guests. Donovan had no concept of the logistics behind feeding large numbers (he was clueless about food ration coupons until Ruth finally explained them to him) and he was constantly springing parties on her. His aides who came to the dinners also soon began to notice that Ruth seemed more distant during these functions, more grim-looking while others were having a gay time. Mary always enjoyed the parties. At Chapel Hill she kept the books for the farm business, helped Ruth with the vegetable gardens and while David was at sea bought and sold livestock. But as Ruth grew less interested in entertaining Donovan's guests, Mary, who looked stunning with her hair dyed blond, began driving to Washington more to replace her mother-in-law as his hostess.

On Wednesday, March 10, however, Ruth and Mary arrived at Georgetown with a rib roast, this time thankfully for a small gathering Bill was hosting for Harold Guinzburg, the founder and publisher of the Literary Guild. But as Donovan carved at the table, a plot was unfolding inside Germany that would later hearten the OSS director. Dissident German officers were planning their first assassination attempt on Adolf Hitler. Three days later on March 13 they planted a pair of limpet mines on a plane flying the führer to Rastenburg, but the devices did not explode. A suicide-bombing attempt a week later also failed as Hitler inspected a cache of captured Russian weapons in Berlin. The OSS had nothing to do with the conspiracies, yet Donovan remained keenly interested in assassinating not just Hitler but anyone in his inner circle. Putzi Hanfstaengl even prepared for him a detailed report on four old Hitler cronies who remained relatively unprotected; if they were kidnapped or killed it would upset the dictator as much as losing Goebbels. One of Hitler's closest confidants was Heinrich Hoffmann, his hunchbacked personal photographer, who "has no bodyguard, drinks heavily, is constantly involved in homosexual scandals and goes out a great deal in Munich," Hanfstaengl wrote. Kill him and "Hitler would go to pieces."

Among the small but growing number of restive German officers who wanted to eliminate Hitler, Donovan became particularly intrigued by one suspected conspirator who also happened to be his professional opposite: Wilhelm Canaris. Fairly fluent in English, prematurely gray, an insomniac and a pessimist by nature, the Abwehr chief also was aggressive and cunning, with a nasty side. The OSS and the State Department monitored practically every step the furtive admiral took overseas. By 1943, he realized it was only a matter of time before Germany would be defeated and began sending out peace feelers to the Allies. Canaris, whom Dulles gave the code number 659, could relay messages to the OSS through Gisevius and later Eduard Waetjen, a Berlin businessman who also was one of Canaris's agents operating undercover in the Germans' Zurich consulate. But since the previous September, Donovan had secretly given the green light to one of his other agents to try to set up a direct meeting between Canaris and the OSS.

Ulius Amoss was a hyperactive Army Air Force officer with a conspiratorial bent who had spent twenty-one years traveling in and out of Greece before he transferred to the OSS. Amoss came across a "sinister Greek magnate" in the United States who knew Canaris well, he wrote Donovan, and "convinced me that he could be used by our organization to contact and pervert Canaris." After the magnate arranged the secret approach, the OSS could always "eliminate him if it is then necessary in the interests of our country," Amoss added.

Donovan never responded to the suggestion that the tycoon might have to be murdered, but before he left the office for his dinner party on March 10, he read an interesting cable from Amoss: Canaris had delivered a message through his intermediaries that he wanted to meet the OSS agent in a neutral country. The meeting never came off, however. Amoss assumed it was because Hitler had sacked Canaris, as the press was reporting. That was not the case, but Canaris was snarled in a fierce bureaucratic war with rivals who suspected he was contacting the Allies. Perhaps he thought a meeting with the OSS too risky at the moment. Donovan, however, never gave up hope that one day he would recruit 659.

BY THE END of May the Joint Chiefs had given Donovan more freedom to dabble in unconventional operations like reaching out to Canaris. Strong still looked for ways to sabotage him, but many lower-ranking officers in Strong's own command admired Donovan's daring style. Some even pulled OSS agents aside and whispered that they wished Wild Bill would replace George the Fifth as the Army's intelligence chief. With the freedom, however, came dangers for Donovan. He set up stations in three other neutral countries important for spying on the Third Reich—Turkey, Portugal, and Spain—but their operations proved far more troublesome than Dulles's in Switzerland.

In April, Donovan sent Lanning "Packy" Macfarland to Istanbul. An Illinois savings and loan executive, Macfarland had been one of Donovan's early hires; the two men had known each other from Republican Party work. Two deputies flew with Macfarland on the plane to Turkey: Archibald Coleman, a former journalist who had been one of Wallace Phillips's spies in his naval unit, and Jerome Sperling, an America archaeologist who had been on numerous digs in Turkey. Their mission: to make Istanbul the base for a bold espionage and subversion operation Donovan wanted to mount into Axis-controlled Bulgaria, Romania, and Hungary.

Macfarland and his men, one of their OSS colleagues recalls, were "bright-eyed Americans in a very complex place." Throughout the war, Turkey professed neutrality but had wavered back and forth from the Axis to the Allies depending on which side she thought had the upper hand at any moment. Hitler wanted Turkey, with her large army and strategic location on the southern flank of the German front with the Soviet Union, to remain neutral and to continue shipping him chrome, which was critical for making steel alloys. Britain and the United States wanted Turkey allied with them and the chrome shipments halted. At least seventeen spy services operated in Istanbul. (Turkish police tolerated foreign agents prowling about as long as they didn't target the Turkish government.) The British had more than two thousand diplomats, military officers, and intelligence agents in the city. The Axis countries had some 1,500 secret operatives. Also mixed in were large colonies of German businessmen, Vichy French, White Russians, hundreds of thousands of Eastern European refugees, and a seemingly endless supply of professional international informants. It made Istanbul a cauldron of snoops, snitches, fabricators, and con men. As Macfarland brought in more OSS staffers the next couple of months, Axis agents had their informants apply for jobs in his office as janitors and drivers.

State Department officials were uneasy about Donovan expanding his espionage operation in Istanbul, fearful it would upset delicate diplomacy to nudge Turkey toward the Allies. They had reason to be nervous. The American spy team was noticeably green. Macfarland was popular among his OSS colleagues, but he had no espionage experience to speak of and soon became laughably casual about his cover. He would stroll into Istanbul nightclubs waving his hands over his head and the band would strike up "Boo Boo Baby I'm a Spy." But the Midwest S&L executive had ambitious plans to make his fledgling network in Turkey as big as his competitors. He gave his agents flower code names. Macfarland became "Juniper." A. V. Walker, an oilman Donovan had recruited in New York, headed the "Rose" chain of informants, who vacuumed bits of information from Istanbul's foreign community and travelers who passed in and out of the city. Archie Coleman, who filled his quarters with Turkish antiques and tended to be a braggart, was put in charge of overseeing another chain of agents code-named "Cereus," after a night-blooming cactus in the American West. Cereus operated out of a front business called Western Electrik Kompani.

The agent who managed the Cereus network for Coleman was Dogwood, a Czech engineer the British spy service turned over to Macfarland in July who had lived in Istanbul for a long time and who claimed his real name was Alfred Schwarz—although the OSS always thought it was an alias. Schwarz, who had passed information to MI6, recruited from scores of disgruntled Germans or well-connected foreigners he told Macfarland and Coleman he knew in Istanbul. They could establish contacts not only in the Balkans but also in Austria and Germany. Dogwood ended up with twenty-nine flowers of all kinds in his garden, such as Begonia (a thirty-eight-year-old Austrian arms buyer in Istanbul eager to eject the Nazis from his country), Hibiscus (a dapper Greek technician to operate their radio sets), and Primrose (a Hungarian pharmacologist expert in Budapest's chemical industry).

Seven months after arriving in Istanbul, Macfarland sent a secret memo to OSS headquarters predicting spectacular results with Cereus. Schwarz's agents had made contact with the Hungarian Army's General Staff, which planned to send a senior intermediary to Istanbul to explore the possibility of Hungary breaking from the Axis. Cereus would soon infiltrate agents into Romania and Bulgaria "to stimulate widespread sabotage" and spark a "revolution." What's more, "we have been successful in developing an elaborate system of espionage, penetrating well into Germany," Packy boasted.

It sounded too good to be true. But Macfarland left important details out of his reports to Donovan. Exactly who were his agents in Cereus? Macfarland didn't tell Donovan because he didn't know. Dogwood, who could be temperamental and intimidating, never told Macfarland the real names behind the flowers he recruited, insisting it had to be kept secret to protect them. That made it impossible for the OSS to vet their intelligence. Who was this Hungarian intermediary? The British had warned Macfarland to beware of Hungarians bearing peace offers. They could well be Nazi plants.

But in the summer of 1943, Donovan had other things on his mind. He was dealing with two crises on the Iberian Peninsula. One was fabricated. The other was real.

THE FABRICATED CRISIS began with crumpled pieces of paper an informant brought Francis "Tony" Di Luca from the Japanese embassy in Lisbon one April day. A former Treasury Department narcotics agent who had joined the OSS, Di Luca was not particularly excited with the find. It was just one more scrap of a blizzard of information that had come into his station the past four months. Stealing secrets also was a cottage industry in Portugal. The Japanese alone had some two hundred undercover agents there, many posing as tie salesmen. Di Luca's informant, a messenger for the naval attaché at the Japanese embassy, was code-named "Z" and he had sticky fingers. The messenger had already purloined Japanese intelligence reports on British mobilization plans and Allied battle strength on the Tunisian front. But as he strolled by a trash can in the naval attaché's office one day, Z noticed two curious-looking pieces of paper balled up in it, which had numbers and Japanese characters written on them that he thought might be some kind of code. Di Luca had not told him to hunt for code material, but Z decided to fish the papers out of the can when no one was looking and stuff them into his pocket.

Di Luca sent his trash can find to Washington and asked headquarters to cable him back on the papers' value so he would know what to pay Z for his troubles. When the sheets arrived, Whitney Shepardson, now the agency's chief of Secret Intelligence, walked into Donovan's office and laid them on his desk. The papers, he told Donovan, "may prove to be of enormous value." The OSS already knew that the Japanese naval attaché was actually the embassy's senior intelligence officer. These scraps of paper may offer "the key to a Japanese code," Shepardson said. Donovan ordered them sent to the Army's cryptoanalysts, hoping to score points with their discovery.

Four days later, he got a disappointing answer from them. The code was for low-grade Japanese naval attaché traffic that the Army Signal Corps had known about for a long time and wasn't interested in. Shepardson cabled Di Luca to tell Z not to grab any more of the sheets; they were not worth the risk. The scraps of paper were filed away—another lead that had not panned out—and Donovan forgot about them. Until a month later.

Strong's aides had been receiving regular reports from the OSS on the documents Z and Di Luca's other mole in the Japanese embassy had been scooping up and they had not been much impressed with the haul. But at the end of June, Strong had on his desk four other intercepted Japanese messages Army code breakers had decrypted. In one of the messages the Japanese embassy in Rome warned Tokyo: "An American espionage agency in Lisbon not only knows to the minutest detail all the activities of the Japanese ministry in Lisbon but is also getting Japanese code books." The Rome embassy's revelation, however, was based on vague reports Italian intelligence had passed on from its sources in Lisbon. The Japanese ambassador in Lisbon in another message assured Tokyo that it was a false alarm; the code books were safe. Japanese Foreign Minister Mamoru Shigemitsu agreed and messaged back it was probably just "planted intelligence of the enemy designed to addle us," but he ordered his embassies to check it out further.

Strong blew up when he read the Japanese messages. On July 6 he began sending Marshall blistering memos accusing Donovan of launching an "ill-advised and amateurish" burglary of the Japanese code books in Lisbon, which threatened to cripple Magic. Once the Japanese realize their codes had been breached they would change them, which would mean Magic would be no good "for months" until the new codes could be broken. Strong demanded a full-scale investigation of the OSS. "The military consequences of the loss would be incalculable," the general darkly warned. Donovan's rogue agents in Lisbon have become "a menace to the security of the nation."

Donovan's aides scrambled to unravel what really happened and get the facts to Marshall. Di Luca wasn't running a rogue operation; Strong knew about his two moles in the Japanese embassy and had never voiced any objection to them being there. Z had not been instructed to steal codes and the sheets he stumbled across were deemed worthless by the Army. It was highly unlikely the Japanese would decide their codes had been compromised from the vague report they got from Italian intelligence—which turned out to be the case. Tokyo eventually concluded they had not been stolen from the embassy. Magic was safe. But Marshall still believed that Donovan had imperiled it.

DONOVAN HAD KNOWN Carlton Joseph Huntley Hayes for a long time and was delighted when Roosevelt made him ambassador to Spain in 1942. The spy chief and the envoy had much in common. Hayes had graduated a year ahead of Donovan from Columbia College and had gone on to earn a Ph.D. and to teach European history at the school. Along the way he had also converted to Catholicism, eventually co-chairing the National Conference of Christians and Jews. In World War I, Hayes had served as a military intelligence officer. It made him amenable now to the Office of Strategic Services coming into Spain, particularly its propaganda experts. "The time is ripe" to separate Spain from Germany, Hayes had written Donovan in June 1942, asking for three psywar agents. "If you can help us in this strategic spot of the Earth's surface, I know you will and I shall be very grateful."

Donovan supplied the agents and many more. His first undercover spy arrived in Madrid in April 1942, renting the second floor of an apartment on the Calle Alcalá Galiano. Within two years, Donovan had about fifty intelligence officers in the Spanish capital, some working under the cover of petroleum attachés in the American oil mission building near the embassy, others under State Department cover out of an attic office in Hayes's official residence, a palace on the Calle Eduardo Dato. For much of the Allies' North Africa campaign Donovan's mission was to watch for signs the Nazis might invade or stage a coup in Spain and to be prepared with subversive operations if they did. As the Allies secured North Africa and fears of an invasion subsided somewhat, Donovan focused more on following Axis agents in Madrid, organizing saboteurs to infiltrate into France, and halting the shipment of Spanish war material, such as tungsten, to Germany.

It became dangerous work, both in Spain and Portugal. The Abwehr closely tracked Spaniards on the OSS payroll. Donovan's officers were threatened, robbed, and shot at by German operatives. Marya Mannes, an OSS agent who operated in Lisbon and Madrid, was even raped by a Portuguese parachute manufacturer she was cultivating after he slipped a potion into her champagne that made her groggy. Mannes still let the rapist show off his factory along the Spanish-Portuguese border to her. The OSS wanted intelligence on his parachute production.

Donovan's relations with his old friend from college days started to go downhill before the Torch invasion, however. By the spring of 1943 the two men were at war with each other. Though Spain had helped the Axis, Hayes believed Franco was now distancing himself from Hitler. The ambassador saw his job as making sure American-Spanish relations were "not disturbed," he argued, so Franco would inch closer to the Allies. Washington also had adopted a policy of not interfering in Spanish affairs, which Hayes intended to follow to the letter. He, therefore, wanted OSS officers in the country to be professional and discreet so the Spanish did not uncover them.

Hayes was convinced Donovan's officers were a bunch of uncouth cowboys and he began firing off angry cables to the State Department. The agents who were posing as petroleum attachés were "woefully" ignorant about their cover jobs, he complained, which meant Spanish and Axis officers could easily spot the phonies. The OSS operatives seemed to Hayes not to know what kind of military intelligence they should collect in their spy jobs. Some of the secret information they bought from informants had actually been copied from local newspapers, he charged. Donovan's operatives also seemed tone deaf to Spain's internal politics. Hayes erupted when he discovered OSS officers contacting Basque separatists to infiltrate them into France. The separatists were enemies of Franco, who had demanded that the United States have nothing to do with them.

Tony Di Luca arrived in Madrid in the fall of 1942 to be Donovan's first station chief. Hayes considered him a disaster. Di Luca passed out lavish tips at restaurants, ran up bills at a tailor shop for expensive suits and shirts, and imported stashes of gourmet foods and silk stockings that Hayes suspected he was selling on the black market. "He threw money around like a drunken sailor," the ambassador griped, so it wasn't long before the former narc "was being watched and shadowed by Spanish police." On November 9, Hayes demanded that Di Luca not only be recalled to Washington but also never be allowed to work in another foreign country. The envoy was outraged when Donovan instead transferred him to Lisbon.

Donovan replaced Di Luca in Madrid with the agent's deputy, Jack Pratt, whose code name was "Silky." He also dispatched Frank Ryan, a waste management businessman before he joined the OSS, to investigate the station's messy finances. Hayes found Pratt an improvement over Di Luca but still considered him a political naïf—Silky refused to halt the OSS contacts with the Basques. The ambassador was shocked when Ryan arrived with silk stockings he wanted to give Franco's wife as a present. Hayes ordered him to stay away from the woman.

Donovan's agents in Madrid groused that Hayes was a meddlesome micromanager, who did not understand that clandestine agents often had to entertain extravagantly and pass out wads of cash to attract informants. Of course the Spanish would be upset with the spy agency's work. "Those engaged in espionage are constantly and regularly violating the laws of the country in which they operate," Ryan told Donovan. Hayes had poisoned the embassy against the OSS officers, he charged. His diplomatic aides even became cavalier about protecting the identities of undercover agents when they chatted with Spanish officials. One OSS officer leaving Washington for the Madrid station was told: "Good luck, you'll probably have more trouble keeping under cover from Americans than from the Gestapo."

Hayes was not allergic to spying; he had set up his own intelligence operation in the embassy to snoop on the Axis in Spain, which was separate from the OSS station and run by his military attaché. Donovan finally proposed sending Gregory Thomas, a large balding man who had worked in the New York office and knew Spain well, to clean up the Madrid mess. But

Hayes wanted no more repairmen. In April he demanded that the entire OSS station be evicted and replaced by General Strong's Army intelligence officers who would work under Hayes's attaché. Though Strong was eager to displace Donovan in Madrid, Marshall opposed such a drastic move and so did Eisenhower. Nevertheless, the Joint Chiefs summoned Donovan to appear before them to respond to the ambassador's charges and make the case for hanging on to his operation in Spain. It amounted to a trial.

At 2:30 on Friday afternoon, April 9, Donovan walked into a basement room at the Public Health Service Building on Constitution Avenue. The Joint Chiefs, who met there regularly with their British counterparts, had nicknamed it "the tank" because that was what the windowless room looked like. Donovan pulled out a chair at the long conference table, wearing his new uniform with the general's stars embroidered on the epaulets and his lone Medal of Honor pinned to his chest.

"At the outset, let me state frankly that Spain has been our greatest difficulty," Donovan admitted as Marshall and the other generals and admirals listened in stony silence. Although he thought this was more a problem of clashing personalities and Hayes had exaggerated OSS misdeeds, Donovan conceded that the agency's intelligence product from Madrid "could be improved both in content and in volume." The station chiefs sent to Madrid have not been the right men for the job, Donovan acknowledged, although Di Luca had performed well in Lisbon. And yes, the other agents sent to Madrid have been amateurs, but "we are all amateurs in this field." America was late to join the intelligence game.

Hayes, however, suffers from a serious case of clientitis, Donovan complained. The ambassador seems more interested in cultivating Franco than in fighting the Nazis. Donovan's marching orders from the Joint Chiefs were to collect intelligence on Hitler's war aims in the Iberian Peninsula and to organize resistance groups there to infiltrate France and Germany. That important mission overrode "the risk of offending the sensibilities of the present Spanish government." The Basques were important for setting up "an underground passage into France" for OSS operatives, Donovan pointed out, and unlike the fascist Franco they could be counted on to fight the Germans if Hitler tried to occupy Spain. "As for the silk stockings," Donovan added, "they are the most valuable informational barter medium in Spain today."

Donovan's presentation was forceful and lawyerly. The next day, the

Joint Chiefs delivered their verdict. Hayes would not be allowed to expel the OSS and take over spying in Spain with Strong's officers. Thomas would be sent to Madrid to fix the problems. But "Ambassador Hayes has considerable justification for his complaints," the service chiefs ruled in a letter sent to the State Department. Donovan had done a poor job of selecting agents for Madrid. Any more OSS officers who embarrass Hayes or anybody else in the embassy will "be summarily withdrawn," the chiefs promised. For Donovan, it amounted to a formal censure—his first as a general—and it stung.

Chapter 17

Infiltration

H IS PRIDE STILL wounded by the Madrid episode, Donovan took off late Monday night, June 21, 1943, for England. At heart he remained an Anglophile. In many instances his intelligence sharing with the British was more intimate than with his own Army and Navy. London opened up its files on German agents to X-2, the name for a new counterespionage branch Donovan had formed earlier, and had begun sharing with the X-2 spy catchers Ultra, its penetration of the German Enigma cipher. Yet tensions still festered in the American-British alliance. At the Trident Conference in Washington the month before, Churchill acceded to a cross-Channel invasion of France in May 1944 and Roosevelt agreed to more operations in the Mediterranean after the Sicily landing. But the decisions came after heated debate and deep suspicion on the American side that Churchill was manipulating them to protect British interests in the Mediterranean.

Donovan arrived in London to confront tensions also building between his OSS and Britain's clandestine services. He hosted a boozy party at Claridge's Wednesday night to lift the spirits of David Bruce's London staff. "The injection of some three hundred cocktails and untold bottles of Scotch into our systems" did the trick, Bruce later wrote. The next two days, however, Donovan held more sobering sessions with his counterparts. The OSS had the Joint Chiefs' approval to mount espionage and subversive operations into Western Europe, the Balkans and southern France from England and North Africa. Donovan was in London now to look for a way to wedge his operations into areas the British secret services controlled. He had decided to exploit the openings the British gave him and seep the few men he could field at the moment into their turf like water looking for cracks.

Donovan's British counterparts, however, knew this was his game plan before he arrived in London. He had a frosty lunch with Menzies as a result. The MI6 chief at first had resisted Donovan's trickle of intelligence agents into Greece and the other Balkan nations, but eventually he went along with them. He had refused, however, to allow OSS espionage agents to take off from England and parachute into France. "Broadway" (the code name for Menzies's Secret Intelligence Service headquarters that came from the street where it was located) had had its own networks in France since 1940. C did not want the Americans now muddying them up with independent operations. Donovan's inexperienced agents would surely "burn" British spies in the field; it was nearly impossible for operatives working the same area not to know each other. General Jacob Devers, the U.S. commander for the European theater, for now was content to rely on Broadway's agents and not let Donovan intrude. Menzies, however, was irritated that Donovan was still looking for ways to sneak his people into France.

Hambro's dinner with Donovan was not much warmer. Hambro had no quarrel with his junior partner trying to organize guerrilla and sabotage operations against the Nazis in Bulgaria and Romania, where his Special Operations Executive agents were not operating. He was also willing to accept OSS subversives perhaps later working on their own in Greece and Albania. But Hambro and Churchill considered Yugoslavia Britain's exclusive preserve and they wanted to keep a short leash on any OSS operations there.

Yugoslavia was a political snake pit. The Croatian Ustasha collaborated with the Nazis. The British at first backed General Draža Mihailović, who led Serbian army forces that were nominally fighting the Germans; but Mihailović's Chetniks were also attacking Josip Broz Tito's communist partisans, who were battling the Germans as well. By the end of March 1943, Churchill had become disenchanted with Mihailović, whose Chetniks increasingly appeared to be collaborating with the Axis. So the prime minister sent a British mission to Tito. As London recalibrated its support between these two factions, Hambro believed now was not the time for Donovan's OSS to be barging in with independent operations that might muddle the British moves to pressure Mihailović back into the Allies' camp. But by May, Hambro's field operatives in North Africa, who were under orders to keep a close eye on their OSS colleagues, began warning CD that Donovan was now scheming to sneak his own commandos into Yugoslavia to hook up with both Mihailović's and Tito's forces. At his dinner with Donovan, Hambro tried diplomatically, but as forcefully as he could, to convince him that in Yugoslavia the OSS must operate under the British.

Donovan listened politely to Hambro and Menzies, but he remained determined to have his own independent operations in Europe. Otherwise London would direct and dominate every move he made and the U.S. military would never take his OSS seriously. The Balkans would be an important battleground for secret warriors. The liberation of France, with its growing underground, was even more important. Donovan did not intend to join in the fight for those prizes as an adjunct to the British.

On Sunday, June 27, he took a jog in Hyde Park and a swim in its Serpentine, then he boarded his aircraft at Hendon. He sat in the co-pilot's seat to try his hand at flying once they were airborne. Eventually tired of gripping the stick he gave control of the plane back to the pilot and browsed through German and French grammar books sitting on his lap. It would be a long flight to Algiers, where he hoped to speed up the infiltrations into Europe that made his British cousins so nervous.

DONOVAN SETTLED INTO the St. George Hotel on a hilltop overlooking Algiers Harbor on Monday, June 28. He had a masseur rub the soreness out of his body from the long flight. The radio by the massage table broadcast news while Donovan alternatively read reports and dictated cables to a secretary Eddy had sent from his headquarters at the nearby Villa Magnol, a palatial nineteenth-century Arab estate.

Getting his men to work was the problem Donovan had to tackle at the moment. He had three hundred spies, commandos, and support personnel he wanted to move to the Mediterranean along with their tons of weapons and supplies, but the OSS was no higher on the shipping priority list than civilian organizations like Davis's Office of War Information. Once his force finally arrived in the Mediterranean, Donovan also needed planes. The Royal Air Force had assigned two squadrons of Halifax bombers for infiltrating their agents and supplies into Southern Europe, but the British were being stingy about lending aircraft for his OSS missions. For France alone, he needed a squadron to haul more than three million pounds of war supplies to some fifty thousand French guerrillas he hoped to equip, plus another three long-range bombers for delivering his para-chuting spies.

Donovan had his own personnel problems as well. Snug with his North Africa operations, Eddy showed little interest in expanding to Southern Europe. For most of the OSS officers sent so far to mount missions into France, Eddy had relegated them to shuffling papers at desks in Algiers. So before leaving Washington, Donovan ordered Eddy to focus on operations in North Africa and Italy. To lead the penetration of France, Donovan brought in more energetic agents. The day he arrived in Algiers, Donovan met briefly with one of them.

At twenty-eight, Henry Hyde was terribly young to take over Donovan's secret intelligence missions that would be launched from North Africa into France. He had no experience with spying save for the short course the OSS gave him before his posting to Algiers. But the forceful, bright, and boyish-looking Hyde would become one of Donovan's most skilled operators and the perfect man to manage espionage in France. The grand-son of the founder of the Equitable Life Insurance Company, Hyde had been born in Paris, educated throughout Europe, and after a law degree from Harvard had been working in a New York firm when Allen Dulles recruited him. Hammertoes he developed climbing the Swiss Alps kept Hyde out of the Army. He spoke French fluently enough to pass himself off as a native, but more importantly he knew intimately the French char-acter, which proved complicated in this war.

The first two missions Donovan's men had dispatched to southern France produced mixed results. Hyde spent more time training his agents for the third infiltration, code-named Penny Farthing. General Giraud, North Africa's high commissioner after Darlan, had handed over seven French exiles for the job. Hyde planned to infiltrate them as two-man teams to organize spy networks in the southeast, central, and southwest regions of France, through which the Allied armies might have to move. The day Donovan arrived in Algiers, Hyde was ready with his first team. "Jacques," who would organize the spy network, was the code name for Jacques de Rocquefort, a frail, thirty-year-old former French army reserve officer who had worked as an Agriculture Ministry civil servant before the war and had been one of Robert Murphy's coup plotters during Torch. "Toto" was twenty-three-year-old Mario Marret, a tough high school dropout from a peasant family in central France's Auvergne region, who would serve as the team's radio operator. There was no aircraft available in Algiers to parachute Jacques and Toto into France. But the Special Operations Executive station chief there, Douglas Dodds-Parker, had agreed to sneak Hyde and his two French agents, dressed as British officers, aboard a regular flight to one of his agency's London bases, where an SOE plane was available to airlift them to France. In agreeing to this circuitous and clandestine bit of transportation, Dodds-Parker, who Donovan thought was crafty "like a fox," was risking the wrath of the SOE's bitter rival, the British Secret Intelligence Service and its chief, Menzies.

C was furious when he learned that the Special Operations Executive had let in Donovan's trespassers against his express wishes. But after a week of tense negotiations behind closed doors between Bruce and MI6, Menzies finally relented. On the morning of July 17, Hyde, Rocquefort, and Marret were driven to a safe house near Cambridge. Rocquefort and Marret would be dropped over Clermont-Ferrand near Lyon in central France's Rhône Valley. Lyon was a key hub for German transportation routes into southern France. Rocquefort's mission was to organize a spy network to report on enemy train and truck traffic into the city as well as Nazi troop concentrations in the area.

The two men had been given fake identities. Rocquefort was posing as a visitor to a sanatorium, which was not a stretch since he actually suffered from a tubercular condition in his left lung, while Marret would be a farm machinery salesman. They had been grilled for hours on their covers in mock police interrogations. British officers lent them the latest reference books for businesses, restaurants, and shops in the Clermont-Ferrand and nearby Lyon areas so the men could brush up on everyday details of French life since they were last there. British officers had also supplied them French banknotes with serial numbers that would not arouse police suspicion, French identity cards, clothing cards, workers' registration and food cards, along with two French suitcases with false bottoms for storing documents and weapons.

An hour before their 9 P.M. takeoff, the spies were taken to a nearby Royal Air Force base under heavy British guard. In a hut near the runway they put camouflaged jumpsuits over their civilian clothes, strapped on crash helmets, and fitted snow-boot-type overshoes over their regular shoes. They would likely be parachuting into muddy fields and would shed the overshoes, along with their jumpsuits, when they reached a road. That way if they ran into police, there would be no suspicious mud cakes on their regular shoes to conflict with their cover story that they had just left a friend's house. Finally they received their poison tablets in case suicide became necessary.

Hyde rode with Jacques and Toto in the car that took them to a Halifax bomber revving up on the runway. Later, when he had more teams infiltrating into southern France, Hyde had "Joe-handlers" assigned to this job: OSS men who would tend to the nervous agents like parents with children—fielding last-minute requests to contact their wives, to pass along a final letter, to buy milk for their babies—until the spies climbed into the plane.

The noise now made small talk impossible. Forty-two bombers with engines gunning were preparing for takeoff that night for missions over France. Jacques and Toto did not want a long goodbye anyway. Hyde shook their hands quickly, and because they were Frenchmen, gave them a peck on each cheek. Donovan's first two agents to parachute into France from England hurried to climb aboard the plane.

AUGUST 17, 1943, the early morning hours before dawn. Rocquefort and Marret quickly gathered up their parachutes and their two suitcases in the open field. Rocquefort's ankle throbbed from the airdrop. He thought he might have sprained it when he landed.

The July 17 drop had to be aborted. Looking out the belly hatch of the Halifax that night, Jacques and Toto had spotted lights flickering on the ground from the resistance fighters waiting near Clermont-Ferrand to receive them. But just as the two men prepared to jump, the lights went off. Jacques and Toto held back. The pilots circled the bomber twice over the target to see if the lights came on again, but they did not so the plane returned to England with the two French agents. The pilots had been told not to drop the agents unless they saw the lights from the reception committee below, which turned out to be wise instructions; the British later learned from one of their other teams on the ground that the Germans had spotted the guerrillas waiting for the spies and had arrested them. The drop had to be postponed until August during the next full moon.

This time, Jacques and Toto made a "blind drop" southeast of Clermont-Ferrand, with no reception committee on the ground that the enemy might find. The dispatcher in the bomber, however, had pushed them out early and they had landed three miles from their "pinpoint," spy jargon for the spot on the ground where a parachuting agent was supposed to land. Three miles off might not seem like much, but Jacques and Toto had spent hours studying their pinpoint on a map before leaving England. All the landmarks they had memorized to give them their bearings in the dark— the church steeples, hills, road crossing—were now not there. It took them several hours to get oriented.

Weight was another problem. One of their suitcases contained two radios and spare parts. The other had their clothing, money, and weapons. Lugging the heavy bags the more than nine miles to Clermont-Ferrand would be impossible, so they decided to bury the suitcase with the radios in a vineyard they saw near their pinpoint, whose earth had been freshly turned. They would carry the lighter bag with the clothes and weapons.

Dawn had broken by the time they finished burying the first suitcase. The spies were too exhausted to walk further to Clermont-Ferrand. Fortunately, Toto knew a farm family near the pinpoint who let them hide the suitcase in their house and sleep for a while. Later that afternoon, Jacques, his sore ankle aching, set out for Clermont-Ferrand. Despite wearing the jumpsuit his civilian clothes had been splattered with mud and he was worried he would attract attention along the way.

Beginning an agent network in Lyon, their final destination, was not easy. Rocquefort and Marret did not yet know what kind of reports hotel or apartment owners were required to file with the Vichy police on renters, so they took a room in a private house, but dared not pull their radios out of the suitcase for fear the nosy landlord might report them. The old friends they first tried to track down were either on vacation, in prison for anti-occupation crimes, or hiding out with the resistance. Jacques finally located an attorney he had known and a Jesuit priest for a Catholic student association he had once belonged to. They and the young woman in Clermont-Ferrand "were the only connections I had with which to begin organizing my intelligence service," he later recalled.

But he had to move carefully and slowly with them. You don't just drop into the lives of ordinary civilians and the next day ask them to be espionage agents collecting military secrets. Jacques kept his contacts with the three social at first. But he lucked out a week or so later. The girl from Cler-mont-Ferrand, out of the blue, introduced him to three friends: a major in the Vichy army, a Michelin tire factory engineer, and the engineer's brother, who was an artillery captain. He now had three more people who had the professional background to know the kind of military or industrial information that might be important. At the same time the Jesuit priest on his own initiative put him in touch with two of his students who were in their mid-twenties. Rocquefort gave them the code names "Jacques II" and "Petit Jean." They helped him find a private apartment where Toto could set up his radio with no questions asked.

Henry Hyde and other OSS officers gathered anxiously around the radio at their station in Algiers on Wednesday morning, September 15. Before Rocquefort and Marret had left England on August 17, Hyde had arranged for them to transmit their first message to Algiers thirty days later at 8:30 A.M. on that Wednesday. The silence the last month—not knowing if his two agents had succeeded in infiltrating into Lyon, if they had begun their network, or if they had been captured or killed—had been agonizing. One minute past the designated hour a faint voice over the radio's crackle could be heard. It was Toto. They had arrived safely, he told them, and had begun building their network. But it would be slow going at the out-set. Hyde breathed a sigh of relief. "The cornerstone of our house was in place," he would report later.

Chapter 18

—◦◦◦—

Sicily and Italy

DAVID DONOVAN had become an exemplary naval officer. His eyesight remained poor by service standards but his superior officers found that it in no way hampered him in performing his duties managing amphibious vessels. He had also displayed "remarkable judgment in emergency operations," one of his commanders noted in a fitness report. David would have preferred duty in the Pacific, where the Navy was doing the real fighting, rather than being a taxi service for Army soldiers landing at the shore. But for now he was satisfied serving as a staff officer aboard the USS *Samuel Chase*, the flagship for the admiral commanding the amphibious force putting troops ashore on July 10 for Operation Husky, the invasion of Sicily. David had been promoted to lieutenant two months earlier. Senior naval officers knew he was Donovan's son and had pushed for speedy promotions, although David would have earned them on his own merit. In fact, wanting to keep as much distance from Donovan as he could, David had never told his shipmates he had a famous father.

It explained why he was both embarrassed and angry when the day before the Sicily invasion, Donovan was piped aboard the *Samuel Chase* as it prepared to get underway from the port of Algiers. He was there to visit David and to join the troops in landing on the beach. Donovan could not be faulted for wanting to see him. Senior officers routinely checked on their sons and the sons of others in war zones. As another ship's officer shot a home movie, David stood awkwardly by his father on deck, forcing a smile. The *Buffalo Evening News* learned of the reunion and published a glowing story on "father and son landing from the same ship for the invasion of Sicily." But David hated the attention Donovan's presence brought him.

David also didn't believe his father had any business being in a war zone at his age. Donovan, who was sixty, had passed his Army physical three months earlier but his body was showing signs of wear and tear from being on the go constantly. He weighed two hundred pounds, too much for his five-foot-nine-inch frame, and his waistline had grown to forty inches. Both legs bore scars from war wounds or football injuries, and he had astigmatism in his right eye. His blood pressure thankfully was low but an X-ray revealed that he had "moderate cardiac hypertrophy," a thickening of the heart muscle from too much stress on the organ. It was not life-threatening though it had to be watched. But oblivious to danger as he always had been, Donovan was eager to make this landing.

In April the Joint Chiefs approved an aggressive $3 million covert operation for Sicily. Donovan, who had begun studying Italian, wanted to shower the island with black propaganda broadcasts, infiltrate spies to supply the Army and Navy intelligence for the beach landings, and organize partisan guerrilla bands to harass the 300,000 Italian and German soldiers who defended it. A year earlier, a twenty-two-year-old Sicilian American named Biagio Max Corvo, who had worked on a Connecticut newspaper and was just a private in the Army, walked into OSS headquarters in Washington and convinced Donovan's officers he had a plan to recruit Sicilian Americans from around the country to infiltrate into Sicily and organize a rebellion among antifascists on the island. They hired the young supply clerk and sent him out to begin recruiting. At one point, Army counterintelligence officers in New York grabbed him, wondering why a lowly private was roaming the city trying to enlist agents for a secret mission. Corvo eventually was commissioned a second lieutenant and sent to Algiers in May with the Sicilian Americans he had rounded up; they included Vincent Scamporino, a Connecticut lawyer who served as his deputy. Before Corvo left, Donovan told him to get a haircut so he would look more military. In North Africa, Corvo and Scamporino recruited more Sicilian refugees for their penetration. The British suspected that some of the men Scamporino found in Tunis were Mafia foot soldiers who had fled the island, although Scamporino assured them that was not the case.

Two weeks before the Sicily invasion, Donovan's Morale Operations branch set up a radio station in Tunis that beamed in broadcasts mixing facts with phony news and urging Sicilians to rise up against the Germans and the Italians who had "sold out to the Nazis." But otherwise, the invasion moved too quickly for the rest of Donovan's covert plan. Corvo finally had a team ready to penetrate the island by early June but Husky's commanders canceled the mission at the last minute, fearing at that late date it might alert Sicily's coastal defenses that an invasion was imminent.

So except for one of his officers assigned to a division to interrogate prisoners, Donovan was the only OSS man going ashore on Saturday, July 10. The night before D-Day, as the *Samuel Chase* steamed through stormy weather to the southwestern beaches at Gela, Sicily, he had slept in a bunk on the weather deck. The ship's other berths were crammed with officers and soldiers from the 1st Division. The next morning after the first wave of Big Red One division soldiers had debarked, Donovan borrowed camouflage fatigues from the crew and climbed down the ship's rope ladder to a landing craft, which took him to Gela's beach.

The invasion caught the Axis defenders by surprise. General Sir Bernard Montgomery's 8th Army had landed on the southeastern side of the island and met little opposition. Patton's 7th Army, assigned the south side, at first came under fire from coastal artillery and Italian and German planes strafing the Gulf of Gela and its beaches. But the U.S. Navy's heavy guns soon obliterated the coastal defenses and by mid-morning Patton's army had begun to move inland. Once ashore, Donovan found the Big Red One's temporary headquarters off the crowded beach. Its assistant division commander, General Theodore Roosevelt Jr., lent him a jeep and one of his aides, Captain Paul Gale, to give him a tour of the operation. Donovan wanted to drive inland, which made Gale nervous because the enemy was not far ahead, but the captain obliged and the two sped down a road away from the beach.

Sure enough, they soon ran into an Italian patrol, which opened fire on the vehicle. Donovan grabbed the light machine gun Gale had brought along and began firing back. "He shot up the Italians single-handed," recalled Gale, a combat veteran from Torch who nevertheless found this firefight a bit unnerving. "He was happy as a clam."

The next day, as the Hermann Göring Panzer Division moved south to counterattack, Donovan caught up with Patton in the town of Gela and the two shared a K ration lunch. They were old friends from Virginia's horse country. Patton owned a Middleburg home near Chapel Hill. "You know,

Bill," Patton had once roared at one of their Middleburg get-togethers, "there are two things in life that I love to do—fucking and fighting." "Yes, George," Donovan roared back, "and in that order, too." Patton had been impressed with the intelligence Eddy's men had fed him for the Torch campaign, but as the two men spooned out cold K rations from cans at Gela, he proved a tough bargainer when they started talking business. Eddy had found that Patton could be prickly and more than willing to throw units like the OSS out of his theater if they crossed him. Patton now agreed to have more of Donovan's espionage and sabotage teams join him in Sicily. But when Donovan asked if two of the 7th Army's officers who were expert in French affairs could be transferred to the OSS, Patton refused to let him raid his staff.

Corvo and his nine-man team were not able to wedge their way onto a Navy transport ship to Sicily until three days after the first landing. Once there, they tried to cross enemy lines riding mules or on foot to collect intelligence but usually found the Axis forces retreating and Patton's army overrunning them before they could return with any worthwhile information. Since his team all spoke the Sicilian dialect they became more useful interrogating POWs. When Donovan left on July 18, his parting orders to Corvo were: "plan for the invasion of Italy." Operating out of a walled villa in Palermo after Patton captured the northwest city on July 22, Corvo's men began collecting intelligence from Sicilians, including Mafia gunmen, who had connections on the Italian mainland. Donovan also dispatched one of Langer's research analysts from Washington to set up what he called the "OSS University of Palermo" in an abandoned country club. Local professors and college students were brought in to analyze the mass of documents seized from the fascist headquarters around the island and to write military and political reports on Italy.

Donovan returned to Washington on August 4, his face sunburned from tromping through Sicily with the troops. Aides thought he had shed a few pounds from his adventure. He also came back with a GI crew cut a ship's barber on the *Samuel Chase* had given him, which earned him a little teasing. "That's sure as hell some haircut you've got there, mister," Wallace Deuel joked when he poked his head into Donovan's office. Agent 109 laughed. He intended to crop his hair closely for more landings.

DONOVAN SPENT ONLY a week back in Washington before boarding a train for Quebec late Thursday night, August 12. He paid the $38.88 out of his own pocket for a sleeping compartment in the Pullman. He stopped in Nonquitt for a brief visit Friday afternoon with Ruth, who was on her regular summer vacation, but was back on the train headed north the next day.

Events were moving quickly in Europe. Patton and Montgomery had ground their armies forward to take Sicily but tragically had allowed more than 100,000 Axis soldiers on the island to escape across the Strait of Messina to the Italian mainland. On July 25, the Fascist Grand Council had ousted Mussolini. King Vittorio Emanuele III had the dictator arrested and made Marshal Badoglio, who had impressed Donovan in the 1936 Ethiopian campaign, the new head of the Italian government. Badoglio soon dissolved the National Fascist Party and opened secret negotiations with the Allies for an armistice. But already Hitler had begun moving German soldiers from France and the Russian front into Italy, as well as into the Balkans, to block the Allies from seizing them. Roosevelt and Churchill would be making important decisions at their Quebec conference, code-named Quadrant, which began on August 17. "Action will follow quickly," warned Lieutenant Colonel Ellery Huntington, a former Yale all-American quarterback and now Donovan's Special Operations chief. Donovan's men had been unprepared for the Sicily invasion. He did not want the war to pass them by in Italy or the Balkans.

Over the next week in Quebec's historic Citadelle, Roosevelt and Marshall managed to quash Churchill's proposal for an Allied army to invade the Balkans. No more diversions beyond an Italian campaign, the Americans insisted. The cross-Channel invasion of France, under the command of an American, would be the priority for the next year. Instead of a Balkans offensive, the president and prime minister agreed the Allies would back the region's guerrilla movements with arms and operatives from the British secret services and Donovan's OSS.

Donovan also convinced Marshall that the OSS and British special operations might be able to capture the Italian island of Sardinia and the French territorial island of Corsica just north of it. Six Italian divisions along with German garrisons held the two islands. In December 1942, the OSS had infiltrated a four-man team into Corsica, which radioed back intelligence on the strength of Axis forces on the island for six months before occupation troops captured and killed the men. On June 23, a five-man team slipped into Sardinia but was captured by Italian sentries the next day. The Allies did not consider the two islands valuable enough prizes to warrant a conventional invasion. But Marshall was willing to let Donovan's fifth column subversives sneak in to try to convince the Italian defenders to give up Sardinia and Corsica without a fight. Eisenhower doubted the covert operatives could pull it off, particularly on the more heavily defended Sardinia. But Marshall cabled him from Quebec that it would "give Donovan a chance to do his stuff without fear of compromising" Eisenhower's other operations. "If he succeeds, fine, if not, nothing would be lost," Marshall reasoned. Ike agreed to give it a try.

Churchill and Roosevelt had also agreed to appoint Admiral Lord Louis Mountbatten the top commander for Southeast Asia, whose theater would also include India and China. After being told of the appointment, Mountbatten walked back to his quarters at the Château Frontenac and found Donovan sitting in his room. Donovan had done small favors for Mountbatten in the past, such as helping his wife, Edwina, arrange a tour of the United States on behalf of the British Red Cross.

"How did you get in?" Mountbatten asked, a bit irritated. "It was locked."

"The OSS can get in anywhere," Donovan said smugly. "Let me be the first to congratulate you on being appointed Supreme Allied Commander Southeast Asia."

"I don't know what you're talking about!" Mountbatten, appalled, nearly shouted. The appointment was still a closely guarded secret.

"You can't fool me," Donovan said. "I've got spies everywhere."

"Well supposing you're right," Mountbatten said gruffly. "Why do you come and worry me about it?"

"Because I want your permission to operate in Southeast Asia," Donovan replied quickly.

"Are you any good?" Mountbatten shot back.

"You bet we're good."

"Then I'm going to test you," Mountbatten said. He would be in New York with his flag lieutenant in a couple of days. *Oklahoma!* had opened on Broadway in March. Donovan's test: "Get me two of the best seats" for the musical, Mountbatten demanded.

"Goddamn it, that's impossible!" Donovan yelped. "There are absolutely no seats for six months. How do you expect me—?"

"No seats for *Oklahoma!*, no operations in Southeast Asia," Mountbatten interrupted. Then he threw Donovan out.

Two days later, Donovan showed up at Mountbatten's New York hotel with six tickets plus three beautiful young women to help the admiral, the flag lieutenant, and the spy chief enjoy the play and a nightclub afterward. (Lord and Lady Mountbatten had what could charitably be called an open marriage.) A news photographer, however, intercepted the party as they walked out of the club later that night and snapped photos of Mountbatten with his date.

"If those photographs are published," Mountbatten told Donovan, not only will the OSS be out of Southeast Asia, "I'll probably be out, too!" Suddenly two burly agents protecting Donovan appeared, grabbed the photographer by both elbows and carried him off. The shots never made the papers. "Bill, you are in," Mountbatten said, smiling.

AS THE NAVAL armada of 642 ships loitered in the calm waters of the Gulf of Salerno early Thursday morning, September 9, waiting to disgorge their 55,000 assault troops for Operation Avalanche, Donovan stood on the flag bridge of the USS *Ancon* command ship with Admiral Kent Hewitt and the 5th Army's commander, Mark Clark. (David also was in the Gulf of Salerno aboard the *Samuel Chase*, but, much to his relief, his father did not drop in on him this time.) Donovan sported combat fatigues and a helmet and planned to smear black camouflage paint over his face when he went ashore after the initial wave. Donald Downes, who had led the embassy break-ins in Washington, was also on the *Ancon* in charge of a twenty-man OSS detachment wading ashore with the first wave. He had arranged for a Navy PT boat to ferry Donovan to the beach later. German warplanes began strafing the fleet shortly after 4 A.M., but Donovan remained on deck to watch out of curiosity. Donovan's senior aides had tried admonishing him about being too close to the line of fire. His head was filled with the knowledge of Magic and Ultra and countless other sensitive Allied secrets, which risked exposure if he was captured at a beach landing. But Donovan had no intention of missing the Allied invasion at Salerno.

Clark saw no problem with the spy chief making the landing. Once Donovan reached the beach, he told Clark: "If you can give me a jeep and a gun I won't bother you further." Clark was willing to provide the weapon and vehicle, but he balked on other matters. With Ultra already giving him a detailed picture of enemy forces in Italy, the 5th Army commander refused to let Donovan's agents infiltrate into Salerno before D-Day and risk compromise of Operation Avalanche's timing if they were discovered. Since May, however, Marshall and Eisenhower had approved Donovan's broadcasting bare-knuckled propaganda messages into Italian radio sets to convince their listeners that alliance with Germany would set Italy back a hundred years.

Italy did not need Donovan's propaganda to convince her that breaking from the Axis was the only way she could survive. On September 3, Badoglio's representative signed unconditional surrender documents at the Allied forward headquarters in Sicily. Just eight hours before the Salerno invasion Eisenhower and Badoglio announced the Italian capitulation over Rome and Algiers radio. Soldiers on the ships floating in the Gulf of Salerno were euphoric, believing that the landing would be a cakewalk. It was anything but. Anticipating an Allied landing somewhere in the Salerno area, the German 16th Panzer Division nearby rushed to counterattack while German reinforcements further south moved toward the city. Clark landed his force in short order but it stalled within several miles of the beachhead as the Germans fought ferociously to drive his army back into the sea. Finally after ten days of intense fighting and some nine thousand British and American casualties, the 5th Army managed to hold, then push back the Germans, eventually with the help of Montgomery's slowly arriving force.

As Donovan watched from the shore, Downes's detachment interrogated enemy POWs and began sending small intelligence-gathering teams ten to fifty miles behind German lines. They were guided often by antifascist Italian soldiers and civilians from the Salerno area, whom the OSS men hired on the spot. Two days after the first landings, Downes and three other OSS officers sped in a PT boat to the small beachhead Lieutenant Colonel William O. Darby's Army Ranger battalions had carved out at the coastal resort villages of Maiori, Minori, and Amalfi on the Sorrento Peninsula jutting west of Salerno. The agents rounded up some four hundred raggedy-looking men and boys from the villages who hauled ammunition, fuel cans, and food that Navy amphibious ships off-loaded at the beach to Darby's force fighting at the front. Downes paid the men of this makeshift stevedore gang fifty lire a day and the boys thirty-seven lire along with two cans of C rations for each from the boxes they toted.

As Darby's Rangers pushed northward, Downes, who also had a nose for fine living, commandeered the Hotel Luna in Amalfi as his headquarters. He drove Donovan there and had the hotel's waiters serve them a seven-course dinner in black tie. The boss was nonplussed by this ostentatious display. Donovan had begun receiving disturbing reports from other OSS officers that his protégé from the Spanish embassy break-ins was in over his head at Salerno. "Downes and his staff were acting like bandits, requisitioning everything, including cars, without rhyme or reason," one OSS officer complained in an after-action report. Downes's agents looted one Italian villa of its personal effects. Predictably many of the locals his men hurriedly hired to infiltrate the German lines proved to be "of doubtful character," the report continued. "Lack of discipline was the rule of the day. The [OSS] personnel behaved much as they pleased." Donovan knew he had a potential mess on his hands.

But before he tackled the Downes problem, Donovan returned to Algiers to launch the two missions Marshall had approved at Quebec. He sprung the Sardinia operation on Serge Obolensky, the dashing czarist officer who had been one of his early hires in New York and who had just arrived in Algiers to train OSS commandos. Donovan wanted him to parachute onto the island with surrender letters from Eisenhower and the new Badoglio government and convince the commander of the 270,000 Italian soldiers there, many perhaps still loyal to Mussolini, to surrender and begin attacking the nineteen thousand Germans in Sardinia as they evacuated north into Corsica. "Oboe," the nickname Obolensky's comrades had given him, was less than enthusiastic at first. "General, I don't speak Italian," he pointed out. "I know France and speak French fluently . . ."

"I know you can do it, Oboe," Donovan kept repeating with his soft, soothing voice. "I have confidence in you." Donovan had a way of making an agent feel that the mission he was going on was "perfectly simple," as he always put it. "Believe me, I wish I were going with you."

Oboe took the bait. A half hour before midnight on September 13, with his weak ankles heavily taped so he hopefully wouldn't sprain them, the Russian cavalryman jumped out of a Halifax bomber along with two other OSS commandos and a British radio operator and floated down to the foot-

Fourteen-year-old Will Donovan (top line, third from the right), on the Saint Joseph's Collegiate Institute football team, was an average student and a scrappy athlete, who fought to control his temper as a boy. *Saint Joseph's Collegiate Institute*

The handsome Donovan rose out of the poverty of Buffalo, New York's Irish First Ward to become one of the city's prominent lawyers. He was also one of its most eligible bachelors. *David G. and Teresa Y. Donovan Collection*

Ruth Rumsey was the beautiful daughter of one of Buffalo's wealthiest businessmen. Although her family at first disapproved of her suitor from First Ward, Ruth was captivated by Donovan and married him in 1914. But she soon found that Donovan would be an absent husband for much of their marriage and he would have affairs with other women. *Molly Mugler Collection*

Donovan, with young Patricia and David after World War I, was away for long stretches, so much of his children's upbringing was left to Ruth. *Molly Mugler Collection*

Donovan was closer to his daughter, Patricia, whose outgoing personality was much like his. But she died in an auto accident at age twenty-two, which devastated Donovan. *Molly Mugler Collection*

David, who was far closer to Ruth, shunned the spotlight his father commanded and preferred running the family farm in Virginia. His wife, Mary, was captivated by Donovan's celebrity status and often filled in as his hostess at parties in Ruth's absence. Mary, however, also met a tragic end at a relatively young age. *Patricia Gilbert Collection*

Donovan, right, began his military career in 1912, leading Troop I, a National Guard cavalry unit made up of young professionals and businessmen from Buffalo who volunteered for weekend duty and became known as the "Silk Stocking Boys." *Buffalo Cavalry Association*

A French officer pins the Croix de Guerre on Donovan, one of many awards he received for heroism in World War I. It was during the First World War that Donovan earned his nickname "Wild Bill," given to him by his men because he put them through grueling training for battle. *U.S. Army Military History Institute*

Donovan (left) and Father Francis Duffy, the chaplain of the 165th Regiment (originally the 69th), became as close as brothers during World War I. Donovan thought that Father Duffy was as near a saint as he would ever see. The politically savvy chaplain, who thought Donovan was the bravest man he had ever met, lobbied to have him made commander of the Irish Regiment. *National Archives*

Donovan, sporting a mustache, posed for this photo in the field during World War I. He eventually won the Medal of Honor for leading his men in the murderous battle at Landres-et-Saint-Georges, while suffering a severe wound to his leg. *U.S. Army Military History Institute*

Promoted to colonel, Donovan (on the ship returning from Europe) came back to New York a war hero, touted as a possible candidate for governor. Ruth had sent his letters describing the combat to New York newspapers, which were eager to publish them. *U.S. Army Military History Institute*

Donovan, speaking at a rally, ran for governor of New York in 1932 as a Republican. But he proved to be a lackluster campaigner and was handily defeated in the Democratic sweep that year. *Georgetown University Library*

Ruth and the children, now in their teens, posed for a campaign photo in 1932. Though she wanted to be the first lady of New York, Ruth did little campaigning for her husband. With Donovan gone so much, Ruth began to carve out a life for herself. *Molly Mugler Collection*

For much of their marriage, Ruth went on many vacations without her husband, who was always preoccupied with business. But occasionally they traveled overseas together, such as this trip to North Africa and the Middle East, where they toured the pyramids of Egypt. *David G. and Teresa Y. Donovan Collection*

During an unofficial diplomatic mission for Franklin Roosevelt in the winter of 1940–41, Donovan confers with Yugoslav military officials. Donovan pressured wavering Balkan leaders not to side with Adolf Hitler, warning that FDR did not intend to let Great Britain lose the war. *U.S. Army Military History Institute*

Donovan huddles with foreign correspondents on his Balkans diplomatic tour in the winter of 1940–41. He made a point of cultivating reporters, whom he found useful as intelligence sources and propagandists during World War II. *U.S. Army Military History Institute*

The OSS Washington headquarters (currently a U.S. government facility) was located at 25th and E Streets atop Navy Hill in a building the Public Health Service had been using for animal research. Berlin radio mocked it as the home of "50 professors, 10 goats, 12 guinea pigs, a sheep, and a staff of Jewish scribblers." *Author Photo*

William Stephenson, head of British intelligence operations in the United States and Latin America, became a close Donovan friend, helping him set up the OSS and supplying him with intelligence reports and expertise from London's spy service. *U.S. Army Military History Institute, Sam Morse-Brown portrait*

Donovan, on one of two phones connecting him to the White House and U.S. military leaders, had his office in Room 109 of OSS headquarters. He used 109 as his code number in all secret cable traffic. *U.S. Army Military History Institute*

Donovan and Franklin Roosevelt had been political enemies in New York in the 1930s, but by 1940 FDR found his Republican rival useful in preparing the country for war against the Axis. A spy buff, Roosevelt approved Donovan's setting up the Office of Strategic Services but never allowed him to oversee intelligence operations in the military or other government agencies. *Franklin D. Roosevelt Presidential Library*

Donovan fought fierce bureaucratic battles. General George C. Marshall, Army chief of staff (center), at first opposed the OSS but eventually came to see its value and protected it from enemies in the military. General George Patton (left) was a Donovan friend, as was General Henry "Hap" Arnold (right), the chief of the Army Air Forces. *Franklin D. Roosevelt Presidential Library*

Winston Churchill found Donovan an important ally in his early drive to have the United States join Britain in the war against the Axis. But the two men soured on each other as Donovan's OSS and British intelligence squabbled over which service controlled secret operations in overseas theaters. They patched things up after the war. *Franklin D. Roosevelt Presidential Library*

hills of Sardinia about fifteen miles from Cagliari, its capital in the south. The mission turned out to be as simple as Donovan had predicted. General Alberto Basso, the island's courtly Italian commander, read Obolensky's two surrender letters the next afternoon and courteously agreed to "push the Germans out of Sardinia." Instead of fighting the Nazis, however, Basso's divisions merely followed them up the island and watched as they all crossed the narrow Strait of Bonifacio into Corsica by September 18.

The Corsica operation, which Donovan sprang on anthropology professor Carleton Coon, proved to be not as easy. At midnight September 13, the French warships *Fantasque* and *Terrible* pulled up to the docks at Corsica's east coast capital of Ajaccio and deposited Coon, his small contingent of OSS intelligence agents and commandos plus a reinforced brigade of French, Moroccan, and Algerian colonial soldiers the French headquarters in Algiers had cobbled together to liberate the island. They were greeted by a noisy crowd of Corsicans dancing, singing the "Marseillaise," and firing shotguns in the air. After the Italian surrender had been announced September 8, Corsican resistance bands around the island had begun seizing towns and enemy barracks. But the clannish Corsicans fought the hated Italians on the island and one another as much as the Germans. The eighty thousand Italians on Corsica who had been expected to join the Allies in capturing the Germans instead blew up bridges and threw up roadblocks in front of French convoys moving to the front.

At any time, the island's Nazi garrison reinforced by the nineteen thousand well-trained German soldiers who had arrived from Sardinia could have turned around and wiped out the ragtag band of invaders. Instead they conducted a fighting withdrawal to the northern town of Bastia, where ships evacuated the force to the Italian mainland on October 4. Coon's intelligence team spied on the retreating Germans and his thirty-four commandos harassed them with guerrilla attacks. Three of his men died in a crossfire. Donovan, who dropped in on Coon's villa headquarters at one point before the battle ended, now had a base on the two islands for launching covert operations into Italy and southern France. But "far from being a great victory," the invasion of Corsica "was largely an act of occupying territory which the Germans did not want," Coon later admitted. His OSS army ended up "simply annoying them on their way out."

On a PT boat ride with Downes in late September to the resort island of Capri just off the Sorrento Peninsula, Donovan finally dealt with his

Salerno problem. Ellery Huntington, the Special Operations chief from Washington, will take over the OSS detachment assigned to Clark's army, he told the agent. Downes could remain as Huntington's counterintelligence officer. And before the British grabbed it, Donovan also wanted Downes to secure a plush Capri villa that had been vacated during the war by his friend Mona Williams, a New York fashion icon married to a public utilities millionaire. Donovan wanted to use Villa Fortino as a rest camp for OSS agents.

Downes blew up. He angrily declared that he would not work for Huntington, who he claimed was incompetent and had risen this far in the OSS only because he had been one of Donovan's campaign contributors. As for the villa, Downes said huffily, he wasn't fighting this war to protect Donovan's clients. It was all Donovan could do to keep from throwing Downes overboard. Instead, he calmly told his agent he looked exhausted and needed to come home for a rest. Downes did need a rest. He was suffering from amoebic dysentery. Donovan was prone to relieve an officer from one position, then find another job for him to do in the OSS. But the man he had considered a superstar for the embassy break-ins left Italy and never returned to the field as a secret agent.

Chapter 19

—◦◦◦—

The Balkans

DONOVAN ROAMED the Mediterranean region until October 2, seeding ideas and rearranging his personnel. The briefcase he carried with him also bulged with secret plans for the Balkans. The region was not a primary war theater for Roosevelt, whose generals wanted no part of invading it with a conventional force, nor for Hitler, whose troops there were mostly too old or unfit for duty on the Eastern or Western Fronts. For outsiders, it was forbidding territory. The incessant infighting among countless Balkan factions became a constant headache for the German occupiers. For the Allies, organizing a unified resistance against the Germans became filthy work as well. The indigenous guerrillas, often more intent on battling rival factions than the Nazis, wanted American and British arms but no meddling in their internal affairs. Yet the Balkans became a key theater for Donovan's war. By the fall of 1943 both he and the Joint Chiefs believed the time was "ripe" for intensive subversion and propaganda operations to peel off countries such as Bulgaria, Romania, and Hungary. With Italy's surrender and German defeats on the Soviet front, the Nazi satellites had begun looking for ways to wiggle out of an alliance with what would likely be the losing side. If it did not cause a breach, "subversive pressure" would at least "cause difficulties for the Axis," Donovan reasoned.

The Balkans would also be the place for Donovan's most intense battles with the British. He had finally reached an accord with Sir Charles Hambro on July 26, which allowed his men to work jointly under the SOE missions already in Yugoslavia and Greece. In Yugoslavia, he agreed that both outfits would use the same cipher system to encode their radio messages transmitted from the field. (That would also conveniently enable Hambro's men to monitor OSS communications.) But Donovan had no intention of merely servicing London in Yugoslavia or Greece. He drew up detailed plans for OSS-organized commando attacks on rail lines, bridges, and tele- phone exchanges the Germans used in both countries. The guerrilla upris- ings would make life miserable for the Nazis, Donovan envisioned, forcing them to withdraw, or at least to drain soldiers from France and the Eastern Front to fight the rebellions. Donovan ordered a "supreme effort" to put more American operatives than the British wanted into both Yugoslavia and Greece.

In mid-August, Walter Mansfield, a thirty-two-year-old Marine lieuten- ant who had worked in Donovan's law firm, parachuted into the moun- tain headquarters of Draža Mihailović, who commanded some seventy thousand Chetnik fighters in central and eastern Serbia. Army Lieutenant Colonel Albert Seitz, a tall Virginian and Mansfield's friend from para- chute training, joined him the next month. Mihailović, a middle-aged stocky man who sported an iron-gray beard, black cap, and leather jacket, gave Mansfield and Seitz the royal treatment, much to the chagrin of the British.

For six months, Mansfield and Seitz interviewed Mihailović and hiked through his command, sleeping under tents made of torn parachutes, eat- ing black bread and lamb stew with his soldiers (who all had heavy black beards and skull-and-bones insignias sewn onto their frayed uniforms), and dodging German patrols hunting for guerrillas. They came away convinced that while Mihailović hated Tito's communist partisans far more than the Germans, the Serbian nationalist would start killing more Nazis if the Americans gave his threadbare army weapons. Even if Churchill prevailed and convinced Roosevelt to cut off all arms to Mihailović, Mansfield and Seitz argued that it still made sense to keep OSS officers in the Serb's tent camp to exploit him "as a source of intelligence" on the German occupiers.

Donovan was not convinced Mihailović was the man to back with American arms. He had other senior advisers warning him that the Chet- niks were killing more communist partisans than Germans and that Mihailović often was collaborating with the Nazis in his power struggle with Tito. But he believed that OSS agents should remain with Mihailović to spy and to work with the Chetnik warlord evacuating Allied pilots whose planes were shot down over his territory. By the end of 1943, however, Churchill convinced Roosevelt that the British and American officers at Mihailović's headquarters should leave and all Allied arms and advisers should be shifted to Tito. Donovan bitterly fought the move, but Churchill, who did not want to alienate Tito by continuing ties with his hated rival, prevailed. The British mission pulled up stakes by February 1944. Donovan reluctantly ordered his officers at Draža's headquarters to leave as well.

Before he left North Africa after the Salerno landing, however, Donovan was intent on throwing the full weight of the OSS behind Tito. The communist commander's army of some 180,000 occupied most of Bosnia-Herzegovina, Dalmatia, Slovenia, and a chunk of Croatia-Slavonia. Though they were fighting a civil war with the Chetniks, Tito's partisans were also violently anti-Nazi and inflicting far more damage on the thirteen German divisions occupying Yugoslavia. On September 14 during a stop in Algiers, Donovan huddled at Villa Magnol with two young aides to Louis Huot, his Cairo special operations officer, who offered up a new operation code-named Audrey (after the name of Huot's wife) to ship massive amounts of supplies to Tito. The British still controlled the planes for special operations but with the Allies now occupying half of southern Italy, Huot proposed another way of moving men and supplies to Tito—by boat on the relatively short hop over the Adriatic Sea from Italy's eastern coast to Yugoslavia's western coast. John Toulmin, a former Boston bank executive Donovan had recently made his Cairo station chief, had a queasy feeling about the headstrong Huot, who tended to jump the gun on operations. But for now, Donovan was enthusiastic about Audrey. He ordered Huot "to push ahead full speed."

Huot did just that. He set up his secret naval base at Bari, an Italian fishing town on the Adriatic coast whose boutique shops, opera house, and a strategically more important deepwater port had been left intact by the departing Germans. By mid-October, Huot had a fleet of seventeen small steamers and schooners there, which began sailing fuel, food, weapons, uniforms, and medical supplies to Vis Island, south of the coastal town of Split, where Tito's men off-loaded the cargo by hand. Later, however, it became an open and hotly disputed question whether Huot had obtained the proper authorizations from the theater command to mount a major supply operation into a country London considered its turf. Huot insisted he had the clearances. Before leaving North Africa, Donovan also had told British General Henry Maitland Wilson, the Middle East commander, that he wanted to set up an OSS "advanced base" on southern Italy's Adriatic coast to mount covert operations into the Balkans. "Jumbo," the nickname Wilson had earned because he was huge, saw no problem with the base, according to Donovan. The British later howled that Huot never told them he was convoying hundreds of tons of supplies to Tito, which amounted to a smuggling operation behind their backs.

On October 23, however, Huot clearly did wander off the reservation. He sneaked into Tito's mountain headquarters at Jajce in Bosnia-Herzegovina, without the prior approval of higher headquarters or the chief of the British mission to Tito, Brigadier Fitzroy Maclean. A lanky thirty-two-year-old Churchill confidant, Maclean had once been a Conservative Party member of Parliament. The brigadier was away from the camp when Huot showed up for a long chat about guerrilla operations and American supplies with Tito in his office, a bare-wood shed under a stand of cedar trees. The handsome and manicured Tito, dressed in a gray tunic and breeches with black riding boots that clinked with spurs, chain-smoked cigarettes perched in what Huot thought was a ridiculous-looking miniature pipe adorned with silver filigree. But over a simple dinner washed down with schnapps and a light rosé, the charismatic Croatian wowed Huot, who called him "a man of action rather than polemics." The major left with a long shopping list from the communist warlord. Maclean, who was supposed to clear all British and American visits to Tito's headquarters, was livid when he learned of the protocol breach. The British soon took over the convoying and Huot was eventually sent home.

Huot left behind bruised feelings. Fitz Maclean became a bitter Donovan enemy. Over the next three months the British brigadier tried to block more OSS commandos and intelligence agents from entering Yugoslavia. Maclean ordered that not only did the Americans have to encode their radio messages using British ciphers but that he also must read their intelligence reports before they were transmitted. Any OSS officer who violated these draconian rules would be arrested and evicted.

But Huot's china-breaking behavior merely mirrored Donovan's basic instinct. By the fall of 1943, the OSS director was intent on busting up the British monopoly in the Balkans. On his return to Washington from his Salerno adventure, Donovan made a stop in London to visit Major General Colin McVean Gubbins at Baker Street. A war-seasoned officer and resourceful guerrilla organizer, Gubbins had just replaced Hambro as the head of the Special Operations Executive. He knew he had to keep a close eye on Donovan's requests to infiltrate OSS men into British territory. That was why Gubbins's ears perked up when Donovan mentioned casually at the end of their meeting that he hoped the two sides did not become too "legalistic" about the wording of previous OSS-SOE agreements dividing up the world's turf. The new CD took the passing remark from the New York lawyer as a signal that Donovan intended to abrogate their contract—which was exactly what Donovan planned to do.

Overall, the United States, Great Britain, and the Soviet Union—each with competing postwar goals—were finding it more difficult to manage their alliance. Donovan's mood and moves reflected a broader tension between British colonial aims and American anticolonial sentiments. When he later learned that Maclean wanted to make his OSS officers in Yugoslavia subjects of the crown, Donovan angrily informed Gubbins that the deal was off. The OSS would not use British ciphers in the Balkans, his officers at Jajce would not clear their reports with Maclean, and, if he had to, he would treat the British there like the Nazis and sneak his secret agents into Yugoslavia behind Maclean's back. Donovan's "violent attack" on Fiztroy and his rules, as one secret SOE memo termed it, stunned the British.

Churchill was even more flabbergasted with an October 22 cable from Roosevelt, which Donovan had convinced FDR to send. "The chaotic conditions developing in the Balkans causes me concern," Roosevelt's "Personal and Most Secret" message to Churchill began. "And I am sure you are also worried. In both Yugoslavia and Greece the guerrilla forces appear to be engaged largely in fighting each other and not the Germans." FDR had ceded Nazi-occupied Greece to Churchill as a British theater of operations. The prime minister was committed to restoring exiled King George II to the Hellenic throne and his Special Operations Executive favored the more conservative National Republican Greek League (EDES) and its some 6,500 guerrillas. Donovan's OSS, which considered the senior ministers who fled Greece with the fascist-prone king mostly a bunch of crooks, leaned more toward the leftist National Liberation Front (EAM) and its military corps, the Greek People's Liberation Army (ELAS), whose 17,500 guerrillas were communist-led and, as was the case in Yugoslavia, appeared to be doing most of the fighting against the Germans. "In the present confused condition," Roosevelt's cable continued, "the only hope I see for immediate favorable action is the presence of an aggressive and qualified officer." Why not send Donovan to take charge of covert operations and unify the feuding parties in the countries? "I do not believe he can do any harm," FDR wrote his friend, "and being a fearless and aggressive character he might do much good."

Churchill contained his fury over Donovan's blatant power grab. The next day, the "Former Naval Person," as Churchill always called himself in his private messages to Roosevelt, wrote FDR in the most diplomatic words he could summon that the Yugoslav and Greek civil wars indeed were "vexatious," but Jumbo Wilson, the region's British commander, had matters well in hand. "Some of our officers there of Brigadier's rank are very capable and have in numerous cases been there for two years," Churchill gently lectured the President. "I have great admiration for Donovan, but I do not see any centre in the Balkans from which he could grip the situation." In other words, butt out. Roosevelt dropped the idea.

By late fall of 1943, however, Churchill's intelligence and special operations chiefs had accepted the fact that they could no longer hold back the OSS in the Balkans or the rest of Europe for that matter. By the time Donovan flew back to Washington in early October he had finally secured for his exclusive use nine American bombers and cargo planes for his infiltrations. The OSS would not be where it is today if London had not freely lent its considerable expertise in espionage and covert warfare, the British correctly believed. But like a teenager eager to escape his parents, the OSS now wanted "to break away from the existing tutelage," in Gubbins's words. It left his Baker Street Irregulars both nervous and bitter. The British effort "to work as one" with Donovan's organization "has proved a failure," an SOE representative in North Africa wrote CD at the end of September. "The American temperament demands quick and spectacular results, while the British policy is generally speaking long-term and plodding." The dangers to His Majesty's Government in assuaging their "inferiority complex" and granting the Americans independence, the memo indignantly warned, are obvious:

1. The irresponsibility of the OSS.
2. Their permanent hankering after playing cowboys and red Indians.
3. Their unlimited dollars.
4. The political necessity of paying spectacular dividends.
5. Their capacity for blundering into delicate European situations about which they understand little.

Gubbins agreed.

Chapter 20

Peace Feelers

DONOVAN BOOKED a late lunch October 13 with Roosevelt, who was eager to hear his war stories from Salerno and an update on the rest of the Mediterranean theater. After two years of near immobility, his OSS was finally being assigned aircraft for its missions, Donovan proudly told the president. He had men in Yugoslavia and more on the way. Covert operatives would be infiltrated into Greece by planes and caique fishing boats. As soon as Coon finished work in Corsica, he was headed to Albania. As for a large relief map of Italy that Roosevelt had told him at the Quebec conference he wanted in order to follow Clark's campaign, Donovan said his cartographers were putting the finishing touches to a sheet they had been coloring by hand—scaled one inch to eight miles. Donovan did not mention it to Roosevelt but peace feelers were also percolating. They would confound his agency for many months.

Although Hitler would hold together his army through intimidation and rewards, a growing number of senior Wehrmacht officers believed by the fall of 1943 that Germany had no hope of winning the war. Europe became alive with reports of an impending German officer coup or peace emissaries looking to gain concessions for Germany in the future. Many of Donovan's advisers were skeptical. "There is no cause for undue optimism," Putzi Hanfstaengl wrote on September 10, "for although fortress Europe may be cracking, Hitler himself is not." Expect "much hard fighting" ahead, he warned. Though their declared position was to accept nothing less than unconditional German surrender, the Allied leaders remained wary that the Nazis or other factions within Germany might attempt a separate peace with one country to break up the alliance. No one more so than Stalin, paranoid that Churchill and Roosevelt would strike a deal behind his back leaving him fighting the Germans alone on the Eastern Front.

Enter Count Helmuth Graf von Moltke, descended from one of the most revered military families in Germany. His great-uncle, General Field Marshall Helmuth Karl Bernhard Graf von Moltke, had been the innovative strategist who had defeated France in the 1870 Franco-Prussian War, and Helmut Johann Ludwig von Moltke, known as "Moltke the Younger," had been chief of the German General Staff at the outbreak of World War I. Thirty-seven-year-old Helmuth von Moltke had inherited the family estate in Silesia but instead of the military had pursued international law. At least six-feet-five-inches tall, Moltke was well read, well educated, and well traveled, having made a number of friends in American circles, such as Alexander Kirk (the U.S. ambassador to Cairo), journalist Dorothy Thompson, and Donovan. The young count also was a liberal, who became part of what would be called the Kreisau Circle after the Silesian city near Moltke's estate. It was a loose pro-West and anticommunist association of left-wing civil servants, doctors, lawyers, labor leaders, and anti-Nazi military staff officers, all determined to defeat the regime as the only way to save Germany from annihilation.

In the summer of 1943, Moltke had traveled to Istanbul both as a Kreisau Circle emissary and as an Abwehr agent for Canaris, hoping to use his American connections to make contact with U.S. representatives. He met with two members of Alfred Schwarz's chain of Dogwood agents: Hans Wilbrandt, an economist code-named "Hyacinth," and Alexander Rustov, a sociologist code-named "Magnolia," both of whom were members of the German Freedom Movement in Istanbul, which collaborated with the OSS. Moltke, who assumed the code name "Hermann," read Hyacinth and Magnolia his written peace plan. The Kreisau Circle accepted the "unequivocal military defeat and occupation of Germany." But the Hermann Plan, as it came to be called, was Russophobic. The Kreisau Circle proposed to overthrow Hitler and establish a "provisional anti-Nazi government," which would help the Western Allies invade quickly by having the German army shift east to hold the Red Army at the Tilsit-to-Lemberg line in Poland. Moltke offered an unnamed "high officer" of the Wehrmacht to meet with Eisenhower's representative and work out this complicated military dance.

Packy Macfarland, the OSS Istanbul station chief, urged Donovan to take Moltke seriously. The count wanted to present the Hermann Plan to Alexander Kirk, whom he had known intimately from the envoy's prewar posting in Berlin, but Kirk begged off, insisting that the war could not end by "dickering" with German factions. Dejected he could not meet Kirk, Moltke returned to Berlin. He wanted to fly back to Istanbul in January 1944, when Macfarland hoped to have convinced the Cairo ambassador to change his mind and meet the count, joined by an Eisenhower representative authorized to negotiate the deal.

Donovan was cautious. In October 1943, Theodore Morde, a fast-talking correspondent for *Reader's Digest* who fashioned himself a spy and diplomatic dabbler, arranged a meeting on his own in Turkey with Franz von Papen, Hitler's crafty ambassador there. Papen, who told Morde "the time had come when the war must stop," floated a proposal to overthrow Hitler and head a new government that would make peace with the West but maintain the German army on the Eastern Front to "keep guard" against the Russians. Morde brought Papen's peace offer back to Washington, where Donovan urged Roosevelt to "carefully" consider it. But FDR was horrified when he learned of the freelance diplomacy. In late November he planned to travel to Tehran for the first Big Three conference with Churchill and Stalin to coordinate the Allied offensive against Hitler. If word leaked—and it surely would—that an American emissary was negotiating a secret deal behind the Russian dictator's back, which was far less than unconditional surrender and left intact the German army facing Stalin's force, it could blow the Tehran talks sky high. Roosevelt shut down the line to Papen, ordering the State Department to revoke Morde's passport so he could not return to Turkey or travel anywhere else overseas.

Smarting from FDR's rebuke in the Morde gambit, Donovan ordered Macfarland to keep a tight leash on Dogwood and any of his agents talking to Moltke. No "loose talk" that even hinted at how Washington might react to the Hermann Plan, he demanded. Meanwhile, a top secret debate raged within his headquarters over how the OSS should treat the offer. Whitney Shepardson, Donovan's intelligence chief, believed Moltke was "one of the most influential individuals" of a powerful and broad-based anti-Nazi group that Hitler had not yet liquidated. The Hermann Plan was a way to short-circuit the war as well as liberate Western Europe—and to occupy Germany ahead of the Russian army. Others weren't so sure. Except for Moltke, the OSS did not know the names of anyone else in the Kreisau Circle. The Hermann Plan could be a Nazi plant deviously designed to split the alliance. Even if genuine, the plan was disturbingly short on specifics, such as exactly how this little group would move Hitler's massive army in France and Western Europe's other occupied countries, along with the German home forces, to the Eastern Front. William Langer, Donovan's research director, continued to "find it extremely difficult to believe" that any well-organized opposition existed in Germany, as Moltke claimed. "Certainly it would be a vast mistake for any military commander to count upon such inside aid" from the Kreisau Circle and change his battle plans.

Donovan tended to agree with the pessimists. He drafted a lengthy memo to the Joint Chiefs detailing objectively the pros and cons of the Hermann Plan and recommended that Washington should consult Churchill and Stalin over what was obviously "an anti-Russian proposal." But after rereading the draft and chewing it over with his staff once more, Donovan shelved the document. He ordered Macfarland just to keep in touch with Moltke to see what intelligence he could provide for the Allied invasion of France. Perhaps the Kreisau Circle could offer spies for the OSS in Berlin.

Macfarland, however, never again heard from Moltke after he left Istanbul in December. Donovan would learn later that the Gestapo had grabbed the count shortly after he returned to Berlin and had executed him soon after. It was disturbing news. Why the sudden arrest? Had the Gestapo been tipped off to agent Hermann? Was there a leak in Macfarland's chain?

DONOVAN RECEIVED encouraging news from one operation to pry a satellite from the Axis. He had attended his law firm's annual dinner at the River Club of New York on Friday night, March 17, 1944, then hopped on the last train to Washington so he could put in a full day's work on Saturday. As Donovan sipped his breakfast coffee at his Georgetown home Arthur Goldberg phoned with the report headquarters had just received from an overseas station. "The Sparrow team has been dropped success-fully," was all Goldberg would tell him over the open line. Later from his office, Donovan delivered the top secret news to the Joint Chiefs: Hungary had been penetrated.

Four hours before dawn on Thursday, March 16, Colonel Florimund DuSossoit Duke and his two subordinates—Major Alfred Suarez and Lieu-tenant Guy Nunn—feverishly shoveled holes in a forest field near the junc-tion of the Mura and Drava Rivers. Short and muscular, Duke had been a football star at Dartmouth College and had fought in World War I. He had been *Time* magazine's advertising manager before he joined Dono-van's organization as a Balkans operative. Duke was not a particularly subtle thinker, but he was a bullheaded leader who kept his cool under pressure. Arthur Goldberg's Labor Section, set up to organize European unions against the Nazis, had recruited Nunn, a freelance writer educated at Stanford University, and Suarez, who had served in the Spanish Civil War with the anti-Franco Republicans as a radio operator. The OSS team, code-named Sparrow, had parachuted from a British Halifax to a plowed field and the exact spot they wanted to be—just over the border from north-ern Croatia in Hungary. But they had a lot of digging to do before sunup. The bomber had also dumped out three parachuted containers crammed with clothing, food, and radios that needed to be buried along with the chutes and their jumpsuits. Exhausted, they finally finished about 6 A.M. and began walking to a village Duke spied a mile and a half away, where he hoped the Sparrow team would be captured by the Hungarian military.

It took a while to find someone awake but Duke finally convinced the friendly villagers to have a teenage boy bicycle to the military barracks six miles away and alert it that the Americans had landed.

Duke calmly told the squad of Hungarian soldiers who arrived that their plane had been hit by antiaircraft fire and they had to bail out to lighten the load so the aircraft could return to base. The enlisted soldiers, not sure they should buy this story, radioed for officers to come to the village. By 11 A.M., Duke and his Sparrows had more than a dozen Hungarian authori-ties milling about them when one, dressed in civilian clothes, finally pulled the colonel aside and whispered in English: "I've been waiting for you for three days." He identified himself only as Major Kirali from the Hungarian air force and told Duke to let the soldiers process them through the army's regular security channels so they could eventually meet the man they had come to see. That person was General Stephen Ujszaszi, the army's chief of intelligence.

The Sparrow team had an unusual infiltration plan. They would become prisoners of war of the Hungarian army, which would take them to Ujszaszi, who had secretly agreed to be their go-between in peace talks with the Hungarian cabinet. Part One of the operation went off without a hitch. By the next evening, Duke, Suarez, and Nunn sat comfortably in a jail cell in the basement of Budapest's Internal Security Police headquarters building, enjoying a delicious dinner from the restaurant around the corner and waiting for General Ujszaszi.

Donovan began mulling the idea for Sparrow in the summer of 1943. Hungary had joined the Axis to be part of Hitler's land grab and win territory from Romania. The Hungarian regent, Admiral Miklós Horthy, hoped to do it with as little of his force fighting the Red Army as he could get away with and not anger the führer. But as Hungarian losses on the Eastern Front mounted in 1943 and public resentment over Nazi exploitation of Hungary's oil industry grew, Horthy and his new anti-German prime minister, Miklós Kallay, began casting out soundings in the West. Hungarian intermediaries in Bern and Stockholm had approached British envoys and OSS officers about a separate peace with the Allies.

In July 1943, Alfred Schwarz offered up "a grandiose program," as one top secret OSS report put it, to penetrate Hungary with espionage agents both to steal secrets and attempt to break the country away from the Axis. Schwarz had an agent who would serve as the key intermediary for this operation: Trillium, the flower code for a reputed Zionist named Andor Gross, alias Andre György, a chatty and somewhat disreputable intriguer who over the years had been a freelance courier for both the Allied and Axis intelligence services in Istanbul. In September, Trillium, who traveled freely between Istanbul and Budapest, reported to Schwarz that Lieutenant Colonel Otto von Hatz, a top aide from the Hungarian General Staff, would soon arrive in Istanbul as his country's military attaché and was eager to establish a secret line to the Americans. On one of Trillium's visits to Budapest, Hatz had promised him a pardon from smuggling charges Gross faced in Hungary if he could set up the communications link with the OSS. Schwarz gave his courier a radio set with an OSS cipher for sending coded messages, which he passed to Hatz. The colonel then told Trillium to tell Schwarz that the Hungarian General Staff was willing to slip intelligence to the OSS on the German army and that Prime Minister Kal-lay had personally instructed Hatz to report that Hungary was willing to join the Allies. By mid-December, Schwarz was meeting secretly with Hatz, who had arrived for his attaché job in Istanbul, and now proposed that the OSS infiltrate an agent into Budapest to be the conduit for the General Staff's secrets on the German army and for negotiations to shift Hungary to the alliance.

Donovan monitored the Hatz meetings closely from Washington. MI6, which had sneaked two agents into southwestern Hungary in November, also kept an eye on Hatz and wanted in on the secret conferences the OSS was having with him. Hatz, however, balked at another intelligence service being looped into his sensitive talks and Donovan saw no need to share him with the British, who hadn't told the OSS about their two spies in Hungary. On December 5, the Joint Chiefs approved Donovan's plan to infiltrate a team into Budapest, but with the proviso that they be under strict orders to make no promises on behalf of the United States.

Alarm bells, however, began to tinkle ever so slightly. Dulles, who had long harbored doubts that the Allies could win over the Hungarians, warned on January 2, 1944, that Kolbe had delivered a Foreign Office report, which revealed Hatz was really working for the Nazis and stringing along Macfarland's agents to feed the Germans intelligence on the Ameri-cans. Hatz also had a number of mistresses in Istanbul, Kolbe claimed, as well as a currency smuggling operation on the side because he was always personally short of cash. Donovan cabled Macfarland on January 7: Hatz "is working under orders to double-cross you." Macfarland, however, insisted Hatz was an honest broker "not in sympathy with Nazi ideals," he wrote Donovan. Yes, the Hungarian colonel has been talking to German intelligence, but he is actually a double agent, Packy believed, "only paying lip service" to the Nazis "in order to cover up his negotiations with us." Macfarland convinced Donovan to let the Sparrow team jump.

Friday night, March 17, Major Kirali fetched Duke and his comrades from their basement cell and escorted them upstairs to Ujszaszi's office. The cordial intelligence chief, speaking in French, welcomed the men to Hungary and asked Duke for the American peace proposal. We have none, Duke told him as he was supposed to, "other than our regular terms of unconditional surrender." The Sparrow team was there only to learn of the government's plans and relay them along with any useful intelligence to

Washington. Duke will be allowed to set up his radio at a secret location to begin transmitting, Ujszaszi told them. In the meantime, he had arranged a meeting on Monday with two cabinet members, who would lay out the government's offer to switch sides. The men returned to their cells to wait.

Before dawn Sunday morning, however, they were rousted from their beds and ordered to dress quickly for a meeting upstairs with Ujszaszi. The general, who had not slept all night, looked white as a sheet and on the verge of tears when they walked into his office. Three German panzer divisions have just crossed the Austrian border into Hungary and will soon be in Budapest along with 240 Gestapo agents, Ujszaszi told the Americans. Escape at this point was impossible. The best he could do was hide their radio sets and code books and have the agents mixed in with the other Allied aviators the Hungarians held as war prisoners to pretend they had been shot down—which hopefully would keep them from being arrested and tortured by the Gestapo as spies.

German intelligence, which knew of Ujszaszi's contacts with Duke, had kept Hitler fully informed of the Hungarian government's peace feelers to the West. The führer had earlier summoned Horthy to Berchtesgaden and bluntly told him he could no longer "stand aside and watch the Hungarian government make attempt after attempt to come to terms" with the enemy. He browbeat Horthy into accepting the German divisions and replacing his prime minister with a Nazi sympathizer.

In Istanbul, Macfarland hustled to contain the damage. Hatz, who had been in Budapest when the German divisions entered, returned to Turkey on March 28, but showed no interest in talking to Schwarz any longer about Hungary leaving the Axis. He had a few army documents on Hungarian troop deployments at the Eastern Front to pass to Dogwood, but they appeared to be "chicken feed," spy jargon for worthless intelligence a service's double agent supplied to the enemy to make it appear he was cooperating. Otherwise, Hatz dropped suspiciously out of sight. Macfarland worried about Andor Gross as much as he did the Sparrow team. Trillium had been trapped in Budapest when the Germans invaded and Macfarland knew the shady courier would sell out the OSS operation if the Gestapo captured him. Schwarz finally arranged for a friendly Turkish transport company in Budapest to vouch that Trillium was an employee so he could obtain a visa and be smuggled out.

The Sparrow team's ruse worked only for a week. As Duke, Suarez,

and Nunn boarded a bus with other airmen for the ride to Frankfurt and
the Luftwaffe's interrogation center, a Gestapo agent arrived and ordered
them off. They were taken away handcuffed and eventually delivered to a
Budapest jail the Nazis had commandeered. Duke stuck to his cover story
through several interrogations until his Gestapo questioner, tired of the
lies, finally said: "You look like an intelligent guy. There is no use kidding
each other and beating about the bush. Here is the story." He tossed across
the table a twenty-page typewritten statement made by Ujszaszi, who had
been imprisoned. Duke read it carefully. The document spelled out the
entire Sparrow operation. But Ujszaszi had not told them the team was
from the OSS because Duke had never disclosed that to him. Thinking
through his next move quickly, Duke looked up from the pages and confirmed what Ujszaszi had already revealed, but he stayed vague about his
organizational affiliation, claiming their team was from Air Force intelligence on a special diplomatic mission for the Joint Chiefs of Staff and
State Department.

That line appeared to work. An intelligence officer from Vienna arrived
two weeks later to interrogate Duke on the OSS. "It's a well-known organization in America run by 'Wild Bill' Donovan," he told the Vienna
officer. As far as he knew they specialized in collecting economic and political information from around the world, like a research company. "This
seemed to satisfy him and he went away happy," Duke recalled. A Berlin
Wehrmacht officer who specialized in the American army showed up next
with questions on how many soldiers the United States had in England.
Duke didn't have a clue, but by now he had become adept at spinning
yarns for his interrogators. As the officer furiously scribbled notes, Duke
told him in as much detail as he could dream up that England probably
had three million soldiers who would launch against France in a simulta-
neous attack with the Soviets marching west from the Eastern Front and
the Allies moving north from Italy, so "Germany will be squeezed in from
all sides." That turned out to be the Allied strategy but Duke had not told
him anything the German high command didn't already know. The officer left satisfied but skeptical the Americans could pull off the landing in
France.

By May 1944, the Gestapo had tired of questioning Duke and his team.
They were shuffled off to Colditz Castle, a comfortable but heavily guarded
prison near Leipzig for VIPs, where they remained until a U.S. Army divi-

sion finally liberated them on April 16, 1945. Duke had a lot of time sitting in his cell to think about the blown operation. It was clear to him that Hitler's intelligence operatives knew early on about the Sparrow mission and that the leak likely came from Turkey. Who had compromised them, he wondered?

The fear that operations in Turkey had been compromised grew in Donovan as well. But in late fall 1943, he was preoccupied with conspiracies in his own organization as well as the other war in Asia.

Chapter 21

—⦿—

Asia

A FTER HIS LONG journey abroad for the Salerno landing and visits to his Mediterranean stations, Donovan stayed at his desk in Washington for just a month. Late Tuesday morning, November 9, 1943, he boarded his plane once more for a flight to his first important stop, Cairo. Roosevelt planned to meet Churchill and Chinese Nationalist leader Chiang Kai-shek in the Egyptian capital before the president and prime minister conferred with Stalin in Tehran on November 28. From Cairo, Donovan planned to fly to Asia.

Back in Washington, a joke began making the rounds at headquarters. If the flag in front of the Q Building were raised and lowered every time Donovan "packed his flight bag, it would require a full-time color guard operating on day and night shifts." Midlevel employees in OSS headquarters hardly knew their director, who seemed to be an absentee landlord. Donovan's visits to his overseas stations proved to be terrific morale builders. Donovan also became an important umbilical cord for them to decision makers in Washington. With an Air Force plane at his disposal, long-distance travel no longer was a barrier for a man who loved to jump aboard it at a moment's notice and fly to an exotic spot. Word soon spread among OSS officers abroad that Donovan also liked a female for the night during his foreign stops. "You knew to have women at the receptions Donovan attended," recalled Rolfe Kingsley, one of his Middle East operatives. "He'd take care of the rest of it."

Donovan was as chaotic a manager as could be found. Sherman Kent, a Yale historian in the research office, once found a line from Shakespeare that read: "Confusion now has made its masterpiece!" "That's us!" he exclaimed. Agents in the field overlooked 109's lack of organizational skills because he was such an overwhelmingly charismatic leader. Back in Washington, however, Donovan's inner circle had begun grumbling by the fall of 1943 about the work piling up on his desk while he was away. The OSS was growing into a large government bureaucracy with 4,500 employees by August. More than four thousand cables soon sailed back and forth between headquarters and overseas posts every month.

When Donovan was away, he put Ned Buxton, his World War I comrade and a deputy director, nominally in charge, but Buxton, though competent and levelheaded, was not a forceful or energetic man. By August 1943, complaints began to pile up over how the organization was being run. Donovan knew he had a problem. Buxton on August 25 sent him an unsettling memo from George Platt. Because he prepared monthly intelligence summaries for Donovan, Platt was plugged into scuttlebutt from all quarters and he warned of "a deterioration of morale in OSS." The reason: No one "with the exception of those who are very close to the General can put his finger on anything concrete that the organization has accomplished." The OSS started out as a "closely-knit family bristling with ideas" but with the influx of people and wide-ranging missions, that esprit de corps has faded and "apathy toward this endeavor" has seeped in. Ellery Huntington warned his boss that the organization suffers from "a dangerous lack of cohesion," which "will require some changes at the top." Reorganization plans had been bumping around headquarters since spring. Most of the proposals from his advisers recommended reducing the flood of people with direct access to Donovan. Brigadier General John Magruder, a thin and nervous man with a bulbous nose and trembling hands, had been brought in to oversee the Secret Intelligence, X-2 counterintelligence, and Research and Analysis branches. Magruder also was a meticulous Army officer, convinced from the first day he walked into OSS headquarters that the agency was spread too thinly and Donovan had his finger in too many pies.

Donovan took the suggestions for improving morale and operations to heart. He had his own ideas for streamlining intelligence gathering overseas, based on what he had seen during his travels. Before he left for the Salerno landing in September he asked his executive committee, composed of his top advisers, to respond to an idea he had for freeing up his branch chiefs in Washington from the paperwork burying them so they could pay more attention to operations and long-range planning. When he returned to Washington in early October a six-page memo sat on his desk, drafted by a half dozen top advisers on this committee. In addition to Magruder, they included Donovan's pollster and organizational guru, Elmo Roper, and Charles Cheston, a strong-willed Smith Barney executive Donovan had hired earlier in the year as another deputy director to deal with personnel problems.

But the memo was not what he hoped for. As he read each page Donovan scrawled angry notes on the side with his pencil. Magruder & Co. had ignored his ideas for tinkering with the organization and instead they proposed radical surgery that he felt would strip the agency down and move him out. "The plain facts are that the OSS has grown too big and is engaged in too many diverse activities," the memo asserted. The sprawling growth was causing "a morale problem within the agency" and would eventually lead to embarrassments with the OSS "undertaking operations, which may exceed its capabilities." What was supposed to be a small cohesive unit had become "a holding company" with a hodgepodge of different endeavors that Donovan had put together, bearing no relation to one another save for the fact that they all reported to him. For example, the Operational Group, which launched commando attacks abroad, and the Foreign Nationalities branch, which interviewed refugees in the United States for intelligence, had about as much in common as Mark Clark's "5th Army and Chase National Bank," according to the memo. It recommended the reorganization Magruder wanted. The OSS would return to its espionage and research roots: collecting and analyzing intelligence for the military and spying on the Axis services. Units like the Foreign Nationalities branch would be sent to the State Department and the Operational Group commandos to the military, where they logically belonged.

Then came the real punch in the gut, which Magruder spelled out in a more detailed memo lying underneath the first one. Donovan would become what amounted to a chairman of the board, dictating broad policy for an OSS whose spy operations would be organized and run by Magruder and other deputies. A military-like chain of command would be put in place. Donovan's days of personally running spy networks, swooping into overseas stations to shake them up, issuing direct orders to agents, bypassing branch chiefs to phone underlings, allowing practically anyone to walk into his office with an idea, and landing at beaches would be over.

Donovan had hatched enough coup attempts overseas to smell one in his own organization. He learned that other senior OSS aides, such as Huntington, backed Magruder and his gang of six. The spymaster huddled with loyalists, who included Ed Putzell (his gatekeeper) and Ole Doering (his general counsel and confidant). The day before he boarded his flight for Cairo, Donovan summoned his secretary, Eloise, to his office and dictated one of the most biting memos he had ever written, which he had her deliver to Magruder. He began by sarcastically saying that whoever dreamed up the analogy that the OSS was like a holding company "knows nothing about a holding company." The gang of six's proposed organization "is one way of running the show, but it is not the way that considered experience over a period of months indicates is the best way to run it," he continued. The OSS "is not a bank and should not be run as a bank. It is not a War Department and should not be run as that." The agency was an unconventional warfare outfit, which had to remain "flexible to meet any particular ends, and so long as I have anything to say about it, it is not going to be wed to any particular scheme or put in any particular niche." Donovan refused to slim down his organization or distance himself from his agents and the details of their operations. He was open to any reorganization plan that would make the OSS more effective, "but this report does not do it."

Donovan had a right to be angry. For the entire U.S. military, key war fighting decisions were being made not by Marshall but by Eisenhower, MacArthur, and the other theater commanders in the field. For the OSS, the center of gravity had shifted as well from Washington to the overseas stations in London, Cairo, Algiers, and Chungking. Donovan's instinct to be abroad rather than chained to his desk with his headquarters staff was justified. A war leader leads from the front. Donovan had glaring managerial weaknesses, to be sure, but the fact remained—and he knew it—that without his enthusiasm, aggressiveness, and charisma the OSS would not have gotten this far. And it would make little headway in the future if he were gone. Donovan later made minor organizational changes, delegating some of his authority and giving top aides more power in his absence. But he refused to release his reins on the organization or to ground his plane. He squelched what Doering nicknamed the "Palace Revolt"—for the moment.

———————

DONOVAN'S PLANE LANDED in Cairo at midday on Monday, November 15, a week before the conference, code-named Sextant. He settled into the OSS's Cairo headquarters, a walled-in villa with a broad veranda and manicured lawn, which looked like a "bastard version of the Taj Mahal," according to Hollywood actor Sterling Hayden, who had joined the OSS as a Mediterranean operative. Meeting in the luxury Mena House Hotel at the base of the Great Pyramids, Roosevelt, Churchill, and Chiang agreed to accept only unconditional surrender from Japan and to strip her of land she had seized from China and Russia. Donovan briefed Roosevelt on the Far East intelligence the OSS possessed and lobbied Chiang on the covert operations his agency could mount to help the Generalissimo evict the Japanese from his territory. The OSS Map Division, which Donovan's coup plotters preferred to be rid of, also delivered some three thousand maps weighing more than seven hundred pounds to Sextant.

When Roosevelt flew to Tehran on November 27 for the Big Three meeting with Churchill and Stalin, Donovan broke off and took his plane east to Asia. He stopped first at Mountbatten's Southeast Asia Command headquarters in New Delhi. In the Far East, Donovan was hemmed in. Douglas MacArthur, who commanded the Southwest Pacific forces, and Admiral Chester Nimitz, in charge of the Pacific Ocean Areas to the north, were waging their wars with the brute force of naval ships, airpower, and troops storming tropical beaches. Neither saw much need for Donovan's covert operatives. That left the OSS confined to the strategically minor theaters of China and Southeast Asia. To flatter Mountbatten, Donovan had sent Ford ahead of him with a film crew to shoot a propaganda movie on the British admiral. But the movie and the tickets to *Oklahoma!* turned out to go only so far with Mountbatten. Donovan's aides in the region warned him that the admiral and his staff "were laying plans to dominate OSS activities in Southeast Asia."

On a windy Sunday afternoon, November 28, Donovan stepped off his plane at New Delhi's airport. Colonel Richard Heppner, a law partner from New York who now served as Donovan's representative on Mountbatten's staff, greeted him, along with Edmond Taylor, a reporter who had worked on Donovan's headquarters staff but later left to be Mountbatten's personal adviser on covert warfare. Though fresh and alert from his overnight flight, Donovan looked "incorrigibly civilian," Taylor observed. He had a "barbershop glow" and "fleshy jowls" and was dressed in a "carelessly worn, slightly rumpled khaki uniform with the blue ribbon of the Medal of Honor sewn on the breast of his tunic." In a Wall Street office or a conference room in the Pentagon, Donovan always was impeccably tailored, but in the field he dispensed with spit and polish, which conveyed the impression he was not, and had no intention of being, a conventional soldier.

Heppner and Taylor drove Donovan to Faridkot House, a gaudy palace that served as Mountbatten's official residence. Ragged Indian servants padded into and out of the admiral's office as he sipped tea and chatted about clandestine operations with the spy chief—neither man particularly concerned about foreign ears listening in on their conversation. Donovan bragged that if Mountbatten couldn't spare two or three thousand soldiers for an operation "just call on OSS, which would send twenty or thirty men to do the job." Mountbatten wasn't impressed. After a friendly but tough round of bargaining, he allowed Donovan to create a new detachment in his command, which would organize all OSS operations in Southeast Asia. But always wary of mischief from Donovan's men, Dickie Mountbatten kept a firm hand on the detachment. Like Churchill, he viewed Wild Bill and the other enthusiastic Americans both as allies and threats to British colonial interests—which was true in the spymaster's case. Donovan flew to Agra in the northern state of Uttar Pradesh for a tour of the Taj Mahal before heading to China. He filed a five-page report with his Washington headquarters on the grinding poverty he witnessed. British colonial rule, Donovan concluded, "stands in the way of any immediate economic development."

CHINA HAD BEEN savaged by war since 1937. Twenty-five Japanese divisions now controlled vital industries, ports, and cities in the country's center. They had successfully bottled up Mao Tse-tung's communist force in the northwest and pinned down Chiang's nationalist army in the south. Roosevelt had sent General Joseph "Vinegar Joe" Stilwell to China in early 1942 as Chiang's nominal chief of staff to keep supply routes open to the Kuomintang army and train it to fight the Japanese. A rumpled and caustic officer who had spent years in China and spoke the language, Stilwell found Chiang so frustrating to work with he considered at one point having him assassinated. The generalissimo was a brutal, corrupt, and ineffective commander who wanted the Americans to fight his war with the

Japanese while he husbanded his army to battle Mao's communists. His cunning intelligence chief was General Tai Li, a short and stocky man always dressed in a khaki coat buttoned tightly at the collar, whose teeth were laced with gold bridgework that he exposed during the rare times he smiled. Reputedly wealthy from his private monopoly of China's opium trade, Tai Li had been dubbed Chiang's "Heinrich Himmler" by the OSS officers who knew him. An obsessive xenophobe, he commanded over 300,000 secret agents more preoccupied with spying on the communists and repressing internal dissent than fighting the Japanese.

Within a month after the Pearl Harbor attack Donovan had ambitious plans for moving into China quickly with a large force of covert operatives. He wanted to develop a vast OSS intelligence network on the mainland married with Tai Li's operatives. Since Chiang could not field an effective conventional army, Donovan envisioned a guerrilla force of Kuomintang commandos molded and led by the OSS, who would take the war to the Japanese. Stilwell approved his proposal to set up an espionage and sabotage school in Chungking, Chiang's provisional capital, to train subversives not only for China but also to infiltrate throughout Korea and Southeast Asia. Donovan, who had been brainstorming ideas for unconventional warfare with Stilwell since their first meeting New Year's Day 1942, found him to be an able but old-fashioned troop commander, open to bringing in the OSS but never really understanding, or caring to understand, what the operatives could do for him.

Donovan, however, was just as clueless about the problems he would face in a country so vast with a culture so alien to him and most of his men. Chiang wanted no foreigners operating independently in the territory he controlled. Donovan had to live with a fact of life: Tai Li ran espionage in Nationalist China. So far, the intelligence he doled out to Stilwell and Washington had been too little, too late, and largely irrelevant. For the United States to have the information it wanted, Tai Li had to be reoriented to spy on the Japanese instead of on his own people. American diplomats in China believed only one man could change Tai Li's ways: Mary Miles.

Milton "Mary" Miles had enlisted in the Navy as a sailor in 1917 but had proved adept enough to win an appointment at Annapolis and become an officer. Now a captain, he would have preferred to have been in command of a ship but saluted and followed orders for land duty in China to collect intelligence for the Navy. Weather patterns that formed over the Asian mainland swept east across the Pacific where they could spell success or failure for Nimitz's fleet operations. With Japan holding the Malay Peninsula, French Indochina, and the resource-rich Dutch East Indies, she also depended on secure shipping lanes along the coast of China. Miles set up weather stations to radio reports to U.S. warships in the Pacific and had coast watchers track Japanese cargo vessels for Allied submarines to sink. The Navy captain also became the lone American Tai Li would talk to. In short order, Miles considered Tai Li like an older brother—China's greatest patriot behind the generalissimo and a man of "indomitable spirit," he declared. Tai Li considered Miles and the money he could draw from the U.S. Navy a cash cow for his secret operations and gave the officer a special nickname to flatter him: "Mei Lo Shi," after a winter plum.

With no other way to wedge his force into China, Donovan joined Miles, who had struck a deal with Tai Li, called the Friendship Project, for the Chinese spy chief to share intelligence with the U.S. Navy. Donovan made Miles his Far East director for the OSS, and by April 1943 the Navy captain and the Chinese spymaster had set up the Sino-American Cooperative Organization (SACO) at Tai Li's headquarters in Friendship Valley outside Chungking. Tai Li ran the show—he was named director of SACO and Miles was made his deputy—but Miles promised Donovan the arrangement would solve all his problems in China. The organization would collect not only weather and shipping information but also mount OSS espionage and guerrilla operations against the Japanese. Tai Li's covert army was the best he had ever seen, Miles wrote Donovan, and "I want you to know that I will turn this outfit inside out, if necessary, to produce" for the OSS. Miles demanded complete independence in working with his Chinese friend. Any meddling by Donovan's headquarters and he would "sever" his connection with the OSS, the captain announced at the outset. Donovan would never put up with that kind of declaration from any other subordinate, but he realized that for now Miles could dictate his terms. Stilwell received almost no intelligence that wasn't handed to him by Chiang's army. Donovan had to work in China through Miles and Tai Li, or not at all.

Donovan's aides started out optimistic. With enough money and equipment from the OSS "Miles will be of tremendous assistance," one wrote him. Donovan flew to China on December 6, 1943, however, to fire Mary Miles.

The Sino-American Cooperative Organization proved a boon for the Navy. Miles eventually assembled 2,500 officers and enlisted men in China, who collected reams of weather and targeting information for the sea service. It was intelligence Tai Li had no interest in so he gave the captain a free hand to collect it. Miles boasted that he knew every enemy harbor, river, and port in China and Southeast Asia like the back of his hand. But Donovan soon realized he was being shortchanged. Miles did not send a single intelligence report to OSS headquarters until four months after the joint organization with Tai Li had been formed and what finally trickled into Washington and Stilwell's command was inconsequential, such as Japanese magazines and digests from Indian newspaper articles, or intelligence summaries edited by Tai Li with no way for Donovan's men to determine their credibility. Tai Li refused to let the OSS officers interview his agents or observe the guerrilla attacks he claimed they were carrying out against the Japanese. He also blocked Donovan's men from launching independent espionage operations in China against the Japanese. Tai Li feared the OSS agents might dig up political and military secrets on the Kuomintang along the way, which Chiang did not want them to see.

Donovan was in a straitjacket. Tai Li acted like a little dictator and Miles did nothing to discourage him. John Davies, who was detailed to Stilwell as his diplomatic officer, warned Donovan in a memo before he flew to Asia that the Navy captain had proven to be an "excessively naive" American planted in a country he did not understand, who was being played for a sucker by Tai Li. While Donovan wanted to take the fight to the Japanese, Tai Li still ran what amounted to a "racketeer mob"—now with better training and more sophisticated equipment from the OSS. Stilwell had already concluded the joint intelligence operation wasn't "worth a damn." Donovan found the situation even more galling because by the end of August he had poured twenty-five intelligence officers, research analysts, and propagandists into Friendship Valley along with $110,000 for Miles's expenses and had gotten practically nothing in return. For Donovan, the final insult came when Miles wrote him that even with the open bank account Tai Li enjoyed from the OSS, the Chinese general kept "a little black book" on foreigners he distrusted, which included many of Donovan's officers. Donovan thought it was time to confront Tai Li and be rid of his sidekick, Mary Miles.

Donovan, in fact, had already begun working around the Chinese gen-

eral. In early 1943, he had sounded out the State Department about sending one of his officers to Mao's communists in the north. State blocked
this for the moment for fear of antagonizing Chiang. Donovan's China
officers who did not work under the Sino-American Cooperative Organization tried to recruit their own agents, paying some with opium and at
one point even running a bordello to ply sex for secrets. Before he landed
in Chungking, Donovan had his plane stop at Kunming in southwestern
China to arrange for an OSS detachment to provide targeting intelligence
to Brigadier General Claire Chennault, the maverick Flying Tigers commander who now led the 14th Air Force attacking Japanese troops on the
mainland. But as far back as April 1942, Donovan had begun his most
secret operation behind Tai Li's back.

Cornelius Vander Starr was a New York insurance magnate and international investor who had spent two decades in Shanghai. Among the
many businesses Starr had accumulated by his early fifties was the English-
language *Shanghai Evening Post and Mercury*, which he founded in 1931 and
which the Japanese seized in 1939 after they swept through the east coast
metropolis at the mouth of the Yangtze River. Donovan, an old friend, had
asked Starr to join his operation in January 1942 as his top intelligence
officer for Asia. Starr had begged off because of the demands of his multi-
national enterprise, but he passed along the names of other international
businessmen Donovan could hire and helped him set up an insurance unit
to mine the records insurance companies had on buildings in Axis countries, which helped the Air Force select bombing targets. Starr also wrote
a memo to Donovan on how to organize business covers in Asia for his
intelligence.

By the end of 1942, however, Starr took his intelligence work for Donovan an important step further. He formed a front company for the OSS,
called Metropolitan Motors Overseas Incorporated, and arranged for one
of his associates, a Canadian named James Arthur Duff, who had been
born in China, to return to Kunming as its president and pretend to
import cars. Duff's real job, along with another OSS undercover agent and
a Hong Kong smuggler he brought with him, was to recruit snitches to feed
intelligence on the Japanese.

Starr formed another, even bigger, front company for Donovan: the
Shanghai Evening Post and Mercury, which he reconstituted with editions
published in New York and Chungking. Donovan kept it one of the most

tightly held secrets in his organization. Again, little paperwork was produced on this operation and Donovan ordered that few people in headquarters be cleared to know about it. The "S Project," as it became known, "can be blown sky-high if dealt with lightly and treated in a careless manner," one highly classified memo warned. Donovan had good reason for concern over leaks. Beyond the danger exposure posed for Starr's newspaper, the spymaster was circumventing Tai Li and Chiang with his own clandestine intelligence organization in their country. Stilwell was briefed but Donovan kept the project secret from Miles.

The OSS put up $350,000 to start the New York and China editions and Donovan eventually agreed to subsidize the Chungking paper to the tune of $500,000 a year, a huge sum in that day. His agents posed as reporters on the news staffs for the New York paper, which started publishing New Year's Day 1943, and for the Chungking paper, whose first edition rolled off the press on October 31, 1943, less than a fortnight before Donovan left for Asia. The Metropolitan Motors and *Shanghai Evening Post* fronts ended up with mixed results. The agents on the New York paper compiled dossiers on five thousand Asians or Americans with Asia connections in the United States who could help Donovan's organizations with information. Duff, who eventually had a falling out with Starr, tried to collect military information under his business cover but admitted later that the product was paltry and not worth the money Donovan paid for it. Like all Westerners in China, Duff and the other American agents in Starr's two networks stood out and were kept under close watch by Tai Li's men. They were reduced to collecting largely "rumors and tall tales," Duff believed. "They would have done just as well if they were sent to the South Pole to gather intelligence amongst the penguins." The reporters in Chungking, who divided their time between writing real news for the paper and filing secret cables to Stilwell's headquarters and the OSS in Washington, produced 1,500 reports over two years, practically all of which dealt with political and economic conditions in China or Japan. William Langer's academics in the research department found their reports on such subjects as "Japanese Banking Institutions" and "Chinese Communications Facilities" valuable, but none of them much help for "immediate war operations." Tai Li, not Donovan's reporters, held the key to military secrets.

Shortly before two o'clock on Thursday afternoon, December 2, 1943, Donovan's B-24 Liberator bomber, with a full combat crew and .50-caliber machine guns bristling from four turrets, landed at the military airport along the bank of the Jialing River, which with the upper reaches of the Yangtze intersected Chungking. Encased in a wall built during the Ming Dynasty, Chungking was a fortress city atop a cliff, protected from Japanese invasion by mountains and impenetrable gorges to the east. Fertile rice paddies and vegetable gardens stretched up to the wall, while inside, the city teemed with fresh fruit stands and squealing pigs brought in from the countryside and sedan chairs and rickshaws lifted and pulled by coolies. A quarter-million refugees from Chiang's Nationalist government who fled the Japanese had invaded the city of 300,000 and taken over hotels and office buildings for their ministries as well as the best villas outside the walls for their military headquarters and private residences.

Tai Li and Miles stood on the airport tarmac waiting as the fuselage door opened and Donovan climbed down the ladder from the bomber. The Chinese spy chief knew his American counterpart was coming with a long list of complaints about the product being delivered to the Office of Strategic Services. Donovan had no grounds to gripe, Tai Li thought; the Chinese had been more than generous with the Americans. Tai Li decided to smother the OSS director with Oriental civility and send him on his way. He had a motorcade whisk Donovan to a sumptuous house in Jarling Village outside the city and offered him the run of nearby Friendship Valley, where Tai Li kept his mansion and office.

Donovan wasted no time getting down to business. In their first meeting at Friendship Valley, he gave Tai Li an earful. He was not happy with the way the Sino-American Cooperative Organization was treating the OSS. The "person at 1600 Pennsylvania Avenue" had ordered him to collect intelligence in China and fight the Japanese, Donovan told the general, and that's what he intended to do with or without Tai Li's help. If the regime did not let the OSS expand its operations in China and have a voice in deciding what spying would be done by both sides, Donovan bluntly warned, he would shut off the OSS money spigot and equipment pipeline to Tai Li's intelligence service.

Tai Li arranged a dog-and-pony show for the American delegation the next day—tables in the Friendship Valley headquarters stacked with documents, uniforms, and weapons captured from Japanese soldiers—but the OSS director was not impressed. Later Friday afternoon, Donovan sat down for a private meeting with Mary Miles to break the news he had for him. The naval officer could not hide his nervousness at being in the room alone with Donovan. Though he was contemptuous of other OSS agents, Miles still told friends that from the first day he had met Donovan he "liked the cut of his jib." But the captain knew the ax was falling. Donovan did his best to soften the blow with kind words. He still hoped to salvage an accord with Tai Li, who, after all, held the monopoly on Chinese espionage, and Miles continued to be the only American close to him. Miles's workload was "far too heavy for any one man to carry," Donovan gently told him. He was relieving him as the OSS officer for the Far East. Miles could still spy for the Navy in China and be the sea service's representative in the Sino-American Cooperative Organization. But to run China operations for the OSS, Donovan was bringing in one of his trusted officers, Lieutenant Colonel John Coughlin, a thirty-six-year-old West Pointer from Arizona who was currently working in Burma. Coughlin would look out for the agency's interests with Tai Li's group, not Miles. To Donovan's relief, Miles appeared to meekly accept the decision.

Friday night, Tai Li hosted a large banquet in Donovan's honor at the French Group House in Friendship Valley, hoping that a seven-course meal, free-flowing wine, and pretty young Chinese women among the men would loosen him up—or perhaps catch him in an indiscretion. Tai Li's spies didn't tell him that Donovan did not drink and he was not interested in these girls. Up to that point, Tai Li did not impress Donovan as being all that sinister. Donovan could clearly see that the Chinese general was "a mediocre policeman with medieval ideas of intelligence work," he later told Mountbatten, "but apart from that a rather likeable fellow." As more bottles drained at the banquet, however, and the two men resumed their argument over Donovan's freedom to operate in China, Tai Li began to bare his talons.

"General, I want you to know that I am going to send my men into China whether you like it or not," Donovan finally said.

"If OSS tries to operate outside of SACO I will kill your agents," Tai Li answered, his eyes flaring.

"For every one of our agents you kill, we will kill one of your generals," Donovan said, pounding the table with his fist and clanking the dishware.

"You can't talk to me like that!" Tai Li shouted.

"I am talking to you like that!" Donovan shouted back.

A deathly silence fell over the banquet room. Donovan and Tai Li locked their eyes on each other. Miles sat horrified. He knew Tai Li was seething over this serious breach of protocol. Tai Li visited Miles's quarters later and vented that "General Donovan could not get away with those things in China." But for now, Tai forced a thin smile. Donovan did as well. Others in the room strained to resume conversations.

Over the next three days, Donovan and Tai Li finally reached a peace agreement. The Chinese spymaster promised to give the OSS more free-dom to operate in China. Miles no longer could block Donovan's agents from coming into the country. Tai Li would share more useful intelligence with Donovan's men and point his spies more at the Japanese.

Before Donovan left China Monday evening, December 6, Tai Li drove him up the mountains overlooking Chungking past two sentries guarding an entrance to Chiang's rock-walled compound, which Japanese bombers had never been able to find. Chiang, who spoke no English and met with only a few Americans, pointed Donovan to a chair beside his desk, which had a sign over it with the motto: "All officials must serve the people." Donovan didn't believe it for a minute. His aides had given him a secret memo ahead of time warning that Chiang was a "narrow and limited" leader who maintained power by ruthlessly repressing dissent. The result: a brain drain of talented civil servants and intellectuals from his govern-ment, Donovan's memo warned, which meant "less and less hope of [the regime] being able to meet current problems."

Tai Li had already alerted Chiang to the American's rude behavior at the banquet. Speaking through an interpreter, the generalissimo began with a stern lecture. Donovan was operating in a land "both foreign and friendly to you," Chiang said. "We Chinese are a sovereign country and expect you to recognize that. We expect you Americans to behave in the same manner as you would expect other allies to behave in your country. You do not expect a secret service from another country to go into the United States and start operations." We, likewise, object to the American spies "working without the knowledge of the Chinese." So "please conduct yourself accordingly," the warlord warned. Donovan replied (more politely than he had to Chiang's spy chief): FDR ordered him to place agents in China and he intended to follow those orders. And he will "replace" each agent Tai Li killed with another one. This time, Donovan considered it best to leave out the eye-for-an-eye threat to kill Chiang's generals. But Tai Li still thought he acted impudently in front of the generalissimo.

Donovan boarded his B-24 Monday evening confident he had broken the logjam in China. But soon that would prove not to be the case. Donovan left Mary Miles in a vengeful mood. He later told one of Hoover's agents that Donovan had fired him because Miles refused to accept "communists, pinks and sexual perverts" the OSS wanted to foist on his operation, which was hardly the case. Miles told friends he still intended to make life "difficult" for the OSS in China. So did Tai Li.

John Ford and his movie crew, which had accompanied Donovan to China, boarded the bomber to film him at his next important stop: Nazira in the east Indian state of Assam. He had a base camp there launching operations into nearby Burma, the only place on the Asian mainland where he was actually fighting the Japanese at this point. But Donovan had another disagreeable chore to take care of at Nazira out of view of the cameras: sending Carl Eifler home.

AFTER THE JAPANESE gained control of China's eastern coast in 1937 and the Nationalist government had fled to Chungking in the interior, Chiang depended on a western artery to supply his poorly equipped army of four million men. Ships docked at the southern Burmese port of Rangoon and off-loaded weapons and matériel onto trains that chugged northeast to the town of Lashio, where the precious cargo was transferred to trucks. The vehicles then trekked east over a windy seven-hundred-mile mountain highway Chiang had drafted more than a hundred thousand Chinese laborers to build to Kunming. The entire route became known as the Burma Road, but by spring 1942 the Japanese had cut that lifeline as well with four divisions occupying all but the northern tip of Burma. Cargo planes valiantly flew tons of supplies over "the Hump"—the eastern end of the rugged Himalayan mountain range between India and China—but Japanese fighter aircraft based at the northern Burmese town of Myitkyina shot down many of them. Stilwell was desperate to close the Japanese base and open a northern ground corridor to Chiang's army—a road stretching from Ledo at the eastern tip of India south into Burma to hook up with the Chinese leg of the Burma Road at the border below Myitkyina.

Carl Eifler was commanding a detention camp in Hawaii for Japanese Americans when a cable from Washington arrived February 17, 1942, asking if he was available for duty in the Far East. A hulk of a man over six feet tall and 250 pounds with ham hocks for arms and gigantic hands, Eifler had been a U.S. Customs agent rounding up bootleggers in San Diego when he decided to return to active duty in the Army. He had served before as a reserve officer. When Stilwell was a lieutenant colonel, he had commanded Eifler in a San Diego reserve unit and had been impressed with the thoroughness of his reports before the Pearl Harbor attack on Japanese officers who roamed in Mexico. Skilled in jujitsu, Eifler also was as smart and imaginative as he was loud and domineering. And he was willing to stick his neck out to tackle risky projects, which Stilwell liked. When Donovan's men approached Stilwell about having a small OSS detachment sent to spy and launch guerrilla strikes behind Japanese lines, Vinegar Joe demanded that it be commanded by Major Eifler and that his team be sent to Nazira to attack the Myitkyina airbase and reopen the Burma Road. He gave Eifler a free hand to carry out the espionage and guerrilla operations as he saw fit. All Stilwell said he wanted to hear were "booms" from the Burmese jungle.

Eifler became one of the most colorful guerrilla leaders in the Office of Strategic Services. For Detachment 101, the name given his unit, he assembled nearly two dozen American officers and soldiers he had recruited stateside. To penetrate deep behind enemy lines, Eifler's men trained thousands of Burmese agents drawn from the Indian army, refugee camps, and the Kachin tribes of northern Burma. The sign at their Nazira camp read "The U.S. Army Experimental Station," which made any curious locals think it was a research facility studying tropical diseases. Inside, Eifler kept a pet bear for roughhousing during his free time. He used magic tricks to convince superstitious Kachins the spirits wanted them to fight the Japanese and he often paid the small wiry tribesmen with opium. His agent training was rigorous, often dangerous—Eifler liked to pull out his .45 and fire rounds several inches from recruits crawling through obstacle courses to see how they reacted—and he ruled Detachment 101 with an iron hand. But his men grew intensely loyal to him. The few who became insubordinate literally got the back of his hand across their faces. Burmese agents who betrayed him were taken out to the jungle and beheaded.

By the end of 1943, Detachment 101 was showing results, which delighted Donovan. Promoted to lieutenant colonel, Eifler had six camps hidden in northern Burma's jungles, which were sending out agents to spy on the Japanese and harass their bases and troop trains with guerrilla attacks. A maritime team also patrolled Burma's Indian Ocean coast to scout Japanese defenses and insert agents.

It was during one of those coastal infiltrations in March 1943, however, that Eifler's head slammed against a rock when his rubber boat crashed in pounding surf near the shore. The accident left him deaf in one ear and with a ringing noise and excruciating pain in his head. Eifler tried to cope with painkillers, but the symptoms worsened over the months. He could not sleep and grew more nervous, irritable, and forgetful. Heppner was stunned when in one meeting the detachment chief broke out crying for no reason.

Eifler clung stubbornly to his command, checking himself into a hospital for a while, then checking out when he thought he had the pain under control. Donovan dispatched aides to Burma to investigate his troubled warrior. They reported back that Eifler seemed mentally unbalanced and increasingly acting irrationally.

Donovan arrived at Nazira on Tuesday, December 7. Eifler thought the day went well. He gave his general a personal tour of the camp, impressed that Donovan had memorized the names of Eifler's officers from the cables he had read and chatted with them as if they were old friends. Donovan probed Eifler on the supplies and personnel he needed and the morale of his troops. That night, after a hearty meal, the two men sat in Eifler's war room and the lieutenant colonel pulled back the curtain to seven tactical maps marked with positions for his field units. Eifler began explaining the seven routes into Burma he said Stilwell wanted him to carve. "I was supposed to organize each one of them, and I did," he began proudly, but Donovan interrupted.

"That's what I mean about you, Carl," Donovan said frostily, barely looking at the maps. "You are too goddamn ambiguous about organizing. What do you mean by organizing?"

Eifler was taken aback. The day had gone so pleasantly. Donovan's visit had been a tremendous morale boost for his men, and for Eifler. But the tone of Donovan's voice and the almost belligerent way he had interrupted with his question told Eifler that the OSS director was here for another reason besides a guided tour.

Eifler kept his cool and asked in a soft voice: "Would the General like to go behind the lines and see for himself?" It was as juvenile as a high school dare. Eifler knew the Medal of Honor winner, who itched to be at the front, would take it. He was practically challenging Donovan's manhood.

"When do we leave?" Donovan asked calmly.

"First thing in the morning," Eifler replied, a thin smile creeping across his face.

Shortly before ten o'clock Wednesday morning Eifler stepped into his parachute straps next to the de Havilland Tiger Moth. Eifler knew how to pilot the lightweight single-prop biplane, which he had bought from the British to fly his agents to remote jungle landing strips. Ford's crew filmed the scene. Donovan at first refused to wear his chute, believing it would be far better for him to go down with the plane than to be captured by the Japanese, but Eifler, sensibly for once, talked him into strapping it on. The men climbed into the Moth's two front-and-back seats.

Eifler had picked "Knothead" for their visit, the code name for one of his jungle camps 150 miles behind Japanese lines and almost 275 miles from Nazira. The little Moth did not have that kind of range for a round-trip so Eifler had an Air Force cargo plane air-drop drums of gasoline onto the Knothead camp ahead of time so they could fill up for the return flight.

The Moth rumbled down the dirt landing strip and strained to clear the bushes and trees at the end. The mechanics worried that the more than 450 pounds Eifler and Donovan added would give the plane's four-cylinder engine a hernia lifting off. Talking was impossible in the open cockpits so Donovan enjoyed the view as Eifler in the front seat followed a river below flowing east into Burma and kept his head on a swivel for the enemy. Japanese warplanes routinely prowled the skies, their antiaircraft batteries on the ground dotted the path the Moth was taking, and enemy soldiers bivouacked close to Knothead's secret headquarters. Two hours into the flight, Eifler twisted his body back and pointed down. Donovan could see only thatched roofs tucked into dense jungle foliage. Then suddenly the roofs began to move and Donovan realized they were props to camouflage a crude airstrip.

Eifler made a perfect landing and while he taxied to the jungle on the side, where men would cover his plane with branches to hide it, natives had already begun moving the fake huts back over the strip to conceal it. Scruffy-looking OSS officers and Burmese agents crowded around Donovan saluting and shaking his hand, as if he were MacArthur come to liber-

ate. They showed him around the camp. Donovan interviewed, through
an interpreter, skinny Kachin guerrillas, some barely taller than the U.S.
rifles they toted. Eifler, meanwhile, paced off the crooked landing strip. He
calculated that his plane had to rise into the air 80 percent of the way down
the path to clear the trees at the end. If the Moth couldn't by that point he
decided his only recourse was to tilt the aircraft sharply right to slip almost
sideways through a break in the trees.

After an hour and a half on the ground, Eifler pulled Donovan away
from his Kachin entourage and told him they needed to climb into the
now refueled plane so they could make it back to Nazira before dusk. The
strip was cleared of the huts. Natives gripped the wings tightly to hold the
plane in place while Eifler revved up its engine. They let the aircraft go
and the Moth raced down the runway. But it did not have enough speed
at the 80 percent mark to go airborne. Eifler quickly had to switch to his
alternate plan. When the Moth finally lifted off further down the runway,
he banked it violently to the right. Flying sideways, the aircraft squeezed
through the break in the trees, dipped down the hill past them, and came
to within five feet of the surface of the river beyond when Eifler leveled it
and managed to gain altitude.

"You didn't think you were going to make it, did you?" Donovan said
calmly after they climbed out of the aircraft at Nazira.

"General, I knew we were going to make it," Eifler said with a cocky
grin. But the harrowing flight demonstrated that he needed more powerful
planes to stay connected with his remote bases, Eifler added.

Donovan approved better aircraft along with other supplies the detachment desperately needed. But that evening he broached the main reason
for his visit. "Carl, I think it is time for you to return to America," Donovan said gently but firmly. He was cutting the orders "immediately," he
said, replacing Eifler with one of the detachment's senior officers, William Peers. Eifler stood stunned. (Later he broke down in tears over being
relieved of command.) He tried to talk Donovan out of it. Donovan had
actually been impressed with what he saw at Nazira and the Knothead
camp, but his decision remained firm.

Donovan left Burma thrilled over his trip behind enemy lines. His
senior aides were horrified when they learned of the escapade. Donovan
knew Eifler had taken a serious blow to his head but he did not know how
serious it was. Eifler was suffering from traumatic brain injury and taking

morphine for the pain when he climbed into the cockpit the day before. He had no business operating an aircraft, much less flying the leader of America's intelligence service over Japanese territory. For both men, the trip had been a reckless display of bravado.

Edmond Taylor and Richard Heppner met Donovan when his plane landed in New Delhi shortly before 11:30, Thursday night, December 9. They thought he would want to head straight to bed after his exhausting flight, but Donovan was charged up and eager to go to Faridkot House to regale Mountbatten with his stories from Burma and China. Lord Louis stood with his back to the fireplace in his drawing room sipping a highball with his senior aides as Donovan launched into the tale of how he confronted Tai Li. The Chinese general had been told he had six months to produce worthwhile intelligence for the OSS, Donovan recounted to Mountbatten, after that no more "wampum"—tommy guns, radio sets, and other toys from the OSS. Donovan bragged how he had threatened to secretly infiltrate his agents into China behind Tai Li's back if that was the only way they could get into the country.

Mountbatten chuckled, but only lightly. Donovan had an ulterior motive for sharing the gossip with the Southeast Asia commander. If his OSS agents weren't allowed to enter a war theater "through the front door," recalled Taylor, who sipped his cocktail quietly in the drawing room, they would "slip in through the transom." That rule applied to the British as well as to the Chinese. "There was no doubt that Lord Louis got the point," said Taylor, "but he seemed amused rather than offended by his guest's colossal cheek."

Donovan's next stop: Moscow.

Chapter 22

—⦿—

The Russians

TWO DAYS BEFORE Christmas 1943, a brutal winter blanketed Russia as Donovan's aircraft struggled to stay just above the tree-tops on its approach to Moscow. Ice caked on the wings dragged down the plane's lifting power. A Russian navigator and radio operator had come aboard during a stopover in Tehran. The Soviets required that every foreign plane entering their airspace have the two Russian airmen aboard to guide it, which made Donovan's aircrew even more nervous. The navigator and radio operator were both armed with revolvers and proved to be little help for the tense flying. The crew, nevertheless, made a perfect landing at a Moscow military airport and Donovan climbed out carrying a case of Scotch for the U.S. embassy. The Christmas gift brightened the eyes of John Deane, the American general greeting him. Before taking over the U.S. military mission in Moscow, Deane had been secretary of the Joint Chiefs of Staff and a Donovan friend during his bureaucratic battles. Donovan needed Deane's help once more—to establish a working relationship between the OSS and Russia's intelligence service.

Within months after the Pearl Harbor attack, Donovan had begun probing for ways to slip his spies into the Soviet Union. It would not be easy, he realized; Russia was a closed society with foreigners' movements severely restricted and closely monitored by "the best counter-espionage system in the world," one secret memo warned him. A clandestine infiltration would likely fail and when the agents were inevitably caught it would disrupt an already strained alliance between Roosevelt and Stalin. Donovan hunted for a State Department officer seasoned in Russian affairs to be posted in Moscow as his spy. He inquired about placing one of his agents there as a Lend-Lease representative and even considered having an OSS man sneaked in with Britain's embassy, which already had four special operations officers in its Moscow delegation. The ideas were all dropped by Donovan or rejected by the State Department as too risky. By October 1943, Donovan decided on the direct approach: flying to Russia and offering a deal to the People's Commissariat for State Security, the Soviet secret service that went by the initials NKGB. The two sides would share intelligence. An OSS officer would be posted in Moscow in exchange for an NKGB officer in Washington. The Joint Chiefs, who suspected that Stalin already had a robust covert operation to steal military secrets from the Allies, slapped tight restrictions on the intelligence to be shared with the Russians. Roosevelt approved Donovan's Russia mission before he flew to Tehran.

From what little he knew of Russia's covert force, Donovan was impressed. The NKGB had planted an extensive espionage network in Germany before the war and organized hundreds of thousands of partisan guerrillas who harassed Wehrmacht occupation forces and cut rail lines supplying them on the Eastern Front. Soviet psychological warriors showered enemy territory with propaganda and aggressively indoctrinated POWs to defect. "The Russians never miss an opportunity to undermine the morale of the German people and of the German Army," an August OSS memo to Donovan concluded, which he passed on to Deane.

Donovan flew to Moscow with his eyes wide open, however. He knew the Soviet alliance was critical to winning the war and had ordered William Langer's research analysts to study intensely how the Red Army matched up with the Wehrmacht. Donovan also knew the Russians could play hardball with their allies. One of his OSS men had already been targeted by the *Daily Worker*, the Communist Party USA propaganda organ, which accused him of being anti-Soviet. Another adviser sent him an intercepted report from the Comintern, the international communist organization Moscow sponsored, boasting that after the war the Soviets planned to "let loose a Communist revolution on Germany in order to neutralize the effect of a victory by the Allies." Though he came to Moscow with an offer for an open exchange of intelligence officers, Donovan did not intend to miss any opportunity to spy behind the NKGB's back. In September he secretly arranged for four American engineers traveling to the Soviet Union under

Lend-Lease to feed him any intelligence they picked up helping the Russians build oil refineries.

Christmas Day, Averell Harriman escorted Donovan into the Kremlin office of Vyacheslav Mikhailovich Molotov, Stalin's loyal foreign minister. The son of a railroad baron and a banking scion in his own right, the courtly Harriman had become Roosevelt's ambassador in Moscow three months earlier. At first, he had been wary of Donovan's men barging in; coordination of American and Russian military operations had been nil so far. The Soviets always were wary of any foreign government's motives. The introduction of an American spy service would elevate suspicions even more, which Harriman did not need as he tried to build trust early in his ambassadorship. But Harriman mellowed and even became impressed by the operations Donovan had carried out, such as the capture of Corsica and Sardinia. Intelligence collaboration might be a helpful icebreaker, he decided.

It was seven o'clock in the evening, the sky black outside, when Donovan and Harriman settled into their chairs in Molotov's dimly lit office. Donovan's analysts believed Molotov was the most Westernized of Stalin's inner circle, a teetotaler like him and perhaps a vegetarian, who had a reputation as a tough but reliable negotiator. The NKGB had given the foreign minister a full dossier on the American spy chief. Molotov now used it to compliment Donovan on his military record in World War I and his career in New York politics. Pretending to be flattered, Donovan outlined in broad strokes how the Office of Strategic Services was set up and the secret operations it was conducting in Balkan nations, such as Bulgaria and Yugoslavia. The OSS, he told Molotov, was prepared to give Russia's intelligence agency "full details" on its covert missions. He hoped the two services could operate together "inside Germany." Harriman then chimed in with the exchange offer: Donovan was also prepared to send an OSS officer to work with the Russian secret service. "A Soviet representative" was welcome in Washington.

Stalin unfortunately had left that day for the front, Molotov told the Americans, so he could not "consult" with him, but he promised to take the matter up with "the Soviet military authorities." Harriman thought that meant Donovan would have to cool his heels for a while, but to his surprise Molotov sent a message after they left that a meeting had been arranged two days later with two top officers in the NKGB. Stalin must have already been consulted and approved the intelligence collaboration, because Harriman knew that decisions in Moscow never were made with this blinding speed.

Monday night, December 27, Donovan, Deane, and Charles "Chip" Bohlen, who came along to act as an interpreter, walked into the front entrance of the NKGB's grim-looking headquarters on Lubyanka Square. Guards whisked the three to an upstairs conference room where two Russians, who introduced themselves as Lieutenant General Pavel Fitin and Colonel Alexandr Ossipov, sat alone. Fitin, who headed the foreign intelligence department that spied overseas, seemed to Deane to be in his late thirties, with long blond hair, bright blue eyes, and a pleasant smile that made him look more like a cruise director than a spy chief. Only the blue piping on his army uniform gave away that he belonged to the secret police. Ossipov wore a civilian suit and had brown eyes, wavy brown hair, and a sallow complexion that made him look like a ringer for Boris Karloff. Ossipov, however, spoke fluent English with no trace of an accent, which would not have been a surprise if Donovan had known why—a subversive warfare expert, Ossipov's real name was Gaik Ovakimyan, a former New York station chief and veteran of spying in North America.

A lamp beamed a harsh light on an empty chair at the conference table as if it were the seat for an interrogation victim. Donovan walked around the long table and sat in the chair. "I'm ready for the third degree," he announced, squinting his eyes. The Russians smiled and turned off the lamp. Donovan again described his organization and offered to deliver intelligence on the Germans that he knew would interest Fitin. The Soviets likewise had information that "would be of great value to the United States," Donovan said. Fitin paid close attention. Could the OSS help drop Soviet agents into western Germany or France, he asked? "That would be entirely possible," Donovan replied. Donovan also dangled as bait the gadgets the OSS might be able to offer the NKGB if the services cooperated, such as suitcase radios and plastic explosives. Ossipov suddenly showed interest.

Are you here just to offer cooperation or have you come "with some other intentions?" Fitin asked, his voice dripping with suspicion.

"No other intentions!" Donovan answered indignantly, although he was lying and both men knew it. Donovan fully intended to milk the Russians for as much information as he could and to spy on them every chance he had. Fitin planned the same, which was why one of the NKGB's best American penetration agents sat in the room with him.

Donovan and Fitin let the brief moment of tension pass. They quickly agreed to an exchange. Donovan would send a small OSS team headed by Colonel John Haskell, a former vice president of the New York Stock Exchange and the son of one of Donovan's World War I comrades. Haskell had flown to Moscow with him. Fitin's Washington team would be led by Colonel A. G. Grauer.

Donovan did not leave Moscow until January 6. Soviet bureaucratic hurdles flying out of Russia turned out to be far more maddening than flying in. But he left confident he had achieved a major intelligence break-through. He decided to remain in the Middle East and send Haskell to Washington to explain the logic behind it. The OSS would have access to Soviet intelligence from German-occupied countries in which Dono-van had agents, such as the Balkans, and from countries where he had no agents at the moment, such as Japan. Donovan's propagandists could learn a lot from Moscow's psychological experts. As for exchanging intel-ligence officers, England had such an agreement with the Russians the past two years and British counterespionage agents had little difficulty keeping watch on the three NKGB officers roaming London. Most importantly, the deal finally put OSS officers into Russia with the opportunity to spy. Harriman thought the arrangement made good sense. After hearing Don-ovan's arguments, the Joint Chiefs were inclined to agree as well.

Not J. Edgar Hoover. The FBI director protested loudly when he learned of Donovan's deal. Hoover's men had their hands full tracking NKGB operatives already in the United States who were "attempting to obtain highly confidential information concerning War Department secrets," he wrote Francis Biddle, Roosevelt's aristocratic attorney general who sported a thin mustache, wore spats to work, and liked Hoover. The FBI did not need Donovan adding more Soviet agents to that list. Frenchy Grombach, who ran Strong's secret spy unit, also believed the Soviets would end up infiltrating the OSS as much as the British had. Hoover lobbied the White House, warning in a strongly worded letter "it will be highly dangerous to our government operations to have an agency such as the NKGB offi-cially authorized to operate in the United States." Hoover also paid Roos-evelt a visit and told him point-blank he would be opening the door to Russian spies. Biddle worried that in an election year the political fallout would be toxic if conservative Republicans discovered the administration had allowed communist espionage agents to enter the United States. So did Harry Hopkins and Admiral William Leahy, FDR's chief of staff. Roosevelt also knew that the man most likely to leak the arrangement to the Republicans was Hoover.

Donovan could barely contain his outrage over what he considered baseless paranoia. When he returned from overseas the next month he fired off angry memos to the White House and marched into a meeting of the Joint Chiefs on Tuesday afternoon February 22 to argue his case. The Russians already had spies in the United States working undercover in their embassy and in the many trade delegations they have sent here. Donovan didn't know that Moscow, in fact, had begun aggressive clandestine operations in both the United States and Great Britain to steal atomic secrets. But he did know that Roosevelt wanted the Soviets treated as allies, which they were, and that senior administration officials, Hopkins included, had traded secrets with Russia. It was ludicrous to contend "that the addition of four or five other representatives on an open basis to work with the OSS on matters concerning our joint operations against a common enemy would provide any greater facilities for undercover activities than are already in existence," he wrote Leahy. "For the first time, we have an opportunity to find out just how our strongest ally carries on important agencies in its war effort." It is just as critical "to know how your allies conduct their subversive work as to know how your enemy does it." To hell with politics, "this is entirely a matter of prosecuting the war," Donovan maintained. Collaborating with the Russians "in the fields of intelligence and subversion is as essential as collaborating in other types of military and naval operations against the enemy." Reject this exchange and the U.S. military "would be the only loser."

Roosevelt killed the exchange, and Hoover bragged to aides that he deserved the credit for its death. Leahy cabled the decision to a dismayed Harriman on March 15. The ambassador dispatched Deane to break the news to Fitin. Meeting in a seedy Moscow apartment late at night, Deane told Fitin and Ossipov that trading intelligence missions had to be postponed, most likely until after the November elections. Fitin did not appear to be all that bothered, perhaps because he knew he already had enough spies in the United States, including moles in the OSS, while Donovan had virtually no assets in the Soviet Union. The canceled exchange meant his counterintelligence agents did not have to worry about following a few OSS officers in his country.

Deane, however, assured Fitin and Ossipov that Donovan still wanted to swap intelligence with them—which happened over the next year and a half with Washington's approval. Donovan delivered more than he received from Fitin; he sent the Russian reports on oil terminals in Romania, the location of German spare parts depots, Abwehr spying on the Soviets in Turkey, gossip Dulles picked up on Hitler and Göring, along with a sampling of OSS toys, such as the suitcase radio, pistol silencers, pocket incendiaries, and a portable microfilm set with miniature camera for agents photographing documents in the field. For his part, Fitin responded to long lists of questions Donovan had on German industrial plans. He provided reports on Bulgarian raw material production, on Nazi torpedo and chemical plants in occupied territories that Donovan passed along to General Hap Arnold for his Air Force to bomb. He also alerted Donovan to agents the OSS had recruited in Switzerland and the Balkans, whom his NKGB men considered unreliable. Even the questions Fitin sent gave OSS analysts important insights into "the things the Russians look for" and "the way they work," Donovan told Roosevelt.

THE DAY AFTER finally escaping Moscow on January 6, Donovan's plane stopped in Cairo. He ordered Rolfe Kingsley and several other men from the OSS station to meet him at the airport. Donovan had earlier sent a stuffed-shirt admiral the Pentagon had foisted on him to the Middle East for an inspection tour. The admiral had reported back that the Cairo station had the finest group of officers he had ever met. "I want to know what you did to him?" Donovan asked suspiciously. The admiral had been terrorizing stations all over the theater, Kingsley explained, so when he arrived in Cairo they convinced him to go with them to a nightclub, where they tanked him up with martinis and had a belly dancer escort him back to their quarters. The admiral woke up the next morning stretched out on a dining room table, his head throbbing, with no memory of his night with the belly dancer. He was no trouble after that. Donovan roared with laughter.

While Washington churned over his Soviet mission, Donovan spent much of January country hopping in the Mediterranean. By the second week of January, however, the grueling pace of Donovan's trip finally caught up with him. He arrived at Mark Clark's 5th Army headquarters in Caserta just north of Naples with a raging case of the flu. Clark's army had settled into a slow, grinding war of attrition against nearly two dozen Wehrmacht divisions, eight of which General Albert Kesselring had deployed in three fortified lines across Italy's narrowest point south of Rome. In addition to coastal attacks by Donovan's Operational Group commandos from Corsica, Italian agents were sent across enemy lines along the 5th Army front or infiltrated deeper into Rome and northern Italy, where a resistance movement began to blossom by the fall of 1943. After Clark captured Caserta he planted his headquarters in the city's Royal Palace, a majestic eighteenth-century compound with more than a thousand rooms, which the OSS also used as the headquarters for its detachment assigned to Clark's army. Donovan now lay writhing in a bed in one of the palace's rooms, delirious with a high fever from the potent virus. He refused to go to the hospital or bother with doctors, insisting he could ride out the bug. David Crockett, a Harvard man and Boston department store owner who now managed OSS finances at the Caserta station, sat up with the spy chief for two nights terrified he would blurt out secrets in his crazed state of mind.

Donovan soon recovered enough to make a short flight south to Naples and drop a surprise on Peter Tompkins. The son of artists (his father was a New York sculptor), Tompkins had lived much of his life in Italy and spoke the language fluently. Until 1940, he had been a Rome reporter for the *Herald Tribune,* but after being recruited by the OSS Tompkins found himself speeding in a PT boat to the Salerno beach for the landing. He ended up sending Italian recruits short distances across enemy lines around Naples to collect combat intelligence for what became largely suicidal missions. Nazi troopers always infested the territory just ahead.

After Clark took Naples, Tompkins commandeered for his OSS headquarters a four-story palazzo with a shabby garden off one of the city's back streets, which a Neapolitan duke had once owned. He filled up its warren of rooms, cellars, and attics with radios, high explosives, and Italians of different political stripes preparing for infiltrations. On Saturday evening, January 15, Donovan showed up at his doorstep. He hardly knew this twenty-four-year-old officer, but, typical of his operating style, he had read his dossier on the plane trip and been impressed with his family background and experience in Italy. Donovan now treated the agent like an old friend. The instant intimacy had the same effect on Tompkins as it did on every other OSS officer who got the treatment; it melted all his frustrations with the Naples assignment and made him intensely devoted to his boss. Tompkins ushered the spymaster into his candlelit dining room for bowlfuls of fettuccine his Posilipan cook had whipped up with flour and GI powdered eggs. "You are the host," Donovan said, acting like a humble guest. "I shall sit at your right." Sipping coffee and Strega liqueur in the sitting room later, Donovan dropped the news he came to deliver. He wanted Tompkins to go to Rome immediately.

After occupying Naples, Clark demanded more intelligence on the Eternal City, the next prize he lusted. On October 12, Donovan's OSS detachment with the 5th Army had infiltrated into Rome a six-man Italian team, headed by "Coniglio," the code name for Clemente Menicanti, a Neapolitan resistance leader. Coniglio hooked up with the senior Italian intelligence officer remaining in Rome, along with assorted communist, socialist, and Social Democratic factions in the city. By late November he had begun sending back intelligence reports over a clandestine radio station code-named Vittoria. Now, with Clark's surprise landing of 56,000 men at Anzio just a week away, Donovan wanted an American OSS officer in Rome to run the Vittoria operation the Italian team had set up.

Early Sunday morning Tompkins drove Donovan in his battered jeep to the Naples airfield where his plane's engines warmed up. Again typical for Donovan, who regularly swooped into overseas stations and turned things upside down, Tompkins had no signed military orders, no protocols written out with the 5th Army, no coordinating cables sent to the Rome team. Just go, Donovan told him over the prop noise, contact the Vittoria station, act as an intelligence officer for the 5th Army in Rome, and launch sabotage attacks when the Allies land at Anzio. "Then he shook me by the hand," Tompkins recalled, "climbed into the hatch and took off into the chill north wind, leaving me alone on the airstrip with that feeling of dedication which comes when one has been entrusted with a mission by a superior being."

Late Thursday night, January 20, a captured Italian torpedo boat deposited Tompkins and a bodyguard near the coastal town of Civitavecchia north of Rome. The two men reached the capital early the next morning, the day before the Anzio landing. Rome teemed with secret Italian resistance cells and some six thousand German counterespionage agents who ruthlessly hunted, tortured, and killed the dissidents. Tompkins, who expected Clark's invasion force to speed to the capital, found Menicanti in a flat near the Littorio airfield along with other members of the Vittoria team: Maurizio Giglio (code name Cervo, whose day job was a mounted police officer in Rome), Franco Malfatti (a military intelligence officer for the Italian Socialist Party), Elio Gambareri (a Unione Democratica party member and Menicanti's paymaster). Tompkins explained his mission.

CLARK HAD BEEN ambivalent about the Anzio landing Churchill had pushed to leapfrog Kesselring's defenses to the south, but he was delighted Saturday morning, January 22, when Operation Shingle met little resistance at what had once been a resort beach. The Germans were blindsided. As usual, Donovan was on hand, speeding in Clark's landing craft to the beach mid-morning after the early waves had landed. OSS officers began to worry that the Germans would be tipped off that a landing was coming anyplace Donovan showed up. Washington columnist Drew Pearson, in fact, suspected that as well and later tucked a note in one of his pieces that Donovan "always goes ashore with every invasion." Clark now thought it somewhat humorous that Donovan always popped up at these operations, but not so amusing when Donovan walked up to him on the beach, poked a finger at his chest, and said: "Hey, old boy, what are your plans?" Donovan didn't care if it irritated Clark. He thought the Army commander had botched the previous Salerno landing, which proved bloody.

Donovan had his own PT boat, which zipped him back and forth from Anzio to the OSS station in Bastia, where he wolfed down flapjacks and bacon in the dining hall with his men in the morning and sang Irish songs with them in the evening by a fireplace. At Corsica and back at Clark's beachhead, Donovan also began firing off cables to the Vittoria station demanding constant updates on any German troop movements toward Anzio.

Tompkins had quickly set up an elaborate system to transmit cables out of the Vittoria station. His Italian agents delivered their reports to radio operators written on thin tissue paper balled up so it could be easily swallowed if the Germans intercepted them. He had road watchers posted along the routes south toward Anzio. They counted vehicles in German convoys and recorded the directions they traveled. The traffic reports confirmed what Ultra intercepts already told Clark, that Kesselring was rushing rein-forcements to the beach. Tompkins organized minor acts of sabotage, cut-ting phone lines and defusing mines the Germans laid at choke points into the city. Eventually, he had a spy planted inside Kesselring's headquarters, feeding him intelligence on German military plans for Anzio.

But all was not well for the Vittoria station. As German resistance stiff-ened, Clark's invaders stalled at Anzio. Tompkins dejectedly realized they would not reach Rome anytime soon. A bitter feud erupted between him and Menicanti over who controlled clandestine operations in the capital. The OSS command with Clark did little to referee the dispute, but Dono-van was to blame as well, for jumping in and rushing Tompkins to Rome without sorting out the jurisdictional questions ahead of time. Meanwhile, German agents penetrated the Vittoria network. Giglio was arrested, horri-bly tortured for six days, then executed when he refused to talk. By March, Tompkins was on the run as the Germans recruited informants in his net-work and rounded up others.

WHEN DONOVAN FINALLY returned home, trouble was waiting for him. Shortly after 5 P.M., Monday, April 3, he and Edwin Putzell boarded the train at Union Station for Chicago. Putzell was far more than the sched-uler and paper flow manager for Donovan, a man he had known since joining his law firm in 1938. They had developed practically a father-son relationship. Putzell became Donovan's traveling companion, attending to the minutest details of his trips. Donovan's two most trusted assistants became Putzell on the road and Doering in Washington. They watched his back, handled the dirty administrative chores of enforcing his orders and easing out poor performers.

Before they boarded the train, a messenger from headquarters ran up to Donovan and handed him an envelope from his deputy, John Magruder. Donovan tucked it into his coat pocket to read later. After the train had pulled out and he had settled comfortably into the Pullman car with Put-zell, Donovan pulled the envelope out of his coat pocket, ripped it open, and began reading.

His hands trembled. Putzell thought he was about to have an apoplectic fit. Magruder and the gang of six were back at it, this time with a memo even more explicit than the one they sent six months earlier. The note bluntly criticized his "ineffectual administration of day-by-day affairs of OSS." The agency needed better leadership at the top. Donovan should step aside and give Magruder and the other senior managers more power. "It really hurt him to the quick," Putzell recalled. "Here were men he thought were supporters and here they were in a cabal."

Donovan wanted to stop the train immediately, climb off, and march back to Washington to have it out with them. Putzell talked him out of it. "You can't do anything in the heat of the moment," he said. Wait until we arrive in Chicago and you've calmed down.

The next morning in Chicago, Donovan got off the train and found a phone in the station. With Doering listening in, he had the headquarters operator round up Magruder, Cheston, and several of the other coup plotters who could be found. He gave them an old fashioned Army ass chewing. "Donovan really crawled all over them," Putzell said. The power they had was all he would allow them to have. "The chain of command is what I want it to be!" Donovan angrily declared. Donovan did not fire the gang of six, although Putzell thought he should have. He made Charles Cheston a deputy director along with Magruder and the nominal chief in his absence. But he never again trusted them and kept the entire junta at arm's length.

Donovan climbed aboard another train, which now traveled west. Just two months before the Allied invasion of France, Magruder and the other members of the junta thought he was headed in the wrong direction—and on a hopeless mission.

THE TRAIN ARRIVED in San Francisco on Friday, April 7, and the next day Donovan and Putzell boarded a plane that would eventually land them in Brisbane, Australia. He brought along two books for the long flight: one an impenetrable tome in German to brush up on his language skills, the other an advanced physics textbook. An FBI agent in Honolulu spotted Donovan, whose plane landed in Hawaii for a refueling stop, and messaged Hoover. But the agent could not figure out why the OSS director was in the Pacific. Donovan, in fact, was flying to Brisbane for what his aides dubbed "Project Penetrate MacArthur"—a mission Donovan privately gave low odds for success.

After the decisive Battle of Midway in June 1942, Nimitz and MacArthur went on the offensive with an expanded carrier force, ground army, and superior pilots. Their strategy: island-hop in the Pacific to capture strategic stepping-stones to Japan and leave starving enemy garrisons behind. By the time Donovan arrived in Brisbane, a number of the islands had fallen to overwhelming American firepower. The geography of the Pacific alone was daunting enough, but the hostility of the theater's two commanders had made OSS operations impossible. Donovan sent Nimitz one of Stanley Lovell's pistols with a silencer, which the admiral enjoyed shooting at targets. But during Donovan's visit to Nimitz's Hawaii headquarters while his plane refueled, the Pacific Ocean Areas commander made it clear he didn't want much else from the OSS.

Donovan had a complicated relationship with MacArthur. Though the two made a point of being cordial to each other after World War I, Donovan confided to Putzell that he always resented MacArthur being so slow to protect his right flank from the murderous enfilade at Landres-et-Saint-Georges. With large armies MacArthur was a brilliant strategist and a grand showman, Donovan told another friend, but on the ground with a small unit he was a timid tactician. Many OSS officers were convinced MacArthur kept their organization out of his theater because he was jealous that Donovan had won the Medal of Honor in the Great War and he had not. They had no proof for their theory, though MacArthur *was* infamously vain. What was undeniable was that MacArthur was constitutionally incapable of working jointly with almost everybody—Nimitz, the British, outsiders like Donovan—and he demanded total control of every outfit in his theater.

MacArthur also thought that he was more than ably served by his own intensely loyal intelligence officer, General Charles Willoughby, a German American who had his uniforms custom-tailored and often wore a monocle that earned him the nickname "Sir Charles" behind his back. Willoughby, who also was as close-minded to outsiders as MacArthur, vied "for the title of stupidest intelligence chief of World War II," one military historian has written. He habitually produced faulty reports on the condition of beaches MacArthur's forces stormed and underestimated the strength of Japanese defenders they faced on the islands.

Donovan had dispatched emissaries to MacArthur's Brisbane headquarters and peppered him with written requests the past two years to send spies, commandos, and research analysts to his theater. MacArthur turned them all down and the Joint Chiefs refused to overrule MacArthur's rejections. William Langer thought his research analysts could provide valuable intelligence on the beaches that would save lives. Willoughby considered them a bunch of academic pinheads ransacking libraries for worthless information. But Donovan had a standing invitation from MacArthur to visit his theater. He decided to take him up on the offer and try to crack the wall himself. He arrived in Brisbane the second week in April for the invasion of Hollandia.

The landing at Hollandia on the northern coast of New Guinea was a MacArthur masterstroke. His army and the Australians' had captured bits of southeastern New Guinea and advanced as far as Saidor on the northern coast. But forty thousand well-armed and dug-in Japanese soldiers in between prepared to make the 550 miles between Saidor and Hollandia a killing ground as the Americans slogged northwest. Hollandia, however, was lightly defended with eleven thousand mostly rear-echelon enemy troops. MacArthur decided to leapfrog the Japanese defenses just ahead and land two divisions with 55,000 GIs at Hollandia, then move inland behind the enemy.

On April 19, Donovan boarded MacArthur's command ship, the USS *Nashville* cruiser, docked at Finschhafen on the Huon Peninsula, which the Americans held, in southeast New Guinea. His briefcase bulged with memos from advisers on how best to approach MacArthur along with lists of gadgets from Lovell that might impress him. As the *Nashville* and the invasion convoy sailed circuitously to fool the Japanese, MacArthur, like an emperor on a galley, spent much of the next two days lounging on a deck chair outside his cabin chatting with aides, snoozing, and signing autographs for crewmen brave enough to approach him. Between the stream of interruptions, Donovan made his pitch. He said he had "no wish to compete with or disturb" Willoughby's intelligence network and proposed a small team be sent to MacArthur as a sort of pilot project to show what the OSS could do: a research officer who could draw on the "voluminous data" the agency had collected on the Pacific region, a couple of propagandists expert in "the demoralization of enemy troops," a training officer to instruct Asia operatives in clandestine techniques, an intelligence and special operations officer who could scout opportunities for spying and sabotage plus acquaint MacArthur with Lovell's exotic gadgets. MacArthur would have complete control of the OSS officers sent to his command.

Donovan sat back and waited for a response. He could see no reason why the man would not at least give it a try.

Willoughby, however, had alerted his boss ahead of time to the bill of goods he thought Donovan would be selling. The cagey MacArthur came back with a counteroffer. He would take Donovan's team, but only if they checked out of the OSS and became members of his staff. That killed the deal as far as Donovan was concerned, although he did not tell MacArthur aboard the *Nashville* that he had no intention of letting his men be absorbed by the Southwest Pacific Command. The other theater commands had accepted OSS detachments. Caving in to MacArthur's demand "would destroy all that we have built," Donovan told his senior advisers later, particularly if the other commands then demanded the same treatment. "It would mean that we would be only a recruiting agency for each theater."

The Hollandia landing was a resounding success, catching the Japanese completely by surprise as MacArthur had predicted. The American assault troops began hitting the beaches north and south of the town on Saturday morning, April 22, and lost only 150 lives in scattered fighting. At 11 A.M., MacArthur went ashore at the Humboldt Bay beach just south of Hollandia with his staff officers and Donovan in tow. Army photographers scurried ahead to snap photos of him with his trademark corncob pipe, aviator glasses, and gold-embroidered crush cap. The sun beat down, the humid tropical air was stifling, and the beach's soft squishy sand had Donovan and the others panting and their uniforms soaked with perspiration. The sixty-four-year-old MacArthur walked at a fast clip and, to the astonishment of Donovan and everyone else, did not sweat a drop. His khakis remained dry and crisp. Putzell thought the only thing he and his boss had accomplished with this jaunt halfway around the world was being props for MacArthur's photo op. Ultimately his command accepted only a smattering of operatives from the OSS.

Chapter 23

—◦◦◦◦—

Normandy

C LARIDGE'S WAS HALF EMPTY when Donovan arrived on May 14, 1944. The London bombing had made it easy to book rooms at high-end hotels and grab reservations at the priciest restaurants. Donovan had spent less than a fortnight in Washington after his Hollandia landing. As he had with most overseas trips, he told Ruth nothing about where he was headed on this one. Secrecy was now even more paramount for the Allied invasion of France's northern coast, code-named Overlord.

Donovan arrived in London near the top of his game. His organization was still the "junior partner" in its alliance with the British, as one memo he read on the plane trip over cautioned, mainly because London had such a head start in Europe's shadow war. But Donovan's contribution was substantial, and growing every day. He now had nearly three years' experience under his belt and a worldwide network of some eleven thousand American officers and foreign agents scattered in every important capital. The OSS even had begun to accumulate its own ditties and songs. The last stanza to the irreverent "OSS Hymn" went:

> The brass hats don't know "F" all, the rest are snafu too,
> It takes a damned magician to know just what to do.
> An order here, an order there, it's anybody's guess.
> You too can be a fubar if you join the OSS.

("Snafu" was the GI acronym for "situation normal, all fucked up," while "fubar" stood for "fucked up beyond all repair.") Donovan enjoyed hearing all the tunes.

David Bruce's London station had grown to more than 2,900 OSS men and women. He had a clothing shop, complete with a cobbler Polish intelligence supplied and tailors who paid attention to the minutest details dressing agents for foreign countries so they did not stand out. Buttons had to be sewn onto coats by threading the holes parallel, the European style, instead of crisscrossing them. A photoengraving plant the British loaned him printed phony identification documents for agents. A special mill supplied the paper whose watermarks matched continental Europe's. Potential commandos from the United States went first to a reception center Bruce set up at Franklin House in Ruislip outside London, where British special operations officers helped screen them for clandestine duty in France. More than a third washed out; the rest went to five-week guerrilla warfare "finishing schools" in the English countryside.

Bruce had become another of Donovan's trusted aides, which was not surprising. They were a lot alike. Bruce tended to be disorganized with administration and enjoyed landing at beaches with the troops as much as Donovan. One of Bruce's favorite moments occurred in the summer of 1943 when Donovan had slipped unnoticed into a meeting General Jacob Devers, the commander of U.S. Army forces in Europe, was holding at his military headquarters on Grosvenor Square with his senior officers. Bruce, a lowly lieutenant colonel, was being dressed down by Devers's G-2, also a general, who accused the OSS of being "a dangerous intruder" into the military intelligence system he'd set up. Bruce tried the best he could to defend his agency but the G-2 got wound up and finally declared loudly that Donovan was "tricky" and he didn't trust him "or his ideas." Donovan walked quietly to the front of the room where Devers sat at a table and said in a clear but absolutely calm voice the entire room could hear that unless the intelligence chief "withdraws this slur on me and apologizes I shall tear him to pieces and throw what is left of him through these windows into Grosvenor Square." A barely audible gasp could be heard from the gaggle of generals in the room because Donovan seemed ready to do exactly that. The intelligence chief "made a handsome apology," Bruce recalled.

Hitler had ordered German defenses bulked up all along the northern French and Belgian coasts. The buildup included Normandy to the southwest; the extensive Allied deception campaign for the most part convinced the führer and German military leaders that the main landing would be northeast at Pas de Calais. Putzi Hanfstaengl predicted to his OSS debriefers that if Hitler threw back his invaders at the French coast he would quickly "drive through Spain to Gibraltar with the object of immediately cutting off our North African and Italian forces." If the Allies gained a foothold on the French coast and moved inland, Hitler, who envisioned himself a twentieth-century Frederick the Great, "will fight to the utmost limit of his resources," Putzi predicted.

Dulles thought otherwise. Fritz Kolbe, one of his key spies, had supplied him four hundred pages of Foreign Office documents that convinced the Bern station chief Nazi Germany was near "imminent doom," he cabled Donovan. D-Day might well prove easy for the Allies. Donovan passed Dulles's cable to Roosevelt, Marshall, and Eisenhower. He would have been better served sending them Hanfstaengl's. Marshall's intelligence aides saw no evidence the offensive would be a cakewalk. "It would be extremely unwise from the military standpoint to count on an imminent collapse of the Nazis," one adviser warned. With the Army scoffing at Dulles's bold prediction, Donovan queried his Bern chief to see if he wished "to modify" it. Dulles backpedaled some, predicting the Wehrmacht might fiercely fight an invasion attempt. But he continued to insist that "a collapse of Germany might follow . . . a few months after" the Allies established "a firm toe-hold" in France. Dulles could not have been more wrong.

Donovan had a wide range of OSS operations underway for D-Day. Langer's research analysts sent the Army and Navy lengthy topographic studies of the Normandy coast and analyzed German targets in France for Arnold's 8th Air Force. By the time Donovan arrived in London, Bruce had parachuted nearly twenty-five two-man spy teams into France, under a joint American-British project code-named "Sussex" to collect military intelligence for the invaders. Menzies had dropped thirty-five of the French teams. Another eighty-five OSS special operations commandos infiltrated behind enemy lines to organize the French resistance fighters who had fled to the forests and mountains and became known as the Maquis—the "men of the underbrush" its literal translation. They cut telephone lines, sabotaged factories, blew up bridges and fuel dumps, mined roads, derailed trains, and eventually captured ten thousand German prisoners. (One of the OSS infiltrators was Virginia Hall, who had lost part of her leg in a hunting accident before the war and wore a wooden prosthetic; she arrived on the Brittany coast in March to supply the Maquis with money and arms.) All told, the OSS and British Special Operations Executive dropped ten thousand tons of weapons and equipment to the Maquis before and after the Normandy invasion. The British grew nervous the massive supply operation would end up arming different Maquis factions to fight one another after the war but Donovan pressed to keep up the airdrops. A typical two-and-a-half-ton load in a bomber, he wrote Roosevelt, included four machine guns, forty-four rifles, fifty-five Sten guns, and 41,000 rounds of ammunition.

The clandestine penetrations were not uniformly successful. The Sussex teams did radio back eight hundred intelligence reports, which Eisenhower's staff found helpful. But because they were rushed into the field with little advance preparation, only a quarter of the Sussex teams succeeded in their missions. Two men air-dropped into Le Blanc in central France on April 10 transmitted 127 messages on Panzer deployments, V-1 rocket launching ramps, and enemy convoy routes out of Paris they had gleaned from a stolen German map. Another team, which parachuted into Rochefort-sur-Loire in western France on June 1, had its radio dumped into a well by panicky Maquis guerrillas fleeing the Germans and became totally useless because it could not transmit any information it found.

Eisenhower also questioned whether guerrilla attacks should be attempted at all for the Normandy invasion. By March de Gaulle had successfully united under his Forces Française de l'Intérieur headquartered in London the two other Maquis factions: the Organisation de la Résistance dans l'Armée controlled by North Africa's General Henri Giraud and the communist Francs Tireurs et Partisans. But Overlord's planners still found the maverick French general difficult to deal with and Ike worried that partisan warfare at D-Day would result in the useless slaughter of de Gaulle's Maquis and French civilians by the enemy. Hitler's occupation already had been brutal. Determined to crush all resistance, the SS mauled the Maquis forces they found and the Gestapo methodically terrorized the French population. Donovan's men and the British special operations commanders also worried about the heavy partisan casualties that would surely result from a French national insurrection. But Eisenhower finally softened his opposition to a Maquis revolt. The French will rise up whether he wanted them to or not, his advisers told him. The Allies might as well exploit the Maquis as best they could to harass and help delay German reinforcements that will surely rush to Normandy when they land.

While waiting in London for the invasion, Donovan busied himself with chores. He fired cables back to Washington ordering more assets transferred to Europe and flew to the Home Counties around London to inspect the men and equipment being parachuted in for Sussex. He booked a lunch at Chequers with Churchill, who did not relish a session suffering Donovan's pushy views on the Balkans. Churchill arranged for Fitzroy Maclean to drive to the prime minister's country estate in the same car with Donovan. The two men remained frosty but civil toward each other during the awkward trip and the meal. David Donovan dropped by Claridge's for a visit with his father. Now a full lieutenant, he was about to board the flagship of the imposing Admiral John "Viking" Hall Jr., who commanded the 11th Amphibious Force and thousands of landing craft for the Normandy invasion. Donovan also had one more loose end to tie up before Overlord commenced—obtaining permission to be in on the Normandy landing.

Marshall, who by now had his fill of Donovan's escapades at Salerno, Anzio, and Hollandia, ordered that he not be allowed to join in Overlord. Eisenhower agreed that the Normandy beach was no place for America's top intelligence officer. James Forrestal had sent Bruce a cable he wanted passed on to Donovan telling him "he was not to board any U.S. Naval craft." (Forrestal had just been installed as navy secretary after Knox died from a massive heart attack on April 28.) Bruce tried to hand his boss Forrestal's message but Donovan brushed him off and told him to put the paper in his pocket. "I'll read it later," he said. Instead he took Bruce with him to a luxurious apartment on Grosvenor Square occupied by Admiral Harold "Betty" Stark, the commander of U.S. Naval Forces in Europe.

Donovan turned on the Irish charm. He begged his old Navy pal to cut orders attaching him to one of the ships making the landing. Stark, who had been alerted by Ike's staff about what Donovan was up to, said absolutely not. The Army had barred Donovan from going in with any of its contingents, no way a Navy admiral would countermand orders from a sister service and take a stowaway, Stark told him.

Stark stood up to warm his backside in front of the fire crackling in his living room's fireplace. Donovan jumped out of his easy chair and sprung at him, poking his stubby forefinger into Stark's midriff, almost toppling him into the flames. "Betty, you and I are old and expendable," he told the white-haired admiral. "We ought to die together on the beach with enemy bullets through our bellies!"

That did not seem like a pleasant prospect to Stark, who still wouldn't change his mind. Donovan returned to Claridge's to brood over another solution to his problem.

Bruce never learned how Donovan found it, but on late Tuesday night, May 30, the two of them boarded the train at London's Paddington Station for Plymouth in southern England. Donovan told the London OSS office they would be visiting friends at British army units. He knew his habit of attending landings had made it into the papers, which the Abwehr read. He decided to keep his staff in the dark about his movements so Overlord's timing wasn't leaked from his end. It was curious that Donovan and his partner decided to take what amounted to a week-long excursion instead of sticking to their headquarters desks and monitoring their secret forces in the biggest invasion of the war. To Donovan's detractors it seemed like a joy ride. But at this point all the preparations had been completed, the OSS penetration agents were in place or on their way, and the rest of Donovan's secret army for Overlord was now under the command of generals at the front. At the outset of a great campaign, the most useless officer is the headquarters commander who must sit and wait for field reports on how his plan is being carried out. The ever restless Donovan did not intend to wait at headquarters for his reports.

Their train arrived in Plymouth early Wednesday morning and the two boarded the destroyer USS *Davis*, which pushed away from the pier shortly after noon. The next morning, June 1, when the *Davis* dropped anchor off Belfast, Donovan and Bruce hopped into a launch that took them to the USS *Tuscaloosa*, a heavy cruiser that soon would be parked off Utah Beach for the invasion. Donovan was comfortably installed next to the cabin of Vice Admiral Morton Deyo, the deputy commander of U.S. Naval Forces for Normandy. Bruce, who landed a berth in the ship captain's emergency cabin, finally guessed how Donovan had wangled his passage. During the visit Donovan and Knox had made to Pearl Harbor before the war, he had struck up a friendship with Deyo.

While the *Tuscaloosa* remained anchored with an Allied flotilla off the Irish coast the next two days, Donovan motored back and forth in the launch from the cruiser to the docks. He met with Britain's Northern Ireland commanders in Belfast Castle, sipped port wine with the Duke of Abercorn (the charming seventy-five-year-old governor of Northern Ireland whose purple nose showed he had drunk a lot of port), paid a courtesy call to Sir Basil Brooke (the Northern Ireland prime minister judged to be amiable but far lazier than his famous uncle, Field Marshal Sir Alan Francis Brooke), and took tea, jam, and cakes with the Marquis of Dufferin and Ava at their Clandeboye estate. Between idle chitchat he also caught up on the intelligence both Northern Ireland's officers and diplomats from the Republic of Ireland to the south had secretly fed the OSS the past year on Nazi agents and sympathizers infesting the island.

Donovan and Bruce returned to the ship each evening for long dinners with Deyo, his staff officers, and Willard Shadel, a CBS radio correspondent on board for the landing. Shadel shared gossip reporters had picked up on Mark Clark's arrogance and George Patton's bombast, which Donovan was eager to hear. After dinner each night Donovan slipped into the ship's combat information center to study the invasion plans for Overlord, which Deyo's officers scrambled through the wee hours to update with last-minute changes. He was struck by the complexity of the plan. Donovan had always favored Churchill's idea to invade Germany with a thrust from the Mediterranean through the Balkans. He thought too much optimism infected Overlord's architects. They did not realize the multitude of battle hazards that might confront the Allies with this amphibious attack.

Early Sunday morning, June 4, the *Tuscaloosa* arrived off Falmouth at England's southwest tip. By 6:30 A.M., the ship's radio shack had received orders that bad weather in the Channel had forced postponement of the invasion for twenty-four hours. It further heightened Donovan's fears. Only for a few days in each month were the moon, tides, weather, and sea conditions right for the long cross-Channel invasion. Choppy seas like what he now saw from the *Tuscaloosa*'s deck could toss landing boats about "like cockleshells," he told Bruce, throwing off the carefully choreographed schedule and hurtling seasick "human freight" to the shore to be mowed down by the enemy. The Germans, too, would consider Normandy a favorable point of attack and have its coast heavily fortified, he thought. So much of the plan he now read depended on surprise, but how could you keep a huge armada like this one secret? German espionage agents are bound to have picked up its breadcrumbs, he worried.

The weather mercifully improved on Monday, June 5. As the *Tuscaloosa* steamed back around the southeast tip toward Plymouth, Donovan spent much of the day leaning over a deck rail watching the majestic armada of over six thousand ships and landing craft assembled before him: cruisers and battleships in line, flanked by destroyers, long convoys of transports crammed with hundreds of thousands of troops, barrage balloons floating overhead. "The firepower of this fleet will be immense," Bruce recorded in his diary. On the *Tuscaloosa* alone Donovan counted nine eight-inch guns, eight five-and-a-quarter-inch guns, six forty-millimeter antiaircraft quads, and eighteen twenty-millimeter pieces.

By 9 P.M., the winds picked up and the seas churned higher, but Eisenhower's weathermen predicted an interval of calmer skies into the night and by next morning. The *Tuscaloosa* set its course for the beaches designated Utah at the coastal village of La Madeleine on the western leg of the ninety-mile landing front. Sailors stood watch wearing helmets and nervously chain-smoking cigarettes. Admiral Deyo pounded a punching bag in his cabin to vent his pent-up energy, while Donovan cheerily shaved and showered next door. After he dried off and wiped the foam from his pink cheeks, he dressed in his fatigues, buttoning his trousers around his ankles, and slipping on rubber-soled shoes. He took an olive wool cap out of his duffel bag, perched it on his head, and began calmly munching an apple. Other OSS officers had told Bruce this was his routine before going into a combat zone. Shortly before midnight, Donovan made his way to the officers mess and ate a plate of bacon and eggs. He was ready to storm the beach.

The *Tuscaloosa*'s heavy guns opened fire shortly before 6 A.M. on Tuesday, June 6. Donovan could feel the deck tremble under his feet and hear ship joints creak. His own teeth rattled in his head from the discharges. The air around him smelled acrid with powder from the yellow clouds of smoke billowing out of the guns while a fine mist of disintegrated wadding fell around him like lava ash. Spouts of water gushed near the cruiser as German long-range batteries off Utah Beach tried to zero in on their vessel. An Allied fighter was hit by antiaircraft fire and skidded along the ocean in front of them before bursting into a ball of flame. The USS *Corry* destroyer nearby struck a mine, then took shore battery rounds and had to be abandoned by its crew. A sailor on watch spotted a periscope pop up out of the water a thousand yards from the *Tuscaloosa* so depth charges were readied. Something—the crew could never determine exactly what it was—made a direct hit on Deyo's flagship, which shattered the water closet Donovan had been using adjoining the admiral's cabin.

The troops began wading ashore at Utah at 6:30 A.M., undaunted by four heavy enemy guns shelling the beach. Donovan heard over German radio the cruiser monitored the announcement that American paratroopers had landed in France. BBC radio ordered French resistance troops to await further instructions. An OSS photo unit covered the Normandy landings, shooting four reels of film that were later screened for Roosevelt, Churchill, and Stalin. Donovan also succeeded in having a spy and sabotage detachment landed with Bradley's army to link up with the guerrillas ahead. Even Bill Stephenson, who had accompanied Donovan to London, managed to snare a rear gunner's seat in a British bomber and was now flying over the Normandy coast.

But the OSS director was stuck on the ship. Donovan had sidled up to Deyo throughout the day, hinting about how "interesting" it would be to wade ashore soon after the landings to check up on what his agents were doing near the beach, but the admiral ignored him. It was clear to Bruce that Deyo had been told by his superiors he could give Donovan the run of ship, but he was not to let him leave it.

By Wednesday afternoon, June 7, Donovan could no longer be caged. Deyo flatly refused to lend him a boat to go ashore, but if Donovan could hail a passerby, the admiral said he could not stop him. That was enough for Donovan to escape. He strapped on his helmet and battle kit and pinned his Medal of Honor ribbon to his fatigues. With Bruce and Shadel, he clambered down a swinging rope ladder and fell part of the way, plopping into a launch that happened by filled with aviators shot down over the beach and three corpses. The launch helmsman agreed to take Donovan further in, where he climbed aboard a destroyer escort and convinced its bewildered skipper he had urgent spy business ashore where his agents awaited him. The lieutenant commander sailed his ship as close to the beach as he safely could so this mysterious general with a Medal of Honor pinned to his chest could hail an empty landing craft vehicle passing by and order it to lay alongside the destroyer. A swarthy-looking sailor from Chicago manned the LCV. Donovan perched up on a ledge next to the helmsman for a better view and traded stories with him about Chicago gangsters. It looked as if he and Bruce would have to swim the last twenty yards to shore, but Donovan spotted a DUKW amphibious truck and shouted at the Duck driver to draw near. Donovan and Bruce climbed onto the front hood of the DUKW for the ride to dry land.

The battle at the three eastern beaches assigned to British and Canadian forces—Sword, Juno and Gold—had gone pretty well the first and second days. A seasoned German division had just arrived at Omaha Beach in the center, however, and turned the shore into a murderous killing field for the wet and frightened infantrymen struggling through frigid surf and maddening obstacles to reach the shelter of dunes and cliffs. Nearly three thousand lay dead, wounded, or missing after the first day. But the 7th Corps (part of Lieutenant General Omar Bradley's American 1st Army) had landed at Utah Beach, where Donovan's DUKW sat parked, and suffered only about two hundred casualties, far below what had been expected, and the corps had already begun to march inland. Even so, the beach, now in a state of organized chaos as equipment and men streamed ashore, remained a hot zone as Donovan sat with Bruce on the DUKW's hood scanning his field map.

Donovan heard the drone of a plane motor along with the thudding sound of machine gun fire and looked up. Four German Messerschmitts approached, strafing the beach. He rolled nimbly off the hood to the sand beside the DUKW for cover. Bruce was slower to react and fell on top of Donovan. He discovered to his horror that the rim of his steel helmet had gashed Donovan's chin, and blood now gushed down his neck. Bruce was terrified he had cut a vital artery and was about to kill the leader of America's spy service. Donovan, however, cheerily got up after the planes passed, dusted the sand off his uniform, and dabbed his chin with a handkerchief.

Donovan ditched the DUKW and began to trudge inland with Bruce, hoping he could catch up with OSS agents or French guerrillas he felt sure were nearby. After several miles of walking they were halted by a young Army lieutenant in command of a forward antiaircraft battery, who demanded to know what they were doing out there. Eyeing the stars on Donovan's collar, the Medal of Honor on his chest, and the dried blood on his neck, the lieutenant asked it respectfully. Donovan told the incredulous officer he was hunting for secret agents. He spotted three French peasants a couple hundred yards ahead digging up roots and vegetables in a large open field enclosed at the far end by a thick hedge. "Those are some of my boys and I must interrogate them," Donovan told the lieutenant.

The officer thought waltzing into an open field with German soldiers still around was a crazy idea but Donovan practically sprinted off before he could stop him. With Bruce running to catch up, Donovan reached the far end of the field near the hedgerow, but by then the Frenchmen had disappeared. Suddenly enemy machine gun fire erupted not far from the hedgerow. Donovan and Bruce dove to the ground. With bullets whizzing overhead, Donovan turned to Bruce and said in a whisper: "You understand, of course, David, that neither of us must be captured. We know too much."

"Yes, sir," Bruce dutifully answered. Each of them had only a revolver strapped to his waist.

"Have you your pills with you?" Donovan asked in a low voice.

Bruce had been issued the poison tablets but hadn't brought them along, thinking the last place he'd be was flat on his stomach with Germans firing at him. He apologized profusely.

"Never mind, I have two of them," Donovan whispered and began hunting for his L tablets while Bruce peered through a hole in the hedge looking for the machine gun nest.

Donovan disgorged everything from his pockets onto the ground beside him: hotel keys, passport, currency of several nationalities, photographs of his granddaughter, travel orders, newspaper clippings. Then he realized he had left his pills in the medicine cabinet in his room at Claridge's. If we get out of this jam, he told Bruce, "you must send a message" to the hall porter at Claridge's and tell him not "to allow the servants in the hotel to touch some dangerous medicines in my bathroom."

Donovan took his revolver out of his holster and looked through the hole in the hedgerow. "I must shoot first," he whispered to Bruce.

"Yes, sir," Bruce answered, almost breathlessly. "But can we do much against machine guns with our pistols?"

"Oh, you don't understand," Donovan explained. "I mean if we are about to be captured I'll shoot you first. After all, I am your commanding officer." Then, Donovan said, he would shoot himself.

Bruce was not particularly enthralled with that prospect. Fortunately, American and British warplanes roared above and they soon heard the whine of artillery shells streaking over them and exploding ahead. Crouching down, Donovan and Bruce ran across the field to safety.

On their way back they stumbled onto the 7th Corps command post in a deserted barn. General Bradley stood inside, bleary-eyed from little sleep the night before with staff officers and newsmen crowded around him as he pored over tactical maps of the inland terrain. He had had a busy day racing from one field headquarters to another bucking up the morale of his commanders, visiting the wounded at aid stations and dodging German artillery fire along the way. He now was intent on joining the Utah and Omaha landing forces at all cost to form a single beachhead. Bruce thought they should turn around and leave the harried Army commander alone. Bradley had grudgingly accepted the OSS detachment but thought it would prove useless. He believed the British spy service was far superior not only to Donovan's organization, but also to his own Army intelligence, which he complained was a "dumping ground for officers ill-suited to line command."

Donovan, however, strutted up to Bradley and delivered a polite salute. "General," he began, interrupting the briefing Bradley had been receiving at the map table. "Colonel Bruce and I have just been trying to establish contact with some of our agents. As I have always predicted, it is going to be easy to get intelligence from behind German lines. I would like to send Bruce to spend some time with the First Army as soon as possible, and I've instructed him to give you all the help he can."

Donovan's chutzpah flabbergasted Bruce. Bradley had more important things on his mind at the moment than visiting firemen from the OSS and Bruce was sure he knew Donovan had been banned from Normandy. He thought Bradley would erupt now. But the Army commander answered in an even voice: "Bill, I would be very glad to have Bruce at my headquarters later on. But suppose you now go back to wherever you came from." Bradley returned his attention to the tactical maps on the table.

It was almost dark when Donovan reached the beach. He was delighted with what he thought had been a diplomatic breakthrough with Bradley. Bruce didn't have the same impression from their curt encounter with the 1st Army commander, but he decided not to dampen his boss's enthusiasm. Donovan vacuumed intelligence on the way to the shore and scribbled impressions into a notebook, which he later put in a thoughtful six-page memo to Roosevelt. Clearly his earlier misgivings had been unwarranted, he concluded; the Germans did not have the resources to meet the Allied attack at every landing point. He had stopped along the way to interrogate a prisoner and try out his German. The Wehrmacht captain told him he was "overwhelmed" at the sight of the Allied armada and realized he was witnessing a historic event. Despite his close call with a Messerschmitt, Donovan noticed that the Luftwaffe had managed to put only a small contingent into the air, which told him "the Germans no longer have an air force that belongs in the Big League," he wrote FDR. Likewise, the fact that the Germans could muster only a few submarines to harass the invasion fleet demonstrated they were no longer a naval power as well. In the months ahead, "there will be a lot of hard going," Donovan wrote another friend, "but something has died in the German machine."

Donovan walked up to the only DUKW he could see on the beach. The driver, a Brooklyn boy, told him he had been sent there to wait for Bradley. "He's in the field and won't be back for a long time," Donovan told the GI. "Meanwhile, Colonel Bruce and I are on urgent business for the President and must rejoin our ship at once." To Bruce's amazement Donovan also convinced the Brooklyn driver he had once defended a friend of his in a New York criminal case. He succeeded in commandeering Bradley's ride. The DUKW took them to a landing craft and they began vessel hopping until they finally reached the *Tuscaloosa*.

Donovan eventually managed to debark the cruiser with Bruce when it weighed anchor the evening of June 9 off Plymouth. By the third day of Overlord, the window for the Germans repulsing the invaders had shut. Allied soldiers and supplies poured in. They struggled the first month to seize ground and break out of the Normandy pocket, but break out they did. Another 276 OSS, British, and French commandos, called Jedburghs for their training site near Jedburgh, Scotland, would be air-dropped in three-man teams the next four months to organize more than twenty thousand French guerrillas cutting tracks, derailing trains, and ambushing German truck convoys. All told, 523 OSS commandos fought behind enemy lines in France during 1944. Eighteen of them died, fifty-one were wounded, and seventeen were missing in action or captured by the Nazis. Allied aerial bombing and the Maquis's sabotage and guerrilla attacks succeeded in delaying for two days German reinforcements from arriving at the Normandy front, which Eisenhower considered critical to establishing a beachhead—although Donovan confided to Roosevelt that he thought the Army Air Force's destruction of French bridges and oil installations did far more to slow the German counterattack than the Maquis.

By itself, the French resistance amounted to only pinpricks against the better armed and trained Germans, who continued to make the Maquis pay dearly for their attacks. Donovan ended up believing the French resistance had been a mixed blessing. After Normandy, the Maquis ranks swelled and "everyone was climbing on the bandwagon," he said. Some fought well. "In other places their value was nil." But though their physical strength was puny, the Maquis still wielded symbolic power. They gave their countrymen hope and self-respect. They also reminded those who collaborated that the day would come when traitors would be held accountable.

DONOVAN LEFT LONDON on June 13. He asked Bruce for a copy of everything in his station files so he could catch up on European operations during the flight back. Bruce talked him out of it by saying that the plane would never lift off the ground with that many documents. Back in Washington, Donovan made the rounds with stories about what he saw during the landing. Roosevelt booked a lunch, eager to hear about the fighting at Normandy. The signs he saw of German "disintegration, spiritual as well as physical" made him optimistic, Donovan told FDR. Even the normally reserved Stimson recorded in his diary that Donovan "gave us some very interesting points and comments from his observations." The spy chief had been struck by the power and accuracy of naval gunfire during Overlord, which became the artillery batteries for Bradley's Army divisions as they moved forward from the beach, he told the war secretary. Donovan also sent a letter to Forrestal with his observations from the *Tuscaloosa* bridge and Utah Beach—a not so subtle notice to the new Navy secretary that he didn't have enough clout yet to keep Donovan from the front.

Chapter 24

━━∽∾∿∿∾∽━━

Intelligence Failures

TOWARD THE LAST week in June 1944, Donovan bumped along in a jeep on a southern highway leading into Rome. David Crockett, who had tended to him in Caserta when he had the flu, drove. In the back seat Putzell sat crammed between bags with Colonel Edward Glavin, a West Pointer and seasoned military man Donovan had just brought in to head the OSS's Italian operations. Donovan, who had spent only a week back in Washington after the Normandy landing, was eager to reach the Italian capital, which Clark had finally liberated at the beginning of June after a slow and bloody campaign in the south. Hitler had ordered Kesselring not to raze Rome when he retreated; it was strategically unimportant. The German occupation soldiers streamed north out of the city in convoy trucks, stolen cars, motorcycles, bicycles, pushcarts, or anything else they could find on wheels. Peter Tompkins had his agents track stay-behind Nazi spies and compiled long lists of collaborators who would need to be rounded up. As Clark's soldiers entered on June 4, Tompkins also became an unofficial intermediary in the turnover of law enforcement in Rome between the Italian police chief and the city's German commander, who was stinking drunk that day.

Crockett pulled the jeep up to the ornate Grand Hotel Plaza in the city's historical center. The doorman at the front instantly recognized Donovan, and they were ushered to a second-floor suite, where porters brought up pails filled from a nearby fountain for washing because the hotel had no running water. The dining room's waiters served the few customers at tables full-course meals. The soup du jour, the boeuf à la mode, and fruits

249

de saison were all made from black market Army rations the cooks had doc-
tored. Word spread like wildfire that Donovan was in town; Crockett was
sure that all manner of enemy agents had quickly booked rooms around
their suite to plant listening devices in the walls, floors, and ceilings, so
Donovan conducted all his sensitive business in the street outside. "Italy is
the cesspool of intelligence," he told Crockett. But Donovan was there to
clean up his own dirty pond.

His operation in Italy was a mess. Glavin and Putzell launched an intensive probe of all the intelligence activities the OSS had in the country. Donovan assigned Crockett to look into the compromise of the Vittoria station
in Rome. They came back with a long list of problems. The men running
Donovan's Italian operations were enthusiastic but amateurish, his advisers told him. He had three separate intelligence programs underway in
the country: some seventy Italian and Sicilian Americans Max Corvo and
Vincent Scamporino first brought to Algiers who were now at Brindisi in
southern Italy, the OSS intelligence detachment assigned to Clark's 5th
Army further north at Caserta, and a group of OSS special operations
commandos in Corsica who were organizing partisans in northern Italy.
The three worked independently, at times they feuded with one another,
and generally they created bureaucratic chaos in the field, Glavin found.
A lot of the military intelligence Corvo's outfit at Brindisi collected was
vague. The political intelligence the OSS outposts in Palermo and Naples
gathered was worthless. Money was being wasted. Some OSS officers were
even pocketing cash on the side, speculating on fluctuating exchange rates
among the Italian lira, the Algerian franc, and the U.S. dollar.

In Rome, Donovan had two competing and overlapping operations—
Menicanti's and Tompkins's—with each man insisting that he was the head
of the city's clandestine operations and no one at headquarters settling the
dispute. Crockett reported that Menicanti was a "very rough, ruthless gangster type." Tompkins, he concluded, was courageous and sincere, but the
young man was in way over his head and "did a very sloppy job of security."
Counterintelligence officers sifting through the Vittoria station wreckage
concluded that the Germans knew about Tompkins before he even arrived
in Rome and by March they had a good read on his activities in the city.
The ridiculous-looking beard he grew as a disguise instead made him stand
out in the capital city, they decided, and made it easier for the Gestapo to
track him. "It seems quite probable," the OSS security men theorized in a

later report, that the Germans let Tompkins roam freely so they could follow him and gather up the Italians he recruited as agents. By early spring, the Germans, in fact, had convinced four of the snitches they captured by following Tompkins to work for them as double agents. The most important turncoat in Tompkins's network turned out to be Franco Malfatti, the Socialist Party's military intelligence officer, who "betrayed OSS to the SD," the security officers reported.

The British were angry over what they considered a slipshod OSS operation in Italy. Even reputable Italian politicians complained to Donovan that "any scoundrel" in their country could get the ear of an OSS officer and sell him worthless information or a shady spy mission. Personnel problems had grown acute for the entire U.S. Army in Italy, with poorly trained replacements arriving from stateside, almost mutinous morale among weary front-line troops, and an alarming number of desertions or GIs shooting themselves in the foot to escape combat. Even so, the OSS operational breakdowns and security lapses in Italy had become a black eye for the agency. "Our Italian intelligence units have given me cause for anxiety," Donovan admitted in one cable to Glavin. He blamed his troubles on the Italian Americans Corvo had recruited. He thought they were mostly unreliable and addicted to political intrigue. Corvo thought Donovan and other snobby WASPs in the OSS were prejudiced against Italian Americans. But Donovan was as much at fault for the mess. The jumbled OSS organization in the country, after all, was his creation.

By April the problems had begun to leak into the press. The *New York Post* speculated that FDR was unhappy "with our intelligence work in the Italian theater" and "Bill Donovan's OSS may soon be on their way out." Roosevelt was not actually paying attention to the OSS in Italy, but a senior U.S. Army officer was: General Jacob Devers, whose G-2 Donovan had threatened to throw out of a window the year before. Now the deputy supreme allied commander for the Mediterranean, Devers was convinced the OSS had wasted millions of tax dollars in Italy. He demanded "a thorough accounting" of everything Donovan had spent there. What's more, Devers intended to send his inspector general to the OSS to examine its ledgers and in the future he wanted Donovan to get his approval for every nickel the OSS spent in Italy.

Mark Clark thought Devers was "a dope" and Donovan was now inclined to agree. Donovan was accountable to the president of the United

States, to the Joint Chiefs of Staff, and to the U.S. Congress; opening his books to any other military outsider with a beef would mean baring complex financial arrangements for covert activities, exposing sensitive operations, revealing the names of undercover agents. No spy organization could operate under those conditions. Donovan politely but firmly refused to let Devers have a peek at his accounts. The general soon backed off.

Donovan instead did his own housecleaning in Italy. In addition to making Glavin the head of all Italian operations he brought in two other Army officers: Lieutenant Colonel William Suhling, to be Glavin's deputy for special operations, and Colonel Thomas Early as his executive officer. Glavin, whom Donovan knew from the officer's connections in New York Republican circles, eventually turned out to be a weak administrator as well, but at the outset he sent half of the intelligence officers in Italy home. He banned political activity among the ones who remained and tightened security and the vetting of agents. Donovan also had an audit team come in to police the Italian finances. Tompkins, who wanted to stay in the field as a spy, fought to defend his record in Rome, pointing to the valuable intelligence he provided Clark during the Anzio offensive. But Donovan decided he had become a liability and ordered him home. Tompkins was a courageous and brilliant young man, but the Germans had a full dossier on him, which made it impossible for him to maintain a cover in the field, Donovan knew. Moreover, Donovan wrote his deputy Ned Buxton, lives were lost "as a result of his inexperience and poor handling of people." Angry Italians might kill him if he remained.

Donovan's reforms improved his agency's performance in Italy. As Clark's army ground slowly forward the OSS dropped seventy-five commando teams and two thousand tons of arms, food, and equipment into northern Italy, whose partisan force grew to 85,000. By February 1945, Kesselring warned his generals that guerrilla attacks in the north had "spread like lightning." He ordered brutal reprisals. But the partisans eventually succeeded in taking forty thousand enemy prisoners, killing or wounding thousands more, and liberating over a hundred cities and towns, including Genoa, Milan, Venice, and Turin. In another operation launched shortly after Donovan left Rome, OSS agents recruited disaffected German soldiers from POW camps and slipped them behind enemy lines in their Wehrmacht uniforms to plant subversive propaganda, gather intelligence, and mingle with their old comrades to gauge morale. "Sauerkraut," the code name for the operation, was legally questionable—the Geneva Convention prohibited using war prisoners as spies—but the higher command looked the other way. Striking up conversations with German soldiers, the infiltrators detected subtle signs of deteriorating morale: complaints growing about no mail coming from home and cigarette rations being cut. Soon the infiltrations got under Kesselring's skin. At one point he was forced to deny authorship of a phony proclamation Sauerkraut agents spread among his troops with his forged signature, which denounced "Hitler's policy of destroying the German Wehrmacht for the sake of the party."

AS HE SHOOK UP his operation in Rome, Donovan was also cleaning house in another country: Turkey. There had been such high hopes that Packy Macfarland would tunnel critical intelligence pipelines into Bulgaria, Hungary, Austria, and even Germany. But problems with his Istanbul station had begun to pile up. The Pentagon complained about the quality of the intelligence coming out of Turkey. The reports from Alfred Schwarz's Dogwood chain, which Archie Coleman oversaw, were "regarded as erratic— sometimes extraordinarily good, often extraordinarily poor," a memo warned Putzell, who had Donovan's ear. Nearly two thirds of the intelligence reports sent by the Rose chain, which was led by Donovan's New York friend A. V. Walker, were not even delivered to the military because OSS headquarters considered them worthless. By early 1944, Donovan and his senior advisers also became increasingly suspicious that covert projects such as Sparrow to separate Hungary from the Axis and the Hermann Plan to topple Hitler had been the victims of more than just bad luck.

Packy Macfarland was loved by everyone in Istanbul, but respected by no one. Visitors such as John Toulmin, the top OSS Middle East officer in Cairo, found him appallingly lackadaisical in running his operations, "and very slow to realize that the intelligence received from his two chains is practically valueless," Toulmin wrote Donovan. The American ambassador in Turkey considered Macfarland incompetent. The embassy's naval attaché refused to work with him. British special operations officers in Istanbul cabled London in February 1944 that the security problems they saw with Macfarland's station had become "alarming." London relayed that warning to Donovan through back channels. A month later, Donovan asked his X-2 counterintelligence branch for a report on anything they had on the Abwehr tracking OSS agents in Turkey. Their answer hardly calmed his nerves. The X-2 men thought the Germans knew little about the OSS operations, but they had to admit this was only a guess; Donovan's counterintelligence team hadn't even set up an office in Istanbul until January and had not vetted any of Macfarland's foreign agents.

Macfarland could be glaringly cavalier about security. Turkish intelligence officers finally informed him that two of his chauffeurs worked for the Russian secret service. When Hildegarde Reilly, the Germans' most successful female agent in Istanbul, struck up a friendship with one of Macfarland's men, Macfarland ordered the OSS officer to continue seeing her, naively believing he could glean information on the Germans. Macfarland's man proved no match for Hildegarde, who weaseled far more intelligence out of him about OSS employees in the station and their activities. By May 1944 the British services in Istanbul decided to cut back their dealings with the OSS station until Macfarland's men could demonstrate they were "actually serious and organized to do the job." Donovan and his top intelligence officers were stunned when they learned of the demarche.

Donovan sent Toulmin and counterintelligence investigators to Istanbul to assess the damage. The biggest problem, they reported back, was Alfred Schwarz's Dogwood chain and its more than two dozen flower-named agents. "It was completely infiltrated by the Germans," Toulmin concluded. The Abwehr, Gestapo, and SD had complete dossiers on the Czech engineer and closely watched the Western Electrik office, his front company. Double agents in the chain not only spied for the enemy, they also fed Nazi propaganda and disinformation to Schwarz.

Macfarland supervised this most important chain in his operation like an absentee landlord. He rarely talked to Dogwood. Instead, Macfarland delegated that job largely to Archie Coleman and his assistant, Lansing Williams, who both found Schwarz nearly impossible to manage. Strong-willed, egocentric, and domineering, the Czech "fancied himself to be a practicing psychologist and had the utmost confidence in his ability to make friends and influence people," one investigator reported to Donovan. "He was interested in grandiose political schemes involving individuals only in high echelon." Coleman complained that Schwarz was "an egomaniac," with a "big-shot-dreams-of-glory complex." He also brooked no interference in his intelligence operation, flying into a rage and threatening to quit every time Coleman or Williams tried to supervise him or question his authority.

Schwarz got his way. Because his chain produced the largest volume of reports for the Istanbul station, "it was impossible to call the Dogwood bluff and he knew it," one secret postmortem report concluded. His operation became "almost entirely independent." All intelligence from Central Europe came through the Dogwood network. Schwarz insisted that he was the only one who could talk to his agents. He dictated and edited each of their reports, which came to Coleman and Macfarland identified only as from a "sub-source." Donovan's investigators found "evidence that Dogwood colored intelligence he received to conform to his own ideas," as one report stated. "There is evidence that he withheld material from us for personal and, perhaps, less obvious reasons" and concocted phony reports that he attributed to his agents, which were "subsequently found inaccurate."

Of the twenty-eight original flower operatives in Dogwood's chain, only five were now deemed credible enough to keep on the payroll, Donovan's investigators decided. The network was riddled with double agents. Andor Gross, the smuggler code-named Trillium who was Schwarz's courier for contacts with Hungarian Lieutenant Colonel Otto von Hatz, was a Nazi informer, the counterintelligence team concluded. So was Iris, the code name for Friedrich Laufer, another intermediary with the Hungarian General Staff. Iris reported to the Gestapo in Budapest. Hatz as well kept the Nazis posted on Donovan's infiltration of Florimund Duke into Budapest and his plot to entice the Hungarian regime to part with the Axis.

Incredibly, Dogwood knew that many of his spies were double agents. But he believed that he still commanded their loyalty and that they paid only lip service to their Nazi employers. It proved hardly the case. Donovan's investigators concluded that Nazi informers in Dogwood's chain betrayed the Sparrow mission, the Hermann Plan, and other operations. Virtually all the agents the Istanbul station developed in Central Europe ended up killed (like Moltke) or arrested (like Duke's team).

Some of Donovan's counterintelligence officers suspected that even Schwarz was a double agent the Nazis planted to feed the OSS "worthless intelligence" and render "our Central European operations ineffective," as one top secret report theorized. Others disagreed. Dogwood, they argued, was an arrogant and garrulous fool who meant well but ended up unwittingly being a tool of the Nazis. Either way, Donovan's men realized the Czech agent was part of a larger failure. The Istanbul "organization we set up to handle Central European intelligence was unwisely conceived, badly staffed, and directed in the first instance by mediocrities," admitted one confidential report that landed on Donovan's desk. Moreover, "this organization was given a free hand with no direction" from anyone above. The report did not name the guilty at the top, but it had to include Donovan.

By late June 1944, Donovan had moved to shut down Macfarland's network, much of which had already collapsed. Packy was sent home. Schwarz was fired. To rescue what he could from the wreckage in Istanbul, Donovan brought in a four-man team, headed by Frank Wisner, a thirty-five-year-old Mississippian and former Wall Street lawyer who spoke with a Southern drawl and had a level head. But Wisner found little he could salvage. "All our Central European eggs had been placed in the Dogwood basket," a confidential memo glumly told Donovan. In Turkey, the OSS now had to start all over from scratch.

BEFORE HE LEFT ROME, Donovan paid a visit to the Vatican to huddle with Pope Pius XII. Donovan had devoted a lot of time to cultivating and encouraging spying by the Catholic Church. Vincent had vetted priests for him who might be useful as agents. The apostolic delegate Cardinal Spellman had introduced to Donovan three years earlier dropped by his office frequently with political reports papal envoys filed from foreign posts where Donovan had no agents, such as in Tokyo. Donovan also had another Catholic intelligence network he kept hidden from the apostolic delegate and all but a few of his trusted advisers. It was known as the "Pro Deo" project and it was run for him by Father Felix Morlion, whose code name became "Blackie."

Morlion was a Belgian Dominican priest Vincent had known who had run a press and propaganda service since the 1930s in Breda, Holland, and Brussels with Catholic correspondents scattered around Europe feeding him reports that he distributed in two dozen countries on the continent. The uncensored stories Morlion's correspondents smuggled out of Germany particularly irritated Goebbels and the Gestapo. When the Germans overran Europe, Morlion relocated his service to Lisbon in July 1940 and continued to print his anti-Nazi and anticommunist news stories for what he now called the Pro Deo Movement. But fearing the Germans would also invade Portugal, Morlion moved once more, this time to New York City in September 1941 with the help of Donovan and Dulles. He set up the Center of Information Pro Deo and soon had his presses rolling with reports from Europe. But Morlion's network of Pro Deo correspondents around Europe also became a private intelligence service for Donovan.

By April 1944, he was secretly paying Blackie almost $2,000 a month to help maintain his New York office as well as bureaus overseas. In return, Morlion funneled to him cables his European correspondents filed, which became known as the Black Reports. Many of the files, which were written by reporters instead of trained spies, were too general or opinionated or had too many errors to be of use. But other Black Reports contained intelligence Donovan's analysts deemed valuable on the mood and thinking of Catholics in Germany and other countries. One file analyzed the "fate of the Catholic Church in Russia." Another, which Donovan relayed to Roosevelt, gauged "German Catholic resistance to the Nazis." Pro Deo, one classified OSS memo concluded, "is one of the few sources from which an approximation may be made of what the common man and woman are thinking."

Donovan ordered that the Black Reports be sent to him and only to a select few in his organization, not because the information in them was so secret, but because of the danger Morlion's correspondents faced if it became known they were working for an American intelligence service. The reporters, who were given code names like "Hank Judah," were never told their cables also ended up in the hands of the OSS.

Donovan soon had bigger plans for Morlion. Within four months he would have Blackie planted in the Holy See and feeding him Vatican gossip on the man in whose private chamber he now sat: Pope Pius XII.

Pius had been one of the war's most cunning fence straddlers. The Allies seethed at his silence over German atrocities and his willingness to have a Japanese embassy in the Vatican. A racist, the pontiff asked the Allies not to have black soldiers posted in Rome. (The Allies ignored the request when they entered the city.) After Axis soldiers were expelled from North Africa in May of 1943, Hanfstaengl reported to Donovan that Pius felt the wind shift and became more critical of fascism and National Socialism in his speeches, which Putzi knew would irritate Hitler. Donovan also knew that Pius so far had refused to authorize priests to serve as chaplains with the northern Italian partisans; the pope thought the bands were infested with anticlerical communists and discounted their strength. He reversed himself later in 1944 when he realized the guerrillas had clout.

But Donovan told friends he liked Pius "immensely as a person." He did not mind Tokyo having a delegation in the Vatican as long as the pontiff's emissaries continued to feed him tidbits on what they picked up from Japanese ambassador Ken Harada and his underlings. But after the two men settled into their chairs and the pope's aides had left the room, Donovan told Pius that espionage agents hidden in Harada's diplomatic mission soon planned to install a radio transmitter in their office to beam intelligence back to Japan. Pius promised to shut it down.

The pope and the spymaster chatted about American politics. Pius let Donovan know that he was pulling for Roosevelt's reelection. He told Donovan to send FDR "all my heart's affection." Donovan said he would. The Catholic Church had become a trusted and valuable ally in his secret war against the Nazis.

Chapter 25

The Plot

D ONOVAN WAS FINISHING dinner in his Georgetown home the night of July 20 with Lieutenant Colonel Hsiao Po and his wife when a servant whispered into his ear that he had a phone call from his office. Hsiao was Chiang Kai-shek's military attaché as well as Tai Li's Washington representative for the Sino-American Cooperative Organization. Though Donovan had traded threats with Tai during his Chungking visit, he remained on cordial terms with Hsiao and occasionally had him for dinner.

Donovan excused himself from the table and took the call in another room. The message center was on the line to relay a report Dulles had just delivered by radio-telephone. The Bern station chief was intentionally vague and cryptic. He knew both the Swiss and the Germans listened in on all his calls. There had been "an attempt on Hitler's life" that day, Dulles told Donovan. "I presume you all have the news we have on this. We haven't very much except the names of the various generals and admirals who were wounded." But Hitler survived the attack, Dulles said. "The man seems to have a charmed life."

The next morning Dulles began sending Donovan lengthier coded cables with all the details he had so far been able to piece together on Valkyrie, the name given for the plot to remove Hitler. Some of the German generals who were in on the conspiracy had been at Hitler's Wolf's Lair headquarters near Rastenburg in East Prussia "when the bomb went off because the only chance for planting the bomb was in conjunction with a conference attended by many of the chief military leaders," Dulles cabled

Donovan. Even though Hitler survived the blast, Dulles believed the conspirators could still have carried out the coup, but "one of the disheartening facts seems to be that the participants in the revolt did not have adequate radio facilities at their command" to mobilize the Home Army against the Nazi regime. Dulles had dossiers on most of the senior officers who were part of the conspiracy. "Various members of the Canaris organization were also giving their assistance," he wrote Donovan. But he did not have much on the obscure colonel who actually planted the bomb, Claus Schenk von Stauffenberg. He checked his files and discovered Stauffenberg's name on an earlier list of dissident officers, "but at that time we did not realize the part he would play," Dulles wrote.

Stauffenberg, in fact, had become the engine behind the assassination plot. A Catholic aristocrat who had lost his left eye and right hand in the Tunisia campaign, he had become deeply disillusioned with the war and had joined the conspirators. Now as chief of staff for the Replacement Army, which trained soldiers for the front, he had been under orders to report to Hitler personally at Wolf's Lair. Stauffenberg had entered the wooden hut where the noon meeting was held and placed a briefcase containing a small bomb under the heavy oak conference table as near as he could to the führer. He then had excused himself and watched from a nearby knoll when the explosion nearly demolished the hut. Stauffenberg had immediately flown to Berlin to help organize the coup against the remaining Nazi leadership, certain that Hitler had been killed. Four officers did die in the room and most of the others had been severely injured, but Stauffenberg's briefcase had been pushed from one side of the heavy oak table to the other, shielding Hitler from the brunt of the blast. He had escaped with only bruises, wooden splinters all over his body, and a concussion.

Although Stauffenberg's heavy involvement surprised Donovan, the Valkyrie plot itself did not. Dulles, who had given the conspirators the code name "Breakers," had kept Donovan fully informed of almost every move they had made the past six months. In January 1944, Hans Gisevius and Eduard Waetjen, Canaris's emissaries from his Abwehr station in Zurich and two of Dulles's best informants, had quietly approached him about the coup plotters. The Breakers conspirators, they told Dulles, were heavyweights in military and government circles. They included: General Ludwig Beck, the former chief of the German General Staff, who resigned in 1938; Carl Friedrich Goerdeler, the former mayor of Leipzig, who was prepared to be chancellor of a new government; Brigadier General Hans Oster, Canaris's former deputy, who had been arrested by the Gestapo in 1943 for helping rescue Jews and later released; and Colonel General Franz Halder, head of the army General Staff until 1942, when Hitler dismissed him in a dispute over strategy for the Eastern Front.

The peace plan the Breakers group offered was almost a carbon copy of the one Helmuth von Moltke had brought to Istanbul a month earlier. All negotiations would be with the Western powers, not the Soviets. The Breakers group would topple Hitler, allow the Americans and British to sweep through the west and three Allied parachute divisions to drop into Berlin, while the Wehrmacht shifted its force east to defend against the Russians. Donovan immediately suspected that some of the Breakers members had been in Moltke's Kreisau Circle. They were offering an anti-Russian peace proposal as diplomatically unworkable as the count's Hermann Plan had been.

But by April, Gisevius and Waetjen returned with news that the Breakers conspirators were ready to "to take steps to oust the Nazis and eliminate Hitler." Breakers was the only group "with personal access to Hitler," the emissaries said, "and with enough power in the army to make a coup feasible." A month later, Gisevius and Waetjen came back with the names of senior active duty officers who had joined the conspiracy. They included General Alexander von Falkenhausen, head of the military government of Belgium, and General Friedrich Olbricht, deputy commander of the Replacement Army. Dulles, however, told Gisevius and Waetjen that the United States and Great Britain would never negotiate with the plotters unless the Soviets were in on the talks. Dulles was skeptical Breakers could pull off the coup. Even if they succeeded, Donovan told him he did not want Breakers replacing a Nazi regime with a military junta just as odious. The Gestapo also had to be aware of what these conspirators were up to, Dulles thought.

With the Americans unwilling to exclude the Soviets, the Breakers group decided to move on its own. In early July, Dulles alerted Donovan that a courier from the conspirators had arrived in Bern with news that the strength of Breakers continued to grow. Colonel General Fritz Fromm, the commander of the Replacement Army and Stauffenberg's superior, had joined the cabal as had Wolf-Heinrich Graf von Helldorf, the Berlin police chief and a longtime Nazi. Donovan sent the update to Roosevelt. If the courier is to be believed, Dulles cabled Donovan on July 12, "there is a possibility that a dramatic event may take place" in Germany within the next few weeks.

The courier's message was the last report Dulles received from Breakers. Gisevius returned to Berlin to be with the coup plotters. Waetjen remained in Switzerland to serve as the Breakers' link with the outside world.

The day after the failed assassination, Dulles hunted for any bits of intelligence he could find for what happened. He noticed that photos in a German newspaper of Hitler with Mussolini after the attack showed the führer offering his left hand to Il Duce to shake. It "may indicate that Hitler's right hand has been wounded," Dulles cabled Donovan. Likewise, the carefully staged photo shows "only the left side of Hitler's face," Dulles noted. "Possibly the right side of the face is wounded." Donovan forwarded everything his Bern agent turned up to Hull, Marshall, and Roosevelt. Dulles meanwhile looked for a way to evacuate his mole in the Breakers group. When he learned that the coup had failed and Stauffenberg and other plotters had been arrested and executed at Bendlerblock military headquarters that same night, Gisevius had fled to a Berlin suburb. He hid out for six months until the OSS could sneak to him phony travel documents to make his way back to Switzerland, his nerves shattered from the experience.

With news coming out of Germany slowly, Dulles admitted he did not yet have a "very clear picture," but it seemed to him that the conspirators may have launched their plot prematurely because Hitler was about to award Himmler new powers over the government, he told Donovan. Dulles also suspected the Gestapo knew of the impending coup by the first week of July. "Naturally, the blood purge will be unmerciful," he now predicted, but the rebellion may not have been "put down at once." The crucial question was whether the Home Army would "follow Himmler as their chief or whether they will stick to their old commanders, some of whom appear to be involved in the plot." If the outcome of the conspiracy was still up in the air, there were many things the United States could do to nudge it in the right direction, Dulles advised. Roosevelt could issue words of encouragement, the OSS could air-drop leaflets, the Air Force could bomb Nazi strongholds around Hitler's Berchtesgaden retreat or "announce that any German town which sides with the opposition would not be attacked."

Donovan relayed Dulles's suggestion to Roosevelt and Air Force planes dropped leaflets over Germany. But Hitler quickly regained control. Four days after the assassination attempt, Dulles cabled Donovan that "it seems clear now that any prospects of an armed military revolt growing out of the Putsch against Hitler have been crushed." Over the next two months, the Bern chief sent Donovan periodic cables on the net "being pulled tighter around Breakers." Hitler eventually executed nearly five thousand.

Donovan took a particular interest in one Breakers casualty—Wilhelm Canaris, the man with whom he had played a cat-and-mouse game the past three years. The Abwehr chief, whom Hitler fired in February 1944 for intelligence failures, had not been personally involved in the plot, but he knew of its preparations and the Gestapo soon discovered Canaris aides who were conspirators. Canaris was arrested on July 23 and eventually taken to the Flossenbürg concentration camp, where he was brutally tortured then hanged on April 9, 1945. Treating Canaris as if he had been an American collaborator, Donovan tracked down his wife, Erika, after the war and dispatched an OSS officer to help her settle her personal affairs. He also asked her to write him a long letter about her husband so he could gain a better sense of the man who had been his opposite. Erika complied. "My husband's chief aim," she wrote Donovan, "was to get good intelligence from abroad in order to try to convince the powers that be" that Hitler had embarked on a "mad adventure."

Walter Langer, William Langer's brother and the top psychologist on Donovan's staff, sent him a memo speculating that Hitler may have "staged" the assassination attempt to demonstrate he was invincible and lift German morale. That was not the case. Johanna Wolf, the führer's personal secretary, told U.S. Army interrogators after the war that "July 20 left Hitler a broken man." Dulles predicted to Donovan that Breakers would "undermine the will of the German Army to keep up the struggle." More coup conspiracies would emerge. William Langer's research analysts, however, produced a twenty-six-page study seven days after the assassination attempt, which forecast accurately that the Nazis would use the plot to clean up the few dissidents remaining while the party's grip on the army would tighten even more. Tragically, William Langer's experts warned, "the collapse of Germany may be retarded" because of Breakers.

Though Donovan at the outset had been excited about Breakers' potential, he came to the conclusion that it was a clumsy, rushed job—bound to fail. Eight days after the assassination attempt he put OSS coup plotting into lockdown. He ordered his men not to share any of the Breakers material with the Soviets, knowing it would just stoke their suspicions that the Americans were plotting behind their backs. For the moment he decided it was best for his agency not to become entangled in any more of these conspiracies. "If the Germans battle it out inside Germany without help from us," he cabled David Bruce in London, "it will be of more benefit to humanity."

THE AMERICAN 7th Army under the command of General Alexander Patch had landed at France's Mediterranean coast between Nice and Marseille on August 15, 1944, and facing little enemy resistance quickly moved north. Marshall had insisted on Operation Anvil to link up with Overlord in northern France. Churchill bitterly fought what he considered a militarily worthless invasion; when Eisenhower and Roosevelt overruled him the story went that Churchill had the operation renamed Dragoon because he had been "dragooned" into accepting it. But Anvil-Dragoon was an intelligence triumph for the OSS.

As usual, Donovan showed up for the landing, wading ashore at the beach near Saint-Tropez. He found his OSS officers in a dither because their vehicles and equipment had been deposited at another beach. Donovan listened to their complaints for a few minutes, then cut them off. "Any man who can't get transportation somehow, doesn't belong in this outfit!" he declared. But in the next breath, he said with a smile: "And I'll fire the first man caught stealing a car."

The landing glitch, however, was insignificant compared to what the OSS had accomplished in the preparations for the invasion of southern France. Colonel William Quinn, Patch's senior intelligence officer, was stunned when Donovan and Henry Hyde walked into his office at the 7th Army's Algiers headquarters one day in the spring of 1944 and revealed that in southern France the OSS had twenty-eight agent networks operating, such as the one Rocquefort and Marret ran for the Penny Farthing mission. Quinn knew nothing about the espionage chains or the hundreds of reports they had been radioing back on German troop dispositions and fortifications in territory Patch's army would soon be attacking. The OSS reports were all sent to Patch's higher command at the Allied Forces Headquarters, where they disappeared into a black hole never to be seen by Quinn. Donovan offered to deliver the raw agent reports directly to the

Army colonel, who was eager to get his hands on them. When the Allied Forces Headquarters discovered the end run it dispatched a British briga- dier and two staff officers to Quinn. They huffily ordered him to halt this serious breach of protocol or he would be fired. Quinn threw them out of his office with a string of expletives.

Patch made sure Quinn wasn't fired and his intelligence chief reaped a windfall from Donovan. During the next five months, Hyde's networks delivered him more than eight thousand reports on enemy troop concen- trations, airfields, convoy routes, roadblocks, rail yards, coastal defenses, minefields, beach obstacles, submarine pens, antiaircraft gun emplace- ments, searchlights, and even dummy defenses the Germans built to try to fool Air Force bombers. (Prostitutes servicing German soldiers in Lyon's bordellos gave Rocquefort details on their units from military identifica- tion documents in their customers' pockets.) It all represented half the intelligence Patch's army used for Anvil-Dragoon. "We knew everything about that beach and where every German was," Quinn recalled. "And we clobbered them." The 94,000 soldiers Patch landed the first days suffered fewer than five hundred casualties and captured 57,000 Axis prisoners in the next two weeks.

AFTER THE Anvil-Dragoon landing, Donovan flew back to Rome for a secret meeting with a German diplomat. Hitler had made Baron Ernst von Weizsäcker his ambassador to the Vatican the year before because he wanted a seasoned and loyal diplomat for that important post. Born into German nobility and a naval lieutenant commander in the First World War, Weizsäcker had joined the Nazi Party in 1938 to further his career in the Foreign Office and became friends with Himmler, who awarded him an honorary rank in the SS. At one point helping with diplomatic arrange- ments to deport Slovakian Jews to Auschwitz, Weizsäcker rose to secretary of state under Ribbentrop. At the Vatican he tried to cultivate cardinals with the line that Germany was "a bulwark against communism."

Hugh Wilson, one of Donovan's senior aides, had known Weizsäcker before the war and had arranged a secret meeting with him during a visit to the Vatican earlier in August. For three quarters of an hour behind closed doors, Weizsäcker and Wilson discussed the war. The German public real- izes it is lost, Weizsäcker told Wilson, and now regards the fighting as a race to see which enemy army arrives in Germany first, the Americans and British or the dreaded Russians. "I found him in despair," Wilson later wrote Donovan, "but still unwilling to give full vent to his personal feelings." Wilson could not tell if Weizsäcker was a true dissident or still a loyal Nazi but he suggested to the German envoy that he meet with his "good friend," Bill Donovan, who would be in Rome in ten days. Weizsäcker liked that idea. "He said it would be excellent if there were some American source with whom he could remain in touch," Wilson wrote Donovan. The OSS gave Weizsäcker the code name "Jackpot II."

As de Gaulle triumphantly rode into Paris on August 26, Donovan sat down with the German ambassador at a secret location in the Vatican compound. Weizsäcker had snow-white hair brushed neatly across his high forehead with warm expressive eyes set into a gentle face. Only a small Nazi Party Eagle pin on the lapel of his tailored pinstriped suit indicated he was the enemy. Colonel Joseph Rodrigo, an OSS officer in Rome, had arranged the meeting through Weizsäcker's consul, Albrecht von Kessel, who Rodrigo believed harbored anti-Nazi sentiments. Weizsäcker had told Wilson he knew little about Donovan, which very likely was a lie.

The American spy chief mostly listened as the Nazi envoy launched into a long and somewhat mournful monologue. It had been ages since he had heard from his family, Jackpot II said; he was rarely in radio contact with his own Foreign Office, so he kept up with war news mostly from *Stars and Stripes* and other Allied newspapers that cutouts smuggled to him. Weizsäcker adamantly opposed the partition of Germany into American, British, and Soviet zones after the war, he told Donovan. It was "incomprehensible" to him why Roosevelt "did not want to dicker" with the generals who had previously approached him with peace offers.

Donovan offered Jackpot II nothing more than FDR's terms: unconditional surrender. But he told the German he wanted to set up a back channel to him. Rodrigo, Donovan said, would deal with any intermediary Weizsäcker designated for exchanging messages. He did not know what to make of this ambassador. Weizsäcker certainly did not sound like a Hitler loyalist, Donovan later wrote Roosevelt, but "his own nationalist aspirations for Germany and his long experience as a diplomat make him very useful to the Nazis." Donovan, nevertheless, thought Weizsäcker could be of value to him as an informant or perhaps in helping him infiltrate agents into Germany and Austria.

Peace offers continued to dribble in until the war's end. Nothing ever came of them, and by August, Donovan's interest had shifted from talking peace with the Germans to infiltrating agents into their country.

AFTER HIS MEETING with Weizsäcker, Donovan hopped into his plane and flew back to southern France, where he picked up an energetic thirty-one-year-old OSS officer named William Casey at an airstrip near Lyon. Patch's 7th Army had captured the city in early September and soon would link up with Patton's 3rd Army to form a broad Allied front stretching from Switzerland to Belgium and marching east toward Germany. Before he went to Rome to meet with Weizsäcker, Donovan had flown to Grenoble southwest of Lyon, where the OSS had commandeered a tree-shaded château with a glorious view of the Alps. Over a fine French meal prepared by the house cook and several bottles of excellent Burgundy he had brainstormed with Casey future operations into Germany.

Bill Casey was a lot like his boss, whom he worshipped. Born to a poor Irish Catholic family, fiercely Republican, and a successful lawyer before the war like Donovan, Casey had joined the OSS in the summer of 1943 as a Navy lieutenant eager to see action overseas. He reached London in November of that year. Colleagues found Casey to be genial if a bit rumpled, often hard to understand because he mumbled when he spoke, and a rabid anticommunist. He also had a healthy disdain for bureaucracy and a can-do spirit that impressed Donovan, who soon made him a troubleshooter for European operations.

Casey now boarded Donovan's DC-3 at the Lyon airstrip for the flight back to London. In his briefcase he had a plan for infiltrating OSS agents into Germany. But also climbing aboard the plane with him was an OSS officer with a reputation now as large as Donovan's: Allen Dulles. When Patch's army moved north and broke through the Swiss border near Geneva, Dulles was finally able to liberate himself after more than a year and a half of seclusion in Bern and reunite with Donovan in Lyon.

The slow-flying DC-3 lumbered north along the Loire Valley, which soon made everyone in the cabin nervous except Donovan because Luftwaffe warplanes with the retreating German army still roamed the skies and the transport aircraft had no fighter escort to protect it. Dulles ignored the young OSS officer from London whom he had never before met and began updating Donovan on the latest details he had picked up on the July 20 assassination attempt. Despite Hitler's brutal response, Dulles told Donovan he was still convinced that German opposition to the regime was growing, which the OSS could accelerate. Donovan agreed but then dropped a question Dulles knew would be coming, which he dreaded. "I wonder if the time isn't ripe for penetration en masse?" he asked. "Agent drops from England—the way we infiltrated France." Dulles considered the idea a fool's errand. It was too late to send OSS agents into Germany, he thought, networks have to be organized in an enemy country before a war breaks out. After the fighting starts, a hostile nation locks down. The agents Donovan parachuted into France succeeded because they had the Maquis on the ground to protect them and help them transmit out their reports. Friendly French civilians brought them food and hid them in safe houses. None of that existed in Germany, Dulles knew. Far better, he argued as they flew to London, to recruit Germans already in the country to spy for the OSS, as he had done with agents such as Hans Gisevius and Fritz Kolbe.

Other OSS officers agreed with Dulles. "Germany is a fortress—a besieged fortress," an earlier secret memo from Donovan's intelligence branch warned. OSS operatives sneaking into it will face "a generally hostile population—almost if not entirely mobilized for war and literally linked house by house, if not person by person, to the secret police in one form or another. A pretty formidable picture!" It was one reason Donovan's operation to put his agents into Germany had moved so slowly. Arthur Goldberg, whose Labor Section in London had been largely ignored by Donovan's senior intelligence staff, had begun a makeshift infiltration project, code-named "Faust," in October 1943. Goldberg had been funneling money and equipment to underground labor organizations in Germany and German-occupied territories the past year and a half. By February 1944, he had ten agents in training to penetrate the Fatherland. But his operation moved at a snail's pace. The British showed no interest in infiltrating agents into Germany, a country they also considered too difficult to crack, and soon their secret forces, as well as Donovan's, were preoccupied with the Normandy landings.

But in his briefcase for the plane ride to London, Casey had the Faust Plan, which he, Goldberg, and David Bruce had been polishing and which

Eisenhower's staff had approved two weeks before. Faust now had an ambitious goal: infiltrating at least thirty OSS agents into Germany to collect political and military intelligence and spy on Hitler's espionage organizations. As the DC-3 sped toward London, Dulles tried to smother Faust with evidence he had that a viable underground remained in Germany with agents already in place, which the OSS could exploit.

But Donovan's mind was already made up. The agency must rethink the way it operates, he told Dulles in a loud voice so he could be heard over the engine noise in the cabin. He knew full well that his spies and commandos operating in occupied countries such as France had enjoyed the benefit of resistance groups sustaining them and fighting alongside, and that Germany would be different. "We can no longer count on the presence of friendly forces in the rear of enemy lines to give us a welcome," Donovan said. There will be no civilian population "wishing us well." The agency's covert warriors will have to treat everyone around them as the enemy and "bring all our skill and ingenuity to bear on the problem," he told Dulles.

Donovan envisioned nothing less than a "rebirth" of OSS operations "in their truest sense—that of bold raids and nicely carried out attacks from hideouts, of patrolling by small groups, of destroying industrial installations." He now wanted Dulles to use his Bern station as "a salient" for launching intelligence and subversive teams into Germany and Austria.

Donovan's plane landed in London on Friday evening, September 8, shortly before the Germans' first V-2 ballistic missile slammed into the city, gouging a giant crater in Chiswick that killed three people. Donovan bounded up the stairs to the rooftop of the OSS station hoping to catch a glimpse of any more of Hitler's "vengeance weapons" that might streak by. On previous London visits he had stood on the roof like a curious boy watching the stars as V-1 buzz bombs that were crude cruise missiles rained down on the city.

Dulles returned to Washington to begin drafting plans for infiltrating agents from Switzerland into Germany although he remained pessimistic about Donovan's venture. Before they left Lyon, Donovan had given Dulles another piece of distasteful news. He would not get the job he now craved. Dulles had heard the rumors that Bruce wanted to leave London and he wanted to replace him as chief of the most important station in the OSS empire. But before they boarded the plane, Donovan had pulled Dulles aside and told him no moves would be made. With the war reaching a crucial turning point, this was not the time to change chiefs at two critical stations. "I'm ordering David to stay on, just as I'm asking you to do the same," Donovan told him. "God knows what would happen if we had a change in Bern at this juncture. We just can't afford to lose you."

Although he did not reveal it to Dulles, Donovan always considered Bruce the better station chief of the two, particularly for the wide-ranging operations in Europe. Despite Dulles's intelligence triumphs at Bern, Donovan thought he was a poor administrator, who, unlike Bruce, did not command the loyalty of the people who served under him. Donovan also suspected that Dulles coveted his job, which was true. Dulles thought he was the better leader for the OSS and that Donovan was jealous of what he had accomplished in Bern. Donovan's misgivings about Dulles soon proved justified, however. When the Swiss border opened that fall and OSS staffers poured into Bern for the final push against Germany, Dulles, who thrived as a lone wolf, had trouble managing the ballooning bureaucracy. Donovan became frustrated over the growing disorder he saw in Bern and began scribbling hostile notes on some of Dulles's cables. After the European war ended, he again refused to promote Dulles to the job he wanted. He made him head of the OSS mission in Germany instead of all operations in Europe.

FOR THE ALLIED advance through France, Donovan had OSS detachments with the American armies to feed them intelligence the resistance fighters collected just ahead and to recover the agency's spies who were overrun by the U.S. divisions—although the promise he thought he had from Bradley at the Normandy beach to welcome his men with open arms never panned out. Bradley still balked at having OSS officers assigned to his staff and his senior intelligence aide treated the ones who were grudgingly accepted as if they were Abwehr agents. Even the more congenial Patton, who appreciated Donovan's men organizing guerrillas to guard his southern and western flanks as he swept through France, became irritated at times when Bruce and other OSS officers showed up for what his staff thought were nothing more than sightseeing tours. While the Allied armies marched east, OSS counterintelligence teams also prowled the rear to round up German sabotage agents left behind, some dressed in American uniforms. Many agreed to work for the American side. An Abwehr radioman the OSS nabbed in Verdun began transmitting back to his base phony information Donovan's agents concocted on Allied troop movements. The reports pleased his unwitting German superiors so much they awarded him the Iron Cross.

Donovan was convinced, however, that he needed to step up the infiltration of agents into Germany. Otherwise, he feared, the Allied armies would be blind to what lay ahead as they advanced east. A few days before Christmas, Donovan promoted Casey to be his chief of secret intelligence for the European theater with orders to launch a full-scale invasion of Germany with covert warriors. Casey did just that, over the next six months infiltrating 150 agents into Germany. Anti-Nazi Germans who were physically fit to parachute in but not so young that they would be drafted by the Wehrmacht as soon as they landed were in short supply, so Casey recruited his agents from German-speaking foreign laborers who could blend in, from German and Austrian POWs willing to spy on the Reich, and from German communist refugees (Donovan ordered him to overcome his ideological repugnance and hire them). Casey, however, soon abandoned Donovan's visions of having teams launch commando attacks; what little was left to be destroyed in Germany could be more safely and efficiently flattened by American bombers. Instead, Casey sent in spy teams—the ones collecting intelligence about German military movements were given alcoholic code names, such as "Martini" and "Daiquiri."

Donovan's penetration of Germany had mixed results. The Faust teams managed some successes. Agents who were overrun by the quickly advancing Allied armies alerted commanders to enemy threats ahead. Some operatives rescued war prisoners or convinced local German commanders to quit fighting. Three teams penetrated Gestapo organizations in Munich and Berlin while other agents identified local Nazi chiefs for American soldiers. But the Faust spies ended up delivering only bits and pieces of intelligence. Only about half of Casey's infiltration missions were successful. Because of nagging equipment problems, just seven of the thirty-four intelligence teams that he did safely infiltrate radioed back reports. "I don't think they did very much good," said Richard Helms, a young naval officer who worked on the OSS infiltrations into Germany and who one day would be director of the Central Intelligence Agency. Even Casey, who also would later become a CIA director, conceded the penetrations did nothing to shorten the war. At best, "we probably saved some lives," he said.

After the Wehrmacht surrendered, all but seven of the spies infiltrated into Germany were recovered. Casey expected to lose far more. For many of those who did survive, life behind German lines had been harrowing. Leon Adrian, one of Casey's Polish-born agents in the Martini operation, parachuted into Germany on March 19, 1945, pretending to be a foreign railroad worker. Though he had a limited education, Adrian possessed street smarts and he was a skilled observer of military hardware traveling on trains. But at a rail station at Altenburg in eastern Germany, an official in the military recruiting office noticed a slight discrepancy in Adrian's war service papers and called the police, who arrested him. Adrian managed to tear a drawing he had made of a nearby military airport into small pieces and swallow them before two Gestapo agents arrived. At their station in nearby Halle, the two Gestapo men stripped him and searched every inch of his clothes, then plunged a hypodermic needle into his arm and injected him with a solution to make him throw up. When Adrian refused to drink a second concoction to induce vomiting, they knocked out five of his front teeth with a rifle butt and forced the noxious liquid down his throat. He began to heave violently, but suspecting his stomach still wasn't empty, the agents started rolling two rubber cylindrical pins up and down his body from his knees to his ribs as if he were a lump of dough. Adrian finally threw up everything and with a magnifying glass the agents picked out the bits of paper.

Convinced he was a spy they beat him mercilessly with rubber clubs nearly eight hours a day for the next five days, but Adrian, barely able to remain conscious, never talked. On the morning of the sixth day, when he was sure he would be dragged out of his cell and executed, American B-17s dropped bombs over Halle, one of which blew open the door to his prison cell. His face bruised and bloated and his legs nearly crippled from the beatings, Adrian hobbled out and managed to escape to a nearby forest, where American GIs eventually picked him up on April 15. For the next three weeks, he helped an Army counterintelligence team round up Gestapo men in the region.

As Army officers processed a group of Gestapo prisoners in a room, Adrian spotted the two thugs who had tortured him. He silently sidled up to one of the American guards and pulled the pistol out of the soldier's holster without him realizing it. Adrian walked up to the two Gestapo men, whose faces he would never forget, and calmly fired two bullets into each of them. The Army planned to ship the two brutes along with the other Gestapo officers to a prison camp and they would likely get away with their cruelty, Adrian later told his OSS superiors. Now "they won't beat anyone else."

Chapter 26

The Sideshow

B Y THE SUMMER of 1944, Donovan had built a formidable covert operation in the Balkans. The Allied command estimated that by spring the resistance forces Donovan and the British backed in the region were killing 4,700 Axis soldiers a month. That was likely an overestimate. Churchill and Donovan were never able to set the area ablaze to make life unbearable for Hitler though the resistance movements at least made the Germans bleed and Donovan was proud of what he had accomplished so far. In his Georgetown house he kept a collection of guerrilla weapons to show off to visitors—like the Smatchet, a combination machete and Roman short sword for knife fighting. At dinner parties he read in a loud and dramatic voice for his enthralled tablemates after-action reports filed by OSS commandos. But the war Donovan's men fought in what both the Allies and the Axis considered a strategic sideshow could be brutal and coldhearted, and he agonized over the human loss. For Donovan, fighting in the Balkans also continued to be a political jousting match with his allies.

By November 1944 he had almost sixty OSS agents with Tito, led by one of his most senior aides, Colonel Ellery Huntington, and was pouring arms and propaganda kits into the partisan camps. The leaflets OSS officers prepared for the kits urging Axis troops to desert ended up backfiring; when enemy soldiers arrived with their hands up, the vengeful partisans executed them, which soon convinced the Germans never to surrender. But Ultra intercepted complaints Wehrmacht commanders in Yugoslavia radioed back to Berlin that Tito's fighters appeared to be better clothed and armed because of the OSS supplies. Donovan's buildup made Churchill nervous as well. To add prestige to the British delegation with Tito, Churchill dispatched his son, Randolph, to the partisan headquarters, giving the communist warlord a direct pipeline to the prime minister. The Russians also beefed up their Yugoslav mission, which was now led by two seasoned generals, one whom, N. V. Korneyev, was a confidant of Stalin's. It also soon became clear to Donovan's men that Tito treated the Soviet delegation as the first among equals.

Donovan chuckled when the Chetnik press reported that he had sent his son, David, to Mihailović's headquarters in late February 1944. The story was false. Donovan, to his great annoyance, had no one with Mihailović after he had bowed to Churchill's demands and pulled out his lone OSS officer with the Chetniks that month. Ever since, he had been lobbying the Joint Chiefs and State Department to put his intelligence agents back with Mihailović and use his base for infiltrating into Germany and Austria. Roosevelt finally agreed at the end of March to allow OSS officers to return to the Chetniks as long as they made it clear to Mihailović they were there only to collect intelligence and not to lend him any military or political support. Churchill was furious when he learned Donovan planned to slip his men back into the Chetnik camp. While Donovan trekked to the Pacific to be with MacArthur at the Hollandia landing in early April, Churchill fired off a cable to FDR pleading with him to reverse his decision. "If, at this very time, an American Mission arrives at Mihailović's headquarters, it will show throughout the Balkans a complete and contrariety of action between Britain and the United States." Roosevelt complied and ordered the team not to be sent.

With Mihailović and his Chetniks out of the way, Churchill was intent on dancing alone with the communists in Yugoslavia. His goal: to preserve the country's monarchy by forming a postwar unity government between Tito and the young King Peter exiled in London—with Ivan Šubašić serving as prime minister. Donovan knew exactly what Churchill was up to because Šubašić was his mole among the four men. The project was code-named "Shepherd" and it was a sensitive intelligence operation because it violated the agreement the United States and Great Britain had that they would not spy on each other. Both did, of course, but the Shepherd Project was one of the more blatant breaches of the accord. Šubašić had been the prewar Ban of Croatia. Though exiled in the United States, Donovan's men believed he remained a revered figure among the some five million Croats he once governed, many of whom sympathized with the Allies instead of the pro-Axis Croatian regime that now ruled over them. With the help of Bernard Yarrow, a Russian-born New York lawyer on his staff, Donovan had recruited Šubašić in August 1943 to infiltrate into Yugoslavia to spy on the Germans for the OSS and stir up an anti-Nazi rebellion among the Croats. He had given Šubašić the code name Shepherd and approved $53,000 for his covert operation. Šubašić instead ended up in London, where Churchill browbeat Peter into dumping Mihailović as an ally and accepting the Croation governor as prime minister of his exiled government. But with Yarrow as his handler, Šubašić continued to spy for Donovan, sending him detailed reports, which he relayed to Roosevelt, on the private talks Churchill had with Peter, Tito, and Stalin to form a unity government in Yugoslavia.

Donovan, however, still believed he needed agents with Mihailović and true to his MO he did not intend taking Roosevelt's no as the final answer. While he was untangling his messy Italian operation in June, he paid a visit to Jumbo Wilson, the supreme commander for the Mediterranean theater, and cajoled the amiable British general into agreeing that, despite the objections of Churchill and his Foreign Office, there was really no harm in the OSS sending an intelligence team to Mihailović, particularly if it helped hunt for Allied pilots shot down over Chetnik territory. Donovan passed along Wilson's green light, such as it was, to Roosevelt, who reversed himself once more and approved the OSS team joining Mihailović.

It was a nifty piece of diplomatic maneuvering on the spy chief's part. Even before FDR reauthorized the mission in early August, Donovan had already begun preparations in July for a six-man team to slip into Mihailović's headquarters, headed by Lieutenant Colonel Robert McDowell, who had taught Balkan history before the war as a college professor. Donovan ordered that "Ranger," the code name for the operation, be kept secret at that point from both Tito and Churchill. After FDR changed his mind in early August, Donovan had his aides inform Wilson's Mediterranean command and Fiztroy Maclean, who led the British mission to Tito, that he planned to send his team to the Chetniks.

Donovan decided to tell Tito himself. Five days before the Anvil-Dragoon invasion of southern France, he flew to Caserta, where Tito was visiting Jumbo Wilson. The Yugoslav marshal was settled comfortably in a hunting lodge near Wilson's quarters with his son, a secretary named Olga, an aide, two guards, and an Alsatian dog. Thursday afternoon, August 10, Donovan was ushered into the lodge's sitting room. He had brought with him Maclean, in a display of British-American unity, and Huntington, to introduce him to the marshal as the new chief of the American mission at his headquarters. Tito received the delegation alone, except for the large hound sleeping at his feet.

The OSS was interested only in fighting the Germans, Donovan told the partisan commander, reminding him that "a large percentage of the supplies" he now received from the Allies came from the Americans and more was on the way. Tito nodded. He was aware of that fact, he said. The OSS mission also "is purely military in character," Donovan told him. "It is to serve no political ends. We are neither making nor requesting political or territorial commitments of any kind." Tito nodded again, although he knew the OSS arms certainly served his political aims. Donovan nevertheless insisted that his agency would work with any faction "which can aid us in our struggle against the enemy." That included the Chetniks, although Donovan decided to wait and break that news to Tito over a sumptuous lunch the next day at Mona Williams's luxury home on Capri.

The Friday lunch at Villa Fortino lasted more than three hours. After the war, Williams sent Donovan a bill for all the furniture that had been damaged by OSS officers on R&R there and the silver that was missing from the estate. The long list also included the bottles of vintage wine in her cellar that had been drained. Donovan and Tito decided to take their coffee on the terrace. Maclean, Olga, and the Alsatian joined them. As they sipped and enjoyed the view, Donovan finally broached the Mihailović mission. McDowell's team would be going in only to collect intelligence. Donovan already had a small team, code-named "Halyard," near Belgrade, where Mihailović had delivered more than 250 Allied airmen shot down over Chetnik territory and he planned to keep his officers there to receive more pilots, he told Tito. "In no sense of the word" would the Ranger or Halyard missions provide the Chetnik leader arms or political support, he assured the marshal.

To Donovan's surprise, Tito did not appear angry. He nodded once more and simply warned Donovan that McDowell's stay with Mihailović "might not be too pleasant." Donovan should give him the names of the Halyard and Ranger team members so his partisans don't accidentally shoot the OSS officers if they run into them with the Chetniks, the marshal said.

But although he did not let his true feelings show on the terrace, Tito was annoyed with the news. Fighting between the communist partisans and the Chetniks had intensified lately and for Tito the civil war had become personal. Not only was Mihailović collaborating with the enemy, Donovan also knew that Tito was convinced the Chetnik chief had fed the Nazis information to try to have him assassinated three months earlier. There was also no doubt in Tito's mind as they finished their coffee on the terrace that Mihailović would consider the McDowell mission proof the Americans backed him instead of the communists and that he would try to manipulate the team for his own political advantage. As Donovan and the marshal got up to put on their bathing suits for a swim in Villa Fortino's pool, the long tail of the happy Alsatian swept over the small tea table in front of them, sending the expensive china cups and saucers crashing to the ground. Mona Williams would add them to the bill.

McDowell's Ranger team parachuted into Mihailović's camp on August 26. Tito's wariness quickly proved warranted. Though McDowell had dutifully told Mihailović that Ranger was there only to collect intelligence, Draža released a propaganda leaflet written in Serbo-Croatian proclaiming that the lieutenant colonel had come as Roosevelt's personal representative with an endorsement letter from the president clearly demonstrating U.S. support for the "freedom loving" Chetniks. Tito was furious when he read the flyer. He stopped cooperating with the American and British missions at his headquarters and slapped travel restrictions on OSS officers in his domain. He also demanded that the McDowell mission be removed.

Churchill, who had been fuming ever since the Ranger team parachuted in, was also outraged. On September 1, he sent a testy cable to Roosevelt. He had worked hard cultivating Tito to form a pro-British alliance with King Peter and Šubašić. After their April exchange of messages he thought Roosevelt had agreed not to send the OSS mission to Mihailović, he wrote FDR. But lo and behold, he now discovered that Donovan has a team with the Chetnik warlord, which meant "complete chaos will ensue," Churchill complained. "I was rather hoping things were going to get a bit smoother in these parts, but if we each back different sides we lay the scene for a fine civil war. General Donovan is running a strong Mihailović lobby, just when we have persuaded King Peter to break decisively with him."

Like a boy taken to the woodshed, Roosevelt cabled back: "The mission of OSS is my mistake. I did not check with my previous action of last April 8th. I am directing Donovan to withdraw his mission."

Donovan was livid when he learned that Roosevelt had yanked his chain once more. He protested as diplomatically as he could. "I am happy to accept, at your hands, repudiation of any act of mine when you think it may be necessary," he wrote the president. "It is not my function to make policy decisions." But nearly sixty more airmen had come out of Yugoslavia by the first week of September, bringing the total number retrieved by the Halyard operation to over three hundred. Ranger had collected valuable intelligence on German divisions in Chetnik territory and fielded peace offers from Nazi representatives in Yugoslavia. Donovan hated abandoning either operation when they had so much more to accomplish. But Roosevelt would not change his mind again. The Ranger and Halyard missions were pulled out in early November.

Donovan ordered his men with Tito to make no apologies over the two missions to Mihailović. "It is important for us not to be stampeded or bluffed or intimidated," he told Huntington. The marshal had acted boorishly, Donovan thought, likely because the communist chief knew he had the civil war under control. By the end of September 1944, Mihailović's army had begun disintegrating, with thousands of Serbs once loyal to him joining the partisans. (Tito's men later rounded up the Chetnik leader and his loyalists, executing Mihailović and throwing the others into prison after hasty trials.) Tito would not need British and American help much longer. Churchill's vision of Yugoslavia becoming both a British and a Soviet sphere of influence proved to be an illusion. Negotiations to restore Peter to the throne with Šubašić as his prime minister and Tito his military commander collapsed. Yugoslavia would belong to Tito as a communist and somewhat nonaligned state. The OSS passed along to Roosevelt Tito's wishes for a happy New Year in 1945, but the marshal did not remain long in the holiday spirit. By early October 1944 he had invited the Red Army in to "liberate" Yugoslavia. Huntington cabled Donovan on November 3 that a convoy of Soviet troops, most riding in American-made vehicles, was approaching Belgrade, the nearby villages welcoming them with "triumphal arches." The OSS brought in ten tons of medical supplies for the partisans and retrieved another hundred airmen by the beginning of 1945, but their relations with the new Yugoslav regime became more strained as Tito imposed further travel restrictions to keep the American agents from roaming the country and spying.

On May 11, 1945, Arso Jovanović, Tito's chief of staff, finally summoned an OSS officer and a British special operations representative to his Belgrade office and curtly told them their teams must leave the country. The OSS man reminded Jovanović of all the help the Americans and British had given the partisans. "We would have won the war with or without your support," Jovanović told them haughtily. "The materials you provided were our right to receive."

Donovan believed Churchill deserved no apology either over the OSS missions to Mihailović. Yugoslavia had caused a serious rift between the two men. But it was not the only country in the region where they clashed.

WHILE CHURCHILL TRIED to work with the communists in Yugoslavia he was fighting them in Greece. The prime minister, who wanted to restore the Greek monarchy, had become increasingly irritated with Donovan's OSS aiding the royalists' enemy, the leftist National Liberation Front and its People's Liberation Army, known as the ELAS. Reflecting Roosevelt's view, not to mention American pubic opinion, Donovan cared little about propping up Greece's King George II and had sent his men to aid ELAS because their communist-led guerrillas, not the royalists, were doing most of the fighting against the Germans. The tension between Donovan and Churchill, however, reached a boiling point when the August 19, 1944, edition of the *Washington Post* hit the stands.

Drew Pearson was the richest journalist in the United States, with more pipelines in Washington, so the joke went, than Standard Oil. The U.S. military looked for ways to block Pearson's sources in the Pentagon but failed. Roosevelt detested Pearson and had once called him a liar. So did Churchill, who considered the newsman a bitter enemy of the United Kingdom after he published an article critical of British rule in India. Citing "uncensored diplomatic reports" as sources for his August 19 "Washington Merry-Go-Round" column in the *Post*, Pearson delivered a blistering attack against Churchill, who "insists on keeping King George of Greece on the throne, despite the opposition of a great majority of the Greek people." While brave Americans were fighting the Nazis, Pearson charged, Churchill was conniving to save the British Empire and keep a royal crony in power. When aides showed the prime minister the column he flew into a rage. Churchill immediately suspected that Donovan, who shared Pearson's contempt for British policy toward Greece, had planted the hostile story.

Churchill had no proof, but reason to be suspicious. Pearson had written snide columns about the OSS, calling it the "Oh, so social" organization, and Donovan suspected he had a plant in his agency slipping him sensitive material, but Donovan also had his own pipeline to the columnist. Ernest Cuneo, Donovan's liaison officer with the Roosevelt administration and the British, was a Pearson pal who regularly fed him scoops. When Donald Downes returned to Washington the year before, he told Cuneo the story circulating in Italy that Patton had slapped two soldiers in evacuation hospitals who were suffering from shell shock. Cuneo sent Downes to Pearson with the story, which he published later in November 1943, sparking a political firestorm for Patton as well as for Marshall and Eisenhower.

Five days after Pearson's column attacking him, Churchill sent a private telegram to Donovan. He asked General Walter Bedell "Beetle" Smith, Ike's chief of staff, to deliver the note; he was sure that Smith would share its contents with Eisenhower and Marshall, which Beetle did. Churchill couched his incoming round for Donovan in sugary language. "I must tell you that there is very formidable trouble brewing in the Middle East against OSS, which is doing everything in its power to throw our policy towards Greece, for which we have been accorded the main responsibility, into confusion," he wrote. "I grieve greatly to see that your name is brought into all this because of our agreeable acquaintance in the past. Drew Pearson's article is a specimen of the kind of stuff that fits in with the campaign of the OSS against the British." Churchill said he was about to cable FDR "when I realized that you were involved and in view of our association I should not like to put this matter on the highest level without asking you whether there is anything you can do to help." If Donovan could not be of assistance in Britain's Hellenic affairs then "the whole issue must be raised as between governments." Translated: I know you leaked that story to Pearson. Don't mess with me in Greece or I'll have you crushed.

Churchill's threat was crystal clear to Beetle Smith, who moved quickly to put some distance between Eisenhower's command and the spymaster. "I have forwarded your message on to Donovan," he wrote the prime minister two days later, adding: "I have always been worried by his predilection for political intrigue, and have kept a firm hand on him when I could, so he keeps away from me as much as possible."

Churchill could not stem the chaos that followed after German troops evacuated Greece in October and British forces moved in. Civil war broke out between the royalists and communists by early December 1944. It took the British occupation force about two months to beat back the communists. From his OSS officers in Greece, who spied on the British as well as the Soviet agents in the country, Donovan filed regular reports to FDR on Churchill's struggle to put the royalists on top. Churchill could be a bully when he wanted to, notorious for sacking military commanders so often it surprised even Hitler, who had fired a few in his day. The prime minister had even tried to browbeat senior American officers like Marshall and Admiral King. But in the Balkans, Donovan would not be intimidated.

Chapter 27

⟨◦⟩

Stockholm

ONOVAN SENT ROOSEVELT a warm note after he was reelected
to an unprecedented fourth term on November 7. It "clearly
shows the determination of the great majority of the American
people to support you in the conduct of the war," he wrote. And he meant
it. Working for Roosevelt had its frustrations, but he could think of no
Republican qualified to be commander-in-chief at this point—certainly not
New York governor Thomas Dewey, whom he was privately glad FDR had
defeated. Frenchy Grombach, who ran the G-2's secret spy unit nicknamed
the Pond, told his Army superiors Donovan was having a law partner slip
Dewey classified information to "butter up" the governor in case he won.
Grombach had no evidence to back up his charge. What was true was that
three weeks before the election, Donovan had quietly passed to Roosevelt
an analysis Elmo Roper had prepared for him of survey results. It showed
Republicans had gained ground from public concerns over the president's
health, his choice of Harry Truman as his running mate, and his willingness to work with Stalin. Donovan also passed the survey reports to Bill
Stephenson, who cabled them to London.

By the fall, Mary Donovan's name had begun to crop up more in the
society columns, which gushed that the spy chief's daughter-in-law was one
of Washington's "out-of-the-ordinary beauties." Mary had moved into the
Georgetown house with her daughter, Patricia, who was now three years
old. With David at sea, farm life in Berryville had become insufferably dull
compared to the limelight surrounding her father-in-law. Mary also now
had a job in the capital. In early October, Donovan had hired her to be

a clerk in the OSS secretariat and one of his personal assistants at a start-ing salary of $1,440 a year. She answered phones, took messages, booked appointments for him, and sometimes helped female agents overseas with personal problems. Occasionally, Mary also began traveling abroad with Donovan to handle secretarial chores.

Gossip soon spread from Berryville to OSS and society circles in Wash-ington that Donovan was having an affair with her. The same rumor cir-culated in Nonquitt, where neighbors noticed on several occasions that Donovan arrived there with Mary and they did not see Ruth in the sum-mer home. Questions were whispered in Rumsey family circles: Had Donovan—who they knew enjoyed the pleasures of other women—taken his daughter-in-law as a lover? But no one had any proof, because there was none. Mary was twenty-seven years old and her father-in-law was now sixty-one. Their relationship was odd, and it would become more so over the years, but it was not sexual. Moreover, Ruth was practically as close to Mary as Donovan was. Never once did she even hint to family or friends suspicion that anything unusual was going on between her daughter-in-law and husband—whose philandering with other women Ruth knew full well.

Donovan had enough rank in the military he could ignore the rumors, as well as complaints from some in the Pentagon of nepotism in his orga-nization. After his reelection, Roosevelt promoted his spymaster to major general. Congratulations poured in from other flag officers who had treated him warily in the past, such as Omar Bradley and Beetle Smith. He was now moving up the ladder in their exclusive club. His pay increased to $10,200, which he needed. Soon he had a new Cadillac to drive around Washington, with license plates displaying the two stars for his new rank. Donovan also requisitioned an M1 .30-caliber rifle with ten clips of ammu-nition. He planned to keep it at his side during overseas trips.

AFTER GERMAN DEFEATS on the Russian front in the spring of 1944, Hungary, Bulgaria, and Romania looked for the exit doors. But as all three countries tried to pull out of the Axis alliance, the Red Army moved in. Donovan wanted to maintain good relations with Fitin, hoping it would grease the way for OSS teams to remain in the Balkan and Eastern Euro-pean nations coming under Russian control so his spies could continue snooping on the Germans—and the Soviets replacing them. The NKGB general was still eager for OSS technology and intelligence reports so he continued to exchange information with Donovan and help him find downed pilots and missing agents in the territory the Soviets occupied.

Romania became what OSS officers called a "dry run" for how they planned to spy under Stalin's nose in the region. Just before Soviet divisions arrived in late August, Donovan rushed in Frank Wisner, who had cleaned up his Turkey station, with an OSS team that eventually retrieved 1,350 Allied airmen and nearly a ton of German documents. Wisner's men passed out cigarettes to Russian soldiers, presented a matched pen and pencil set to one of their generals, and traded intelligence reports with NKGB agents, whose numbers in Bucharest swelled to 1,200 by November. A month after his arrival, Wisner reported to Donovan that he thought the team's rescue work and cooperation with the Russians had provided good cover to spy on the Red Army.

But not for long. Soviet military commanders moving in assumed that any foreign intelligence service in their midst would spy on them, so soon they began to put the squeeze on Donovan's operations. Moscow refused to allow OSS contingents to enter Budapest and Warsaw and forced a team in Sofia to leave after it evacuated 335 airmen. Donovan quickly realized what the Red Army did not want his agents to see in their occupation zones. His OSS officers who remained reported that Soviet troops were looting millions of tons of grain from the Balkans and shipping it back to Russia. Wisner cabled that Romanian factory and refinery equipment was being loaded onto rail cars headed for the Soviet Union. Meanwhile, communist thugs had moved into the capitals to hunt down intellectuals and political opponents. OSS men soon became harassment targets. Donovan was outraged when Russian soldiers roughed up several of his officers who were filming a communist rally in Bucharest from a nearby rooftop and confiscated their film.

Donovan invited Fitin to meet with him in the Balkans, or anywhere in Europe convenient for the spy chief, to discuss how the OSS and NKGB might work together in enemy territory either side occupied. Fitin begged off, claiming "a number of important duties" prevented him from leaving Moscow.

Soon after the war ended in Europe, the Soviets forced the remaining OSS teams out of countries they occupied. But long before that, Donovan had grown suspicious of the Russians and increasingly alarmed over

Stalin's aggressive moves. In August of 1944, he notified Marshall that he already had nearly three dozen Russia experts on his research staff preparing a comprehensive intelligence estimate on "Soviet intentions and capabilities." After Germany's defeat, "the United States and the Soviet Union will become, and will long remain, by far the strongest nations in the world," he predicted. And though Donovan was willing to work with the Soviets if he thought it was in his country's interest, he was also ready to treat them as an intelligence target before many in the American government were. In August, he quietly arranged for the Italian government to have its military intelligence service, the SIM, spy on Moscow for the OSS under the diplomatic cover of its overseas embassies. "The handling of Russia is a very delicate matter at this time," a secret OSS memo acknowledged, "and it is thus considered advantageous to have a second power perform the basic work of securing the necessary intelligence."

Within months, Donovan would discover just how delicate collecting intelligence on the Soviets could be.

THOUGH SHE DECLARED herself neutral, Sweden had at first collaborated with the Nazis, shipping them high-grade iron ore and allowing tens of thousands of Wehrmacht troops to cross her territory to attack the Soviet Union. Only when the Germans began losing the war did the nimble Swedish government begin tilting toward the Allies. Stockholm, like Bern and Istanbul, became a major espionage outpost for the OSS and other foreign intelligence services. Donovan had seventy-five officers in Stockholm collecting information on the Nazis and the help they received from the Swedes. He also used the capital as a launching pad for agents infiltrating into Germany and German-occupied Norway and Denmark. His Stockholm officers eventually had a code clerk in the German embassy on the OSS payroll feeding them secret diplomatic cables while the Swedish intelligence service provided them transcripts from their phone taps at the Japanese embassy.

Wilho "Ty" Tikander was a former Justice Department antitrust lawyer whose father had emigrated from Finland in the 1880s and set up a country store in northern Minnesota to sell dry goods to local miners. Tikander knew nothing about spying except for a quickie OSS tradecraft course he had taken in Washington and he spoke no Swedish. But he was fluent in

Finnish, a difficult language to master, so he was packed off in the fall of 1942 to Stockholm, the key OSS post for vacuuming intelligence out of war-torn Finland. Donovan at first had been wary of promoting Tikander to station chief. Stockholm was a difficult assignment, and Donovan wanted a seasoned OSS officer in charge there, who would be as skilled a diplomat as he was a spy so he did not anger the Swedes or the U.S. ambassador, Herschel Johnson. Johnson seemed to be allergic to espionage operations. Tikander soon proved adept at cultivating the Swedes and staying on Johnson's friendly side, so Donovan finally put him in charge of the station in April 1944. But he kept Tikander on a short tether, demanding to be "kept fully informed" of his most sensitive missions and sending him nasty notes when he held back details from OSS headquarters in Washington.

One of Tikander's most delicate operations, which Donovan knew could be diplomatic dynamite, began when four battered Finnish steamboats sailed into Swedish harbors on September 21, 1944. Among the 750 refugees on the vessels fleeing the Russian army was the entire Finnish intelligence service along with crates of their most secret documents stored in the cargo holds. The Finns had one of the best spy organizations in Europe. Already they had broken a State Department code for cables coming from many U.S. embassies overseas. The Swedish intelligence service, which had arranged for the evacuation in an operation code-named "Stella Polaris," put their Finnish colleagues in downtown Stockholm's Hotel Anston, where they stored the crates in the basement under heavy guard and soon opened for business to sell their precious documents to the highest bidders. Despite their country's alliance with the Nazis, military and diplomatic officers in Finland's Stockholm embassy had handed the OSS station a steady stream of reports under the table the past two years on German and Russian forces. Tikander became a prime customer for one of the choice items the Stella Polaris gang had for sale on the black market: 1,500 pages containing keys to decipher the codes the Russian army and NKGB used for their cables, plus a trove of sensitive Finnish intelligence documents on the Red Army, all gift-wrapped in two hundred boxes. The price: $62,500. (The entrepreneurial Finns did not tell Tikander that they later sold copies of the same material to the Japanese military attaché in Stockholm for $75,000.)

Tikander cabled Donovan in October with the Finnish offer. Donovan was enthusiastic and ran the sale by Roosevelt, Marshall, and Undersecretary of State Edward Stettinius. A New Dealer whose hair had grown prematurely white but whose dark eyebrows and bright blue eyes made him strikingly handsome, Stettinius was to replace the ailing Hull as secretary at the end of November. He had been impressed in the past with the intelligence he had received from the OSS, but not always with the agency's political acumen; this deal was a perfect example of Donovan's tin ear for international politics, Stettinius thought. The Soviet Union was still an ally and if it ever came to light that the United States had stolen the Russians' communication code there would be diplomatic hell to pay, he knew. Stettinius protested so forcefully, Donovan sent a top secret cable to Tikander: "Do not undertake to secure or indicate interest in any Russian material now in the hands of your Finnish friends. There are impelling political reasons for this prohibition, which must under no circumstance be violated."

The Finns, however, kept dangling the documents before Tikander. In early December he flew to Washington to lobby Donovan and finally convinced him the Finnish offer was too valuable to pass up. Donovan approved the $62,500 payment. In Stockholm, Tikander's officers loaded the two hundred boxes onto a plane for Washington. Ned Buxton, one of the OSS deputies, told the State Department Donovan felt the purchase "was of such importance, that he was willing to take the entire responsibility for dealing with this matter." He sent Roosevelt a short top secret note on December 11 informing him that his Stockholm chief had bought the codes.

Even for Donovan, this was an audacious move. Stettinius, now the secretary, was livid at being overruled. Two days before Christmas he walked into the Oval Office to plead with FDR to order Donovan to turn the code material over to the Russians. Roosevelt had become increasingly irritated with Donovan's intelligence escapades that gave him political headaches at home or abroad. He ordered the code books delivered to the Russians. Donovan cabled Deane in Moscow to tell Fitin one of the biggest cock-and-bull stories one spymaster has ever sent to another spymaster. The OSS had discovered that "enemy sources" were selling some 1,500 pages of Russian codes on the black market, so "General Donovan took the only course open to a loyal ally in accepting this material as soon as he found it was procurable," General Deane was to inform the NKGB chief. Donovan now wanted to turn the documents over to a Russian representative in Washington and assure Fitin that the OSS had not read a single page.

Fitin did not quite know what to make of this tale—except that it was likely not the truth—but he arranged for the handover. In late January 1945, Putzell showed up at the Soviet embassy on 16th Street with several OSS security officers lugging the boxes. Andrei Gromyko, who had taken over as ambassador just a year earlier and at thirty-five was the youngest Russian ever to assume such an important post, had Putzell's men stack the boxes near his office. Gromyko was tall, dark, and wore horn-rimmed glasses. The OSS dossier on him was thin because he kept to himself in Washington and rarely talked to neighbors around his home in the suburbs. "He is modest, bookish and speaks English well," an agency report noted. Putzell found Gromyko noticeably disdainful when he presented him the documents. The Soviets had already changed the codes since they obviously had been compromised. Gromyko likely had a disparaging look on his face because he probably suspected he still was not the only one who had custody of the material. Donovan was bound to have had his men photograph the papers before he gave them to the Russians—although copies have never turned up in the OSS archives.

Though he told Tikander to back away from more Finnish offers from the Stella Polaris trove, Donovan continued to build up his spy operation against the Soviets. By December he had begun tapering off the number of OSS research reports sent to Fitin. Several weeks before Putzell visited the Russian embassy, Donovan told Dulles to prepare agents to penetrate the occupation zone the Soviets would control in Germany after the war. He wanted his spies in the British sector as well. Donovan assumed those two countries would plant their agents in the American zone. Donovan also ordered his men to look for NKGB agents to recruit as informers as they had with German moles.

BY THE END of 1944, Donovan's men noticed other enemies circling as victory in Europe seemed near. In Washington, the OSS and FBI fielded basketball teams that played each other regularly in a city league. Both agencies brought in college players for the games. The OSS had the services of George Glamack, a six-foot-seven-inch all-American from the University of North Carolina at Chapel Hill. But the friendly rivalry stopped at the court's edge. Hoover had put FBI agents in the U.S. embassies in Paris, Madrid, Lisbon, Rome, and Manila. He insisted his men were acting only as legal attachés to track international criminals and communist agitators who threatened the United States, but Donovan's officers knew better. Hoover was laying the groundwork for a worldwide intelligence network after the war to replace the OSS, they warned their boss. Donovan's counterintelligence agents had made a "good-faith" effort to cooperate with the FBI, they wrote him in early 1945, while Hoover's cooperation had been "half-hearted" at best. By their count, over the past two years the OSS had sent the FBI 615 intelligence reports, but had received only 398 in return. Hoover still believed that most OSS intelligence reports were rewrites from the British. Donovan thought Hoover's much ballyhooed spy-catching record also was a lot of smoke and mirrors. He sent an acid memo to Roosevelt in early 1945 pointing out that of the twenty espionage and sabotage cases Hoover had brought to trial, in a dozen of them "the original tip-off that the individual was a German agent came . . . from the British." Four of the other big busts benefited indirectly from information the Brits had supplied. Hoover's men had solved only four cases on their own.

Then there was John "Frenchy" Grombach, the Army major Donovan had eased out of the OSS two years earlier. No one in the OSS could determine exactly what the Pond's band of spies was doing for the Army's G-2, but Grombach, now a colonel, kept popping up on Donovan's radar screen. At one point Frenchy breezed into London, where Bruce's men found him the same conspiratorial oddball they had known when he was in the OSS. But now he was secretive and vague about his job for the Army. As near as Donovan's officers could tell, Grombach had operatives roaming Portugal, Sweden, Hungary, and Romania. By December 1944, Donovan's senior advisers discovered he was also trying to recruit former OSS officers with experience in Turkey and Greece. "He is extremely ambitious and tough-minded," one OSS officer warned headquarters.

Indeed he was. Operating out of front companies in Washington and New York that were kept hidden from Donovan, Grombach had assembled a network of more than forty military intelligence agents spread out in over thirty countries with some six hundred foreign informants on their payroll. They secretly fed thousands of intelligence reports on the Axis to Marshall and other top officers. The Pond's spies also mounted a major espionage operation against the "Dons," their nickname for Donovan and his agents. Grombach's snitches overseas kept him regularly posted on any missteps Donovan and his men made. Grombach kept tabs on Donovan's affairs with other women, suspecting he "freely talked about secret matters" with some, as he put it in one report. He even looked for dirt on the theft of Donovan's traveling bag from the Sofia hotel in 1941, believing the bag contained more sensitive material than Donovan acknowledged and the Nazi line that he had been carousing with nightclub dancers. The colonel also collected dossiers on hundreds of OSS officers. Sometimes, wives of the Dons were watched.

Frenchy clearly was treading on Donovan's turf. The G-2 had no authority that he knew of to launch a worldwide espionage service. But Buxton advised Donovan not to confront the Army just yet on Grombach's bigfooting. We'll collect more intelligence on this colonel, he wrote Donovan, "and continue to assemble a file for use at the right time."

Chapter 28

The Vatican

DONOVAN SPENT Christmas Eve 1944 in New York but took the train the next morning to have Christmas dinner at the Georgetown house with Ruth, Mary, and his granddaughter. It was a miracle for Ruth that Bill had showed up at all. With the war, holidays had been just another workday for him and Christmas this year fell on a Monday. But Donovan took the rest of the afternoon off to relax at home and play with his granddaughter, who delighted him. Little Patricia was a rambunctious and assertive three-year-old who did not like the stern French governess Mary had brought in to care for her when she was at work at OSS headquarters. The little girl had marched into Donovan's study one day and declared that she was sure she could fly and planned to test her wings by jumping out of a third-story window and onto the awning over the porch below.

"I don't think you should try that," Donovan said with a chuckle and finally talked her out of the flight. Patricia and the grandchildren born later called Donovan "Faddy." They called Ruth "Num Num," which was what her children had called their grandmother.

Donovan's holiday respite was brief. The morning after Christmas he boarded a plane with almost a dozen senior aides and flew to Paris for another month-long trip that again would take him around the world to Asia. David Bruce, who had moved to the French capital to direct OSS operations as the Allied armies pushed east, met Donovan's plane at the Paris airport. He was grappling with a serious security breach when the boss arrived.

On the morning of September 26, Gertrude Legendre, a glamorous New York socialite on Donovan's payroll, had been riding in a jeep near the German-Luxembourg border with Navy Lieutenant Commander Robert Jennings (an OSS secret intelligence officer), Army Major Maxwell Papurt (an OSS counterintelligence officer), and Private Doyle Dickson, their driver. As their jeep approached Wallendorf on the German side of the border an enemy patrol spotted them and opened fire with their machine guns. Dickson and Papurt were shot in the legs, but along with Legendre and Jennings they managed to escape the vehicle and dive into a shallow ditch, burning their identification cards with a cigarette lighter and concocting a cover story before the German soldiers captured them. The four were herded off to the Wallendorf village, where Legendre and Jennings eventually were separated from their wounded comrades.

Panic swept through the OSS over Gertrude Legendre's capture. An old Donovan friend, the forty-two-year-old heiress hailed from one of South Carolina's most prominent families and had married a sugar baron from New Orleans before moving into New York's best social circles. When war broke out, Legendre wanted to serve her country, believing that her world travels, her fluency in French, and the fact that she could shoot a rifle as good as any man qualified her for something. Donovan hired her in August 1942 as a cable clerk in Washington, where she routed the secret intelligence messages from overseas stations to the people who needed to read them. A year later, Legendre was transferred to London's message center and then followed Bruce to Paris doing the same job.

When Legendre's jeep did not return to base the evening of September 26, OSS security officers dispatched a search team to hunt for the four but it found nothing. Donovan finally learned what happened to them on October 21 when German radio announced their capture. The propaganda broadcast hailed Legendre as "the first American woman to be made a prisoner of war on the Western Front." Thankfully, Legendre had the good sense to tell her captors that she was just a Red Cross worker with the Allied Expeditionary Forces Club, which the Germans apparently bought for the moment because that was how they had identified her in the broadcast.

American newspapers soon were crawling all over the story that a New York society matron was a Nazi prisoner. So far, the Western media had bought the line that Legendre was just a Red Cross volunteer. Donovan had the War Department confirm to reporters the cover story Legendre had put out. But he feared it might be only a matter of time before the Germans discovered her true employer. Legendre was a lowly clerk but what she had read in the messages that had crossed her desk gave her "a tremendous fund of information concerning the OSS operations in the European Theater," Donovan warned the War Department before he flew to Paris. "Any discovery by the Germans that she possesses such information would have grave consequences not only for her personally but also for this organization." Dickson was just a driver who knew nothing even if he talked. Papurt and Jennings were skilled enough intelligence agents they could probably bluff their way out of having to admit they belonged to the OSS, Donovan's security officers thought. But they did not have the same faith in Legendre. Eisenhower's staff and Menzies at MI6 were briefed on what a top secret OSS memo acknowledged could be "one of the disasters of the war."

There was another even more sensitive secret in her case that eventually Donovan wanted to keep hidden—not from the Nazis, but from the press corps. The reason Legendre and her comrades had been captured was because they had been out on a joy ride. In the bar at Paris's Ritz Hotel several days before October 26, Legendre and Jennings had decided as a lark to drive to the 3rd Army headquarters just outside Wallendorf. George Patton was a friend of Legendre's and she wanted to catch up. Legendre and Jennings made it as far as Luxembourg, where their Peugeot broke down, and then hitched a ride with Papurt to Wallendorf, where he said he had business to attend to at Patton's command post. All three cavalierly ignored the fact that the area around Wallendorf was still infested with Germans.

Major Papurt died on November 29 when a bomb from an Allied air raid struck his prison camp. Private Dickson, of no value to German intelligence, was sent to a POW camp. Wehrmacht officers rigorously interrogated Lieutenant Commander Jennings but he managed to convince them he was simply a naval observer, so he was packed off to a dreary Stalag as well. For Gertrude Legendre, however, being a POW turned out to be a delightful excursion. The Germans moved her from prison to prison. One was a baroque seventeenth-century castle, another a comfortable room in a hotel. She befriended her guards, who sometimes brought her beer, cognac, and apple strudel. When a Gestapo interrogator asked her what OSS stood for, she chirped: "God, I haven't the slightest idea. Probably Office of Social Club or something." Legendre's questioners soon lost interest in her. Convinced a German surrender could not be far off, one interrogator toward the end of March 1945 had a guard dump her near the Swiss border. Dulles eventually retrieved Legendre and ordered her not to talk to the press because Dickson and Jennings had not been recovered. Dulles also found a note sewn in the lining of her raincoat from the guards at her last prison wishing her well.

When counterintelligence officers in London learned of the friendly German note they sent a for-your-eyes-only cable to Donovan questioning whether Legendre had been turned into a double agent or at best a propaganda pawn for German intelligence. Donovan knew she was neither, but he ordered her hustled back to the States and kept under wraps. "She is to give no interviews, make no statements and remain completely silent in getting from Switzerland to Washington," Donovan cabled Dulles on March 27. By then he knew the real story behind the Legendre party's capture and he was furious.

When Legendre finally reached Washington the first week of April 1945, Donovan personally moved to bury the fiasco in a deep hole. He sat her down in his office and dictated to her the cover story she would continue to keep if anyone asked. She was a Red Cross volunteer for the Allied Club. Otherwise, she shuts up. Donovan ordered Legendre to go underground. Because she was a civilian, Donovan could not bring military charges against her for the escapade and even if he could it would have leaked to the press because Legendre was now a celebrity. New York gossip columns already were reporting she had returned. Donovan had to treat Legendre with kid gloves. But he had to keep her quiet. When his security officers discovered she had brought back a long diary written during her imprisonment, they impounded it and ordered it not returned to her until after the war.

Lieutenant Commander Jennings *was* subject to military law and after he was freed on March 28, 1945, by Allied troops liberating his POW camp, Donovan lowered the boom on him. When Jennings arrived back in Washington, Donovan treated him like a sailor who had deserted his station. He placed him under house arrest and ordered that no one talk to him and that he not be allowed to set foot inside OSS headquarters. Not only did he kick Jennings out of his agency, he ordered him drummed out of the Navy. "He was absent without leave and had no orders whatever permitting him to make [that] trip," Donovan angrily wrote. "His action exposed [the] OSS to great criticism and discredit."

———————

AFTER PARIS, Donovan flew to Cairo and Caserta before heading east to Asia. He caught another nasty flu bug in Italy, which this time put him in the Army infirmary in Caserta for several days. But his doctor still could not keep OSS officers from surrounding his bed for business. Vincent Scamporino, the former Connecticut lawyer who was now his chief of secret intelligence for Italy, arrived from Rome. "Scamp," as everyone called him, was in his late thirties with a dark complexion and a heavy beard that he had to shave twice a day. His winning smile, however, masked a fierce determination to keep Washington meddlers out of his hair while he built up his Italian network. As the Germans evacuated north the OSS had harvested thousands of Italian documents on the Axis. By the time Donovan arrived, Scamporino had nearly thirty informants in the top echelons of the new Italian government. Propped up in his hospital bed, Donovan told Scamp he wanted him to manage the alliance the OSS had set up with the SIM, Italy's military intelligence service, to spy on both the Axis and the Russians for the agency. Scamporino questioned whether it was proper, or even legal, for the OSS to be using military agents who had been on Mussolini's payroll. Donovan had no qualms. "The British have been using SIM for six months," he said.

Donovan recovered enough from the flu to make a side trip to Rome and meet with a young counterintelligence officer who had become a rising star in his organization. Only twenty-eight years old, James Jesus Angleton already had enough quirks for a man twice his age. He chain-smoked, spoke with a slight British accent, was a chronic insomniac, quoted T. S. Eliot to relax, refused to sit beside a colleague in a restaurant booth, struck his OSS friends as overly secretive even for their profession, could be irrationally paranoid about communists, and liked to prowl Rome's streets in a black cape. After graduating with poor grades from Yale, Angleton joined the OSS and was sent to London as a counterintelligence corporal. From his first day in the London station, Angleton was a human tornado, quickly learning street skills for spy catching. Within six months he was commissioned a second lieutenant and by October 1944 he had been transferred to Rome to clean up counterintelligence operations in Italy, using the code name "Artifice."

By the time Donovan met with him that January, Angleton had set himself up in Rome's five-star hotel district off Via Veneto with an impressive network of moles in Italy's spy services. Though he had exchanged only a few words with Donovan during the director's previous swings through London and Rome, Angleton, like most field agents, worshipped the ground he walked on. Donovan, too, was impressed with the moles Artifice had cultivated and the fact that he also seemed to have a well-grounded skepticism of foreigners who walked in bearing gifts of secrets.

BUT WITH THE new year, Donovan could see that the European war was reaching its end, which was the reason his plane flew from the Mediterranean to the Far East the first week in January. His future battles would be there, he believed. Since he waded ashore at Hollandia the previous April, the Marines had taken Saipan, Tinian, and Guam. MacArthur had returned to the Philippines and U.S. strategy had shifted to launching large Navy and ground amphibious operations against the outlying Japanese islands, the assault on Iwo Jima and Okinawa the most important ones to come. From mid-January until the first week of February 1945, Donovan toured his outposts scattered in the Burma-China theater, still the only place in Asia his covert forces were allowed to fight. But China remained a troubled land for the OSS. Even after Donovan fired Mary Miles and won what he thought were concessions from Tai Li to allow the OSS more independence, progress on the mainland remained slow. Tai Li still restricted his agency's operations. When he arrived in Chiang's military headquarters in mid-January, the OSS was only beginning to assemble a viable intelligence and commando operation. Two precious years had been wasted squabbling with the Chinese.

Consumed with clearing the thicket in Chungking, Donovan had paid only scant attention to a cable that arrived the second week in January from the Washington headquarters. Charles Cheston was letting him know that he planned to send Roosevelt a report from an important informant the OSS now had deep in the Vatican. The source had been given the code name "Vessel" and Cheston was sure his latest report would interest the president. It was a snippet of a private conversation Pope Pius had a month earlier with Father Norbert de Boyne, his vicar general of the Jesuits. The two men were mulling the possibility of the Vatican mediating a peace agreement between Japan and the Allies. Pius, according to the Vessel report, asked his Tokyo envoy to find out how receptive the Japanese government would be to laying down its arms "before determining whether our intervention is opportune." A pope interested in peace talks was not headline news, but what was startling was the fact that Roosevelt was reading parts of a verbatim transcript from a meeting in the Vatican, one of the most impenetrable institutions in the world where private papal conversations rarely seep out.

In November 1944, a Russian émigré named Dubinin had approached Scamporino in Rome with an offer to sell transcripts of papal meetings that were being supplied to him by a well-placed official inside the Vatican. Since Donovan cleaned house, OSS operatives in Italy were under pressure to produce. Scamporino wanted to show results. Through the Vatican passed international gossip and power brokering at the highest level. Vessel's pipeline to what went on behind its walls could be priceless. Shortly after the Russian approached Scamporino, an Italian named Fillippo Setaccioli offered the identical material from what appeared to be the same Vatican source to Angleton, who was just as eager to please Donovan. Because of distrust and bureaucratic rivalry between them, Scamporino refused to cede control of Vessel to Angleton and have his reports come through just Setaccioli. The Rome station ended up paying two intermediaries for the same intelligence.

In any other case the double billing would have been considered a waste of money except that the reports the OSS was receiving from Vessel were spectacular. This mysterious source in the Vatican—neither Scamporino nor Angleton at first knew his name—was revealing intelligence the pope had on Roosevelt's upcoming Yalta summit with Churchill and Stalin, a peace offer Japanese industrialists were pressuring their military to make, the damage a B-29 air raid had inflicted on an Osaka armored car plant. Donovan had been only mildly impressed when Scamporino and Angleton briefed him on Vessel during his stopover in Italy; it looked promising yet there were many promising sources coming out of Rome. But while he toured Asia, Vessel began attracting high-level attention in his Washington headquarters. The Vatican source "offers great promise," John Magruder, Donovan's senior deputy for intelligence, cabled Scamporino—almost too good to be true. How credible is Vessel? Magruder asked. Scamporino admitted that he was obtaining the reports through a cutout but he rated them "very reliable." So did Angleton. Donovan's Reporting Board, a panel of experts that evaluated intelligence from overseas stations, also pronounced the Vatican reports sound enough to pass around. The Vessel cables were assigned a special "Control-Secret" classification so they were at first delivered only to FDR and a select group of his senior officials.

By the second week of January, a half dozen Vatican reports landed on Magruder's desk each day. Vessel provided a pessimistic telegram from the pope's Madrid envoy on the political health of the Franco regime in Spain, details on Japanese shipbuilding, and the location of her key war vessels. As Roosevelt prepared for his conference at the Crimean resort city of Yalta with Churchill and Stalin to decide the partition of postwar Europe and the final offensive against Japan, Buxton and Cheston rushed two Vessel reports to his desk with what they thought were explosive diplomatic revelations. The Vatican's Tokyo envoy, according to the OSS source, had received the "minimum demands" from the Japanese government "for a negotiated peace" with the Allies, which included her army's withdrawal from China and most other occupied territories in exchange for U.S. recognition of "Japan's privileged position in the Far East." Just as significant, Vessel reported, the emperor had been informed on January 10 that unofficial Japanese intermediaries had been trying to arrange a papal mediation of the war and "the Emperor did not express any disapproval of these efforts." On January 20, Magruder cabled a list of Vessel's revealing intelligence on Japan's recent war losses to Donovan, who was visiting Detachment 101's Nazira base camp in East India. Donovan was impressed with what he read and ordered the Asia material delivered to Nimitz in Hawaii.

Roosevelt sailed on the USS *Quincy* for the Crimea on January 25, intent on having Stalin join the war in the Pacific against Japan. Vessel revealed that Ken Harada, Japan's Vatican ambassador, had told Pius's private secretary the Kremlin had secretly assured Tokyo that at the Yalta conference "Russia will continue to define Japan as [the] aggressor but will not go beyond this" and declare war. Instead, Vessel disclosed that Moscow and Tokyo were negotiating a private agreement to continue their nonaggression pact in exchange for Japan breaking with Germany and removing "all anti-communist controls" in her country. Roosevelt was beginning to find the Vessel reports "most interesting," Grace Tully, his White House secretary, told the OSS.

But how much credence FDR gave the Vatican reports, Magruder did not know. For that matter, he and other officers in headquarters were still unsure about how much faith they should have in Vessel. Scamporino was now dealing directly with his prized source. Vessel was Virgilio Scattolini, a short, fat, timid man with a sallow face and a slight twitch in one arm, who stuttered somewhat when he spoke. A former journalist, Scattolini claimed he worked for a Vatican agency that gave him access to the sensitive documents. Scamporino was still convinced the material was authentic, but he told Washington there was an easy way to establish Scattolini's bona fides. Vessel had also reported on diplomatic positions the White House had told the Vatican that Roosevelt would take at Yalta and on conversations Myron Taylor, the U.S. envoy at the Vatican, had with Pius on papal mediation in the Pacific war. They would certainly know whether Vessel's reports on their diplomatic moves were accurate. But verification was easier said than done. Roosevelt, who was too busy with Yalta to be vetting an OSS source, raised no red flags about the reports mentioning him. Donovan's officers in Rome and Washington, meanwhile, could not get a straight answer from Taylor or other White House and State Department officials on whether Vessel's intelligence on them was correct.

But by the time Donovan returned to Washington the first week of February, other government agencies had begun to raise questions about Vessel's veracity. Two days before the Yalta conference began on February 4, Scattolini claimed Tokyo had told the Vatican that Stalin definitely would not abrogate Russia's nonaggression treaty with Japan and would pressure Churchill and Roosevelt to negotiate a peace treaty in the Pacific. The Army's military intelligence section dismissed the Vessel report as nothing more than "straight propaganda" the Japanese must be planting with the OSS to sow dissent among the Allies.

The warning shot from the G-2 should have made Donovan more wary of Vessel, but it did not. He remained an eager customer for Scattolini's wares. On February 9, another Vessel report arrived claiming Taylor had met with Harada, who declared that if the Americans and British offered "acceptable" peace terms Japan might agree to them. Taylor, according to Vessel's report, reminded Harada that Americans had not forgotten Pearl Harbor, but he said he would ask Washington if it was interested in negotiations. A peace feeler from a senior Japanese envoy was big news. At the very least, Vessel's report indicated that a secret meeting between Taylor and Harada had been leaked to the Vatican. Donovan should have checked Scattolini's story first with Taylor, a former U.S. Steel executive who was close to FDR and a favorite of Pius's. Instead, he rashly cabled the unverified report on February 16 to Roosevelt, who was sailing to Algiers after the Yalta conference.

It was a foolish move for Donovan, who should have been paying more attention to the misgivings his aides had begun having. The day before he sent FDR the Vessel report on Taylor, Scamporino had warned him that the enterprising Scattolini appeared to be selling his documents to several other governments, some of which were likely leaking them to the enemy. Magruder realized that the Italian's intelligence on secret Soviet-Japanese peace negotiations did not square with the facts. Stalin at Yalta had agreed to join the Pacific war two to three months after Germany was defeated. The Vessel material, Magruder wrote Scamporino on February 17, seems to be "a mixture of the obvious, the unimportant if true, and plants" by the enemy. Magruder, for the moment, stopped distributing Vessel reports, which was a good idea. When the State Department received Donovan's surprising news that its Vatican envoy had conferred with the Japanese ambassador on peace negotiations, James Dunn, the assistant secretary for European affairs, immediately fired off a telegram to Taylor asking what in the world he was doing. Dunn sent Donovan Taylor's reply: Not only had he not talked to Harada, he had never met the man. The evidence was now clear, Magruder cabled Scamporino. Vessel has "manufactured" intelligence "out of whole cloth."

Donovan sent a disingenuous "Dear Jimmie" letter to Dunn pretending to be one of the skeptics all along. Dunn's news that Vessel had fabricated the Taylor-Harada meeting merely "confirmed . . . our suspicions of the source of this material," he claimed. That was hardly the case. Donovan, Scamporino, Angleton, and everyone else in his agency had been conned by Vessel. If the OSS had done its homework it would have discovered that transcripts were never made of the audiences Pius had with visitors. Suspecting the Italian might be fabricating reports because he was an Axis agent trying to confuse the Americans, Donovan kept Scattolini on the payroll and Angleton plotted ways he might feed Vessel disinformation to pass on to the enemy. Holding out hope that Scattolini's Asia information might still be reliable, Donovan also continued to send occasional Vessel reports to Roosevelt on peace feelers from Tokyo.

Only later did Donovan's men discover they had been victims of an old-fashioned swindle. The Vatican, which wanted to throw Scattolini in jail when it learned of his scam, let the Americans in on a little secret. Fabricating papal documents was a lucrative business in Rome that dated back to 1883. Scattolini was a fairly successful pornographic novelist who found religion, then went to work for the semiofficial Vatican newspaper *Osservatore Romano* until the editors discovered he had written dirty books and fired him. But Scattolini left the paper with a warehouse of Vatican political trivia in his head, a playwright's talent for concocting dialogue, and a vivid imagination. To feed his family, he penned Vatican political documents and reports, which he began selling to such news outlets as the *New York Times*, Agence France-Presse and TASS, the Russian press service. Scattolini soon had a collection of middlemen, such as Dubinin and Setaccioli, who found the British, Polish, Argentine, and Spanish embassies also eager to shell out money for his phony intelligence reports and transcripts of papal conversations. Donovan eventually determined that the only reason his agency became one of Scattolini's suckers was that Dubinin had mistakenly approached Scamporino with material that was intended for another client.

Vessel arrived at Donovan's doorstep around the time he was dealing with the Legendre scandal. Fortunately, he was able to keep her embarrassing case in-house. But many top people in Washington's national security community knew about the Vessel debacle—including the president of the United States. Curiously, Roosevelt had been intrigued by the Vatican memos but not particularly bothered when it became clear to him later that they were bogus. He may have simply read the Vessel reports and ignored their information. By January when these memos began pouring in, Roosevelt was in desperately poor health with heart disease and distracted by preparations for Yalta. When he returned from the Crimea he was physically exhausted, in no condition to pay much attention to a Donovan gambit gone haywire. Whatever the reason, Roosevelt never reacted one way or the other to the memos the OSS sent him throughout the Vessel episode. Vessel, however, did not help Donovan with another more important initiative he wanted Roosevelt and other top administration officials to approve—a future CIA.

Chapter 29

———

The Leak

E ARLY FRIDAY MORNING, February 9, 1945, was frigid and dark outside as a servant padded down to the front of the driveway of the
Georgetown house to scoop up the newspapers and deliver them to
Donovan, who was eating his breakfast. He had kept a light schedule since
arriving in Washington Wednesday from his grueling Asia trip. There had
been meetings through Thursday to catch up with senior aides and branch
chiefs. He found time to phone Ruth, who was in Buffalo with her family.
Donovan also phoned Grace Tully at the White House for the latest news
from the Yalta conference at Livadia Palace. The Big Three had settled on
demilitarization of Germany and occupation zones after the war. Stalin
promised to join the Far East campaign, but his concessions came with a
price. He won postwar territory in Asia and two extra votes for the Ukrainian and Belorussian Soviet Socialist Republics in the new United Nations
General Assembly. Stalin also agreed to eventual democratic governments
in Poland and the other Eastern European countries his army occupied,
but there was no enforcement mechanism to guarantee that the communist regimes he had installed would allow free elections. Conservative
Republicans later denounced Yalta as a "sellout" and Donovan privately
disparaged the accord when he reviewed its details. "The Russians have
robbed us blind," he complained to friends. Donovan was being unfair.
Stalin's extra votes mattered little in the large General Assembly and he
was accorded in Eastern Europe what he had already won on the battlefield. Churchill and Roosevelt were not prepared to fight another war to

take it back. The Yalta sellout came only later, when Stalin reneged on what he had agreed to for Eastern Europe.

What the three leaders could not agree on at their Crimea meeting was a coordinated final offensive against Germany. As the Allied armies raced across West Germany, the Eastern Front collapsed and the Red Army advanced toward Berlin, where Hitler had moved his headquarters to his Führerbunker under the New Reich Chancellery for the final siege. Dulles cabled Donovan Berlin updates he received from Fritz Kolbe and Swiss intelligence, which Donovan relayed to the White House. Hitler is "suffering from depression and works only at night," Dulles cabled. He has "opposed any evacuation measures for Berlin."

It was only a matter of time before the German capital fell, Donovan knew. But he now became convinced that the Nazis would never surrender and instead would fight on with an underground force left behind in Austria and southern Germany. The Alpine redoubt turned out to be a German-inspired myth—and an intelligence failure Donovan's OSS shared with most other Allied spy agencies. By February, however, Donovan was trumpeting the redoubt theory as one of many reasons Roosevelt needed the OSS or some type of spy and subversion service after the cease-fire—to combat not just a German guerrilla threat but also future international dangers to the United States.

But when he read the front page of the *Washington Times-Herald* at his breakfast table the morning of February 9, he realized his vision of a future central intelligence agency had taken a serious body blow. Eleanor "Cissy" Patterson, who published the *Times-Herald*, was as rabidly anti-Roosevelt as her cousin, Colonel Robert McCormick, who ran the *Chicago Tribune*, a sister paper in the McCormick-Patterson chain along with the *New York Daily News*. Donovan stared in disbelief at a headline blaring from the front page of the Friday *Times-Herald*: "Donovan Proposes Super Spy System for Postwar New Deal." The story, which also ran in the *Tribune* and *Daily News* that day, was written by Walter Trohan, the chain's White House correspondent, who shared his publishers' contempt for Roosevelt. Trohan had crossed paths with Donovan after his 1940 trip to England for Roosevelt, and in the four years since he had not been impressed with the Republican lawyer or the spy agency he had created for the Democrats.

Donovan knew from the first sentence of Trohan's story that he was in for a hatchet job. "Creation of an all-powerful intelligence service to spy on the postwar world and to pry into the lives of citizens at home is under consideration by the New Deal," the reporter declared. The New Deal reference made it sound as if this was another intrusive government scheme cooked up by Roosevelt liberals McCormick and the conservatives hated. Donovan, the story alleged, wanted to create a "super-intelligence unit" after the war ended, not only to spy on America's "good neighbors throughout the world" but also to snoop on citizens "at home," commandeering the "police powers" of the FBI and other law enforcement agencies "whenever needed." The plan Donovan had drafted for a postwar espionage organization would give him "tremendous power" over how intelligence was gathered and analyzed, Trohan darkly wrote, with a hidden hand "to determine American foreign policy by weeding out, withholding or coloring information gathered at his direction." In sentences he knew would inflame Republicans who hated FDR loyalist Felix Frankfurter, Trohan claimed unnamed Washington "high circles" had dubbed Donovan's postwar intelligence organization "Frankfurter's Gestapo" because the Supreme Court justice's sister, Estelle, worked for the OSS and was picking "key personnel" for the new agency "at the suggestion of her brother."

Equating the postwar intelligence agency Donovan wanted to create with the dreaded German Gestapo was as incendiary an attack as Trohan could make—sure to spark panic in Washington and across the country. But the Trohan article had two other bombshells that jolted Donovan as he read the piece. The newspaper had printed verbatim a secret memo Donovan had written to Roosevelt on November 18 proposing the postwar central intelligence agency along with an executive order he had drafted for the President to sign setting up the service. This was a major leak of two highly classified OSS documents. It exposed, not only to Americans, but also to the Germans, the Soviets, and other foreign governments a secret initiative Donovan had been formulating since the previous fall.

Donovan had been informally brainstorming ideas with his staff for a postwar intelligence agency since May 1943. By the end of September 1944, he had firmly in his mind the type of postwar service he wanted, which was not much different from what he envisioned when he got into the spy business in 1941. It should be an independent organization reporting directly to the president, collecting foreign intelligence and conducting secret operations for the entire government, and focused on the big picture to help the future leader of the free world make sound foreign policy decisions. The military services could still collect intelligence for their battle-field needs, but Donovan would coordinate their activities and those of other civilian agencies like the FBI—although he was emphatic that this new spy outfit not operate at home or have police functions.

In October, Donovan began quietly lobbying the White House for his plan. He assigned two aides, Louis Ream and Joseph Rosenbaum, to begin shopping his plan with key FDR staffers. Harold Smith, the Budget Bureau chief preoccupied with shrinking postwar agencies, not expanding them, was hostile. Harry Hopkins, the most powerful adviser, was noncommittal. But other senior White House aides were more encouraging. The most important ally became Isadore Lubin, a small, bespectacled, and bald New Deal economist close to Roosevelt who had been his point man on labor and war production issues. Lubin had been appalled by the worthless mili-tary intelligence reports piled on his desk, but the OSS product impressed him. "Bill Donovan's Office of Strategic Services has been doing some swell work," he wrote FDR on October 25, strongly endorsing the post-war plan. Lubin convinced the president to request a memo from Dono-van on his proposal, then advised Donovan on Roosevelt's hot buttons to push when he wrote it—for example, that the plan would "eliminate a lot of duplication between agencies" (Roosevelt was obsessed with downsizing after the war). Lubin joked with Donovan that when Roosevelt approved his program, "I want 10% of your salary increase."

Lubin should not have been so cocky. Roosevelt was far from sold on Donovan's idea. Correctly sensing the mood of the country, he wanted government to contract after the war and the military to demobilize. FDR had already ordered Smith to think about agencies to cut and the budget czar had the OSS high on his list. As he prowled the White House lobby-ing, Rosenbaum also sensed that Roosevelt had become disenchanted with his spy chief. Donovan had accumulated too many political enemies to lead a central intelligence service in peacetime, White House aides whis-pered to Rosenbaum, and there was still the problem that he was a Repub-lican, which made him suspect.

On November 18, Donovan finally sent his memo to Roosevelt out-lining his arguments for "an intelligence service for the postwar period" along with a draft executive order to set it up. FDR would pick the intelli-gence director and supervise him. The State Department, Navy, and Army, which would keep their own intelligence operations, would lend Donovan men and equipment when he needed them and form a board to advise him. But the central intelligence service, drawn from what already existed in the OSS, would coordinate the spying of other agencies, collect and evaluate intelligence of strategic value to the government, and perform any other "subversive operations abroad" that a president wanted done. Roosevelt sent Donovan's draft order to the Army, Navy, Air Force, and State Department and asked for their opinions on it. He was tossing it into the shark tank.

Donovan, it turned out, was not the only one thinking ahead. The Army, Navy, and State Department were hatching their own plans for postwar intelligence services. Major General Clayton Bissell had been a young pilot and acolyte of air maverick Billy Mitchell in the 1920s. But by the time he pinned on his second star and replaced Strong as the Army's military intelligence director in early 1944, Bissell had grown more conservative and as hostile to Donovan as George the Fifth. Grombach already was plotting to have the Pond take over postwar espionage. Frenchy fretted that Roosevelt would promote Donovan to lieutenant general and his OSS would be controlled by the British and Soviets after the war.

John Franklin Carter, who had picked up rumors the month before that Donovan was preparing a postwar intelligence plan, launched a preemptive strike, sending Roosevelt a poison-pen memo on October 26, which warned that the British had "already penetrated the Donovan organization" and would control the OSS if it ran intelligence after the war. Instead, Carter proposed that his tiny and less expensive outfit be the spy agency of the future sending out "look-see agents in special circumstances" to steal secrets overseas and report back to the State Department, FBI, and the military. Roosevelt sent Carter's memo to Donovan for his reaction, which he could have already guessed. Donovan, who did not appreciate being called a British dupe, fired back that Carter was "in the horse and buggy stage of intelligence thinking." Roosevelt never followed up on the newsman's plan.

But J. Edgar Hoover was a more formidable foe. The FBI director also wanted to be the spy czar after the war, expanding his Latin America intelligence operation to the rest of the world. Hoover's informants in the White House, Pentagon, and Congress kept him posted on Donovan's plan and every move he made to sell it in the administration. The director did not like what he saw. Donovan's expensive worldwide intelligence organization would be accountable to no one and run out of the White House by a "party man," he complained to Attorney General Biddle. Hoover did not believe for one minute that Donovan's new agency wouldn't be a secret police force operating in the United States like a Gestapo and taking over the FBI. The only agents Hoover wanted spying on Americans were his.

Hoover's most powerful ally became Harry Hopkins, who had grown increasingly disenchanted with Donovan and irritated by his secretiveness. Hoover, meanwhile, had edged closer to Roosevelt's consigliere. Hopkins slipped the FBI director all the memos Donovan had submitted to the White House on his postwar plan, while Hoover alerted Hopkins to the publicity campaign Donovan was planning to promote the OSS. By the end of November, Hoover was on the phone with his important friend or dropping by the White House for private chats with him practically every week.

Donovan spent the month of December 1944 fighting for his plan behind closed doors, compromising where he had to. The Pentagon adamantly opposed an independent intelligence organization reporting directly to the president. But feeling confident the military would bend to his will and Roosevelt would eventually back him, Donovan had boarded his plane for his Asia trip the day after Christmas. He left Magruder and other senior aides in Washington to thrash out the final wording of an executive order. Administrative chores and bureaucratic dickering still bored him to tears. Donovan possessed a restless energy and an almost evangelical conviction that on the big things, like a new central intelligence agency, his ideas would be accepted. But flying to Asia, with the future of his organization at stake in a white-hot Washington war, was a tactical blunder.

Magruder kept his boss posted as best he could by cable on the bureaucratic haggling. As he prepared to leave Europe for the Far East, the Joint Chiefs' staff came up with a counteroffer for the White House. Roosevelt could still pick a spy director, but a National Intelligence Authority (made up of the Army, Navy, and State Department secretaries plus a Joint Chiefs representative) would control his espionage operations and his budget. Donovan hated the plan. Instead of the president, he would be reporting to a committee, and one that could keep him on a very short leash. But Magruder cabled him that it was the best they could get out of the Pentagon. He advised Donovan to accept the military's plan for now. At least the

Pentagon recognized that the intelligence system needed overhaul. When Donovan returned to Washington he could maneuver to have some of its more offensive provisions changed as the White House considered the measure.

But as Donovan sat at his breakfast table on February 9 reading the *Times-Herald* with his November 18 memo and draft executive order printed on a back page, he knew his plan for a central intelligence agency was in mortal danger of never making it out of the Pentagon, much less being approved by the White House. Donovan phoned Doering at 6 A.M., ordering him to begin an immediate investigation into who leaked the sensitive documents and to report back to him in three hours. He then rushed to the office and huddled with his senior staff on damage control. Donovan had good relations with many Washington reporters so he cleared his afternoon schedule and began phoning them while aides set up dinner roundtables with bureau chiefs.

Donovan's media blitz worked to a degree. The Copley newspaper chain, a McCormick-Patterson rival, declared Donovan's plan one of the most "important postwar programs under consideration by President Roosevelt." The *New York Times* ridiculed the notion that Donovan was setting up an American Gestapo, while the *Washington Post* hailed him as "one of the trail blazers in our war organization." After the fighting ended, the United States will need "reliable intelligence from all over the world" with an agency like Donovan's, his friend, Ed Murrow, told radio listeners.

But Trohan wasn't finished. On February 11, he dropped his second bombshell, printing verbatim the intelligence plan the Joint Chiefs had drafted as an alternative for Roosevelt along with a Pentagon memo trashing the Donovan proposal. The *Tribune's* editorial page charged that Roosevelt needed his secret spy service to play his "dirty" political games "all around the world," while the *Times-Herald* ran a cartoon with the caption "Life in the Brave New World" showing FDR peeling off dollars for greedy, black-bearded spies to snoop on American taxpayers.

The White House became deathly silent on Donovan's plan and its leak. Delighted, Hoover cabled the *Tribune* stories to his agents in the field. Donovan, meanwhile, worried about international fallout from the leak. German propaganda had a field day, accusing him of conspiring to set up "a net of Jewish informers" to spy on "good neighbors throughout the world" with a plan that leaves "even the most hard-boiled gangsters of New

York and Chicago wondering." Cables went out to OSS stations abroad to be on the lookout for foreign reaction. The French remained silent while some British intelligence officers refused to send their OSS cousins classified documents for fear they could not keep them secret. London privately worried Donovan would not recover. Trohan's "characteristic piece of misreporting," a confidential Foreign Office note warned, "shows what opposition there is going to be to any extension of war agencies into peacetime."

Donovan began a massive investigation to uncover how the classified documents ended up in Trohan's hands. It was evident from the rapid-fire series of hostile articles that "the disclosure was no mere leak but a deliberate plan to sabotage any attempt at reorganization of this government's intelligence services," Donovan angrily wrote Roosevelt. And it was also crystal clear that this was "an inside job," he added. Ole Doering had not come up with a culprit three hours after Donovan's 6 A.M. call but he believed it had to be Hoover. He couldn't prove it but he thought the signs certainly pointed to the FBI director. The month before, a Navy source had tipped him off that Edward Tamm, Hoover's deputy, had used such vile language denouncing Donovan and his intelligence plan at a Pentagon meeting that the note taker decided not to record what he said.

To try to narrow the universe of leakers, the Pentagon and OSS security officers began the painstaking exercise of tracking down everyone who had been given copies of Donovan's November 18 memo to Roosevelt with its draft executive order or the intelligence plan the Joint Chiefs had drafted. Donovan scribbled on pads at his desk the names of staffers in his own organization and officials in other agencies who had seen the documents. It turned out to be a large universe. Nearly eighty copies had been made of Donovan's memo, which had been seen by more than two hundred people, while some 175 had seen nearly fifty copies of the Joint Chiefs' plan. Donovan could account for the memos in his own agency so he was pretty sure the leak did not come from there. But when the security officers did a word-by-word review of the *Times-Herald* stories they came up with an important clue. Trohan had printed copies the Joint Chiefs' aides had made of Donovan's memo, which contained a few minor word changes from the original version sent out by his agency. That meant the leak had come from the Pentagon or from another agency that had received a Pentagon copy of Donovan's memo.

Donovan had plenty of enemies in the military like Bissell who wanted to sink his plan. But Hoover hated him, his plan, and the military's alternative the most. The FBI was not on the original military distribution list, but Doering, whom Donovan had sent to the Pentagon in early March to scour its records, discovered that Hoover's agents had gotten copies of the two documents there. Hoover hotly denied he was the leaker and claimed that the FBI had returned its copies of the two documents to the Pentagon on February 17. But there was some question whether the bureau actually did. Tamm confessed to Hoover in a later internal memo on March 13 that the FBI's records section had never been able to find the two documents.

Donovan was now convinced that Hoover was guilty. He demanded that the Pentagon launch a full-scale criminal probe. The leak "strikes at the heart of military security," he told the Joint Chiefs. But the only agency with the authority to conduct a criminal investigation was the Justice Department and its FBI—Donovan's enemies. So many people had access to the documents it was impossible to determine how they got out. The Pentagon managed to retrieve all but one set of memos, which had been checked out by the Joint Intelligence Staff, but a copy of a copy could have been made and slipped to Trohan so accounting for the originals was no help. The Pentagon eventually abandoned its inquiry. It left Donovan bitter. He confronted Trohan at a later Gridiron dinner and accused him of aiding and abetting the enemy.

But who leaked the material? Many years later, Trohan told a CIA historian that it was not Hoover. None other than Franklin Roosevelt had leaked the memos. Trohan claimed that Steve Early, the White House press secretary, had given him the Donovan and Pentagon documents and told him FDR "wanted the story out." Roosevelt had grown distant from Donovan, Trohan said, and along with Hopkins did not want the Republican taking on a prominent position in the postwar administration. So in one of the most Machiavellian maneuvers a White House could make, FDR and Hopkins decided to leak Donovan's proposal to the McCormick-Patterson papers to kill it. Early had always been friendly with Trohan and the crafty Roosevelt knew that no one would ever suspect him of leaking the documents if they appeared in a newspaper chain that was his political enemy.

Trohan wasn't the first reporter to lie about the identity of a source and in this case he likely did to the CIA. It would take a monumental effort on Roosevelt's part to overcome his visceral hatred for Robert McCormick and Cissy Patterson and leak secret documents to their newspaper chain, which would end up painting him as a power-hungry politician intent on establishing an American Gestapo. It also defied credulity that Roosevelt would engineer to have a story damaging to him as well as to Donovan come out as he was immersed in sensitive talks at Yalta. Moreover, there was no record of Roosevelt, Hopkins, or Early receiving the Joint Chiefs' copy of the documents, which Trohan printed. Donovan had sent the White House his original version, which the reporter did not have. The biggest hole in Trohan's cover story, however, was that at the time he claimed he received the documents in Washington from Early, the press secretary was five thousand miles away with Hopkins and Roosevelt in Yalta. Though he tried to keep the relationship secret, Trohan had long been close to Hoover. The two had done favors for each other over the years. FBI agents had fed Trohan stories and considered him a bureau loyalist. The odds that Hoover was the leaker were high.

But neither Donovan nor anyone else who investigated the case could ever be sure. By the end of March, however, the question became moot even for Donovan. Marshall and the other service chiefs decided that with all the negative publicity it was best to shelve consideration of a future central intelligence agency for now. Roosevelt, who had remained silent through-out the controversy, agreed. Exhausted from his Yalta trip and preoccupied with the speech he had to give before Congress justifying the conference's result, FDR had ignored Donovan's memos complaining about Trohan. He made a point of acknowledging a gold cigarette case one of Donovan's officers had delivered as a gift from the regent of Thailand, but he said nothing to his spy chief about the leak. Harold Smith, meanwhile, moved quickly to take control. He sent Roosevelt a memo letting him know that the Budget Bureau was working on a "comprehensive study" of a future intelligence system. Smith advised his boss not to commit to Donovan's scheme or anyone else's until his number crunchers had sorted out the "tug-of-war going on between some of the agencies." Roosevelt agreed.

DONOVAN LUNCHED WITH Roosevelt at the White House on March 15. He was horrified at how feeble and exhausted the president appeared. Roosevelt had lost weight and showed no appetite for their meal. "He looks like he is on his last leg," Donovan later told Putzell. The two men did not discuss the Trohan leak or Donovan's CIA plan. Most of the lunch was spent with small talk. Donovan told Roosevelt of his plans to fly to Europe to organize OSS operations in the areas of Germany the Allies occupied or soon would occupy. The agency intended to have a large mission in Berlin once the Russians captured the city. Roosevelt planned to take the train down to Warm Springs, Georgia, for a much needed rest. After that, he said, he was looking forward to the first organizing conference of the new United Nations, which would be held in San Francisco. He planned to attend. After he retired, he told friends, he even wanted to be secretary-general of the world body one day. Donovan planned to go to the U.N. conference as well, along with a large delegation of more than eighty OSS officers. His Presentation Branch and foreign experts in William Langer's research department had been assigned to help the State Department with displays and position papers. Donovan's graphics shop had even designed the United Nations emblem. The mission of others in Donovan's party, however, was quietly to spy on the foreign delegations attending the conference and look for informants to recruit among them—which made the State Department nervous. This was supposed to be a diplomatic meeting to chart an enduring peace and Stettinius did not want its atmosphere fouled with a large OSS contingent the other delegations were sure to suspect was snooping on them. The Russians, assuming Donovan was up to no good, did object to the large contingent he wanted to bring to San Francisco, so he had to scale back his group.

Before he boarded his plane for Europe on April 6, Donovan deftly engineered a last gasp for his central intelligence agency plan. He got Isadore Lubin, one of his staunchest allies in the White House, to breach the wall Harold Smith thought he had firmly erected around Roosevelt to prevent anyone from foisting an intelligence proposal on the president. On April 4, Lubin rushed a memo to Warm Springs, where Roosevelt was now resting, which Donovan had helped him draft. Donovan's central intelligence idea "has stalled" in the Pentagon, Lubin wrote FDR. "Personally, I think that this is the time to have a definite plan formulated. The difficulty seems to lie in the fear of certain agencies of the government that they will not be permitted to play their part in the proposed setup." Why not have all the agencies come together for "a frank, across-the-table discussion" of Donovan's plan, Lubin suggested. He was sure their differences could be resolved. Lubin attached to his note the draft for a memo to Donovan—

which Donovan also helped Lubin write—ordering the OSS director to call together the one dozen intelligence agencies in the U.S. government, ask for their suggestions on how a centralized service might be set up, and reach "a consensus of opinion" from them on a new agency. Roosevelt signed the order.

Even in a town where skilled bureaucratic fighters never let an issue die, this was a brassy move. The twelve agencies had already reached consensus the previous winter and that consensus was anything but Donovan's plan. But Roosevelt was giving him a second chance. Donovan phoned Grace Tully in Warm Springs to make sure the president's order was rushed back in the April 5 pouch to the White House. The next day, he dashed off letters to the twelve cabinet departments and executive agencies with a copy of FDR's order attached, notifying them that after he received their opinions on his intelligence plan he would gather them together to hammer out an agreement, as the president wanted. Donovan boarded his flight for London that night confident he still had a fighting chance for his intelligence agency when he returned to Washington on April 25—particularly with Franklin Roosevelt in the White House to back him up.

Chapter 30

—◦◦◦—

Harry Truman

A S DONOVAN SETTLED into his suite at Claridge's Saturday evening, April 7, eight American, British, and Canadian armies raced toward the River Elbe west of Berlin. The Red Army prepared to jump across the Oder east of the German capital. Wehrmacht forces were now in such a confused state, Allied intelligence knew their positions on the battlefield better than German generals did. Dulles cabled to Washington regular reports from his informants on Hitler's eleventh-hour moves to shore up his crumbling lines. An OSS source in Berlin reported that "supplies of bread and potatoes are virtually exhausted" sparking food riots, while "conditions in the hospitals are hopeless" with no medicines to treat the sick or injured. "People's nerves are at an end," the agent noted. "Hysterical outbursts over trifling incidents are common."

Donovan transformed one floor of the London hotel into a command post. Rooms were set aside for secretaries, staff officers, and clattering typewriters, closets were stuffed with classified documents, and aides scurried into the suites twenty-four hours a day with reports and cables. The spy chief held round after round of meetings with his OSS team and with Menzies and his top MI6 officers to plot operations in Europe after the war. Donovan had twenty-one more intelligence missions being launched into the central slice of Germany that Hitler still controlled. To uncover Gestapo officers trying to blend in with civilians in the parts of Germany the Allies controlled, Donovan told aides he wanted to send out teams of French, Danish, Norwegian, and Polish nationals who had been tortured by the goons and survived. They would remember their faces.

Donovan was eager for practically any new mission launched into Germany. But he began to have second thoughts about one of the projects his aides briefed to him at Claridge's. Its code name was "Cross." Among the many resistance factions fighting the German occupation of France had been the communist-leaning German nationals of CALPO (for the Comité de l'Allemagne Libre pour l'Ouest or Free Germany Committee for the West). They were political refugees or Wehrmacht deserters. The OSS found them to be capable and courageous operatives. In February Donovan's special operations officers began training one hundred of the CALPO guerrillas to take their subversive war back to the Fatherland for the Cross Project. Once in the field, the Cross agents were promised what at the time was the princely sum of $200 a month. They were to carry out sabotage missions against Nazi strongholds in southern Germany including Hitler's retreat at Berchtesgaden. But the other mission Donovan had assigned the Cross team was assassinations. Their targets: Hitler, Himmler, Göring, and the other top Nazis, along with every Gestapo official or SS and SD officer with a rank of major or higher. One memo to Eisenhower termed them "organized killings." High-paid death squads would roam Germany looking for Hitler and his henchmen. The Cross teams received detailed briefings on who to pick as their prey; anyone wearing the "Golden Party Badge, the Order of Blood medal, the Guerrilla Warfare medal, or SS number lower than 125,000 should be disposed of without formality," one secret memo advised—in other words, executed on the spot.

Twenty-two assassins had been trained by the time Donovan received his final briefing at Claridge's. A top secret memo had been delivered to Ike asking for his approval. But as he sat in his suite and mulled the full scope of Cross, Donovan got cold feet. He had the good sense to realize that at this late stage of the war, launching a "wholesale assassination" program "would invite only trouble for the OSS," as he told his staff. Top Nazis such as Hitler and Göring were more valuable alive and brought to trial. Donovan canceled the execution plan. The Cross teams could be sent out for sabotage missions and if they ran across German leaders they should kidnap them, he instead ordered. Bad weather, however, delayed airdrops for Cross before the war ended so Donovan eventually scrubbed the sabotage and kidnap missions.

WEDNESDAY, APRIL 11, was busy at the Little White House in Warm Springs. Roosevelt endured another sitting with Madame Elizabeth Shoumatoff for his watercolor portrait that left his neck stiff. He settled on his schedule for the next week, dictated his Jefferson Day speech, took a long drive through the rural hill country, and met with Henry Morgenthau, who dropped by to lobby once more for Germany being broken up into small agricultural states after the war. The secretaries who traveled south with the president thought he did not look as deathly feeble as when he first arrived at the west Georgia retreat on March 30. He had even gained a few pounds. But his blood pressure remained dangerously high and his enlarged heart strained to keep pumping.

Buxton had three OSS memos pouched to Warm Springs by Wednesday so Grace Tully could place them in Roosevelt's overflowing in-box. Over the four years, Donovan or his senior aides had sent Roosevelt 7,500 pages of memos, cables, reports, and studies. One document now in the in-box updated Roosevelt on a surrender offer Dulles was negotiating. Karl Wolff, the Waffen SS chief for Italy, and Heinrich von Vietinghoff, who had replaced Kesselring as overall military commander, were proposing to surrender the hundreds of thousands of German soldiers who still occupied northern Italy. "Wolff recognizes the futility of further fighting," Dulles reported in the memo sent to Roosevelt. All that remained was haggling over the details. The two German generals had agreed to the Allied demand for unconditional surrender, Dulles cabled, but they wanted the language in the final document they signed "dressed up" so it looked like they had capitulated with "military honor."

The OSS had given the secret talks the code name "Sunrise." The first peace feeler had arrived in November 1944 and Wolff finally met Dulles secretly in his Bern apartment on March 8 to begin serious talks. Dulles believed the SS general was "probably the most dynamic personality in North Italy," as he wrote in one top secret memo to Donovan. Wolff was also a war criminal, complicit in the extermination of 300,000 Jews, who calculated that successful surrender negotiations would save Germany's Army Group C—and his skin. But there were delays on the German side while indecision gripped Washington and London. The Soviets were informed of the Wolff contacts but not brought into the early negotiations. Stalin complained that the Germans were exploiting the lengthy talks to move three divisions from northern Italy to the Eastern Front and demanded that they be broken off. Fearing Sunrise seriously undermined relations with Moscow, Churchill at one point succeeded in having the operation suspended. Not until April 29 was a surrender finally signed in Caserta. It went into effect May 2, five days before all German forces gave up.

Those five days saved hundreds, perhaps thousands, of lives. But they came at the price of further straining U.S. relations with the Russians, who remained indignant at being cut out of the operation. Donovan considered it one of the most successful diplomatic missions his agency carried out.

DONOVAN FLEW TO Paris on Thursday evening, April 12. He had stored among the classified documents packed in the plane's cargo hold a piece of war booty he planned to take back to Washington. Among the hundreds of subjects he dealt with during his London meetings was the disposal of the Abyssinian Treasure Trove, found after the Allies liberated Ethiopia in 1941. Donovan ordered all of the artifacts returned to Emperor Haile Selassie, who had been restored to power. But he decided to take home one item he knew Selassie did not want—a silver casket containing the baton of the hated Marshal Rodolfo Graziani, who had brutally ruled Ethiopia at one point during the Italian occupation.

Donovan settled his traveling headquarters into a suite Hermann Göring once occupied at the Ritz Hotel. He planned to breakfast with Casey the next morning for an update on his penetrations into Germany. He went to bed not knowing the momentous news Steve Early had released to the press in Washington at 5:48 P.M., which was almost midnight Paris time.

Early the next morning, Donovan was shaving in the bathroom when Russell Forgan, his London counterintelligence chief, rushed into the suite with the news bulletin that the sixty-three-year-old president had died of a massive cerebral hemorrhage Thursday afternoon at Warm Springs. Donovan raced out of the bathroom, wiping the shaving cream off his face with a towel, and told Forgan to get him an open line to Washington. He then dashed off a condolence cable to Eleanor—so sorry, he wrote, for the "crushing loss" she and the nation have suffered. It came from the heart. Back in Washington, many staffers at OSS headquarters were in tears, grief-stricken like the rest of country. "We felt the end of the world had come," recalled Margaret Tibbetts, a research analyst covering Great Britain.

For three hours, Donovan sat on the edge of the bed in his Paris suite, his elbows propped on his knees, his head slumped down. Some of the time he just talked to himself, or when Forgan, Casey, and other officers walked into the bedroom he looked up and pondered the loss with them. "This is the most terrible news I've ever had," he said at one point. Roosevelt was the last person protecting his agency. Donovan hardly knew Truman. It probably means, he told his aides, that their dream of a postwar central intelligence service has died as well.

BY MAY 1, the Red Army occupied practically all of Berlin. British forces neared Lubeck and Hamburg while the U.S. armies stood at the Elbe and Mulde Rivers and, to the south, moved into Austria. That Tuesday evening, Ruth had brought a rib roast from Chapel Hill to their Georgetown home for a dinner party Donovan was throwing in honor of Victor Cavendish-Bentinck, who chaired Britain's Joint Intelligence Committee. After dessert, cars took the group of more than a dozen American and British intelligence officers to OSS headquarters where they watched a movie in the basement theater. Ruth found the musical boring. But midway through the show, Donovan ordered the projectionist to halt the film. An aide had just passed him a news bulletin from Hamburg radio. Hitler was dead. With the fighting drawing near to his Berlin Führerbunker, Hitler married his mistress, Eva Braun, on April 29 and the two committed suicide the next day. Their bodies were burned but the remains later found by the Soviets. Grand Admiral Karl Dönitz, whom Hitler had appointed to succeed him as head of state, announced that "the struggle against the Bolsheviks" would continue and exhorted every German soldier to "do your duty!"

The final days of the Axis leaders had been on Donovan's mind lately. He read with interest grisly details in the autopsy report for Mussolini, whom Italian partisans had captured and executed on April 28. Il Duce's head had been beaten and shot so many times his face was "almost unrecognizable," the report noted. Donovan had earlier ordered Dulles to have an agent search Munich's police headquarters, where he knew Hitler's fingerprints were on file when he had to register there as a nonresident in

1921—just in case the dictator sent an impostor out to be captured while he fled. He later gave Pavel Fitin, the Russian intelligence chief, Hitler's dental records to help the Soviets identify the corpse. OSS counterintelligence officers had gotten their hands on the chart when they captured the führer's personal SS dentist in April.

The projectionist did not restart the film after Donovan read the news report. Everyone stood up. A few shook hands. Then silently they filed out of the theater and climbed into their cars for home and bed—a feeling of both relief and exhaustion overpowering them all.

Donovan was in a more festive mood after Dönitz signed the unconditional surrender of all German forces at Eisenhower's Rheims headquarters on May 7. At a raucous private dinner at New York's St. Regis Hotel with Bill Stephenson, the two men shouted toasts and danced about like bears in triumph. Donovan had had his squabbles with the British, but he realized full well the contribution they had made to his organization.

DONOVAN HAD RETURNED to Washington from his Europe trip two weeks after Roosevelt died. His most important task now was developing some type of relationship with Harry Truman. Like many FDR aides and Washington political pundits, Donovan thought the Missourian was a provincial politician unqualified to be president. Truman, in fact, had assumed the nation's highest office unprepared for it, but he was not cowed by the tremendous responsibility dumped into his lap. An internationalist, he had read a lot about foreign affairs before joining the administration. Once he solved his immediate transition problems, "there'll be no more to this job," he wrote his wife, Bess, "than there was to running Jackson County," Missouri, when he was its commissioner. Truman quickly developed a firm sense of the FDR men he could trust—such as Early and Harold Smith at the Budget Bureau—and those he could not. He could spot a phony a mile away, and prima donnas in the military—MacArthur was already on his list—did not impress him.

Truman intended to bring organization to an executive branch he found shockingly disorganized. Unlike Roosevelt, he did not encourage rivalries among his top people and he did not intend to run cabinet agencies as if he were their secretary. Truman liked order and delegating authority, and he quickly halted the haphazard access to the Oval Office his predecessor had encouraged. Unlike Roosevelt, he had no use for secret operations run out of the White House and shut down John Franklin Carter's spy unit.

Truman also began his new job with a healthy distrust of J. Edgar Hoover. Hoover tried to cultivate Truman early on. He arranged for an FBI agent who hailed from Independence, Missouri, to drop by the Oval Office to swap family stories and plug his plan for heading a worldwide intelligence service. The new president was willing to open his door for a hometown neighbor, but not for Hoover. Roosevelt had encouraged the FBI's domestic spying, but Truman feared the bureau had become a Gestapo-like secret police force and he wanted no part of it. From his days in Congress, he also knew that Hoover kept files on the sex lives of lawmakers to blackmail them. From now on, Truman ordered that anything Hoover wanted to say or report to him first had to go through his new military assistant, Harry Vaughan, a garrulous, blustery, and often comical Army colonel he had known since World War I. Hoover detested the arrangement and tried to bypass Vaughan, but Truman still refused to give him direct access.

Donovan and Truman had more in common. Both had fought in World War I. Donovan saw more intense combat, but Truman had been a conscientious artillery captain, receiving commendations from his superiors and reacting coolly when German field guns and planes rained counterfire on the battery he commanded. Truman also revered soldiers who received the Medal of Honor for valor, as Donovan had. But there was a lot with Wild Bill that Truman did not like. Donovan was a smooth-talking and successful Wall Street lawyer from New York, not the kind of person a failed Missouri haberdasher identified with. Truman fought to make government more open when he chaired a special Senate committee probing waste. Donovan worked to increase secrecy. The spy chief also was a Republican and Truman did not believe he had been completely loyal to the Democratic administration.

Donovan brainstormed with his staff about how to cozy up to the new president. Putzell phoned Rose Conway, Truman's personal secretary, to arrange for Donovan's secret intelligence memos to be placed on his desk without being seen by intermediaries, as Grace Tully had done with FDR. A small, shy woman who could outwork any man, Conway agreed to the same procedure. Donovan tried the tricks he had used to schmooze Roosevelt. He sent Truman a framed map of Belgian territory the 2nd Armored Division had recaptured, a warm letter addressed to the president that he had received from twenty thousand workmen in the Netherlands, and accounts of the daring exploits of agents like Virginia Hall behind enemy lines in France. He worked hometown connections as well, sending Truman reports from two Missourians recovering Americans from Japanese POW camps in China. Truman thanked Donovan for the map and, unlike for Hoover, allowed the OSS reports to come directly to him. But he did not respond to the war stories.

Donovan also sent Truman his proposal for a postwar intelligence service, along with the April 4 Roosevelt memo directing him to shop it with the twelve other agencies. The responses Donovan got from the twelve were disheartening but not unexpected. The five most important organizations—War, Navy, State, Justice, and FBI—shot down the plan once more. Almost all the others rejected it or had no comment. The only one backing Donovan was the Foreign Economic Administration, an insignificant outfit for his purposes. Over long lunches or private meetings in their offices, Donovan promoted his plan with Truman's Senate pals, such as Illinois's Scott Lucas (a rising liberal star and Truman favorite), West Virginian Harley Kilgore (a key Military Affairs Committee member who had befriended Truman), and South Carolina's James F. Byrnes (whom Truman would soon make his secretary of state). But the person to convince was Harry Truman.

After almost a month of begging for time on Truman's crowded schedule, Donovan finally walked into the Oval Office on Monday morning, May 14, for his first meeting. Truman already knew his other national security agencies opposed Donovan's postwar intelligence plan. Harold Smith, who developed almost an instant rapport with the new president, also had convinced him to keep both Donovan and Hoover at arm's length until the Budget Bureau came up with a postwar intelligence plan.

Truman gave Donovan just fifteen minutes for their first meeting—what a president usually affords visiting firemen. It was the chilliest session the spymaster had ever had in the White House. Donovan tried his best in the cramped time slot to make his pitch for a postwar intelligence agency, but Truman did little to hide his lack of interest in the proposal. Afterward the president noted mockingly in his diary that Donovan "came in to tell how important the Secret Service [sic] is and how much he could do to run the government on an even basis."

Donovan continued to pepper Truman with memos: on future U.S.

relations with Russia, on Axis espionage agents remaining undercover after the war, on peace feelers the Japanese sent through intermediaries to OSS officers overseas. Truman was too busy to respond to most of the reports but he did scan them and was quick to react when he saw something he did not like. On August 18, Donovan sent him an offer of cooperation from Kim Ku, who he identified as chairman of the Korean Provisional Government, a loosely organized group of exiles holed up in Chungking with visions of governing Korea after the war. The OSS's Asia experts did not think the uneducated Kim or his cronies could run the country, but Donovan told Truman he had been working with the man to install agents in Korea. The only problem: The State Department knew nothing about Kim Ku or his group and White House aides thought it highly improper for a spy chief to be dealing with them. Truman agreed. He dressed down Donovan in a snippy note, telling him he had no business "acting as a channel for the transmission to me of messages from representatives of self-styled governments which are not recognized by the Government of the United States."

THREE DAYS AFTER his frosty meeting with Truman, Donovan took what amounted to a short break from his own agency. Bureaucratically it was not a particularly smart move with the OSS on life support in Washington. But Donovan boarded his plane for Europe on May 17 to become what he had been twenty-three years earlier—a prosecutor. This time the criminals were the Nazis of Germany.

Though he had been largely indifferent to collecting wartime intelligence on the Holocaust, Donovan had been ahead of the rest of the U.S. government in making preparations to bring Axis leaders to justice for their crimes. As early as August 1942 he had ordered his staff to begin looking into Japanese atrocities against civilians and POWs. By October 1943, he was urging Roosevelt and others in the administration to set up the legal machinery for extraditing and prosecuting Axis war criminals. The military, State Department, and the British paid little attention to the subject, but Roosevelt was interested and told Donovan to begin investigating how the accused could be brought to trial. John Ciechanowski, the Polish ambassador to Washington, sent him the names of the top Nazis ruling Poland and Donovan cabled his OSS teams in the Balkans for the

Germans there who should be on the war crimes list. He gathered up affidavits from Norwegian doctors who had treated victims of Gestapo torture in German prisons and news stories on the liberation of death camps such as Treblinka, where nearly a million Jews had been gassed. Finally on December 15, 1944, the War Department's judge advocate general formally assigned to the OSS the job of collecting evidence against suspects and researching international law to bring them to justice. Donovan plunged into the mission as if he were launching a covert operation. He ordered his aides to put together "a top-flight staff on war crimes." Donovan envisioned the Germans bringing the men to trial so the country could "purge itself of its blood guilt and punish its own criminals," he said. Other officers, like Dulles, thought that was a bad idea; the Allies should control the prosecution.

There were practical reasons for Donovan's interest in going after war criminals—he wanted payback for the torture and murder of his agents. He had personally interviewed a female OSS operative raped and beaten by her German guards and was shocked by what he heard. He had not forgotten the commandos from a team code-named "Ginny" who were captured by the Germans in Italy and gunned down by a firing squad or the fifteen OSS and British operatives captured in Czechoslovakia who had been taken to the Mauthausen concentration camp, where they were brutally tortured for eight days, then executed naked with bullets to the back of their heads. Both teams' members had been wearing their U.S. Army uniforms and should have enjoyed the Geneva Convention protections for war prisoners. Donovan, Dulles, and British intelligence also wanted to protect German spies who had worked for the Allies from being swept up in war crimes prosecutions, although Roosevelt resisted offering blanket immunity. FDR suspected a number of guilty Germans would try to save themselves by coming over to the winning side at the last moment.

After the European war ended, Truman picked Supreme Court Justice Robert Jackson to be America's chief counsel for the prosecution of Nazi war criminals. Jackson was a handsome and courtly man who had taught himself law to pass the bar exam instead of graduating from law school. Both he and Donovan came from western New York and had become able lawyers, but that was about all they had in common. The two had been political rivals in the state. Jackson, a Roosevelt Democrat, did not think much of Donovan's conservative Republican positions and both men had been mentioned as presidential prospects for their parties. But Jackson, who took a leave of absence from the Supreme Court, quickly discovered the OSS was the only agency in the U.S. government seriously working on war crimes. He asked Donovan to join his trial staff, clearing it first with Truman, who thought having a prominent Republican on the legal team was a good idea.

On May 15, Donovan huddled with Jackson in the justice's chambers. He offered the full resources of his spy agency. Jackson was grateful; he had only a handful of loyalists to call on, including his son who was a lawyer, and none was experienced in war crimes prosecutions. Donovan also said he knew Jackson would be "the captain of the team" and he "would play wherever" the Justice could use him. Donovan didn't really mean that. He intended to play a star role in the trials. He wanted to put Hermann Göring, who had just surrendered to the Allies, on the stand for a dramatic cross-examination. Jackson was intrigued and told Donovan he should send agents to interview the Reichsmarschall.

Donovan flew to Europe on May 17 eager to move quickly to trial. It was important to show progress at the outset, he warned Jackson before boarding his plane, not only to generate public support for the historic proceedings but also to keep on board the Russians, who would have a say in the prosecution. Jackson agreed. Over the next six months, 172 OSS staffers would join the justice's team. Navy Lieutenant James Donovan, the OSS's general counsel, became one of Jackson's key trial tacticians. (OSS critics used James Donovan as an example of nepotism in the spy agency, which was not true in his case; the general counsel and his boss were not related.) Donovan and his investigators began piecing together the many parts of the Nazi Holocaust machine, unearthing SS documents on "death vans" used to asphyxiate Jews, collecting testimony from Auschwitz survivors on its gas chambers. Dulles's key Abwehr informant, Hans Gisevius, sketched out the organization of the Nazi Party. William Langer's researchers in Washington and London provided mountains of reports on such topics as the inner workings of the German General Staff and analyzed captured documents plotting the religious and ethnic cleansing of Europe. Donovan assembled a panel of psychiatrists to rule on Nazis who might plead insanity as a defense and briefed Jackson on the agency's highly secret research into truth drugs, which the justice agreed might be useful in getting defendants to talk. No detail was ignored. The OSS Presentation

Branch designed the courtroom for the tribunals (one innovation put the judges on the right facing the defendants in a box on the left), while John Ford's film unit produced movies of the concentration camp horrors.

Jackson later had second thoughts about making the proceedings a media spectacle. But for now he was eager to have Donovan's agency at his disposal. He flew to London to join the spymaster, impressed with the luxury suite he commanded at Claridge's and the Dewar's White Label Scotch he had stocked in the rooms. Jackson was even more impressed with the doors Donovan opened for him in the British government, foreign embassies, and Eisenhower's command. The two men paid a visit to Fedor Gusev, the Soviet ambassador in London, who was cordial but secretive about Soviet plans for the tribunal. They flew in Donovan's plane to Frankfurt, where Beetle Smith manned Ike's forward headquarters in the former I. G. Farben building, one of the few left standing in a city that to Jackson seemed nothing but "a mass of rubble." Smith was skeptical about the value of the tribunals. The Soviets, he told them, had a far more efficient system for dealing with undesirable Germans in their sector; they just shot them on the spot.

Donovan soon became Jackson's most trusted emissary, with the OSS insinuated into every aspect of the justice's operation. He gave Jackson's lawyers OSS office space in Paris, brought in his propagandists to write press releases, covered the prosecution team's expenses with money from the agency's accounts so Jackson did not have to haggle with Congress, and helped him screen American judges for the tribunal. By mid-June Donovan had presented his team captain a detailed plan for organizing the prosecution staff with the spy chief acting as his deputy and his star attorney during the trial. Jackson, who thought Donovan and his OSS had been a godsend, agreed to practically all of the suggestions.

DONOVAN FLEW BACK to Washington on Monday, June 11, and made a rare weekday excursion to Nonquitt, where Ruth, Mary, and Patricia were vacationing. But as usual, he became bored and spent most of his two days at the retreat on the phone to headquarters or New York. Back in Washington, Jackson returned Donovan's favors and lobbied for his postwar central intelligence service. "It's none of my business," Jackson had already told Truman in one meeting, but Donovan seems to be the only person in town who has paid much attention to collecting foreign intelligence. "Perhaps there is some way" his large organization could continue after the war, Jackson said. "It would be very useful." Truman was noncommittal, repeating once more that he did not want to see "the beginning of a Gestapo" in the country.

Jackson let Donovan tag along on another visit the justice made to the Oval Office on Saturday, June 16, shortly after noon. Truman was in a cheerier mood than the last time Donovan had been to the White House. Jackson began by catching him up on the war crimes prosecution; he was having to treat the Russians with kid gloves in organizing the tribunal. He handed Truman a draft executive order directing other agencies to work with his team. Don't be too solicitous toward the Soviets, Truman cautioned. "They have more respect for people who stand up to them." Truman summoned an appointments secretary and told him to have an aide put the draft order "in shape to sign." And "if he can add any forty-dollar words to make it more effective, do so."

Jackson planned to fly to Rome and pay Pope Pius a visit to solicit his cooperation with the war crimes trials. Truman thought that was a good idea. "You and I are Masons," Jackson pointed out. Just as that fraternal organization binds together millions of Americans, "the two most cohesive forces in Europe are the Communist Party and the Catholic Church." Truman understood and stood up to fetch from a cabinet the gavel the grand master of Missouri's Masons had given him. Maybe they should take it as a gift for the pontiff, he said with a chuckle. It might be better to take Donovan with me to the meeting since he is a Catholic, Jackson suggested. Looking at Donovan with a smile, Truman thought that was a good idea as well.

Donovan recounted stories about the high-value Nazis now in custody for trial. Göring was ingesting large dosages of codeine, he said. Truman got up once more and retrieved another souvenir from the cabinet: Göring's gaudy Reichsmarschall baton covered with Nazi symbols and inlaid diamonds, which the U.S. Army had delivered to him.

Jackson finally moved the conversation to the direction Donovan wanted it to go. As the justice had mentioned to Truman before, he and Donovan both believed that someone in the new administration should be assigned to work "more closely" with the OSS and "to know what it is doing." Donovan's intelligence agency had been vital for the prosecution team, Jackson said, and he thought it could be useful for Truman. It was important for a president to have an outfit collecting political intelligence overseas in addition to military secrets gathered by the Pentagon; it was also important that the intelligence agency be independent and its "reports not pass through some department for screening, which would have a special interest in slanting the information." Truman agreed.

Donovan sat there somewhat stunned. Jackson was the best lobbyist he could have ever found for his organization; the justice was one of the most well-connected Democrats in town, close to many people who were becoming key players in this new administration, and here he was promoting— quite effectively—a role for the OSS after the war ended. And Truman, who had given Donovan nothing but a cold shoulder so far, seemed amenable to the idea of a peacetime intelligence service—at least in principle.

Donovan took over the pitch at this point. Truman might want to consider sending one of his most trusted aides to the OSS, he told the president, and Donovan would give him "complete access" to the agency's secrets. He zeroed in on the all-important political problem he knew Democrats had with him and his organization. Donovan believed in party government, he told Truman, and he recognized that Democrats were in power. Yes, there were "a good many" Republicans in the OSS, but "about seventy percent of the staff are Democrats and many of them New Dealers," he said. Domestic policy will be run by Democrats as long as he is president, Truman told Donovan. But party affiliation "should make no difference in foreign affairs," the president said. The country comes first.

Donovan drove back to the Supreme Court with Jackson elated over their Oval Office meeting. But whatever goodwill the justice had built for him with Truman was being eaten away by more hostile news stories, which were painting for the new president a portrait of a rogue intelligence chief. Donovan had enjoyed cozy relations with many reporters, but now he found elements of the media a powerful enemy helping to nail the coffin of the OSS.

Walter Trohan reported that day in the *Washington Times-Herald* that MacArthur had refused to allow Donovan's men into his theater and followed up with a second story four days later that Nimitz had barred the OSS from his operation as well. The House Appropriations Committee, which was considering Donovan's budget for the next year, decided to poll the Joint Chiefs and all the theater commanders on the value of the OSS. Donovan scrambled to contain the damage. He ordered his overseas stations to do all they could to massage the answers the theater commands cabled to Washington. In many cases the station chiefs were allowed to edit the responses before they were sent. MacArthur and Nimitz wrote back that they could not evaluate the OSS's performance because neither had asked for its services. The Joint Chiefs delivered a qualified verdict, acknowledging both the agency's successes and failures. But Eisenhower and the commanders for the China, India-Burma, and Mediterranean theaters turned in glowing reviews. The value of the OSS in Europe "has been so great that there should be no thought of its elimination as an activity," Ike declared.

Trohan wasn't through. Citing unnamed congressional sources, he followed up with two more stories, which charged that the OSS was riddled with communists and "scarcely more than an arm of the British Intelligence Service." Donovan managed to get some of his news friends, such as *New York Times* Washington bureau chief Arthur Krock, to defend him in print. But their voices were drowned out by bigger media stars.

One of the most negative stories came from a leak in Donovan's own organization while he was in Europe with Jackson. On May 25, Drew Pearson published an April cable Donovan had sent Russell Forgan, his counterintelligence officer in Paris, ordering him to keep three I. G. Farben executives the OSS had in custody isolated and to make sure the tons of files that had been seized, which incriminated the company in the Nazi war buildup, were shipped to Paris. Pearson suggested that Donovan and Forgan, a former Chicago banker, had a sinister motive: keeping the Farben executives away from Justice and Army investigators to protect the giant German chemical manufacturer for American business interests after the war. But Pearson was taking what he read in the one cable out of context. If the columnist had had a dozen other OSS messages in the case, he would have discovered that Donovan wanted the Farben execs sequestered so they could be interrogated properly for Jackson's war crimes prosecution and their documents analyzed by a skilled OSS team that included representatives from his George Project, which had been carefully tracking Farben's infiltration into Latin America. Donovan had asked Beetle Smith to hold off having untrained military investigators question the suspects. Angry Army intelligence officers in Washington, however, believed the OSS was pampering the Farben execs while aides for Biddle complained that Donovan should not be allowed to corner the interrogations.

Donovan was furious that Pearson had gotten hold of even one of the secret cables. He had sent his message to Forgan encrypted in what he thought was an unbreakable code and he now feared Pearson had found a way to decipher it with the help of someone inside the OSS. He ordered another internal probe into what could be a serious security breach. His investigators eventually concluded that someone in the message center passed a copy of the cable to the columnist before it was encoded but they could not pinpoint the leaker. The affair, however, took another twist typical for Washington political intrigue. Ole Doering turned up what Donovan suspected might be a shady connection between Francis Biddle and the leak to Pearson. When Donovan returned from his Europe trip with Jackson, he placed an angry phone call to the attorney general. Biddle sheepishly admitted that Pearson had shown him the cable during a visit to his office.

Did you tell Pentagon security officers that Pearson had the classified cable "or did you tell this office?" Donovan asked, his voice rising in indignation.

"No. No reason why I should have," Biddle answered just as indignantly.

"Did Pearson tell you where he got it?" Donovan asked.

"No, you'll have to ask him," Biddle answered smugly.

Donovan fought to control the rage boiling in him. Biddle was the nation's top law enforcement officer. He had been presented with evidence that a highly classified document had been stolen from the U.S. government and he sat on his hands. It further convinced Donovan that Biddle, Hoover, and enemies in the Pentagon were in cahoots with Trohan, Pearson, and other hostile journalists intent on destroying his agency.

DONOVAN BOARDED his plane on June 22 for another trip to Europe with Jackson. It was almost as if he were trying to escape his enemies in Washington. The two men did their best to entertain Ambassador Gusev and other members of the Soviet prosecution team at a private dinner at Claridge's. Donovan, who would have preferred to run the tribunal without them, stood up and gave a solemn speech extolling the American-Soviet alliance. Gusev and the other Russians toasted Truman, but they sipped little of the yellowish liquid the hotel claimed was vodka.

A fortnight later Donovan and Jackson flew to the Bavarian city of Nuremberg, the cultural home for National Socialism, where Hitler staged his grandest propaganda rallies and the Reichstag convened to pass the horrid anti-Semitic laws. The Russians wanted the war crimes trials held in Berlin, which they controlled. Donovan pressed for Nuremberg, not just because of its symbolic importance to the Nazis, but also because it was in the American zone and had the spacious Palace of Justice, damaged but still intact, with a large prison near the courthouse. Jackson agreed. The two picked their way through piles of brick and debris over barely recognized roads and sidewalks near the medieval city center to reach the palace. Allied bombers had destroyed practically all of the city and the stink of corpses rotting under rubble still hung in the air. Inside the palace they took out tape measures to plot the dimensions of the courtrooms, checked out the badly damaged library, and inspected the jail. The trial rooms were small, but with repairs and a few walls knocked out one in the east wing would do. The jail, by Jackson's count, seemed to have room for about a thousand prisoners.

Casey and Forgan flew back with Donovan to Washington on July 13. Between rounds of gin rummy in the passenger cabin, they brainstormed operations in Asia where the costly war still raged. Donovan had ambitious plans for infiltrating agents into Japan's home islands, but ultimately no operatives ended up reaching them so he had to settle for collecting intelligence through intermediaries, such as Vatican diplomats and visiting Thai students. He was just as enthusiastic about anti-Japanese propaganda. But because of cultural differences and a dearth of long-range radio transmitters those initiatives also ended up being small-time, such as fake surrender orders from their commanders dropped on Japanese troops in Burma or rumors spread that their quinine, which comes from the cinchona, was made from the worthless bark of other trees. Donovan did feel some sense of pride over his China operation, however. After interminable haggling with Chiang and his generals, his OSS officers had managed to mount credible guerrilla attacks that had inflicted more than six thousand Japanese casualties. Five thousand Chinese airborne commandos were being trained and hundreds of OSS operatives from Europe were being transferred to the mainland to expand that mission.

After less than two weeks in Washington, Donovan boarded his plane with more than a dozen senior aides for one last tour of the Asian war. Even his son, David, finally got his wish to serve there. The Navy assigned him to the USS *Avoyel*, a fleet tug towing ships and clearing mines in the

Pacific, where he became its executive officer and later its skipper. Bureau-cratically, it was probably safe for Donovan to be overseas once more; the person who would decide the fate of his organization, Harry Truman, was out of town as well, preoccupied with Churchill and Stalin at the Potsdam conference in the Brandenburg state, where the three powers were decid-ing on punishment for occupied Germany and strategy for finally defeating Japan. On the way to Potsdam, Truman learned of the successful atomic bomb test in New Mexico and informed Stalin of the development when he arrived. Stalin did not appear surprised.

DONOVAN WAS IN rain-soaked Kunming, arguing with Chiang over his generals who still did not cooperate with the OSS station, when news came of the atomic bombs dropped on Hiroshima and Nagasaki August 6 and 9. His Far East officers immediately queried the few Japanese sources they had to gauge the government's reaction to the devastation.

Donovan took a side trip to the ancient city of X'ian north of Kunming where an OSS team was located at a remote U.S. Army base. He kept to a leisurely pace, rising early before the summer heat became oppressive and sitting on the porch at his quarters, where he read a prayer book, fingered a rosary, and meditated. During his morning meditation, OSS officers gath-ered around the steps to the porch and listened quietly as Donovan turned philosophical. He was sure the atomic bombs would soon end the fighting in Asia. (Japan formally surrendered on September 2.) Our possession of these terrifying weapons meant there would be a "peaceful interlude," but sooner or later America would have a showdown with the communist world, he predicted, and it would be a nuclear showdown. It was only a matter of time before Russia acquired atomic arms. (Two months later, Donovan phoned Jackson and told him U.S. intelligence had "incontestable proof" the Soviets were in "complete possession of the secret of the atomic bomb," which explains "their stiff and aloof position in international affairs.") The OSS would be needed in Europe to spy on the Russians, Donovan believed, and in Asia to police the Japanese and monitor communist advances in China, Manchuria, and Korea. "You must understand," he told his men on the porch, "America has won a war but not a peace."

WHEN DONOVAN RETURNED to Washington on August 14, he immediately launched an eleventh-hour publicity campaign to save his spy organization. Wallace Deuel, an OSS propaganda adviser, had already left the agency to rejoin the *Chicago Daily News*, but Donovan enlisted him to write a series of articles in the paper touting OSS accomplishments. Donovan and Doering screened the pieces before Deuel turned them in to his editors. Fisher Howe, who had returned from overseas to be one of Doering's aides, drafted an elaborate twenty-page plan to sell the media. But the OSS had no trained publicity staff. Donovan's aides had always been leery of Pentagon press releases mentioning OSS operations and his agents in the field loathed seeing their names in print for fear it would compromise operations and get someone killed. Donovan, to a large degree, was the agency's public affairs officer, and his dealings with reporters were almost always on background or off the record. Howe dreamed up the PR plan off the top of his head. Deuel, the only one in the group with journalistic experience, was skeptical it would work. Donovan, nevertheless, turned on the spigot. He had his aides declassify more than a hundred secret operations and released accounts of them to reporters—in many cases including their code names and the names of the agents who had performed heroically. British diplomats grew nervous about Donovan taking the wraps off clandestine operations. Truman, who read the flurry of puff pieces in the newspapers, knew what Donovan was up to and he didn't like it.

The press, however, continued sniping. *Newsweek* ran a snide item on the alleged wage scale for Donovan's "cloak and dagger department." An "Eavesdropper" was paid $1,550 a year, a "Rumormonger" received $1,770 annually, and a "Back Stabber" got $4,660, the magazine claimed.

Smelling blood, the House Appropriations Committee slashed Donovan's budget from $38 million to $20 million for the next year. Donovan considered himself lucky to get that much. But he pleaded in memos to both Smith and Truman that it was critical a central intelligence service like the one he proposed to Roosevelt remain in place for peacetime. Donovan told them he intended to resign after the OSS's war assets had been liquidated to return to civilian life. (That was just a ploy on his part to keep from being a lightning rod as he maneuvered to put his central intelligence plan in place. Donovan wanted to run the postwar CIA.)

But Truman and Harold Smith, who faced the daunting task of demobilizing millions of soldiers, sailors, airmen, and marines, had other plans for Donovan's spy agency by late August. Smith's budget staff began quietly working on a proposal for a new intelligence organization in the future; the OSS would be disbanded and its operations parceled out to the military and the State Department. By the second week of September, however, Donovan had picked up the rumors that his agency would be dismembered and he was furious that Smith had hatched this plot without consulting him—or anyone else in the Pentagon for that matter. He could not believe Smith had foisted such a naively dumb idea on the president, he angrily told the budget chief.

Donovan fired off an angry memo to Truman on September 13. "I hope that in the national interest, and in your own interest as the Chief Executive, that you will not permit this to be done," he wrote, practically accusing Truman's budget director of treason. That same day he had managed to schedule an appointment with Truman to bring in Henri Laussucq, a Pittsburgh artist who had fought bravely for the French underground. But Donovan sat dour-faced as Truman listened to a few war stories from Laussucq, pinned a Silver Star medal on his chest, posed for photos, then hustled the two men out before Donovan could get in a word about his agency. Later in the afternoon, Smith slipped into Truman's office to let him know that Donovan was "storming about our proposal to divide his intelligence service."

I know, Truman told Smith. Donovan had brought one of his agents in earlier that morning but Truman said he didn't give him a chance to bring up the subject. Continue with your plan to dissolve the OSS, he told his budget director, "even if Donovan did not like it," Smith recorded in his diary.

Ironically, Truman actually wanted some kind of "broad intelligence service" set up in the future, as he told Smith, and he wanted it reporting directly to him, not to the Pentagon, as Donovan advocated. But he was firm in the belief that neither Donovan's OSS nor Hoover's FBI should head it. Hoover launched his own publicity campaign to show how the bureau had won the war. His agents regularly took Harry Vaughan, Truman's military aide, out to dinner and Hoover became a lunch buddy with the jolly but well-connected officer, who swapped dirty jokes and played poker with Truman. But the director had no luck cultivating the president. Truman told Smith to cut the 8,223 employees in the FBI to its prewar level of about six thousand and he ordered a scale-back of the bureau's spy operation in Latin America. He worried that gringo agents roaming the region threatened Roosevelt's old Good Neighbor Policy.

Hoover, whose sources in the administration kept him informed of every move Donovan made with Truman to save his agency, took one more important step to make sure his nemesis failed. The unfounded rumor floating around Washington and Berryville that Donovan was having an affair with his daughter-in-law had no difficulty making its way to FBI agents. Hoover ordered an aide to pass the rumor on to Vaughan, who in turn passed it on to the president. Truman, who was prudish about sex and totally devoted to Bess, was offended. But the rumor was far from being the final death blow for Donovan's organization. Truman had another equally derogatory report on his desk.

Richard Park Jr. had been an Army brat from Washington, D.C., who followed his father's footsteps and graduated from West Point. Though trained as an artillery officer, Park eventually gravitated to military intelligence and became devoted to George Strong, who reciprocated and sent him to Moscow in 1941 as a military attaché. It was a prestige post and Park sent back a vivid report to Washington on his month-long tour of the Russian front, which even reached Donovan. In March 1944, Park was assigned to the White House as an assistant to Pa Watson, Roosevelt's military adviser and appointments secretary. Park had little to do with military advice for Roosevelt. Watson handled that himself. Park's real job was being the Army's representative in FDR's map room, where he sometimes funneled OSS reports to the Oval Office or handled chores Watson didn't have time for. But Park made important friends during his White House tour, such as Hopkins. The Army officer lunched with him occasionally and traveled with Hopkins to Yalta. After the ailing Watson died on the return voyage from Yalta, Park was named to succeed him. But he was just a placeholder at this point, and did not have the access to the physically weak president that Watson had. After FDR died, Vaughan kept Park on as his assistant for a few months.

Shortly after Roosevelt's death, Truman had on his desk a scathing fifty-nine-page indictment of the OSS written by Richard Park. How he came to write this detailed study of OSS misdeeds remains a mystery. Park claimed in a cover memo to Truman that Roosevelt ordered him to produce the report before he died and that he collected much of his information on the OSS from a tour he made of the Italian and Western fronts. But the evidence that Roosevelt gave him the assignment is flimsy. George Elsey, a Navy officer who worked with Park in the map room, did not believe his Army colleague knew enough about the OSS to put together a top secret report with more than one hundred charges in it. Based on the gossip Elsey heard from Park and from Vaughan, he suspected General Bissell's G-2 minions had written the document and put the lieutenant colonel's name on it to give it the appearance of being a White House paper so it got into the hands of Vaughan and then Truman.

Elsey's suspicions proved valid. Bissell tried to distance himself from the enterprise, but it turned out that the hidden hand behind the Park report was the man who ran the general's secret espionage unit, John Grombach. Most of Park's information on Donovan's organization came not from any tour he had taken of war fronts, but rather from a fifty-two-page memo Grombach had slipped to him with every damaging rumor the Pond had collected on the OSS. Park spliced page after page from Grombach's memo into his report. Hoover's men helped as well. Park lifted one paragraph practically verbatim from a letter the FBI director had written ridiculing Donovan.

Frenchy later bragged that they all had been part of a "a top secret ex-parte investigation of the OSS." The Park report they put on Truman's desk ended up being a cut-and-paste collection of accusations of petty graft, rule infractions, scandalous behavior, and communist infiltration in the OSS, with practically every complaint the FBI, Pentagon, and State Department had ever lodged against the agency included. It claimed one of Donovan's officers got drunk and spilled secrets, money was wasted on worthless agents in Portugal, the Turkey station hosted lavish parties, and OSS agents in Bombay staged an orgy in their offices (all with no names or evidence to substantiate the charges). It rehashed Hoover's irritation with Donovan's students trying to infiltrate U.S. factories on training exercises, the Pentagon's grousing about overpaid OSS officers, and Ambassador Carlton Hayes's gripes about cowboy operatives in Spain. Some of the mishaps the report raised were true. But other allegations distorted the facts. The report claimed Tony Di Luca's infiltration of the Japanese embassy in Portugal caused Tokyo to change its codes, costing "many American lives in the Pacific," which was not the case. It cited British help for the OSS and the cooperation of the two intelligence agencies before the Normandy landing as if that were something evil.

Some of Donovan's activities "have not been harmful," such as William Langer's research branch, the Park report grudgingly acknowledged. But overall the OSS "is the most expensive and wasteful agency of the government." That was a gross exaggeration. In unconventional warfare, petty graft came with the territory and thievery among a spy agency's foreign sources had to be expected because they were often disreputable characters. The OSS had elaborate accounting procedures for its secret funds, detailed rules for entertainment expenses, and Donovan wasn't shy about disciplining officers he caught dipping into the till. The agency's infractions turned out to be no more or less than for other American units. The Army's top supply officer estimated that pilferage and waste in the Mediterranean theater alone had been so rampant, it amounted to "one ship out of every five" lost.

Oddly enough, the Park report did not alert Truman to the OSS's larger debacles, such as the Dogwood case in Istanbul, likely because its writers knew little about them, and it ignored an even more important question: How much did Axis intelligence know about what the OSS was doing? Donovan's organization performed detailed postmortems on blown operations and agents nabbed by the enemy who were forced to talk. Yet for all the operatives captured and successfully interrogated in Europe, all the OSS documents seized and codes broken, counterintelligence officers in London concluded in one top secret report that the Wehrmacht "failed to make worthwhile use" of what they got. "German knowledge of [the] OSS was fragmentary, uncollated, incorrect and diffuse." Abwehr charts on the agency were riddled with errors. Some of Donovan's officers who had been captured were shocked that their Gestapo interrogators did not even know what the letters OSS stood for.

DONOVAN SPENT THE weekend of September 15 with Ruth in Nonquitt. This time, he made no phone calls back to Washington. He seemed to be marking the last days of his agency in serene calm—something he had not done in four years.

By the time he returned to Washington Sunday evening, September 16, the machinery to close down his operation was moving quickly behind his back. Smith had all the pieces in place—beginning in October, Langer would move his Research and Analysis branch, which Smith considered the crown jewel of the OSS, to the State Department. The intelligence and special operations units would go to the War Department and be headed by Magruder, Donovan's deputy. Truman ordered his new secretary of state, Jimmy Byrnes, to form an interdepartmental group to thrash out a new plan to coordinate the intelligence arms of the State Department, military, and FBI. If Byrnes wasn't up to that job—his State Department bureaucracy certainly wasn't suited for it considering its cultural aversion to espionage—Truman left open the option of having the White House do it. Smith quickly got the parties to agree to this setup. The Pentagon brass never had an opportunity to present their alternative. Truman did not intend to give them that chance—this was a president taking over the decision-making process that had snarled the agencies since last November and imposing his will. On Tuesday, Smith told Donovan the White House's plans. Donovan protested once more but Smith didn't much care at this point what he thought. Donovan was history.

Thursday afternoon, September 20, Smith walked into the Oval Office with all the paperwork for Truman to sign. The president was not in a particularly good mood. It had been a trying week and Truman was feeling sorry for himself. War agencies balked over downsizing. "It is almost impossible to get any action around here even from the most loyal of the close-in helpers," he wrote in his diary that day. "Well, this terrible job was virtually crammed down my throat." He intended to do it as he saw fit. "No pressure group need apply," he wrote. And that included Wild Bill Donovan.

Smith handed him the executive order abolishing the Office of Strategic Services. The plan to have its functions divided between the War and State Departments while Byrnes worked out the coordination was the best the Budget Bureau could come up with at the moment, he said. "Donovan will not like it," he warned. Truman could care less what Donovan liked or didn't like. He scanned the order and signed it.

Smith put another page in front of him to sign. A perfunctory thank-you note to Donovan for heading up the agency the past four years. It was insulting—the kind of form letter written for a low-level civil servant leaving his job. Truman acknowledged only that Donovan had provided "capable leadership" of the OSS.

Donovan took the train to New York that morning, not bothering to be at his desk when the letter arrived.

PART III

AFTERMATH

Chapter 31

——❧❦❧——

Nuremberg

D ONOVAN SAT ACROSS the table from Hermann Göring in one of the Palace of Justice's bare and cramped interrogation rooms. Dressed in a plain gray uniform shorn of military insignia, the Reichsmarschall spent most of each day reading and writing intently in his prison cell next to the palace, a dingy and chilly cinder block room with a metal cot, crude commode, washstand, small desk, single wood chair, and heavy steel door. The only breaks from monotony were lonely walks in the prison's exercise yard (Donovan could see him from his nearby office window), Sunday services in the Protestant chapel (which Göring attended for the music, not to confess his sins), and the interrogation sessions, like the one he was having this Tuesday evening, November 6, with the American spy chief.

Since his surrender six months earlier at his Bavarian villa near Berchtesgaden, Göring had lost his swagger and joviality, as well as some of his 340-pound girth. Donovan and the other prosecutors found the Reichsmarschall more serious now, alternating between fits of cockiness and deep depression. But his mind remained quick and his heart, as one of the American attorneys put it, was still "cold, brutal and murderous." The Army soldiers who detained him relieved him of 485 tons of documents the prosecution team found useful, a vial of potassium cyanide concealed in a coffee can, and several thousand paracodeine tablets. OSS researchers had compiled a lengthy dossier on Göring's many war crimes. An art looting unit Donovan had formed with ten investigators and analysts to track stolen treasures in Europe also soon discovered Göring was the Reich's biggest thief.

A large military detail mingled outside the interrogation room. Rumors had circulated in Nuremberg that Nazi diehards still at large were hatching a plot to spring Göring from jail, so he was under heavy guard. Inside the room only an Army private sat with Donovan to translate—although both men could have dispensed with the interpreter. Göring understood English well and Donovan had been practicing his German for the cross-examinations he planned at trial. The Reichsmarschall insisted that no official reporter record their meetings. Donovan obliged. (After he left the room, however, he always promptly wrote down the conversation for the prosecution team.) Donovan had worked hard to cultivate the Reichsmarschall. He wore his uniform each time pinned with every medal he had received to impress Göring, who liked to drape himself with military decorations. Göring believed the spymaster was approachable and had sent word he was open to cooperating. The two had a total of ten private meetings. Donovan, who had always been intensely curious about what made evil men like Göring and Hitler tick, found the sessions fascinating. The Reichsmarschall seemed to Donovan only too willing to regale him with inside stories, such as Hitler's early diplomatic bluffs to win European territory before the war's outbreak. Like a skilled intelligence operative, Donovan eventually convinced Göring they were both like-minded conspirators who could share secrets. This Tuesday evening, Göring had salacious details he wanted Donovan to keep hush-hush about generals in the early years of the regime. Hitler, for example, had attended the 1937 wedding of his field marshal, Werner von Blomberg, to a young woman the führer thought was "of simple background but of fine character," Göring told Donovan. The bride turned out to be a porn model, so Göring engineered Blomberg's dismissal.

Donovan filed a report on Göring's sex stories, but he had a bolder legal gambit in mind. There was no way Göring could escape death, Donovan told him in one of their meetings. But he could "die like a man" after a full confession, Donovan said. The egotistical Göring, who knew the only question remaining was how he met his end, was intrigued with the idea of copping a plea and ratting on his comrades—if the price were right. Donovan was after what could be the world's most sensational plea bargain. Göring would accept full responsibility for the war crimes, which would dramatically shorten the trial, and would take the stand to sell out Dönitz and the other top Nazis under indictment with testimony on their complicity. In return, the Reichsmarschall would be executed as a soldier before a firing squad instead of suffering the humiliation of hanging as a common criminal. The scene in the courtroom with Donovan as the star prosecutor and Göring on the witness stand could be dramatic, the spy chief knew—if he could pull it off, which on November 6 was far from certain.

DONOVAN HAD FLOWN to Nuremberg two days after the OSS closed down on October 1. Mary, who had given birth two months earlier to her second daughter, joined him for the trial as a confidential secretary. She left Patricia and the baby, whom they named Deirdre, with Ruth at Chapel Hill. (David had been home on leave for the conception nine months earlier but was now in the Pacific with the *Avoyel*.) Putzell, who also traveled with Donovan, did not see any useful purpose for Mary being there, but she "elbowed her way in," he griped. The beautiful daughter-in-law quickly caught the eye of other prosecutors.

Donovan could still drive in any direction for ten minutes and see few buildings standing in Nuremberg. Where the residents who survived now lived was a mystery to the prosecutors but they always managed to appear magically for bread lines with dazed and haggard looks on their faces. Donovan commandeered for his quarters a bürgermeister's home, one of the grander structures left standing, which came with servants and GI sentries to guard against saboteurs. The Palace of Justice had been renovated using hundreds of SS prisoners as laborers. Donovan's drafty dank office was located near Jackson's in what used to be chambers for appeals court judges.

Donovan expected to take up the star prosecution role he envisioned for himself before he left Jackson's team to fly to Asia and then fight for his agency's survival back in Washington. Jackson's son, Bill, suspected from the first day Donovan returned that he wanted to take over his father's job as part of a scheme to revive the OSS. But Donovan had been away from Nuremberg for nearly four months. He was out of the loop and did not command the influence he once had over the tribunal. Jackson no longer needed the spymaster or his organization as much. Research material had already been assembled for the trial, the indictment had been drafted, and the prosecution staff had grown to some 650, only a quarter of whom were former OSS members.

Jackson still found uses for Donovan's tradecraft. When Rudolf Hess, Hitler's onetime deputy, developed a convenient case of amnesia, claiming he could not remember his Nazi past, Donovan had a team of OSS psychologists and psychiatrists try to trick him. They showed Hess newsreels of him with Hitler and Göring at a Nazi Party rally and beamed a light at his face to study his reactions. The haggard-looking Hess, who was handcuffed to a guard, continued to feign his memory loss. But tension between Donovan and Jackson soon surfaced. It had as much to do with different personalities and lawyering styles. Jackson found Donovan's behavior often erratic, and temperamental when he didn't get his way. Donovan, he feared, was a manipulator trying to trap him in schemes for the trial that suited his personal agenda but not what was best for the prosecution. Donovan thought Jackson was a poor administrator (even the justice's loyalists admitted he was hopeless on that score) and weak in the courtroom. Jackson was skilled at preparing trial briefs and analyzing arguments lawyers presented to him on the High Court. But he had no experience handling witnesses and criminals before a jury and Donovan thought he should have paid more attention to someone who had actually prosecuted cases in Buffalo as a U.S. attorney.

Jackson thought the prosecution strategy should depend heavily on the thousands of documents he had accumulated to demonstrate Nazi guilt rather than on the flashy examinations and cross-examinations Donovan envisioned. Donovan argued intensely that the case needed live Germans and Holocaust victims to testify instead of Jackson spending days reading dreary records to the judges. Sensitive to image, he feared the press would grow bored and the Nazi defendants would turn public opinion against the tribunal if a dramatic case were not presented against them. Other lawyers on the team agreed with Donovan; Germans on the stand would counter the impression among their countrymen that Nuremberg was nothing more than "victor's justice."

The targets of the prosecution also divided the two men. Donovan believed that Germany's top officers should be charged with the war crimes they actually committed. He was nervous about Jackson's intention to prosecute the entire German High Command collectively as members of a "criminal organization," with simply proof of membership enough to convict an officer. Under that standard Donovan could have been prosecuted for war crimes in World War I because his men had killed surrendering Germans, while senior Wehrmacht officers like Canaris, who supported the resistance, could be charged in this conflict.

Convinced that Jackson's approach was wrong, Donovan went off the reservation and began organizing his own prosecution strategy for the trial. He started negotiating with Walter Warlimont, whom he had known before the war, and four other senior Wehrmacht generals, hoping to have them admit their guilt and testify against two top men, Field Marshal Wilhelm Keitel, the head of the armed forces high command, and his deputy, Alfred Jodl. Donovan sounded out another Nuremberg defendant—Hjalmar Schacht, the former economics minister and Reichsbank president who financed Hitler's arms buildup in the 1930s and was a loyal Nazi until 1943. The ambitious Schacht, who later was arrested by the Gestapo for being part of the Stauffenberg plot and sent to a prison camp, was eager to distance himself from his co-defendants and work with Donovan. Though the German economist had been the financial wizard behind Hitler's aggression, Donovan was convinced Schacht could be a valuable witness and he sorely wanted to question him on the stand. But Göring was the biggest prize, Donovan thought. He began private negotiations with the Reichsmarschall and his lawyer to have him testify for the prosecution. Donovan prepared a lengthy pretrial questionnaire for Göring and the Reichsmarschall promised he would give truthful written answers to the questions. Schacht and Göring, Donovan told the other attorneys, would be the "big rabbits out of a hat."

Robert Jackson was no fool. He knew what Donovan was up to and deeply resented the challenge to his authority. Jackson eventually was persuaded he would need some witnesses on the stand, but he moved to shut down Donovan's negotiations with defendants such as Schacht and Göring. The economist was one of the most guilty Nazis, Jackson argued, because he had financed Hitler's war making. Striking a deal with the devious Reichsmarschall was fraught with danger, Jackson correctly worried. Neither would testify for the prosecution, he ruled.

By early November, Jackson and Donovan were barely on speaking terms—their communication handled with testy memos back and forth—and Donovan was openly ridiculing the trial tactics in staff meetings, calling them "utterly foolish." Other lawyers on the team began taking sides

and the feuding bogged down preparations for trial. "What this organization needs is about six tickets—one way—to New York," complained
Thomas Dodd, a young attorney who had not worked for the OSS and
one day would be a senator from Connecticut. Jackson began to shrink
Donovan's role in the tribunal, which infuriated Donovan. Jackson, who
had depended on him so much in the prosecution team's early days, now
hoped the spymaster would take one of those tickets to New York.

As the trial opened the third week in November and Jackson began
plodding through a reading of his documents, another clash with Donovan outside the courtroom erupted that caused the final breach in their
relationship.

Mary looked glamorous in her red cocktail dress that Thursday evening
November 22. Sitting across from her at the dinner table was an enemy
POW, Major General Erwin Lahousen, who was enchanted with Mary, but
had no idea why he was dining in Donovan's plush quarters with her, three
other OSS women also in stylish dresses, a couple of U.S. naval officers,
and Paul Leverkühn, who had extended him the invitation. Leverkühn, the
Berlin lawyer who had introduced Donovan to Warlimont and other German officers during the 1930s and had served as a Canaris intermediary in
Istanbul, had been advising Donovan at Nuremberg on how to handle the
defendants. Lahousen was an Austrian Abwehr officer who had also been
close to Canaris and had crossed paths with Leverkühn in Turkey. Donovan
considered them both valuable sources and had them put up in guesthouses
reserved for prosecution witnesses. He did not arrive at the dinner party
until later that night, stayed just for a short while, and made only small talk
with the German general. Lahousen assumed this was a social affair and
enjoyed the meal, the wine, and the company of Mary and three other pretty
women. Clinking glasses with a top German spy thrilled Mary.

Jackson was irritated enough with Donovan's freelance interrogations
of Germans. When he discovered that Donovan had wined and dined two
of them in his quarters he was outraged. Jackson had not settled in his own
mind whether Lahousen was a valuable witness or a future criminal defendant and he was not sure that Leverkühn wasn't a hostile spy. If the press
found out the prosecution team was throwing dinner parties for German
suspects, it would raise a huge stink, Jackson knew. He fired off a terse note
to his senior prosecutors, ordering that "no social entertaining of any prisoner of war shall be undertaken." The memo did not mention the dinner

party incident but everyone knew it was aimed at Donovan. An OSS aide put a smiley face on the copy the spymaster received and underlined the order. Jackson finally sent a letter directly to Donovan on November 26, one of the most hostile he had ever put to paper. "You and I appear to have developed certain fundamental differences," he wrote. "Frankly, Bill, your views and mine appear to be so far apart that I do not consider it possible to assign you examination or cross-examination of witnesses." Jackson, in effect, was firing him.

Enraged, Donovan shot back a letter just as pointed. Indicting the entire German high command is "unbecoming" of "our country," he bluntly wrote. Relying "exclusively on documents" is a mistake. Getting Göring, "the last sane leader of the gang," to confess on the stand "was not intended as a 'stunt' or as a dramatic episode, but as a very practical means of bringing home to the German people the guilt of these men." The case Jackson has assembled sorely lacks "central administrative control" or "intellectual direction." Donovan, in effect, accused him of being an incompetent lawyer. He told Jackson he was leaving Nuremberg.

DODD SAW MARY and Donovan off at the airport on November 30, sad to see them leave. Donovan, he thought, was a skilled trial lawyer and Jackson should have paid more attention to his ideas. Donovan left Nuremberg as bitter as he had ever been. He packed up the thousands of pages of court papers and classified documents he had collected there and put them on his plane, further angering Jackson, who believed he had stolen government documents. The justice thought Donovan was a shallow, social-climbing headline grabber. He didn't intend to get into a "pissing contest" with the "skunk," he told Dodd, but he suspected Donovan was planting stories in the press to smear him. The *Washington Times-Herald* carried a piece complaining that Jackson's "inefficient and undramatic presentation of evidence" was boring everyone silly. To preempt any damage the negative publicity might cause him with the White House, Jackson rushed a letter and thick file to Truman with an account of the Lahousen dinner party and copies of Donovan's most pungent notes. Friends had warned him Donovan "would not work in second place with anybody," Jackson wrote Truman, and he had found that to be the case. The package further convinced Truman he was right to be rid of the bad apple.

Donovan's allies on the prosecution team continued to feed him inside information on the mistakes they thought Jackson was making throughout the ten-month trial. With the plea deal fallen through, Göring took the stand defiantly unrepentant and tried to rally the other defendants against the prosecution. But Göring and twenty-one others were convicted. Three were acquitted, including Schacht. Of the six groups Jackson had targeted as criminal organizations, three were found guilty: the Nazi Party, SS, and Gestapo. Hitler's cabinet, the SA paramilitary "brown shirts," and the German high command were found not guilty. His suit hanging limply from him, Göring, who was found guilty of "crimes unique in their enormity," gave his judges a cynical look when the death sentence was read and turned on his heel to follow two white-helmeted guards out of the courtroom. He managed to cheat the hangman by swallowing a potassium cyanide capsule in his cell. He claimed to the end that Donovan was one prosecutor he could trust. As Donovan had warned, the tribunal and Jackson's prosecution were accused of dispensing victor's justice. But though the legal basis for the proceedings may have been flawed and Jackson's prosecution less than spectacular, the eleven ordered to the gallows and the rest who were sentenced to prison richly deserved the punishment they got.

Chapter 32

—⟨⟨⟩⟩—

Recovery

REPORTERS STAKED OUT La Guardia Airport when Donovan and Mary finally arrived from Europe in mid-December, hoping he would comment on the press stories about his feud with Jackson. Donovan disappointed them, claiming he planned all along to return by Christmas. The next month, he took the train to Washington to receive an Oak Leaf Cluster to his Distinguished Service Medal, which Truman pinned on him in a largely private and stilted ceremony. As Donovan walked out of the Oval Office, Truman let slip that he was having trouble setting up a new intelligence system and mentioned, almost as an after-thought, that it would be nice to have Donovan's views before he finally decided on one. It lifted Donovan's spirits. But Truman never called back. Decompressing from the last four years, Donovan soon realized he was on the periphery of that debate and other foreign policy issues. He lamented to friends about no longer being a part of major decisions for the country. "What good am I doing?" he sometimes asked plaintively.

Donovan's more immediate problem was recovering from four years liv-ing the lifestyle of the rich on an Army salary. He was nearly broke. Debts had piled up and he owed more than a quarter of a million dollars in back taxes to the Internal Revenue Service. He still had Ruth's family money as a cushion, but to raise cash he sold their Georgetown home to Katharine and Phil Graham, who had just taken over the *Washington Post*. Chapel Hill was put into a trust and they moved out of the Beekman Place flat and into a less expensive New York apartment on Sutton Place. To make money, Donovan took on antitrust cases, his bread-and-butter work in prewar years. But he had been too long absent from the courtroom to be the major litigator he once was. Colleagues began to complain that he was overconfident with cases, did not do his homework, and tried to ad-lib at trial, which didn't serve his clients well in high venues like the Supreme Court. The firm, which emerged from the war financially strapped as well, found Donovan's biggest value now was as a rainmaker, bringing in clients from the intelligence and foreign contacts he had accumulated.

But the legal work was merely a way to pay the bills so Donovan could pursue his eclectic interests. He hired a researcher who began collecting thousands of documents for a massive tome he wanted to write on the history of American intelligence since the Revolution. (The project dragged on for ten years and never resulted in a book.) He told a friend he also wanted to write children's books—an odd admission considering he had done so little to raise his own children and, except for Patricia, had even less contact with his grandchildren. Donovan wanted to assume the role of elder statesman after the war. Often with Ruth and Mary he toured Europe and Asia for months at a time, interviewing old foreign sources on the emerging Soviet threat. Donovan chaired the American Committee for United Europe to promote the political and economic integration of the continent, an idea Truman supported that eventually resulted in the European Union decades later. Through that committee work he was able to patch up his strained relations with Churchill, who had been voted out of office in July 1945 and now was an honorary president of the European Movement, which also lobbied for integration. In exchange for a $25,000 donation to the Movement from the American Committee, Churchill agreed to speak at a kick-off fund-raising luncheon in New York for Donovan's group. Before the event, the two men sat in the Sutton Place apartment reminiscing about the war years, Churchill bouncing Patricia on his knee.

Donovan also could not resist another try at elective office. Within months after returning from Nuremberg, Republican Party operatives convinced him he had a shot at winning the New York Senate seat in the 1946 congressional elections. Donovan—foolishly, it turned out—mounted a late-starting campaign to secure the nomination at the party's convention in Saratoga Springs on September 9. A few editorial writers and a sprinkling of county Republican chairmen endorsed his candidacy, but one important person did not: Thomas Dewey, New York's progressive governor who was running for reelection and had a lock on the state GOP. New York's labor unions, which had fought Donovan's bid for governor in 1932, opposed him again and Dewey did not want to alienate that constituency important for his campaign by backing Donovan. He also told friends the former OSS commander was "too reactionary" for his taste. But the most important reason Dewey opposed Donovan's nomination was because the general had snubbed him at the outset, refusing to endorse Dewey for reelection when he announced he was running for the Senate. The snub was intentional. Donovan *was* more conservative than Dewey and always thought the governor was trying to stab him in the back.

By the time the Saratoga convention rolled around Donovan had the backing of young Republicans, World War I veterans groups, and the upstate county chairmen. He boasted that he had the momentum and promised to wage a spirited floor fight to win the nomination. He also reluctantly endorsed Dewey two days before the convention, hoping that would mollify him. It did not. Dewey, who kept the delegates tightly under his control, had no problem securing the nomination for his man, New York assemblyman Irving M. Ives. A loyal Republican, Donovan campaigned for Ives and Dewey, praising them and denouncing Truman as a "tragic figure of good intent but poor comprehension in the White House."

A MONTH AFTER Donovan returned from Nuremberg, Truman had two Navy admirals in for lunch and a bit of fun. William Leahy, who had been Roosevelt's no-nonsense chief of staff, had stayed on in that position with Truman. Sidney Souers had achieved little distinction as a Naval Reserve officer, but he was sitting at the table with Leahy and Truman because in his day job he was a high-powered Missouri insurance executive and a campaign contributor. After the plates were cleared, Truman playfully hauled out black coats, black hats, and wooden daggers and presented them to the admirals, proclaiming that the two were now officially anointed the leaders of the "Cloak and Dagger Group of Snoopers."

It was the only light moment Truman had enjoyed with intelligence since he disbanded the OSS and divided its functions between the War and State Departments. The parts sent to the Pentagon were renamed the Strategic Services Unit and shrunk to just a shell of their original size. Langer's researchers had their funding slashed by Byrnes at the State Department, who proved incapable of carrying out the other assignment Truman had given him to forge a coordinated foreign intelligence program. Truman still had no such spy operation abroad, no organization to warn him of strategic threats from the Soviet Union or other enemies. He went back to the drawing board.

After more months of cajoling and arm twisting his agencies, he managed to cobble together another plan, this one a watered-down version of the Pentagon compromise Donovan had been forced to accept before the Trohan leak blew everything out of the water in February 1945. Leahy would form a National Intelligence Authority with the Pentagon and State Department that would oversee a new Central Intelligence Group. This intelligence group, which Souers would manage as an executive secretary (not really its leader), would spy overseas with employees lent to it from the Army, Navy, and State Department.

It was sort of a car pool arrangement. Donovan, who had been following the travails of his old units and keeping tabs on the formation of this new Central Intelligence Group, ridiculed it as little better than "a good debating society." Which it turned out to be. Souers, who admitted he never really wanted the job, proved to be a disinterested leader whom Hoover found easy to bully. He lasted only six months. The director who succeeded him—a handsome and well-connected air general named Hoyt Vandenberg—stood up to Hoover but still became bogged down in bureaucratic battles with the military. With the Cold War heating up, Truman in February 1947 asked Congress to approve a new Central Intelligence Agency as part of a larger reorganization of the armed forces into a Department of Defense. With Allen Dulles's help, Lawrence Houston, a young lawyer who had spied in the Middle East for the OSS and now worked for Vandenberg, wrote the provision setting up the CIA. They slipped Donovan copies of their drafts and he privately lobbied Congress on behalf of the spy unit. Donovan was not completely happy with the organization the lawmakers finally approved in July; the new agency reported to a National Security Council instead of directly to the president, as Donovan wanted. But in most other respects, the CIA resembled closely the proposal he first brought to Roosevelt. It would be an independent outfit controlled by the White House, conducting espionage and covert operations overseas with the analysis of intelligence centralized in one organization. The new CIA was a vindication of Donovan's vision.

He wanted to lead it. Friends lobbied Truman to appoint him the agency's chief. Even Vaughan, who had passed on the damaging gossip about his sex life, eventually told Truman he ought to consider him for the job. But it was unrealistic for Donovan to expect that a president he had called a "tragic figure" on the campaign trail would name him to such a sensitive post. Truman appointed Admiral Roscoe Hillenkoetter, who had been Vandenberg's lackluster deputy, to be the CIA's first director. The best Truman offered Donovan was chairman of an inconsequential committee studying the nation's firefighting departments. Donovan bit his lip and accepted the humiliating appointment.

But he was determined to keep dabbling in spy work. Donovan sent Hillenkoetter and Beetle Smith (who succeeded the admiral three years later as CIA director) notes on former OSS officers to hire, such as Dulles and Casey, and scouted overseas operatives who might be useful. He showered them with ideas for covert operations, such as secret programs to recruit Russian defectors and arm French mercenaries to attack communist agitators. Donovan mined old contacts for covers CIA agents could use infiltrating into the Soviet Union and passed along plans Eastern European exiles gave him to spy on Russian troops occupying their countries. Hillenkoetter and Smith dutifully listened to the suggestions along with leads he brought back from foreign trips about black marketeers shipping strategic goods to communist countries. But Truman was furious when he learned about Donovan's meddling in CIA affairs, calling him a "prying S.O.B."

Donovan eventually set up what amounted to a private intelligence operation of his own. He regularly debriefed lawyers and businessmen traveling overseas for their observations. Friendly American ambassadors slipped him classified cables on communist activity in Europe. Gisevius kept him posted on politics in Germany. An Italian journalist touring the Persian Gulf briefed him on the quality of Soviet troops he saw at the Russian-Iranian border. Soon New York gossip columnists were alive with speculation about the secret comings and goings at Donovan's law firm, one writer calling him "one of the most influential behind-the-scenes men in the country today." That was hardly the case, but the FBI grew suspicious. The bureau's snitches warned that the CIA was slipping Donovan secret documents by the pound.

MARY GARDNER JONES had worked as an OSS research analyst and after the war became one of a few women to graduate from Yale Law School in 1948. But no New York law firm would take her until she applied to Donovan's. Others in the firm thought a female attorney should not be hired when men returned from the war needed jobs, but Donovan never gave it a second thought and made her his assistant. Jones answered his mail and wrote him memos on legal and foreign policy questions. She also became his partner for dinner parties when Ruth was not there, which was often. Jones had heard stories from the secretaries about Donovan's affairs. Women noticed that even in his mid-sixties, the general still had a sparkle in his eye for the ladies. But Donovan treated Jones practically as another surrogate daughter. Soon she was having lively debates with him on issues of the day. Jones found her boss open-minded and willing to listen to her arguments. They co-authored a *Yale Law Review* article on civil rights and national security; Jones managed to edge Donovan more toward the civil rights side by the time they finished writing the piece.

But she could push him to the left only so far. With the onset of the Cold War, Donovan became a conservative hawk. He did not believe the Soviet Union would risk attacking the United States with nuclear weapons—America's retaliatory capability made that unthinkable—but he was convinced the Cold War was becoming "hot as hell," as he liked to tell reporters, and that the communists were moving to dominate the world by every other means. The State Department, however, was meeting the Red menace with "basic timidity," he complained to a friend, and Dean Acheson, who became its secretary in 1949, was a "pantywaist," he told Jones.

Donovan's strident anticommunism also helped inoculate him from attacks by his political enemies. Hoover had no luck uncovering a nest of communists among the OSS officers who transferred to the Pentagon after the war, but he remained convinced that Donovan was a closet commie— or, at the very least, a sympathizer. Security guards one day found electronic bugs hidden in Donovan's law firm; a rival firm may have planted them, but Ole Doering, who returned to the practice after the war, suspected it was Hoover's men. Donovan and Dick Heppner, another OSS officer who rejoined the firm, were outraged when two FBI agents knocked on the door of Heppner's New Jersey home one day and told his wife, Betty, they were there to search the library. Betty let them in and the agents took away two books from the room: Hitler's *Mein Kampf* and *Quotations from Chair-*

man *Mao Tse-tung.* For his part, Donovan continued to gig Hoover, accusing him in magazine articles and letters to the Truman administration of running an amateur intelligence agency during the war and being just as inept at battling communists afterward. The attacks infuriated Hoover. "My, my," he scrawled on one memo about Donovan's bad-mouthing, "Col. Bill knows all the answers but few of the facts."

Hoover had better luck dredging up the past. Elizabeth Bentley, a Vassar College graduate and disillusioned NKGB courier, had gone to the FBI in 1945 and identified over twenty-eight Soviet informants in the U.S. government—five of whom worked for Donovan. Hoover thought they were the tip of the iceberg. But the bureau did not have enough corroborative evidence to prosecute the OSS officers Bentley fingered so she was paraded before the House Committee on Un-American Activities in 1948, where the "Spy Queen," as she became known in the press, named Donovan's executive secretary, Duncan Lee, and the four other OSS analysts. Other OSS officers were swept up by Joseph McCarthy, a junior senator from Wisconsin beginning to make a name for himself ferreting out Reds.

Under fire from conservatives for lax hiring, Donovan stood up for his old agency and denied it had been infiltrated by Russian intelligence—although he knew it had been. In the summer of 1944, his security office had sent him a memo with the names of forty-seven OSS employees suspected of being communists or party sympathizers. Moscow had begun its effort to penetrate the OSS in 1942 and soon had a dozen snitches planted in OSS stations in England, Spain, and Yugoslavia. Lee denied the charges, although the evidence is now clear that he was one of a half dozen NKGB informants in the Washington headquarters. Privately, Donovan did not believe that Lee and the other Soviet moles posed any danger to U.S. national security—they were, after all, passing secrets to an ally at the time—and, in fact, there was no evidence that the information they delivered to the NKGB did any damage to Donovan's wartime operations. But in public, Donovan stood by the adviser who had been in his inner circle. Duncan Lee is "a Rhodes scholar and a very high principled boy," he told reporters. "I believe he would be very loyal and not disclose any classified material." Nevertheless, Donovan now let his fear of communism cloud the better judgment he should have had as a lawyer in one high-profile court case.

On June 10, 1948, Donovan arrived in Athens to browbeat Themistocles Sophoulis, the frail eighty-eight-year-old prime minister of Greece. A month earlier, on May 8, the body of CBS correspondent George Polk had washed ashore at Salonika Bay, his hands and feet bound by hemp rope with a bullet hole in the back of the head. A former World War II Navy pilot with a daring streak as a reporter, the thirty-four-year-old Polk had visited Salonika in northern Greece to interview communist leader Markos Vafiadis, whose guerrillas controlled the surrounding countryside. The city dwellers and Salonika's police, however, had grown hostile to American journalists like Polk, who had filed stories critical of the Greek government in the past. Truman was committed to helping the Greek military fight the communist insurgency raging in the north. Athens now wanted a solution to the crime that did not incriminate the Hellenic government and endanger U.S. aid. So it was little wonder that Greek officials and the U.S. embassy were convinced at the outset that the communists, not Greek rightists, were responsible for the murder. Salonika's police began their investigation assuming that Polk had been in a boat motoring across the bay to meet Vafiadis when communists on board shot him and threw his body into the water. The murder would be blamed on the Greek government to embarrass it.

That theory seemed a stretch. Vafiadis had every reason to want to keep Polk alive to broadcast the guerrillas' story to the world, while Greece's right-wing extremists had good reason to want him killed as a warning to any other network reporter thinking about putting communists on the air. Suspecting the Greek government would whitewash the case, American journalists formed the Overseas Writers Special Committee of Inquiry, led by Walter Lippmann, to monitor the investigation. The respected columnist recruited Donovan, an old friend, to be the panel's chief counsel. During two trips to Athens and Salonika, Donovan bluntly warned Sophoulis, the local prosecutor, and police that the American press expected an honest probe and a speedy arrest.

On August 18, the Salonika authorities produced their culprit: Gregory Staktopoulos, a thirty-eight-year-old stringer for the Reuters news service who had joined Greece's communist-leaning National Liberation Front (EAM) during the war. At first, Staktopoulos told the police he had talked to Polk for only five minutes before the American went missing. But after forty-five days in custody, the Greek newsman finally signed a lengthy confession, admitting that he had been Polk's translator and intermediary, taking him to the boat with two of Vafiadis's communist saboteurs aboard as escorts. About a mile from shore, Staktopoulos's statement claimed, one of the communists shot Polk, who had agreed to be blindfolded for the trip. Donovan and the State Department accepted the police version of events and backed Staktopoulos's arrest. But there was a problem with the confession. After being starved and beaten with brass knuckles for weeks, Staktopoulos signed a statement that had been fabricated by the Salonika police. Donovan was kept in the dark about the torture, although as an experienced lawyer and seasoned OSS man who had seen his share of captured agents confessing to anything to stop the pain, he should have suspected it.

Donovan attended Staktopoulos's nine-day trial, which began on April 12, 1949, in a drab courtroom in Salonika. He told reporters he was there to make sure the proceedings were fair. He should have realized they were rigged. Staktopoulos kept his mouth shut about the torture. The police, who had arrested his mother as an accomplice, told him the only way he could keep her out of jail was to stick to the confession they had written for him. The law officers also handpicked Staktopoulos's lawyers, whose weak defense of their client boiled down to arguing that he was probably mentally ill and just a small part of a larger communist conspiracy to kill Polk. On April 21, the jury freed Staktopoulos's mother, but gave him life in prison and sentenced the two communists he had identified on the boat to death in absentia. Donovan told the newsmen gathered around him in the courtroom afterward that the trial "was honestly and efficiently conducted." The final report he drafted for the Lippmann committee concluded that the Greeks had convicted the right men. They had not. Who killed George Polk remains a mystery, but the evidence clearly pointed to someone besides Staktopoulos and the communists. Donovan, however, saw Greece as a critical battleground between the United States and Russia. Prosecuting rightists for the crime would be a setback for that war. In his mind now, the communists had to be guilty.

He had plenty of company. The U.S. embassy praised Athens's handling of the case. Greek and American reporters covering the trial never seriously questioned its fairness. Lippmann and the other members of the Overseas Committee accepted Donovan's conclusion that Staktopoulos and the communists were guilty. Even Ed Murrow, Polk's colleague at CBS, went along with the verdict. The trial of Gregory Staktopoulos was not a proud moment for Greek justice, U.S. diplomacy, American journalism, or for Donovan.

IN 1949, Ruth and Mary brought Patricia to spend her third-grade year with Donovan at the Sutton Place apartment. It was a special time for her. They rode horses in Central Park and listened to the big dance bands play at the St. Regis. In the afternoons when Donovan came home from work he flipped on the television in the living room to the Arthur Murray show and practiced dancing with his granddaughter, who stood on the toes of his shoes. It surprised Mary Gardner Jones, who was in and out of the apartment all the time with memos for the boss to read and letters for him to sign. Donovan did not strike her as a kid person.

Jones never saw Mary's husband, who had no interest in joining them. David finally processed out of the Navy as a lieutenant commander on April 28, 1946. He became a gentleman farmer in love with Berryville's peaceful life that Mary found boring. Chapel Hill became a major agricultural operation, marketing 450 head of cattle, hogs, and lambs each year, and David soon branched out, trying his hand at running a trucking line for ten states. Though he kept his feelings mostly to himself, David was increasingly unhappy with Mary spending so much time away from Chapel Hill and leaving him to care for the children with the nanny. By 1949, their brood had grown to six: Patricia the oldest, Deirdre now four, Bill who was three, two-year-old Sheilah, and the twin babies David and Mary. But his wife's absences had begun to put strains on the marriage. Donovan did not help; he may have been a doting father-in-law but he was a poor father to his son, encouraging Mary to be away for long stretches to keep him company and be his hostess.

When they were together Bill could still be a tender husband to Ruth. Sometimes they dined with Donovan's old war comrades such as Allen Dulles and his wife, Clover. On a walk down a New York City sidewalk to a party being thrown for Louis Mountbatten, Heppner's wife, Betty, was struck by how Donovan fussed over Ruth when she slipped and fell. But they were rarely together. If not by law then by practice, Bill and Ruth were separated. She had succeeded in walling him out of her life and building one for herself. She rarely talked about her husband to friends or relatives and kept her unhappiness with the failed marriage to herself. In Berryville, she took on civic projects and hosted at Chapel Hill the U.S. equestrian trials for the Olympics. To friends, Ruth Donovan seemed reserved and distinguished as she began her sixties, yet strong-willed and determined.

For the grandchildren, Chapel Hill became a magical place, filled with horses, dairy cows, sheep, pigs, and all manner of dogs, with pastures for roaming and forests for hunting and two donkeys named Fearless Flannigan and Sneaky Pete for riding. The floors in the house creaked, a grizzly bear rug stared up at them in the living room, and a mounted ram's head looked down from a basement wall. Donovan visited Chapel Hill more often after the war but it was still infrequent, so holidays like Christmas were always a treat because they were the few days the grandchildren could count on Faddy being there, always in his coat and tie with presents for them.

New Year's Eve 1951 began as one of those special days. Grandchildren played outside as the sun set in late afternoon while parents and grandparents scurried about inside the house dressing and primping for the Blue Ridge Hunt Club Ball that night. Mary and David were being honored at the event. Four-year-old Sheilah raced into the kitchen at one point thirsty for a drink of water. But in the confusion the little girl reached for a cup of silver polish that had been set out for Ruth and drank it. Sheilah collapsed unconscious almost immediately. The silver polish contained potassium cyanide. David and Mary rushed her to the Winchester hospital twelve miles away but she was pronounced dead on arrival.

David and Mary were devastated. The pain of losing her daughter lingered long for Mary and her marriage with David also deteriorated after the death. From 1952 on, the two became unofficially separated, as Bill and Ruth were. While David worked the farm, Mary pursued her own social life in Berryville performing regularly in the local theater or entertaining her father-in-law's guests in New York and traveling with him overseas.

Ruth took the death hard as well, but typical of her personality she soldiered on and never complained. Donovan was crushed. A daughter and now a granddaughter lost. He was not prone to introspection but he realized how distant he had been from his family while the personal tragedies seemed to him to be piling up. After Sheilah's death, Mary Gardner Jones found him sometimes in his Sutton Place apartment muttering to himself: "What have I done with my life?"

Chapter 33

Thailand

DONOVAN CAMPAIGNED HARD for Eisenhower in the 1952 presidential race. The two men had become good friends during Ike's short tenure as president of Columbia University from 1948 to 1950. Donovan was an eager fund-raiser for his alma mater, which Eisenhower appreciated. Early in 1952, Donovan joined other prominent Republicans pressing him to enter the race. He helped line up GOP support among his political friends and fed Ike memos on how to outmaneuver Ohio senator Robert Taft for the nomination at the Chicago convention. Donovan insisted to Ike that he wanted nothing in return, but he did. He wanted to be the CIA director. He thought he had his best chance at the job now that his Republican friend was in the White House.

News reports circulated that General Beetle Smith would soon resign as the CIA's chief, which could not come too quickly for Donovan. He feared that Smith had ruined the CIA, sapping it of the esprit de corps that existed under the OSS; the agency needed an infusion of outsiders and a leader who was a civilian like him, not a career military man. Donovan began a quiet campaign for the directorship. The Veterans of OSS, an organization of ex-OSS officers that Donovan controlled, lobbied Eisenhower on behalf of their old boss. The national commander of the American Legion, which Donovan helped found, told Ike the OSS chief was now the man with the "knowledge, experience and passion" to wage a subversive war against the Soviets.

Men more powerful mobilized against Donovan, however. Tipped off early by his agents that Donovan wanted the CIA job, Hoover paid a visit to the president-elect on the morning of December 30. Unlike Truman, Eisenhower harbored no doubts about retaining the FBI director and he was anxious at the outset to have good relations with him. But Hoover soon learned he had to tread carefully with Ike. The president-elect started off their meeting in his transition headquarters ordering Hoover not to send him uncorroborated rumors about the sex lives of people he was thinking of appointing to his administration. Eisenhower wanted just the facts, which eliminated the best trash Hoover had on Donovan. But he still managed to work in a shot. Beetle Smith was a "sincere and earnest man," Hoover told Eisenhower, but he had been hobbled by bad elements from Donovan's old organization. His agents followed up with more derogatory information slipped to the transition team on Donovan's OSS years.

Even if Hoover had kept his mouth shut, Donovan was not in the running to be CIA director. Allen Dulles had the inside track. The former Bern station chief had joined the CIA in October 1950, in charge of its clandestine operations, and within a year became its deputy director under Smith. Dulles considered himself the natural heir to the top job and he had an advocate who had the new president's ear on foreign policy: his brother, John Foster Dulles, whom Eisenhower tapped to be his secretary of state. Ike moved Smith, his loyal staff chief during World War II, to the State Department to keep an eye on Foster as the undersecretary of state. That conveniently opened the door for Allen to lead the CIA, which his brother and Eisenhower wanted.

The appointment left Donovan bitter. He still believed Dulles was a poor administrator, although his low opinion of him was tinged by jealousy that his underling had jumped ahead of him after the war. To friends, Donovan continued to predict that Dulles would be a disaster as director of central intelligence. As a consolation prize, Eisenhower offered Donovan the ambassadorship to France. Ike was surprised and irked when Donovan summarily rejected the prestigious post. But Donovan knew that John Foster Dulles was deeply interested in Europe, as any secretary of state would be. Foster would hover over him if he took the Paris post, and Donovan could not stomach being his errand boy. He thought Eisenhower's secretary of state was sanctimonious and as weak-kneed as Acheson. Donovan, however, was willing to serve elsewhere as a diplomat.

———

HIS PLANE touched down at Bangkok's airport early Thursday morning, August 27, 1953. Weary from little sleep on the long flight, Donovan was the first to leave the aircraft, Thailand's baking tropical heat enveloping him instantly and taking out what starch was left in his summer suit. A large welcoming party of some 150 stood on the tarmac at the end of the ladder along with a battery of Thai reporters shouting questions and photographers jostling for position to snare the best shots. When Donovan's feet touched ground, General Phao Sriyanon, the country's police chief, stepped forward and placed a lei in his hand. The chief of protocol for the king and a senior officer representing Field Marshal Phibun Songkhram, the prime minister, approached with stiff bows and handshakes. In the terminal, Donovan sat briefly for the ceremonial tea and delicacies always offered high-level visitors while the photographers crowded around for more pictures. A large contingent of Americans from the U.S. embassy stood by as well, along with a handful of former OSS officers who had remained in Southeast Asia after the war. They finally managed to pry Donovan loose from the newsmen and bundle him into a limousine for the motor convoy to his new home: the palatial U.S. ambassador's residence, a rambling two-story structure with an immense pagoda, magnificent green lawns, and lush gardens.

Donovan had been in chilly Oslo, Norway, three months earlier when an urgent cable arrived from Beetle Smith asking him to return to Washington immediately. The Truman administration had worried about Red China's domination of Southeast Asia by invasion or subversion. Though Thailand shared no border with China, Truman feared it was vulnerable to communist infiltration from Vietnam—a prospect not helped by the fact that the Bangkok government was run by "a small group of conniving and often venal upper-class politicians," as one secret National Security Council memo warned. With the Korean War a stalemate, Mao's takeover of China in 1949 still a fresh wound, and the Viet Minh unraveling French control of Vietnam, Eisenhower entered office at the beginning of 1953 even more intent on blocking further communist advances in the Far East. Ike viewed Thailand not only as a bulwark against the Reds but also as a base for operations to roll back communism in the rest of Southeast Asia. Thailand would be the launching pad for America's propaganda, paramilitary, and covert missions in the region.

Donovan was not the State Department bureaucracy's first choice to be ambassador to Thailand. But Foster told his aides he wanted a "big man" for what he thought might be "a real hot spot," and Donovan, who loved adventure, seemed to him ideal for the assignment. When Donovan arrived in New York on Sunday, May 17, he phoned Smith at his home.

"I have a tough dirty job for you," the undersecretary said, not revealing on an open line what it was.

Donovan took the train to Washington the next day and met Smith at the State Department. "I am authorized by the President to offer you the ambassadorship of Siam," Smith began their conversation. Donovan accepted on the spot. In Thailand he would be far more independent of Foster, who he thought would be preoccupied with Europe.

But typical of Donovan, he soon made a counteroffer. The communists threatened all of Southeast Asia, he told Smith. Ike should make him not just an ambassador to Thailand but also a regional envoy, perhaps restoring his general's rank, with a beefed-up staff, plenty of money, a plane always at his disposal to roam through other countries, and a direct phone line to the White House. Donovan envisioned using Thailand as his base for dabbling in the Malayan guerrilla conflict, in Vietnam's counterinsurgency, in Taiwanese covert operations into China, even the Korean War nearing its end.

John Foster Dulles wanted no part of Donovan becoming a second secretary of state for Asia. Neither did the Defense Department, the CIA, or the White House. Donovan was "grabbing off much too much territory," one White House memo warned. Smith drafted a letter Eisenhower was happy to sign, which squelched the scheme. "You are the man best qualified" to be the envoy to Thailand, Ike's confidential note to Donovan read. "However, I want you to do it in the capacity of Ambassador, under the direction of the Secretary of State and within State Department channels of control." Donovan agreed to the conditions—but he was intent on breaking them when he arrived in Thailand.

Before he could leave, Donovan's nomination had to be confirmed by Congress. Dulles asked the FBI to conduct a background check, which the Senate Foreign Relations Committee required for ambassadorial nominees. Hoover now had a precious opportunity and he did not intend to waste it. Donovan had been chief of the nation's intelligence service with access to its most sensitive secrets, but Hoover treated him like a first-time applicant for a government job—and a suspicious one at that. He put his best men on the case and for a month they scoured the country. FBI agents investigated the loyalty of Donovan's parents and dug up his school records. They interviewed his law partners, business associates, judges he had appeared before, former colleagues in the intelligence world, political enemies in Washington, residents of Berryville, even the doorman at his Sutton Place apartment. For the most part the agents came back with positive reports. Even men Donovan had clashed with in the past, such as Herbert Hoover, recommended him for the job. But the FBI investigators also turned up nasty allegations and rumors from informants, two of whom were New York newspaper columnists. As the Elizabeth Bentley hearings had revealed, Donovan's OSS had been infested with communists, the sources reported. Staffers in the agency's Presentation Branch once held a collection "for Russian war relief," another report alleged, and "were anxious to hire colored personnel." Pro-communists had infiltrated Donovan's law office. When it comes to fighting Reds, Donovan was a "bubblehead," one of the columnists told the agents. He had even joined an effort to oust Joe McCarthy from the Senate.

On July 15, Hoover sent the White House a twenty-page report on Donovan. The first eleven pages dutifully acknowledged the rave reviews the agents had received. But the next seven dwelled on what Hoover had to be sure would scare any administration away from a nomination—particularly in the McCarthy era. The FBI director practically accused Donovan of being a traitor. The OSS chief "has always been 'soft and mushy' in his treatment of Communists," Hoover reported, quoting "an informant of known reliability." (The informant was one of the New York columnists.)

Hoover's report did not scare off Eisenhower or his secretary of state. The Senate quickly confirmed Donovan. Three days before taking off for Bangkok, he held another meeting with Smith to receive the top secret mission Eisenhower wanted him to carry out. He was to "quietly" assume command not only of the embassy but also the propaganda, military aid, and CIA operations for Thailand. He was to build "a bastion" for democracy there, Smith told him, and use it to fight communists overtly and covertly in the neighboring countries. Donovan already was on board. He had huddled with OSS officers who spied in Thailand during the war and had just returned from a visit to Fort Bragg, North Carolina, to scout out Green Beret guerrilla fighters and Army psychological operations officers he wanted for the embassy.

Sloppy research, Pres. Kennedy created Spec. Forces

RUTH, MARY, AND PATRICIA (who was now twelve) arrived in Thailand on a later flight. The other grandchildren remained with David at Chapel Hill. Ruth was not particularly thrilled with her husband's foreign posting or eager to join him but she agreed to stay in Bangkok for at least three months. Mary still had not recovered from Sheilah's death and Donovan thought Thailand might get her mind off the tragic accident. Patricia was enthralled with her new exotic home. Funny-looking insects always crawled across the dinner table, snakes slithered through the gardens, and gibbons roamed the yard and hopped on the handlebars of her bicycle when she rode it or sneaked into Ruth's room and stole underwear from her drawer.

Dressed in formal morning clothes and a top hat, Donovan on September 4 presented his credentials to King Phumiphon Adunyadet at the Grand Palace along the Chao Phraya River. The lighting in the court chamber was dim. Donovan had difficulty reading from the sheets of paper he held so he ad-libbed parts of his speech. The twenty-five-year-old king paid no mind and read the speech the government had written for him thanking Donovan profusely for American cooperation and aid. The Bangkok press hailed Donovan's arrival, which gratified the State Department. Appointing an ambassador as high-profile as the former director of the OSS carried considerable symbolic weight with the Thai public.

But officers at the U.S. embassy in Bangkok remained leery of Donovan's arrival. Demoralized by the McCarthy witch hunts at the State Department, the embassy staff feared Donovan was invading with a planeload of OSS spooks to take over the diplomatic mission. Donovan sensed the nervousness the minute he walked through the front door of the embassy and worked hard to cultivate his new employees. But he did intend to run the embassy as an OSS outpost. He brought with him an energetic young Air Force lawyer named William vanden Heuvel, who had been an associate in his law firm. Vanden Heuvel, whose assignment was to keep watch over the intelligence operations Donovan planned to jump-start, soon became his confidant and sounding board for ideas. Donovan began consulting closely with old OSS comrades, such as Jim Thompson, who remained in Bangkok after the war to make his fortune in the silk trade. Donovan hired an Army lieutenant as his personal bodyguard and was quick to dress down embassy employees he thought were too lax with security. He also got the White House to agree to beef up the number of U.S. military advisers assigned to the country to four hundred.

Five days after he landed in Bangkok, Donovan sat down with the embassy staff to outline his vision for the post—which was now Washington's vision. The line against communism would be drawn at Thailand's border. Eisenhower had ordered him "to create a bastion of resistance in this area of the world," he told them. "The battle that has to be won need not employ only machine guns as weapons," he said, although there would be more of them coming from the United States. He also planned to push for more American business investment and to "harness the minds of free men . . . to devise the imaginative means to preserve the meaning of democracy." With its three million ethnic Chinese and fifty thousand Vietnamese refugees, the country was ripe for subversion, he warned his staff. And if Thailand falls, "all of Southeast Asia might be lost." Ike believed the domino theory as well.

Some of the seasoned foreign service officers in the Bangkok embassy thought Donovan's thinking far too simplistic. Nationalism drove politics in Southeast Asia more than communism, they believed. The Joint Chiefs thought the communist presence in Thailand too puny to warrant it becoming a base for the U.S. military. Moreover, the bastion Donovan wanted to create there protected the ruthless and corrupt men who ran the country. Prime Minister Phibun had grown wealthy from businesses on the side. His hard-drinking army chief, General Sarit Thanarat, ran whorehouses and raked off money from the national lottery. Phao, the charming yet cunning police chief, controlled the opium trade. And to keep a firm grip on the nation, Phibun and Sarit rigged elections while Phao's security agents efficiently rounded up dissidents and threw them in jail.

Donovan knew the three men were brutal and crooked but he cozied up to them nonetheless. The triumvirate served the Eisenhower administration's higher cause. Donovan convinced the White House to spend more than a million dollars for propaganda in Thailand—among its projects, the *Handbook of Communism*, which was passed out to Thais and was of dubious value. He pushed for tens of millions of dollars to expand the Thai army, navy, and air force, which delighted Phibun. Donovan organized an intelligence unit in the army and the Green Berets he scouted at Fort Bragg arrived to train Thai soldiers in counterguerrilla tactics. He trudged through steamy jungles to watch their training and inspect their camps.

It left him dripping wet and panting for breath. But it was important to him to be out in the field in command once more of his warriors. He envisioned covert commando outfits being organized not only in Thailand but also in the Philippines and Taiwan to sneak into other Southeast Asian nations and harass the communists.

Donovan also dialed up the CIA's operations. At first Allen Dulles had not wanted Donovan in Thailand. He ordered his officers there to watch the new ambassador closely and report back to him every move he made. But Donovan was intent on leading the CIA in Thailand instead of the agency leading him. Dulles eventually sent him money from the CIA's account for an embassy "nest egg," as Donovan called it, to use for emergencies. Donovan pushed the CIA station to supply Phao more weapons for his police and had it assign bodyguards to protect King Phumiphon. He had the agency launch a covert operation to rid Thai newspapers of communist infiltrators and CIA spies sneaked into the Russian embassy in Bangkok to bug it. He also tried to clean up one agency misadventure in the region before it became a major embarrassment for the U.S. government.

Less than a week after he had arrived in Bangkok, Donovan had been briefed on the CIA debacle with General Li Mi. Defeated by Mao's communists in 1949, the Nationalist general had evacuated remnants of his force to Burma's Shan State near the Thai border. But the CIA, in Operation Paper, continued to fund and arm Li Mi's ragtag army, hoping it would launch guerrilla attacks against the communist Chinese in Yunnan, forcing them to divert troops from the Korean War. Li Mi mounted several cross-border raids into southern China, which Mao had no trouble beating back. The Kuomintang mercenaries, however, proved to be far more successful setting up their own narco-state in southeast Burma, plundering local villagers and smuggling out opium by the ton. Finally fed up with the criminal force, Burma took its case to the United Nations, which pressured the United States to evacuate Li Mi's gang to Chiang Kai-shek's exile island of Taiwan. Donovan did not have an exact count of how many Kuomintang soldiers were hidden in the jungle—he had been given estimates ranging from 1,200 to 20,000—but he now had the miserable job of flying out the bandits in planeloads of several dozen to several hundred. Not all the soldiers brought their weapons with them but they were all forced to leave their opium behind. Fifteen tons piled up at one airport. It was a slow headache-filled operation that took months. Donovan, with a .38-caliber pistol strapped to his waist, had to make several trips to the dense Burmese jungle just off the northern Thai border to unsnarl problems with the flights. Eventually more than 5,500 mercenaries were airlifted out but thousands more remained behind exporting heroin for decades from the Golden Triangle, much of it pumped into American veins.

THAILAND HAD MORE pleasurable moments for Donovan than dealing with drugs and thugs. A parade of VIPs came through. California Republican Bill Knowland, the hard-line Senate majority leader who backed Chiang, dropped by and offered over a whiskey and soda to float Donovan's name with Ike to fill the vacant chief justice seat on the Supreme Court. Donovan thought he was ill-suited for that job and told Knowland not to pursue the matter with Ike. Richard and Pat Nixon arrived at the end of October for a three-day visit as part of a world tour. Donovan escorted the vice president to his meetings with the regime and sent a gushy cable to the State Department afterward, claiming that the "warmth" of Nixon's personality had bowled over his Thai hosts. But he wrote it only because he knew that was what the administration wanted to hear. Later Ruth confessed to him: "I just didn't like Nixon." Donovan agreed that he was a ruthless and charmless man.

At first, Donovan had boundless energy. He swam and played tennis in the embassy compound, worked on his intelligence history book at night, and took regular French classes from a beautiful instructor named Claire Bouchet. Many evenings he ducked out of diplomatic parties, preferring rounds of bridge with Ruth, Mary, and vanden Heuvel. Ruth and Bill were the happiest they had been together in a long time. Ruth found Thailand more enjoyable than she expected and earned high marks from the embassy staff for her eagerness to explore the country. She attended Thai weddings with Bill, hunted tigers on a safari with Jim Thompson, and rode elephants to an archaeological site with Carleton Coon, Donovan's OSS agent from North Africa, who came for a visit.

Mary was erratic throughout her stay in Bangkok. She had bouts of depression over Sheilah's death. She went on shopping binges in Hong Kong. Sometimes she reverted to her role as Donovan's confidential assistant, passing along to him intelligence she picked up from the diplomatic circuit on the Viet Minh. Other times she became a party animal; she passed out after dancing through the night at one Thai event and Bill and Ruth stayed up to nurse her hangover. She seemed to vanden Heuvel never to be physically well, always heavily medicated. Sometimes she wore a neck brace to relieve pain from a bad back. Mary, Ruth, and even granddaughter Patricia became Donovan's traveling partners for the many trips he took outside Thailand. Donovan ignored the restrictions Eisenhower and his secretary of state had placed on him and became a de facto regional diplomat for Southeast Asia, and even beyond. He also routinely bypassed John Foster Dulles and reported directly to Ike on diplomatic initiatives he had not discussed with the secretary. It irritated Foster but Donovan did not care. His contempt for the man only grew as the months passed. At one point he considered complaining to Nixon about what he perceived to be Foster's weak leadership fighting communism in Southeast Asia, but thought better of it because he did not trust the vice president. Dulles finally demanded that Donovan get State Department approval every time he wanted to set foot out of Thailand. When the department then claimed it had no money for plane travel, hoping that would discourage his wanderlust, Donovan paid for the tickets out of his own pocket.

The nation outside of Thailand that commanded most of Donovan's attention was Vietnam. He practically became Washington's second ambassador there. Donovan traveled frequently to Saigon, touring the battlefields outside the city, huddling with top Vietnamese and French officials, and receiving regular briefings from the man who was its U.S. ambassador, Donald Heath, a career diplomat who had been at the post since 1950. Soon Donovan had a network of military and intelligence sources in the country almost as wide as Heath's. He became close friends with General John "Iron Mike" O'Daniel, the stumpy, gravel-voiced American military adviser in Vietnam who at first had been optimistic about French prospects for holding on to its colony. On Donovan's visits to Saigon and secret trips O'Daniel made to Bangkok, the two brainstormed ways to turn the war around and weaken Ho Chi Minh, the Viet Minh's leader. It wasn't long before Heath, who could be prickly over protocol, began to resent his intruder, but Donovan continued to poach. He believed Heath lacked the energy and vision to save Vietnam from the communists. Senior officials in Washington agreed. Nixon thought Heath had been in the country too long and had become co-opted by the French.

Beetle Smith lamented that the department should have posted Donovan to Saigon instead of to Bangkok.

Toward the end of World War II, an OSS team code-named "Deer" made brief contact with Ho Chi Minh, who was fighting the Japanese in the north, and had supplied him with a few weapons. An OSS medic even treated the guerrilla leader for malaria and dysentery. Ho pressed for more OSS help and American recognition of his movement, which Donovan relayed to Truman. But after the war, Truman ceded Indochina to the French, who were intent on crushing both its communists and nationalists to restore colonial rule. Eisenhower believed the French had handled Vietnam miserably and refused to rescue them with American troops. But Ike also believed that if the country fell to the communists the rest of Southeast Asia would be imperiled, which was why he dispatched American military aid, Iron Mike, and a large contingent of U.S. trainers to Saigon.

Immediately after World War II, Donovan felt that Ho was a nationalist and had the potential to be a Tito-like ally of the United States. But he had changed his mind by the time he arrived in Thailand. America's job, he believed, was finding a graceful exit for the French and not letting the Viet Minh come in as they left.

On May 8, 1954, vanden Heuvel ordered the Marine guards to lower the Bangkok embassy's American flag to half-mast the next day to mark the Viet Minh's capture of the French garrison at Dien Bien Phu. At Donovan's staff meeting later that afternoon, the aides around the conference table were gloomy over the news. "I think it is a disgrace that we should sit in this room as Americans and feel so deeply the responsibility for the tragedy of Indochina," vanden Heuvel finally blurted out. The French had brought this on themselves. They had refused "to recognize the nationalistic aspirations of the Vietnamese" and to get out of the country, he argued. Donovan's face flushed and his eyes flashed with anger. "It is an American responsibility," he said coldly, glaring at his young officer. Donovan, like Eisenhower, did not want to send in American forces after the fall of Dien Bien Phu. Instead, he pushed for propaganda and covert operations to keep Ho from taking over. He lobbied Phao to commit his secret police to the Saigon government fighting the Viet Minh and pressed the CIA station chief in Bangkok to step up supply flights into Vietnam.

Donovan also looked for a true nationalist leader to unify the nation. He believed he found that man in Ngo Dinh Diem, who was appointed prime minister of South Vietnam after the Dien Bien Phu defeat by Bao Dai, the puppet emperor for the French. An anti-Viet Minh politician who had lived in exile in Europe since 1950, Diem had become a favorite with conservative Republicans in Washington. He also was a Catholic and came highly recommended to Donovan by clerics. Donovan met with Diem frequently in Washington and Saigon and became convinced he was the Catholic alternative to Ho and worth supporting. He plugged Diem with lawmakers visiting Bangkok and in letters to Eisenhower. South Vietnam's new leader is "an intense nationalist and an incorruptible man," he declared in speeches.

Donovan proved a poor judge of character in this case. Diem, who became president of Vietnam in 1955, turned out to be a corrupt, nepotistic dictator who was eventually assassinated in a 1963 coup given the green light by the administration of John F. Kennedy.

SIX DAYS AFTER the fall of Dien Bien Phu, vanden Heuvel walked into Donovan's embassy office and could tell he was in a bad mood that morning. Why, he didn't know. The first piece of business they had to deal with was a top secret telegram that had come in from the State Department on Donovan's proposal to have the U.S. Air Force's Strategic Air Command put long-range bombers in Thailand. Accepting the SAC bombers, which were capable of carrying nuclear weapons, would be a politically sensitive move for the Thai government and a provocative one for the region. But Donovan was enthusiastic about a SAC squadron coming to Thailand and John Foster Dulles backed it. The Joint Chiefs were balking, however. Donovan had drafted a memo to the Pentagon arguing his case and vanden Heuvel began making editing suggestions. Donovan suddenly blew up. He rose from his chair, eyes wide, face flushed, swearing at his Air Force aide for trying to rewrite his copy, and stormed out of the room. The venting was totally out of character for Donovan, who prided himself on keeping his emotions under control, particularly with subordinates. Vanden Heuvel, who worshipped Donovan and had been a devoted aide, was deeply wounded. But lately he had noticed more of these outbursts from the boss—against him, against other members of the embassy staff, even toward Ruth.

Donovan was starting to look old and weak. The oppressive jungle heat and the strain of constant travel had begun to take a toll on his seventy-year-old body. He tried to exercise in the embassy gymnasium, but the sessions became more infrequent and he had begun to gain more weight. Other diplomats in the region noticed that Donovan's memory had begun to fade and his mind was not as sharp in meetings.

Three months earlier, John Foster Dulles had asked his staff for evaluations of the ambassadors in Asia. The Thais had nothing but praise for Donovan. Walter Robertson, the assistant secretary for Asia, sent Dulles a glowing evaluation. "There were many misgivings" about sending the former spy chief to Thailand, Robertson acknowledged, but "I believe Ambassador Donovan has been a stimulating and dynamic factor." Donovan, however, cared nothing about an evaluation. By the spring of 1954, he was ready to leave Thailand.

Donovan wrote Eisenhower that he wanted to go on August 1. He had planned to stay in Thailand for only a year, he reminded him. Ike understood all along that it would be a one-year appointment but he was truly distraught when he learned that Donovan intended to keep to that schedule. "It was with a feeling closely akin to dismay when I read your letter," the president wrote back. Eisenhower and Dulles also worried that Donovan's abrupt resignation might rattle the Thai government. They asked him to remain at his post longer to give them time to find a replacement with as high a profile. Donovan agreed to stay on until the end of August, although he was not happy about it.

Predictably, there were murmurs in Thai government circles at the end of August that Donovan had been recalled for being too aggressive in fighting the communists and that his departure signaled Washington was scaling back its commitment to Bangkok and the rest of the region. Donovan knew that would be the reaction and he pressed Eisenhower to keep him as a special adviser to the region. That way he could travel about Southeast Asia as a diplomatic troubleshooter, as he had before, with his expenses paid by the State Department, but he would be free to make money as a lawyer to refill his bank account.

Once more, he was nearly broke. The law firm's partners had cautioned vanden Heuvel to keep a careful eye on Donovan's spending while he was in Thailand but that became an impossible job for the Air Force lieutenant. Donovan often dipped into firm money or his own to pay for his many trips throughout the region and again he owed back taxes to the IRS.

Donovan inspects a German Tiger tank destroyed at Gela when the Allies landed at Sicily in July 1943. Eager to be close to the action, Donovan went in on all the major Allied landings, which made top generals like Marshall and Donovan's own OSS officers nervous. With all the intelligence secrets in his head, he would be a valuable prize if captured by the enemy. *U.S. Army Military History Institute*

Donovan joined 5th Army Commander General Mark Clark in his patrol boat for one of the Italian landings. A controversial World War II commander, Clark found the OSS valuable for his operations. Donovan told aides he thought Clark was vain and superficial. *U.S. Army Military History Institute*

Donovan confers with his men in X'ian, China, on special operations plans for the OSS. China was one of a few countries in Asia in which the OSS was allowed to operate. But it took more than two years of haggling with Chinese Nationalist leader Chiang Kai-shek and his intelligence chief before Donovan was able to launch credible guerrilla attacks against the Japanese. *U.S. Army Military History Institute*

In Washington, whether he was in a civilian suit or his uniform, Donovan was always impeccably tailored. But in the field with his men he appeared "incorrigibly civilian," as one friend put it, with his uniform "carelessly worn"— as if he wanted to convey the impression that he was an unconventional soldier. Here he sports an unmilitary ascot. *U.S. Army Military History Institute*

In the four years he commanded the OSS, Donovan spent much of his time in a plane, flying to his far-flung stations overseas. Soon, members of his inner circle began to grumble that he was not spending enough time at his desk in Washington. They tried to stage what became know as the "Palace Revolt" to have him made a broad overseer of the OSS while others ran it. Donovan squelched the move. *U.S. Army Military History Institute*

Donovan, shown here inspecting an OSS field station in Kandy, Ceylon (now Sri Lanka), was a charismatic leader revered by his agents in the field. But he had a penchant for swooping into OSS stations abroad and launching covert operations or shaking up personnel assignments, which sometimes left administrative chaos in his wake. *National Archives*

Donovan inspects an OSS propaganda office overseas. Many of his senior aides were skeptical of the value of psychological operations. But Donovan was enthusiastic about them and fought bitter bureaucratic battles with other agencies to control wartime propaganda. *U.S. Army Military History Institute*

Francis Cardinal Spellman, an old friend, pins the Order of Saint Sylvester on Donovan after the war. Donovan enlisted the Catholic Church and its emissaries overseas to feed him intelligence in places his OSS agents could not penetrate. Donovan also thought he had a prized source within the Vatican, who slipped him purported transcripts of papal conversations, but the man turned out to be a fabricator. *U.S. Army Military History Institute*

Allen Dulles, who would one day lead the CIA, headed the OSS station in Bern, Switzerland, one of Donovan's most successful intelligence operations. But Donovan considered Dulles a poor administrator and did not promote him. Dulles believed he was more qualified than Donovan to run the OSS. *CIA Photo*

Harry Hopkins (left), Roosevelt's closest adviser, stands with White House press secretary Stephen Early (center) and Charles "Chip" Bohlen (right), a U.S. diplomat in Moscow, at the Livadia Palace during the Yalta Conference. Hopkins, the second most powerful man in the country after FDR, was irritated with Donovan's secretiveness and became one of his political enemies. *Franklin D. Roosevelt Presidential Library*

Roosevelt gave J. Edgar Hoover (shown second from the left during the signing of a 1934 crime bill) wide latitude to battle Axis agents in the United States and spy on FDR's political enemies. Hoover and Donovan were intense bureaucratic enemies—the FBI director thought the OSS was a band of amateurs—and each fought the other for control of espionage operations. *National Archives*

Thrust into the presidency after Roosevelt's death, Harry S. Truman knew he needed a central intelligence service after the war. But he did not want Donovan heading it. Truman closed down Donovan's OSS after Japan surrendered and parceled its functions out to other agencies. Truman finally created the CIA in 1947, modeled after Donovan's proposal for a postwar service. *National Archives*

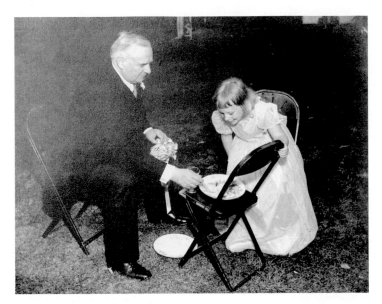

Donovan doted on granddaughter Patricia, named after his daughter who died in a car crash. Patricia spent a lot of time with Donovan, but for the most part the other grandchildren saw him only when he showed up at the family's Virginia farm for holidays. *U.S. Army Military History Institute*

Dwight Eisenhower (pinning the National Security Medal on Hoover in 1955) thought highly of the work the OSS did in his European theater during the war. But he made Allen Dulles CIA director, which disappointed Donovan, who wanted the job. As a consolation prize, Ike made Donovan ambassador to Thailand. Donovan thought Richard Nixon (to the right of Eisenhower) was a ruthless and charmless man and John Foster Dulles (right of Nixon) was a weak secretary of state. *National Archives*

Donovan, shown here at a George Polk Award Dinner with George Marshall (left) and columnist Walter Lippmann (right), became a staunch anticommunist after World War II. But his hawkish views clouded his objectivity when Lippmann, who led a reporters' group, commissioned him to monitor Greece's investigation of the 1948 murder of Polk, a CBS correspondent. Donovan accepted the Greek government's verdict that communists had killed Polk when the more likely culprits were Greek rightists. *U.S. Army Military History Institute*

Colleagues were struck by Donovan's mental and physical deterioration after he returned from his Thailand ambassadorship in 1954 at age seventy-one. In 1957, Admiral Jack Bergen (left), an old friend, took him to the Mayo Clinic, where doctors discovered Donovan suffered from a severe form of dementia. He died two years later at Walter Reed Army Medical Center. *U.S. Army Military History Institute*

Donovan eventually settled his tax problems with the IRS. To help replenish his finances he registered as a lobbyist for the Thai government, collecting a $50,000 fee; Eisenhower was irritated that he became an influence peddler for the Thais so soon after his ambassadorship. Ike and John Foster Dulles also cooled to the idea of sending Donovan back to Asia as a roving diplomat. Thailand would be his last major public assignment.

Chapter 34

———ↄﮫﮮↄ———

Walter Reed

W HEN DONOVAN RETURNED to Washington, Eisenhower gave him the attention typically afforded to men put out to pasture. He sent Donovan to Europe to represent him at ceremonies dedicating cemeteries and memorials for the World War II dead, appointed him to a commission studying veterans' pensions, and made sure he was on the A-list for tickets to his second inauguration in January 1957. Occasionally, Donovan sent Ike notes with foreign policy or political advice. Eisenhower always sent back polite responses.

Donovan's relations with Truman, who had retired to Independence, remained in a deep freeze. When Ike made Donovan chairman of the People to People Foundation to promote citizen exchanges with countries overseas, he had him go to Truman to ask him to serve as an honorary chairman. There was bad blood between Eisenhower and his predecessor, but Donovan knew Truman would be no more receptive to him so he sent vanden Heuvel to Independence with the invitation in January 1957. Truman politely listened to the young lawyer but refused to join People to People. The same month, Donovan asked Truman to sign a petition to Russia demanding justice for Hungarians, whose revolt from the Warsaw Pact had just been crushed by Soviet tanks. Truman refused, sending back an insulting letter that these kinds of petitions were worthless and only designed "to get the names of the people who signed them in the papers."

Donovan kept traveling in Europe and Asia to drum up business for the law firm. He also continued to pursue his anticommunist causes with a passion. He resumed his work with the International Rescue Committee, a refugee organization that had supplied the OSS with intelligence from European exiles during World War II. Donovan now arranged for the committee to help the CIA as well with refugees bringing out information from the Eastern bloc and joining covert operations to destabilize Soviet rule. He toured Europe for a month as an IRC representative, sounding the alarm over a Soviet program to convince refugees to return home. The bribes and threats from Moscow resulted only in a trickle of redefections, but Donovan condemned it as an intimidation tactic to break resistance movements behind the Iron Curtain. After the Russian invasion of Hungary in 1956, he tirelessly raised $1.5 million to aid more than ten thousand refugees streaming into Austria. He flew to the Hungarian border to supervise personally the relief operation—a grueling trip that exhausted him.

Donovan also continued to believe that Diem was Vietnam's savior. On his Asia trips, he often stopped in Saigon for long talks with the South's president. Back in Washington he joined Iron Mike O'Daniel, who had retired as chief of the U.S. military assistance group, in forming American Friends of Vietnam. The Friends became a propaganda organ for Diem, extolling the "fine progress" Washington's "staunch ally" had made.

BILL AND RUTH retreated to their separate worlds after Thailand. Donovan visited Chapel Hill and Nonquitt only occasionally. Ruth's trips to New York were rare. David had even less contact with his father and preferred to keep it that way; Donovan's fame had been too overpowering. "He stole the sun from anyone around him," a friend of David's said. After Sheilah's death, David had demanded that Mary spend more time at home taking care of the other children, but she ignored him, continuing to serve as Donovan's hostess in New York when he needed her. When she was in Berryville she carved out a social life separate from her husband.

After she returned from Thailand, Mary, who had never been particularly good with horses, took a bad spill from one. It aggravated the neck pain she had suffered overseas and forced her to wear the brace more. She began taking heavy doses of painkillers during the day and sleeping pills to help her rest at night. By the summer of 1955, her Berryville friends worried that she had an alcohol and prescription drug problem. In July, Ruth, Mary, and the grandchildren took their annual summer vacation at Nonquitt. Mary by then was mixing alcohol and barbiturates in dangerous quantities. She made fewer entries in her appointment diary and the ones that were written were in a nearly illegible scrawl.

Sunday night, July 24, Mary went to bed doped up on liquor and sedatives. She may have awoken in the middle of the night and swallowed more pills. The next morning, Ruth knocked on her bedroom door but got no answer. She walked in and found Mary dead on the bed. Donovan rushed to Nonquitt the next day. He arrived at the morgue as the medical examiner finished his autopsy. The coroner concluded in his report that this thirty-seven-year-old woman had died of "barbiturate poisoning" under "circumstances undetermined"—a polite way of saying he didn't know if the overdose had been accidental or intentional. Some friends in Berryville, as well as OSS colleagues who knew Donovan's daughter-in-law, suspected she had committed suicide for a number of reasons: boredom, feelings of unfulfillment, lingering grief over Sheilah's death. Donovan believed the overdose had been accidental, but the pain for him was no less profound. When he returned to the Nonquitt cottage after visiting the coroner he sat alone on its wide front porch as a warm sea breeze washed over him—and cried.

Mary was buried in Arlington National Cemetery next to Patricia and Sheilah. Because David had also served in the military, the cemetery allowed his wife and children to be interred there. David, who had not been at Nonquitt, stoically accepted Mary's death. Ruth now became the grandchildren's surrogate mother at Chapel Hill. She was kind and gentle with them. She always spoke quietly and never raised her voice to discipline them. But she could be stern when she had to. She demanded obedience and good behavior. Rooms must be clean. Beds made. Grandchildren must arrive well dressed and on time for dinner. They knew not to cross their Num Num. And they never really wanted to because they also knew misbehavior would hurt her feelings.

Donovan returned to the lonely Sutton Place apartment in New York.

IN MID-FEBRUARY 1957, Ruth was visiting her brother, Dexter, in Buffalo when a phone call came from Jane Smith, Donovan's secretary at the law firm, who had been frantic trying to track her down. Donovan is at the Mayo Clinic in Rochester, Minnesota, Smith told her. You must fly there immediately.

"What in the world is he doing out there?" Ruth asked. The question startled Smith. Donovan was at the Mayo Clinic because he was gravely ill and his wife appeared to know nothing about his condition. But Ruth's surprise was understandable. In the past seven months she had rarely seen Bill.

After his return from Thailand, Donovan's colleagues were struck by his physical and mental deterioration. Jim Murphy, one of his senior aides in the OSS, could tell he was definitely slowing down. He had serious memory lapses. Ralstone Irvine, one of the firm's partners, was shocked how Donovan rambled on like a befuddled old man during a dinner with Hollywood movie company presidents. Friends suspected he may have had a series of mild strokes beginning in Thailand and later in New York. If Donovan knew he had experienced them, he kept it secret from his family and colleagues.

Mary Lasker decided her old friend did not look or act well. She had been a client of Donovan's since the 1920s. He had introduced her to her late husband, Albert, an advertising executive. With Ruth not around, Mary took over the medical care of her seventy-four-year-old friend. She thought Donovan's doctor was incompetent and sent him to her physicians, who immediately recommended that he visit the Mayo Clinic. Jack Bergen, a retired admiral and another old friend, flew with him to Rochester. Donovan lied to Jane about where he was going, telling her it was to the Midwest for a speech. After several days at Mayo, Bergen phoned the secretary and told her to find Ruth. The doctors might have to operate and they wanted her permission.

When Ruth landed at the Rochester airport, however, she was startled to find Donovan there to greet her and looking fit. Mayo's doctors decided he did not need an operation. Their diagnosis was that his condition was impossible to treat. It was arteriosclerotic atrophy of the brain—a form of dementia. Donovan's brain was literally shrinking. He was losing his mind, which would eventually kill him. For a man so intellectually and physically vibrant, it was a cruel sentence.

Donovan returned to New York understandably depressed. He tried to resume his usual workload at the office, but that soon became impossible. Jane Smith would look down the hallway and see him swerving from wall to wall as if he were drunk. By the end of March, Donovan was confined to his bed at Sutton Place with round-the-clock nursing care. He had suffered a cerebral hemorrhage. His mind remained alert most of the time but the stroke had left him often unable to speak clearly.

On March 27, George Leisure, Donovan's mild-mannered senior partner in the firm who had loyally held it together for so many years as his friend pursued his other interests, phoned Colonel Robert Schulz, a military aide at the White House, and asked him to slip a confidential note to Eisenhower. "Your old friend, Bill Donovan, is, to use his language, 'approaching the end of the trail,'" Leisure wrote. Would the president consider one last honor—the National Security Medal, which Truman had created four years earlier to be the nation's fourth highest award, for "distinguished achievement" in the field of intelligence. That medal, Leisure knew, would put Donovan in the record books, making him the only man to win the nation's four highest decorations. Fearing Donovan might die before the medal was approved, Sherman Adams, Eisenhower's chief of staff, quickly cleared it on April 1 with Allen Dulles. Two days later, Larry Houston, the CIA's general counsel, arrived at Sutton Place, where Donovan lay in bed with Leisure and Ruth at his side. He pinned the medal on Donovan's pajama top. It had been a bad day for her husband and Ruth was not sure he understood what was happening. But the next day he asked to see the medal and brightened when the nurse laid it in his hand. When Doering and another partner arrived to congratulate him, the nurse asked Donovan if he wanted her to pin it on his top. "No, that would be out of character," he said, but continued looking at the medal, beaming.

Leisure had another private request when he phoned Schulz. Donovan's illness had become more serious. Soon, the nurse would not be able to care for him at home. Would Eisenhower consider putting Donovan in Washington's Walter Reed Army Medical Center? Leisure did not reveal it to Schulz but one of the reasons he was asking for the favor was because Donovan's finances were still in poor shape. The law firm, whose earnings had been flat since Donovan returned from Thailand, was paying his medical bills, but the expenses would soar if he was admitted to a private hospital and the firm could not afford it. Walter Reed was free for active duty service members, who were its priority patients. Eisenhower did not know if an ex-service member could be admitted, but he told Leisure he would have his staff investigate. Ike felt truly sorry for his old war comrade and penned him a note trying to lift his spirits. "I do recommend most highly that you cooperate fully with the doctors," he wrote. "I need not tell you that the country needs you back on the active list." Ruth read the letter to Bill during one of his lucid moments and it did cheer him.

Miraculously, Donovan improved for a while from late April to May. Ruth and his partners held out hope he might even be able to return to work. But it was only a brief interlude. Donovan's condition soon worsened and his lucid moments became more infrequent. The White House finally made the arrangements for him to be admitted to Walter Reed on September 23, 1957. He was seventy-four years old.

The Walter Reed complex took up 113 acres in northwest Washington. The Old Main Hospital, now designated Building Number One, was the first to be constructed on the campus in 1909—a new Georgian revival structure with a cupola on top, stately columns at the front entrance, and high ceilings in the rooms inside. Donovan was placed in Ward Four on the second floor in a small private room with a freestanding closet for his clothes and a small bathroom. The walls were bare. Ruth at one point placed a watercolor portrait done of him on the top of the closet. Another time, a colleague tacked a photo of a pinup onto the wall to get a smile out of him. Across the hall from his room were the nursing station and a small kitchen that prepared meals for the patients. To the right, double doors opened to a day room. From his window Donovan could see the circular driveway in the front and the lush green lawn stretching out beyond it. Eisenhower routinely visited Walter Reed for his medical check-ups. Movie stars like Bob Hope and Red Buttons dropped by to entertain the patients. In the summer months, Donovan could hear the Army band play marches and classical tunes every Wednesday evening in the formal gardens also at Building One's front entrance. But for him, Walter Reed became his prison.

A stream of men and women from Donovan's past visited him at Walter Reed. Richard O'Neill, an Irish Regiment comrade who had also won a Medal of Honor in World War I, dropped by. So did Mountbatten, who came two months after Donovan was admitted. The two shared a laugh over the evening they spent at the *Oklahoma!* play. David Crockett, the OSS finance officer who had sat up with Donovan the night he had a raging case of the flu in Caserta, was amused the boss still had enough spunk to flirt with nurses at Walter Reed. Donovan also became animated when William vanden Heuvel, his devoted aide in Thailand who also was a regular visitor, brought his fiancée one time to introduce her to him.

Donovan struggled to recognize friends and maintain his dignity. Armando Chacon, the Army medic who cared for him, helped him put on his coat and tie to receive visitors. He also insisted on wearing a suit when Chacon walked him down the hallway for exercise. But his mind began to fail him far more frequently. He mixed up Mary Gardner Jones in time, believing she had served under him in the Far East during the war. Betty Heppner found it heartbreaking to see him no longer in command of the people around him or of himself, those captivating blue eyes now straining to identify her. Jim Murphy, who had headed X-2 counterintelligence, came away from his visits angry that his OSS comrade was condemned to end his life this way. Jane Smith left the room in tears. When Grayson Kirk, the president of Columbia University and a friend, came by, Donovan stood up in the middle of their conversation, looked out the window for several minutes, then turned to him asking angrily: "Who the hell are you? What are you doing here?"

Ruth rented an apartment near the Walter Reed campus so she could be near him. She grew closer to her husband in these final months. As he slowly drifted away from her, she began to read a lot about death. It was strange that the interest would come to her now after a daughter and granddaughter had already died. Ruth still did not believe in the hereafter although she was finding more comfort now in religious teachings. Vincent also kept regular watch. Only in his moments of clarity did Donovan know his wife and brother were there. Often in his addled state he became cold and angry with them, turning his head to the side of his bed and refusing to look at them. It would take a while after they left for the nurses to calm him down. For dementia patients, hostility to loved ones was common, but his reaction hurt his wife and brother nonetheless. Three times Vincent gave him the last rites when he thought he was about to die. But Donovan clung to life tenaciously through 1957 and into the next year.

Chacon discovered he had to keep a close watch on his patient when he escorted him along the hall. Donovan was still strong and there was still spring in his legs. If the Army medic looked away, in an instant the general would slip through an exit and bound down the stairs to another floor. One day, fully dressed in his coat and tie, he scampered out of the building. Orderlies found him walking briskly to Delano Hall, the nurses' residence, and coaxed him gently back to Building One and his bed. At times, the nurses and friends found Donovan in his room hallucinating. He feared communists lurking in dark corners. He relived in rambling monologues the World War I battles he fought at Ourcq River and Landres-et-Saint-Georges, the daring flight he took over the jungles of Burma, the landing at Utah Beach during the Normandy invasion. In his rare lucid moments, he often became depressed. "This is a hell of a way to die," he told Leisure during one.

But 1958 passed and Donovan refused to surrender. In late January 1959, a CIA car pulled up to Building One. The nurses had brushed Donovan's white hair and helped him into his major general's uniform, making sure all the buttons were buttoned and the ribbons were in their proper place. Larry Houston helped him to the automobile, which drove them to the CIA's headquarters, housed in the old OSS compound on E Street. Inside the foyer of the South Building, agents unveiled an oil portrait of him that would be hung there. Donovan's eyes widened and he tried to come to attention, but his legs began to wobble under the strain. The officers gathered around started to applaud but Donovan looked like he was going to buckle. Houston and another aide grabbed him by the arms before he could fall and took him back down the steps to the waiting car.

NINE-YEAR-OLD DAVID GRANDIN Donovan sat in his nanny's Oldsmobile convertible late Sunday afternoon, February 8, listening to the radio. Ruth let him drive her car down the long dirt driveway from the farmhouse and when she wasn't looking he'd speed up with a cloud of dust behind him. The nanny would only let him listen to the radio in her car, which was parked in front of the garage at Chapel Hill. David had not seen his grandfather Faddy in the hospital. Patricia, the oldest, was the only grandchild allowed to visit him at Walter Reed. In fact, David hardly knew his grandfather. He was a kind old man and it was fun when he showed up at Christmas. David remembered the holiday two years ago when Faddy sat in one of Num Num's favorite wooden chairs, which cracked and broke, and everybody laughed when he fell down.

David now sat staring at the car radio, startled at what he was hearing. The broadcast was interrupted for a news bulletin from the Associated Press. "Major General William J. 'Wild Bill' Donovan, lawyer-soldier-diplomat and World War II director of the Office of Strategic Services, died today," the voice on the radio announced.

Crockett had dropped by Walter Reed on Saturday. Donovan had awoken from a deep sleep and tried hard to speak to him but he couldn't. The nurse said he had suffered another stroke. Crockett told her he would return the next day to check on his general. After he left, Donovan muttered softly to the nurse, "Good boy, Good boy," then drifted back to sleep.

The last week had been quiet. Donovan never got out of bed. He slept most of the time, awaking only occasionally to mumble something, then closing his eyes. His blood pressure had started to drop, his body organs began to shut down, and his breathing became labored. Dr. Harry Daniel, the attending physician, told Ruth Sunday morning he probably would not last through the day. Vanden Heuvel rushed to the hospital. By noon they stood at both sides of his bed, Ruth holding one of Donovan's hands, vanden Heuvel the other. At 2 P.M., Donovan died—a little more than a month after his seventy-sixth birthday. Dr. Daniel marked on his chart "pulmonary embolism" as the immediate cause of death—a fatal blood clot blocking the main artery of the lung.

SAINT MATTHEW'S CATHEDRAL in Washington was filled to capacity for the solemn Requiem Mass on Wednesday morning, February 11. Donovan and Rumsey family members, old pals from Buffalo, Troop I cavalrymen, Irish Regiment comrades, law partners, New York matrons, Ruth's Berryville friends, OSS colleagues, and British spies filled the pews. Allen Dulles and a delegation from the CIA attended. A military aide from the White House came for Eisenhower. The army chief of staff and army secretary sent generals. The archbishop of Washington represented the church hierarchy. Small laminated cards were passed out to congregants inscribed with biblical passages—"Blessed are they that mourn, for they shall be comforted"—and a student choir from Catholic University sang Mass. Vincent officiated over the ceremony and the Right Reverend John Cartwright, Saint Matthew's pastor, delivered the eulogy. Donovan's "life of combat and leadership, of service and example is ended now," he said in a loud voice. "He has gone from the scene of his success to meet his final judgment, his final reward, his final destiny."

The funeral cortege gathered at the ceremonial gate and marched slowly into Arlington Cemetery, six black horses drawing the caisson bearing the flag-draped coffin, an Army band playing sad music to the muffled beat of drums, Donovan's red pennant with the two stars on it for his general's rank fluttering in the icy breeze. Donovan's gravesite was a choice spot at the foot of the slope to the Lee Mansion. Ruth had arranged for forty-five of his friends from his law firm, from New York society, Hollywood, the military, and his spy world to be his honorary pallbearers. They included Frank Raichle (who had stuck with him after the Saturn Club raid), director John Ford, *Time* publisher Henry Luce, David Bruce (his London station chief), and Bill Stephenson (the British agent who helped him set up the OSS). Patricia and the other grandchildren flinched when cannons boomed a thirteen-gun salute and a line of Army soldiers in dress blues fired off three volleys from their rifles. As Vincent said a final prayer, an honor guard from the 3rd Infantry Division lifted the flag from the coffin, folded it smartly, and handed it to Ruth, who sat bundled up and grim beside her son, David, in the front row.

Newspapers around the country printed tributes in their editorial pages. The *New York Times* called Donovan "a living symbol of what we think of as plain, simple, unadulterated courage." "Most of the O.S.S. story is still untold," reported the *New York Herald Tribune*, "but it is not too much to say that General Donovan created America's first world-wide intelligence force." "His imagination was unlimited," Bruce wrote in a letter to the editor. "Ideas were his plaything. Excitement made him snort like a race horse." Allen Dulles the next month sent a dispatch to his branch chiefs and the CIA stations overseas. "The greatest tribute of all can be paid by us in the organization that Bill Donovan helped create," he wrote. "He will know his life's work has been well done if the CIA can help assure the nation's security by keeping the Government fully informed of world developments."

Hoover mailed a condolence letter to Chapel Hill the day after Donovan's death. "His life's work, devoted as it was to service of others, should be a source of gratification to all who were honored to know him," the FBI director wrote Ruth. "If I can be of any assistance, I hope you will let me know." Ruth had the grace to respond to the note from the man who was her husband's enemy. "I thank you for your kind expression of sympathy, which I appreciate very much," was all she wrote back.

Yet Hoover remained wary that his rival could remain a threat even from his grave. The director's press handlers predicted that there would be a biography written on Donovan, surely followed by a movie. Dulles, one bureau memo warned, "will likely take every opportunity to make certain the movie places the CIA in a favorable light." Hoover tried to head that off. He spread a false rumor that Donovan had died of syphilis.

Epilogue

———◦◦◦———

T HE ESTATE DONOVAN left behind was modest. Most of the money and all of the property belonged to Ruth. His assets totaled just $136,587.72 and almost a quarter of it had to go to settling tax bills. When she finished paying all his other bills, Ruth had $83,438.53 left. A month after burying her husband, Ruth flew to St. Croix in the U.S. Virgin Islands to relax and clear her head of Donovan's passing. When she returned in mid-April 1959, she was her old self, determined not to let the tragedies in her life—the failed marriage, the deaths of her daughter, her granddaughter, her daughter-in-law, and her husband—weigh her down.

Seven months later on Tuesday morning, November 3, a CIA car drove up the driveway to Chapel Hill. It was a cool, crisp day, the autumn leaves turned to shades of brown, bright orange, and yellow. Larry Houston, the agency's lawyer, and Robert Murphy, who had led the Twelve Apostles for Torch, climbed out of the car to fetch Ruth and drive her east to a construction site near Langley, Virginia.

They arrived at a 140-acre tract of government land on the south bank of the Potomac River. A hastily constructed wooden podium with an American flag fluttering to the side had been set up next to the partially completed building. It was the Central Intelligence Agency's new headquarters. The eight-story, $44 million complex would have more than a million square feet of space, sixteen high-speed elevators, a cafeteria to serve 1,400 at a time, a labyrinth of pneumatic tubes and conveyor trays to whisk secret documents from office to office, and a freestanding, dome-shaped auditorium to seat five hundred.

Ruth was ushered to a folding metal chair on the back row of the podium, which held a dozen VIPs. Some five thousand CIA officers, administration officials, and workers in hard hats gathered around for the cornerstone-laying ceremony. An Air Force band played marching music.

Eisenhower stood up for a short speech. When Ike finished, he and Allen Dulles placed a copper box inside the large white cornerstone a workman held with a pulley at the building. Among the treasured items inside the metal time capsule were Donovan's original November 18, 1944, memo to Roosevelt proposing a central intelligence service and FDR's April 5, 1945, memo after the disastrous Trohan leak directing him to poll the other agencies on his plan. With silver-plated trowels, Eisenhower and Dulles patted over the cornerstone symbolic cement, which was actually a mixture of water, sand, and sugar. (The cornerstone and capsule were removed after the ceremony and anchored permanently a year later when the building was finished.) The Air Force band played the National Anthem, then Ruth was ushered to the staff car for the drive home.

Stonecutters chiseled into the marble wall of the building's foyer a verse from John 8:32 that Dulles liked: "And Ye Shall Know the Truth and the Truth Shall Make You Free." In the decades to come the CIA did not always live up to that biblical ideal. Like its predecessor, the agency has had its share of intelligence failures along with the successes. When Bill Casey, who led the OSS penetrations into Germany, took over the CIA in 1981, he commissioned a bronze statue of Donovan, which was placed in the foyer. Donovan's grandson, David, who was in his thirties by then, posed for it to help the sculptor get the proportions right.

RUTH REMAINED IN control of the Rumsey family trust money and the farm. She stayed active in community work and the garden clubs of Clarke County. Until she was seventy, she rode with the Blue Ridge Hunt Club chasing foxes. David ran the farm and became a prominent businessman in Clarke County. He eventually remarried, but Ruth continued to live in a wing off the main Chapel Hill house.

Ruth never remarried. She never had a boyfriend. Looking after her grandchildren kept her too busy. She did have men friends. They escorted her to the annual Master of Foxhounds Ball in New York, the white-tie dances for hunt clubs. But they were only friends.

It was somewhat ironic. During Donovan's lifetime, his quest for adventure, his political ambitions, his determination to build a world-class spy agency, and his infidelities had ruined his marriage and left Ruth to live much of her adult life alone with her children and grandchildren. "Sometimes I wonder how well I really did know the general," Ruth confessed at one point. But after Donovan's death, Ruth set his personal failings aside and devoted herself to airbrushing his image and making sure he had his place in history. She conscientiously attended functions of the Veterans of OSS, set up to preserve the memory of the World War II agency and its leader. The group created a William J. Donovan Award and Ruth always showed up for its presentation, even arriving the year Casey received it with a painful broken collarbone she had suffered from a riding accident.

Ruth also hunted for an author to write a complimentary book on Donovan. While he lay in Walter Reed his last year, she and Doering had begun carefully screening potential biographers. They finally commissioned Corey Ford, a writer who had helped Donovan with his last-ditch propaganda campaign to save the OSS in 1945. Ford dutifully produced a biography, which Doering carefully edited. It portrayed Donovan and his agency in glowing terms, as Ruth wanted.

Donovan's true legacy, and that of his OSS, was far more nuanced. During World War II, he created a large and far-flung intelligence operation while fighting a war at the same time. That alone was not exceptional. So unprepared was the United States for war, most of its military leaders were building their organizations and fighting at the same time. But the Army, Navy, and Air Force at the start did have tanks, ships, and planes, as well as a small cadre of professional soldiers. Donovan began practically from scratch. The institutional and cultural resistance he faced from the national security establishment of his day *was* exceptional. Commanders fight among themselves in every war and they did so with no less passion and vindictiveness in World War II. But so foreign were Donovan's concepts for intelligence and unconventional warfare to the prevailing military and political mind-set, his intramural battles took on an added ferocity. Early on, he was spending as much time fighting his allies as he did the enemy. As a result, it was not until more than a year and a half after America's entry into the war that the OSS really got into the battle.

The agency Donovan created would send an organizational theorist into convulsions. It became a Rube Goldberg collection of disparate programs, functions, and initiatives whose common denominator sometimes was only that Donovan had dreamed them up. By any measure he was a bad manager. At one time or another during his reign over the OSS, Donovan violated practically every rule taught in business or public administration schools. His own men recognized the organizational failures. In one confidential survey of them after the war, they acknowledged he was a poor administrator, often a "terrible judge of human beings," as one put it, which led to bungled operations. But practically all of them praised him as a remarkable leader—which he was. Without Donovan's creativity, his charisma, his intelligence, his open-mindedness, his personal courage, and his vision for the future, an unconventional organization like the OSS would likely not have been organized or sustained throughout the war.

Did the OSS contribute to the war effort? Yes. His operatives earned more than two thousand medals for bravery and suffered relatively few casualties. Was Donovan's organization key to winning the war? No. Did his shadow operation even shorten the conflict appreciably? Again, no. But that may be setting the bar too high for his agency. Far more powerful forces were at work defeating the Axis: Russian and American women in the 1920s who delivered more male babies for the future fight than German, Italian, and Japanese mothers could hope to produce, American industry and Roosevelt's mobilization of it for war, vast oceans that made Axis attack of that industrial base impossible, the Merchant Marine force, Army Quartermaster, and Navy Supply Corps that could move more arms and machinery to the front than the Axis could. The atomic bomb. The OSS agent played his part, just as the infantryman on the front line in Europe, the sailor at sea in the Pacific, the sergeant in the motor pool in Detroit, the riveter on the plane assembly line in Los Angeles. Donovan's vision of covert warfare winning major battles on its own, making conventional operations unnecessary, proved illusory. His heroic guerrilla raids were a bother for Adolf Hitler, not a strategic threat. Shadow warfare was no match for brute force.

Donovan and his men began their work as rank amateurs. "The personnel of OSS, recruited and brought together in haste under the stress of the emergency, tended to be uneven in quality," his deputy, John Magruder, concluded in a candid after-action report. (Fortunately for Donovan, Germany's spies proved to be far worse.) But most of the U.S. Army also began World War II as rank amateurs. Donovan's OSS made horrible mistakes, had disastrous operations. But their mistakes and botched missions were no more or less than for other parts of the American military. As the war progressed they improved as the rest of the Army did. Donovan's spies gained experience. They produced better intelligence and reams of it, which earned them more plaudits from conventional commanders. The dull work—agents counting vehicles in enemy convoys, experts reading Axis newspapers, economists poring over building records and government reports to select bombing targets—proved to be of far more value than the cloak-and-dagger spying. Donovan recognized that. And all the intelligence the OSS produced never matched the value of the Ultra electronic intercepts in Europe and Magic in the Pacific. Donovan's men recognized that as well.

Donovan's other major goal was having his OSS survive after the war. His organization did not, but his ideas did. Even his critics—and they argue over his legacy to this day—concede that his OSS was the Petri dish for the spies who later ran the CIA. Allen Dulles, Richard Helms, William Colby, Bill Casey—men who cut their teeth under Donovan—became future directors. The daring, the risk taking, the unconventional thinking, the élan and esprit de corps of the OSS would permeate the new agency. The failings of the OSS would, too—the delusions that covert operations, like magic bullets, could produce spectacular results, that legal or ethical corners could be cut for a higher cause, infected the CIA as well. Donovan, nevertheless, was one of the men who shaped modern warfare. For that, Ruth was justified in making sure he was remembered.

Selected Bibliography for Source Notes

MANUSCRIPT COLLECTIONS

Abbreviations are used for manuscript collections in the source notes.

BCA — Buffalo Cavalry Association Archives
BECPL — Buffalo Erie County Public Library
BEH — Buffalo and Erie County Historical Society, William J. Donovan Collection
CA — Churchill Archives Centre
  CHAR — Chartwell Papers
  CHUR — Churchill Papers
COR — Cornell University Law Library, Donovan Archive
CU — Columbia University Archives
  DP — Manuscript Collection, Donovan Project
DDEL — Dwight D. Eisenhower Presidential Library
  AWF — Ann Whitman File
  AWP — Albert C. Wedemeyer Papers
  CF — Central File
  ELP — Edward P. Lilly Papers
  JFDP — John Foster Dulles Papers
  NSCP — White House Office, National Security Council Staff Papers, NSC Registry Series
  PF — Principal File
  PPP — Pre-Presidential Papers
  WHCF — White House Central Files
  WSP — Walter Bedell Smith Papers
  WSPWWII — Walter Bedell Smith Collection of World War II Documents
FBI — Federal Bureau of Investigation, Freedom of Information Act, File on William J. Donovan, Parts 1a-d, 2a-c, http://foia.fbi.gov/foiaindex/donovan.htm
FDRL — Franklin D. Roosevelt Presidential Library
  ABP — Adolf Berle Papers, Adolf Berle Diaries
  ECP — Ernest Cuneo Papers
  HHP — Harry L. Hopkins Papers
  HMD — Henry Morgenthau Jr. Diaries
  HSP — Harold Smith Papers
    HSD — Harold Smith Diaries, Conferences with President Roosevelt Files, 1941–45, and Conferences with President Truman File, 1945
  HWP — Henry Wallace Papers
  OF — Official File
  PPF — President's Personal File
  PSF — President's Secretary File

SEP	Stephen T. Early Papers
SF	Safe File
SWP	Sumner Welles Papers
WSP	Whitney H. Shepardson Papers
GU	Georgetown University Library Special Collections Division, Anthony Cave Brown Papers
HLHP	Harry L. Hopkins Papers
HHL	Herbert Hoover Presidential Library
JM	James MacLafferty Papers
HIA	Hoover Institution Archives
ADP	Arthur Duff Papers
AWP	Albert C. Wedemeyer Papers
CEP	Carl F. Eifler Papers
GSP	George E. Sokolsky Papers
HGP	Hermann Göring Papers
JDP	James B. Donovan Papers
JRFP	J. Russell Forgan Papers
MMP	Milton E. Miles Papers
MPGP	M. Preston Goodfellow Papers
PGP	Perrin C. Galpin Papers
RMP	Robert D. Murphy Papers
TGP	T. T. C. Gregory Papers
HSTL	Harry S. Truman Presidential Library
CF	Confidential File
EAP	Eban A. Ayers Papers
GF	General File
HSTP	Harry S. Truman Papers Pertaining to Family, Business, and Personal Affairs
OF	Official File
PPF	President's Personal File
PSF	President's Secretary's File
SMOF	Staff Member and Office Files
SRP	Samuel I. Rosenman Papers
VF	Vertical file
WHCF	White House Central Files
LOC	Library of Congress
CHP	Cordell Hull Papers
CLP	Clare Booth Luce Papers
CS	Charles P. Summerall Papers
EBP	Edward L. Bernays Papers
EC	Edward T. Clark Papers
EKP	Ernest J. King Papers
EMP	Edgar A. and Lillian T. Mowrer Papers
FKP	Frank Knox Papers
GMP	George C. Marshall Papers
HIP	Harold L. Ickes Papers
HVP	Hoyt S. Vandenberg Papers
JP	General John J. Pershing Papers
KRP	Kermit and Belle Roosevelt Papers
LRP	Lessing J. Rosenwald Papers
RJP	Robert H. Jackson Papers
RPP	Robert Porter Patterson Papers
TCP	Thomas G. Corcoran Papers

WDP	Wallace R. Deuel Papers
WLP	William D. Leahy Papers
MHI	U.S. Army Military History Institute, Army War College
CHP	Chester B. Hansen Papers
IYP	Ivan D. Yeaton Papers
RDP	Richard Dunlop Papers
WJDP	William J. Donovan Papers
WVHD	William vanden Heuvel Diary, last unnumbered box in the Donovan collection
WQP	William W. Quinn Papers
NA	National Archives and Records Administration
M1270	Reports, Interrogations, and Other Records Received from Various Allied Military Agencies, 1945–48
RG59	General Records of the Department of State, 1763–2002
RG65	Records of the Federal Bureau of Investigation, 1896–2008
RG117	Records of the American Battle Monuments Commission
RG120	Records of the American Expeditionary Forces (World War I), 1848–1928
RG165	Records of the War Department and General and Special Staffs 1860–1952
RG226	Record Group 226, Records of the Office of Strategic Services
A-3304	Original Microfilm of Washington Director's Office Administrative Files held by the Donovan-Leisure law firm
M1642	Microfilm of Washington Director's Office Administrative Files
RG263	Records of the CIA
GP	Records of the Grombach Organization ("the Pond")
TTP	Thomas Troy Papers
RG319	Records of the Army Staff, 1903–2009
RG407	Records of the Adjutant General's Office, 1909–81
RG457	Records of the National Security Agency/Central Security Service, 1917–88
T-77	Records of the OKW, German Armed Forces High Command
T-78	Records of the OKH, Germany Army High Command
T-84	Miscellaneous German Records Collection
T-120	Records of the German Foreign Office Received from the Department of State
NAUK	The National Archives United Kingdom
CAB	Records of the Cabinet Office
FO	Foreign Office Records
HS	Records of the Special Operations Executive
PREM	Records of the Prime Minister's Office
NPRC	National Personnel Records Center, David Rumsey Donovan Official Military Personnel File
NU	Niagara University Archives
PU	Public Policy Papers, Department of Rare Books, Princeton University Library
ADP	Allen W. Dulles Papers
AKP	Arthur Krock Papers
DLP	David Lawrence Papers
HAP	Hamilton Fish Armstrong Papers
WEP	Walter E. Edge Papers
SJCI	Saint Joseph's Collegiate Institute Archives
VHS	Virginia Historical Society
YU	Yale University Library
HSP	Henry L. Stimson Papers

PERSONAL COLLECTIONS

DGD   David G. Donovan Personal Collection
EMC   Elizabeth McIntosh Personal Collection
KNP   Kay Nelson Personal Collection
MMP   Molly Mugler Personal Collection

REMINISCENCES

Abbreviations are used for the oral history collections in the source notes. Only the last name will be listed, preceded by the abbreviation for the oral history collection. For example, the reminiscences of Edwin Putzell in the OSS Oral History Project will be listed in the source notes as "Putzell, OHP, page number."

FAOH: Foreign Affairs Oral History Collection of the Association for Diplomatic Studies and Training, American Memory from the Library of Congress, http://memory.loc.gov. Interviews with Samuel D. Eaton, James J. Halsema, Kempton B. Jenkins, and William W. Thomas Jr.

OHC: Columbia University Oral History Research Office Collection. Reminiscences of the Donovan, Leisure, Newton, and Irvine Oral History Project: Judge Joseph Edward Lumbard, Thomas J. McFadden, John Lord O'Brian, Frank G. Raichle, Jane Smith, Harold C. Train, Bethuel M. Webster, and James T. Williams. Also reminiscences of Sidney S. Alderman, Mary Bancroft, Adolf A. Berle Jr., F. Trubee Davison, Bernard L. Gladieux, Averell Harriman (Arnold Project), Robert H. Jackson, Alan Goodrich Kirk (Columbia University Sesquibicentennial Oral History Project), Grayson L. Kirk, Mary Lasker, Judge Joseph Edward Lumbard (New York Bar Foundation Project), Marya Mannes, William Phillips, Samuel I. Rosenman, Frank Stanton, Admiral Harold C. Train, James W. Wadsworth, and Henry A. Wallace.

OHP: OSS Oral History Project, National Archives and Records Administration, Record Group 263, Records of the CIA. Interviews with Charlotte Bowman, Frederick Burkhardt, David Crockett, Roger Gorian, Samuel Halpern, August Heckscher, Richard Helms, H. Stuart Hughes, Charles P. Kindleberger, Gertrude Legendre, Elizabeth McIntosh, Donal McLaughlin, Eloise Page, Barbara Podoski, Edwin Putzell, and Arthur Schlesinger Jr.

OTHER ABBREVIATIONS USED

AB	Adolf Berle	HS	Henry L. Stimson
AWD	Allen W. Dulles	HST	Harry S. Truman
B	Box for an entry or collection	JCS	Joint Chiefs of Staff (U.S.)
CC	Charles Cheston	JEH	J. Edgar Hoover
CH	Cordell Hull	JFC	John Franklin Carter
CIA	Central Intelligence Agency	JFD	John Foster Dulles
DB	David K. E. Bruce	JM	John Magruder
DDE	Dwight D. Eisenhower	NSC	National Security Council
E	Entry for a collection	OCD	Otto C. "Ole" Doering
EB	Edward G. Buxton	R	Microfilm reel
EH	Ellery C. Huntington	RG	Record Group for a collection
EP	Edwin Putzell	RRD	Ruth Rumsey Donovan
ES	Edward Stettinius	SW	Sumner Welles
EW	Edwin M. "Pa" Watson	WBS	Walter Bedell Smith
FK	Frank Knox	WC	Winston Churchill
Fr	Frame on a microfilm reel	WJD	William Joseph Donovan
FDR	Franklin Delano Roosevelt	WL	William L. Langer
GCM	George C. Marshall	WS	Whitney Shepardson
HH	Harry Hopkins		

AUTHOR INTERVIEWS

In the source notes only the last name of the interviewee will be listed followed by the date of the interview. For example, author interview with Patricia Gilbert on October 29, 2007, will appear in the source notes as "Gilbert, Oct. 29, 2007."

Cicely Angleton, Margot Rumsey Banta, Judy Beecher, Joseph F. Bieron, Armando Chacon, David G. Donovan, Tippaparn Weam Donovan, Mary Jean Eisenhower, George Elsey, Robert H. Ferrell, John R. Friant, Curt Gentry, Patricia Gilbert, Lucia Henderson, Cordelia Hood, Fisher Howe, Mary Gardiner Jones, Gordon Joost, Rolfe Kingsley, Sal Martoche, Elizabeth McIntosh, Louise McKay, Margot Mugler, Kay Nelson, Henry Putzell Jr., David Robarge, Charles Schulte, Susan Spaulding, Marsha Joy Sullivan, Thomas F. Troy, William J. vanden Heuvel, Michael Warner, Betty Wise, and James R. York.

BOOKS, PERIODICALS, DISSERTATIONS, AND GOVERNMENT REPORTS

To avoid repetition, the full citation of the work is given here, but in the source notes it will appear in second reference form.

Aid, Matthew M. "'Stella Polaris' and the Secret Code Battle in Postwar Europe," *Intelligence and National Security* 17, no. 3 (Autumn 2002): 17–86.

Allen Welsh Dulles as Director of Central Intelligence: 26 February 1953–29 November 1961. Monograph. Vol. 1, Allen Dulles, The Man, DCI-2, July 1973, Series B, Central Intelligence Agency.

Alvarez, David. "Tempest in an Embassy Trash Can," *World War II*. January/February 2008, pp. 55–59.

Atkinson, Rick. *An Army at Dawn: The War in North Africa, 1942–1943*. New York: Henry Holt, 2002.

———. *The Day of Battle: The War in Sicily and Italy, 1943–1944*. New York: Henry Holt, 2007.

Bancroft, Mary. *Autobiography of a Spy: Debutante, Writer, Confidante, Secret Agent. The True Story of Her Extraordinary Life*. New York: Morrow, 1983.

Batvinis, Raymond J. *The Origins of FBI Counter-Intelligence*. Lawrence: University Press of Kansas, 2007.

Belmont, Eleanor Robson. *The Fabric of Memory*. New York: Farrar, Straus, 1957.

Bennett, Gill. *Churchill's Man of Mystery: Desmond Morton and the World of Intelligence*. New York: Routledge, 2007.

Bess, Demaree. "Our Frontier on the Danube: The Appalling Story of Our Meddling in the Balkans," *Saturday Evening Post*, May 24, 1941, pp. 9, 118–21.

Bischof, Günter, and Anton Prelinka, eds. *Austrian Historical Memory and National Identity: Contemporary Austrian Studies*, vol. 5. New Brunswick, Conn.: Transaction, 1979.

Bishop, Jim. *FDR's Last Year: April 1944-April 1945*. New York: Morrow, 1974.

Blair, Anne. *There to the Bitter End: Ted Serong in Vietnam*. Australia: Allen & Unwin, 2001.

The Blue Book Buffalo 1905. Buffalo: Dau Publishing Co., 1905.

Boll, Michael M. *Cold War in the Balkans: American Foreign Policy and the Emergence of Communist Bulgaria, 1943–1947*. Lexington: University Press of Kentucky, 1984.

Bower, Tom. *The Red Web: MI6 and the KGB Master Coup*. London: Mandarin, 1993.

Braden, Tom. "The Birth of the CIA." *American Heritage* 28, no. 2 (February 1977): 4–13.

Bratzel, John F., and Leslie B. Rout, Jr. "FDR and the 'Secret Map,'" *Wilson Quarterly*, New Year's 1985, pp. 167–73.

Brinkley, David. *Washington Goes to War: The Extraordinary Story of the Transformation of a City and a Nation*. New York: Knopf, 1988.

Brown, Anthony Cave. *The Last Hero: Wild Bill Donovan*. New York: Vintage, 1982.

Brunner, John W. *OSS Weapons*. 2nd edition. Williamstown, N.J.: Phillips, 2005.

Buffalo City Directory 1891. Buffalo: Courier Company, 1891.

Caldwell, Oliver J. A Secret War: Americans in China, 1944–1945. Carbondale: Southern Illinois University Press, 1973.

Casey, William. The Secret War Against Hitler. Washington: Regnery Gateway, 1988.

Chalou, George C., ed. The Secret War: The Office of Strategic Services in World War II. Washington: National Archives and Records Administration, 1992.

Charles, Douglas M. "'Before the Colonel Arrived: Hoover, Donovan, Roosevelt, and the Origins of American Central Intelligence, 1940–41." Intelligence and National Security, June 2005, pp. 225–37.

Chernow, Ron. The House of Morgan: An American Banking Dynasty and the Rise of Modern Finance. New York: Atlantic Monthly Press, 1990.

Chester, Eric Thomas. Covert Network: Progressives, the International Rescue Committee and the CIA. New York: M. E. Sharpe, 1995.

Churchill, Winston S. The Second World War: the Grand Alliance. Boston: Houghton Mifflin, 1950.

———. The Second World War: Closing the Ring. Boston: Houghton Mifflin, 1951.

Clark, Mark W. Calculated Risk. New York: Harper, 1950.

Coffman, Edward M. The War to End All Wars: The American Experience in World War I. Lexington: University Press of Kentucky, 1998.

Colville, John. The Fringes of Power. London: Weidenfeld & Nicolson, 2004.

Conant, Jennet. The Irregulars: Roald Dahl and the British Spy Ring in Wartime Washington. New York: Simon & Schuster, 2008.

Cooke, James J. The Rainbow Division in the Great War, 1917–1919. Westport, Conn.: Praeger, 1994.

Coon, Carleton S. A North Africa Story. Ipswich, Mass.: Gambit, 1980.

Corson, William R. The Armies of Ignorance: The Rise of the American Intelligence Empire. New York: Dial, 1977.

Corvo, Max. The O.S.S. in Italy, 1942–1945: A Personal Memoir. New York: Praeger, 1990.

Darling, Frank C. Thailand and the United States. Washington, D.C.: Public Affairs Press, 1965.

Deane, John R. The Strange Alliance: The Story of Our Efforts at Wartime Co-operation with Russia. New York: Viking, 1946.

Demaris, Ovid. The Director. New York: Harper's Magazine Press, 1975.

D'Este, Carlo. Eisenhower: A Soldier's Life. New York: Henry Holt, 2002.

Deutsch, James I. "'I Was a Hollywood Agent': Cinematic Representations of the Office of Strategic Services in 1946." Intelligence and National Security 13, no. 2 (Summer 1998): 85–99.

Documents on German Foreign Policy: 1918–1945, Series D (1937–1945), vol. 11, The War Years. Washington: Government Printing Office, 1960.

Dodd, Christopher J., with Larry Bloom. Letters from Nuremberg: My Father's Narrative of a Quest for Justice. New York: Crown, 2007.

Donovan, Robert J. Conflict and Crisis: The Presidency of Harry S. Truman, 1945–1948. New York: Norton, 1977.

Donovan, William J. "A Central Intelligence Agency: Foreign Policy Must Be Based on Facts," Vital Speeches, May 1946, pp. 446–48.

———. "Intelligence: Key to Defense." Life, Sept. 30, 1946, pp. 108–20.

———. "Our Stake in Thailand." Fortune, July 1955, pp. 94–95.

———. "Religion—The Need of the Hour." Niagara Index 34, no. 17 (June 15, 1902): 166–67.

———. "Should Men of 50 Fight Our Wars?" Reader's Digest, June 1940, pp. 30–32.

———. "Stop Russia's Subversive War." Atlantic Monthly, May 1948, pp. 27–30.

———. "Who Says We're Soft." Reader's Digest, April 1941, pp. 66–68.

———, and Mary Gardner Jones. "Program for a Democratic Counter Attack to Communist Penetration of Government Service." Yale Law Journal 58, no. 8 (July, 1949): 1211–41.

Downes, Donald. The Scarlet Thread: Adventures in Wartime Espionage. London: Derek Verschoyle, 1953.

Duffy, Francis P. *Father Duffy's Story: A Tale of Humor and Heroism, of Life and Death with the Fighting Sixty-Ninth.* New York: George H. Doran, 1919.

Dunlop, Richard. *Donovan: America's Master Spy.* New York: Rand McNally, 1982.

Dunn, Edward T. *Buffalo's Delaware Avenue: Mansions and Families.* Buffalo: Canisius College Press, 2003.

Elsey, George McKee. *An Unplanned Life.* Columbia: University of Missouri Press, 2005.

Fausold, Martin L. *James W. Wadsworth, Jr.: The Gentleman from New York.* Syracuse: Syracuse University Press, 1975.

Ferrell, Robert H., ed. *The Eisenhower Diaries.* New York: Norton, 1981.

——, ed. *Off the Record: The Private Papers of Harry S. Truman.* New York: Harper & Row, 1980.

——. *The Question of MacArthur's Reputation, Côte de Châtillon, October 14–16, 1918.* Columbia: University of Missouri Press, 2008.

Fischer, Benjamin B. "Dirty Tricks and Deadly Devices: OSS, SOE, NDRC and the Development of Special Weapons and Equipment." *Journal of Intelligence History* 2 (Summer 2002): 1–20.

Foot, M. R. D. *Resistance: European Resistance to Nazism.* New York: McGraw-Hill, 1977.

Ford, Corey. *Donovan of OSS.* Boston: Little, Brown, 1970.

Furgurson, Ernest B. "Back Channels." *The Washingtonian*, June 1996, pp. 57–59, 102–14.

Gentry, Curt. *J. Edgar Hoover: The Man and the Secrets.* New York: Norton, 1991.

Goldman, Mark. *City on the Edge: Buffalo, New York.* Amherst, N.Y.: Prometheus, 2007.

Graham, Robert A. "Notes and Comments: Virgilio Scattolini, The Prince of Vatican Misinformers, A Bibliographical Note." *The Catholic Historical Review* 59, no. 4 (January 1974): 719–21.

Grose, Peter. *Gentleman Spy: The Life of Allen Dulles.* New York: Houghton Mifflin, 1994.

Gunther, John. *Roosevelt in Retrospect.* New York: Harper Brothers, 1950.

Hamby, Alonzo L. *Man of the People: A Life of Harry S. Truman.* New York: Oxford University Press, 1995.

Harriman, Averell W., and Elie Abel. *Special Envoy to Churchill and Stalin, 1941–1946.* New York: Random House, 1975.

Harris, Stephen L. *Duffy's War: Fr. Francis Duffy, Wild Bill Donovan, and the Irish Fighting 69th in World War I.* Washington: Potomac, 2006.

Hersh, Burton. *The Old Boys: The American Elite and the Origins of the CIA.* New York: Scribner's, 1992.

Hoettl, Wilhelm. *The Secret Front: The Story of Nazi Political Espionage.* New York: Praeger, 1954.

Hough, Richard. *Mountbatten.* New York: Random House, 1981.

Hyde, H. Montgomery. *Cynthia: The Spy Who Changed the Course of the War.* London: Hamish Hamilton, 1966.

Kahn, David. *Hitler's Spies: German Military Intelligence in World War II.* New York: Macmillan, 1978.

Keegan, John. *The Second World War.* New York: Viking, 1989.

Keeley, Edmund. *The Salonika Bay Murder: Cold War Politics and the Polk Affair.* Princeton: Princeton University Press, 1989.

Kent, George O. *Historians and Archivists: Essays in Modern History.* Fairfax, Va.: George Mason University Press, 1991.

Kessler, Pamela. *Undercover Washington: Touring the Sites Where Famous Spies Lived, Worked and Loved.* McLean, Va.: EPM, 1992.

Kimball, Warren F. *Churchill and Roosevelt: The Complete Correspondence*, vols. 1–3. Princeton: Princeton University Press, 1984.

Klurfeld, Herman. *Behind the Lines: The World of Drew Pearson.* Englewood Cliffs, N.J.: Prentice Hall, 1968.

Lagemann, John K. "'Wild Bill' Donovan." *Current History*, April 1941, pp. 23–25, 55–56.

Lankford, Nelson D. OSS Against the Reich: The World War II Diaries of Colonel David K. E. Bruce. Kent, Ohio: Kent State University Press, 1991.

Laurie, Clayton D. "Black Games, Subversions, and Dirty Tricks: The OSS Morale Operations Branch in Europe, 1943–1945." Prologue: Quarterly of the National Archives, Fall 1993, pp. 269–71.

Lay, Shawn. Hooded Knights on the Niagara: The Ku Klux Klan in Buffalo. New York: New York University Press, 1995.

Leary, William M. Perilous Mission: Civil Air Patrol and CIA Covert Operations in Asia. Tuscaloosa: University of Alabama Press, 1984.

Lewin, Ronald. The American Magic: Codes, Ciphers and the Defeat of Japan. New York: Farrar, Straus & Giroux, 1982.

Lindbergh, Charles A. The Wartime Journals of Charles A. Lindbergh. New York: Harcourt Brace, 1970.

Lochner, Louis P., ed. The Goebbels Diaries. New York: Charter, 1948.

Lovell, Stanley P. Of Spies and Stratagems. Englewood Cliffs, N.J.: Prentice Hall, 1963.

Lyell, Anne Morse. Nonquitt: A Summer Album, 1872–1984. South Dartmouth, Mass.: Barekneed, 1987.

MacDonald, Elizabeth P. Undercover Girl. New York: Macmillan, 1947.

Manchester, William. American Caesar: Douglas MacArthur, 1880–1964. Boston: Little, Brown, 1978.

Mangold, Tom. Cold Warrior: James Jesus Angleton: The CIA's Master Spy Hunter. New York: Simon & Schuster, 1991.

Martoche, Sal. "William J. Donovan: More to Remember." Western New York Heritage 6, no. 2 (Spring 2003): 4–15.

———. "Lest We Forget: William J. Donovan." Western New York Heritage 6, no. 1 (Winter 2003): 5–23.

Mauch, Christof. The Shadow War Against Hitler: The Covert Operations of America's Wartime Secret Intelligence Service. New York: Columbia University Press, 1983.

McCullough, David. Truman. New York: Simon & Schuster, 1992.

Miles, Milton E. "U.S. Naval Group, China." United States Naval Institute Proceedings. July 1946, pp. 921–31.

Miller, Merle. Plain Speaking: An Oral Biography of Harry S. Truman. New York: Berkley, 1973.

Miller, Richard Lawrence. Truman: The Rise to Power. New York: McGraw-Hill, 1986.

Montague, Ludwell Lee. General Walter Bedell Smith as Director of Central Intelligence: October 1950–February 1953. University Park: Pennsylvania State University Press, 1992.

Moon, Tom. This Grim and Savage Game: OSS and the Beginning of U.S. Covert Operations in World War II. Los Angeles: Burning Gate, 1991.

———, and Carl F. Eifler. The Deadliest Colonel. New York: Vantage, 1975.

Morris, Joe Alex. Nelson Rockefeller: A Biography. New York: Harper & Brothers, 1960.

Mosley, Leonard. Dulles: A Biography of Eleanor, Allen and John Foster Dulles and Their Family Network. New York: Dial, 1978.

Mueller, Michael. Canaris: The Life and Death of Hitler's Spymaster. Annapolis: Naval Institute Press, 2007.

Mulligan, Timothy P. "'According to Colonel Donovan': A Document from the Records of German Military Intelligence." The Historian, November 1983, pp. 78–86.

Murphy, Robert. Diplomat Among Warriors. New York: Doubleday, 1964.

O'Donnell, Patrick K. Operatives, Spies and Saboteurs: The Unknown Story of the Men and Women of WW II's OSS. New York: Free Press, 2004.

One Hundred Years, 1885–1985: The Saturn Club of Buffalo, New York. Kenmore, N.Y.: Partners' Press, 1985.

Ormsby, Linus, "The University on the Banks of the Niagara." Western New York Heritage, Fall 2006, pp. 1–8.

O'Toole, J. J. A. Honorable Treachery: A History of U.S. Intelligence, Espionage, and Covert Action from the American Revolution to the CIA. New York: Atlantic Monthly Press, 1991.

The Overseas Targets: War Report of the OSS, vol. 2. New York: Walker, 1976.

Peake, Hayden B. "OSS and the Venona Decrypts." *Intelligence and National Security* 12, no. 3 (July 1997): 14–34.

Peers, William R., and Dan Brelis. *Behind the Burma Road: The Story of America's Most Successful Guerrilla Force.* New York: Atlantic Monthly Press, 1963.

Perret, Geoffrey. *Old Soldiers Never Die: The Life of Douglas MacArthur.* New York: Random House, 1996.

Persico, Joseph E. *Casey: The Lives and Secrets of William J. Casey: From the OSS to the CIA.* New York: Viking, 1990.

———. *Nuremberg: Infamy on Trial.* New York: Viking, 1994.

———. *Roosevelt's Secret War: FDR and World War II Espionage.* New York: Random House, 2002.

Peterson, Neal H. *From Hitler's Doorstep: The Wartime Intelligence Reports of Allen Dulles, 1942–1945.* University Park: Pennsylvania State University Press, 1996.

Petrov, Vladimir. *A Study in Diplomacy: The Story of Arthur Bliss Lane.* Chicago: Henry Regency, 1971.

Powers, Richard Gid. *Secrecy and Power: The Life of J. Edgar Hoover.* New York: Free Press, 1987.

Ranelagh, John. *The Agency: The Rise and Decline of the CIA.* New York: Simon & Schuster, 1986.

Riebling, Mark. *Wedge: The Secret War Between the FBI and CIA.* New York: Knopf, 1994.

Salter, Michael. *Nazi War Crimes, U.S. Intelligence and Selective Prosecution at Nuremberg.* New York: Routledge-Cavendish, 2007.

von Schlabrendorff, Fabian. *The Secret War Against Hitler.* Boulder, Co.: Westview, 1994.

Scott-Smith, Giles, and Hans Krabbendam, eds. *The Cultural Cold War in Western Europe 1945–1960.* Portland: Frank Cass, 2003.

Sherwood, Robert E. *Roosevelt and Hopkins.* New York: Harper, 1948.

Singlaub, John K. *Hazardous Duty: An American Soldier in the Twentieth Century.* New York: Summit, 1991.

Smith, Bradley F. *The Shadow Warriors: O.S.S. and the Origins of the C.I.A.* New York: Basic Books, 1983.

———, and Elena Agarossi. *Operation Sunrise: The Secret Surrender.* New York: Basic Books, 1979.

Smith, Richard Harris. *OSS: The Secret History of America's First Central Intelligence Agency.* Guilford, Conn.: Lyons, 1972.

Sperber, A. M. *Murrow: His Life and Times.* New York: Freundlich, 1986.

Storey, Robert G. *The Final Judgment? Pearl Harbor to Nuremberg.* San Antonio: Naylor, 1968.

Stout, Mark. "The Pond: Running Agents for State, War, and the CIA." Center for the Study of Intelligence, CIA, www.cia.gov.

Stranges, John B. *The Rainbow Never Fades: Niagara University, 1856–2006.* New York: Peter Lang, 2007.

Sulzberger, C. L. *World War II.* Boston: Houghton Mifflin, 1985.

Taylor, Edmond. *Awakening from History.* London: Chatto & Windus, 1971.

Tompkins, Peter. *A Spy in Rome.* New York: Simon & Schuster, 1962.

Trevor-Roper, Hugh, ed. *Final Entries 1945: The Diaries of Joseph Goebbels.* New York: Putnam, 1978.

Troy, Thomas F. "The British Assault on J. Edgar Hoover: The Tricycle Case." *International Journal of Intelligence and Counterintelligence* 3, no. 2 (1989): 169–209.

———. *Donovan and the CIA: A History of the Establishment of the Central Intelligence Agency.* Frederick, Md.: University Publications of America, 1981.

———. "Knifing of the OSS." *International Journal of Intelligence and Counterintelligence* 1, no. 3 (1986): 95–108.

———. *Wild Bill and Intrepid: Donovan, Stephenson and the Origin of the CIA.* New Haven: Yale University Press, 1996.

Vaughan, Hal. *FDR's 12 Apostles: The Spies Who Paved the Way for the Invasion of North Africa.* Guilford, Conn.: Lyons, 2006.

Walker, David A. "OSS and Operation Torch." *Journal of Contemporary History* 22, no. 4 (October 1987): 667–79.

War Report of the OSS. New York: Walker, 1976.

Warner, Michael. "The Office of Strategic Services: America's First Intelligence Agency." Monograph posted March 15, 2007, Public Affairs, Central Intelligence Agency.

———. "Salvage and Liquidation: The Creation of the Central Intelligence Group." CIA History Staff Monograph, pp. 111–20.

———, and Robert Louis Benson. "Venona and Beyond: Thoughts on Work Undone." *Intelligence and National Security* 12, no. 3 (July 1997): 1–13.

Weinberg, Gerhard L. *A World at Arms: A Global History of World War II.* New York: Cambridge University Press, 2005.

Weinstein, Allen, and Alexander Vassilev. *The Haunted Wood: Soviet Espionage in America–The Stalin Era.* New York: Random House, 1999.

Weintraub, Stanley. *Long Day's Journey into War, December 7, 1941.* New York: Dutton, 1991.

White, Theodore H. *In Search of History: A Personal Adventure.* New York: Warner, 1978.

Whitehead, Don. *The FBI Story: A Report to the People.* New York: Random House, 1956.

Willoughby, Charles A., and John Chamberlain. *MacArthur: 1941–1951.* New York: McGraw-Hill, 1954.

Winks, Robin W. *Cloak and Gown: Scholars in the Secret War, 1939–1961.* New York: Morrow, 1987.

Source Notes

In many instances a source note covers several paragraphs. Unless otherwise indicated, each source lists material cited up to the previous source note.

PROLOGUE

1   *for $1.25:* Washington Post, Sept. 29, 1945; Brinkley, pp. 119–20, 277–28.

2   *for the pin:* WJD memo to former members of the OSS, Sept. 28, 1945, Fr: 439–40, R: 135, M1642, RG226, NA.

2   *glamorous spymaster:* McIntosh, Aug. 29, 2007; Bancroft, OHC, pp. 196–97; David G. Donovan, Nov. 15, 2007.

2–3   *Donovan's life to "will endure":* OSS Personnel Analysis, Fr: 86, R: 113, WJD Remarks at Final Gathering of OSS Employees, Sept. 28, 1945, Fr: 441–43, R: 69, M1642, RG226, NA; "Donovan Gives Farewell Talk to OSS Crew," Washington Post, Sept. 28, 1945.

4   *to come:* Unsigned OSS letter in Latin, Safe File, OSS, 1945, PSF, FDRL; WJD letter to Arthur Krock, Sept. 29, 1945, B: 24, AKP, PU; Col. J. G. Coughlin memo to WJD, Aug. 18, 1945, Fr: 449–53, R: 3, ECONIC memo to JM, Oct. 30, 1945, Fr: 348–49, R: 45, M1642, RG226, NA.

4   *many times:* Warner, "Salvage and Liquidation," pp. 112–18; Gentry, Dec. 1, 2008; Confidential interviews by author.

5   *out his name:* Col. Richard Park Memorandum for the President, B: 6, TTP, RG 263, NA; Draft HST speech, March 3, 1948, Speech File 1945-53, Jan.–March 1948, PSF, HSTL.

5   *"to haunt you":* L. M. Ream memo to WJD, Sept. 12, 1945, Fr: 559–61, R: 77, Maj. Delafield memo to WJD, Sept. 10, 1945, Fr: 1355, R: 77, Memo to WJD, "Liquidation Problems—UK," May 1, 1945, Fr: 841–52, R: 69, M1642, RG226, NA; John M. Jeffries memo to WJD, Aug. 27, 1945, R: 86, A-3304, RG226, NA; "Summary of New OSS Weapons," B: 311, E: 210, RG226, NA; Kingsley, Jan. 1, 2008.

5   *"in wartime":* WJD letter to James K. Yardsman, Sept. 29, 1945, Fr: 804, R: 3, M1642, RG226, NA; Nature of M. O. Set II, No. 2: With Comments by Gen. William Donovan, 9/2/1945, ARC Identifier 102071/Local Identifier 226.15, Motion Picture, Sound and Video Records Section, RG226, NA.

6   *the organization:* Brown, pp. xi, xii; Putzell, OHP, p. 72.

6   *shades of gray:* Harper & Brothers letter to WJD, Aug. 12, 1943, and WJD response, Aug. 20, 1943, Fr: 1096–98, R: 39, Memos on OSS history, Fr: 748–948, R: 55, M1642, RG226, NA; Deutsch, pp. 85–99; WJD letter to Louis de Rochemont, July 3, 1946, B: 1, JRFP, HIA.

CHAPTER 1: FIRST WARD

10   *Irish Republic:* Corey Ford interview with Vincent Donovan, November 1967, pp. 6–8, 11, B: 1, Part 1, GU; Notes on W.J.D., B: 137C, WJDP, MHI; Lay, p. 14; Beecher, Sept. 25 and 26, 2008; Brown, pp. 15–16; Memorandum on lunch with OCD and Father Vincent Donovan, Sept. 25, 1958, B: 18, WJDP, MHI; Goldman, pp. 39, 75.

10   *Democratic Party:* King letter to Edward H. Butler, Oct. 2, 1980, B: 19, RDP, MHI.

10 *fine literature: Buffalo Courier & Republic,* July 20, 1868; Corey Ford interview with Vincent Donovan, November 1967, pp. 33-34, B: 1, Part 1, GU.

11 *"Need Apply": Buffalo City Directory 1891,* p. 421; *The Blue Book Buffalo 1905,* p. 166.

11 *was fifteen:* State of New York, County of Erie, City of Buffalo, Birth Certificate for Jan. 1, 1883, WJD Birth Certificate File, BEH; Corey Ford interview with Vincent Donovan, November 1967, pp. 8, 33-34, B: 1, Part 1, GU.

11 *on the bar:* Beecher, Sept. 11, 2007, Sept. 25 and 26, 2008; Corey Ford interview with Vincent Donovan, November 1967, pp. 18, 34-35, B: 1, Part 1, GU.

12 *or orations:* Corey Ford interview with Vincent Donovan, November 1967, pp. 1, 22, 25, 38-39, B: 1, Part 1, GU; Memorandum on lunch with OCD and Father Vincent Donovan, Sept. 25, 1958, B: 18, WJDP, MHI; Beecher, Sept. 25, 2007; Sullivan, Sept. 25, 2008; Nardin Academy school records for WJD, 1895.

12 *on the field:* Saint Joseph's Collegiate Institute brochure, B: 2, RDP, MHI; Bieron, Sept. 24, 2008; History of Saint Joseph's Collegiate Institute, SJCI; Saint Joseph's commencement program brochures, 1898-99, SJCI; "The Quigley Medal," news clipping, May 1899, SJCI.

12 *Donovan railed:* Corey Ford interview with Vincent Donovan, November 1967, pp. 3-5, B:1, Part 1, GU; Stranges, p. 1; Ormsby, pp. 1-8; WJD grades in Records of the Collegiate and Academic Departments of Niagara University, September 1898 to June 1910, NU; WJD, "Religion—The Need of the Hour," pp. 166-67.

13 *the "handsomest":* Newton D. Baker Memorial Lecture by WJD, May 3, 1946, p. 68, B: 3A, WJDP, MHI; Corey Ford interview with Vincent Donovan, November 1967, pp. 4, 43, B: 1, Part 1, GU; Notes on WJD, B: 137C, WJDP, MHI; Interview with RRD, March 6, 1972, B: 7, Troy Papers, RG 263, NA; Donovan Football Record, unnumbered box, WJDP, MHI; M. Halsey Thomas letter to WS, Dec. 19, 1958, B: 80, Historical Background Files, CU; The Columbian 1905: The Year Book of the Junior Class, p. 272, C722, CPI, CU; The Senior-Year Book of the Class of 1905, Record of the Senior Class of Columbia College, pp. 127-28, CU.

14 *from Hyde Park:* Kyle Bradford Smith, "Remember 109—Recollections of OSSers," OSS Society Newsletter, Winter 2007, p. 14; Brown, p. 20; Newton D. Baker Memorial Lecture by WJD, May 3, 1946, p. 68, B: 3A, WJDP, MHI.

14 *defense issues:* Notes on W.J.D., B: 137C, WJDP, MHI; "The Rise of Wm. J. Donovan," undated newspaper article, B: "World War I, Political Campaigns, etc.," WJDP, MHI; "William J. Donovan," undated newspaper article, B: 135, WJDP, MHI, MIH; WJD letter to Donnelly & O'Neil, Jan. 2, 1914, B: 1, BEH.

15 *his way up:* WJD letter to Saturn Club, Dec. 24, 1914, B: 1, BEH; Baker & Watson letter to WJD, Feb. 17, 1915, B: 1, BEH.

15 *music harmony:* Bing & Nathan letter to WJD, Dec. 7, 1915, WJD to Brother Clement Donovan, Dec. 22, 1915, B: 1, BEH; WJD letter to Loretta Donovan, Dec. 16, 1915, Immaculata Seminary Report Card for Loretta Donovan, November 1915, B: 1, BEH.

15 *military neophytes:* WJD letter to Col. Charles I. DeBevoise, Nov. 15, 1913, B: 128A, WJDP, MHI.

16 *wanting to join:* WJD letter to David H. Biddle, Dec. 11, 1915, WJD letter to John M. Scopes & Co., Feb. 17, 1916, WJD letter to Maj. J. Leslie Kincaid, Dec. 17, 1915, WJD letter to Cpt. Chester King, March 13, 1916, WJD letter to Lt. Col. Henry A. Bostwick, Dec. 21, 1915, B: 128A, Troop I bylaws, B: 137B, WJDP, MHI.

16 *amateur productions:* Corey Ford interview with Vincent Donovan, November 1967, pp. 25, 48-49, B: 1, Part 1, GU; WVHD, p. 34, WJDP, MHI; Unidentified newspaper obituary for Eleanor R. Belmont, B: 135, WJDP, MHI; Belmont, pp. 77-79, 95, 100, 111-12; Donald S. Rumsey letter to David Donovan, Dec. 5, 1982, Part 3, B: 1, GU.

16 *a millionaire:* Beecher, Sept. 25, 2008; Brown, pp. 27-29; "Death of Aaron Rumsey," Buffalo Commercial Advertiser, April 6, 1864, p. 3; Dunn, pp. 155-56; "D. P. Rumsey Dead," Buffalo Commercial Advertiser, April 5 and 11, 1906, p. 14 and p. 8; RRD letters to Susan Rumsey, B: 2, GU; Rosemary Hall report card for RRD, December 1908, B: 135, WJDP, MHI; Mugler, Jan. 21, 2008.

17 *her daughter*: Banta, Jan. 28, 2008; Spaulding, Feb. 18, 2008; Corey Ford interview with Vincent Donovan, November 1967, p. 11, B: 1, Part 1, GU.

17 *"own class"*: WJD letter to RRD, undated, B: 135, WJDP, MHI.

17 *his fiancée*: Corey Ford interview with Vincent Donovan, November 1967, p. 11, B: 1, Part 1, GU; "I Remember," unidentified newspaper article from Buffalo, MMP.

18 *them a car*: "Donovan-Rumsey," *Buffalo Evening News*, July 16, 1914, p. 18; WJD letter to John T. Ryan, March 27, 1915, B: 1, BEH; WJD letter to Susan Rumsey, B: 135, WJDP, MHI.

18 *"your manners"*: Notes on W.J.D., B: 137C, WJDP, MHI; Donald Rumsey interview, B: Interviews—Teitelbaum to Withrow, 1975-undated, WJDP, MHI; Guy Martin interview, April 28, 1941, B: 6, RDP, MHI; Dunlop, pp. 171-72; WVHD, p. 12, WJDP, MHI.

18 *across the border*: C. P. Franchot cable to Robert Lansing, June 22, 1916, B: 137B, WJDP, MHI. There has been wild speculation by Anthony Cave Brown and other OSS writers that during his European tour with the Rockefeller Foundation Donovan met British agent William Stephenson and was secretly recruited and trained by British intelligence. There is no credible evidence that was the case. Donovan was working only for the Rockefeller Foundation. See Troy, *Wild Bill and Intrepid*, pp. 165-77.

19 *his father*: Corey Ford interview with Vincent Donovan, November 1967, p. 11, B: 1, Part 1, GU; WJD letter to RRD, May 12, 1916, B: 135, WJDP, MHI; Corey Ford interview with Vincent Donovan, November 1967, pp. 31-32, B: 1, Part 1, GU.

19 *"to get well"*: "Troop I Gets Invitation to Private Lake," unidentified news article July 24, 1916, and other news clips, BCA; WJD letter to RRD, Oct. 2, 1916, B: 135, WJDP, MHI; WJD letter to RRD, Fall 1916, EMC.

20 *loyal soldier*: Harris, pp. 2-3, 17-41, 50-60, 73-74, 96-99, 198, 285; WJD letter to RRD, circa August 1917, B: 135, WJDP, MHI; WVHD, p. 12, WJDP, MHI; "69th Has New War Game, 'Bucking the Line,' to Harden Men for French Trenches," unidentified news article, Aug. 28, 1917, B: 137C, WJDP, MHI.

20 *and wife*: WJD letter to RRD, Sept. 12, 1917, B: 134, WJDP, MHI; WJD letter to Susan Rumsey, 1917, WJD letters to RRD Aug. 2, 8, 21, and 30, 1917, B: 135, WJDP, MHI; Corey Ford interview with Vincent Donovan, November 1967, pp. 14, B: 1, Part 1, GU.

CHAPTER 2: THE GREAT WAR

21 *that day*: Duffy, p. 271; WJD letters to RRD, Sept. 17, 21, and 25, 1918, B: 132A, WJDP, MHI; Cooke, pp. 133-34.

22 *he told Ruth*: WJD letters to RRD, Dec. 26, 1917, Jan. 1, Feb. 7, March 11, March 28, April 4, May 7, 1918, B: 132A, WJDP, MHI; Harris, pp. 150-78.

23 *he loved it*: WVHD, p. 24, WJDP, MHI; Dunlop, pp. 58-59; Interview with Mrs. William J. Donovan, March 6, 1972, B: 7, TTP, RG263, NA; WJD to RRD, Nov. 11, 1917, B: 132A, WJDP, MHI; WJD to C.O. Co. C, 165th Inf., Jan. 16, 1918, WJD memo to CO Medical Detachment, March 4, 1918, WJD memo to C. O. Co. C, March 4, 1918, and Oliver Ames memo to Platoon Commanders, March 4, 1918, B: 26, E: 1241, RG120, NA.

23 *published them*: Sept. 13, 1918, Donovan, 1/165, B: 230, RG117, NA; Cooke, p. 164; Sen. Wadsworth letter to WJD, Aug. 9, 1918, and King letter to WJD, Sept. 1, 1918, B: 137B, WJDP, MIII; Notes on W.J.D., B: 137C, WJDP, MIII; Sen. Wadsworth letter to WJD, May 18, 1918, B: 129, WJDP, MHI; "Major Donovan's War Diary," *New York Sun* Magazine Section, Sept. 22, 1918; WJD to RRD, Aug. 7, 1918, Box 132A, WJDP, MHI.

23 *abandon God*: Sen. Wadsworth letter to WJD, Aug. 9, 1918, B: 137B, WJDP, MHI; letter to RRD, Feb. 28, 1918, B: 1, BEC; Goldman, pp. 75-76; WJD letters to RRD, April 4, Aug. 7 and 26, Sept. 5, 9, and 21, 1918, and March 27, 1919, B: 132A, WJPD, MHI; Corey Ford interview with Vincent Donovan, November 1967, pp. 13, 19, 21, B: 1, Part 1, GU; Beecher, Sept. 26 and 26, 2008; McIntosh, April 7, 2009; Vincent Donovan letter to RRD, November 1918, B: 137D, WJDP, MIII; Memo of conversation with Betty McIntosh, April 26, 1973, B: 7, TTP, RG263, NA; Donald Rumsey interview, B: Interviews—Teitelbaum to Withrow, 1979-undated, WJDP, MHI.

24   *through forces:* Coffman, p. 255; Ferrell, *The Question of MacArthur's Reputation,* p. 11;
        Cooke, pp. 134, 163–69.

25   *right flank:* Ferrell, *The Question of MacArthur's Reputation,* pp. 13–22, 82–83; Cooke, pp.
        167–70; Harris, pp. 336–39.

25–29   *With rain to carry it out:* Ferrell, *The Question of MacArthur's Reputation,* pp. 22–42, 52,
        81–88; Ferrell, Dec. 22, 2008; 201–Bootz, Henry A. testimony, April 14, 1930, B: 232,
        RG117, NA; Harris, p. 341; WJD letter to RRD, Oct. 15 and 23, 1918, B: 132A, WJDP,
        MHI; 42nd Division Inspector report to Commanding General on WJD countermand-
        ing order, Oct. 25, 1918, B: 94, HDQRS.—Dec. File 331.5-350, E: 1241, RG120, NA;
        AEF and 5th Corps Records of the relief of Brig. Gen. Michael J. Lenihan and Col.
        Harry D. Mitchell, B: 85, World War I Organization Records 5th Corps, RG120, NA;
        Cooke, pp. 174–81; Harris, pp. 349–60; Duffy, pp. 275–78, 284–85. One story that
        has refused to die over the years is that the battery Harry Truman commanded was sup-
        posed to provide artillery support for Donovan's attacking regiment October 14 and 15.
        When it did not do so, Donovan allegedly complained, earning the everlasting enmity
        of Truman, who eventually retaliated by closing down Donovan's OSS. Nothing could
        be further from the truth. Truman's battery was nowhere near the Landres-et-Saint-
        Georges battle.

29   *fight again:* Duffy, pp. 325–26; WJD letters to RRD, Nov. 11 and Dec. 7, 1918, Jan. 15,
        1918, B: 132A, WJDP, MHI; WVHD, p. 22, WJDP, MHI.

30   *ever met:* Duffy, pp. 326–27; Harris, pp. 375–77.

30   *AEF headquarters:* WJD letters to RRD, Nov. 24 and 28, Dec. 6, 1918; Harris, pp. 375–
        79; Affidavits collected by Father Duffy for WJD Medal of Honor, B: 129 and 136A,
        WJDP, MHI; C.O. 165th Infantry memo to Adjutant General of the Army, Feb. 22,
        1919, B: 136A, WJDP, MHI.

30   *Ourcq River:* John J. Pershing letter to Newton D. Baker, June 13, 1919, and memo to
        Pershing from the Adjutant General AEF, June 8, 1919, B: 19, JP, LOC; Ferrell, Dec. 22,
        2008.

31   *would follow:* WJD letters to RRD, Oct. 8 and Dec. 22, 1918, Jan. 17–28, Feb. 15, March
        7, 23, and 27, 1919, B: 132A and 135, WJDP, MHI.

31   *and wept:* Donovan scrapbook of welcome home news articles, B: 131A, WJDP, MHI;
        Corey Ford interview with Vincent Donovan, November 1967, pp. 25–26, 53, B:1, Part
        1, GU.

CHAPTER 3: THE PROSECUTOR

32   *with details:* Donovan diary, June 8, 14, and 16, 1919, Box 132A, WJDP, MHI; RRD let-
        ter to Susan Rumsey, June 26, 1919, B: 3, BEC.

33   *in Washington:* WJD letter to Roland Morris, Nov. 16, 1919, B: 19, RDP, MHI; F. C.
        MacDonald diary, The Omsk Journey, B: 95B, WJDP, MHI; WJD letter to William J.
        Eagan, Oct. 23, 1919, B: 2, BEC.

33   *the picture:* Vincent Donovan letter to WJD, Sept. 6, 1919, B: 1, BEC.

33   *North Shore:* Lay, pp. 11–18; WJD letter to Reginald D. Boardman, Nov. 17, 1919, B: 2,
        BEC; Raichle, OHC, pp. 1–3, 20.

34   *billion-dollar plans:* WJD letter to Col. Frank McCoy, July 30, 1920, B: 128B, WJDP,
        MHI; Chernow, pp. 210–11.

34   *delicately put it:* WJD letter to RRD, March 9, 1920, B: 135, WJDP, MHI; Brown, p. 78;
        Donald Rumsey interview, p. 10, B: Interviews—Teitelbaum to Withrow, 1979-undated,
        WJDP, MHI; Notes on W.J.D., B: 137C, WJDP, MHI.

35   *violation charges:* Lay, pp. 19–37, 76–77, 143–44; "Buffalo Bombers Phone Threat to Get
        Col. Donovan," *New York American,* April 20, 1924; "To Close This Chapter," unidenti-
        fied news article, "Donovan Asks Strict Regard for All Laws," unidentified news article,
        B: 130B, WJDP, MHI.

35   *in Munich:* WJD diary entry, March 21, 1923, B: 132B, WJDP, MHI; WJD letter to John
        J. Larkin, Sept. 16, 1922, WJD letter to Col. William Haskell, Nov. 22, 1922, B: 130C,

WJDP, MHI. Previous biographers (Dunlop, p. 151) have speculated that Donovan met Hitler during his 1923 trip to Germany. But Donovan's itinerary and diary for the trip clearly show that no such meeting took place.

35   *the armory:* Ferrell, Dec. 22, 2008; "Col. 'Wild Bill' Donovan of Old 69th Gives His Honor Medal to Regiment," unidentified news article, B: 130B, WJDP, MHI; Sen. James Wadsworth letter to Maj. Gen. P. C. Harris, Feb. 28, 1921, B: 426, AGO 1917-25, 220.515-52, RG407, NA; WJD letter to Francis P. Duffy, Nov. 6, 1919, B: 2, BEC; "Col. Donovan Gets Congress Medal," *New York Times,* Dec. 8, 1922, p. 16.

36–37   *Donovan stood to for the raid:* Alex H. Griffin letter to Herbert Hoover, Feb. 26, 1929, B: 1, Part 5, GU; Raichle, OHC, pp. 5–7; "The Night They Raided the Saturn Club," Dick Hirsch, *Buffalo Courier Express,* Aug. 24, 1980; "Raid Saturn Club, Arrest Bartender," *Buffalo Courier,* Aug. 24, 1923, p. 1; "Raid Country Club; Others to Follow," *Buffalo Evening News,* Aug. 24, 1923, p. 1; Notes on W.J.D., B: 137C, WJDP, MHI; Report #5 (10/16/42), B: 3, Downes Papers, E: 136A, RG226, NA; Martoche, p. 22; *One Hundred Years,* p. 295.

CHAPTER 4: POLITICS

38   *high society:* Memorandum on lunch with OCD and Father Vincent Donovan, Sept. 25, 1958, B: 18, WJDP, MHI; Mugler, Jan. 21, 2008; "The Catholic Viewpoint," R. C. Gleaner, unidentified news article, August 1924, "Donovan Appointed Stone's Assistant," Aug. 15, 1924, unidentified news article, B: 130B, WJDP, MHI; "The Underworld Awaits the Word," unidentified news article, B: 103C, WJDP, MHI; Kessler, pp. 15–16.

38–39   *Donovan who to Bureau of Investigation:* WJD Appointment diary, Sept. 13, Oct. 5, 1924, July 5, 1925, B: 132B, WJDP, MHI; Lyell, pp. 11–13, 246, 259; Gilbert, Sept. 29 and Nov. 11, 2007.

40   *Donovan's life:* Gentry, pp. 20–21, 63–69, 74, 80, 101, 103, 111, 117, 122–31, 133–36, 280; Batvinis, pp. 42–46; Letter from George H. Wark, Sept. 15, 1924, 61-0-662(77), Newspaper clippings on WJD, March 23, 1930, July 5, 1932, and Aug. 1, 1932, 66-1897-26X (71), 66-1897-97(71), 60-1553-37(71), Oct. 18, 1924, JEH letter to WJD, 62-25733-326, encl. pp. 299, 430, 554 (109), FBI; Dunlop. p. 153.

40   *the justices:* Gentry, pp. 142–45; McFadden, OHC, p. 2; 1925–1928 Reports of the Attorney General, Office of the Assistant to the Attorney General, Antitrust Division, B: 130B, WJDP, MHI; interview with Bethuel M. Webster, p. 9, B: Interviews–Teitelbaum to Withrow 1979-undated, WJDP, MHI.

41   *double-crossing him:* "Donovan Retires from State Race," *New York Evening Post,* Sept. 21, 1926; Douglas MacArthur letter to WJD, June 21, 1928, B: 137C, WJDP, MHI; "Boom for Donovan Likely Tomorrow," *New York Times,* May 24, 1928; William J. McEvoy memo, March 1, 1929, B: 1, MacLafferty Diaries, JM, HHL; Raichle, OHC, p. 20; Gentry, pp. 147–48; Hoover notes on reasons Donovan was not taken into the cabinet, B: 1038, Individual Name Files, HHL; Mabel Willenbrandt memo to Herbert Hoover, Feb. 8, 1920, B: 69, Presidential Papers Subject Files, HHL; WJD diary entry, March 2, 1929, File: WJD Diary, 1929, B: 2, Part 1, GU; WVDH, p. 3, WJDP, MHI; Interview with Mrs. William J. Donovan, March 6, 1972, B: 7, TTP, RG263, NA.

42   *at night:* History of the William J. Donovan Law Firm, pp. 1–2, 4–6-10, B: Donovan Firm History, WJDP, MHI; Smith, OHC, pp. 9–13, 40, 57; Gilbert, Oct. 29, 2007; Interview with John E. Tobin, June 30, 1980, pp. 5, 29, B: Interviews–Teitelbaum to Withrow Jr. 1979-undated, WJDP, MHI; Interview with J. Edward Lumbard, May 20, 1980, B: Interviews–Teitelbaum to Withrow 1979-undated, WJDP, MHI; Lagemann, pp. 25, 55; Raichle, OHC, p. 19; Donald Rumsey interview, p. 5, B: Interviews–Teitelbaum to Withrow, 1979-undated, WJDP, MHI.

42   now sought: WJD letter to Walter E. Edge, June 9, 1932, B: 3, WEP, PU; "Bitter Race for Governor by Buffalo's 'Wild Bill' Donovan," Buffalo News, March 29, 1992.

43   the nomination: WJD address before the Women's University Club, Oct. 29, 1930, B: 2A, WJDP, MHI; Notes on W.J.D., B: 137C, WJDP, MHI; vanden Heuvel, Jan. 7, 2008; letter to WJD, Aug. 16, 1932, B: 1, TGP, HIA.

43   husband's side: Edward Clark letter to WJD, July 5, 1932, B: 4, EC, LOC; Win Donovan and Davison Committee flyer, B: 4, EC, LOC; "Donovan Youngsters Lead Normal Lives," Buffalo Times, October 1932, "Hundreds of Delegates Throng Rumsey Tea," Buffalo Times, Oct. 4, 1932, B: 130B and B: "World War I, Political Campaigns, etc.," WJDP, MHI.

43   for winning: Edward T. Clark letter to WJD, Oct. 13, 1932, B: 4, EC, LOC; "Victory Song" of Campaign for Republican Candidate for Governorship: "Wild Bill" Donovan, B: "World War I, Political Campaigns, etc.," WJDP, MHI; Davison, OHC, pp. 189–90; William Donovan 1932, B: 458, EBP, LOC.

44   U.S. attorney: Win Donovan and Davison Committee flyer, B: 4, EC, LOC; "Donovan Says Rougher Man than Lehman Is State Need," unidentified news article, "Donovan Gives Lie to Charge Made by Smith," unidentified news article, Oct. 25, 1932, "'Persecution' Charge Hurled at Candidate," unidentified news article, "Mrs. Roosevelt Defends State Administration," Buffalo Courier-Express, Oct. 27, 1932, B: 130B and B: "World War I, Political Campaigns, etc.," WJDP, MHI.

44   been forgotten: "Donovan Starts on Final Drive, Sure of Victory," New York Herald Tribune, Oct. 31, 1932; "Donovan Retires to Quiet of Home," unidentified news article, Nov. 8, 1932, B: 130B and B: "World War I, Political Campaigns, etc.," WJDP, MHI; "Donovan Concedes Defeat and Congratulates Lehman," New York Times, Nov. 9, 1932, p. 2; "State Victory Solid," New York Times, Nov. 9, 1932, p. 15.

CHAPTER 5: FAMILY

45   on the go: Gilbert, Jan. 12, 2008; David G. Donovan, Nov. 4, 2007; Interview with Jim Murphy, April 28, 1981, B: 6, RDP, MHI.

45–47   As a teenager to of business: Beecher, Sept. 25, 2008; Gilbert, Oct. 29, 2007; RRD letters to WJD, Jan. 31, Feb. 6, 23, and 30, March 2, 1930, B: 135, WJDP, MHI; WJD letter to RRD, March 12, 1929, WJD letter to RRD, Feb. 28, 1930, RRD letter to WJD, 1930, B: 137C, WJDP, MHI; National Register of Historic Places Registration Form for Chapel Hill Farm, DHR # 021-0014; Henderson, Nov. 11, 2008; Gilbert, Oct. 29, 2007, Jan. 12, 2008; Memorandum for the Record on James R. Murphy, Jan. 10, 1969, Memo of Conversation with Betty McIntosh, April 26, 1973, B: 7, TTP, RG263, NA; WJD letter to RRD, late 1930s, B: 137C, WJDP, MHI; Application for Commission in U.S. Naval Reserve from David Rumsey Donovan, Oct. 20, 1940, NPRC; Bancroft, OHC, pp. 337–41; "Home Bridal Held for Mary Grandin," New York Times, June 19, 1939, p. 18; Dunlop, p. 197; Gilbert, Sept. 29, 2007, Jan. 12, 2008; Tippaparn Donovan, Jan. 24, 2008.

47–48   After David's to serious affair: "Yankee Back Home After Third World Cruise," unidentified news article, B: unnumbered third and fourth boxes from the end of the collection, WJDP, MHI; Application for Commission in U.S. Naval Reserve from David Rumsey Donovan, Oct. 20, 1940, NPRC; Gilbert, Sept. 29, 2007, Jan. 12, 2008; WJD to RRD undated letter, B: 135, WJDP, MHI; WJD undated letters to RRD, B: 137C, WJDP, MHI; Brown, pp. 139–41; Interview with Guy Martin, April 28, 1981, B: 6, RDP, MHI; RRD letter to WJD, Jan. 26, 1930, B: 137C, WJDP, MHI; New York Times reprint unidentified, B: 119A, WJDP, MHI; EP interview, B: 6, RDP, MHI; Interview with Mrs. William J. Donovan, March 6, 1972, B: 7, TTP, RG263, NA; Interview with OCD, p. 416, B: "Oral History Interviews—OCD, Activities in Europe, 1941–89," WJDP, MHI; Kingsley, Jan. 7, 2008.

48–49   The midnight to a contract: "Mrs. Vanderbilt Enjoys Midnight Reception," unidentified news article, B: 137C, WJDP, MHI; "Pierpont M. Hamilton Weds Miss Stickney," Jan.

5, 1930, "P. M. Hamilton Asks Divorce," July 24, 1946, *New York Times*; Bancroft, OHC, pp. 201–4, 337–41; Bancroft, pp. 59, 73–89, 91, 138; Memo of conversation with Betty McIntosh, April 26, 1973, B: 7, TTP, RG263, NA; vanden Heuvel, April 15, 2009.

CHAPTER 6: WAR CLOUDS

51   *America intervened:* WVHD, pp. 29, 61, WJDP, MHI; Personal Records of Alaska and the Yukon Hunting Trip 1939 by H. Wendell Endicott, Box 132C, WJDP, MHI.

51   *"look at it":* Smith, OHC, pp. 57–58; David G. Donovan, Nov. 11, 2007; "Coffee, Tea or Turtle Soup?," *U.S. News & World Report* Web site, posted Dec. 12, 2009; Lumbard, OHC, p. 13; "Remembering 109," by Guy Martin, OSS Society Newsletter, Spring 2003.

52   *to answer:* WJD diary entry, Nov. 27, 1935, B: 132C, WJDP, MHI; WJD letter to Douglas MacArthur, Sept. 17, 1935, George S. Simonds letter to WJD, Sept. 30, 1935, Ambassador Augusto Rosso letter to WJD, Dec. 2, 1935, B: 8A-Part 1, WJDP, MHI.

52–53   *The day after* to *Il Duce insisted:* WJD Diary of Trip to Ethiopia, Dec. 26, 1935, B: 96A, WJDP, MHI; WVHD, p. 10, WJDP, MHI.

54   *gatherer overseas:* WJD Diary of Trip to Ethiopia, Jan. 4–15, 1936, B: 96A, WJDP, MHI; WJD letter to Marshal Pietro Badoglio, March 11, 1936, WJD letter to Ambassador Augusto Rosso, March 23, 1936, B: 8A-Part 1, WJDP, MHI; Desmond Morton memo, Feb. 9, 1936, memo to private secretary of WC, Feb. 7, 1936, 2-251-30-33, CHAR, CA.

54   *from the Nazis:* "Nazi Judicial Curb Protested by Bar," May 29, 1933, *New York Times*; NY Rpt. 1/2/42, 65-3108-17 (27), Letter to Richmond 8/21/40 61-5062-5 (28), FBI; Dunlop, p. 191.

54   *quietly listened:* Detailed Interrogation Report on Gen. Warlimont, CCPWE #32/ DI-18, June 29, 1945, Vol. VII-13-08, COR.

55   *political purposes:* "Donovan of the 69th," unidentified news article, Feb. 17, 1940, Local Biographies, A-J, BECPL; *We the People* radio program transcript, Jan. 23, 1940, B: 2B, WJDP, MHI; Harris, pp. xvii, xx–xxi.

55   *White House:* WJD address before the Women's Republican Club Albany County, July 23, 1935, B: 2A, WJDP, MHI; WJD address at the Illinois Favorite Son Homecoming Celebration, April 4, 1934, B: 2B, WJDP, MHI; WJD address before the State Convention of the American Legion at Fairmont, W. Va., Sept. 1, 1936, B: 2A, WJDP, MHI; Troy, *Donovan and the CIA*, p. 28; Wadsworth, OHC, 433–39; Donovan, "Should Men of 50 Fight Our Wars?," p. 30; WJD letter to James A. Farley for the Paderewski Fund, March 25, 1940, PPF 6558, FDRL; Persico, *Roosevelt's Secret War*, pp. 91, 94; interview with OCD, p. 40, B: "Oral History Interviews–OCD, Activities in Europe 1941–89," WJDP, MHI; WVHD, pp. 29, 62, WJDP, MHI.

56   *other Republicans:* FK letter to FDR, Dec. 15, 1939, and FDR response, Dec. 29, 1939, Departmental File Navy, Knox, Frank, 1939–41, PSF, FDRL; FK letter to Annie Knox, 1940, B: 3, FKP, LOC; Harold Ickes diaries, entry Dec. 24, 1939, HIP, LOC; vanden Heuvel, Jan. 1, 2008.

56–57   *A heavy* to *he lost:* "Miss Donovan Killed in Crash," *Buffalo Evening News*, April 9, 1940; "Former Buffalo Girl Dies in Virginia Auto Accident," *Buffalo Courier Express*, April 9, 1940; "Patricia Donovan Is Killed When Car Crashes into Tree," unidentified news article, Fr: 258–60, R: 14, GMP, LOC; "Donovan Rites Set for Today at Washington," *Buffalo Courier Express*, April 10, 1940; "Patricia Donovan," April 10, 1940, "Mrs. Donovan Receives Word of Death by Radio," April 11, 1940, *Buffalo News*; Smith, OHC, pp. 34–35; McFadden, OHC, p. 6; WVHD, p. 30, WJDP, MHI; vanden Heuvel, April 15, 2009; Tippaparn Donovan, Jan. 24, 2008; Gilbert, Oct. 29, 2007, April 10, 2009.

CHAPTER 7: ENVOY

58   *confirmation hearing:* FK letter to Annie Knox, July 6, 1940, B: 3, FKP, LOC; Henry Green letter to WJD, June 24, 1940, B: 234, HIP, LOC.

59   *Patricia's death:* Troy, *Donovan and the CIA,* p. 31; WVHD, p. 3, WJDP, MHI; FK letter to CH, Oct. 25, 1938, Fr: 1089, R: 16, CHP, LOC; Smith, *Shadow Warriors,* pp. 25–34; vanden Heuvel, Jan. 7, 2008.

59   *get-acquainted chat:* RRD to Thomas Troy, May 20, 1968, B: 7, TTP, RG263, NA; Dunlop, pp. 206, 208–9; Churchill appointment calendar, July 25, 1940, CHAR-19-2, CA; Troy, *Wild Bill and Intrepid,* p. 55; J. B. 16/7, American Department, Marquess of Lothian cables, July 10 and 13, 1940, FO 371-24237, NAUK.

60   *be anticipated:* Brendan Bracken cable to Lord Lothian, Aug. 29, 1940, FO 371-24237, NAUK; "Enemy Aliens in the United Kingdom July 1940, File on Great Britain War Time Documents, Vol. 3, B: 97A, WJDP, MHI; Troy, *Wild Bill and Intrepid,* pp. 52–54; WJD letter to FDR, Oct. 1, 1940, PPF 6558, FDRL; Corson, pp. 119–20; WJD schedule in London, July 22–Aug. 1, 1940, letter to WJD on Menzies, July 25, 1940, B: 81B, WJDP, MHI; WJD letter to S. G. Menzies, Aug. 27, 1940, WJDP, MHI; L.A. Hince memo to JEH, Sept. 18, 1942, B: 8, TTP, RG263, NA, FOIA NW 31095.

60   *sea lanes:* Air Ministry memo, July 31, 1940, B: 81B, WJDP, MHI; WJD letter to Brendan Bracken, Aug. 27, 1940, B: 81B, WJDP, MHI; WJD speech to the Union League of Philadelphia, B: 2B, WJDP, MHI; Marquess of Lothian cable, Aug. 7, 1940, FO 371-24237, NAUK; Cable to Lord Lothian, November 1940, FO 317-2451, NAUK.

61   *Back in to be sent:* "Today and Tomorrow," by Walter Lippmann, *New York Herald Tribune,* Feb. 11, 1941; HS diary entry, Aug. 6, 1940, Film HM 51, HSP, YU; "Defense Program Hitting Its Stride, President Asserts," *New York Times,* Aug. 11, 1940; White House telegram, Aug. 6, 1940, Schedule of Trip of the President, Aug. 9–13, 1940, Members of the presidential party list, Fishing Grounds memo for Massachusetts Bay, Pouch to Poughkeepsie, New York, Aug. 7, 1940, File on Hyde Park, N.Y.–New England Navy Yards, Aug. 3–12, 1940, OF 200-PPP, FDRL; WJD letter to Sir Cyril Newall, Aug. 27, 1940, B: 81B, WJDP, MHI; Account of Balfour conversation with Whitehead, Dec. 19, 1940, FO 371-2463, NAUK; Transcript of presidential press conference, Aug. 10, 1940, FDRL.

62   *several years:* Account of Balfour conversation with Whitehead, Dec. 19, 1940, FO 371-2463, NAUK; Transcript of presidential press conferences, July 14, 1936, Aug. 6 and 9, 1940, FDRL; Oral History Interview with Walter Trohan, pp. 1–4, 69–74, 113–15, HSTL; Samuel I. Rosenman interview, Nov. 11, 1971, B: 7, TTP, RG263, NA; "Donovan Confident of Britain," *New York Post,* Aug. 12, 1940; Steve Early correspondence with Walter Trohan, File: Correspondence TR-WAK, Walter Trohan, SEP, FDRL.

62   *wrote a friend:* WJD letter to Raymond Lee, Aug. 28, 1940, B: 81B, WJDP, MHI; WJD Speech before the Union League of Philadelphia, B: 2B, WJDP, MHI; C. A. Powell letter to WJD, Oct. 9, 1940, Schedule of Navy Secretary, Sept. 9–13, 1940, and Navy narrative of Hawaii trip, B: "United Kingdom, the Balkans, etc.," WJDP, MHI.

62   *New York lawyer:* "U.S. Survey of Hitler Conquests Reveals '5th Column' Spearhead," by William J. Donovan and Edgar Mowrer, Aug. 20, 1940, "Germans Said to Spend Vast Sums Abroad to Pave Way for Conquest," by William J. Donovan and Edgar Mowrer, Aug. 23, 1940, *New York Times;* JEH Confidential Memorandum, Aug. 24, 1936, B: 8, TTP, RG263, NA; Dunlop, p. 225; WJD letter to Robert Van Sittart, Sept. 21, 1940, B: 81B, WJDP, MHI.

63   *into the war:* WJD corrections of Conyers Read history, B: 1, TTP, RG263, NA; Gene Tunney letter to Thomas Troy, Aug. 6, 1969, B: 7, TTP, RG263, NA; Ernest Cuneo Manuscript on the OSS and BSC, File: N-P, ECP, FDRL; Troy, *Wild Bill and Intrepid,* pp. 31–32, 67; Charles, p. 227.

63   *private lunch:* Photo captioned "In London on a Mission for the U.S.," *New York Times,* Dec. 19, 1940; Telegram 1 . 7Ifl. (geh. Chiff. Verf.), Dec. 14, 1940, Fr: 587613–14, R: 1442, T-120, NA; A. G. cable to Secretary of State, Dec. 17, 1940, Marquess of Lothian cable, Nov. 28, 1940, V. G. Lawford letter, Dec. 18, 1940, FO 371-24263, NAUK; "Very Secret—But Sure We'll Win," *Daily Mirror,* Dec. 21, 1940.

64   *Donovan agreed:* WJD speech to the Empire Club of Canada, April 10, 1941, B: 2B, WJDP, MHI; Churchill, *The Grand Alliance,* pp. 28–37.

64–65   *Cables went to foreign countries:* WJD briefing to War Department officers on his London trip, March 17, 1941, B: 89, E: 99, RG226, NA; Cipher telegram to Sir M. Lampson (Cairo), No. 1608, Dec. 24, 1940, FO 371-24263, NAUK; Troy, *Wild Bill and Intrepid*, p. 87; Sir M. Palairet cable to Sofia, Jan. 18, 1941, FO 371-29792, NAUK; Memorandum of Conversation by WJD with King Boris, Jan. 22, 1941, FO 371-29721, NAUK; Foreign Office telegram to Halifax, March 10, 1941, PREM 4-25-5, NAUK; Wallace Murray cable to AB, Feb. 15, 1941, EW 101-200, 740.00118, RG59, NA.

65–66   *Berlin grew to inside it:* "Donovan Tour 'Impudent,'" Jan. 29, 1941, *New York Herald Tribune*; WJD briefing to War Department officers on his London trip, March 17, 1941, B: 89, E: 99, RG226, NA; Sofia to Foreign Office cable, Jan. 27, 1941, FO 371-29721, NAUK; State Department cable, March 29, 1941, B: 137B, WJDP, MHI; Cablegram received from London, Feb. 2, 1941, No. 729, File 2257-22-325, MID, E: 65, RG165, NA; *Documents on German Foreign Policy,* pp. 1201–3; Aussen-und militaerpolitische Nachrichten, Feb. 21, 1941, Fr: 6583368-69, R: 933, T-77, NA; Mrs. William J. Donovan interview, March 6, 1972, B: 7, TTP, GR263, NA.

66   *a celebrity:* "Donovan Back with Advice for Defense of U.S.," *New York Herald Tribune,* March 19, 1941; Gilbert, Sept. 29, 2007, Jan. 12, 2008; David G. Donovan, Nov. 15, 2007; Wise, Jan. 27, 2008; Report of Investigation of Applicant for Appointment in U.S. Naval Reserve for David Rumsey Donovan, Feb. 12, 1941, John F. O'Keefe memo to Commander Ihrig, Feb. 26, 1941, NPRC; Wise, Jan. 27, 2008.

66   *"the President":* WJD Cable to FK, Feb. 20, 1941, Fr: 1150-59, R: 3, M1642, NA; WJD letter to FK, April 26, 1941, B: 139A, WJDP, MHI.

67   *"materials required":* "Roosevelt Sees Donovan: Goes South Today," *New York Journal American,* March 19, 1941; E.M.W. memo to FDR, March 18, 1941, PPF 6558, FDRL; Hopkins cable to WC, March 19, 1941, Winston S. Churchill File, HHP, FDRL.

67   *"is going on":* Henry Morgenthau Jr. diary entry, March 20, 1941, Book 384, pp. 14–25, HMD, FDRL; Batvinis, pp. 98–100, 120–22.

68   *to make:* Weinberg, p. 522; WJD broadcast press release, March 26, 1941, B: 1B, WJDP, MHI; Letters to WJD on March 26, 1941, radio address, B: 2B, WJDP, MHI; "Col. Donovan to Make Reply to Lindbergh," *Pittsburgh Post Gazette,* June 18, 1941; "Germans Renew War Zone Threat," *New York Times,* April 26, 1941; "Italians Assail Donovan's Tour," *New York Sun,* April 11, 1941; "Washington Glum over Balkan War," *New York Times,* April 12, 1941; Bess, pp. 9, 118–21.

68   *targeting Donovan:* JEH note on Memo for the Director, Nov. 11, 29, 1941, 62-64427-76 (118), Memorandum RE: William J. Donovan and the Office of the Coordinator of Information, Jan. 5, 1942, FBI; Batvinis, pp. 192–96; Charles, p. 233; JEH letter to EW with memo, March 5, 1941, Rpt. No. 669, DOJ, JEH memo to EW, March 17, 1941, Rpt. No. 687, DOF, OF 10B, FDRL; Troy, *Wild Bill and Intrepid,* p. 82.

CHAPTER 8: SPY SERVICE

69   *Marshall agreed:* WJD letter to Vivian Dykes, May 9, 1941, B: 104B, WJDP, MHI; WJD letter to FK, July 3, 1941, B: 119A, WJDP, MHI; Sherman Miles memo to Chief of Staff, April 8, 1941, File: 310.11, B: 423, E: 47, RG319, NA.

70   *"effectively employed":* Persico, *Roosevelt's Secret War,* pp. xii, 3–9, 96, 181; Notes from WJD, April 5, 1949, B: "Bomb Fuses, Admiral Darlan, etc.," WJDP, MHI; Brig. Gen. Sherman Miles memo on Area Controller for the New York Area, April 3, 1941, B: 1, TTP, RG263, NA; Chalou, p. 13; Batvinis, p. 32; WJD Memorandum on Establishment of Service of Strategic Information, June 10, 1941, B: 89, E: 47, RG226, NA.

71   *"I want":* WJD address before the Economic Policy Club of Detroit, Dec. 2, 1946, B: 3A, WJDP, MHI; Ian Fleming memo to WJD, June 27, 1941, B: 2, TTP, RG263, NA; AB diary entry, Sept. 27, 1941, ABP, FDRL; James Wright letter to A. W. Kirchhofer, June 16, 1942, B: 19, RDP, MHI; WJD letter to Bill Whitney, Aug. 19, 1941, Fr: 373–74, R: 123, M1642, RG226, NA; Smith, *Shadow Warriors,* p. 64.

71   *operations now:* St. Paul letter, July 7, 1936, 62-43010-1-45X(59), FBI; Batvinis, pp. 77–80, 197; JEH letter to EW, June 2, 1941, Rpt. No. 796-A, DOJ, 10B, OF, FDRL; Gentry, pp. 223–29.

72   *intelligence operations:* interview with James G. Rogers, Oct. 5, 1944, B: unnumbered third and fourth boxes from the end of the collection, WJDP, MHI; HS diary entries, June 22–July 1, 1941, Film HM 51, HSP, YU; Gladieux, OHC, pp. 187–91; Brig. Gen. Sherman Miles memo for the Chief of Staff, May 22, 1941, B: 1, TTP, RG263, NA; Designating a Coordinator of Information, FDR, July 11, 1941, Fr: 43, R: 4, M1642, RG226, NA; FDR memo to Director of the Budget, June 28, 1941, PPF 6558, FDRL.

72   *prove true:* Viscount Halifax cable to War Cabinet, June 26, 1941, FO 371-26231, NAUK; Telegram (Geh. CH. V.), Thomsen to Berlin, Aug. 9, 1941, Fr: 375592-95, R: 782, T-120, NA, Harold L. Ickes diary entry, June 6, 1941, HIP, LOC.

72–73   *Around the to on the road:* Rosenman, OHC, p. 181; Notes on Discussion between Mr. Elmo Roper and Mr. A. M. Wilson, Jan. 8, 1945, B: German Documents, Elmo Roper, etc., WJDP, MHI; Interview with Robert E. Sherwood, Jan. 10, 1945, B: Interviews— Bancroft to Sherwood 1945-undated, WHDP, MHI; Interview with Dr. J. P. Baxter, Oct. 25, 1944, Col. Thomas Early's dictated report, Dec. 12, 1044, B: unnumbered third and fourth boxes from the end of the collection, WJDP, MHI; Bob Sherwood letter to WJD, June 16, 1941, B: 99B, WJDP, MHI; E. F. McDonald letter to WJD, Feb. 20, 1942, and WJD response, March 9, 1942, Fr: 3–4, R: 70, M1642, RG226, NA; Harold Smith letter to WJD, July 30, 1941, B: 1, TTP, RG263, NA.

73–74   *Donovan made to spy agency:* Author tour of former OSS headquarters on Navy Hill, Sept. 27, 2007; "Washington Merry-Go-Round," by Drew Pearson and Robert S. Allen, *Washington Times-Herald*, Dec. 3, 1941; Bowman, OHP, p. 22; Dunlop, p. 175; Telegram (Geh. CH. V.) by Ambassador Thomsen, Washington, Aug. 27, 1941, Fr: 37685, R: 782, T-120, NA.

74   *bureaucratic competitor:* Memorandum on Office of Coordination, April 5, 1963, B: 19, RDP, MHI; Persico, *Roosevelt's Secret War*, pp. 56–58; JFC memo to FDR, Dec. 18, 1941, JFC, Nov.–Dec. 1941 File, Subject File, PSF, FDRL; Memo to SW, Feb. 10, 1941, State Department File, 1938-45, JFC, ABP, FDRL; "Changed Donovan Works in Capital," by Jay Franklin (pen name for John Franklin Carter), *Newark Evening News*, Sept. 8, 1941; JEH memo to Clyde Tolson, Nov. 17, 1941, War File, B: 20, E: 14B, RG65, NA.

75   *"amicable relationships":* Notes on Discussion between Elmo Roper and A. M. Wilson, Jan. 8, 1952, B: German Documents, Elmo Roper, etc., WJDP, interview with Robert Sherwood, Jan. 10, 1945, B: Interviews—Bancroft to Sherwood 1945-undated, WJDP, MH; "A Look at 'Invisible' C.O.I.," Oct. 5, 1941, *True Comics*, Nov. 30 and Dec. 7, 1941, *Washington Star*; Viscount Halifax cable to Foreign Office, Oct. 31, 1941, FO 954-24A, NAUK.

75   *foreign policy:* HS diary entry, Nov. 12, 1941, Film HM 51, HSP, YU; Sherman Miles memo to Chief of Staff, Dec. 5, 1941, B: 2, TTP, RG263, NA; Hamilton Fish Armstrong letter to SW, Sept. 17, 1941, B: 24, HAP, PU.

76   *he deserved:* Gladieux, OHC, pp. 270–78; Harold Smith letter to WJD, Dec. 8, 1941, WJD letter to Lindsey C. Warren, Dec. 24, 1941, Fr: 373-415, R: 27, Robert Sherwood memo to WJD, Oct. 20, 1941, Fr: 92–100, R: 123, M1642, RG226, NA; Morris, pp. 162–67; White House memo to WJD, Oct. 15, 1951, OSS, 1940-Oct. 1941 File, OF 4485, FDRL.

76   *was false:* Sherman Miles letter to Major Goodfellow, Nov. 7, 1941, B: 632, E: 47, RG319, NA; WL letter to WJD, Nov. 23, 1941, with Walter Winchell "On Broadway" column, Nov. 23, 1941, Fr: 544–46, R: 136, M1642, RG226, NA.

77   *Donovan refused:* Collier's news item, Nov. 22, 1941, JEH letter to WJD, Nov. 21, 1941, Fr: 511–12, R: 46, M1642, RG226, NA; JEH letter to WJD, Oct. 22, 1941, Fr: 596–602, R: 46, M1642, RG226, NA; Putzell, OHP, pp. 39–40; Memo for the Director, July 19, 1941, 62-63816-2 (81), Bureau letter, Dec. 2, 1941, 62-64427-75 (118), FBI.

77   *"secret legs":* Ernest Cuneo Manuscript on the OSS and BSC, N-P File, ECP, FDRL; interview with WL, Feb. 5, 1969, B: 136B, WJDP, MHI; Troy, *Donovan and the CIA*, pp.

111-15; Mauch, pp. 35-42; Dunlop, p. 199; James L. Wright letter to A. M. Kirchhofer, June 16, 1942, B: 19, RDP, MHI; WJD memo to FDR, Dec. 22, 1941, OSS, Reports 12-22 to 31-41 File, Subject File, PSF, FDRL.

78   *to Hopkins:* Oberleutnant report, Nov. 29, 1941, Fr: 205460-62, R: 275, T-120, NA; Brinkley, p. 36; Kent, pp. 124-26.

78   *even-numbered ones:* Summary of Present System of Collecting Military Information from Abroad, June 15, 1941, B: 1, TTP, RG263, NA; Ranelagh, p. 58; Weinberg, p. 312; Persico, *Roosevelt's Secret War,* pp. 102-3.

78   *newspaper features:* Edgar Mowrer letter to WJD, Sept. 30, 1941, $1,880 COI invoice for Edgar Mowrer, Fr: 338-51, R: 75, Fr: 1064, R: 46, M1642, RG 226, NA; DB memo, Dec. 2, 1941; Dunlop, pp. 329-30.

78-80   *At 1 P.M. to that speech:* Donovan appointment book, Dec. 5, 1941, B: 98A & B, WJDP, MHI; EP letter to S/Sgt. Kisner, Dec. 3, 1944, Fr: 480, R: 45, M1642, RG226, NA; Page, OHP, pp. 22, 47; MacDonald, p. 22; Bowman, OHP, p. 18; Smith, *Shadow Warriors,* pp. 378-79; Interview with Wayne Nelson, Nov. 28, 1961, B: 4A, WJDP, MHI; Nelson Poynter memo to Archibald MacLeish, Dec. 4, 1941, Fr: 327-30, R: 121, Nelson Poynter memo with FDR speech draft to WJD, Dec. 4, 1941, Fr: 1393-1402, Nelson Poynter memo to WJD, Dec. 6, 1941, Fr: 1403, R: 48, M1642, RG226, NA; Kent, pp. 115-17.

CHAPTER 9: PEARL HARBOR

83-84   *Donovan sat to "United States":* "55,051 See Dodgers Beat Giants; Bears Win, Tie Packers for Western Title," "Tuffy Leemans Receives the Gifts, but Two Dodgers Steal Spotlight," *New York Times,* Dec. 8, 1941, p. 32; "Football Sunday, Dec. 7, 1941: Suddenly the Games Didn't Matter," *New York Times,* Dec. 7, 1980, p. S6; Gentry, pp. 277-78; Churchill, *The Grand Alliance,* p. 605; Nelson Poynter memo to WJD, Nov. 15, 1941, Fr: 385-88, R: 48, WJD memo to FDR, Feb. 14, 1942, Fr: 1029-32, R: 22, John Elwood letter to WJD, Nov. 6, 1941, Fr: 543-46, R: 49, M1642, RG226, NA; Ralph Nafziger memo on CBS Shortwave Department, Sept. 20, 1941, B: 16, ELP, DDEL; Nelson Poynter memo to WJD, Dec. 7, 1941, Fr: 1404-8, R: 48, M1642, RG226, NA.

84-85   *Donovan walked to intelligence agency:* The President's Appointments, Dec. 7, 1941, Book 4, Sherwood Collection, HHP, FDRL; Gunther, pp. 361-62; Weintraub, pp. 327-33; Sperber, pp. 206-7; Whitney memo to Sherwood, Nov. 21, 1941, Fr: 546, Pflaum memo to Winner, Jan. 22, 1942, Fr: 954, R: 123, Edward R. Murrow letter to WJD, Jan. 31, 1945, Fr: 673, 675, R: 71, M1642, RG226, NA; Notes from WJD—April 5, 1949, B: "Bomb Fuses, Admiral Darlan, etc.," WJDP, MHI.

86   *"was firm":* "Germany Delays Axis Pact Action," *New York Times,* Dec. 8, 1941; Brinkley, p. 92; WJD letter to James Forrestal, Dec. 10, 1941, HS letter to WJD, Feb. 2, 1942, Fr: 1167-85, R: 46, M1642, RG226, NA; AB diary entries, Dec. 7 and 10, 1941, ABP, FDRL; Irving Pflaum memo to WJD, Dec. 9, 1941, Fr: 331-35, R: 121, M1642, RG226, NA; Atherton Richards memo to WJD, Dec. 27, 1941, Fr: 404-6, R: 55, William Kimbel memo, Dec. 20, 1941, Fr: 374-75, R: 66, Memo for U.S. Ambassador, Chunking, China, Dec. 16, 1941, Fr: 718-25, R: 48, M1642, RG226, NA.

86   *Great Britain:* Elsey, p. 19; Gilbert, Feb. 1, 2008; Memos to FDR, Dec. 13, 1941, Report on the Current Situation in Baja California, Dec. 15, 1941, OSS, Reports 12-12 to 17-41, Subject File, PSF, FDRL; W. B. Phillips memo to WJD, Dec. 23, 1941, Fr: 253-55, R: 73, Dec. 10, 1941 memo, Fr: 292-93, R: 123, WL memo, Dec. 9, 1941, Fr: 336-38, R: 121, M1642, RG226, NA; JEH letter to EW, March 11, 1942, Rpt. No. 2013, OF 10B, FDRL.

87   *to do so:* Nelson Poynter memo to Robert Sherwood, Dec. 9, 1941, B: 16, ELP, DDEL; WJD memo to Capt. Roosevelt, Dec. 9, 1941, Fr: 1227, R: 100, WJD memo to FDR, Dec. 9, 1941, Fr: 123, R: 123, M1642, RG226, NA; Mulligan, p. 82; WJD speech before the Canadian Club, April 10, 1941, B: 2B, WJDP, MHI; "Germany and Italy Declare War on U.S.," *New York Times,* Dec. 12, 1941.

88   *her vulnerability:* William Kimbel memo to Victor Sheronas, Dec. 22, 1941, Fr: 633-44, R: 1, M1642, RG226, NA; Putzell, OHP, pp. 50-51; WJD memos to FDR, Dec. 17

and 18, 1941 Fr: 714, 782–89, 733, R: 22, WJD memo to FDR, March 11, 1942, Fr: 1135–36, R: 75, M1642, RG226, NA; WJD memo to White House, December 1941, Diplomatic Correspondence Spain, 1940–45, PSF, FDRL; "Boiler Explodes at Spanish Embassy," *Washington Post*, Dec. 26, 1941; WJD memo to FDR, Dec. 30, 1941, OSS, Reports 12-22 to 30-41, Subject Files, PSF, FDRL; WJD memo to FDR, Dec. 22, 1941, Fr: 857–67, WJD memo to FDR, Dec. 18, 1941, Fr: 790–91, R: 22, M1642, RG226, NA.

88   *to defect:* WJD memo to FDR, March 11, 1942, Fr: 1243–50, R: 22, M1642, RG226, NA; Memo for Chief of Staff, March 13, 1942, B: 10, EKP, LOC; WJD memos to FDR, Feb. 19 and 21, 1942, FDR memo to WJD, Feb. 25, 1942, GCM letter to WJD, Feb. 27, 1942, Fr: 177–213, R: 97, Fr: 573, 578, 1061–63, R: 22, M1642, RG226, NA.

89   *German invaders:* Notes regarding the Nazi Organization for Sabotage in the United States, Fr: 590–91, R: 97, WJD memo to FDR, Feb. 17, 1942, Fr: 1036, R: 22, John Wiley memo to WJD, March 7, 1942, Fr: 1159–61, R: 49, Political Tendencies Amongst the Population of Ukrainian Descent in the United States, Fr: 955–68, R: 104, Lowman memo to WJD, Feb. 16, 1942, Fr: 1149–63, R: 39, M1642, RG226, NA.

89   *the internment:* WJD memo to FDR, Dec. 15, 1941, OSS, Reports 12-12 to 17-41, Subject File, PSF, FDRL; Pearl Buck memo to WJD, Fr: 456–77, R: 36, EB letter to WJD, Feb. 20, 1942, Fr: 372–74, R: 39, M1642, RG226, NA.

89–91   *Sporting a to inner sanctum:* FDR Day by Day–The Pare Lorentz Chronology, Jan. 11, 1942, FDRL; Brown, pp. 200–202; WVHD, p. 3, WJDP, MHI; Notes from WJD–April 5, 1949, B: "Bomb Fuses, Admiral Darlan, etc.," WJDP, MHI; Elsey, pp. 18–21; HS diary entry, Jan. 12, 1942, Film HM 51, HSP, YU; Irving Pflaum letter to William Hassett, Dec. 23, 1941, OSS, Nov.–Dec. 1941, OF 4485, FDRL; WJD memos to FDR, Dec. 21, 1941, Fr: 448–49, 838–47, WJD letter to Harold Smith, Dec. 26, 1942, Fr: 451–57, R: 22, M1642, RG226, NA; WJD memo to FDR, Dec. 22, 1941, OSS, 12-22 to 30-1941 File, Subject File, PSF, FDRL; Persico, *Roosevelt's Secret War*, pp. 208, 239; Sherwood, p. 202; Gen. Albert C. Wedemeyer oral history, p. 13, HIA; HH memo, Dec. 17, 1941, Hopkins, Harry, SF, PSF, FDRL; Elsey, July 24, 2008.

CHAPTER 10: THE BEEHIVE

93   *the capital:* "Col. Donovan Is Wild Chief of Mysterious U.S. Army," *Washington Post*, Jan. 20, 1942; Donovan's Undertaking, *Munchner Neueste Nachrichten*, Dec. 23, 1941, B: Press Statements on OSS, 1942–45, WJDP, MHI; WJD letter to Leonard Lindas, Feb. 20, 1943, and Lindas reply, Feb. 26, 1942, Fr: 1280–84, R: 92, M1642, RG226, NA; Friant, Feb. 18, 2008; Lumbard, OHC, p. 15; Gilbert, Oct. 29, 2007, Jan. 12, 2008; McKay, Feb. 18, 2008; David G. Donovan, Nov. 11, 2007; Mugler, Jan. 21, 2008.

93   *"never-mind":* Ford, pp. 239–40; Putzell, OHP, p. 20; Peers and Brelis, pp. 29–30; interview with WL, Feb. 5, 1969, B: 136B, WJDP, MHI; Vincent Lassiter, The General Donovan Story, B: 1A, WJDP, MHI.

93–94   *By the end to as well:* Troy, *Donovan and the CIA*, pp. 77–80; Ford, pp. 132–34; Kingsley, Jan. 7, 2008; John Pershing letter to WJD, Feb. 16, 1943 Fr: 883–84, R: 119, Analysis of Security Office File Relating to Karl L. Falk, May 11, 1943, Fr: 590–96, R: 136, M1642, RG226, NA; Vincent Donovan letter to Jim Murphy, July 15, 1943, B: 379, E: 92, RG226, NA; Harold Ickes letter to WJD, July 21, 1941, B: 180, HIP, LOC; Notes on Discussion between Mr. Elmo Roper and Mr. A. M. Wilson, Jan. 8, 1945, B: German Documents, Elmo Roper, etc., WJDP, MHI; FDR memo to EW, Oct. 2, 1941, EW memo to James Roosevelt, Oct. 7, 1941, OSS, 1940–Oct. 1941, OF 4485, FDRL; Kingsley, Jan. 7, 2008; John Weitz interview, B: Interviews–Teitelbaum to Withrow Jr. 1979-undated, WJDP, MHI; Chalou, pp. 20, 24; Interview with OCD, pp. 150, 425, B: "Oral History Interviews–OCD, Activities in Europe 1941–89," WJDP, MHI; "Senate Votes Inquiry into U.S. Bureaucracy," *Chicago Tribune*, Feb. 19, 1942; James Wright letter to A. M. Kirchhofer, June 16, 1942, B: 19, RDP, MHI; WJD memo to FDR, April 22, 1942, Fr: 139–42, R: 23, letter to Robert Sherwood, May 23, 1942, Security Office memo to WJD, May 28, 1942, Fr: 13–33, R: 49, Fr: 82, R: 109, M1642, RG226, NA.

94   *the schemes:* OSS Assessment Program, Fr: 618-704, R: 33, M1642, RG226, NA; JEH letter to WJD, July 13, 1945, Fr: 1149-56, R: 46, M1642, RG226, NA.

95   *set up for it:* War Report of the OSS, pp. 70-73; Chief of Naval Operations memo to FK, Sept. 25, 1941, B: 1, TTP, RG263, NA; WJD memo to Wallace Phillips, Nov. 17, 1941, Fr: 462-503, R: 97, NA; Agent telegram to Phillips, Nov. 15, 1941, WJD letter to Atherton Richards, Nov. 24, 1941, Fr: 462-503, R: 97, M1642, RG226, NA; Wallace Phillips memo to WJD, Nov. 18, 1941, B: 361, E: 210, RG226; WJD undated memo to Wallace Phillips, Fr: 462-503, R: 97, M1642, RG226, NA; J.B. memo on Danger of German Infiltration into North Africa, March 13, 1941, FO 371-28378, NAUK.

95   *they collected:* WJD memo to FDR, Feb. 18, 1942, Fr: 1059, R: 22, DB memo to WJD, Nov. 10, 1941, Fr: 63-67, R: 33, Norman Davis letter to WJD, Nov. 19, 1941, Fr: 936-41, R: 104, WJD letters to A. Stuber, May 6 and 11, 1942, Fr: 327-31, R: 48, M1642, RG226, NA; DB memo to WJD, July 21, 1942, B: 350, E: 210, RG226, NA; DB memo to H. Watson Starcher, March 26, 1942, B: 386, E: 210, RG226, NA; WJD memo to JCS, Jan. 22, 1943, B: 251, E: 210, RG226, NA.

96   *"the trees":* Mauch, pp. 43-44; War Report of the OSS, pp. 61-63; Serge Obolensky letter to FDR, June 24, 1941, Fr: 754-59, R: 120, Eve Curie letter to WJD, Aug. 7, 1941, WJD draft letter to Trippe, Fr: 746-75, R: 38, WJD memos to FDR, April 30, 1942, Fr: 147, 193-96, R: 23, M1642, RG226, NA; Harold Ickes diaries, entry March 3, 1943, HIP, LOC; WJD letter to FDR, Nov. 17, 1941, B: 16, E: 211, RG226, NA; Armand Denis letter to DB, Sept. 17, 1942, B: 352, E: 210, RG226, NA.

97   *"bill of goods":* Chalou, p. 46; Donovan, "A Central Intelligence Agency," p. 446; Donovan, "Intelligence: Key to Defense," p. 114; Coordinator of Information Budget Proposal for 1943, Fr: 190, R: 43, M1642, RG226, NA; Harold Smith diary entry, Jan. 6, 1942, HSP, FDRL.

98   *troublesome rival:* George H. Muhle Report on Office of Economic Intelligence, Propaganda and Similar Action, B: 4, E: 210, RG226, NA; German Bayer Aspirin memo to WJD, May 26, 1943, B: 11, E: 157, George Office Records, RG226, NA; George memo to Francis, Aug. 16, 1943, B: 6, E: 157, George Office Records, RG226, NA; Dun & Bradstreet report, April 7, 1944, B: 344, E: 210, RG226, NA; War Report of the OSS, p. 142; Preston Goodfellow memo to J. V. Grombach, March 18, 1942, John Grombach memo to Preston Goodfellow, May 7, 1942, B: 4, Almet Latson letter to Preston Goodfellow, June 17, 1942, Box 2, MPGP, HIA; Profile of John V. Grombach sent to author by Thomas Troy; WJD memo to Preston Goodfellow, April 28, 1942, Fr: 1096, R: 123, M1642, RG226, NA; Stout, p. 2; John Grombach letter to George Sokolsky, May 28, 1953, B: 57, GSP, HIA.

98-99 *Donovan's headquarters to traffic cop:* James Murphy memo to EH, July 24, 1942, Fr: 1334-42, R: 92, WJD letter to Rowland, Oct. 22, 1942, Fr: 754, R: 45, William Kimbel memo to WJD, Feb. 8, 1943, Fr: 859-64, R: 65, M1642, RG226, NA; "Remembering 109," by Julia Child, OSS Society Newsletter, Spring 2001, p. 5; OCD memo to WJD, Oct. 29, 1942, Fr: 839-44, R: 56, M1642, RG226, NA; HRW's memo of his talk with the Secretary of State, June 4, 1042 Fr: 339-40, R: 112, M1642, RG226, NA; Calvin Hoover memo to WJD, Aug. 21, 1942, B: 362, E: 210, RG226, NA; Harold Ickes letter to WJD, Sept. 15, 1942, Fr: 832-35, R: 56, Secretariat memo to Scars, Jan. 13, 1944, Fr: 924-28, R: 56, M1642, RG226, NA.

100   *personal sources:* WJD letter to Daniel Bell, Oct. 26, 1942, Fr: 1177, R: 117, Stanton Griffis memo to WJD, Sept. 15, 1942, Fr: 1168, R: 92, Stanley Lovell memo to WJD, Feb. 22, 1943, WJD letter to John Deane, March 10, 1943, Fr: 462-81, R: 96, M1642, RG226, NA; War Report of the OSS, pp. 85, 129-55; Garland Williams memo to Goodfellow, April 28, 1942, Fr: 50-51, R: 45, M1642, RG226, NA; Page, OHP, p. 21.

100   *the novelist:* WJD letter to FDR, Nov. 17, 1941, Fr: 430-33, R: 22, WJD memo to FDR, April 21, 1942, Fr: 120, R: 23, M1642, RG226, NA; Memos to WJD on scopolamine, Nov. 11-12, 1941, R: 76, A-3304, RG226, NA; Halpern, OHP, p. 13; Gladieux, OHC, pp. 393-95; Wesley McQueen memo to Early, Oct. 21, 1941, B: 89, E: 47, RG226, NA;

Trumbrill Marshall letter to WJD, July 31, 1941, Fr: 649–51, R: 113, John Steinbeck letter to WJD, Aug. 19, 1941, Fr: 1015–17, R: 104, M1642, RG226, NA.

101   *American people:* WJD memo to FDR, May 5, 1942, FDR memo to S.T.E., May 6, 1942, OSS Reports 4-29 to 5-9-42, Subject File, PSF, FDRL; W. Don Clawson letter to A. S. Watt, Dec. 8, 1942, and WJD response, Dec. 31, Fr: 109–15, R: 33, WJD memos to FDR, Feb. 10 and 18, 1942, Fr: 442–45, R: 75, M1642, RG226, NA; HS diary entry, Dec. 20, 1942, Film HM 51, HSP, YU.

101–102   *Stanley P. Lovell to one memo:* Lovell, pp. 35–58, 167, 183–88; Persico, *Roosevelt's Secret War*, pp. 165–66; Dunlop, pp. 377–78; Fischer, pp. 10–11; R. Mazzarini memo to H. P. DeVries, June 2, 1944, B: 366, E: 210, RG226, NA; Lt. Macdonald memo to Major Shepard, Aug. 29, 1941, B: 207, E: 210, RG226, NA; Warren Lothrop letter to Stanley Lovell, Nov. 11, 1942, B: 207, E: 210, GR226, NA; Amendments to OSS 1942 Catalogue of Materiel, Fr: 1776–77, R: 14, Sylvester Missal memo to WJD, May 31, 1944, Fr: 201–2, 113–14, R: 73, M1642, RG226, NA; *War Report of the OSS*, pp. 83, 159; General Counsel memo to Rex Keller, July 16, 1945, B: 37, JDP, HIA; James Hamilton memo to Edmond Taylor, Aug. 29, 1943, B: 361, E: 210, RG226, NA.

102–103   *Smoke swirled to the experiments:* Truth Drug Preliminary Report, Oct. 13, 1943, Part 2, B: 2, GU; Allen Abrams memos to WJD, June 4 and 21, 1943, Memorandum on T.D. June 2, 1943 (Withheld), Item 1, R: 86, 89-0067R Donovan Microfilm RG226, NA; WJD memo to OCD, May 10, 1944, B: "United Kingdom—OSS Training School 1040-60," WJDP, MHI; WJD memo to Cornell University Medical College, March 26, 1945, B: 344, E: 21, RG225, NA; H. G. Wolff letter to WJD, Sept. 21, 1946, B: 364, E: 210, RG226, NA; Lovell, pp. 57–58.

104   *and Navy:* William Whitney memo to WJD, Jan. 8, 1952, and WJD Reply, Fr: 411–20, R: 123, WJD letter to Robert Sherwood, Feb. 23, 1942, Fr: 10, R: 106, WJD memo to Robert Sherwood, May 5, 1942, Fr: 1053–55, R: 49, M1642, RG226, NA; Elmo Roper letter to WJD, May 13, 1942, B: 3, TTP, RG263, NA; Troy, *Donovan and the CIA*, pp. 120–47; Interview with OCD, pp. 378–79, box labeled "Oral History Interviews—OCD, Activities in Europe 1941-89, WJDP," MHI.

104–105   *Roosevelt, who to his adventures:* WJD memo to FDR, March 6, 1942, OSS, Reports 3-1 to 9-42, Subject File, PSF, FDRL; WJD memo to FDR, May 26, 1942, Fr: 569, R: 63, WJD memo to FDR, Feb. 28, 1942, Fr: 272–73, R: 32, M1642, RG226, NA; FDR memo to WJD, Feb. 9, 1942, OSS Confidential File, PSF, FDRL; Lovell, pp. 61–63; Tolstoy-Dolan Mission B: 99B, WJDP, MHI; WJD letter to FDR, March 24, 1943, and FDR response, March 26, 1943, the Dalai Lama, PPF 8108, FDRL.

CHAPTER 11: ADOLF HITLER

106–107   *Donovan's Coordinator to of evil:* Irving Pflaum memo with transcript to WJD, Sept. 29, 1941, Fr: 1154–55, R: 52, R. A. Pfaff memo to EB, Jan. 16, 1945, Fr: 1020–21, R: 99, M1642, RG226, NA; Weinberg, pp. 305, 481–83; vanden Heuvel, Jan. 7, 2008.

107   *the sex: Psychological Analysis of Adolf Hitler: His Life and Legend,* by Walter C. Langer, *Analysis of the Personality of Adolf Hitler,* by Henry A. Murray, October 1943, B: 188, E: 139, RG226, NA; General Counsel memo to WJD, Nov. 11, 1944, Fr: 1016–19, R: 38, M1642, RG226, NA.

107–108   *An important to "bedtime stories":* Persico, *Roosevelt's Secret War,* pp. 191, 233, 330–31; Mauch, pp. 48, 50, 56; Grose, pp. 112–16; WJD letter to John McCloy, March 26, 1942, Fr: 30–33, R: 54, Special Sedgewick Report, Dec. 9, 1943, Fr: 374–76, R: 109, M1642, RG226, NA; J. F. Carter letter to Gerald Campbell, May 26, 1942, R. Campbell letter to Carter, FDR memo to Secretary of State, Dec. 3, 1942, Subject File Carter, John F., PSF, FDRL; Memo to Miss Clarkson with memo to SW, July 4, 1942, Memorandum on E.S., July 7, 1942, JFC memo to SW, Nov. 3, 1942F: Carter, John Franklin, 1942, Office Correspondence 1920-1943, SWP, FDRL.

108   *"with longing":* Douglas Miller memo to WJD, Oct. 6, 1941, with Notes for a strategic plan, Fr: 1163–67, R: 52, J. P. Warburg memo to Barnes, Dec. 19, 1941, Fr: 88, R: 36,

Nelson Poynter memo to WJD, Aug. 7, 1941, Fr: 411, R: 49, M1642, RG226, NA; Interview with Dr. J. P. Baxter, Oct. 25, 1944, Col. Thomas Early's dictated report, Dec. 12, 1044, B: unnumbered third and fourth boxes from the end of the collection, WJDP, MHI.

108-109   *Donovan became to back to Donovan:* Donovan appointment book, Sept. 30, 1941, B: 98A & B, WJDP, MHI; Malcolm Lovell and Hans Thomsen files, B: 355, E: 210 and B: 312, E: 92, RG226, NA; Brinkley, pp. 37-39; Interrogation Report on Hans Thomsen, Oct. 10, 1945, B: 337, E: 19, RG226, NA; Bureau Memo Re: Malcolm Lovell, March 14, 1946, 100-25944-47 (19), FBI.

109   *an assassination:* Dec. 10, 1941 memo, Fr: 1219-24, R: 52, WJD memo to James Dunn, Jan. 13, 1941, Fr: 446-51, R: 75, M1642, RG226, NA.

110   *of Austria:* AWD memo to WJD, April 8, 1942, Fr: 810, R: 48, AWD memo to Hugh Wilson, June 3, 1942, Fr: 375-79, R: 68, M1642, RG226, NA; WJD memo to FDR, March 26, 1942, Fr: 1360-61, R: 22, M1642, RG226, NA; George Bowden memo to Donald Downes, Oct. 19, 1942, B: 4, Memo for AWD on Father Odo, April 17, 1941, B: 4, E: 136A, Donald Downes Papers, RG226, NA; AWD memo to Hugh Wilson, May 29, 1942, B: 346, E: 210, RG226, NA; WJD memo to FDR, April 21, 1942, Fr: 111-17, R: 23, Michael Williams letter to WJD, March 18, 1943 Fr: 1046-53, R: 119, M1642, RG226, NA; WJD memo to FDR, March 26, 1942, OSS Reports 3-16 to 26-42 Subject File, PSF, FDRL; SW letter to FDR, March 31, 1942, Coordinator of Information 1942, Office Correspondence, 1920-43, SWP, FDRL; Brinkley, p. 143.

111   *Donovan agreed:* Donald Downes memos to WJD, Aug. 18 and Oct. 1, 1942, Confidential memo on Treviranus, Jan. 27, 1943, Robert Ullman memo to Sidney Clark, Jan. 20, 1942, B: 1, E: 183, RG226, NA; "Strategic Services," B: 8, E: 136A Donald Downes Papers, RG226, NA.

CHAPTER 12: ENEMIES

113   *to himself:* Interview with Wayne Nelson, Nov. 28, 1961, B: 4A, WJDP, MHI; Interview with EB, March 3, 1945, B: unnumbered third and fourth boxes from the end of the collection, WJDP, MHI; Brinkley, pp. 139-40, 156-63; Wallace, OHC, pp. 1476-77, 2147.

113   *husbands' ears:* Train, OHC, p. 296; Dunlop, p. 348; WJD memo to Chief of Naval Personnel, May 3, 1943, Fr: 589-91, R: 19, M1642, RG226, NA; Howe, July 19, 2009; Kingsley, Jan. 7, 2008; Interview with Mary Bancroft, p. 20, July 16, 1980, B: Interviews—Bancroft to Sherwood 1945-undated, WJDP, MHI; Report #5 (10/16/42) B: 3, E: 136A, RG226, NA.

113   *circling now:* WJD letter to Lincoln MacVeigh, April 19, 1942, Fr: 808-11, R: 56, M1642, RG226, NA; Interview with Wayne Nelson, Nov. 28, 1961, B: 4A, WJDP, MHI; Interview with OCD, p. 364, B: "Oral History Interviews—OCD, Activities in Europe 1941-89," WJDP, MHI; interview with WL, Feb. 5, 1969, B: 136B, WJDP, MHI; Howe, Sept. 25, 2007.

114   *"anyone else":* WJD memo to FDR, April 27, 1942, Fr: 172-73, R: 23, David Williamson memo to DB, Feb. 19, 1942, Fr: 581-89, R: 97, W. B. Phillips memo to WJD, Dec. 19, 1941, Fr: 483-536, R: 97, William Kimbell letters to WJD, May 20 and 23, 1942, Fr: 982-94, R: 68, WJD memo to FDR, May 9, 1942, Fr: 238-43, R: 23, M1642, RG226, NA; SW letter to WJD, March 25, 1942, and WJD reply, March 26, 1941, Coordinator of Information 1942, Office Correspondence, SWP, FDRL; AB memo to SW, April 29, 1942, OSS Reports, 4-29 to 5-9-42, Subject File, PSF, FDRL; Harold Smith diary entry, April 10, 1942, HSD, FDRL.

115   *was lying:* Harold Smith diary entry, Nov. 16, 1944, HSD, FDRL; WJD letter to Davis P. Barrows, July 9, 1942, Fr: 624-33, R: 68, M1642, RG226, NA; WJD memo to FDR, Dec. 30, 1941, OSS, Reports 12-22 to 30-41, PSF, FDRL; National City Bank letter to WJD, Oct. 23, 1942, Fr: 650-55, R: 68, Report of Meeting in WJD's office, March 13, 1942, Fr: 996-1003, R: 68, M1642, RG226, NA; Secretariat memo to WJD, June 18, 1943, Items of Information, Kangaroo Project, June 25, 1943, Summary Kangaroo,

Spencer Phenix memo to R. C. Foster, Sept. 28, 1943, B: 365 and 366, E: 210, RG226, NA; Thomas Troy letter to author, Feb. 12, 2008; Preston James memo to WL, Feb. 18, 1943, Fr: 901–2, R: 102, M1642, RG226, NA; FBI , memo for Mr. Ladd, B: 8, TTP, RG263, NA, FOIA NW31095.

115   *than not:* War Report of the OSS, p. 20; Notes from WJD, April 5, 1949, B: "Bomb Fuses, Admiral Darlan, etc.," WJDP, MHI; WJD memo to FDR, April 14, 1942, Fr: 231, R: 43, M1642, RG226, NA; Gladieux, OHC, pp. 364–75; Smith, *Shadow Warriors,* pp. 118–19.

116   *Roosevelt's order:* John Wiley interview, Sept. 27, 1944, B: unnumbered third and fourth boxes from the end of the collection, WJDP, MHI; WJD memo to FDR, May 16, 1942, Fr: 309-13, R: 23, FDR Military Order, June 13, 1942, Fr: 44, R: 4, M1642, RG226, NA; Troy, *Donovan and the CIA,* pp. 148–53; Memo to Bruce Lockhart, June 15, 1942, FO 898-102, NAUK.

117   *military's machine:* W. B. memo to GCM, May 2, 1942, George Strong memos to GCM, May 11, 1942, B: 632, E: 47, RG319, NA; War Report of the OSS, pp. 99, 101; Smith, *Shadow Warriors,* pp. 141–44, 158–67.

117   *any salary:* FDR letter to Secretary of the Treasury, July 3, 1942, Fr: 14–15, B: 27, M1642, RG226, NA; Notes on Discussion between Mr. Elmo Roper and Mr. A. M. Wilson, Jan. 8, 1945, B: "German Documents, Elmo Roper, etc.," WJDP, MHI.

117–118   *He soon to John Grombach:* Lovell, pp. 164–69; Memoirs of Ivan D. Yeaton, pp. 1, 58, IYP, MHI; Putzell, OHP, p. 42; Troy, *Donovan and the CIA,* p. 150; Kingsley, Jan. 7, 2008; WJD Letter to George Strong, Nov. 4, 1942, EB memo to John Deane, Nov. 21, 1942, B: 120B, WJDP, MHI; Memorandum for the files, Nov. 17, 1942, Fr: 577, R: 113, M1642, RG226, NA; John Grombach memo to G-2 with enclosure, Dec. 4, 1945, B: 1, History, Background and Current Status of Secret Intelligence Organization, April 15, 1953, B: 7, E: 12, GP, RG263, NA; Interview with OCD, p. 75, B: "Oral History Interviews— OCD, Activities in Europe 1941–89," WJDP, MHI.

118   *held secrets:* WJD memo to C. W. Horn, June 12, 1942, Fr: 818, R: 56, Memorandum for Joint Staff Planners, March 11, 1943, Fr: 24–31, R: 32, WJD memo to George Strong, Oct. 21, 1942, Fr: 996–1003, R: 64, M1642, RG226, NA.

118   *foreign sources:* Memo for WJD on Operational Security, B: 126A, WJDP, MHI; Henry Field Memorandum on Office of Coordinator of Information, April 5, 1963, B: 19, RDP, MHI; EH memo to EB, June 4, 1942, M1642, NA.

119   *sensitive material:* McIntosh, OHP, p. 33; Legendre, OHP, p. 41; Lovell, pp. 182–83; Interview with Wayne Nelson, Nov. 28, 1961, B: 4A, WJDP, MHI; David Williamson interview, Jan. 25, 1945, B: unnumbered third and fourth boxes from the end of the collection, WJDP, MHI.

119   *matched Donovan's:* Mulligan, pp. 79–86; Telegram (Geh. Ch. V.) Nr. 2241 vom 10.7.42, July 10, 1942, Fr: 79016–18, R: 165, T-120, NA; Detr. 1 Sowjetunion, Polen. May 26, 1942, Fr: 713–14, R: 574, T-78, NA; Telegram (Geh. Ch. V.) Nr. 1933 vom 16.6, June 17, 1942, Fr: 39152, R: 48, T-120, NA.

119   *be successful:* Dunlop, pp. 352–53; Ernest Cuneo Manuscript on the OSS and BSC, N-P File, ECP, FDRL; WVHD, p. 26, WJDP, MHI; WJD memo to FDR, Sept. 29, 1944, Fr: 367, R: 24, WJD memo to FDR, Feb. 14, 1942, Fr: 1034, R: 22, M1642, RG226, NA.

CHAPTER 13: THE EMBASSIES

120–121   *Cynthia rose to for work:* Hyde, pp. 149–56; R. A. Newby memo to D. M. Ladd, Jan. 21, 1943, B: 119, E: 38B, RG226, NA; Charles Brousse letters to Admiral Leahy, Dec. 28, 1942, and to FDR, Jan. 7, 1943, B: 344, E: 210, RG226, NA.

121–122   *The Asia war to North Africa landing:* WJD memo to FDR, April 7, 1942, Fr: 151, R: 34, M1642, RG226, NA; Gentry, pp. 229, 281–87; WJD letter to F. J. Bailey, April 22, 1942, Fr: 807, R: 56, WJD memos to FDR, April 27 and June 1, 1942, Fr: 174–76, Fr: 469–72, R: 23, M1642, RG226, NA.

122–123 *Donovan had to his mistress:* WJD memo to FDR and FDR response, Jan. 26, 1942, Fr: 528–31, R: 22, Whitney memo to WJD, Jan. 12, 1942, Fr: 427–32, R: 123, M1642, RG226, NA; Hyde, pp. 11–148, 160; AB diary entries, Jan. 28, 1942, Feb. 1, 5, 13, and 14, March 5 and 10, 1942, ABP, FDRL; Cynthia letter to Downes, Nov. 23, 1942, B: 6, E: 136A, RG226, NA; Memo for A.D. concerning Mrs. D, April 26, 1942, B: 4, E: 136A, RG226, NA; JEH memo to Tolson, Feb. 13, 1942, B: 8, TTP, RG263, NA, FOIA NW31095.

123–124 *Donald Downes to phone line:* Putzell, OHP, p. 26; Winks, pp. 152–71; Downes, pp. 63–79, 87; DB memo to Robert Cresswell, Dec. 21, 1942, B: 140, E: 92, RG226, NA; FBI memo on Donald Chase Downes, June 29, 1956, B: 201, E: A1-36M, RG226, NA; S. K. McKee letter to JEH, Aug. 8, 1942, JEH letter to Special Agent in Charge, Washington, D.C., Aug. 14, 1942, B: 119, E: 38B, RG65.

125 *breaking into:* WJD letter to C. M. Cook Jr., Nov. 9, 1942, Fr: 1166, R: 75, EB letter to WJD with enclosure, Oct. 22, 1941, Fr: 138–39, 150–51, R: 123, Early memo to J. Freeman Lincoln, Feb. 18, 1942, Fr: 620–23, R: 1, M1642, RG226, NA; Memorandum to Colonel Donovan Concerning Spanish Material, Jan. 9, 1943, B: 340, E: 210, RG226, NA; Memo on Ambassador de Cardenas, March 20, 1942, B: 2 and B: 4, E: 136A, RG226, NA.

125–127 *Since he to their compound:* Report #3, March 28, 1942, Floor Diagram of Spanish Embassy, Safe Combination Instructions, Shaw Walker safe specifications, B: 25 and B: 4, E: 136A, RG226, NA; Interview with OCD, pp. 57–59, B: "Oral History Interviews–OCD, Activities in Europe 1941–89," WJDP, MHI; Downes, pp. 87–97; Winks, pp. 171–79; Brown, pp. 226–34; Memo to JEH Jan. 10, 1956, B: 201, E: A1-36M, RG65, NA; Ernest Cuneo manuscript on the OSS and BSC, N-P File, ECP, FDRL; C. Dallas Mobley memo to SAC, Aug. 17, 1953; FBI memo on "The Scarlet Thread," Sept 8, 1953; L. B. Nichols memo to Mr. Tolson, Sept. 9, 1953; A. H. Belmont memo to D. M. Ladd, Aug. 28, 1953; SAC, Washington Field (BSM) Aug. 11, 1953, FBI FOIA No. 1131282-000.

127 *in Washington:* Donald Downes memo to WJD, Oct. 16, 1942, B: 3, E: 136A, RG226, NA; Memorandum to Colonel Donovan Concerning Spanish Material, Jan. 9, 1943, B: 340, E: 210, RG226, NA.

128 *real enemy:* Interview with OCD, p. 138, 2 (addendum), B: "Oral History Interviews–OCD, Activities in Europe 1941–89," WJDP, MHI; Censorship reports, April 7, 1942, on letters to WJD, 62-62736-2-1533 (105), Bureau memo June 6, 1945, 62-7787-948 (89), FBI; Mosley, pp. 123–25; WJD letter to C&P Telephone Co., April 23, 1942, Fr: 576–79, R: 39, M1642, RG226, NA; Gentry, p. 295.

CHAPTER 14: TORCH

129 *it grew:* Lankford, pp. 3–5, 12–20, 33; OCD memo to C. W. Barnes, Sept. 26, 1942, Fr: 1015–16, R: 69, M1642, RG226, NA; Visit of G and G.50,000 memo, June 6, 1942, HS 4–143, NAUK; OSS Exhibit B, July 17, 1942, B: 344, E: 210, RG226, NA.

130 *North Africa:* Howe, Dec. 20, 2007; Notes on Conversation with G.50,000, June 15, 1942, HS 8-115, NAUK; Summary of Agreement between British SOE and American OSS, Fr: 1333–45, R: 11, M1642, RG226, NA.

131 *covert operatives:* WJD memo to FDR, Feb. 2, 1942, Fr: 887–88, R: 22, Establishment of Operational Base for Southwestern Europe and French North Africa, Fr: 425–34, R: 64, WJD letter to National Geographic Society, Jan. 9, 1942, Fr: 423, R: 75, WJD memo to FDR, Jan. 24, 1942, Fr: 523–27, R: 22, T. S. Wilkinson letter to WJD, Feb. 19, 1942, Fr: 991–1003, R: 50, M1642, RG226, NA; Atkinson, *An Army at Dawn,* pp. 23–28; Kimball, vol. 1, pp. 348–50, 426.

131 *French refugees:* Howe, Dec. 20, 2007; Vaughan, pp. 42, 72–75, 104; Wallace Phillips letter to Preston, May 14, 1942, Fr: 1025–27, R: 44, FDR memo to WJD, Jan. 10, 1942, Fr: 492–93, R: 22, M1642, RG226, NA.

132 *an invasion:* Memorandum of a Conversation between General Weygand and Mr. Murphy, Fr: 438–39, R: 34, Memo to WJD on North Africa, Oct. 9, 1942, Fr: 987–88, R: 33, M1642, RG226, NA; Winks, pp. 153, 179; Vaughan, xiv, pp. 4–32, 50–51, 112–13.

133   *might use:* W. A. Eddy memo to WJD, June 9, 1942, R: 20, A-3304, RG226, NA; Lt. Col. Eddy oral report, June 10, 1942, B: 3, MPGP, HIA; Africa Section memo to DB, Dec. 17, 1942, Fr: 50-53, R: 33, M1642, RG226, NA; Coon, pp. x-xi, 10-32; Torch Anthology, Names and Code Names Torch, p. 10, Pinkeye's Tale, July 15, 1944, B: 49, E: 99, RG226, NA; *The Overseas Targets,* pp. 13-15.

133   *Allied plans:* Abt: Ausland Er. 00 774/41 geh Edos XXL/I E, Feb. 12, 1941, Fr: 26834-63, R: 352, T-120, NA; Vaughan, pp. 60-61; Torch Anthology, Period II, May 1941-March 1942, p. 8, Period II, December 1941-Nov. 8, 1942, p. 14, B: 49, E: 99, RG226, NA; Vaughan, pp. 110-12, 247-49; Memo to WJD, June 4, 1942, Fr: 507-20, R: 122, M1642, RG226, NA; W. A. Roseborough memo to WJD with enclosures, Jan. 1, 1943, B: 63, E: 210, RG226, NA.

134   *another approach:* WJD memo to FDR, May 11, 1942, Fr: 251-53, R: 23, WJD letter to Paul H. Alling, Oct. 27, 1942, Fr: 1053, R: 44, M1642, RG226, NA; Vaughan, pp. 136-37, 154-55.

135   *"considered thought":* EB interview, March 3, 1945, B: unnumbered third and fourth boxes from the end of the collection, WJDP, MHI; Memorandum of Meeting at the St. Regis Hotel, Aug. 21, 1942, R: 20, A-3304, RG226, NA.

135   *the payoffs:* Atkinson, *An Army at Dawn,* pp. 59-61; WVHD, p. 26, WJDP, MHI; FDR press conference, Oct. 13, 1942, FDRL; George Strong memo to WJD, Sept. 11, 1942, Fr: 1-22, R: 34, George Strong memo to WJD, Sept. 30, 1942, Fr: 21-22, R: 34, M1642, RG226, NA.

135-136 The heart to *"little resistance":* Notes on discussion with WJD, Rogers, Taylor, R. Murphy, and DB, Sept. 6, 1942, Fr: 227-34; R: 34, Hugh Wilson memo to OCD with enclosure, Oct. 27, 1942, Fr: 595-623, R: 50, M1642, RG226, NA; Mark Clark letter to Robert Murphy with enclosure, Sept. 23, 1942, Fr: 24-97, M1642, RG226, NA; Clark, pp. 56-89, 121.

137   *being blindsided:* Malvergne case memos, Fr: 1044-48, 1057-59, R: 44, Fr: 905, R: 115, Fr: 47-49, R: 33, M1642, RG226, NA.

137-138 On November 6 to *"or not":* Alfred Gruenther memo to DDE, Sept. 29, 1942, B: 153, PPP, PF, DDEL; Coon, pp. 39-40; Clark, pp. 91-94; Gladieux, OHC, pp. 391-93, 426; Interview with OCD, pp. 125-26, B: "Oral History Interviews—OCD, Activities in Europe 1941-89," WJDP, MHI; Memo to JEH, Jan. 15, 1943, 62-64427-475 (36), FBI.

138   *be the case:* Bowman, OHP, p. 7; Hughes, OHP, p. 23; Brown, p. 253.

139   *nearby airport:* Coon, pp. 41-42; Vaughan, pp. 175-217; Atkinson, *An Army at Dawn,* pp. 62, 145-48; *War Report of the OSS,* p. 175; Smith, *Shadow Warriors,* pp. 151-52; *The Overseas Targets,* pp. 14, 18; J.I.C. Gibraltar, Lomay Operation, Nov. 10, 1942, Fr: 545-52, R: 35, Donald McKay memo to WJD, March 3, 1943, Fr: 1267-1306, R: 33, Factual Account of the Night of Nov. 7-8, 1942, Fr: 1130-38, R: 33, M1642, RG: 226, NA.

139-140 But only to *for North Africa:* David King memo to Robert Murphy, Nov. 18, 1942, Fr: 545-52, R: 35, M1642, RG226, NA; Clark, pp. 95-103; Atkinson, *An Army at Dawn,* pp. 64-159; Vaughan, pp. 201-17; FDR Press Conference, Nov. 10, 1942, FDRL; Lovell, pp. 186-87; Minutes of a Meeting in the St. George Hotel, Algiers, on Nov. 13, 1942, B: 33, PPP, PF, DDEL; Factual Account of the Night of Nov. 7-8, 1942, Fr: 1130-38, R: 33, M1642, RG226, NA.

141   *of the Army:* FDR letter to CH, Nov. 17, 1942, Folder 152, R: 22, CHP, LOC; Donald McKay memo to WJD, March 3, 1943, Fr: 1267-1306, M1642, RG226, NA; Murphy, pp. 139-40; F. L. Meyer memo to WJD, 1942, R: 6, DB memo to WJD with letter and enclosure from William Maddox, Dec. 11, 1942, A-3304, RG226, NA; Atkinson, *An Army at Dawn,* pp. 151-60, 198-99; Walker, p. 673; WJD memo to JCS, Nov. 14, 1942, Fr: 830-31, R: 6, Donald McKay memo to WJD, Fr: 1267-1306, R: 33, Henry Morgenthau letter to WJD with enclosure, June 5, 1943, Fr: 1320-31, R: 33, M1642, RG226, NA.

142   *American cousins:* Spanish Morocco memo, Fr: 43-44, R: 33, M1642, RG226, NA; Richard Heppner letter to WJD, Nov. 18, 1942, B: 340, S.O.E. and S.I.S, pp. 163-66, B: 72, E: 210, RG226, NA; Cipher telegram from New York for CD, Nov. 11, 1942, Telegram

for New York from CD, Nov. 12, 1942, Telegram to New York from CD, Dec. 12, 1942, HS 3-56, NAUK; John Toulmin interview, June 13, 1945, B: unnumbered third and fourth boxes from the end of the collection, WJDP, AWC.

143   *horse to lose*: EH letter to WJD, Feb. 2, 1943, Fr: 603-44, R: 34, WJD memo to FDR, April 25, 1942, John Wiley memo to D. C. Poole, Feb. 18, 1942, W. B. Smith memo to WJD, Aug. 6, 1942, Fr: 1279-1300, R: 1124, M1642, RG226, NA; Note of E.C.H. Jr., Dec. 24, 1942, B: 345, E: 210, RG226, NA; WJD letter to GCM, Nov. 18, 1942, Joseph McNarney letter to WJD, Jan. 25, 1943, Fr: 1118, 1120-21, R: 103, M1642, RG226, NA; Wiley memo to WJD with enclosure, Jan. 12, 1937, B: 344, E: 210, RG226, NA; SOE War Diary 56, OSS/SOE October 1942-June 1943, HS 7-283, NAUK; Notes on SOE's relations with OSS regarding Poland and Czechoslovakia, Aug. 15, 1942, HS 4-151, NAUK.

144   *was dead*: Troy, *Donovan and the CIA*, pp. 181-91; Memoirs of Ivan D. Yeaton, p. 60, IYP, MHI; GCM letter to WJD, Dec. 23, 1942, Fr: 197, R: 126, M1642, RG226, NA; WJD letter to GCM, Dec. 24, 1942, B: 119B, WJDP, MHI; A. C. Bennett memo to Commander Advance Group, Amphibious Force, U.S. Atlantic Fleet, Sept. 30, 1942, DGD; David R. Donovan commission in Naval Reserve, Jan. 3, 1942, Report on the Fitness of Officers for David R. Donovan, May 19, 1943, NPRC.

144   *"Admiral's assassin"*: Murphy, pp. 142-43; *The Assassination of Darlan*, by Peter Dewey, B: 47, E: 99, RG226, NA; Clark, pp. 128-30; WJD memo, Dec. 7, 1942, B: "Bomb Fuses, Admiral Darlan, etc.," WJDP, MHI; Coon report, VIII: Postscript: The World After War: OSS-SOE: *The Invisible Empire*, MEMTO-Torch Anthology, Vol. II, B: 49, E: 99, RG226, NA; Coon, pp. 46-48, 60-61.

CHAPTER 15: BERN

145-146 *At the station* to *isolated Bern*: Grose, pp. 5-141, 150-52; Hugh Wilson memos to James Murphy, July 17, 1942, Fr: 1004-6, R: 114, M1642, RG226, NA; Burns to Victor cable, Nov. 10, 1942, B: 121B, WJDP, MHI; Hood, Dec. 11, 2008; Crockett, OHP, p. 17; Howe, Dec. 12, 2007.

147   *"War Department"*: Burns cable to Victor, Nov. 14, 1942, B: 121B, WJDP, MHI; Mauch, p. 108; Grose, pp. 26-34, 73-107,153-83; Mary Bancroft interview, July 16, 1980, p. 12, B: Interviews—Bancroft to Sherwood 1945-undated, WJDP, MHI; *The Overseas Targets*, pp. 273-80; Allen Dulles interview, Sept. 28, 1944, B: unnumbered third and fourth boxes from the end of the collection, WJDP, MHI; OSS cable to Bern, April 28, 1943, R: 150, A-3304, RG226, NA; *War Report of the OSS*, p. 142.

147-149 *Dulles developed* to *for successes*: JEH letter to HH with enclosure, July 26, 1943, DOJ Rpt. No. 2361-A, OF 10B, FDRL; Breakers cables list 512, B: 9, E: 190C, RG226, NA; W. A. Kimbel memo to Chief, S.I., Jan. 20, 1945, Ferdinand Mayer memo to WS, Dec. 28, 1944, B: 350, E: 210, RG226, NA; The Story of George, B: 7, E: 190C, RG226, NA; W. S. Stephenson letter to WJD, Nov. 15, 1944, B: 1, JRFP, HIA; *The Overseas Targets*, pp. 278-79; WS memo to EB, Jan. 26, 1944, Fr: 1010-16; R: 26, M1642, RG226, NA; A. Ausl. Abw. IM/A, B.Nr. 36 835 Sp, Aug. 11, 1943, Fr: 423-29, R: 539, T-78, NA; Bern cable to WJD, March 15, 1944, B: 469, E: 210, RG226, NA; Memorandum on Penetration and Compromise of OSS in Switzerland and Western Europe (Allen Dulles), May 4, 1948, B: 56, HVP, LOC.

149-150 *Roosevelt and* to *"German resistance"*: William Kimbel memo to WJD with enclosures, March 4, 1943, Fr: 527-31, R: 103, Bern cable to OSS, Aug. 19, 1943, Fr: 817-19, R: 106, M1642, RG226, NA; Lochner, pp. 166-67, 375.

150   *phony mail*: OCD memo to WS, Oct. 21, 1960, B: 126A, WJDP, MHI; Laurie, pp. 259-70.

150-151 *But Morale* to *Army intelligence*: FDR Executive Order, March 9, 1943, Fr: 79-80, R: 4, WJD memo to FDR, Feb. 23, 1943, Fr: 522-25, R: 104, M1642, RG226, NA; Elmer Davis and George Strong appointment with FDR, FDR: Day by Day—The Pare Lorentz Chronology, FDRL; R.N.Y. memo to GCM, Feb. 18, 1943, George Strong memo to GCM, Feb. 18, 1943, B: 346, E: 175, RG165, NA; Troy, *Donovan and the CIA*, pp. 206-

4; Putzell, OHP, p. 42; Interview with Ernest Cuneo, Nov. 27, 1968, B: 7, TTP, RG263, NA.

152   *that counted:* Interview with OCD, pp. 378-79, B: "Oral History Interviews–OCD, Activities in Europe 1941-89," WJDP, MHI; Troy, *Donovan and the CIA,* p. 196; Notes on personnel for Office of Director and Assistant Director, Fr: 403-19, R: 17, M1642, RG226, NA; Wallace Deuel letter to Mom and Dad, April 12, B: 1, 1943, WDP, LOC; Invoice from Wetzel, June 1, 1943, B: 139B, WJDP, MHI; Kingsley, Jan. 7, 2008.

CHAPTER 16: THE NEUTRALS

153   *as his hostess:* Donald Rumsey interview, p. 9, B: Interviews–Teitelbaum to Withrow, 1979-undated, WJDP, MHI; Page, OHP, pp. 23-24; Wise, Jan. 27, 2008; Wallace Deuel letter to Mother and Dad, March 15, 1943, B: 1, WDP, LOC.

154   *and the OSS:* Four Close Associates of Hitler, Dec. 9, 1943, Fr: 379-424, R: 109, M1642, RG226, NA; Notes on Geheime Feldpolizei, Report No. 118888, E: 16, RG226, NA; Mueller, pp. 221-35.

155   *recruit 659:* U.L.A. memos to WJD, Jan. 5 and 11, 1943, Fr: 775, 828, R: 53, WJD memo to Commanding General, Army Air Forces, Oct. 8, 1943, Fr: 426, R: 19, M1642, RG226, NA; U. L. Amoss letter to WJD, March 10, 1943, R: 4, A-3304, RG226, NA; Memo to WJD on OSS Cairo, Aug. 18, 1943, B: "United Kingdom–OSS Training Schools 2940-60, British Influence in Balkans," WJDP, MHI. A number of historians have speculated that Donovan and Canaris met while both were traveling in Europe. But the OSS archives have no record of such a meeting, which would have been an important event and heavily documented. Donovan's own personal papers and the war reminiscences he gave friends also contain nothing about such a meeting. It therefore appears that the closest the OSS ever got to a direct contact with Canaris was through Amoss and even that never occurred.

156   *and drivers:* J. A. Hamilton memo to Edmond Taylor, Sept. 3, 1943, Fr: 838, R: 121, M1642, RG226, NA; WJD memo to Lanning Macfarland, March 5, 1943, B: 340, E: 210, RG226, NA; Weinberg, pp. 196-97; John Riheldaffer memo to Silas Moore, Aug. 17, 1942, Fr: 75-76, R: 36, M1642, RG226, NA; Brown, p. 355.

157   *chemical industry:* Kingsley, Jan. 7, 2008; Dogwood agent profiles, B: 439, E: 210, RG226, NA; Executive Summary of Dogwood report, B: 35, E: 211, RG226, NA.

157   *other was real:* Lanning Macfarland memo to EP with Interim Report from Chief, OSS Mission to Turkey, Nov. 22, 1943, B: 16, E: 211, RG226, NA.

157-159   *The fabricated to imperiled it:* WS memo to WJD, May 3, 1943, Fr: 180, R: 65, M1642, RG226, NA; Alvarez, p. 56; Memorandum on General Background of Japanese Activities in Portugal, B: 355, E: 210, RG226, NA; Milton Katz memo to JM, Dec. 13, 1945, WS memo to WJD on Papers H-361, B: 355, E: 210, RG226, NA; Frank Stoner letter to JM, May 24, 1943, Lisbon to Tokyo cable, June 30, 1943, Tokyo cables to Madrid, Rome, July 1, 1943, Rome to Tokyo cable, June 29, 1943, George Strong memo to GCM, July 7, 1943, George Strong memo to Col. O'Connor, July 8, 1943, SRH-113, B: 31, E: 9002, RG457, NA; George Strong memo to GCM, July 6, 1943, EB memo to C. R. Peck, July 23, 1943, B: 355, E: 210, RG226, NA; Lewin, pp. 11, 293.

160   *parachute production:* WJD memo to FDR, April 22, 1942, Fr: 138, R: 23, M1642, RG226, NA; Carlton Hayes letter to WJD, June 1, 1942, R: 93, A-3304, RG226, NA; Chalou, pp. 122, 124; *The Overseas Targets,* pp. 31-34; Mannes, OHC, pp. 22-24.

160-163   *Donovan's relations to it stung:* Telegram No. 394 from Madrid, Feb. 17, 1943, Madrid memo to Milid, March 6, 1943, Memorandum for the Secretariat, Joint Chiefs of Staff, Memorandum of OSS in Spain, March 8, 1943, George Strong memo to GCM, March 9, 1943, Thomas Handy memo to GCM, March 13, 1943, NATO memo to War Department, March 21, 1943, John Deane memo to WJD, April 8, 1943, Donovan notes on testimony before JCS, April 4, 1943, John Deane letter to AB, April 10, 1943, Frank Ryan memo to WJD, Sept. 25, 1943, Fr: 945-1262, R: 58, Fr: 408-29, R: 110, M1642, RG226, NA.

CHAPTER 17: INFILTRATION

165   *for cracks:* SOE War Diary 56 OSS/SOE, June 1943, HS 7-283, NAUK; WVHD, p. 27, WJDP, MHI; Interview with Wayne Nelson, Nov. 28, 1961, B: 4A, WJDP, MHI; Anthony Eden letter to WJD, March 28, 1943, WJD letter to Earl of Halifax, Nov. 15, 1944, B: 81B, WJDP, MHI; DB letter to EB, June 27, 1943, Fr: 155-64, R: 39, M1642, RG226, NA.

165-166   *Donovan's British* to *so nervous:* EH memo to WJD, May 7, 1943, Fr: 54-62, R: 11, M1642, RG226, NA; DB letter to EB, June 19, 1943, Fr: 155-64, R: 39, M1642, RG226, NA; Dropping OSS men into France, SOE War Diary 56, OSS/SOE, October 1942-June 1943, HS 7-282, NAUK; Draft letter from C.D. to G. 50000 June 2, 1943, HS 5-150, NAUK; Suspected OSS operations to the Balkans, OSS and the Yugoslavs, SOE War Diary 56, OSS/SOE, October 1942-June 1943, HS 7-283, NAUK; SO Operations—Western Europe, April 10, 1943, Fr: 54-62, 1276-1300, R: 111, M1642, RG226, NA.

167   *parachuting spies:* Dunlop, p. 389; WJD memo to John Deane, April 30, 1943, Fr: 929-30, R: 117, WJD letter to John Deane with enclosure, June 13, 1943, Fr: 528, R: 32, Fr: 545-55, R: 18, WJD letter to W. B. Smith, July 21, 1943, and W. B. Smith reply, July 29, 1943, Fr; 320-26; R: 80, M1642, RG226, NA.

167   *in this war:* EH memo to R. Davis Halliwell, June 16, 1943, Fr: 408-11, R: 34, M1642, RG226, NA; Report from Algiers, I and II. The First Recruits, B: 63, E: 210, B: 45, E: 99, RG226, NA; Henry Hyde interview, May 14, 1981, pp. 1-25, B: Interviews—Bancroft to Sherwood-undated, WJDP, MHI; Weinberg, p. 516.

167-169   *The first to* aboard the plane: Report from Algiers, Part One, Operations from October 1943 through January 1944, Part Two The Missions, I. The Penny Farthing Mission, B: 63, E: 210, B: 45, E: 99, RG226, NA; Brown, pp. 328-40; *The Overseas Targets,* pp. 227-30.

169-171   *August 17* to *report later:* Appendix: Jacques' Story, I. The Penny Farthing Mission, Part Two, B: 63, E: 210, B: 45, E: 99, RG226, NA.

CHAPTER 18: SICILY AND ITALY

173   *brought him:* Naval fitness reports for David R. Donovan, April 28, 1942, April 12, 1943, A. C. Bennett memo to Chief of Naval Personnel, July 15, 1942, NPRC; Tippaparn Donovan, Jan. 24, 2008; "Donovan, Father and Son Invaded Sicily Together," *Buffalo Evening News,* Oct. 10, 1943; McIntosh, Aug. 29, 2007.

173   *this landing:* Report of Physical Examination for WJD, April 8, 1943, Personnel File, WJD, RG226, NA.

173-174   *In April* to *Gela's beach:* WJD memo to Dr. Rogers, March 7, 1943, Fr: 524-25, R: 100, James Rogers memo to WJD, March 18, 1943, Fr: 682-760, R: 130, M1642, RG226, NA; Lovell, p. 187; Corvo, pp. 41-42; OSS Working into Sicily, SOE War Diary 56, OSS/SOE, October 1942-June 1943, HS 7-283, NAUK; Pvt. Biagio Max Corvo file, B: 18, E: 92A, RG226, NA; Atkinson, *The Day of Battle,* p. 56; *The Overseas Targets,* pp. 55, 62, 97.

175   *his staff:* Dunlop, p. 399; WVHD, p. 50, WJDP, MHI; John Hughes memo to WJD, Feb. 19, 1943, Fr: 637-41, R: 34, WJD-George Patton letter, July 31 and Aug. 18, 1943, Fr: 33, R: 40, M1642, RG226, NA.

175   *more landings:* WJD letter to John Hilldring, Sept. 3, 1943, Fr: 1097-99, R: 119, M1642, RG226, NA; *The Overseas Targets,* pp. 62-63; Corvo, pp. 80-81; Wallace Deuel letter to Mother and Dad, Sept. 4, 1943, B: 1, WDP, LOC.

176-177   *Donovan spent* to *give it a try:* EH memo to branch chiefs, Aug. 9, 1943, Fr: 577-81, R: 100, M1642, RG226, NA; Spencer Phenix memo dictated Aug. 31, 1943, Fr: 587-600, R: 18, WJD memo on Matters Requested to Be Done for Various of the Service Arms, Aug. 21, 1943, Fr: 1117-18, R: 77, GCM cables to DDE, Aug. 20 and 22, 1943, DDE cables to GCM, Aug. 22 and 28, 1943, Fr: 1314-19, R: 45, M1642, RG226, NA.

177–178   *Churchill and to said, smiling:* Memorandum for WJD, Sept. 26, 1942, OSS, 1942–1945, OF 4486, FDRL; Hough, pp. 94–96, 160–67; Speech by Admiral Louis Mountbatten, March 21, 1966, B: 137A, WJDP, MHI.

178–180   *As the naval to on his hands:* Putzell, OHP, p. 30; Ernest Cuneo Manuscript on the OSS and BSC, N-P File, ECP, FDRL; WJD letter to Mark Clark, Aug. 25, 1943, Fr: 353, R: 53, Mark Clark memo to EH, Nov. 1943, Fr: 334–51, R: 53, M1642, RG226, NA; Dunlop, p. 400; Atkinson, *The Day of Battle,* p. 185; *War Report of the OSS,* p. 209; JEH memo to WJD, June 24, 1943, Fr: 246, 250, R: 51, M1642, RG226, NA; Weinberg, pp. 597–610; *The Overseas Targets,* pp. 65–69; Donald Downes memo to WJD, Oct. 19, 1942, Fr: 86–91, R: 83, Commander Edward Breed Abstract, B: 48, E: 99, RG226, NA.

180–181   *But before to "way out":* Dunlop, pp. 359–60, 389, 417; Corvo, p. 116; W. A. Eddy letter to WJD, March 2, 1943, R: 44, A-3304, RG226, NA; Coon, pp. 138–40; Report of Sardinia Operation, B: 45, OSS Corsica-Phase Two, C.S.C, OSS Activities in Corsica, Sept. 12–Oct. 5, 1943, B: 48, E: 99, RG226, NA.

182   *secret agent:* J. E. Toulmin letter to WJD, Oct. 11, 1943, Fr: 241, R: 41, M1642, RG226, NA; John Toulmin interview, June 13, 1945, B: unnumbered third and fourth boxes from the end of the collection, WJDP, MHI; Peter Karlow memo to Quinn, March 18, 1946, Fr: 1052–55, R: 68, M1642, RG226, NA; Corvo, pp. 112–19; Ernest Cuneo Manuscript on the OSS and BSC, N-P File, ECP, FDRL.

CHAPTER 19: THE BALKANS

184   *and Greece:* SOE/OSS Collaboration in the Middle East, To V/CD from A/D1, Aug. 11, 1943, HS 5-150, NAUK; WJD letter to C.D., July 31, 1943, Fr: 283–93, R: 88, WJD letter to Stuart Menzies, July 28, 1943, Notes on meeting held on July 26, 1943, HS 8-7, NAUK; C letter to C.D. July 30, 1943, HS 3-57, NAUK; OSS Planning Group, Overall Program for Strategic Services Operations in the Balkans Based on Cairo, Egypt, Nov. 9, 1943, Fr: 144–66, 181–215, 250–51, R: 131, WJD memo to Rogers, Oct. 10, 1943, Fr: 555–58, R: 58, M1642, RG226, NA; Weinberg, pp. 460–63.

185   *as well:* Richard Harris Smith, pp. 128–31; "I Fought Beside Mihailovich," by Walter R. Mansfield, *Washington Post,* June 23, 1946; OSS Operations Balkans, May 5, 1944, Fr: 1–217, R: 132, Louis Huot Preliminary Report on a visit to the National Army of Liberation, Yugoslavia, Oct. 29, 1943, Fr: 192–99, R: 132, British request for Concurrent Withdrawal of British and American Officers with Mihailovich, March 2, 1944, Fr: 9–10, R: 84, WJD memo to FDR, Fr: 6828–9, R: 23, M1642, RG226, NA; Churchill, *Closing the Ring,* pp. 461–63.

185–186   *Before he to sent home:* Trip to Tito's HQ in Jajce, Oct. 20–27, 1943, Fr: 1–217, R: 132, WJD memo to Scribner, Oct. 7, 1943, Fr: 1243–49, R: 79, M1642, RG226, NA; Atkinson, *The Day of Battle,* pp. 270–71; Cipher telegram from Massingham, Sept. 18, 1943, HS 3-57, NAUK; Edward Green memo to Deputy Director, SSO, OSS with Final Report on "Operation Audrey," May 20, 1944, B: 36, E: 99, RG226, NA.

186–189   *Huot left to Gubbins agreed:* President to Prime Minister No. 393, Oct. 22, 1943, CHAR 20-121-125, CA; Former Naval Person to President No. 470, Oct. 23, 1943, CHAR 20-122-6, CA; Notes of a Meeting Held at M.O.4. at 1500 Hrs., Nov. 17, 1943, Cipher telegram from Cairo, Nov. 18, 1943, OSS in the Balkans, Nov. 18, 1943, HS 8-7, NAUK; C.D. memo to Cadogan, Oct. 4, 1943, HS 5-150, NAUK; SOE/OSS Relations Nov. 25, 1943, CAB 122-1594, NAUK; SOE/OSS Relations in North Africa, Sept. 27, 1943, CD/6166 to S.O., Sept. 30, 1943, HS 3-57, NAUK.

CHAPTER 20: PEACE FEELERS

190   *many months:* WJD memo to FDR, Oct. 21, 1943, Fr: 664, R: 23, M1642, RG226, NA; WJD memo to FDR, Oct. 5, 1943, OSS, Donovan, William, 1941 to 10-12-43, Subject File, PSF, FDRL.

191   *from annihilation:* Sedgewick report Part XXXVI, Sept. 10, 1943, Fr: 643–45, R: 109, John C. Wiley memos to WJD, Aug. 20 and 23, 1943, Fr: 1305-7, R: 104, M1642, RG226, NA; Mueller, p. 220; Count von Moltke profile, Nov. 2, 1943, B: 18, E: 99, RG226, NA; Letter on meeting with Count von Moltke, Dec. 29, 1943, Fr: 314–95, R: 52, M1642, RG226, NA.

192   *the deal:* Letter on meeting with Count von Moltke, Dec. 29, 1943, A. Kirk letter to Richard Tindall, Jan. 10, 1944, Fr: 314–95, R: 52, M1642, RG226, NA; Memorandum re: German Plan, Jan. 12, 1944, German Plan: Exposé on the Readiness of a Powerful German Group to Prepare and Assist Allied Military Operations Against Nazi Germany, Fr: 314–95, R: 52, M1642, RG226, NA; Mueller, pp. 234–35.

192–193 *Donovan was to Macfarland's chain:* Theodore A. Morde Special Report, Subject: Theodore A. Morde, Fr: 1015–19, R: 125, M1642, RG226, NA; Meeting No. 1—Oct. 5, 1943, Place: German Embassy, Turkey, OSS, Rpt. Donovan, William, 10-19 to 12-17-43, Subject File, FDRL; ES memo to Grace Tully, Nov. 10, 1943, FDR memo to ES, Nov. 8, 1943, WJD memo to FDR, Oct. 29, 1943, OSS, Rpt. Donovan, William, 10-19 to 12-17-43, Subject File, PSF, FDRL; Lanning Macfarland letter to WJD, Feb. 5, 1944, Karl Brandt memo to WJD, Feb. 28, 1944, WS memo to WJD, March 2, 1944, Bern Cable to OSS headquarters, March 5, 1944, Irving Sherman memo to WJD, March 9, 1944, WL memo to WJD, March 15, 1944, F.E.O. memo to WJD, March 19, 1944, WJD memo to JCS on the Hermann Plan, April 2, 1944, WJD letter to Shepard Morgan, April 2, 1944, Acting Chairman, SS Planning Group memo to WJD, April 3, 1944, Fr: 314–95, R: 52, M1642, RG226, NA.

193–199 *Donovan received to war in Asia:* Arthur Goldberg memo to WJD with enclosure, Fr: 817, R: 83, Fr: 450–51, R: 56, Fr: 759, R: 18, M1642, RG226, NA; Watts Hill memo to DB, Dec. 18, 1942, B: 27, E: 92A, RG226, NA; Joint Report on Field Conditions by Florimund Duke, Alfred Suarez, and Guy Nunn, July 11, 1945, B: 27, E: 92A, RG226, NA; Weinberg, pp. 519–20; OSS HQ cable to Bern, Nov. 20, 1943, B: 165, E: 134, RG226, NA; The Istanbul Mission—Certain C-E Aspects, B: 35, E: 211, RG226, NA; Forest Royal memo to WJD, Dec. 5, 1943, WJD memo to JCS, Nov. 20, 1943, B: 181, E: 210, RG226, NA; Peterson, pp. 190–91; WJD cable to Macfarland, Jan. 9, 1944, B: 344, E: 210, RG226, NA; Lanning Macfarland letter to WJD, Jan. 12, 1944, Fr: 245–46, R: 83, M1642, RG226, NA; Hoettl, pp. 195–97; Source: Cereus (59), Sub-Source: Dogwood Oct. 8, 1943, Dogwood Report No. 450, April 4, 1944, B: 447, E: 210, RG226, NA; Dogwood report to Knickerbocker, Memo No. 97, May 30, 1944, B: 447, E: 210, RG226, NA.

CHAPTER 21: ASIA

201   *every month:* Kingsley, Jan. 7, 2008; Dunlop, pp. 392, 469–70; MacDonald, pp. 23–24; Hughes, OHP, p. 13; EP memo to WJD, March 28, 1944, Fr: 850–52, R: 19, Weston Howland memo to WJD, Oct. 24, 1942, Fr: 1116-19, R: 100, M1642, RG226, NA.

201–203 *When Donovan to for the moment:* Liaison Between OSS London and Washington, SOE War Diary 56, OSS/SOE October 1942–June 1943, HS 7-283, NAUK; WL memo to WJD, Aug. 9, 1943, Fr: 1055-56, R: 102, EH memo to WJD, Aug. 26, 1943, Fr: 77, R: 1057-64, G. Platt memo to OCD, Aug. 23, 1934, Fr: 1053-64, R: 77, M1642, RG226, NA; WJD note to EB, Sept. 5, 1943, Fr: 1075-78, R: 77, Memo to Acting Director, Oct. 1, 1943, JM memo to Acting Director, Oct. 2, 1943, WJD memo to JM, Nov. 8, 1943, Fr: 1119-45, R: 77, M1642, RG226, NA.

204   *to Sextant:* Arthur Robinson memo to WL, Jan. 3, 1944, Fr: 439–47, R: 72, M1642, RG226, NA; Sterling Hayden personnel record, B: 320, E: 224, RG226, NA.

204–205 *When Roosevelt to "economic development":* WJD cable to EB and Mrs. Griggs, Dec. 15, 1943, B: 219, E: 134, RG226, NA; R. Davis Halliwell memo to WJD, Jan. 18, 1944, Fr: 248–381, R: 55, R. Davis Halliwell memo to Hugh Wilson, Jan. 13, 1944, Fr: 1262-67, R: 56, M1642, RG226, NA; Taylor, pp. 272–73.

206   *do for him:* Moon, *This Grim and Savage Game,* pp. 147–48, 186, 214–15; Richard Harris Smith, pp. 225–28; *The Overseas Targets,* p. 416; WJD memo to FDR, Jan. 3, 1942, OSS, Reports 1-1 to 15-42, Subject File, PSF, FDRL; WVHD, p. 4, WJDP, MHI.

206   *Mary Miles: The Overseas Targets,* pp. 415–16; Caldwell, p. 56.

207   *fire Mary Miles:* Milton Miles letter to Chiang Kai-shek, March 20, 1946, B: 1, Miles memo to Nimitz, March 1, 1946, B: 9, MMP, HIA; Miles, pp. 921–31; Confidential letter to WJD, Dec. 6, 1942, Fr: 568–639, R: 55, Milton Miles letter to WJD, Fr: 606–6, R: 79, M1642, RG226, NA.

208   *sidekick, Mary Miles:* John Davies letter to WJD, Oct. 6, 1943, Fr: 81–91, R: 91, Carl O. Hoffmann memo to WJD, Sept. 3, 1943, Fr: 317–21, R: 71, Milton Miles letter to Jeff, Aug. 1, 1943, Fr: 82–84, R: 79, WJD memo to Capt. Hoffman, Aug. 30, 1943, Fr: 317–21, R: 71, M1642, RG226, NA; Richard Harris Smith, p. 229.

208–210   *Donovan, in fact to military secrets:* McIntosh, OHP, p. 39; Interview with OCD, pp. 484–85, B: "Oral History Interviews—OCD, Activities in Europe 1941–89," WJDP, MHI; Enclosure "B": Who is C. V. Starr?, J. M. McHugh memo to Chief, SI, July 1, 1944, Charles Fahs memo to WL, July 3, 1944, B: 355, E: 210, RG226, NA; James Arthur Duff profile, James Arthur Duff account, Aug. 8 and 17, 1983, OSS JAD 1942–1943 File, Unprocessed collection for J. Arthur Duff, ADP, HIA.

210–214   *Shortly before to Eifler home:* Caldwell, pp. 56–57; White, pp. 95–103; Major Lee memo to WJD, Feb. 17, 1944, Fr: 841–43, R: 41, R. Davis Halliwell memo to WJD, Jan. 18, 1944, Letter to Admiral Purnell, Dec. 14, 1943, Fr: 248–381, R: 55, M1642, RG226, NA; Milton Miles memo to Chief of Information Branch Central Planning Staff, May 17, 1946, B: 3, MMP, HIA; Memorandum of Conversation, Dec. 5, 1943, B: 327, E: 210, RG226, NA; Bos. Memo, April 6, 1950, 100-24628-606, FBI; Richard Heppner letter to WJD, April 21, 1944, Fr: 306–7, R: 91, M1642, RG226, NA.

214–215   *After the to and beheaded:* Carl Eifler interview, Nov. 20 and 21, 1944, B: unnumbered third and fourth boxes from the end of the collection, WJDP, MHI; Moon, *This Grim and Savage Game,* pp. 1–29, 68–163; Richard Harris Smith, p. 229; MacDonald, pp. 15–16.

215–219   *By the end to of bravado:* R. Davis Halliwell memo to Jan. 18, 1941, with enclosure, Jan. 18, 1941, Fr: 248–381, R: 55, WJD letter to Major Hoffman, December 1943, Fr: 93–104, R: 91, M1642, RG226, NA; Moon, *This Grim and Savage Game,* pp. 133–204; Report to WJD, Dec. 14, 1943, B: 3, Disposition Board Proceedings for Officers, Carl F. Eifler, Jan. 18, 1947, Box 3, Medical Abstract for Carl F. Eifler, B: 4, Dr. Archie Chun-Ming memo on Carl Eifler, May 4, 1943, B: 7, CEP, HIA; Moon, *This Grim and Savage Game,* pp. 105–6, 174–75; Moon and Eifler, *The Deadliest Colonel,* pp. 168–73; Colonel Coughlin interview, Nov. 30, 1944, B: unnumbered third and fourth boxes from the end of the collection, WJDP, MHI.

219   *"colossal cheek":* Taylor, pp. 274–77.

CHAPTER 22: THE RUSSIANS

221   *to Tehran:* Deane, pp. 46, 50–51; William Kimbel memos to WJD, Jan. 23 and Sept. 15, 1943, Fr: 1042–53, R: 104, JSC directive on Disclosure of Technical Information to the USSR, Dec. 12, 1943, Fr: 119–22, R: 5, M1642, RG226, NA; Frederic Dolbeare memo to Calvin Hoover, Oct. 20, 1942, B: 511, E: 210, RG226, NA.

222   *oil refineries:* WJD memo to FDR, Nov. 5, 1943, OSS, 1942–1945, OF 4485, FDRL; Report on the Political Impact of the Formation of the "Committee for Free Germany" in Moscow, and its Appeal to the German People, Aug. 11, 1943, Fr: 260–75, R: 53, JEH memo to WJD, Fr: 162–67, R: 93, Emmy Rado memo to WJD, May 4, 1943, Fr: 1223, R: 104, Col. O'Connor memo to WJD, Sept. 4, 1943, Fr: 1342, R: 104, M1642, RG226, NA.

222–224   *Christmas Day to as well:* Memorandums of Conversation at the Commissariat for Internal Affairs, Dec. 25 and 27, 1943, Fr: 224–69, M1642, RG226, NA; Deane, pp. 51–53; Harriman, p. 292–94; Weinstein and Vassilev, pp. 241–43; Deane, pp. 53–55; Joint Staff Planners meeting minutes, Feb. 17, 1944, Fr: 384–438, R: 79, M1642, RG226, NA.

224–226 *Not J. Edgar Hoover to told Roosevelt:* Whitehead, pp. 228–29; Memo No. 44, Jan. 13, 1944, B: 26, E: 12, GP, RG263, NA; WJD memo to William Leahy, March 7, 1944, William Leahy memo to GCM et al., March 15, 1944, Fr: 384–438, R: 79, Aubrey Harwood memo to Frederick Chaffee, April 17, 1944, Fr: 461–656, 408–14, R: 105, WJD memo to FDR with enclosure, March 9, 1944, Fr: 759–61, R: 23, M1642, RG226, NA; Nichols memo to Tolson, March 15, 1952, 100-364413-56, "The Strange Alliance," by John R. Deane, B: 121B, WJDP, MHI.

227 *state of mind:* Kingsley, Jan. 7, 2008; Atkinson, *The Day of Battle,* p. 372; EH memo to WJD, Dec. 25, 1943, Fr: 553–68, R: 53, M1642, RG226, N; Dunlop, pp. 416–17; Crockett, OHP, pp. 1–2, 52.

227–229 *Donovan soon to his mission:* Tompkins, pp. 17–20; Peter Tompkins interview, Sept. 29, 1944, B: unnumbered third and fourth boxes from the end of the collection, WJDP, MHI.

229 *proved bloody:* Tompkins, p. 17; Drew Pearson news item, *Washington Post,* July 7, 1944; Kingsley, Jan. 7, 2008; War Log, Jan. 24, 1944, Fr: 1046–47, R: 56, M1642, RG226, NA.

229 *toward Anzio:* General Narrative of the Action for Operation "Shingle"—Period Jan. 21–Feb. 1, 1944, B: 4, RDP, MHI; Remembering 109 by Al Materazzi, OSS Society Newsletter, Winter 2004–05, p. 7.

230 *up others:* The OSS Detachment at the Anzio Beachhead, B: 39, E: 99, RG226, NA; Peter Tompkins Report on Missions to Rome, March 1 and June 15, 1945, B: 39 and 48, E: 99, RG226, NA.

230–231 *When Donovan to hopeless mission:* Putzell, OHP, p. 1; WJD letter to JM, April 3, 1944, B: 80A, WJDP, MHI; Putzell, OHP, pp. 14–17, 83–85; Remembering 109, by Edwin J. Putzell, Jr., OSS Society Newsletter, Summer 2001, p. 5.

232 *from the OSS:* Carleton Coon memo to Conyers Read, Feb. 8, 1945, B: 126A, WJDP, MHI; Downes, pp. 82–83; C. W. Nimitz letter to WJD, July 2, 1944, Fr: 68, R: 89, M1642, RG226, NA.

232 *on the islands:* Putzell, OHP, p. 17; WVHD, pp. 29, 62, WJDP, MHI; Singlaub, p. 144; Dunlop, pp. 402–13; Weinberg, pp. xx, 341–47, 553–54, 725, 849–79, 919; Willoughby and Chamberlain, pp. 144–70; Lewin, pp. 140–81.

232–234 *Donovan had to from the OSS:* WL interview, Feb. 5, 1969, B: 136B, WJDP, MHI; J. R. Hayden memo to WJD, April 15, 1943, Fr: 601–31, R: 55, M1642, RG226, NA; WJD memo to Douglas MacArthur, Fr: 854–61, R: 19, Fr: 1312–15, R: 89, C. A. Willoughby memo to the Chief of Staff, April 18, 1944, Fr: 1312–15, R: 89, M1642, RG226, NA; Putzell, OHP, p. 18; WJD cable to EB, May 28, 1944, B: 219, E: 134, RG226, NA; Perret, pp. 379–93; Manchester, pp. 344–48.

CHAPTER 23: NORMANDY

235–236 *Claridge's was to English countryside:* Lankford, pp. 98–136; Edward Green memo to WJD, Aug. 11, 1944, with "OSS Hymn" enclosed, Fr: 1252–56, R: 77, John Wilson memo to WJD, May 6, 1944, Fr: 1164–70, R: 69, M1642, RG226, NA; *The Overseas Targets,* pp. 161–62, 183–87.

236–237 *Bruce had to more wrong:* DB letter to WS, Aug. 16, 1958, Section 12, File WS, DB speech, May 2, 1971, DB, Section 13, 1969–1971, File 14, VHS; Part XLIII, Report of Conversation, Part I, Dec. 31, 1943, Fr: 705–8, R: 109, Bern cable on KAPPA for 105 and Jackpot, April 12, 1944, Fr: 798–805, R: 18, M1642, RG226, NA; John Weckerling memo to GCM, April 16, 1944, Fr: 283–93, R: 14, GMP, LOC.

238 *of ammunition:* WJD memo to GCM, Oct. 20, 1944, Fr: 230, R: 20, WJD memo to FDR, July 8, 1944, Fr: 56, R: 24, M1642, RG226, NA; *The Overseas Targets,* pp. 177–78, 192–99.

238 *when they land:* Smith, *Shadow Warriors,* pp. 245, 252, 291; Final Report of SI Operations Room to Chief, SI Branch, Sept. 30, 1944, Fr: 1193–1208, R: 80, M1642, RG226, NA;

Justin O'Brien memo to Chief, SI, with enclosures on Sussex mission reports, March 1, 1945, B: 16, E: 99, RG226, NA.

239   *Normandy landing:* Brown, pp. 533-34; Private Office memo for WC, May 26, 1944, and McMartin note, May 27, 1944, CHAR 20-141A-69-71, CA; Fitness report for Lt. David R. Donovan, Sept. 20, 1944, NPRC.

239-247   *Marshall, who to the Tuscaloosa:* DB letter to WS, Aug. 16, 1958, Section 12, File WS, DB speech, May 2, 1971, DB, Section 13, 1969-1971, File 14, VHS; Carter Nicholas memo to WJD with enclosure on Irish cooperation with the OSS, March 27, 1944, B: 351, E: 210, RG226, NA; Lankford, pp. 47-71, 220; Chester B. Hansen diary entries for Normandy landing, B: 4, 41, and 42, CHP, MHI; WJD memo to FDR, June 14, 1944, Fr: 896-901, R: 23, M1642, RG226, NA; WJD letter to Evans Carlson, June 17, 1944, B: "United Kingdom—OSS Training School 1940-60," WJDP, MHI.

248   *from the front: The Overseas Targets,* pp. 219-21; WJD lecture for the Army-Navy Staff College, March 12, 1945, B: 119A, WJDP, MHI; Lankford, p. 181; Weinberg, p. 533; Foot, p. 319; Joseph Lynch letter to JEH, July 12, 1945, 94-4-4672-26, FBI; WJD memo to FDR, July 8, 1944, Fr: 460-63, R: 50, WJD memo to FDR, June 14, 1944, Fr: 896-901, R: 23, WJD letter to James Forrestal, June 14, 1944, M1642, RG226, NA; HS diary entry, June 15, 1944, Film HM 51, HSP, YU.

CHAPTER 24: INTELLIGENCE FAILURES

250   *dirty pond:* Atkinson, *The Day of Battle,* pp. 568-75; Crockett, OHP, p. 18; Putzell, OHP, p. 55; Peter Tompkins memo to Frank Mall, Report on Mission to Rome, March 1, 1945, B: 39, E: 99, RG226, NA.

250   *U.S. dollar:* CG allied Mediterranean Forces AFHQ Command memo to War Department, March 18, 1944, Fr: 121-22, R: 83, Fr: 605-7, R: 101, Edward Glavin and Howard Chapin memo to WJD, June 23, 1944, Fr: 140-48, R: 110, M1642, RG226, NA.

251   *officers reported:* Roger Pfaff memo to WJD on Peter Tompkins with enclosure, March 3, 1945, B: 386, E: 210, RG226, NA; Report on Mission to Rome insert, March 1, 1945, B: 39, E: 99, RG226, NA; Italian Operations Centering on Rome, B: 41, E: 99, RG226, NA; Crockett, OHP, p. 45; *The Overseas Targets,* pp. 73-74.

252   *backed off:* Atkinson, *The Day of Battle,* pp. 406-8, 506-8; R&A Branch Naples memo to WJD, Jan. 21, 1944, Fr: 1190, R: 77, M1642, RG226, NA; Corvo, pp. 273-83; "Vanderbilt Writes," *New York Post,* April 6, 1944; WJD cable to Glavin, May 11, 1944, Glavin cable to WJD, April 17, 1944, Crockett and Glavin cable to Rehm and EB, April 25, 1944, Glavin cable to WJD, May 9, 1944, WJD cable to Glavin, May 11, 1944, R: 7 and 10, A-3304, RG226, NA.

252   *if he remained:* William Suhling interview, July 19, 1945, John Toulmin interview, Dec. 5, 1944, Peter Tompkins interview, Sept. 29, 1944, B: unnumbered third and fourth boxes from the end of the collection, WJDP, MHI; WJD cable to 106, Jan. 10, 1945, B: 364, E: 210, RG226, NA.

253   *"of the party":* WJD memo to JCS on OSS Special Operations in Italy, Telegram from C-in-C (Kesselring), South-West, Feb. 26, 1945, B: 66B, WJDP, MHI; Final Report on Sauerkraut Operation #7 (Code-Idaho), March 6, 1945, B: 32, E: 99, RG226, NA; Final Report Operation "Sauerkraut No. 3," B: 27, E: 99, RG226, NA.

253-256   *As he shook to from scratch:* Kingsley, Jan. 7, 2008; *The Overseas Targets,* pp. xiii, 272; The Istanbul Mission—Certain C-E Aspects (addendum No. 1), Chapter XXXIII, Col. Otto von Hatz—A Summary, B: 35, E: 211, RG226, NA; AD/H memo to C.D., Feb. 14, 1944, HS 8-7, NAUK; AG/009 memo to WJD, March 2, 1944, Fr: 180-96, R: 118, OSS headquarters memo to Lanning Macfarland, July 3, 1945, Fr: 1131-35, R: 79, J. E. Toulmin letter to WJD, July 30, 1944, Fr: 319-20, R: 41, M1642, RG226, NA; J. G. O'Connor memo to WS, May 23, 1944, Irving Sherman memo to Hazel Haight, Sept. 26, 1944, with enclosure on "Report on My Istanbul Mission," Aug. 24, 1944, B: 16, E: 211, RG226, NA; Dogwood Requests Allied Protection for His Hungarian Contacts and Collaborators, J. T. Curtiss memo to R. J. Murphy, Sept.

12, 1945, B: 44, E: 211, RG226, NA; The Dogwood Organization, B: 386, E: 210, RG226, NA.

256-258 *Before he to the Nazis:* AWD memo to Hugh Wilson, July 11, 1942, B: 384, E: 210, RG226, NA; Center of Information Pro Deo newsletter, John Hughes memo to WS, April 22, 1941, Lester Houck memo to WS, July 23, 1945, Frederic Dolbeare memo to Alfred Du Pont, Dec. 7, 1943, B: 61 and 62, E: 92, RG226, NA; Frederic Dolbeare memo to Hugh Wilson, Dec. 4, 1943, B: 311, E: 210, RG226, NA; Frederic Dolbeare memos to Ferdinand Mayer, Oct. 20 and 31, and Nov. 7, 1944, to John C. Hughes, May 29, 1945, to AWD, Nov. 9, 1944, and to B. Homer Hall, April 25, 1945, Stephen B. L. Penrose memo to William Gold, Aug. 27, 1945, B: 375, E: 214, B: 121, E: 190, B: 7, E: 214, B: 423-24, E: 210, RG226, NA; WJD memo to FDR, July 3, 1944, Fr: 5, R: 24, The Kulturkampf Flares Up Again: Pius XII Against Mussolini, Hitler and Stalin, June 5, 1943, Fr: 626-42, R: 109, M1642, RG226, NA; Weinberg, p. 677; *The Overseas Targets*, p. 112.

CHAPTER 25: THE PLOT

260 *Dulles wrote:* Mauch, pp. 118-19; Bern cables to OSS headquarters, July 25, 1944, WJD memo to GCM, July 26, 1944, Bern cable to OSS headquarters, July 22, 1944, B: 18, E: 99, RG226, NA.

260-262 *Stauffenberg, in fact, to outside world:* Bern cables to Carib, Jackpot, and 140, April 6 and 7, 1944, Bern cable to OSS headquarters, #4111-12, Breakers, July 15, 1944, B: 235, E: 146, RG226, NA; WJD memos to FDR, July 22 and 29, 1944, Bern cable to OSS headquarters, #4085, Breakers, July 12, 1944, WJD memo to FDR, July 22, 1944, B: 18, E: 99, RG226, NA; Overtures by German Generals and Civilian Opposition for a Separate Armistice, May 16, 1944, Fr: 733, R: 19, Fr: 649-54, R: 125, M1642, RG226, NA.

262-263 *The day after to "mad adventure":* Erika Canaris letter to WJD, Nov. 15, 1945, Vol. XVII, Part 1, COR; WJD memo to FDR, July 26, 1944, Bern cable from 110 to Washington headquarters, Jan. 24, 1945, Bern cable to OSS headquarters #4361, Breakers, Aug. 5, 1944, WJD memo to GCM, July 24, 1944, B: 18, E: 99, RG226, NA.

264 *"to humanity":* WJD memo to GCM, July 24, 1944, The Attempt on Hitler's Life and Its Consequences, R&A No. 2387, July 27, 1944, 109 cable to DB, July 28, 1944, B: 18, E: 99, RG226, NA; Walter C. Langer memo to WJD, July 26, 1944, Fr: 23-27, R: 52, M1642, RG226, NA; Special Interrogation Series No. 10, Miss Johanna Wolf, Hitler's personal secretary since 1928, May 31, 1945, Vol. XCIX, COR; WJD cable to DB, July 28, 1944, B: 18, E: 99, RG226, NA.

264-265 *The American to two weeks:* Allen Dulles speech to the Erie County Bar Association, May 4, 1959, B: 17, ADP, PU; Lt. Gen. William W. Quinn interview, 1981, Senior Officer Oral History Program, pp. 57-63, 133-38, B: 19, WQP, MHI; Memorandum for D/A. C. of S., G-2, Oct. 30, 1944, 103.819/11-244, RG59, NA; Report from Algiers, Jacques' Story, B:63, E: 210 and B: 45, E:99, RG226, NA.

265-267 *After the to their country:* Memo to FDR, Jan. 24, 1945, B: 364, E: 210, RG226, NA; 140, Caserta memo to 106 and 154 Washington, Aug. 18, 1944, Hugh Wilson letter to WJD, Aug. 12, 1944, Joseph Rodrigo memo to Hugh Wilson, Aug. 27, 1944, B: 344, E: 210, RG226, NA.

267 *European operations:* Casey, pp. 142-43; Persico, *Casey*, pp. 53-55, 72; Helms, OHP, p. 8.

268 *Fritz Kolbe:* AWD interview, Sept. 28, 1944, B: unnumbered third and fourth boxes from the end of the collection, WJDP, MHI; AWD speech to the Erie County Bar Association, May 4, 1959, B: 17, ADP, PU; Grose, pp. 205-13; Persico, *Casey*, pp. 62-67; Casey, pp. 144-45.

268-269 *Other OSS to and Austria:* F. L. Mayer memo to Chief, SI, Dec. 13, 1943, B: 428, E: 210, RG226, NA; I. S. Dorfman memo to WJD, Feb. 4, 1944, Fr: 522-43, R: 68, George Pratt memo to WS, Aug. 22, 1944, Fr: 482-85, R: 82, 109 cable to 110, Aug. 2, 1944, Fr: 15-20, R: 81, WJD cable on Future OSS Operations in Central Europe, Sept. 1, 1944, Fr: 63-65, R: 81, M1642, RG226, NA.

270   *in Europe:* Legendre, OHP, p. 12; Chalou, p. 283; Mary Bancroft interview, July 16, 1980, B: Interviews—Bancroft to Sherwood 1945-undated, WJDP, MHI; vanden Heuvel, March 11, 2008; Mosely, pp. 164-65, 223-24; Grose, pp. 209-10, 247-48.

271   *Iron Cross: The Overseas Targets,* pp. 216-19, 250-55; Lankford, pp. 104, 106, 139-43.

272   *he said:* Chief, SI, ETO, memo to CO, OSS, ETO, July 24, 1945, Fr: 555-72, R: 80, M1642, RG226, NA; Casey, pp. 184-85; Persico, *Casey,* pp. 72-73, 83; *The Overseas Targets,* pp. 305-6; Helms, OHP, p. 6; Mauch, pp. 179-81.

273   *"anyone else":* Martini operation report, Leon Adrian and Joseph Bartoszek, Mission Critique: "Martini Team," J. W. Reczkiewiez memo to Joseph Dasher, May 28, 1945, B: 39, E: 115, RG226, NA.

CHAPTER 26: THE SIDESHOW

274   *with his allies:* Smith, *Shadow Warriors,* pp. 244-47; John Toulmin interview, June 13, 1945, B: unnumberd third and fourth boxes from the end of the collection, WJDP, MHI; David Donovan, Sept. 22, 2007; Brown, pp. 431-33.

275   *among equals: The Overseas Targets,* p. 131; WJD memo to FDR, July 8, 1944, Fr: 63, R: 24, Glavin cable to Toulmin, Aug. 23, 1944, Fr: 879, R: 84, T. A. Holdahl memo to WJD, June 6, 1944, Fr: 914-23, R: 84, M1642, RG226, NA.

275   *not to be sent:* "Wild Bill Donovan's Son with Gen. Mikhailovitch," United Press dispatch, March 2, 1944, B: 130, E: 99, RG226, NA; WJD letter to James Dunn, March 15, 1944, Fr: 33-37, R: 84, M1642, RG226, NA; FDR letter to WJD, March 22, 1944, B: 88C, WJDP, MHI; William Leahy memo to JCS, April 8, 1944, Fr: 1201-2, 1197, R: 84, M1642, RG226, NA; Kimball, vol. 3, pp. 80, 82.

276   *in Yugoslavia:* John Hughes memo to EB, Aug. 26, 1943, Penetration of Yugoslavia Project, Memorandum of Conversation with the Shepherd, May 5, 1944, WJD memo to FDR, May 21, 1944, Fr: 273-83, R: 31, Fr: 729, R: 19, Fr: 875-79, 883, R: 23, Fr: 2-912, R: 89, Fr: 883-1325, R: 85, M1642, RG226, NA.

276-278 *Donovan, however,* to *to the bill:* Stephen Penrose memo to Robert Joyce, B: 21 and 23, E: 154, RG226, NA; 109 cable to Maddox, Aug. 23, 1944, Fr: 240-63, R: 120, Memorandum of conversations with Brigadier Maclean and Marshal Tito, Aug. 10 and 11, 1944, Fr: 922-47, R: 84, WJD memo to FDR, July 4, 1944, Fr: 27-28, R: 24, Joyce and Mitchell cable to WS, Aug. 30, 1944, Fr: 230, R: 84, M1642, RG226, NA; Dunlop, pp. 445-46.

278-279 *McDowell's Ranger* to *early November: The Overseas Targets,* pp. 130-32; Robert McDowell's Report on Mission to Yugoslavia, Ranger Unit, Nov. 23, 1944, B: 21 and 23, E: 154, RG226, NA; Marshall Tito memo to U.S.A. Military Mission, Sept. 14, 1944, Fr: 1022-24, 1113, R: 84, Fr: 327-32, R: 24, M1642, RG226, NA; Foreign Office cable to Washington, Prime Minister to President, Sept. 1, 1944, FO 954-34A, NAUK; President Roosevelt to Prime Minister, No. 617, Sept. 4, 1944, CHAR 20-171-38, CA; WJD memo to FDR, Oct. 2, 1944, Fr: 171-73, R: 84, M1642, RG226, NA.

280   *where they clashed:* 109 cable to Glavin and EH, Oct. 5, 1944, Fr: 523, R: 85, 109 cable to Glavin, Sept. 10, 1944, Fr: 467-68, R: 84, WJD memo to CH, Oct. 5, 1944, Fr: 164, R: 20, 1037 cable to 109 and 552, Oct. 9, 1944, EB memo to FDR, Jan. 4, 1943, Fr: 293, 306, 308, R: 31, WJD memo to JCS Nov. 3, 1944, Fr: 1128-30, R: 18, CC memo to Secretary of State, May 3, 1945, Fr: 346-47, R: 31, WJD memo to FDR, May 13, 1945, Fr: 99-100, R: 85, M1642, RG226, NA.

280-282 *While Churchill* to *not be intimidated:* Klurfeld, pp. 66-79; Ernest Cuneo Manuscript on the OSS and BSC, N-P File, ECP, FDRL; Wilson Brown memo for all Map Room personnel, Dec. 18, 1944, Map Room Files, HHP, FDRL; WC cable to Lord Halifax, Sept. 15, 1944, CHAR 20-171-91, CA; "Washington Merry-Go-Round," by Drew Pearson, *Washington Post,* Aug. 19, 1944; Putzell, OHP, p. 40; WC cable to WJD through WBS, Aug. 24, CHAR 20-170-77-78, CA; WBS letter to WC, Aug. 26, 1944, CHAR 20-146B-153, CA; Keegan, pp. 312-13; EB memo to FDR, Dec. 27, 1944, Fr: 1051, R: 24, M1642, RG226, NA.

CHAPTER 27: STOCKHOLM

283   *to London:* WJD note to FDR, Nov. 27, 1944, PPF 6558, FDRL; WJD letter to Grace Tully with Roper analysis enclosed, Oct. 15, 1944, Fr: 997–98, R: 30, M1642, RG226, NA; Memo to Gen. Clarke, Dec. 17, 1945, B: 26, E: 12, GP, RG263, NA.

284   *knew full well:* "The Charming People," by Austine Cassini, *Washington Times-Herald,* Nov. 30, 1944; Tippaparn Donovan, Jan. 24, 2008; Wise, Jan. 27, 2008; Mugler, Jan. 21, 2008; McIntosh, April 7, 2009; Howe, July 19, 2009; Gilbert, April 10, 2009; David G. Donovan, April 25, 2009; Beecher, Sept. 26, 2008; Mary Grandin Donovan Personnel Folder Copy, Oct. 2, 1944, Report of Efficiency Rating for Mary G. Donovan, Aug. 4, 1945, Box 194, Entry 244, RG226, NA.

284   *overseas trips:* WJD memo to Martin McHugh, Dec. 6, 1944, EP memo to McHugh, Dec. 2, 1944, EP memo to Mayo, Dec. 12, 1944, Fr: 479–83, R: 45, M1642, RG226, NA.

285   *the Red Army:* Caserta memo, Nov. 3, 1944, Fr: 517, R: 87, Joseph Rodrigo memo to WJD, Oct. 3, 1944, Fr: 965–66, R: 87, Edward Glavin memo to WJD, Sept. 11, 1944, Fr: 971–73, R: 86, WJD memo to JCS, Nov. 18, 1944, Fr: 1053–55, R: 62, M1642, RG226, NA.

285   *leaving Moscow:* WJD memo to FDR, May 14, 1945, Fr: 314–15, R: 57, Wisner cable to Joyce and Maddox, Nov. 3, 1944, Fr: 511–13, R: 87, Detention of Captain Madison and Captain Kuhn by Russian Soldiers, May 5, 1945, Fr: 233–39, R: 105, CC memo to FDR, Sept. 12, 1944, Fr: 298, R: 24, *The Overseas Targets,* p. 333; P. M. Fitin letter to John Deane, April 9, 1945, B: 18, E: 309, RG226, NA.

286   *"necessary intelligence":* *The Overseas Targets,* pp. 331–35; WJD memo to GCM, Aug. 5, 1944, Fr: 492–94, R: 20, M1642, RG226, NA; Biagio M. Corvo memo to WJD, Sept. 10, 1944, B: 356, E: 210, RG226, NA.

286   *Japanese embassy:* *The Overseas Targets,* pp. 261–67; Wilho Tikander memo to WS, Dec. 10, 1945, B: 435, E: 210, RG226, NA; I. S. Dorfman memo to WJD, May 23, 1945, B: 12, E: 211, RG226, NA; Taylor, Stockholm cable to OSS headquarters, May 26, 1945, B: 379, E: 210, RG226, NA.

287   *in Washington:* WJD memo to A. H. Onthank, March 31, 1944, WJD letter to Wilho Tikander, Sept. 13, 1944, Fr: 465, 480–514, R: 79, M1642, RG226, NA.

287–288   *One of Tikander's to bought the codes:* Memo on WJD conference with ES, Oct. 24, 1944, 109 cable to 155, Nov. 3, 1944, Tikander memo to WJD, Dec. 11, 1944, B: 362, E: 210, RG226, NA; James Dunn memo to ES, Dec. 18, 1944, Box 145, 103.918/12-1844, 1940-44 Central Decimal File, RG59, NA; WJD memo to FDR, Dec. 11, 1944, Subject File OSS, Reports 12-8 to 15-44, FDRL; Aid, pp. 19–37.

289   *OSS archives:* Warner and Benson, pp. 1–13; Matters to Discuss with the President, Dec. 20, 1944, Department File, State, Stettinius, Edward, December 1944, PSF, FDRL; EB letter to John Deane, Jan. 1945, John Deane letters to P. M. Fitin, Jan. 9 and Feb. 15, 1945, B: 18, E: 309, RG226, NA; Weinstein and Vassilev, pp. 246–47; Putzell, OHP, pp. 45–46; Biographical Information About Delegates to the San Francisco Conference, R&A Report 2995, Andrei Gromyko entry, B: 60, WJDP, MHI.

289   *German moles:* Notes on meeting with WJD, Ambassador Murphy, and staff, Jan. 4, 1945, B: 359, E: 210, RG226, NA; Smith, *Shadow Warriors,* pp. 352–53; Kingsley, Jan. 7, 2008.

290   *on their own:* *Washington Evening Star* article, Dec. 14, 1944, B: 130, E: 99, RG226, NA; James Murphy memo to WJD, Nov. 2, 1944, Fr: 1110–20, R: 46, WJD memo to FDR, Feb. 22, 1945, Fr: 226–29, R: 25, M1642, RG226, NA; Roger Pfaff memo to WJD with enclosed report on OSS-FBI Relationships, Feb. 22, 1945, B: 358, E: 210, RG226, NA; Riebling, p. 58.

291   *"the right time":* Stout, pp. 6, 11–12; Howe, July 19, 2009; S. A. Callise to Horace Andrews memos, Nov. 28, 1944, EB memo to WJD, Dec. 6, 1944, Fr: 904-6, 913, R: 121, M1642, RG226, NA; John Grombach memo to G-2, Dec. 4, 1945, with enclosure, B: 1, Draft Pond history, Memo to Director of Information, Feb. 18, 1946, Pond memos on OSS officers, B: 5, 7, 18, and 19, Grombach monograph on OSS, B: 18, E: 12, GP, RG226, NA.

CHAPTER 28: THE VATICAN

292   *their grandmother:* Gilbert, Oct. 29, 2007; Banta, Jan. 28, 2008.
292–295 *Donovan's holiday* to *wishing her well:* Legendre, OHP, pp. 13–37; Lt. Cdr. Robert Jennings statement, April 4, 1945, B: 118, E: 148, RG226, NA; Gertrude Legendre résumé, British Empire Section memo to DB, Jan. 21, 1943, B: 17, E: 92A, RG226, NA; Walter Hochschild memo to CO, SCI, Twelfth AG, Sept. 29, 1944, Norman Holmes Pearson memo to Russell Forgan, Oct. 23, 1944, Allen Dulles memo to WJD with statement made by "Gertrude," March 29, 1945, Fr: 6–255, R: 69, WJD letter to John McCloy, Nov. 4, 1944, Fr: 1299–1300, R: 20, M1642, RG226, NA; Keiste Janulis memo to G-2 Section, Oct. 25, 1944, B: 17, E: 92A, RG226, NA.
295   *"and discredit":* JJ 001, London cable to WJD, April 2, 1945, B: 346, E: 210, RG226, NA; 109 cable to Forgan, March 27, 1945, WJD letter to James Dunn, April 4, 1945, Archbold van Beuren memo to CC, April 13, 1945, WJD letter to Gertrude Legendre, June 18, 1945, WJD cables to Forgan, Armour, Cheston, and Morgan, April 5 and 12, 1945, Fr: 6–255, R: 69, Charles Bane note to WJD, Oct. 27, 1944, Fr: 1273–75, R: 94, M1642, RG226, NA.
296   *he said:* Constantin Bertakis letter to Dunlop, Feb. 17, 1981, B: 19, RDP, MHI; Wayne Nelson interview, Jan. 25, 1984, KNP; Vincent Scamporino memo to W. P. Maddox, Oct. 2, 1944, John Wilson memo to WS with enclosure, Feb. 3, 1945, B: 386, E: 210, RG226, NA.
297   *of secrets:* Mangold, pp. 31–43; 109 cable to 106, Jan. 10, 1945, Fr: 186, R: 114, M1642, RG226, NA; Chalou, pp. 218–30; Gorian, OHP, p. 3; Hood, Dec. 11, 2008; Angleton, Dec. 17, 2008.
297–302 *But with* to *a future CIA:* CC letter to Grace Tully, Jan. 11, 1945, Report No. JR-1358, Dec. 4, 1944, Vessel 6-a. report, Vessel report on Results of B-29 Raid on Armored Car Plant, Jan. 6, 1945, Roger Pfaff memo to JM on Vessel Traffic, March 22, 1945, JM cable to Joyce, Jan. 6, 1945, John Davenport cable to L. C. Houck, Jan. 25, 1945, 622 cables to 154, Jan. 8, 10, 12, 15, and 16, 1945, 109 cable to CC, Jan. 24, 1945, CC memos to FDR, Jan. 24 and 25, 1945, EP memo for files, Jan. 27, 1945, Joyce cable to JM, April 9, 1945, 622 cable to 154 and 198, Jan. 22, 1945, Joyce cable to JM, Jan. 26, 1945, Craig cable to Argonaut for Hall, Feb. 4, 1945, CC memo to JCS, Feb. 2, 1945, CC memo to FDR, Feb. 2, 1945, 109 cable to 148, Feb. 9, 1945, WJD memo to FDR, Feb. 16, 1945, Mero and 148 cable to 109 et al., Feb. 15, 1945, JM and WS cable to 148 and 622, Feb. 17, 1945, James Dunn letter to WJD, March 2, 1945, JM and 154 cable to Glavin et al., March 3, 1945, WJD letter to James Dunn, March 8, 1945, Vessel Traffic, EB memo to FDR, April 11, 1945, JM memo to Director of Naval Intelligence, June 2, 1945, Fr: 2–486, R: 119, M1642, RG226, NA; Rome #284 cable to Saint, July 18, 1945 (Previously Withheld), B: 717, E: 190, RG226, NA; Harold Tittmann letter to Frederick Lyon, April 3, 1945, B: 521, E: 210, RG226, NA; Graham, pp. 719–21; "Leaky Vessel," *Radio Times,* April 10–16, 1982, pp. 17–18; John D. Wilson memo to WS with enclosure on meeting minutes with WJD, B: 386, E: 210, RG226, NA; Chalou, pp. 230–33, 243.

CHAPTER 29: THE LEAK

304   *"for Berlin":* Weinberg, pp. 802–9; WVHD, p. 54, WJDP, MHI; Bern cable to OSS headquarters, March 2, 1945, Fr: 258–59, R: 25, M1642, RG226, NA.
304–305 *It was* to *previous fall:* "Donovan Proposes Super Spy System for Postwar New Deal," by Walter Trohan, *Washington Times-Herald,* Feb. 9, 1945; Walter Trohan interview, Oct. 7, 1970, pp. 15–23, Oral History Interviews, HSTL.
306   *police functions:* Troy, *Donovan and the CIA,* pp. 216–21; The Basis for a Permanent U.S. Foreign Intelligence Service, Oct. 5, 1944, Fr: 1176–91, 1097, R: 3, M1642, RG226, NA.
306   *"salary increase":* Rosenbaum memos to WJD, Oct. 7, 12, 20, 21, and 23, 1944, Louis Ream memo to WJD, Oct. 26, 1944, Fr: 1176–91, 1097, R: 3, Isadore Lubin memo to

FDR, Oct. 25, 1944, Fr: 778–79, R: 3, Fr: 802, R: 24, M1642, RG226, NA; Troy, *Donovan and the CIA*, pp. 221–22; Isadore Lubin interview, Jan. 12, 1972, B: 7, TTP, RG263, NA.

307   *shark tank:* Joseph Rosenbaum interview, Jan. 10, 1972, B: 7, TTP, RG263, NA; WL interview, Feb. 5, 1969, B: 136B, WJDP, MHI; WJD memo to FDR with enclosed Substantive Authority Necessary in Establishment of a Central Intelligence Service, Nov. 18, 1944, Fr: 802–7, R: 24, M1642, RG226, NA.

307   *newsman's plan:* Memo to WJD on Statement of Gen. Bissell in Letter of Nov. 20, 1944, Clayton Bissell letter to WJD, Nov. 20, 1944, Fr: 393–43, R: 121, Fr: 1287–91, R: 20, M1642, RG226, NA; Stout, p. 7; Memo No. 69, July 19, 1944, B: 26, E: 12, GP, RG263, NA; John Franklin Carter's Report on Bill Donovan's Plan for Post-war Secret Intelligence, Oct. 26, 1944, FDR memo to WJD, Oct. 31, 1944, Subject File OSS, Donovan, William, 10-9-44 to 4-11-45, PSF, FDRL; WJD memo to FDR, Nov. 7, 1944, Fr: 1141–49, R: 3, M1642, RG226, NA.

308   *every week:* U.S. Secret Worldwide Intelligence Coverage, Sept. 3, 1945, B: 8, TTP, RG263, NA; FBI; Troy, *Donovan and the CIA*, pp. 252–53; JEH letter to HH, Dec. 29, 1944, DOJ Rpt. No. 2609, OF10B, FDRL; HH diaries 1942–46, HH Appointment Diary 1944, entries for Dec. 5, 11, 16, 1944, HLHP, GU; HH telephone messages, July 27, 1944–July 7, 1945, HHP, FDRL; HH note, Jan. 8, 1945 with two memos, 62-76274-32X (102), N.Y. letter, Feb. 21, 1945, 66-16300 (107), Tamm memo to JEH, Dec. 22, 1944, 94-4-4672-25, FBI.

309   *the measure:* Howe, Sept. 25, 2007; JM cable to 109, Dec. 28, 1944, Fr: 696–705, R: 3, Joint Intelligence Committee Proposed Establishment of a Central Intelligence Service, Dec. 20, 1944, Appendix "A" Draft Memorandum from the JCS to the President, Fr: 1102–4, 1034–63, R: 13, M1642, RG226, NA; Troy, *Donovan and the CIA*, pp. 231–55.

309   *radio listeners:* OCD interview, Jan. 13 and 14, 1972, B: 7, TTP, RG263, NA; "Seeking Correlation of U.S. Intelligence Services," *Illinois State Journal*, March 26, 1945; "Donovan Upheld on Peace Spy Plan," *New York Times*, Feb. 13, 1945; "Donovan's Plan," *Washington Post*, Feb. 16, 1945; Edward R. Murrow script for CBS radio broadcast, Feb. 18, 1943, Fr: 771–885, R: 3, M1642, RG226, NA.

309   *American taxpayers:* "Postwar Spy Plan Assailed by Senators," by Walter Trohan, *Washington Times-Herald*, Feb. 10, 1945; "Army, Navy Want Control of 'Spy' Setup," by Walter Trohan, *Washington Times-Herald*, Feb. 11, 1945, "Bigger and Better Spying," *Chicago Tribune*, Feb. 10, 1945; Editorial cartoon "Life in the Brave New World," *Washington Times-Herald*, Feb. 20, 1945.

310   *"into peacetime":* Bureau letter to all SACs, Feb. 16, 1945, enclosing Trohan newspaper clippings, 66-04-36 (106), FBI; European Section Reference to U.S. Affairs, U.S. to Spy on Allies Through OSS, "A Net of Jewish Informers Throughout the World," *Tagespost* (Graz), Feb. 11, 1945, FB/001 memo to DH/001, March 13, 1945, Fr: 785–871, R: 8, M1642, RG226, NA; Political Situation in the United States, Feb. 17, 1945, Foreign Office report, FO 371-44542.

310   *what he said:* Interview with OCD, pp. 139–40, 338, B: "Oral History Interviews—OCD, Activities in Europe 1941–89," WJDP, MHI; WJD memo to FDR, Feb. 23, 1945, OCD memo to WJD, Feb. 13, 1945, Fr: 785–871, R: 3, M1642, RG226, NA.

311   *two documents:* OCD memo to WJD, Feb. 13, 1945, E. F. Cress memo to WJD with enclosures, Feb. 13, 1943, Fr: 785–871, R: 3, M1642, RG226, NA; Donovan notes on persons who received copies of the postwar CIA plan, OSS word-for-word analysis of Walter Trohan's Feb. 9 and 11, 1945, news stories, B: 222, E: 146, RG226, NA; Hewlett Thebaud and Clayton Bissell memo to JCS, Feb. 13, 1945, F. R. Sweeney memo to Gen. McFarland Feb. 14, 1945, I.G. notes on Trohan article and copies of Donovan plan with the FBI, B: 6, TTP, RG263, NA; Tamm memo to JEH, March 10, 1945, 94-4-4672-24, FBI.

311   *the enemy:* Clayton Bissell memo to JCS, April 10, 1945, B: 6, TTP, RG263, NA; WJD memo to JCS, Feb. 15, 1945, Fr: 785–871, R: 3, M1642, RG226, NA; Walter Trohan letter to Thomas Troy, Feb. 9, 1977, B: 7, TTP, RG263, NA.

312   *leaker were high:* Walter Trohan letter to Thomas Troy, Feb. 9, 1977, B: 7, TTP, RG263, NA; Trohan, "Knifing of the OSS," pp. 95–106; Itinerary of President's Trip to Crimea Conference, Jan. 22–Feb. 28, 1945, members of the President's Party, Subject File, Trips—Crimea Jan.–Feb. 1945, SEP, FDRL; L. B. Nichols memo to Tolson, March 24, 1955, B: 16, E: 14B, RG65, NA; Gentry, pp. 233, 314–15. A number of journalists and historians have concluded that Hoover leaked Donovan's postwar intelligence plan to Trohan; however, there is no documentary evidence in either the extensive OSS records or the FBI records that proves conclusively that Hoover was the leaker. The documents show only that he was likely Trohan's source.

312   *Roosevelt agreed:* GCM memo to JCS, Feb. 22, 1945, B: 6, TTP, RG263, NA; William Leahy memo to FDR, March 6, MR. Naval Aides Files: Intelligence (163), FDRL; Harold Smith memo to FDR, March 2, 1945, White House Memoranda, Jan.–April 1945, HSP, FDRL.

313   *scale back his group:* Putzell, OHP, pp. 76–77; Bishop, p. 440; McLaughlin, OHP, pp. 35–37; Heckscher, OHP, p. 6; Dewitt Poole memos to WJD, March 14 and 16, 1945, Edward Haines memo to E. F. Connely, April 17, 1945, Fr: 1002–1197, R: 107, M1642, RG226, NA.

314   *back him up:* Donovan appointment book, April 2, 4, and 6, 1945, B: 98A & B, WJDP, MHI; Isadore Lubin memo to FDR, April 4, 1945, Subject File OSS Donovan, William, 10-9-44 to 4-11-45, PSF, FDRL; WJD letters to twelve cabinet officers and agency heads, April 6, 1945, Fr: 6–7, R:21, Fr: 415–17, 872–73, 473–74, R: 3, FDR memo to WJD, April 5, 1945, and WJD response, April 6, 1945, Fr: 511, R: 25, Fr: 931, R: 134, M1642, RG226, NA.

CHAPTER 30: HARRY TRUMAN

315   *their faces:* EB memo to JCS, April 13, 1945, Fr: 133–34, R: 22, M1642, RG226, NA; John Wilson memo to EP, July 20, 1946, Claridge's hotel bills for WJD for April 1945, B: 139B, WJDP, MHI; Progress Report memo to Strategic Services Officer, ETO, May 3, 1945, B: 6, E: 99, RG226, NA.

316   *kidnap missions:* Mauch, pp. 175–78; Covering Report for OSS/ETO, April 1–15, 1945, B: 6, E: 99, RG226, NA; Edward Gamble memo to Supreme Commander Allied Expeditionary Forces, March 31, 1945, B: 122, E: 148, RG226, NA; Minutes of Conference of WJD with SO Branch, April 11, 1945, Fr: 1041–52, R: 80, M1642, RG226, NA; Organizational, Administrative and Other Decisions Taken in the European Theater During WJD Visit, April 7–24, 1945, B: 185, E: 210, RG226, NA; Cross Project, SO Branch Paris, Jan.–March 1945, Cross Project Planning, Gerald Miller memo, Feb. 7, 1945, Edward Gamble memo, Feb. 14, 1945, B: 310, E: 210, RG226, NA.

317–318 *Wednesday, April 11 to carried out:* Did FDR actually read the 7,500 pages of material Donovan sent him over four years? Some historians contend the president was too busy to digest much of it. They point to the fact that Roosevelt only occasionally wrote on the margins of Donovan memos or sent him back responses as evidence he read little of them. But FDR made few notations on many of the memos he received. Roosevelt may have read more of the material than he is given credit. Because he was wheelchair-bound, FDR was confined to his desk for long periods and occupied his time reading the piles of documents in his in-box, other historians speculate. Interestingly, many of the Donovan memos that prompted a Roosevelt response dealt with inconsequential subjects, which may indicate that he did read much of what Donovan sent. Bishop, pp. 509–24; Persico, *Roosevelt's Secret War,* p. 434; EB memo to FDR, April 9, 1945, Subject File OSS, Reports, April 1945, PSF, FDRL; EB memo to Grace Tully with memo to FDR enclosed, April 11, 1945, Fr: 533–37, R: 25, EB memo to FDR, April 10, 1945, Fr: 533–37, R: 25, Donovan cables to Glavin, May 12 and June 19, 1945, Fr: 346, R: 114, WJD memo to FDR, March 10, 1945, Fr: 317–23, R: 25, A. J. McFarland memos to WJD, April 20 and 26, 1945, WJD memo to FDR, April 28, 1945, Fr: 1110–1393, R: 113, M1642, RG226, NA; Salter, pp. 109–75; *The Overseas Targets,* pp. xiv, 323–25;

Smith and Agarossi, *Operation Sunrise*, pp. 3–6, 50–51, 184–87. Because Wolff negotiated Sunrise, Dulles managed to shield him from prosecution in the first round of the Nuremberg trials. But justice caught up with the SS general, who was finally convicted of war crimes in 1964.

318–319   *Donovan flew to died as well:* J. R. Murphy memo to WJD, April 20, 1945, B: 185, E: 210, RG226, NA; Casey, p. 201; Women in Federal Government Project Interview with Margaret Joy Tibbetts, Sept. 8 and 9, 1982, pp. iii–iv, 15–16, Schlesinger Library, Radcliffe College; WJD cable to Eleanor Roosevelt, April 13, 1945, Fr: 538–39, R: 25, M1642, RG226, NA; Interview with OCD, p. 230, B: "Oral History Interviews—OCD, Activities in Europe, 1941–89," WJDP, MHI; OCD interview, Jan. 13 and 14, 1972, B: 7, TTP, RG263, NA; Brown, 736–38.

320   *them all:* Brown, pp. 742–44, Benito Mussolini autopsy report, Institute of Legal Medicine and Insurance of the Royal University of Milan, April 30, 1945, B: 69B, WJDP, MHI; 109 cable to 110, April 28, 1945, Fr: 1190, R: 54, JM cable to 109, Aug. 7, 1945, Fr: 1190–97, R: 54, M1642, RG226, NA.

320   *Donovan was to impress him:* Dunlop, p. 467; HST letter to Bess Truman, June 6, 1945, Correspondence with Bess Wallace Truman, 1921–59, HSTP, HSTL; The White House, June 17, 1945, Longhand Notes 1930–55, July 17 and July 4, 1945, PSF, HSTL.

321   *direct access:* McCullough, pp. 365–66; Demaris, pp. 101–3, 281; Harold Smith diary entries, May 11 and Sept. 18, 1945, HSD, HSP, FDRL; Harry Vaughan oral history interview, Jan. 14 and 16, 1963, pp. 85–87, HSTL; HST note, May 12, 1945, Longhand Notes, 1930–55, PSF, HSTL; Morton Chiles memo to JEH, Sept. 22, 1945, B: 8, TTP, RG263, NA; Harry Vaughan letter to JEH, April 23, 1945, OF 10-B, FBI, WHCF, HSTL.

321   *Democratic administration:* Merle Miller, pp. 94–95; Hamby, pp. 77–78, 474; 160: Bureau memo, May 2, 1945, 62-76274-88 (117), FBI.

322   *war stories:* EP letter to Rose Conway, April 19, 1945, Rose Conway Files, OSS-Donovan—War Information Reports, SMOF, HSTL; MJC note to Mrs. Eben, Aug. 23, 1945, PPF 1833, HSTL; WJD memo to HST, May 11, 1945, R: 57, A-3304, RG226, NA; HST note to WJD, Aug. 24, 1945, Fr: 617, R: 72, WJD memo to HST May 12, 1945, Fr: 660–61, R: 3, WJD memo to HST, Aug. 23, 1945, Fr: 691, R: 25, M1642, RG226, NA.

322   *was Harry Truman:* WJD letter to HST, April 30, 1945, Fr: 953–54, R: 25. Letters from the twelve agencies and cabinet departments to WJD's April 6, 1945, memo requesting comment on his postwar intelligence plan can be found in Fr: 419–43, 507–9, Fr: 1015–17, R: 134. WJD letter to Sen. Scott Lucas, Aug. 31, 1945, R: 3, Fr: 677, WJD memo to Sen. Kilgore, Aug. 8, 1945, Fr: 944–51, R: 3, WJD memo to Sen. Byrnes, June 17, 1945, Fr: 374, R: 57, M1642, RG226, NA.

322   *"even basis":* Harold Smith diary entries, April 18 and 26, 1945, HSD, HSP, FDRL; "Gloria's Marriage to 'Stokie' Amazes Her Mother Most," *Washington Daily News*, April 28, 1945; Bureau memo, June 26, 1945, 62-77787-1081, p. 161 (39), FBI; Drew Pearson broadcast transcript, May 6, 1945, memo on Drew Pearson, May 11, 1945, Fr: 888–904, R: 99, M1642, RG226, NA; Brown, p. 638; HST diary entry, May 14, 1945, President's Appointments File 1945–53, Daily Sheets April–Oct. 1945 Files, PSF, HSTL.

323   *"United States":* WJD memo to HST, Aug. 18, 1945, W.D.L. memo to HST, Aug. 22, 1945, HST letter to WJD, Aug. 25, 1945, Confidential File, OSS (Korea, 945), WHCF, HSTL.

324   *the prosecution:* Salter, pp. 2, 5–6, 309; John Ciechanowski letter to WJD with enclosure, Oct. 15, 1943, WJD memo to List S, Dec. 15, 1944, WJD memo to Louis Ream, April 6, 1945, WJD memo to FDR, March 29, 1945, Fr: 44–60, 88–323 R: 121, EB letter to CH with enclosure, Feb. 1, 1944, Fr: 678–80, R: 19, M1642, RG226, NA; Storey, pp. xvii–xviii.

324   *last moment:* Interview with OCD, p. 483, B: "Oral History Interviews—OCD, Activities in Europe, 1941–89," WJDP, MHI; WJD memo to FDR, Fr: 642, R: 81, CC and 154 cable to 110, Feb. 27, 1945, Fr: 874–76, R: 81, M1642, RG226, NA.

325   *the Reichsmarschall:* Salter, pp. 309–33; *Byways of Law,* by James B. Donovan, B: 37, JDP, HIA; Robert Jackson diary entries, May 7, 11, 11, and 15, 1945, B: 95, RJP, LOC.

326   on the spot: Jackson, OHC, pp. 12, 1216; Sheldon Glueck memo to WJD, June 14, 1945, Fr: 88–323, R: 121, M1642, RG226, NA; James Donovan cable to Robert Jackson, June 1, 1945, B: 101, RJP, LOC; Sylvester Missal memo to James Donovan, July 20, 1945, File: WN 6897(10), B: 185, E: 210, RG226, NA; Salter, pp. 247–366; McLaughlin, OHP, p. 38; Alderman, OHC, pp. 914–15; Jackson, OHC, pp. 1234–47.

326   the suggestions: WJD letters to Robert Jackson, June 15, 16 and July 12, 1945, Fr: 88–323, R: 121, M1642, RG226, NA; Robert Jackson diary entries, May 27 and Sept. 5, 1945, B: 95, RJP, LOC; Salter, pp. 340, 362, 368–69; James Wright letter to A. H. Kirchofer, Jan. 11, 1946, B: 19, RDP, MHI.

326–328   Donovan flew back to comes first: Donovan appointment book, July 11–12, 1945, B: 98A & B, WJDP, MHI; Robert Jackson diary entries, June 1 and 16, 1945, B: 95, RJP, LOC.

329   Ike declared: Walter Trohan stories, "MacArthur Rejects Offer of OSS Propaganda Staff," May 16, 1945, and "Rep. Shafer Reveals Nimitz Also Rejected Aid of OSS," May 20, 1945, Washington Times-Herald; 109 cable to EB and CC, May 20, 1945, Fr: 1–230, R: 100, 109 cables to overseas stations, May 25, 1945, Fr: 10–17, R: 28, M1642, RG226, NA. Letters from the JCS and theater commanders to the House Appropriations Committee evaluating the OSS can be found in B: 9, Chairman's File Adm. Leahy 1942–48, RG281, NA, and Fr: 236–37, R: 126, M1642, RG226, NA.

329   media stars: Walter Trohan stories, "OSS Is Branded British Agency to Legislators" and "British Control of OSS Bared in Congress Probe," May 18 and 19, 1945, Washington Times-Herald; "In the Nation," by Walter Krock, New York Times, July 31, 1945.

329–330   One of to his agency: "Washington Merry-Go-Round" columns by Drew Pearson, May 25 and July 9, 1945, Washington Post; 109 cable to CC, April 24, 1945, 109 cable to Forgan, April 30, 1945, James Murphy memo to WJD, May 9, 1945, 109 cable to Forgan, May 12, 1945, Fr: 68, 72–77, 79, 84, R: 46, WJD letter to John McCloy, Fr: 1132–34, R: 21, M1642, RG226, NA; OCD memo to Joint Security Control, July 21, 1945, A. van Beuren memos to WJD, Sept. 7, 1945, OCD memo to WJD, June 15, 1945, WJD memorandum on conversation with Francis Biddle, June 15, 1945, R: 84, A-3304, RG226, NA.

331   thousand prisoners: Jackson, OHC, pp. 1296–99; Salter, pp. 355–62; Storey, p. 87.

331   that mission: Persico, Casey, p. 84; CC memo to GCM, Fr: 1390–94, R: 82, WJD memo to JCS, July 18, 1945, Fr: 589–91, R: 89, M1642, RG226, NA; Rumors Approved by the Rumor Committee, Jan. 20, 1945, B: 185, E: 210, RG226, NA.

332   appear surprised: WJD party for Asia trip, July 22, 1945, Fr: 634–42, R: 32, M1642, RG226, NA; Report of Compliance with Orders for Lt. David R. Donovan, Jan. 9, 1945, Officer's Fitness Report for David R. Donovan, March 1, 1945, NRPC.

332   "not a peace": Coughlin cable to 154, Aug. 10, 1945, Fr: 906, R: 90, M1642, RG226, NA; MacDonald, pp. 221–23; Caldwell, pp. 192–95; Robert Jackson diary entry, Oct. 8, 1945, B: 95, RJP, LOC.

333   didn't like it: John Shaheen memo for files, Oct. 14, 1945, Fr: 232–52, R: 100, Fisher Howe memo to OCD, Aug. 11, 1945, Fr: 267–87, R: 100, M1642, RG226, NA; "Capital Ax Falling on Our Priceless Secret Spy System," by Wallace Deuel, Sept. 4, 1945, Chicago Daily News; Wallace Deuel memo to Fisher Howe, WJD memo to Wallace Deuel, Aug. 15, 1945, with drafts of Deuel's OSS stories, B: 61, WDP, LOC; British embassy Washington cable to Foreign Office, Sept. 15, 1945, FO 371-4453B, NAUK; Troy, Donovan and the CIA, pp. 295–96; Howe, July 19, 2009.

333–334   The press to his diary: "Cloak and Dagger Pay," Newsweek, Aug. 13, 1945; "OSS Fighting to Continue Its Propaganda Program" and "OSS Survival Plan Attacked as Plot for U.S. Super-Gestapo," by Walter Trohan, Sept. 8 and 9, 1945, Washington Times-Herald; WJD letter to Harold Smith with enclosure, Aug. 25, 1945, WJD memo to HST, Aug. 25, 1945, WJD memo to HST, Sept. 13, 1945, WJD memo to JCS, Sept. 13, 1945, Fr: 455–826, R: 3, M1642, RG226, NA; Troy, Donovan and the CIA, p. 296; Harold Smith diary entries, Sept. 13 and 20, 1945, HSD, HSP, FDRL; Harold Smith letter to HST, Aug. 18, 1945, Subject File, 1945, Liquidation of War Agencies, SRP, HSTL.

335   on his desk: Harold Smith diary entries, July 6, Sept. 5, 1945, HSD, HSP, FDRL; Gentry, pp. 325–27; Demaris, pp. 23–24; Harry Vaughan oral history interview, March 20,

1976, HSTL; Troy, *Donovan and the CIA*, pp. 272, 276; Warner, "Salvage and Liquidation," pp. 111, 114; S. J. Tracy memo to Tolson, Oct. 29, 1945, B: 8, TTP, RG263, NA; JEH memo to the Attorney General, Aug. 29, 1945, B: 8, TTP, RG263, NA; Gentry, p. 326; Gentry, Dec. 1, 2008, April 26, 2009; McCullough, pp. 135, 366; Gilbert, April 10, 2009; 1953 FBI background check on WJD, NY 77-16713, FBI; William H. Pryor report on WJD, June 23, 1945, 77-58706-21, FBI.

335–337 *Richard Park Jr. to "every five" lost:* Colonel Richard Park, Jr., Profile, March 15, 1945, Rose Conway Files, OSS-Donovan, William J., SMOF, HSTL; Remarks by Lt. Col. Richard Park, Jr., American Military Attaché in Russia, Jan. 25, 1943, Fr: 1077–81, R: 104, S.T.E. memo to FDR, June 6, 1944, Presidential Memos 1944, SEP, FDRL; Troy, "Knifing of the OSS," pp. 99–102; Clayton Bissell memorandum for the record, March 12, 1845, B: 6, TTP, RG263, NA; Elsey, July 24, 2008; George Elsey letter to author, Aug. 13, 2008; Warner, Nov. 21, 2007; JEH letter to HH, Dec. 29, 1944, DOJ Rpt. No. 2609, OF 10B, FDRL; Richard Park memo to HST with enclosed report, B: 6, TTP, RG263, NA; OSS Monograph, B: 18, Draft memo to National Intelligence Authority, B: 20, E: 12, GP, RG263, NA; Richard Harris Smith, p. 215; Crockett, OHP, p. 44; Rpt. No. 2199, Jan. 30, 1945, Fr: 203–12, R: 109, EB letter to Robert Shutt, June 6, 1944, Fr: 749, R: 19, M1642, RG226, NA; Atkinson, *The Day of Battle*, p. 451.

337 *stood for:* 109 cable to CC, July 1, 1945, German and Japanese Penetration of OSS in ETO, German intelligence charts on Joint Chiefs of Staff and the OSS, Bernd Steinitz memo to Chief, SICE, June 28, 1945, B: 358, E: 210, RG226, NA.

337–338 *Donovan spent to letter arrived:* Donovan appointment book, Sept. 15–16 and 20, 1945 B: 98A & B, WJDP, MHI; Harold Smith, Samuel Rosenman, and John Snyder memo to HST, Acting Secretary of State memo to HST, Sept. 17, 1945, Harold Smith memo to HST, Sept. 18, 1945, Office of Strategic Services, Executive Order Termination of the Office of Strategic Services and Disposition of Its Functions, Sept. 20, 1945, HST letter to WJD, Sept. 20, 1945, OF 128-B, HSTL; HST diary entry, Sept. 20, 1945, Longhand Notes File, PSF, HSTL.

CHAPTER 31: NUREMBERG

342 *biggest thief:* Robert Jackson diary entries, June 14, 1945, B: 95, RJP, LOC; Storey, pp. 85, 122, 137–40; Hermann Göring as a War Criminal, R&A Rept. No. 3152, June 25, 1945, Vol. XCVI, COR; The Göring Collection, OSS Consolidated Interrogation Report No. 2, Sept. 15, 1945, HGP, HIA.

343 *far from certain:* Jackson, OHC, p. 1372; Schlabrendorff, pp. 262–63; James L. Wright letter to A. H. Kirchhofer, Jan. 11, 1946, B: 19, RDP, MHI; Major Kelly memo to WJD, Nov. 9, 1945, Vol. XIX, COR; WVHD, pp. 10, 29, WJDP, MHI; Summary of Interrogation of Hermann Göring, Nov. 6, 1945, Fr: 675–76, R: 5, M1270, NA.

344 *OSS members:* "Berryville Social Events," Aug. 29, 1945, p. 8, "Millwood Social Events," Oct. 31, 1944, p. 6, and Dec. 6, 1944, p. 7, *Winchester Evening Star*; Reports of Compliance with Orders for Lt. David R. Donovan, Nov. 6 and Dec. 11, 1944, and Jan. 4, 1945, NPRC; Personnel Folder Copy for Mary G. Donovan, Sept. 27, 1945, B: 194, E: 244, RG226, NA; EP interview, B: 6, RDP, MHI; Alderman, OHC, pp. 803–4, 1390; James Donovan letter to Mary, Sept. 24, 1945, B: 34, JDP, HIA; "Remembering 109," by George P. Morse, OSS Society Newsletter, Spring 2006, p. 7; Storey, p. 96; Nat S. Finney letter to James Donovan with enclosure, B: 34, JDP, HIA; Salter, pp. 371–79.

344–345 *Jackson still to this conflict;* Putzell, OHP, p. 77; Salter, pp. 374–430; Dodd, p. 180; James Donovan letter to Mary on Thursday, B: 34, JDP, HIA; Jackson, OHC, pp. 1384–87; Storey, pp. 97–98; Alderman, OHC, p. 1389.

345 *"out of a hat":* WJD memo to Robert Jackson, Oct. 20, 1945, WJD memo to Jay Glebb, Nov. 28, 1945, Vol. XIX, COR; Salter, pp. 407, 413; Trial Brief on Hjalmar Schacht, Vol. XVI, Part 2, COR; Hjalmar Schacht letter to WJD with enclosure, Nov. 14, 1945, 48.05, Web site, COR; WJD memo to Robert Jackson, Nov. 14 and 24, 1945, Chief Counsel for Prosecution of Axis Criminality 1945–46 File, CF, WHCF, HSTL; Memo-

randum of interview between WJD and the Defendant Göring, Nov. 12, 1945, Vol. XIV, COR; Alderman, OHC, pp. 1431-33.

345-347 *Robert Jackson to leaving Nuremberg*: Salter, pp. 404, 424; Dodd, p. 186; Robert Jackson letters to WJD, Nov. 8 and 26, 1945, WJD letters to Robert Jackson, Nov. 7 and 27, 1945, Testimony of Erwin Lahousen, Nov. 23, 1945, U.S. Chief Counsel for Prosecution of Axis Criminality 1945-46 File, CF, WHCF, HSTL; Jackson, OHC, p. 1387; Alderman, OHC, pp. 1392-93; Testimony of Erwin Lahousen, B: 98, ADP, PU; Robert Jackson memo to WJD et al., Nov. 24, 1946, Vol. XIX, COR.

347 *bad apple*: Dodd, pp. 190, 201, 204, 208, 255; Salter, pp. 433-47; Jackson, OHC, pp. 1387-88; "Donovan Quits, Revealing Rift in War Trial Staff," *Washington Times-Herald*, Nov. 29, 1945; Robert Jackson letter to Charles Horsky, Dec. 1, 1945, B: 101, RJP, LOC; Robert Jackson letter to HST with enclosures, Dec. 1, 1945, U.S. Chief Counsel for Prosecution of Axis Criminality 1945-46 File, CF, WHCF, HSTL.

348 *they got*: J.E.S. memo to WJD, Vol. XIX, COR; Persico, *Nuremberg*, pp. 324, 406, 430-47; "Washington Merry-Go-Round: Nuremberg Verdict Worries Ike," by Drew Pearson, *Washington Post*, B: 121B, WJDP, MHI; Salter, pp. 6-7, 438; Storey, pp. 125-31; "War Crimes, *Time*, Oct. 7, 1946, p. 14; Martoche, Dec. 3, 2007, Martoche, "William J. Donovan: More to Remember," p. 11. A rumor spread among Donovan's former agents that the poison pill Göring took came from the OSS, which had always been well stocked with the tablets. But the more plausible speculation pointed to a sympathetic U.S. Army lieutenant guarding Göring named Jack Wheelis, who may have retrieved an article with the capsule hidden in it from Göring's bags in the prison luggage compartment, or he let Göring root through the luggage to find it. Wheeler insisted, however, that he never gave Göring access to the baggage room, so the mystery of how the Reichsmarschall got the capsule remains unsolved.

CHAPTER 32: RECOVERY

349 *asked plaintively*: "Donovan Back from Europe," *New York Tribune*, Dec. 17, 1945, WJD letter to Samuel Rosenman, Jan. 13, 1946, Alphabetical File, Donovan, William J., SRP, HSTL; Jones, Sept. 26, 2007; James Wright letter to A. H. Kirchhofer, Jan. 11, 1946, B: 19, RDP, MHI.

350 *had accumulated*: Gilbert, Oct. 19, 2007; John E. Tobin interview, June 30, 1980, pp. 1-4, Donald Rumsey interview, pp. 3-4, B: Interviews—Teitelbaum to Withrow Jr. 1979-undated, WJD, MHI; McIntosh, Aug. 29, 2007, April 7, 2009.

350 *on his knee*: WJD letter to John Forsdyke, Jan. 13, 1948, B: 1, DP, CU; WVHD, pp. 29, 62, WJDP, MHI; "Leaders Hesitant on Idea of Unified Europe," undated news article, B: 137D, WJDP, MHI; Scott-Smith and Krabbendam, eds., pp. 46-47; W.S.C. memos on visit to United States of America, March–April 1949, CHUR 2-266-176-191, CA; Gilbert, Sept. 29, 2007. Donovan worked aggressively on behalf of the American Committee for United Europe, recruiting future CIA chiefs Walter Bedell Smith and Allen Dulles to serve on its board. By the mid-1950s the CIA was funneling about $1 million a year through the committee to promote European unity.

351 *"the White House"*: Notes on WJD, F: 1965, B: 137C, WJDP, MHI; "Politics and Wild Bill Donovan," *New York Daily News*, April 29, 1946; "William J. Donovan for U.S. Senate," *New York Herald-American*, Aug. 11, 1946; "Donovan Backed by Duchess GOP for U.S. Senate," *Syracuse Post-Standard*, Aug. 21, 1946; "Strongest Candidate," *New York World-Telegram*, Aug. 25, 1946; "Report Dewey Finds Donovan 'Reactionary,'" *New York Post*, Aug. 26, 1946; "Stassen Asks Dewey to Back Donovan; Gets Opposite Result," *New York Post*, Aug. 31, 1946; "Donovan Is Sure He'll Win if Free Choice Is Made," Sept. 3, 1946, "Donovan Urges Veterans to Aid Dewey and Ives," Sept. 17, 1946, *New York Herald Tribune*.

351 *"of Snoopers"*: William Leahy diary entry, Jan. 24, 1946, R: 3, WLP, LOC.

352 *Donovan's vision*: Smith, *Shadow Warriors*, p. 408; Warner, "Salvage and Liquidation," p. 11; Troy, *Donovan and the CIA*, pp. 346-47, 402-10; Robert Donovan, pp. 306-7;

"Donovan Tells of Intelligence Agency's Flaws," *New York Herald Tribune*, April 10, 1946; Riebling, pp. 71–77; F. Eberstadt letter to WJD with enclosure, March 6, 1946, B: 80A, WJDP, MHI.

353   *humiliating appointment*: Harry Vaughan letter to HST, Sept. 28, 1951, General File, 1945–53, Vaughan, Harry H., HSTL; Putzell, OHP, p. 67; HST letter to WJD, March 20, 1947, OF File 854 and OF File 148-A, HSTL.

353   *"prying S.O.B."*: WJD letters to WBS with enclosures, Sept. 21 and Dec. 21, 1950, and Nov. 21, 1951, B: 1A, WJDP, MHI; Bureau Memo, March 31, 1949, 62-80750-899 (68), FBI; CIA memo for the record, April 8, 1953, CIA-RDP 79-01206A-0001-0, CIA, CREST, NA.

353   *by the pound*: WJD letter to Robert Patterson, Feb. 8, 1951, B: 35, RPP, LOC; Homer Metz memo to WJD, May 26, 1951, B: 11A, WJDP, MHI; U.S. Embassy Paris memo to WJD, June 9, 1950, B: 10A, WJDP, MHI; "Society as I See It," by Cobina Wright, undated news article, B: 137D, WJDP, MHI; V. P. Keay memo to A. H. Belmont, Aug. 26, 1952, 94-4-4672-45, FBI.

354   *told Jones*: Jones, Sept. 26, 2007, and book manuscript supplied to author; Nelson, Sept. 24, 2007; Donovan and Jones, "Program for a Democratic Counter Attack to Communist Penetration of Government Service," pp. 1211–41; "Cold War Termed Inferno; 'Chips Down,' Wild Bill Says," *Columbus Citizen*, March 2, 1949; WJD letter to Albert Wedemeyer, March 14, 1949, B: 100, AWP, HIA.

355   *"of the facts"*: Lt. Gen. William W. Quinn interview, 1981, Senior Officer Oral History Program, pp. 45–48, 133–38, B: 19, WQP, MHI; Interview with OCD, p. 72, B: "Oral History Interviews—OCD, Activities in Europe, 1941–89," WJDP, MHI; McIntosh, April 7, 2009; D. M. Ladd memo to JEH, Oct. 2, 1946, 94-4-4672-29, FBI.

355   *court case*: William E. Penimore report on WJD, July 3, 1945, 77-58706-43, FBI; Weinstein, pp. 256–61; Peake, pp. 14–34; "Spy Queen Names Aide to F.D.R.," *New York Daily News*, Aug. 1, 1948; Security Office memo to WJD, July 20, 1944, B: 137C, WJDP, MHI; Weinstein and Vassilev, pp. 240, 249, 256–61; Warner and Benson, p. 17; Schlesinger, OHP, p. 10; "Donovan Backs Duncan Lee as Loyal in War," *New York Herald Tribune*, Aug. 31, 1948.

355–358   *On June 10 to for Donovan*: Keeley, pp. 1–370; "Gen. Donovan to Be Counsel in Polk Inquiry," *New York Herald Tribune*, May 25, 1948; Memorandum of Conversation with Major Moushountis et al., July 24, 1948, B: "George Polk Murder 1947–1981" and "George Polk Murder 1948–1953," WJDP, MHI; "Donovan Complains on Polk Case, Calls Greek Inquiry Too One-Sided," *New York Times*, July 29, 1948; "Donovan Back from Greece," *New York Sun*, Oct. 18, 1948; WJD speech before Chicago Council on Foreign Relations, Nov. 29, 1948, B: 3A, WJDP, MHI; E. M. Morgan letter to Walter Lippmann, March 17, 1949, Tentative Draft of the Polk Report, B: "George Polk Murder 1947–1981" and "George Polk Murder 1948–1953," WJDP, MHI; "Donovan Talks to 2 Witnesses in Polk Trial," *New York Herald Tribune*, April 19, 1949; "Staktopoulos Gets Life Term, Mother Acquitted in Polk Case," *New York Herald Tribune*, April 22, 1948.

358   *a kid person*: Gilbert, Oct. 29, 2007, Dec. 12, 2008; Jones, Sept. 26, 2007.

358   *his hostess*: Friant, Feb. 18, 2008; Joost, Jan. 4, 2008; Gilbert, Dec. 12, 2008; Report of Compliance with Orders for Lt. Cdr. David R. Donovan, Feb. 7, 1946, Bureau of Naval Personnel Annual Qualification Questionnaire for David R. Donovan, Aug. 16, 1950, NPRC.

359   *and determined*: Gilbert, Oct. 29, 2007, Jan. 12, 2008; McIntosh, Aug. 29, 2007, Dec. 12, 2008; Tippaparn Donovan, Jan. 24, 2008; Friant, Feb. 18, 2008; McKay, Feb. 18, 2008.

359   *For the grandchildren to "with my life"*: Donovan home movies, DGD; Henderson, Nov. 11, 2008; David G. Donovan, Sept. 22 and Nov. 15, 2007; Gilbert, Oct. 29, 2007; "Cyanide Silver Polish Kills Granddaughter of Gen. Donovan," unidentified news article, B: 56, TCP, LOC; Tippaparn Donovan, Jan. 24, 2008; Gilbert, Oct. 29, 2007, Jan. 1 and Dec. 12, 2008; Jones, Sept. 26, 2007; WVHD, p. 11, WJDP, MHI; Wise, Jan. 27, 2008; Mary G. Donovan appointment diary, April 22, 1953, B: 132C, WJDP, MHI.

CHAPTER 33: THAILAND

360   *the Soviets:* DDE letters to WJD, July 5, 1949 and Jan. 3, 1952, Memo to WJD Re: Status of Republican Pre-Convention, B: 35, PPP, DDEL; WVHD, pp. 29, 62, WJDP, MHI; vanden Heuvel, March 11, 2008; Veterans of OSS letter to DDE, Jan. 8, 1952, B: 8, Name Series, AWF, DDEL; EP letter to L. P. Yandell, Jan. 6, 1953, Sherman Adams letter to EH Jan. 9, 1953, B: 172, Lewis Gough letter to DDE, March 14, 1953, B: 1185, General File, CF, DDEL.

361   *Eisenhower wanted:* Bureau memo, Jan. 17, 1953, 62-80750-2032 (14, 60), FBI; JEH memo to Tolson, Nichols, and Ladd, Jan. 5, 1953, B: 16, E: 14B, RG65, NA; Gentry, pp. 148, 403–4; Montague, pp. 263–66; "Allen Welsh Dulles as Director of Central Intelligence," pp. 14–17; Allen Dulles interview, May 17–June 3, 1965, John Foster Dulles Oral History Project, PU.

361   *as a diplomat:* WVHD, pp. 4–5, WJDP, MHI; Jones, Sept. 26, 2007; McIntosh, Aug. 29, 2007, April 7, 2009; vanden Heuvel, Jan. 7, 2008, March 11, 2008.

362   *in the region:* WVDH, pp. 16–17, WJDP, MHI; WBS telegram to WJD, May 14, 1953, DGD; Staff Study on Psychological Strategy Planning Tasks with Regard to Southeast Asia, Psychological Strategy Board, March 19, 1952, Box 16, PSB Documents, Master of Vol. III (7), NSCP, DDEL; Memorandum on Discussion at the 143rd Meeting of the NSC, May 6, 1953, B: 4, 1-11-54, 1-15-54, in Box 5, NSC Series, AWF, DDEL; vanden Heuvel, March 11, 2008; Darling, pp. 97–99.

363   *with Europe:* John Hines memo to Gen. Smith, May 11, 1953, Subject File (Strictly Confidential)–Chiefs of Mission Discussions (2), B: 1, Name File, Personnel Series, JFDP, DDEL; JFD telephone conversation with WJD, June 11, 1953, B: 1, Telephone Calls Series, JFDP, DDEL; WJD memo to DDE, June 3, 1953, B: 8, Name Series, AWF, DDEL.

363   *in Thailand:* WJD memo to DDE, June 3, 1953, B: 8, Name Series, AWF, DDEL; vanden Heuvel, March 11, 2008; C. D. Jackson letter to WBS, May 25, 1853, B: 588, State Department Decimal Files, RG59, NA; DDE letter to WJD, June 9, 1953, B: 8, Names Series, AWF, DDEL; WVHD, pp. 1, 4–5, WJDP, MHI.

364   *New York columnists:* JEH telegram to FBI field offices, June 19, 1953, V. P. Keay memo to A. H. Belmont, June 26, 1953, SAC New York memo to JEH, June 30, 1953, Rosen memo to Ladd, July 7, 1953, 77-58706-1 through 44, Report of Special Employee Raymond F. Mohr, AL 77-73597, New York interviews on WJD for background check, NY 77-16713, FBI; Thomas J. Lardner report on WJD with enclosures, July 1, 1953, 77-16713, File 77-5876, Section 1, FBI HQ, RG65, NA; JEH letter to Sherman Adams with final background report on WJD enclosed, July 15, 1953, declassified for the author, NLE MR Case No. 2008-32, Doc. 1, DDEL; Frank Raichle interview, March 7, 1981, B: Interviews–Teitelbaum to Withrow Jr. 1979-undated, WJDP, MHI.

364   *for the embassy:* JFD memo to DDE, July 29, 1953, OF 8-F Donovan File, B: 135, Official File, WHCF, DDEL; WBS letter to WJD, Aug. 3, 1953, File "German Documents, Elmo Roper, etc.," 1953–56, unnumbered box, WJDP, MHI; WVHD, pp. 2, 11, WJDP, MHI; WBS memo to Gen. Cutler, Sept. 11, 1953, WJD letter to WBS, Aug. 10, 1953, Alexis Johnson memo to the Acting Secretary, Aug. 14, 1953, B: 588, State Department Decimal File, RG59, NA.

365   *from her drawer:* WVHD, pp. 24, 34, 53–54, 72, WJDP, MHI; vanden Heuvel, Jan. 7, 2007, Jan. 27, 2010; McIntosh, Jan. 1, 2008; Gilbert, Oct. 29, 2007.

365   *Thai public:* WBS letter to WJD with enclosure, Oct. 22, 1953, B: 22, WSP, DDEL; Chalou, p. 344; WVHD, p. 24, WJDP, MHI.

366   *theory as well:* Memo to WBS, June 23, 1953, B: 588, State Department Decimal File, RG59, NA; Robertson memo to JFD, June 2, 1953, Name File D-F, Box 1, Personnel Series, JFDP, DDEL; WVHD, pp. 2–3, 21–30, 94, WJDP, MHI; Thomas, FAOH, p. 6; vanden Heuvel, Jan. 7 and Aug. 13, 2008; James Lay memo to Secretary of Defense, May 8, 1953, B: 62, Disaster File, NSCP, DDEL; Memorandum of Meeting–OCB Working Group on PSB D-23-Thailand, Dec. 28, 1953, B: 79, and Files: 1–6, B: 55, NSCP, DDEL; Donovan, "Our Stake in Thailand," pp. 94–95.

367   *the communists:* Darling, pp. 101-6, 113-30; Thomas, FAOH, p. 4; Jenkins, FAOH, pp. 17, 20; Analysis of Internal Security Situation in Thailand, FE 219-25A, B: 79 and 55, NSCP, DDEL; Discussion at the 159th Meeting of the NSC, Aug. 13, 1953, B: 4 and 1/11/54, 1/15/54 in B: 5, NSC Series, AWF, DDEL; Edwin Carns memo to Secretary of Defense, July 16, 1953, B: 62, Disaster File, NSCP, DDEL; WVHD, pp. 19, 26, 32, 101, 124, 129, WJDP, MHI; Robert Cutler memo to WBS Dec. 28, 1953, B: 16, NSCP, DDEL; Halsema, FAOH, p. 2; Elmer Staats memo to James Lay with Special Report to the NSC, July 12, 1954, B: 55, NSCP, DDEL; vanden Heuvel, Aug. 13, 2008, Feb. 13, 2009; Status Report on NSC 5405, "U.S. Policy with Respect to Southeast Asia," April 20, 1954, B: 55 and 79, NSCP, DDEL.

367   *U.S. government.* WVHD, pp. 4, 19-20, 28, 31, 118, WJDP, MHI; vanden Heuvel, March 11, 2008; Dunlop, p. 502; WJD note to AWD, Jan. 8, 1954, DGD; Joost, Jan. 4, 2008; Grose, p. 338.

368   *American veins:* Leary, pp. 129-31, 195-96; WVHD, pp. 21, 33, 121-22, 125, WJDP, MHI; O'Toole, p. 450; vanden Heuvel, Aug. 13, 2008.

368   *charmless man:* WVHD, pp. 34-38, 42, 71-72, 90-94, WJDP, MHI; vanden Heuvel, Aug. 13, 2008; Lumbard, Donovan Leisure Project, OHC, p. 9, and OHC, New York Bar Foundation Project, pp. 54I, 57; WJD cable to the State Department on CODEL Nixon, Nov. 4, 1953, B: 46, Subject Series, Confidential File, WHCF, DDEL.

368   *for a visit:* WVHD, pp. 12, 55, 85, 146, 151-54, 163, 166, 173, WJDP, MHI; vanden Heuvel, Aug. 13, 2008; McIntosh, April 7, 2009; Gilbert, Oct. 29, 2007; Coon, p. 141.

369   *his own pocket:* WVHD, pp. 101, 104, 107-8, 116, 122, 128, WJDP, MHI; vanden Heuvel, Aug. 13, 2008, April 15, 2009; WVHD, pp. 53, 139-40, 147, 164-66; Gilbert, Oct. 29, 2007; vanden Heuvel, March 11, 2008; JFD cable to WJD, Sept. 25, 1953, B: 588, State Department Decimal File, RG59, NA; WJD letter to JFD, Jan. 8, 1954, DGD; WJD letter to DDE, Jan. 8, 1954, OF 8-F, Official File, WHCF, DDEL.

370   *to Bangkok:* James Stevens memo to George Morgan, July 21, 1953, B: 16, PSB Central Files Series, NSCP, DDEL; Bonsal memo to Robertson, March 12, 1954, B: 1, Personnel Series, JFDP, DDEL; Discussion at the 183rd Meeting of the NSC, Feb. 4, 1954, B: 5, NSC Series, AWF, DDEL; WVHD, pp. 62, 65-66, 108, 127, 155-59; vanden Heuvel, Aug. 13, 2008.

370   *to Saigon:* Warner, "The Office of Strategic Services: America's First Intelligence Agency," p. 22; Richard Harris Smith, pp. 305-8; Smith, *Shadow Warriors,* pp. 326-28; WJD memos to HST, Sept. 27 and 28, 1945, Fr: 549-57, R: 25, M1642, RG226, NA; Paul Helliwell letter to Bernard Fall, Oct. 14, 1954, B: 9A, WJDP, MHI; Dwight D. Eisenhower interview, July 28, 1964, OH-14, DDEL, pp. 24-28; Ferrell, *The Eisenhower Diaries,* p. 190.

370   *into Vietnam:* WVHD, pp. 25-26, 36, 108, 143-45, 152, WJDP, MHI; vanden Heuvel, March 11 and Aug. 13, 2008.

371   *administration of John F. Kennedy:* Vanden Heuvel, March 11 and Aug. 13, 2008; Blair, p. 33; Raymond de Jaegher letter to WJD, April 7, 195, B: 5A, WJDP, MHI; WJD letter to DDE, Feb. 5, 1956, B: 8, Names Series, AWF, DDEL; WJD notes for Speech on April 23, "Speech Material Notes" binder, B: 127A, WJDP, MHI.

371   *toward Ruth:* WVHD, pp. 89, 98, 142-47. The SAC bombers would come to Thailand later in the 1960s, when the United States entered the war in Vietnam.

372   *in meetings:* WVHD, pp. 27, 100-101, 132, WJDP, MHI; vanden Heuvel, Aug. 13, 2008; John E. Tobin interview, June 30, 1980, p. 2, B: Interviews—Teitelbaum to Withrow 1979-undated, WJD, MHI.

372   *leave Thailand:* WVHD, p. 172, WJDP, MHI; Bonsal memo to Walter Robertson, March 12, 1954, Robertson memo to JFD, March 12, 1954, B: 1, Personnel Series, JFDP, DDEL; vanden Heuvel, Aug. 13, 2008.

373   *public assignment:* Vanden Heuvel, Feb. 3 and April 4, 2009; WVHD, pp. 142, 149, 153-54, 161 170, WJDP, MHI; Ford, p. 328; DDE memo to JFD, May, 26, 1954, WJD letter to DDE, May 7, 1954, and DDE response, May 26, 1954, B: 8, Name Series, B: 7, Diary Series, AWF, DDEL; John Hanes letter to Walter Robertson, June 16, 1954, Name File

(Strictly Confidential) D-F, B: 1, Personnel Series, JFDP, DDEL; Memorandum for the President on Resignation of WJD, Sept. 3, 1954, OF 8-F Donovan File, WHCF, DDEL; Bangkok cable to JFD, Nov. 17, 1954, B: 588, State Department Decimal File, RG59, NA; J.W.H. memo to JFD Aug. 30, 1954, B: 1, General Correspondence and Memoranda File, JFDP, DDEL; L. B. Nichols memo to JEH, Jan. 8, 1953, B: 16, E: 14B, RG65, NA; W.K.S. note to WBS, Nov. 9, 1954, B: 6, Personnel Series, JFDP, DDEL; "Bill Donovan, Ex-Envoy, Represents Thai in U.S.," *Washington Star*, Feb. 21, 1956; JFD memorandum of conversation with DDE, April 4, 1955, B: 3, White House Memoranda Series, JFDP, DDEL.

CHAPTER 34: WALTER REED

374   *polite responses:* DDE letter to WJD, May 11, 1956, B: 8, Name Series, AWF, DDEL; WJD Appointment to President's Commission on Veterans' Pensions, March 30, 1956, B: 7, Records of the President's Commission on Veterans' Pensions, DDEL; DDE letter to WJD, Dec. 28, 1956, B: 867, Alphabetical File, WHCF, DDEL.

374   *"in the papers":* Vanden Heuvel, Feb. 3, 2009; Mary Jean Eisenhower, July 31, 2009; Ferrell, *Off the Record*, pp. 347–48.

375   *"staunch ally" had made:* Chester, pp. 1–20, 206–9; "Red 'Come Home' Drive Gaining in Free World, Survey Reveals," *New York Times*, March 28, 1956; Report of Donovan Commission of IRC on Communist Redefection Campaigns, B: 3B, WJDP, MHI; Special Report to the Board of Directors on IRC Hungarian Refugee Relief, Dec. 12, 1956, B: 11, Files of the President's Committee for Hungarian Refugee Relief, DDEL; vanden Heuvel, Aug. 13, 2008; John O'Daniel letters to Jerry Persons, May 20, 1956, and to Adams, May 7, 1956, B: 784, PPF, Central Files, DDEL.

375–376   *Bill and Ruth* to *and cried:* Tippaparn Donovan, Jan. 24, 2008; Gilbert, 2007-9; Friant, Feb. 18, 2008; McKay, Feb. 18, 2008; David G. Donovan, 2007-9; Schulte, March 2, 2008; Wise, Jan. 27, 2008; Mary Donovan appointment diary entries for July 1955, B: 132C, WJDP, MHI; Death certificate for Mary Grandin Donovan, July 26, 1955, Massachusetts Department of Public Health, Registry of Vital Records and Statistics; Estate of Mary Grandin Donovan, Clerk's Office, Clarke County, Va.; Brown, pp. 829–30; vanden Heuvel, April 15, 2009; Banta, Jan. 28, 2008.

376   *in New York:* Gilbert, Oct. 29, 2007; Friant, Feb. 18, 2008; David G. Donovan, Nov. 15, 2007.

377   *and colleagues:* Smith, OHC, pp. 45–47; vanden Heuvel, Feb. 3, 2009; Interview with Ralstone R. Irvine, Aug. 12, 1980, B: Interviews—Bancroft to Sherwood 1945-undated, WJDP, MHI; John E. Tobin interview, June 30, 1980, pp. 1–4, Donald Rumsey interview, pp. 3–4, B: Interviews—Teitelbaum to Withrow 1979-undated, WJD, MHI; James Murphy interview, April 28, 1981, B: 6, RDP, MHI.

377   *cruel sentence:* Lasker, OHC, pp. 63–64, 352, 504; vanden Heuvel, June 10, 2008, Feb. 3, 2009; Brown, pp. 830–33; WJD Death Certificate, District of Columbia Department of Public Health, Feb. 9, 1959.

378   *medal, beaming:* "Gen. Donovan Ill; Condition Is Improving," *Louisville Courier-Express*, April 16, 1957; Robert Schulz note to Ann Whitman with George Leisure letter to DDE, March 27, 1957, RRD letter to DDE, April 6, 1957, George Leisure letter to DDE, April 9, 1957, B: 975, PPF, CF, DDEL; RRD letter to Corey Ford, undated, OCD letter to Corey Ford, Oct. 7, 1968, B: 136B, WJDP, MHI; Citation for WJD for National Security Medal, April 2, 1957, Sherman Adams letter to AWD, April 1, 1957, B: 647, Official File, WHCF, DDEL; Corey Ford interview with Vincent Donovan, November 1967, pp. 6–8, B:1, Part 1, GU.

379   *seventy-four years old:* vanden Heuvel, Feb. 3, 2009; DDE letters to George Leisure, April 2, and to WJD, April 1, 1957, RRD letter to DDE, April 3, 1957, B: 975, PPF, CF, DDEL; Walter Berry letter to Thomas Corcoran, May 17, 1957, B: 56, TCP, LOC.

379   *became his prison:* Chacon, Jan. 11, 2010; author tour of Building One, Walter Reed
       Army Medical Center, Dec. 11, 2008; McIntosh, April 7, 2009. Another myth that
       endures from previous profiles of Donovan (Brown, p. 830): On Eisenhower's orders
       Donovan was placed in the Pershing Suite at Walter Reed. That was not the case. The
       Pershing Suite's three rooms on the third floor of Building One were reserved for gener-
       als more senior than Donovan. He was put in a more modest single room in Ward Four
       on the second floor.

379–381 *A stream to during one:* Chacon, Jan. 11, 2010; Donald Rumsey interview, p. 17, B:
       Interviews–Teitelbaum to Withrow 1979-undated, WJDP, MHI; Corey Ford inter-
       view with Vincent Donovan, November 1967, p. 21, B:1, Part 1, GU; Smith, OHC,
       pp. 47–48; vanden Heuvel, Feb. 3, 2009; Louis Mountbatten Speech, March 21, 1966,
       B: 137A, WJDP, MHI; Hood, Dec. 11, 2008; David Crockett interview, June 16–17,
       1981, B: 6, RDP, MHI; McIntosh, April 7, 2009; Grayson L. Kirk, OHC, p. 17; Jones,
       Sept. 26, 2007, and book manuscript supplied to author. The story of Donovan escap-
       ing Walter Reed became wildly inflated in accounts over the years. Some versions had
       him running down the road from the hospital in his nightgown, believing he was being
       chased by the Nazis or communists (Dunlop, p. 3). The true story was far milder, says
       Armando Chacon, the Army medic who cared for him. Dressed in his suit and tie,
       Donovan was found walking to the nurses' quarters.

381   *waiting car:* Dunlop, pp. 1–2; Robarge, Aug. 21, 2009.

381   *radio announced:* David G. Donovan, Nov. 15, 2007; Associated Press report on WJD
       death, Feb. 8, 1959, DGD.

382   *of the lung:* WJD Death Certificate, District of Columbia Department of Public Health,
       Feb. 9, 1959; Chacon, Jan. 11, 2010; Crockett, OHP, p. 31; vanden Heuvel, June 10,
       2008.

383   *the front row:* "Funeral Services Are Held in Capital for Gen. Donovan," *Buffalo Evening
       News,* Feb. 11, 1959; Excerpts of sermon delivered by the Right Rev. John Cartwright
       Feb. 11, 1959, B: "World War I, Political Campaigns, etc.," WJDP, MHI; Gilbert, Jan.
       12, 2008; David G. Donovan, Nov. 15, 2007.

384   *of syphilis:* "Gen. Donovan's Distinguished Career," *New York Herald Tribune,* Feb. 9,
       1959; "William J. Donovan," *New York Times,* Feb. 10, 1959; DB "Tribute to Wm. Don-
       ovan, Letters to the Editor," *New York Times,* Feb. 15, 1959; AWD, "A Tribute to General
       Donovan," March 30, 1959, Book Dispatch No. 1179, B: "World War I, Political Cam-
       paigns, etc.," WJDP, MHI; JEH letter to RRD, Feb. 9, 1959, 94-4-4672-52, RRD letter to
       JEH, March 11, 1959, 94-4-4672-54, FBI; R. R. Roach memo to A. B. Belmont, Feb. 13,
       1959, 94-4-4672-53, FBI; Gentry, pp. 460–61.

EPILOGUE

385   *weigh her down:* Estate of WJD, Clerk's Office, Clarke County, Va.; Gilbert, Oct. 29,
       2007; RRD letter to Corey Ford, March 18, 1959, B: 136B, WJDP, MHI.

385–386 *Seven months to proportions right:* "No Successes, No Failures and Unsung Heroes–Ded-
       icated, Selfless People Are 'Spies' for America," *Buffalo Evening New,* Nov. 14, 1959;
       Cornerstone Laying of the Central Intelligence Agency Building, Nov. 3, 1959, CIA
       brochure, B: 119A, WJDP, MHI; CIA Observes 50th Anniversary of Original Head-
       quarters Building Cornerstone Laying, CIA Web site, https://www.cia.gov; David G.
       Donovan, Sept. 22, 2007.

386   *only friends:* Estate of Ruth Donovan, Estate of David R. Donovan, Clerk's Office,
       Clarke County, Va.; Tippaparn Donovan, Jan. 24, 2008; OCD letter to RRD, April 18,
       1974, Dick O'Neill letter to RRD, June 17, 1974, B: "World War I, Political Campaigns,
       etc.," WJDP, MHI; Gilbert, Oct. 29, 2007, Jan. 12, 2008; "Ruth Donovan, on Board of
       School, OSS Chief's Widow," *Washington Post,* Dec. 13, 1977.

387   *Ruth wanted:* RRD letter to Cornelius Ryan, B: 1B, WJDP, MHI; Interview with OCD,
       p. 204, B: "Oral History Interviews–OCD, Activities in Europe 1941-89," WJDP,

MHI; OCD letter to William vanden Heuvel, June 17, 1958, letter to RRD, April 21, 1958, B: 136B, WJDP, MHI.

387-389   *Donovan's true to was remembered:* Helms, OHP, p. 7; Hughes, OHP, pp. 19-20; Crockett, OHP, p. 35; Kingsley, Jan. 1, 2008; Schlesinger, OHP, p. 43; Brown, pp. 786-87; Questionnaire of OSS members, B: 120C, WJDP, MHI; JM memo to Robert A. Lovett, Oct. 26, 1945, Fr: 916-51, R: 1, "Failure of the German Intelligence Service," Fr: 737, 740-53, R: 52, M1642, RG226, NA.

Acknowledgments

M ANY HANDS MADE this book a reality. I first want to thank Paul McCarthy, a creative consultant and friend, who helped me conceive the idea for a biography of William J. Donovan. As she has been for my other books, my literary agent, Kristine Dahl, was a steadfast and invaluable adviser in bringing this volume to publication. For the Donovan biography, I also benefited from a number of research grants. I want to thank the U.S. Army Military History Institute, which awarded me a General and Mrs. Matthew B. Ridgway Research Grant to spend nearly two months wading through the voluminous collection of Donovan personal papers at the Institute. A generous grant from the Gilder Lehrman Fellowship Program enabled me to spend a week in New York researching the many reminiscences of people who knew Donovan, which are housed at Columbia University's Oral History Research Office. A Lubin-Winant Research Fellowship from the Franklin and Eleanor Roosevelt Institute helped me spend two weeks at the FDR Presidential Library in Hyde Park, New York, which has a considerable amount of White House material dealing with Donovan and the OSS. I spent several weeks at the Harry S. Truman Presidential Library in Independence, Missouri, thanks to a research grant from the Harry S. Truman Library Institute. The Eisenhower Foundation also helped me with a research grant to travel to Abilene, Kansas, to pore through World War II OSS material and records from Donovan's service as ambassador to Thailand at the Dwight D. Eisenhower Presidential Library.

A lot has been written about William J. Donovan, yet much of his life and work remained shrouded in mystery and myth when I began this project. This book benefited from his three previous biographies, written more than a quarter century ago. Fortunately, the three authors also left their papers and research materials with archives, which I was able to review to check their facts. I soon discovered that all three biographies must be read with caution. Corey Ford, who was selected by the Donovan family and the Donovan-Leisure law firm to write a biography of the general, produced *Donovan of OSS* in 1970, which was largely a hagiography that ended up being edited by the firm. British historian Anthony Cave Brown's *The Last Hero* in 1982 had access for the first time to Donovan's OSS office records, which the general photographed and took to his law firm before Truman closed down the agency. But Brown's book, which was subsidized by the Donovan law firm, contains numerous errors and instances of wild speculation about what Donovan was doing as OSS director. Richard Dunlop's *Donovan: America's Master Spy*, also published in 1982, depends heavily on the reminiscences of former OSS officers and friends to tell Donovan's story. But as any historian or biographer knows, memories of events that happened many decades earlier can often be faulty. I discovered that the documentary evidence sometimes contradicted the recollections in Dunlop's book. The OSS records that have been declassified since these three books were published helped me correct many of the false stories and myths about Donovan that have endured over the years.

A number of valuable histories of the OSS have been written, which helped greatly in my research. (I must caution that this biography could not hope to recount every operation Donovan's agency launched during the war; to do them all justice would take up another book.) In-house government histories must always be viewed with some skepticism, but I found the two-volume *War Report of the OSS* that Donovan's agency produced for the most part to be surprisingly accurate and candid. Richard Harris Smith's *OSS: The Secret History of America's First Central Intelligence Agency* and Christof Mauch's *The Shadow War Against Hitler* were valuable resources. Bradley F. Smith's *The Shadow Warriors* takes a hard, though somewhat harsh, look at OSS failures and successes during the war. CIA historian Thomas F. Troy produced for his agency a comprehensive and densely researched bureaucratic history of the OSS, which was declassified and published in book form in 1981, titled *Donovan and the CIA*. Fortunately I was able to review the thousands of pages of government documents Troy collected for that official history, which are at the National Archives. Before he died, Tom also shared with me other important material on Donovan from his private files. I am also deeply grateful to Curt Gentry, the author of an excellent biography of J. Edgar Hoover, who shared with me a critical aspect of his research into the nasty bureaucratic battle the FBI director waged against Donovan.

A historical biographer soon discovers his best friend is the archivist. I had some of the best in the business helping me in repositories around the United States and in England. Millions of pages of OSS records, including Donovan's office and administrative files, are housed at the National Archives in Suitland, Maryland, where I practically lived for almost a year. I cannot thank enough archivist and OSS expert Larry McDonald for being my guide and mentor, helping me navigate through this complex set of records, and fielding phone calls from me at all hours of the day and night when I couldn't find something. Before he died, John Taylor (the dean of the Archive's OSS records) gave me valuable tips on finding documents buried in the OSS files. Also helping me track down Donovan-related documents in many other National Archives collections were Tim Nenninger, Bill Cunliffe, Mitchell Yockelson, David Langbart, Stephen Underhill, Timothy Mulligan, and Paul Brown. David Keough was indispensable guiding me through Donovan's personal papers at the Army's Military History Institute stored in more than 350 boxes. He also pointed me to other Institute collections that had important OSS material and spent hours sharing with me his insights on military history. At the FDR Library, Robert Clark directed me to many fascinating gems in the collection, which revealed Roosevelt's complicated relationship with Donovan. He also suffered countless e-mails from me after I left with follow-up questions. At the Truman Library, Liz Safly took me under her wing in the reading room (as she had over the years for thousands of other researchers) while Randy Sowell helped me dig up hundreds of pages of documents, many of them not seen by previous biographers, on Truman's chilly relationship with Donovan. At the Eisenhower Library, David Haight enthusiastically tracked down Donovan records from Ike's presidency and his days as supreme allied commander in Europe.

Daun van Ee and the staff in the Library of Congress's Manuscript Division helped me track Donovan-related documents in the papers of nearly twenty military and political figures. Archivist Carol Leadenham helped me hunt for Donovan material (some of it still unprocessed) in the papers of nearly two dozen OSS officers and World War II figures housed at the Hoover Institution Archives. Claire Germain, Thomas Mills, and Brian Eden were my able and enthusiastic guides for the Cornell University Law

Library collection of Donovan's extensive Nuremberg trials papers. William Seibert at the National Personnel Records Center in St. Louis helped me retrieve the military records of Donovan's son, David. I am grateful to Nicholas Scheetz and Scott Taylor at Georgetown University Library's Special Collections Division, who arranged for me to view Anthony Cave Brown's papers on deposit there. The staff at Columbia's Oral History Research Office carted to my desk hundreds of reminiscences by people who knew Donovan. John Fox, the FBI's historian, helped me decipher the Bureau's cataloguing system during the Hoover era for Donovan-related files. David Robarge, the CIA's historian, cheerfully fielded my many questions and requests for information from his agency's files on the OSS. Archivists at the Herbert Hoover Presidential Library, Princeton University Library, Yale University Library, and Virginia Historical Society also found important records for me.

In Buffalo, Marsha Joy Sullivan rooted through boxes and dusty file drawers in the basement of Nardin Academy to find Donovan's elementary school records for me. Joseph Bieron collected for me important school records from Saint Joseph's Collegiate Institute, which Donovan attended as a teenager. Jennifer Potter rummaged through archives at Niagara University to find me Donovan's academic records and articles he wrote for college publications. Cynthia Van Ness at the Buffalo and Erie County Historical Society found for me important files in its archives on Buffalo at the turn of the century, Donovan's parents, his early law practice, and Ruth Rumsey's family. The staff at the Buffalo and Erie County Public Library found city directories, census data, and news clippings for Donovan's years in Buffalo. My thanks also to members of the Buffalo Cavalry Association who provided me news articles and documents from Troop I, which Donovan commanded.

Overseas, the staff at London's National Archives at Kew could not have been more helpful in retrieving records that dealt with Donovan from the Special Operations Executive, Cabinet Office, Foreign Office, and Prime Minister's Office. I also want to thank archivist Neil Cobbett, who helped me hunt through the British collection, and historian Steven Kippax, who shared not only a desk with me at the Archives but also research material he had collected on the SOE. Allen Packwood and the staff of the Churchill Archives Centre in Cambridge helped me find a number of Donovan-related documents in Churchill's government and personal papers. I also want to thank Maria Persinos, who translated for me hundreds of pages of captured German military, intelligence, and foreign office documents on Donovan and the OSS, which the National Archives at Suitland retains in its microfilm collection.

I owe a special debt of gratitude to Donovan and Rumsey family members, whose assistance was critically important for this project. During the three years of research and writing, Patricia Gilbert, Donovan's granddaughter, spent dozens of hours with me being interviewed about her recollections of the general and her grandmother Ruth. She put up with even more phone calls from me to pin down facts about Donovan's personal life. Grandson David G. Donovan was just as generous with his time. David and his wife, Teresa, also sent me hundreds of pages of Donovan documents, press clippings, and letters from their personal collection, as well as home movies and photos from family albums. For both grandchildren, some of the interviews that dealt with Donovan's extramarital affairs were painful, but they were completely candid with me about what they knew or what they had heard. Judy Beecher, who is one of Donovan's cousins, spent days with me recounting family stories she had heard, tracking down family records for me in Buffalo's libraries, museums, and archives, and escorting me around town to Donovan and Rumsey family homes, businesses, and gravesites. My thanks also to Judy's husband, Tom, who hosted a dinner for me with other family members at the Buffalo Club. Margot Rumsey Banta and Margot Mugler were helpful with recollections from the Rumsey side of the family, while Molly Mugler provided me many Donovan and Rumsey family photos.

I also want to thank Charles Pinck, president of the OSS Society, who fielded many questions from me and put me in touch with former members of the OSS. They included Elizabeth McIntosh, Fisher Howe, and Rolfe Kingsley, who knew Donovan well and spent hours with me sharing their recollections. I also appreciate William J. vanden Heuvel enduring many hours of interviews. A Donovan law partner and aide when the general was ambassador to Thailand, Ambassador vanden Heuvel recorded in a lengthy diary, which I read, the private thoughts Donovan shared with him about his life. Kay Nelson, the wife of OSS officer Wayne Nelson, was also generous with recollections and her husband's diaries.

I leaned on a number of colleagues far better versed than I in military and intelligence history for advice and counsel. Rick Atkinson, one of the best military history writers in the country, was a desk mate and lunch companion during months of archival research. He generously shared his World War II research with me and read parts of the manuscript. Gerhard Weinberg, whose *A World at Arms* is the gold standard for World War II histories, answered many questions and read and corrected parts of the manuscript. Military historian Robert Ferrell was also generous with advice, and read and corrected the section on Donovan's World War I battles. Intelligence historian David Kahn spent hours patiently instructing me in the finer points of World War II tactical intelligence, cryptology, and German spying. Intelligence historian Michael Warner also read parts of the manuscript and offered important comments and corrections.

I want to thank my editors at Free Press, Dominick Anfuso, Leah Miller, and Fred Chase, for skillfully getting the manuscript into shape for publication. Colby Cooper and Viveca Novak helped correct the galley proofs. Jenny Woodson came to my rescue with computer advice to process copies of the tens of thousands of documents I collected. Finally, this book could not have been begun or completed without the encouragement, advice, and patience of my wife, Judy. As with all my other books, she is my best editor. And it is to our grandchildren that this volume is dedicated.

Index

Abwehr, 65, 119, 148, 154, 160, 191, 226, 240, 254, 260, 270, 271, 325
Abyssinian Treasure Trove, 318
Acheson, Dean, 354, 361
Adams, Sherman, 378
Adrian, Leon, 272–73
Africa, 95, 96
    see also North Africa; specific places
Air Force, Army or U.S., 104, 198, 200, 209, 217, 226, 237, 247, 262, 265, 307, 371, 387
Aisne-Marne campaign, 22
Alaska, 100–101
Albania, 165, 190
alcohol, 34–37, 39, 164, 212, 375–76
Algeria, 131–34, 136–44
Algiers, 131, 132, 136–42, 147, 168, 171, 173, 179, 181, 203, 250, 264, 301
    Darlan assassinated in, 144
    Darlan's son in, 134
    Donovan in, 166–67, 172, 180, 185
All Arts Club, 17
Alpine redoubt, 304
Amalfi, 179, 180
American Committee for United Europe, 350
American Expeditionary Forces (AEF), 22, 23, 29, 30
American Legion, 29, 360
Amoss, Ulius, 154–55
Ancon, USS, 178
Angleton, James Jesus, 296–97, 298, 301
antitrust cases, 40, 42, 349–50
Anvil-Dragoon operation, 264–65
Anzio, 228, 229, 252
Arcadia conference, 89–91
Argonne Forest, 24, 29
Arlington National Cemetery, 376, 382–83
Armistice Commission, 136, 144
Army, U.S., 35, 39, 41, 52, 66, 77, 85, 88, 100, 198–99, 263, 270, 272–73, 308, 315, 327, 329, 332, 336, 337, 349, 387, 388

Donovan's promotions in, 151–52, 284
Hanfstaengl and, 108
intelligence in, 52, 69–72, 75, 78, 98, 104, 113, 116, 117, 123, 143, 151, 155, 158, 162, 164, 173, 246, 300, 306–7, 329, 352
in invasion of Sicily, 172–75
Normandy invasion and, 237, 239, 243, 244, 246, 247, 248
in Pacific, 204
personnel problems in, 251
Torch and, 130–43
Army National Guard, Troop I of, 15–16, 18, 19
Army Ranger battalions, 179, 180
Arnold, Henry "Hap," 91, 226, 237
Asia, 101, 115, 121, 199, 200, 203–19, 297–301, 308, 331–32, 350, 374, 375
    OSS in, 98, 129, 130, 203, 206–19
    see also Southeast Asia; specific places
Astor, Helen, 47
Astor, Vincent, 47, 63
atomic bomb, 1, 4, 225, 332
Audrey operation, 185
"Aunt Jemima," 101
Australia, 231–33
Austria, 51, 54, 110, 156–57, 197, 256, 271, 304, 319, 375
    OSS in, 266, 275
Austria-Hungary, 110, 146
Avalanche operation, 178–80
Avoyel, USS, 331–32, 343

Badoglio, Pietro, 53, 54, 176, 179, 180
Balkans, 64–68, 110, 130, 142, 146, 149, 156, 183–90, 239, 241, 274–82
    Donovan in, 64–65, 106
    Hitler's aims in, 54, 64, 176
    OSS in, 164–66, 183–99, 222, 224, 226, 274–80, 284, 323–24
    U.S. vs. British in, 143, 164–66, 183–88
Bancroft, Mary, 2, 48, 147
Bangkok, 362, 365–70, 372

Banque Worms et Cie, 133, 141
Basques, 161, 162
Basso, Alberto, 181
Baxter, James Phinney, III, 73, 86
BBC, 138, 243
Belgium, 18, 58, 236, 256, 267
Belgrade, 67–68, 279, 280
Belmont, August, 16
Bentley, Elizabeth, 355, 364
Berchtesgaden, 108, 197, 262, 316
Bergen, Jack, 377
Berle, Adolf, 69, 70–71, 85–86, 119
Berlin, 87, 97, 146, 147, 148, 153, 192, 260,
    261, 262, 271, 315
    Donovan in, 18, 35, 42, 54
    Soviets in, 304, 313, 319, 331
Bern, 145–50, 155, 195, 237, 259–63, 267,
    269, 270, 286, 317
Bernays, Edward, 43
Berryville, Va., 45, 46, 66, 92, 283–84, 335,
    358–59, 364, 375, 376, 382
Biddle, Francis, 224–25, 308, 329, 330
Bissell, Clayton, 307, 310–11, 336
Black Reports, 257
blacks, 92, 257
Blomberg, Werner von, 342
Bohlen, Charles "Chip," 223
Bonnier de la Chapelle, Fernand, 144
bootleggers, 34–35, 36, 38
Boris III, Tsar of Bulgaria, 65, 67
Boyne, Norbert de, 297
Bradley, Omar, 243–48, 270, 284
Braun, Eva, 319
Breakers group, 260–64
Brent, George, 54
bribery, 102, 103, 106, 109, 135, 145
Brisbane, 231–33
British Security Coordination Office, 63
Brousse, Charles, 120–21, 123, 124, 125
Browne, Gordon, 132–33, 137, 140
Browning, Robert, 17
Bruce, David K. E., 73, 78, 96, 129, 164,
    168, 236, 237, 239–48, 264, 268,
    269–70, 290, 383
    in Paris, 292, 293
Brüning, Heinrich, 110
Buck, Pearl, 89
Budapest, 195–98, 255, 285
Budget Bureau, U.S., 76, 95, 97, 100, 115,
    137–38, 306, 312, 320, 322, 334,
    338
Buffalo, N.Y., 2, 9–12, 14–19, 30, 33–39,
    43, 44, 376

law practices in, 14, 31, 33–36, 38, 39
    Saturn Club raid in, 36–37, 38, 41
    society in, 10–11, 14–15, 36
Buffalo Evening News, 172–73
Bulgaria, 65–66, 67, 95, 155, 157, 165, 183,
    222, 226, 256, 284
Bullard, Robert Lee, 35
Burma, 329, 331, 367–68, 381
    OSS in, 214–19, 297
Buxton, Edward "Ned," 73, 75, 89, 94, 201,
    252, 288, 299, 317
Byrnes, James F., 322, 338, 351–52

Cairo, 131, 142
    OSS office in, 129, 203, 204, 226
Cairo conference (Sextant; 1943), 200, 204
CALPO (Comité de l'Allemagne Libre
    pour l'Ouest; Free Germany Com-
    mittee for the West), 316
Camp Mills, 19–20, 31
Canada, 9, 34, 100, 107, 111, 243–44, 315
    Donovan in, 50–51, 176–78
Canaris, Erika, 263
Canaris, Wilhelm Franz, 148, 154–55, 191,
    260, 263, 345, 346
Capri, 181–82, 277–78
Carter, John Franklin, 74, 86, 307, 321
Casablanca, 132, 137–41
Casablanca conference (1943), 149
Caserta, 227, 249, 250, 276–77, 296, 318,
    379
Casey, William, 267–69, 271–72, 318, 319,
    331, 353, 386, 387, 389
Catholics, Catholic Church, 10, 12–13, 23,
    33, 38, 41, 42, 159, 327, 371
    OSS and, 95, 256–58
Cavendish-Bentinck, Victor, 319
CBS, 241, 356, 357
Central Intelligence Agency, see CIA
Central Intelligence Group, 352
Cereus network, 156–57
Chacon, Armando, 380
Chamberlin, Neville, 58
Chapel Hill farm, 45–46, 56, 86, 92–93,
    143, 174, 319, 343, 349, 358–59,
    365, 375, 376, 381, 383, 386
Cheney Brothers, 79–80
Chennault, Claire, 79, 209
Cheston, Charles, 202, 231, 297, 299
Chetniks, 165, 184–85, 275–79
Chiang Kai-shek, 200, 204–7, 210, 213,
    214, 259, 297, 331, 367
Chicago, Ill., 230–31, 360

Chicago Tribune, 61, 304, 309, 311–12
Child, Julia, 98
Chile, 87, 115
China, 4, 32, 79, 85, 104–5, 177, 204–14, 219, 329, 363, 367
  Japanese in, 78, 204–9, 211, 213, 214, 299, 322, 331
  OSS in, 98, 129, 130, 203, 206–14, 297, 331, 332
Chungking, 207, 214, 259
  OSS in, 98, 129, 203, 206, 209–11, 297
Churchill, Randolph, 275
Churchill, Winston, 58–65, 67, 83–84, 108, 131, 191, 193, 229, 241, 350
  Balkans and, 184–85, 187–88, 239, 274–76, 278–82
  at conferences, 149, 164, 176–77, 192, 200, 204, 298, 299, 300, 303–4, 332
  cross-Channel invasion and, 90, 164, 176, 243
  Donovan's meetings with, 59, 63–64, 239
  peripheral strategy of, 64, 89
  SOE and, 129–30, 165, 187
  Washington visits of, 89–91, 164
CIA (Central Intelligence Agency), 5, 271–72, 302, 311, 313, 333, 352, 360–61, 363, 375, 381, 382–86, 389
  Donovan's death and, 382, 383
  Thailand and, 364, 367, 371
Ciechanowski, John, 323
Clare (flying boat), 60
Clark, Eleanor, 125, 126
Clark, Mark, 136, 139, 140, 144, 182, 202, 241
  in invasion and occupation of Italy, 178–79, 190, 227–30, 249–52
Clark, Sidney, 125, 126
Clermont-Ferrand, 168–71
Cloak and Dagger (movie), 6
code numbers, 98–99
coding and decoding, 98, 158–59, 164, 186, 187, 197, 330
  embassy break-ins and, 121–22, 123, 125, 126
  Soviet, 287, 288–89
  see also Magic; Ultra
Cohen, G. B. "Sadie," 126
Colby, William, 389
Colditz Castle, 198–99
Cold War, 352, 354
Coleman, Archibald, 155, 156, 253, 254–55

Columbia College, 13, 15, 159
Columbia Law School, 13–14, 16, 17, 44
Comintern, 34, 221
Communist Party USA, 94, 221
communists, 40, 55, 62, 94, 110, 146, 238, 258, 265, 271, 285, 316, 327, 332, 336, 353–58, 362, 363, 370, 372
  in China, 205–6, 209, 332
  in Greece, 188, 280, 282, 356–58
  in Yugoslavia, 165, 184–86, 275, 279, 280
Congress, U.S., 71, 85, 252, 307, 312, 326, 352, 363
  see also Senate, U.S.
Coniglio (Clemente Menicanti), 228, 250
Conway, Rose, 321
Coolidge, Calvin, 38, 40, 41
Coon, Carleton, 132–33, 137, 138, 144, 181, 190, 368
Cornell University, 46, 47, 103
Corsica, 176–77, 190, 222, 229, 250
Corvo, Biagio Max, 173–75, 250, 251
Costello, Frank, 102
Côte de Châtillon, 24–25, 30
crime, 34–38, 65, 367
  war, 317, 323–27, 329, 330–31, 341–48
Croatia, 165, 194, 275–76
Crockett, David, 227, 249, 250, 379, 382
cross-Channel invasion, 59, 90, 91, 164, 176
  see also Normandy invasion
Cross project, 316
Cuneo, Ernest, 97, 119, 126, 151, 281
Curie, Eve, 96
currencies, foreign, 99–100, 108, 141, 196, 250
Cynthia, *see* Pack, Amy Elizabeth Thorpe
Czechoslovakia, 51, 324

Daniel, Harry, 382
Darby, William O., 179, 180
Darlan, Jean Louis Xavier François (Popeye), 134, 135, 140–41, 144, 149, 167
Daugherty, Harry, 38, 40
Davies, John, 208
Davies, Marion, 47
Davis, Elmer, 116, 138, 140–41, 150–51, 166
Deane, John, 220, 223, 225–26, 288
Deer team, 370
Defense Department, U.S., 352, 363, 371
de Gaulle, Charles, 117, 131, 132, 144, 238, 266

Del Gaizo, August (Little Augie), 102–3
Democrats, Democratic Party, 10, 33, 55–56, 59, 304, 321, 324, 328
    in New York, 35, 41–44
Denis, Armand, 96
Denmark, 58, 286
Dennis, Eugene, 94
Detachment 101, 215–16, 218, 299
Deuel, Wallace, 73, 175, 333
Devers, Jacob, 165, 236, 251–52
Dewey, Thomas, 283, 350–51
Deyo, Morton, 240–43
Dickson, Doyle, 293–95
Diem, Ngo Dinh, 370–71, 375
Dien Bien Phu, 370, 371
Di Luca, Francis "Tony," 157–59, 161, 162, 336
Dodd, Thomas, 346, 347
Doering, Otto, Jr. "Ole," 97, 138, 203, 230, 231, 330, 333, 354, 378, 387
    leak investigation and, 309, 310, 311
"Dog Drag," 101–2
Dogwood (Alfred Schwarz), 156–57, 191, 192, 195, 197, 253–56, 337
Dolan, Brooke, 104–5
Dönitz, Karl, 319, 320, 343
Donovan, Anna Letitia Lennon, 10–11, 12, 14, 364
Donovan, Bill, 358
Donovan, David, Jr., 358, 359, 365, 381, 383, 386
Donovan, David, Sr., 45–47, 57, 66, 275, 383
    at Chapel Hill, 46, 56, 92, 143, 153, 358, 359, 365, 375, 386
    childhood of, 18–19, 20, 32, 33, 39
    education of, 45, 46, 47
    as father, 143, 343, 365
    father's relationship with, 19, 46, 172–73, 358, 375
    Mary's death and, 376
    in Navy, 143, 153, 172–73, 178–79, 239, 283, 331–32, 343, 358
Donovan, Deirdre, 343, 358
Donovan, James (OSS general counsel), 325
Donovan, James (William Donovan's brother), 11
Donovan, Loretta "Loret," 11, 15
Donovan, Mary (David and Mary's daughter), 358
Donovan, Mary (William Donovan's sister), 11

Donovan, Mary Grandin, 46, 56, 57, 66, 283–84, 292, 326, 349, 350, 358
    at Chapel Hill, 46, 92, 143, 153, 359, 375
    drug problem and death of, 375–76, 385
    father-in-law's relationship with, 4, 46, 284, 335, 358, 359, 368–69, 375
    in Nuremberg, 343, 346, 347
Donovan, Mary Mahoney, 9–10
Donovan, Patricia (William Donovan's daughter), 20, 32, 33, 39, 46, 47, 48
    death of, 56–57, 59, 143, 380, 385
Donovan, Patricia (William Donovan's granddaughter), 143, 283, 292, 326, 343, 350, 358, 359, 365, 376, 381, 383
Donovan, Ruth Rumsey, 16–20, 23, 28–35, 38–49, 59, 66, 235, 292, 303, 354, 358, 371, 375–83, 385–87
    at Chapel Hill, 86, 92–93, 143, 153, 319, 343, 358–59, 376, 381, 383, 385, 386
    depression of, 19, 20, 23, 47
    engagement and marriage of, 17–18
    as grandmother, 292, 343, 376, 381
    husband's cheating on, 4, 34, 37, 47–49, 113, 284, 386
    husband's correspondence with, 19, 20, 22, 23, 28–31, 33, 34, 47
    husband's death and, 383, 385, 387, 389
    husband's political ambitions and, 30, 39, 42, 43
    as mother, 18–19, 20, 33
    in Nonquitt, 39, 43, 176, 326, 337, 375–76
    Patricia's death and, 57, 380, 385
    travels of, 32–35, 47, 350, 365, 368, 369, 385
    wealth of, 16, 18, 45, 349, 386
Donovan, Sheilah, 358, 359, 365, 368, 375, 376, 380, 385
Donovan, Timothy, III, 11, 15, 23, 46
Donovan, Timothy, Jr. (Young Tim), 10–11, 12, 14, 364
Donovan, Timothy, Sr. (Big Tim), 9–11
Donovan, Vincent, 11, 12, 15, 31, 33, 34, 46, 93, 110, 127, 256, 380, 382, 383
    Los Angeles ministry of, 42
    Ruth's emotional support from, 23
Donovan, William J. (Wild Bill):
    acting of, 16, 17
    as ambassador to Thailand, 362–73

anticommunism of, 354–55, 357, 362,
364, 369, 374–75
army promotions of, 151–52, 284
Asian travels of, 32–33, 51, 200,
204–19, 259, 297, 298, 299, 308,
331–32, 350, 362–75
as assistant attorney general, 38–41
awards and medals of, 2, 12, 13, 21–22,
30, 35, 152, 162, 232, 243, 245, 321,
349, 378
background of, 2, 9–11, 37, 44, 55
as Catholic, 2, 12–13, 38, 41, 327
celebrity of, 38, 55, 66, 172–73, 375
as charismatic leader, 3, 19–20, 203
charm of, 3, 34, 43, 47, 52, 239
death of, 381–86
economic views of, 43–44, 55
education of, 2, 11–14, 16, 17, 44, 364
in elections, 35, 42–44, 350–51
enemies of, 34–37, 39–41, 68, 71,
75–77, 112–19, 121, 150, 186, 306,
307–8, 310–11, 328–30, 335, 354,
383–84
extramarital affairs of, 4, 34, 37, 47–49,
113, 127, 200, 284, 291, 335, 353,
354, 386
family life of, 45–49, 56–57, 143,
283–84, 292, 350, 358–59
financial problems of, 349, 372–73
as football player, 2, 12, 13, 17, 173
as grandfather, 143, 292, 350, 358, 359,
381
income of, 38, 42, 117, 284, 349
informal intelligence collecting of,
51–54
injuries and health problems of, 21,
26–29, 52, 112–15, 173, 227, 249,
296, 376–82
as Irish American, 2, 5, 37, 64
as lawyer, 2, 14, 31–42, 44, 47, 51–52,
78, 92, 117, 323–24, 344, 349–50,
354, 372
marriage of, 2, 17–18
new spy service planning and, 69–72
in North Africa, 166–67, 172, 180, 185,
200, 204, 226
origin of nickname of, 23
personal items lost by, 65, 118, 291
physical appearance of, 2, 13, 17, 57,
151–52, 162, 173, 175, 178, 204–5,
244
politics considered by, 14, 30, 31, 38, 41,
42, 48, 222

postwar intelligence and, 2–6, 302,
304–14, 322–23, 326–28, 333,
351–53
at Quebec conference, 176–78, 180
as Republican, 13, 15, 33, 35, 41–44,
52, 53, 56, 58, 62, 77, 155, 252, 306,
311, 321, 324, 325, 350–51, 360
resignation considered by, 151
as Roosevelt's envoy, 59–68
rumors and gossip about, 4, 16, 17, 34,
37, 40, 42, 46, 113, 114, 284, 335,
353, 364, 384
in Russia, 219–24
in Saturn Club raid, 36–37, 38, 41, 44
secrecy of, 97, 114–15, 235, 308
spy-service memo of, 70
in Troop I, 15–16, 18, 19
unconventional ideas and projects of,
75, 88, 100–105, 155
war crimes and, 323–27, 330–31,
341–48
in World War I, 2, 19–31, 35, 52, 222,
232, 321, 345, 381
Doolittle, James, 88
Downes, Donald, 111, 121, 123–27,
178–82, 281
drugs, 375–76
illegal, 34, 35, 38, 103, 209, 367–68
OSS, 102, 103–4
Dubinin (Russian émigré), 298, 302
Duff, James Arthur, 209, 210
Duffy, Francis, 2, 19, 20, 27, 29–30, 54
Duke, Florimund DuSossoit, 194–98, 255
Dulles, Allen, 109–10, 124, 154, 167, 196,
226, 257, 267–70, 289, 295, 315,
319, 324, 343, 378
in Bern, 145–50, 155, 237, 259–63,
267, 269, 270, 304, 317
Donovan's death and, 382, 383
FBI investigation of, 127
joke on Donovan by, 118–19
postwar intelligence and, 352, 353, 361,
367, 384, 386, 389
Dulles, Clover, 147, 343
Dulles, John Foster, 146, 361, 363, 369,
371, 372, 373
Dunn, James, 301

Earle, George, 65
Early, Stephen, 61, 75, 93–94, 101, 311,
312, 318, 320
Early, Thomas, 252
Eastern Europe, 119, 284, 303–4, 353, 375

Eddy, William, 131-39, 141, 144, 166, 167, 175
Egan, William, 12, 13
Eifler, Carl, 214-19
8th Army, 174, 176, 179
83rd Brigade, 24-25, 28
84th Brigade, 24-25
Eisenhower, Dwight D., 18, 162, 177, 192, 203, 264, 269, 281, 294, 316, 320, 326, 329, 370
    Normandy invasion and, 237, 238, 247
    as president, 360-64, 366, 368-74, 378-79, 382, 386
    Torch and, 130-31, 133-40
Eisenhower, Milton, 138
elections:
    of 1922, 35
    of 1926, 40-41
    of 1928, 41
    of 1932, 42-44, 351
    of 1936, 52
    of 1940, 59, 61, 66
    of 1944, 258, 283
    of 1946, 350-51
    of 1952, 360
11th Amphibious Force, 239
Ella, 125-26
England, 51, 59, 60, 67, 164-66, 168-69, 198, 224, 304, 355
Ethiopia, 51-54, 176, 318
European Movement, 350

Falkenhausen, Alexander von, 261
Farley, James, 44
Faust project, 268-69, 271
FBI (Federal Bureau of Investigation), 39-40, 68-71, 76, 122, 289-90, 336, 354-55
    Donovan background check by, 363-64
    Donovan's moles in, 127-28
    Donovan spied on by, 4, 40, 76-77, 127, 335, 353, 354
    Ethiopian venture and, 54
    Latin America and, 71, 114, 115, 335
    NKGB and, 224-25
    OSS relations with, 94, 97, 114, 115, 127-28, 307
    Pearl Harbor attack and, 83, 85
    postwar intelligence and, 305-12, 322, 334-35, 338
    Spanish embassy incident and, 126-27
    Truman's relations with, 321, 322
FBQ Incorporated, 98, 118

5th Army, 178-79, 182, 202, 227-30, 249, 250, 252
Fighting 69th, The (movie), 54-55
Finland, 130, 287-88, 289
1st Army, 243, 244, 246
1st Division, 24, 174
Fitin, Pavel, 223-26, 284-85, 288-89, 320
Fleming, Ian, 64, 69, 70
flower code names, 156-57, 191, 195, 253
Ford, Corey, 387
Ford, John, 93, 204, 214, 326, 331, 383
Foreign Office, British, 59, 60, 116, 276, 310
Foreign Office, German, 148, 196, 237, 265
Forgan, Russell, 318, 319, 329-30
Forrestal, James, 239, 248
42nd Division, 19, 23, 24, 26, 28
France, 51, 104, 198, 223, 310, 361
    Anvil-Dragoon in, 264-65
    cross-Channel invasion of, 90, 164
    German occupation of, see Germany, Nazi, France occupied by
    OSS infiltrating of, 95, 161, 162, 164-71, 236, 237, 268, 270, 322
    Overlord and, 235-48, 264, 268, 270
    resistance in, 169, 170, 237-38, 243, 244, 247-48, 268, 269, 270, 316
    Vietnam and, 362, 369, 370, 371
    World War I and, 21-29, 35, 52
    see also Vichy French
Franco, Francisco, 124-25, 160, 161, 162, 299
Francs Tireurs et Partisans, 238
Frankfurter, Estelle, 73, 305
Frankfurter, Felix, 73, 305
Free French, 117, 131, 144
Freeman, James, 5, 92, 93, 112, 118
French navy, 121, 130, 134, 135, 139, 181
Friendship Project, 207
Friendship Valley, 207, 208, 211, 212

Gaevernitz, Gerhart von Schulze-, 146, 147
Gaevernitz, Gero von Schulze-, 147-48
Gale, Paul, 174
Geneva Convention, 253, 324
George II, King of Greece, 187, 280
George project, 329
Georgia Cracker, 120-21, 123
German Americans, 93-94, 106
German army, 50-51, 67, 114, 119, 146, 190, 192, 267

Hungary and, 196, 197
  Soviet undermining of, 221
German Freedom Movement, 191
German High Command, 344–45, 347, 348
Germans:
  in Donovan's network of informants, 54
  in Istanbul, 156, 191
  in Switzerland, 146–49
Germany:
  A. Dulles in, 146, 147, 148
  Donovan in, 18, 34, 35, 42, 54
  Jews in, 54
  in World War I, 21, 22, 24–27, 29, 110, 111, 345
Germany, Nazi, 58–68, 72, 85–91, 98–102, 106–11, 130, 164, 195, 197–98, 249–54, 259–74, 287, 315–16, 317–20, 337
  assassination attempts against Hitler and his inner circle in, 153–54, 259–63
  Balkans and, 54, 64, 165, 176, 183, 184–85, 187, 188, 274–78, 280, 282
  Churchill's invasion plan for, 241
  Corsica, Sardinia, and, 176, 180–81
  defeat of, 91, 286, 301
  dissidents in, 110, 150, 191–93, 260, 263
  Donovan suspected of collaborating with, 54
  on Eastern Front, 77, 86, 108, 119, 141, 155, 176, 183, 184, 191, 192, 193, 284, 304, 317
  France occupied by, 58, 62, 64, 102, 121, 132, 133–34, 140, 146, 168, 169, 176, 184, 193, 238, 264–65, 267, 271
  intelligence of, 63, 65, 133, 136, 145, 197, 199, 295, 388
  in Italy, 176, 179, 185, 229–30, 249–52, 296, 317–18, 324
  Japan's relations with, 78, 299
  leaks to, 119
  mineral needs of, 155, 160, 286
  NKGB in, 221, 223
  Normandy invasion and, 236–37, 238, 241–48
  occupation of, 191, 193, 289, 303, 313, 319, 331, 332
  OSS in, 266–72, 275, 286, 313, 318
  OSS intelligence on, 77, 109, 260, 304
  peace feelers and, 190–93, 261, 266, 317–18
  propaganda and sabotage program of, 62, 65, 70, 98, 106, 108
  in Sicily, 173–74, 176
  Spain's relations with, 121, 124–25, 159, 160
  territories grabbed by, 50–51, 55, 58, 64, 195
  Torch and, 130, 133, 136, 137, 140, 141
  U-boats of, 58, 60, 95
  unconditional surrender and, 149–50, 190, 192, 266, 317, 320
  U.S. postwar intelligence and, 305, 309–10
  war crimes and, 323–27, 330–31, 341–48
  war declared on U.S. by, 87
Gestapo, 98, 133, 137, 193, 238, 250, 254, 255, 256, 271–73, 315, 337, 345, 348
  A. Dulles and, 145, 149
  anti-Hitler coup and, 261, 262, 263
  Legendre and, 294–95
  Sparrow team and, 197, 198
  U.S. postwar intelligence agency compared with, 305, 308, 312, 327
Gibraltar, 136–39, 237
Giglio, Maurizio (Cervo), 229, 230
Ginny team, 324
Giraud, Henri Honoré, 133–36, 138, 139, 140, 144, 167, 238
Gisevius, Hans Bernd (Tiny), 148, 154, 260–62, 268, 325, 353
Glavin, Edward, 249–52
Godfrey, John, 60, 69, 70
Goebbels, Joseph, 106, 107, 150, 154, 256
Goerdeler, Carl Friedrich, 260–61
Goldberg, Arthur, 93, 109, 124, 193–94, 268
Goodyear, Bradley, 14, 15, 33, 35, 36
Goodyear and O'Brien, 14–15, 32
Göring, Hermann, 107, 111, 226, 316, 318, 327
  war crimes and, 325, 341–45, 347, 348
Graham, Katharine, 349
Graham, Phil, 349
Grandin, Mary, *see* Donovan, Mary Grandin
Great Britain, 18, 54, 58–65, 86, 141–44, 154–69, 235, 251, 296, 307, 323, 326
  Balkans and, 143, 164–66, 183–89, 274–82

Great Britain (con't.)
  colonialism of, 187, 205, 280
  Donovan's division of territory with,
    130, 141–42, 164–66, 183–86
  Downes as spy for, 121, 123, 124
  in Germany, 266, 268, 289
  Hanfstaengl and, 107, 108
  intelligence and propaganda operations
    of, 60, 62–63, 66, 68, 70, 71, 76, 77,
    97, 102, 109, 113, 121–24, 141–42,
    143, 148, 164–66, 168, 219, 235–46,
    253, 254, 290, 310, 315, 319, 320,
    324, 329, 336
  Massingham and, 141–42
  Normandy invasion and, 238, 243–44,
    336
  OSS intelligence sharing with, 117, 122,
    129, 164, 186
  peace feelers and, 192, 193, 196, 261,
    300
  Pearl Harbor and, 83–84
  postwar goals of, 187
  Soviet espionage in, 224, 225
  submarines of, 136, 139
  Sussex project and, 237–38
  Turkish policy of, 155–56
  U.S. aid to, 60, 61, 66
Great Depression, 41–44
Greece, 64, 142, 143, 165, 183, 184,
    187–88, 190, 280–82, 290, 355–58
Greek People's Liberation Army (ELAS),
    188, 280
Green Berets, 364, 366
Grombach, John "Frenchy," 98, 118, 224,
    283, 290–91, 307, 336
Gromyko, Andrei, 289
Gross, Andor (Andre György; Trillium),
    195, 197, 255
Group of Five, 133, 135
Gubbins, Colin McVean, 187, 188–89
guerrilla warfare, 144, 169, 176, 215, 221,
    236, 304, 316, 356, 363, 367, 370
  in Balkans, 183, 184, 186, 187, 188,
    274
  in China, 206, 207, 208, 331
  Donovan's plans for, 77, 88, 95, 115,
    116, 142, 143, 165, 167
  in France, 238, 243, 244, 247, 270
  Hambro and, 130, 143
  in Italy, 252, 258
  Torch and, 132, 134, 138, 139
Guinzburg, Harold, 153
Gusev, Fedor, 326, 330

Hagan, Paul, 110, 111
Haile Selassie, 53, 318
Halder, Franz, 261
Hall, Virginia, 237, 322
Halyard, 277–78, 279
Hambro, Sir Charles, 130, 141–43,
    165–66, 183–84, 187
Hamilton, Pierpont Morgan, 48
Hamilton, Rebecca Stickney, 48–49, 147
Hanfstaengl, Ernst "Putzi," 107–8, 154,
    190, 236–37, 257
Harada, Ken, 258, 299, 300, 301
Harding, Warren, 35, 38
Harriman, Averell, 90, 222–25
Harriman, Mary, 13
Harvard University, 46, 107
Hatz, Otto von, 195–96, 197, 255
Hawaii, 57, 62, 232, 299
  Pearl Harbor and, 83–91, 124, 220, 240,
    300
Hayes, Carlton Joseph Huntley, 159–63,
    336
Hearst, William Randolph, 47
Helldorf, Wolf-Heinrich Graf von, 261
Helms, Richard, 271, 389
Henry-Haye, Gaston, 123
Heppner, Betty, 354, 358, 380
Heppner, Richard "Dick," 204–5, 219,
    354–55
Hermann Plan, 191–93, 253, 255, 261
Hess, Rudolf, 344
Hewitt, Kent, 178
Himmler, Heinrich, 108, 262, 265, 316
Hiroshima, 1, 4, 332
Hitler, Adolf, 35, 54, 58, 87, 124, 155, 160,
    176, 226, 238, 249, 253, 257, 265,
    266, 330–31, 342, 344, 345, 354,
    388
  assassination attempts against, 153–54,
    259–63, 268, 345
  Balkans and, 183, 274
  death of, 319–20
  Donovan compared with, 4
  Donovan's views on, 55, 107
  in final siege, 304, 315, 316, 319
  Mediterranean area and, 64–65, 66
  Normandy invasion and, 236–37
  OSS activities against, 101, 106–11, 121,
    144, 150, 253, 263
  peace feelers and, 190–93, 197
  Pearl Harbor and, 85
  territories grabbed by, 51, 55, 58, 64, 195
  unconditional surrender and, 149–50

Ho Chi Minh, 369, 370, 371
Hollandia, 233-34, 275, 297
Hollywood, Calif., 6, 42
Holocaust, 323-25, 344
Home Army, German, 260, 262
homosexuality, 107, 123, 124, 128, 154
Hoover, Herbert, 39, 41, 43, 44, 55, 67, 364
Hoover, J. Edgar, 39-40, 62, 63, 69, 71,
    124, 289-90, 330, 354-55
  Donovan as viewed by, 40, 54, 68
  Donovan's death and, 383-84
  Donovan spied on by, 4, 40, 76-77,
    335, 354
  Donovan's relationship with, 4, 40,
    41, 68, 71, 74-77, 94, 97, 117, 121,
    127-28, 336, 363-64
  Eisenhower's relationship with, 360-61
  gay rumors about, 128
  on Gero Gaevernitz, 148
  Latin America and, 71, 114, 307
  NKGB and, 224-25
  Pearl Harbor attack and, 83, 85, 86
  postwar intelligence and, 307-11,
    334-35, 352
  Spanish embassy incident and, 126-27
  Truman's relationship with, 321, 322,
    361
Hopkins, Harry, 67, 77, 78, 90, 91, 225,
    335
  postwar intelligence and, 306, 308, 311,
    312
Horthy, Miklós, 195, 197
House Appropriations Committee, 328,
    333
House Committee on Un-American Activi-
    ties, 355
Houston, Lawrence, 352, 378, 381, 385
Howe, Fisher, 113, 333
Hull, Cordell, 65, 66, 75, 78, 121, 122, 262
Hungary, 64, 109, 110, 155, 157, 183, 255,
    256, 284, 290, 374
  Sparrow team in, 194-98
Huntington, Ellery, 176, 182, 201, 203,
    274, 277, 279
Huot, Audrey, 185
Huot, Louis, 185-86
Husky operation, 172-75
Hyde, Henry, 167-69, 171, 264, 265
Hylan, John Francis, 31

Iberian Peninsula, 125, 157-63
Ickes, Harold, 56, 72, 93, 96, 99
I.G. Farben, 97, 326, 329

India, 104, 130, 177, 204-5, 214, 219, 280,
    299, 329, 336
Indochina, 78, 121, 207, 370
insurance companies, 99, 209
International Rescue Committee (IRC),
    374-75
International Telephone and Telegraph
    (IT&T), 78, 125
internment camps, 89, 107
Iran, 95, 353
Ireland, 9
Irish Americans, 9-11, 17, 19, 34, 37, 64
Irvine, Ralstone, 377
isolationists, 55, 58, 61, 63, 123
Istanbul, 155-57, 191-93, 195, 196, 197,
    253-56, 261, 286, 337
Italian Americans, 93-94, 142, 250, 251
Italy, 58, 130, 131, 136, 142, 167, 175-83,
    198, 237, 281
  Allied invasion of, 149, 175-82, 185,
    227-30
  Donovan in, 52-53, 249-53, 296-97,
    298
  Ethiopia and, 51-54, 176, 318
  Germans in, 176, 179, 185, 229-30,
    249-52, 296, 317-18, 324
  intelligence of, 158, 286, 296
  Mussolini executed in, 319
  Mussolini's ouster in, 176
  unconditional surrender and, 149, 179,
    180, 181, 183
  war declared on U.S. by, 87
  in World War I, 53, 54
Ives, Irving M., 351

Jackson, Robert, 324-32, 343-49
Japan, 58, 77-80, 100, 104, 121, 204-11,
    215, 224, 232, 233, 286, 287,
    297-301, 323, 331, 370
  atomic bomb used against, 1, 4, 332
  in Burma, 215-17
  in China, 78, 204-9, 211, 213, 214, 299,
    322, 331
  Donovan in, 32-33
  Doolittle's raid over, 88
  intelligence of, 157
  Lisbon embassy of, 157-59, 336
  peace feelers and, 298-301, 323
  Pearl Harbor attack and, 83-86, 300
  propaganda broadcasts of, 98
  unconditional surrender and, 149, 204
  Vatican embassy of, 257, 258
Japanese Americans, 80, 89

Jennings, Robert, 293–95
Jews, Judaism, 13, 21–22, 54, 261, 265,
    309, 317, 324, 331
Jodl, Alfred, 345
Joe-handlers, 169
Johnson, Herschel, 287
Joint Chiefs of Staff, U.S., 122, 125, 129,
    198, 220, 233, 252, 328–29, 366,
    371
    Balkans and, 183, 275
    Donovan given more freedom by, 155,
        164
    Donovan summoned before, 162–63
    Hungary and, 194, 196
    OSS moved to, 115–17, 143
    OSS psychological warfare and, 150, 151
    peace feelers and, 193
    postwar intelligence and, 308–12
    Sicily operation and, 173
    Soviet Union and, 221, 224, 225
    Torch and, 133, 135
Jones, Mary Gardner, 354, 358, 359, 380
Justice Department, U.S., 71, 115, 122, 311,
    322, 329
    Donovan in, 38–41
    see also FBI

Kachins, 215, 218
K activity, 95
Kallay, Miklós, 195–96
Kaltenbach, Fred, 106
Kangaroo project, 115
Keitel, Wilhelm, 345
Kennedy, John F., 371
Kennedy, Joseph, 60, 62
Kent, Sherman, 200–201
Kessel, Albrecht von, 266
Kesselring, Albert, 227, 229, 230, 249, 252,
    253, 317
Kilgore, Harley, 322
Kilmer, Joyce, 19, 22
Kim Ku, 323
King, Ernest, 91, 118, 130, 282
Kingsley, Rolfe, 200
Kirali, Major, 194, 196
Kirk, Alexander, 191–93
Kirk, Grayson, 380
Knothead, 217–18
Knowland, Bill, 368
Knox, Frank, 58–62, 66, 90, 112–13,
    239–40
    new spy operation and, 69, 70–71
    at St. Regis, 114

Kolbe, Fritz (George Wood), 148–49, 196,
    237, 268, 304
Kolchak, Aleksandr Vasilyevich, 33
Korea, 32, 206, 323, 332
Korean Provisional Government, 323
Korean War, 362, 363, 367
Kreisau Circle, 191–93, 261
Kriemhilde Stellung, 24–25, 28
Krock, Arthur, 4, 85, 329
K tablets, 102
Ku Klux Klan, 34, 38, 133
Kunming, 209, 214, 332
Kuomintang, 205–8, 367

labor unions, 44, 194, 351
L activity, 95
Lahousen, Erwin, 346, 347
Landres-et-Saint-Georges, 24, 25, 26, 30,
    35, 232, 381
Langer, Walter, 263
Langer, William, 86, 175, 193, 210, 221,
    233, 237, 263, 313, 325, 337–38,
    351
Lansky, Meyer, 102
Lasker, Albert, 377
Lasker, Mary, 377
Latin America, 71, 97, 109, 307, 329, 335
    Donovan banned from, 75–76, 114–15
Leahy, William, 91, 225, 351, 352
leaks, 119, 192, 199, 210, 225, 240, 251,
    281, 300, 329–30, 386
    postwar intelligence and, 305, 309–13
Lee, Duncan, 97, 355
Legendre, Gertrude, 293–95, 302
Lehman, Herbert, 43, 44
Leisure, George, 378, 381
Lemaigre-Dubreuil, Jacques (Peanuts), 133,
    134, 135, 137, 138, 139, 141
Lend-Lease, 221, 222
Lenihan, Michael, 24–25, 27, 28
Lenin, Vladimir, 33
Leverkühn, Paul, 54, 346
Lindbergh, Charles, 67
Lippmann, Walter, 61, 356, 357
Lisbon, 157–60, 256–57, 289
    Japanese embassy in, 157–59, 336
    OSS office in, 129, 157–59, 161, 162
London, 34, 68, 89, 168, 275, 276, 295
    Claridge's in, 129, 134, 164, 235, 239,
        240, 245, 315–16, 326, 330
    Donovan in, 59, 63–64, 129–30, 135,
        164–66, 187, 235–40, 248, 269, 314,
        315–16, 318, 326, 330

Eisenhower's headquarters in, 138–39
  Malvergne smuggled to, 136–37
  NKGB in, 224
  OSS in, 73, 103–4, 115, 129, 203, 236, 240, 248, 268, 269–70, 290, 325
Lopez, Blanche, 13
Los Angeles, Calif., 42, 57, 86
Lothian, Lord, 59, 63
Lovell, Malcolm, 108–9
Lovell, Stanley P., 101–4, 232, 233
L tablets, 102, 245
Lubin, Isadore, 306, 313–14
Lucas, Scott, 322
Luce, Henry, 383
Luciano, Lucky, 102
Luftwaffe, 58, 59, 60, 198, 246, 267
Luxembourg, 58, 294
Lyon, 134, 147, 168, 170, 171, 267, 269

MacArthur, Douglas, 41, 52, 320
  in World War I, 19, 23–25, 27, 28, 30, 232
  in World War II, 88, 121, 203, 204, 231–34, 275, 297, 328–29
McCarthy, Joseph, 355, 364, 365
McCormick, Robert, 61, 304, 305, 309, 311–12
McDowell, Robert, 276, 277, 278
McFadden, Thomas, 56
Macfarland, Lanning "Packy," 155–57, 192, 193, 196, 197, 253–56
McKellar, Kenneth, 122
McKellar bill, 122
McLean, Evalyn Walsh, 112–13
Maclean, Fitzroy, 186, 187, 276, 277
MacLeish, Archibald, 73, 79
Madrid, 159–63, 289
Magic, 147, 178, 389
  code breakers, 78, 98, 159
  Donovan denied access to, 118, 119
Magruder, John, 201–3, 230–31, 298–99, 301, 308, 338, 388
Malfatti, Franco, 229, 251
Malvergne, René (Victor Prechak), 136–39
Mannes, Marya, 160
Mansfield, Walter, 184
Mao Tse-tung, 205–6, 209, 355, 362, 367
Maquis, 237–38, 247–48, 268
Marines, U.S., 131, 297, 370
Marret, Mario (Toto), 168–71, 264
Marshall, George, 88–91, 98, 118, 119, 121, 203, 262, 281, 282, 286, 287, 290, 312

"Aunt Jemima" and, 101
  Donovan's correspondence with, 143
  Donovan spy service opposed by, 69, 71
  ethnic armies nixed by, 142
  Iberian crises and, 159, 162
  Normandy invasion and, 237, 239
  OSS transfer and, 115–16
  at Quebec conference, 176–77, 180
  Torch and, 135, 136
Martini operation, 271–72
Massingham, 141–42
Mast, Charles Emmanuel, 136, 137, 139
Mayo Clinic, 376–77
Mediterranean region, 35
  in World War II, 60, 64–65, 67, 86, 142–43, 149, 164, 166, 183, 199, 226–29, 241, 251, 264, 276, 297, 329, 337
Menicanti, Clemente, *see* Coniglio
Menoher, Charles, 24, 26, 28
Menzies, Stewart, 60, 62, 63, 64, 66, 70, 143, 165, 166, 168, 237, 294, 315
Metropolitan Motors Overseas Incorporated, 209, 210
Meuse River, 24, 29
Mexico, 86, 114–15, 215
MI5, 60
MI6, 60, 117, 123, 143, 148, 156, 165, 168, 196, 294, 315
Middle East, 65, 67, 130, 224, 226
Mihailović, Draža, 165–66, 184–85, 275–80
Miles, Milton "Mary," 206–8, 211–14, 297
Miles, Sherman, 69, 75, 117
Mitchell, Harry, 24, 27, 28, 29
Mitchell, William, 40, 41
Molotov, Vyacheslav Mikhailovich, 222
Moltke, Helmuth Graf von, 191–93, 255, 261
Moltke, Helmut Johann Ludwig von (Moltke the Younger), 191
Montgomery, Sir Bernard, 174, 176, 179
Morde, Theodore, 192
Morgan, J. P., 48
Morgan, Junius, 93
Morgenthau, Henry, Jr., 67, 317
Morlion, Felix (Blackie), 256–57
Morocco, French, 132–33, 134, 136–37
Morocco, Spanish, 131, 133, 137, 141
Morris, Roland, 33
Moscow, 219–24, 335
Mountbatten, Lady Edwina, 177, 178
Mountbatten, Lord Louis, 177–78, 204–5, 212, 219, 358, 379

movies and film, 6, 54–55, 119, 149, 204, 243, 285, 319, 326, 384
Mowrer, Edgar, 59, 62, 78
Munich, 107, 154, 271, 319–20
Murphy, Jim, 377, 380
Murphy, Robert Daniel, 131–41, 168, 385
Murrow, Edward R., 84–85, 141, 309, 357
Mussolini, Benito, 51–53, 55, 176, 180, 262, 296, 319
Mutual Broadcasting System, 62
Myitkyina, 214, 215

Nagasaki, 1, 332
Naples, 227–28, 250
Nashville, USS, 233–34
National Intelligence Authority, 308, 352
National Liberation Front, Greek (EAM), 187–88, 280, 356
National Parks police, 99
National Republican Greek League (EDES), 187
National Security Council, 352, 362
National Socialist German Workers' Party (Nazis), 35, 42, 54, 148, 257, 265, 330, 348
   see also Germany, Nazi
Navy, U.S., 58, 61–63, 65, 73, 121, 151, 204, 295, 297, 387
   China and, 206–8, 212
   David Donovan, Sr., in, 143, 153, 172–73, 178–79, 239, 283, 331–32, 343, 358
   Donovan's schemes checked by, 88
   intelligence in, 69, 70, 72, 78, 95, 104, 113, 114, 116, 123, 143, 164, 173, 306–7, 352
   in invasion of Sicily, 172–75
   Normandy invasion and, 237, 239–43
   Pearl Harbor and, 84, 85
   postwar intelligence and, 306–7, 308, 310, 322, 352
   Torch and, 136, 143
Nazi agents and sympathizers, in U.S., 62, 71, 88–89, 94, 109
Nazira, 214–18, 299
Netherlands, 58, 119, 256, 322
New Deal, New Dealers, 44, 53, 55, 305, 328
New Delhi, 204–5, 215
New Guinea, 233–34
Newsweek, 333
New York (state), 42–44, 98
New York City, 13–14, 16, 19, 23, 31, 35,

44–48, 54, 66, 79, 83, 124, 177–78, 257, 295, 320, 338, 350, 363
   British intelligence operations in, 62–63
   Donovan's law firm in, 41–42, 47, 56, 92, 109–11, 353, 354
   Donovan's weekend trips to, 78–79, 83
   Nazi attack on, 88
   OSS front company in, 97
   refugees in, 96, 109–11
   St. Regis Hotel in, 112, 113, 114, 118–19, 135
   Shanghai Evening Post and Mercury in, 209, 210
New York Daily News, 304
New York Senate, 350–51
New York Times, 3–4, 41, 85, 125, 309, 329, 383
Niagara University, 12–13
Nimitz, Chester, 1, 204, 231–32, 299, 328–29
Nixon, Pat, 368
Nixon, Richard, 368, 369
NKGB (People's Commissariat for State Security), 221–26, 284–85, 287, 288–89, 355
Nonquitt, Mass., 39, 43, 176, 284, 326, 337, 375–76
Normandy invasion, 235–48, 268, 270, 336, 381
North Africa, 96, 121, 164, 166, 167, 237
   Allied invasion of, 89, 90, 91, 121, 125, 129–45, 160
   French underground in, 133
   Germany in, 86, 125, 133, 136, 257
   Vichy French in, 130–41, 144
   see also specific places
Northern Ireland, 240–41
Norway, Norwegians, 58, 286, 324, 362
Nunn, Guy, 194–98
Nuremberg, 330–31, 341–48

Obolensky, Prince Serge, 96, 180–81
O'Brien, John Lord, 14, 33
O'Brien, Pat, 54
O'Daniel, John "Iron Mike," 369, 370, 375
Odo, Father, 110
Office of Strategic Services, see OSS
Office of War Information, U.S., 116, 138, 150–51, 166
oil, 104, 160, 195, 226
Oklahoma!, 177–78, 204, 379
Omaha Beach, 244, 246

165th Regiment, 19-31, 35
opium, 209, 367
Oran, 137-40
Organisation de la Résistance dans
    l'Armée, 238
OSS (movie), 6
OSS (Office of Strategic Services), 360,
    362, 365, 370, 387-89
  as amateurs, 76, 93-94, 117, 162, 388
  anti-Hitler activities of, 101, 106-11,
    121, 144, 150, 253, 263
  in Bern, 145-50, 237, 267, 269, 270
  British division of territory with, 130,
    141-42, 164-66, 183-86
  British information sharing with, 117,
    122, 129, 164, 186, 290
  Coordinator of Information Office at,
    71-72, 74-75, 99, 106, 107
  Corsica, Sardinia, and, 176-77, 180-81,
    222, 250
  decoding unit of, 118
  development of, 2, 69-74, 203
  Donovan's rifts in, 103-4, 199, 201-3,
    230, 231-32
  embassy break-ins and, 120-28
  end of, 1-6, 333-38, 351-52
  executive committee of, 201-2
  expenses of, 76, 95, 96, 97, 99-100,
    115, 137-38, 173, 210, 251-52, 326,
    333, 336
  faulty intelligence of, 86, 87, 88, 147,
    249-56, 304
  FBI spying on, 4, 76-77, 361
  Foreign Information Service of, 84,
    104, 116
  Foreign Nationalities of, 96, 202
  formal charter of, 143
  front companies for, 97-98, 156,
    209-10, 254
  headquarters of, *see* Washington, D.C.,
    OSS headquarters in
  in Iberian Peninsula, 157-63
  in Italy invasion and occupation,
    178-82, 227-30, 249-53, 298
  K activity of, 95
  Kangaroo project and, 115
  L activity of, 95
  Morale Operations of, 150-51, 173-74
  morale problems in, 201-2
  moved to Joint Chiefs of Staff, 115-17,
    143
  movies about, 6
  naming of, 116

Office of Scientific Research and Devel-
    opment of, 101-4
  Operational Group of, 202, 227
  Oral Intelligence Unit of, 96
  peace feelers and, 190-99
  Presentation Branch of, 313, 325-26,
    364
  propaganda broadcasts and operations
    of, 84, 85, 87, 104, 108, 118, 150-51,
    173-74, 178
  Reporting Board of, 298-99
  Republican color of, 77, 328
  research and analysis section of, 73, 87,
    96, 201, 221, 233, 237, 263, 313,
    325, 337-38
  Russian infiltration of, 355
  Secret Intelligence of, 96, 158, 201
  security at, 94, 118-19
  Sicily invasion and, 172-76
  Special Operations of, 96, 176
  staff recruited for, 73, 93-97
  Torch and, 129-44
  transportation for, 99, 142, 166-67,
    185, 188, 190, 194, 200, 210-11
  unconventional projects of, 100-105
"OSS Hymn," 235
Ossipov, Alexandr (Gaik Ovakimyan), 223,
    225-26
OSS University of Palermo, 175
Otto of Habsburg, Archduke, 110
Ourcq River, 22, 30, 381
Overlord, 235-48, 264
Overseas Writers Special Committee of
    Inquiry, 356, 357

Pacific Fleet, U.S., 86, 88
Pack, Amy Elizabeth Thorpe "Betty" (Cyn-
    thia), 120-24, 127
Pack, Arthur, 122
Pan American Airways, 51, 95
Papen, Franz von, 192
Paper operation, 367
Papurt, Maxwell, 293-94
Paramount Pictures, 99
Paris, 23, 29, 121, 132, 238, 266, 289, 292,
    293, 294, 318-19, 326, 329
Park, Richard, Jr., 335-37
Patch, Alexander, 264-65, 267
Patterson, Eleanor "Cissy," 304, 309,
    311-12
Patton, George, 241, 267, 270, 281, 294
  in invasion of Sicily, 174-75, 176
  Torch and, 134, 137, 140, 141, 175

peace feelers, 190–99, 261, 266, 298–301, 317–18, 323
Pearl Harbor, 83–91, 124, 220, 240, 300
Pearson, Drew, 229, 280–81, 329–30
Penny Farthing, 167–71, 264
People to People Foundation, 374
Perkins, Frances, 83
Pershing, John "Black Jack," 18, 22, 24, 29, 30, 35, 93
Pétain, Philippe, 121, 134, 140
Peter, King of Yugoslavia, 275, 276, 278, 279
Phao Sriyanon, 362, 366, 367, 370
Phibun Songkhram, 362, 366
Philippines, 41, 88, 121, 297, 367
Philips Company, 95, 117
Phillips, Wallace Banta, 95, 114, 131, 155
Phumiphon Adunyadet, King of Thailand, 365, 367
Pius XII, Pope, 256–58, 297–301, 327
Plymouth, 240, 241, 247
Poland, 18, 119, 192, 303, 323
    in World War II, 50–51, 55
Polk, George, 356–57
Pond, the, 117–18, 283, 290, 307, 336
Port Lyautey, 136, 139
Portugal, 89, 157–60, 256–57, 290
    OSS in, 155, 157–59, 161, 162, 336
Potsdam conference (1945), 332
Poynter, Nelson, 86–87
prisoners of war (POWs), 252–53, 271, 293–94, 322, 323
Pro Deo project, 256–57
Prohibition, 34, 36, 41
"Project George," 97
psychological operations, 70, 72, 116, 117, 150–51, 221
Public Enlightenment and Propaganda Ministry, German, 106
Putzell, Edwin, 97, 203, 230–31, 234, 249, 250, 253, 289, 312, 321

Quebec conference (Quadrant; 1943), 176–78, 180, 190
Quinn, William, 264–65

Raichle, Frank, 37, 41, 383
Ranger, 276–79
Rebecca, 137, 140
Red Army, 191–92, 193, 195, 221, 279, 284–87, 304, 315, 319
refugees, 96, 109–11, 131, 156, 173, 202, 211, 271, 287, 366, 375

Reilly, Hildegarde, 254
Replacement Army, German, 260, 261
Republicans, Republican Party, 10, 13, 15, 53, 62, 155, 225, 252, 283, 303, 321, 324, 325, 328, 350–51, 360, 371
    Donovan's speeches to, 42, 43–44, 55
    in election of 1928, 41
    in election of 1936, 52
    in New York, 33, 35, 41–44
    postwar intelligence and, 305, 306, 311
    selected for coalition cabinet, 56, 58
Ribbentrop, Joachim von, 148, 265
Richards, Atherton, 85
Richards, Guy, 88
Robertson, Walter, 372
Robson, Eleanor, 16, 17
Rockefeller, Nelson, 75–76, 97, 115
Rockefeller Foundation, 18
Rocquefort, Jacques de, 167–71, 264, 265
Romania, 64, 65, 154, 155, 165, 183, 195, 226, 284, 285, 290
Rome, 52–53, 158, 179, 227–30, 249–53, 256–58, 265–67, 289, 296–97, 298, 300, 302, 327
Roosevelt, Eleanor, 44, 84, 93, 104, 318
Roosevelt, Franklin Delano, 55–80, 83–91, 104–9, 114–17, 149–51, 159, 213, 222, 251–52, 257, 262, 264, 284, 287, 297–314, 317–21, 335–36
    Balkans and, 142, 183, 184–85, 187–88, 190, 275, 276, 278–79, 280
    Churchill's communications with, 65, 84, 187–88, 275
    coalition cabinet formed by, 55–56
    at conferences, 149, 164, 176–77, 190, 192, 200, 204, 298–304, 312
    death of, 318–19, 320, 335
    declaration of war speech of, 85, 86
    Donovan as envoy of, 59–68
    Donovan compared with, 55
    Donovan's correspondence with, 110, 114, 122, 134, 142, 151, 238, 246–47, 261, 283, 288, 310, 312
    Donovan's memos to, 70, 77, 100–101, 305, 306, 309, 386
    Donovan's relationship with, 2, 14, 44, 55, 77, 94, 104–5, 119, 151, 190, 312–13
    education of, 14, 44
    in elections, 42–44, 59, 61, 66, 258, 283
    executive orders of, 71, 116, 151, 305, 308, 309, 310
    FBI and, 122

fireside chats of, 86–87
French skills of, 104, 134
health problems of, 302, 312, 317
Japanese Americans interned by, 89
McKellar bill and, 122
Normandy invasion and, 237, 238, 243, 246–47, 248
OSS Soviet mission and, 220, 221, 224–25, 226
peace feelers and, 191, 192, 266, 299
postwar intelligence and, 305–14, 333, 352
secret fund of, 71, 73, 74, 95, 96, 99–100, 131
secretiveness of, 69–70
spy service idea and, 69–72
Stalin's strains with, 220
Torch and, 131, 134, 139, 141
Truman compared with, 320–21
unconditional surrender and, 149–50, 266
war crimes and, 323, 324
in Warm Springs, 313, 314, 317, 318
Roosevelt, James, 73, 83, 97
Roosevelt, Theodore, Jr., 174
Roper, Elmo, 72, 73, 117, 202, 283
Rosemary Hall, 16, 46
Rosenbaum, Joseph, 306
Rothschild bankers, 54
Rouge Bouquet, 21–22
Royal Air Force, 64, 166–69
Rumsey, Dexter, Jr., 33, 37, 376
Rumsey, Dexter Phelps, Sr., 16, 17
Rumsey, Ruth, *see* Donovan, Ruth Rumsey
Rumsey, Susan, 16–17, 18, 32, 43
Rustov, Alexander (Magnolia), 191
Ryan, Frank, 161

safes, cracking of, 120–21, 123, 125–26
Saigon, 37, 369–70
Saint-Georges, France, 24, 26
Saint Joseph's Collegiate Institute, 12
Saint Mary's Academy and Industrial Female School (Miss Nardin's Academy), 11–12
Saint-Mihiel offensive, 23, 24
Salerno, 178–79, 182, 190, 227, 229, 239
Samuel Chase, USS, 172–73, 174, 175, 178
Sardinia, 176–77, 222
Sargent, John Garibaldi, 40
Saturn Club, 15, 36–37, 38, 41, 44
Sauerkraut operations, 252–53

Scamporino, Vincent (Scamp), 173, 250, 296, 298, 300, 301
Scattolini, Virgilio (Vessel), 297–302
Schacht, Hjalmar, 345, 348
Schlesinger, Arthur, 93
Schwab, Francis X., 34, 35
Schwarz, Alfred, *see* Dogwood
SD, 254, 316
Secret Intelligence Service, British, 60, 165, 168
Seitz, Albert, 184
Senate, U.S., 35, 38, 41, 321, 363, 364
Serbia, Serbs, 18, 165–66, 184–85, 279
Setaccioli, Fillippo, 298, 302
7th Army, 174, 175, 176, 264–65, 267
7th Corps, 244, 245–46
sex, 150, 321, 335, 342, 353, 361
espionage and, 120, 122, 123, 209
Sextant (Cairo conference; 1943), 200, 204
Sforza, Count Carlo, 96
Shadel, Willard, 241, 243
Shakespeare, William, 2, 200–201
Shanghai Evening Post and Mercury (S project), 209–10
Shepardson, Whitney, 158, 192–93
Shepherd project, 275–76
Sherwood, Robert, 72, 75, 80, 84, 86, 104, 116
Shigemitsu, Mamoru, 158
Shingle operation, 229
Siberia, 33
Sicilian Americans, 173, 250
Sicily, 131, 149, 164, 172–76, 179
SIM, 286, 296
Sino-American Cooperative Organization (SACO), 207, 208, 209, 211, 212, 259
69th "Irish" Regiment, 19
see also 165th Regiment
Skibbereen, 9
Smith, Alfred E., 35, 41
Smith, Harold, 76, 97, 115, 116, 306, 312, 313, 320, 322, 333–34, 337–38
Smith, Jane, 376, 377, 380
Smith, Walter Bedell "Beetle," 281–82, 284, 326, 329, 353, 360–64, 370
Sofia, 65, 285, 291
Sophoulis, Themistocles, 355–56
Souers, Sidney, 351, 352
South America, 75, 87, 89, 115
Southeast Asia, 130, 177–78, 204, 205, 206, 208, 362–73
Southeast Asia Command, 204–5, 219

South Vietnam, 371, 375
Southwest Pacific Command, 204, 234
Soviet Union, 4, 86, 96, 109, 110, 198, 204,
    261, 266, 296, 305, 317-18, 323,
    335
  atomic bomb and, 225, 332
  Donovan in, 219-24
  Eastern Front and, 119, 141, 155, 183,
    191, 192, 284-89, 317
  German occupation zone of, 289, 303,
    313, 319, 320
  intelligence and, 220-26
  Japan's relations with, 299, 300, 301
  OSS and, 117, 219-26, 264, 284-85,
    307
  postwar, 187, 286, 350, 352, 353, 354,
    357, 367, 374
  United Nations and, 303, 313
  war crimes and, 325, 326, 327, 330-31
  Yugoslavia and, 276, 279
Spain, 65, 124-27, 130, 237, 299
  German relations with, 121, 124-25,
    159, 160
  OSS in, 155, 159-63, 336, 355
  Washington embassy of, 87, 121,
    125-27
Spanish Morocco, 125
Sparrow team, 194-99, 253, 255
Special Operations Executive (SOE; Baker
    Street Irregulars), 129-30, 165, 168,
    176, 183-84, 187, 188, 236, 238,
    253
  Maquis and, 237-38
Spellman, Francis Cardinal, 95, 256
sports, 46, 289
  football, 2, 12, 13, 17, 79, 83, 173
SS, 238, 265, 316, 317, 320, 325, 343, 348
Staktopoulos, Gregory, 356-58
Stalin, Joseph, 55, 220-23, 243, 275, 276,
    283, 285, 286
  at conferences, 192, 200, 298-301,
    303-4, 332
  peace feelers and, 191, 192, 193, 317-18
Stark, Harold "Betty," 239-40
Starr, Cornelius Vander, 209-10
State Department, U.S., 18, 33, 60, 73, 87,
    97, 99, 104, 110, 131, 160, 192, 198,
    202, 209, 275, 300, 313, 323, 336,
    354, 357
  A. Dulles in, 146
  ambassador to Thailand and, 362-63,
    365, 368, 371
  Canaris monitored by, 154

codes and, 287, 288
  intelligence in, 2, 69, 70, 306-7
  John Foster Dulles in, 361, 363, 369,
    371, 372, 373
  Latin America and, 109, 115
  Nazi bank accounts and, 109
  Pearl Harbor and, 85-86
  postwar intelligence and, 306-7, 308,
    322, 334, 338, 351-52
  "Project George" and, 97
  Soviet Union and, 220-21
  Turkish policy and, 156
  war crimes and, 323
Stauffenberg, Claus Schenk von, 260, 262,
    345
Steinbeck, John, 100
Stella Polaris, 287, 289
Stephenson, Bill, 62-63, 69, 70-71, 87, 97,
    122-24, 126, 129, 283, 320, 383
  on Kolbe, 149
  Normandy invasion and, 243
Stettinius, Edward, 288, 313
Stilwell, Joseph "Vinegar Joe," 205-8, 210,
    214, 215
Stimson, Henry, 58, 61, 71-72, 75, 77, 90,
    91 101, 248
Stockholm, 148, 195, 286, 287, 288
Stone, Harlan, 13-14, 38, 40
Strategic Air Command (SAC), 371
Strategic Services Unit, 351
Strong, George V., 117-18, 125, 134, 224,
    307, 335
  Donovan sabotage efforts of, 150-51,
    155
  Iberian crises and, 158-59, 162, 163
Suarez, Alfred, 194-98
Šubašić, Ivan, 275-76, 278, 279
Sullivan & Cromwell, 146
Summerall, Charles P., 24, 26-29
Sunrise, 317-18
Supreme Court, U.S., 40, 42, 350, 368
Sussex project, 237-38, 239
Sweden, 87, 286-88, 290
Switzerland, 48, 145-50, 155, 226, 259,
    267, 269, 295, 304

Taft, Robert, 360
Taft, William Howard, 14
Tai Li, 206-14, 219, 259, 297
Taiwan, 363, 367
Tamm, Edward, 310, 311
Tangier, 131, 132, 133, 137, 141, 142
Taylor, Edmond, 204-5, 219

Taylor, Myron, 300–301
Tehran conference (1943), 192, 200, 204, 221
television, 100
Thailand, Thais, 312, 331, 362–73
Third Army, 267, 294
13 Rue Madeleine (movie), 6
Thomas, Gregory, 161–62, 163
Thompson, Dorothy, 47, 191
Thompson, Jim, 365, 368
Thomsen, Hans, 108–9
Tibet, 34, 104–5
Tikander, Wilho "Ty," 286–89
Tito, Josip Broz, 165–66, 184–86, 274–80
Tolstoy, Count Ilya, 104–5
Tompkins, Peter, 227–30, 249–52
Torch, 129–44, 168, 174, 175
    Murphy's request for delay of, 137
    radio broadcasts and, 130, 132, 137, 138
Toulmin, John, 185, 253, 254
T project, 111
Train, Harold, 113
Treasury Department, U.S., 67, 99, 100
Treviranus, Gottfried, 110–11
Trident Conference (1943), 164
Tripartite Pact, 58, 67
Trohan, Walter, 61–62, 304–5, 309–14, 328–29, 330, 352, 386
Truman, Bess, 320, 335
Truman, Harry, 2–6, 283, 320–28, 330, 332–38, 347, 349–53, 356, 363, 370, 378
    Donovan's relationship with, 4–6, 319, 321–22, 374
    OSS disbanded by, 2–5, 351–52
    postwar intelligence and, 322–23, 326–28, 333–35, 338, 349, 351–53, 361
Tully, Grace, 61, 87, 299, 303, 314, 317, 321
Tunis, 132, 138, 173–74
Tunisia, 131–33, 137, 141, 144, 157
Tunney, Gene, 63
Turkey, 65, 191–92, 193, 199, 226
    OSS in, 155–57, 192, 197, 253–55, 285, 290, 336
Tuscaloosa, USS, 240–43, 247, 248
Twelve Apostles, 132, 135

U-boat submarines, 58, 60, 95
Ujszaszi, Stephen, 195–98
Ultra, 60, 147, 164, 178, 179, 230, 274, 389
United Nations (U.N.), 303, 313, 367

Utah Beach, 240, 242–43, 244, 246, 248, 381

Vafiadis, Markos, 356, 357
Valkyrie, 259–60
Vandenberg, Hoyt, 352, 353
vanden Heuvel, William, 365, 368–72, 374, 379, 382
Vanderbilt, William H., III, 93
Vatican, 95, 256–58, 265–66, 297–302, 331
Vaughan, Harry, 321, 334, 335, 336, 353
Vessel, see Scattolini, Virgilio
Veterans of OSS, 360, 387
Vichy, 132, 140
Vichy French, 121–24, 130–41, 144, 156, 170
Viet Minh, 362, 369, 370, 371
Vietnam, 362, 363, 369–71, 375
Villa Fortino, 182, 277–78
Vittoria, 228, 229–30, 250
Vittorio Emanuele III, King of Italy, 176

Wadsworth, James, 23, 34, 35, 40–41
Waetjen, Eduard, 154, 260–62
Walker, A. V., 156, 253
Wallace, Henry, 83, 112–13
Wallendorf, 293, 294
Walter Reed Army Medical Center, 378–82, 387
war crimes, 317, 323–27, 329, 330–31, 341–48
War Department, U.S., 5, 35, 54, 67, 75, 101, 117, 126, 151, 203, 224, 253, 280, 284, 293–94, 324, 330, 336, 351
    A. Dulles's reports to, 147
    postwar intelligence and, 307–11, 313, 322, 334, 338, 352
Warlimont, Walter, 54, 345, 346
Warm Springs, Ga., 313, 314, 317, 318
War Relief Commission, 18
Washington, D.C., 40, 112–13, 382
    Churchill's visit to, 89–91
    embassies in, 68, 72, 74, 75, 77, 78, 87, 90, 108–9, 119–27, 225, 289
    Georgetown home in, 38, 39, 41, 69, 72, 92, 153, 193–94, 259, 274, 283, 292, 303, 319, 349
    OSS headquarters in (the Kremlin), 73–74, 84, 85, 92, 93, 98–99, 100, 118, 138, 173, 193–94, 200, 205, 207, 208, 299–300, 318–19, 355

Washington Post, 280, 309, 349
Washington Star, 75
Washington Times-Herald, 304–5, 309, 310, 328–29, 347
Watson, Pa, 335
Weeks, John, 35
Wehrmacht, 119, 198, 221, 227, 246, 252, 253, 261, 271, 286, 294, 315, 316, 337, 345
  peace feelers and, 190, 192
  surrender of, 272
Weizsäcker, Baron Ernst von (Jackpot II), 265–67
Welles, Sumner, 114
Western Electrik Kompani, 156, 254
White, George, 102–3
Whitney, William "Bill," 73, 103–4
Wilbrandt, Hans (Hyacinth), 191
Williams, Lansing, 254–55
Williams, Mona, 182, 277, 278
Willkie, Wendell, 66
Willoughby, Charles, 232, 233, 234
Wilson, Henry Maitland "Jumbo," 186, 188, 276–77

Wilson, Hugh, 265–66
Wilson, Woodrow, 33
Winchell, Walter, 76
Wisner, Frank, 256, 285
Wolff, Karl, 317
Wolf's Lair headquarters, 259, 260
Wood, Robert E., 50, 51
World War I, 2, 18–31, 52–55, 110, 111, 146, 159, 222, 232, 321, 345, 381
World War II, *see specific combatants, operations, and units*

X-2, 164, 201, 253–54

Yalta conference (1945), 298–304, 312, 335
Yankee, 47, 57, 143
Yarrow, Bernard, 276
Yugoslav Americans, 89, 142
Yugoslavia, 65, 67, 165–66, 183–88, 190, 222, 274–80, 355
Yukon Territory, 50–51

Z, 157–59
Zurich, 148, 154, 260

About the Author

A former veteran correspondent for *Newsweek* and *Time*, Douglas Waller reported on the CIA for six years. A seasoned Washington hand, Waller also covered the Pentagon, State Department, White House, and Congress. Before reporting for *Newsweek* and *Time*, Waller served eight years as a legislative assistant on the staffs of Rep. Edward J. Markey and Sen. William Proxmire. He is the author of the best sellers *The Commandos: The Inside Story of America's Secret Soldiers*, which chronicled U.S. special operations forces, whose lineage goes back to the OSS, and *Big Red: The Three-Month Voyage of a Trident Nuclear Submarine*. He is also the author of *A Question of Loyalty*, the critically acclaimed biography of General Billy Mitchell.

Born in Norfolk, Virginia, in 1949, Waller comes from a military family. He also served as a captain in the U.S. Army Reserves. He lives in Annandale, Virginia, with his wife, Judy, and has three children and two grandchildren.